Purchased with money
from school prize money.

To Samuel

Well

on a

at Sc

Love Father and Mother

THE SPORTS
BOOK

EDITORIAL CONSULTANT **RAY STUBBS**

THE SPORTS BOOK

THE SPORTS • THE RULES • THE TACTICS • THE TECHNIQUES

DK

LONDON, NEW YORK, MUNICH,
MELBOURNE, DELHI

FOURTH EDITION
Editors Ed Wilson
Editorial Assistant Satu Fox
Project Art Editor Katie Cavanagh
Senior Producer (Pre-Production) Ben Marcus
Producer (Pre-Production) Rachel Ng

Managing Editor Stephanie Farrow
Managing Art Editor Lee Griffiths

FIRST EDITION
Senior Art Editor Michael Duffy
Senior Editor David Summers
Project Editors Tarda Davison-Aitkins, Richard Gilbert, Philip Morgan,
Sean O'Connor, Chris Stone
Project Art Editors Adam Walker, Angela Won-Yin Mak,
Phil Fitzgerald, Phil Gamble, Brian Flynn, Anna Hall, Dave Ball

Lead Illustrator Mike Garland

Production Editor Sharon McGoldrick
Senior Production Controller Shane Higgins

Managing Editor Stephanie Farrow
Managing Art Editor Lee Griffiths

Produced with assistance from Brown Reference Group

First edition published in 2007. Fourth edition published in Great Britain
in 2013 by Dorling Kindersley Limited, 80 Strand, London, WC2R 0RL

Penguin Group (UK)

2 4 6 8 10 9 7 5 3
003 – 193825 – Sept/2013

Copyright © 2007, 2009, 2011, 2013 Dorling Kindersley Limited
All rights reserved

A CIP catalogue record for this book is available from the British Library

All rights reserved. No part of this publication may be reproduced,
stored in a retrieval system, or transmitted in any form or by any
means, electronic, mechanical, photocopying or otherwise, without
the prior written permission of the copyright owners

ISBN 978-1-4093-3508-5

Colour proofing by MDP, England

Printed and bound in China by Leo Paper Products

Discover more at **www.dk.com**

KEY Featured alongside each sport in this book is a
series of icons. These either place them in a sporting category
(corresponding to the chapter in which they are featured), or
provide at-a-glance information about the way the sport is
contested and won, how long it lasts, and whether it is
contested by individuals, groups, or teams.

SPORTS CATEGORIES

ATHLETICS

GYMNASTICS

TEAMSPORTS

RACKETSPORTS

COMBATSPORTS

WATERSPORTS

WINTERSPORTS

TARGETSPORTS

ANIMALSPORTS

MOTORSPORTS

**SPORTS ON
WHEELS**

EXTREMESPORTS

TIMED EVENT
Sports that are contested
and decided on the basis of
the fastest completion time.

DISTANCE EVENT
Sports that are contested
and decided on the basis of
the farthest distance gained.

SCORING EVENT
Sports for which the number
of points or goals scored
decides the outcome.

JUDGED EVENT
Sports in which the
performances of competitors
are marked by judges.

TIME PERIOD
Provided for sports, such as
team games, that take place
over a set period.

TEAM AND INDIVIDUAL SPORTS
These icons indicate whether the
sport featured is primarily played
individually or in teams.

CONTENTS

COMBAT SPORTS

WINTER SPORTS

WATER SPORTS

TARGET SPORTS

SPORTS on WHEELS

ANIMAL SPORTS

MOTOR SPORTS

EXTREME SPORTS

INTRODUCTION

"Running", "jumping" and "throwing" have developed somewhat since the Ancient Greeks first established their Games at Olympia. Back then there was only one event, the Stadion race – now there are literally hundreds of sports to choose from. So it's not surprising that you might not know *all* the rules to *all* the sporting disciplines you come across. Which is where this book comes in. We've outlined more than 200 sports in *The Sports Book* so, whether you want to work out what the judges are looking for in a synchronized diving event, or just what on earth's going on in a Madison, not to mention how to argue with the gyoji, this book will provide the answers.

It used to be that every time the Olympics came around you found yourself in front of the television watching sports you knew very little or nothing about, trying to work out the scoring or who was trying to do what. With the explosion in digital television and sports channels, you can now get that same feeling pretty much any hour of any day when you're channel-surfing, encountering a greater variety of sports than you've ever seen before.

In the pages that follow you'll find all the information you need to be right up-to-speed on a multitude of the weird and wonderful sports mankind has invented. You can check out the rules, the statistics, the kit, the whole point of the game, what's legal and what's not, and what on earth the commentator is talking about – enough information to make you the ultimate armchair expert on almost any sport you encounter. You'll never get your migi-men confused with your alley-oop again.

When you're watching something on the screen, being done by a world champion, it's hard to appreciate the skill and difficulty involved – how tricky can it really be to hit that little white ball over those trees and between those three bunkers to the left of that lake? What's the big deal about doing a hands-free back flip on a narrow beam, or launching yourself into the air on the end of a bendy stick? The professionals make it look so easy but often the reality is very different, and I hope this book will give you a bit of an insight into what it's really like to compete in all these different sports. The growth and development of sport over the last century has been immense. Sport has created international incidents and it has helped resolve international disputes. It inspires passion and despair, pride and shame, and its importance for millions of people worldwide is very evident. What I found compiling this book is that sport is also more addictive than even I had thought – not only is there that natural bond with the sports you know and follow avidly; there's another layer of addiction – a fascination that grows as you learn about sports you were less familiar with and start to explore new territory Browsing this book will introduce you to a new spectrum of sports – suddenly you're reading about all sorts of new stuff. If it inspires you into taking up atlatl or land-yachting, that's great; if it means you know what's going on next time it appears on your television screen, I will be delighted.

Just think, thanks to this book you might have the right answer for the tie-breaker question in the sports quiz next time (come on, admit you've entered one!); or finding yourself in pole position when discussing the difference between a behind and a tight end; or even winning your first orange "cheese" at Trivial Pursuit for knowing what to do on a shiajo.

Even better, you might find the perfect sport for you, or broaden already sporty horizons to find yourself trying out new sports. The world doesn't just consist of those who play football and those who prefer rugby, or those who can hit a ball and those who always seem to have a hole in their racket. There are plenty of other sports to choose from, and – who knows – perhaps you'll find the sport that inspires you and I'll find myself commentating on your performance at the next Olympics!

With more than 200 sports to choose from, I hope you find many that grab your interest. Our thanks go to the many governing bodies and sports organizations that helped us compile all the information. And before the Pram Racing Federation throw any toys out of their latest model, I concede that there are bound to be sports that slipped through the net – but that just leaves the door open for a follow-up publication and yet more fun researching more of the weird and wonderful sports in this world (so be ready, bog-snorkelling mountain-bikers of Norfolk, or lawnmower-racers of Wiltshire, your time will come…).

I hope you enjoy this book!

RAY STUBBS

OLYMPIC GAMES

THE OLYMPICS

ANCIENT GAMES

By roughly 500 BCE, athletic festivals were being held throughout Greece. The most famous of these was the Olympic Games, which were held every four years at Olympia, in honour of Zeus. Events in these early games included short-, middle-, and long-distance races, pentathlon, boxing, and wrestling. Most events required athletes – who were male – to compete in the nude.

THE MODERN OLYMPICS

Rome conquered Greece in the 2nd century BCE, and eventually abolished the Olympic Games. But in 1892, Frenchman Pierre de Coubertin – building on the ideas of others – started to campaign for the resurrection of the event. He gave a talk to the Union des Sports Athlétiques in Paris, urging them to support his vision, and emphasizing the potential of the Olympic Games to unite nations around the world under a common cause. He continued his championing of the Olympics at the Congress of Paris – a conference on international sport – in 1894. The result was an emphatic vote in favour of the revival of the Games. The organization of the event was placed in the hands of the International Olympic Committee (IOC). The first president of the IOC was the Greek Demetrius Vikelas, one of de Coubertin's most vocal supporters.

ATHENS

06–15 APRIL 1896 GAMES OF THE I OLYMPIAD

It was initially intended that the Games be staged in Paris in 1900, in association with the World's Fair. However, it was decided that the first Olympics should be an event in its own right. It was brought forward to 1896 and moved to Athens. The revival of the ancient Games attracted athletes from 14 nations including Greece, Germany, France, and Great Britain.

| 14 Number of nations | 241 Number of athletes |
| 9 Number of sports | 43 Number of events |

STAR PROFILE ALFRED HAJOS

Alfred Hajos was 13 years old when he felt compelled to become a good swimmer after his father drowned in the River Danube. The first Olympic swimming contests, at the 1896 Athens Games, were held in the Bay of Zea in water with a temperature of only 13°C (55°F). Hajos won the 100m and the 1,200m freestyle on the same day. For the longer race, the nine entrants were transported by boat to the open water and left alone to swim back to shore.

SPORTING HIGHLIGHTS

→ American James Connolly won the triple jump to become the first Olympic champion in more than 1,500 years.

→ Having already lifted three gymnastics titles, German athlete Carl Schumann added a fourth by taking the wrestling championship title.

→ There was no event that the Greek hosts wanted to win more than the marathon race, because of its historical significance, and they got their wish. Spyridon Louis won the race by more than seven minutes.

PARIS

15 MAY – 28 OCTOBER 1900 GAMES OF THE II OLYMPIAD

| 24 Number of nations | 997 Number of athletes |
| 18 Number of sports | 95 Number of events |

STAR PROFILE ALVIN KRAENZLEIN

At the 1900 Games American Alvin Kraenzlein won the 60m dash, 110m hurdles, 200m hurdles, and the long jump. His four individual gold medals remain the record for a track-and-field athlete at one Games, and he accomplished the feat over a period of only three days. Although a qualified dentist, Kraenzlein never practised, preferring to become a track coach.

The 1900 Games were held in Paris as part of the *Exposition Universelle Internationale* or World's Fair. The exhibition organizers spread the events over five months, the length of the Fair, and de-emphasized their Olympic status. Women took part in the Games for the first time, although only in a limited number of events, including golf and tennis.

SPORTING HIGHLIGHTS

→ American Ray Ewry won three gold medals in one day, yet he is almost unknown today because his unprecedented feats were performed in events that are no longer held: the standing high jump, standing long jump, and standing triple jump.

→ Charlotte Cooper of Great Britain was the first female Olympic champion when she won the singles tennis event. She also won the mixed doubles tournament.

ST LOUIS

01 JULY – 23 NOVEMBER 1904 GAMES OF THE III OLYMPIAD

12 Number of nations **651** Number of athletes
17 Number of sports **91** Number of events

STAR PROFILE MARTIN SHERIDAN

Irish-American Martin Sheridan was the world's finest all-round athlete of his time. As well as winning the discus at the 1904 and 1908 Games, he won the Greek-style discus and took bronze for the standing long jump in 1908. He was at his best before world records were officially recognized but between 1902 and 1911 he set 15 "World Bests" in the discus.

The 1904 St. Louis Olympics organizers repeated all of the mistakes of 1900. The Olympic competitions, spread out over four and a half months, were lost in the chaos of a World's Fair. The general lack of interest was increased by the fact that out of the 94 Olympic events, only 42 included athletes from outside the US.

SPORTING HIGHLIGHTS

→ One of the most remarkable athletes was the American gymnast George Eyser, who won six medals even though his left leg was made of wood.

→ Irishman Thomas Kiely won an early version of the decathlon, completing all 10 events – 100m, 120m hurdles, 800m walk, 1,600m, high jump, long jump, pole vault, shot put, hammer, and 56lbs weight throw – in a single day.

Above (clockwise from left); champion swimmer Alfred Hajos; Alvin Kraenzlein, winner of four individual gold medals in one Games; shooter Oscar Swahn, who was 60 years old at the time of his first gold medal; and all-round Olympian Martin Sheridan.

LONDON

27 APRIL – 31 OCTOBER 1908 GAMES OF THE IV OLYMPIAD

22 Number of nations **2,008** Number of athletes
22 Number of sports **110** Number of events

STAR PROFILE OSCAR SWAHN

In 1908, Swedish shooter Oscar Swahn was already 60 years old when he won his first Olympic gold medal. He won the running deer single-shot event and took a second gold the next day in the team event. Swahn also earned a bronze medal in the running deer double-shot contest. After World War I, Swahn returned to compete in the Olympics at the age of 72 and won a silver medal.

The 1908 London Games were held in the White City Stadium, which had been constructed for the Franco-British exhibition earlier that year. The stadium was equipped with a running track and a velodrome, as well as having a large swimming pool with an adjustable diving board. Women took part in a limited, but increased, number of sports.

SPORTING HIGHLIGHTS

→ When Italian Dorando Pietri entered the stadium at the end of the marathon he went in the wrong direction and collapsed. Officials helped him to reach the finish line, so he was disqualified, but his plucky effort made him famous.

→ American standing jump specialist Ray Ewry added two more gold medals to take his tally to eight; only Michael Phelps has won more individual golds.

STOCKHOLM

05 MAY - 27 JULY 1912   GAMES OF THE V OLYMPIAD

28 Number of nations **2,407** Number of athletes
14 Number of sports **102** Number of events

STAR PROFILE JIM THORPE

Jim Thorpe is often considered the greatest all-round athlete in history. But Thorpe's Olympic medals were taken back after it was revealed he had earlier been paid for playing minor league baseball – only amateur athletes were eligible for the Olympics. It was not until 1982 that the IOC reversed its decision and returned the medals, posthumously, to Thorpe's family.

The organization and sports facilities in Stockholm were both impeccable, making the V Games a model for future Olympic Games. Trailblazing technological innovations at the Stockholm Games included the photo finish for track-and-field events, and the electronic timer to back up the conventional stopwatch.

SPORTING HIGHLIGHTS

→ American Jim Thorpe, of Native American and Irish descent, won the pentathlon and decathlon by huge margins. At the awards ceremony, the King of Sweden told Thorpe, "Sir, you are the greatest athlete in the world."

→ Hannes Kolehmainen of Finland won the 5,000m, 10,000m, and the individual cross-country race. He also won a silver medal in the team cross-country race.

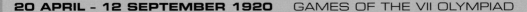

Above (clockwise from left); prolific all-rounder Jim Thorpe; tennis great Suzanne Lenglen; medal-winning speed skater Julius Skutnabb; long-distance champion Paavo Nurmi; and Johnny Weissmuller, Olympic swimmer and film star.

ANTWERP

20 APRIL - 12 SEPTEMBER 1920   GAMES OF THE VII OLYMPIAD

29 Number of nations **2,626** Number of athletes
22 Number of sports **154** Number of events

STAR PROFILE SUZANNE LENGLEN

Suzanne Lenglen of France was one of the greatest women tennis players of all time. Between 1919 and 1926, she lost only one match. In the 10 sets it took her to win the 1920 Olympic title, she lost only four games. Lenglen teamed with Max Decugis to win another gold medal in mixed doubles and with Elisabeth d'Ayen to win a bronze in the women's doubles.

After much debate about whether or not athletes should be admitted from those countries held responsible for the Great War, the IOC excluded delegates from the Central Powers. Spectators witnessed the last tug-of-war, along with a number of other events that were also discontinued, including weight throwing, the 3,000m walk, and the 400m breaststroke.

SPORTING HIGHLIGHTS

→ Hawaii's Duke Kahanamoku won his second consecutive swimming title in the 100m freestyle, and broke his own world record.

→ Italian fencer Nedo Nadi won the individual foil and sabre titles, and led the Italians to victory in all three team events, collecting a record five fencing gold medals at the same Games.

CHAMONIX

25 JANUARY – 05 FEBRUARY 1924 1ST OLYMPIC WINTER GAMES

16 Number of nations **258** Number of athletes
6 Number of sports **16** Number of events

STAR PROFILE **JULIUS SKUTNABB**

Finnish speed skater Julius Skutnabb competed in his first world championship in 1914. At the first Winter Games, aged 34, he took part in every speed skating event. He won a silver medal in the 5,000m race and a gold in the 10,000m, finishing 3 seconds ahead of fellow Finn, Clas Thunberg. Based on his results in the individual races, Skutnabb took a bronze in the combined.

In 1922 a meeting of the French Olympic Committee decided to organize an International Winter Sports Week in Chamonix in 1924. (The IOC did not sanction Winter Games until 1926.) Sadly, the well-organized competitions were beset by poor weather conditions. The Nordic countries demonstrated their dominance in all five disciplines including ice hockey and bobsleigh.

SPORTING HIGHLIGHTS

→ American Charles Jewtraw was the first Winter Olympic champion. He won the gold medal in the first event, which was 500m speed skating.

→ Finnish speed skater Clas Thunberg won 3 gold medals, a silver, and a bronze. Norway's Thorleif Haug won the 18km and 50km cross-country skiing races, and the Nordic combined event.

PARIS

04 MAY – 27 JULY 1924 GAMES OF THE VIII OLYMPIAD

At the 1924 Paris Games, the Olympic motto, "*Citius, Altius, Fortius*", ("Swifter, Higher, Stronger") was introduced, as was the closing ceremony ritual of raising three flags: the flag of the IOC, the flag of the host nation, and the flag of the next host nation. The number of competing nations leapt from 29 to 44, signalling widespread acceptance of the Olympic Games.

SPORTING HIGHLIGHTS

→ American Johnny Weissmuller won two gold medals in swimming and a bronze in water polo all on the same day.

→ Finnish athlete Ville Ritola won the 10,000m, breaking his own world record. He also won gold in the 3,000m steeplechase, along with two silver medals in the 5,000m and 10,000m cross-country races, finishing behind Nurmi.

44 Number of nations **3,089** Number of athletes
17 Number of sports **126** Number of events

STAR PROFILE **PAAVO NURMI**

At the Paris Games, Finnish athlete Paavo Nurmi performed one of the greatest feats in Olympic history. First he won the 1,500m, then with just a two-hour break, he won the 5,000m as well. Two days later, Nurmi won the 10,000m cross-country, earning a team gold at the same time. The next day, he won another gold in the 3,000m team race, bringing his total haul to five gold medals.

AMSTERDAM

17 MAY – 12 AUGUST 1928 GAMES OF THE IX OLYMPIAD

46 Number of nations **2,883** Number of athletes
14 Number of sports **109** Number of events

STAR PROFILE **JOHNNY WEISSMULLER**

At the Amsterdam Games, American swimmer Johnny Weissmuller won the 100m freestyle, as well as being a member of the winning 200m relay team. He is rated by many pundits as the greatest swimmer of all time. Later in life, Weissmuller transferred his sporting success to the silver screen, portraying Tarzan in 12 films between 1932 and 1948.

In 1928, female athletes were allowed to compete in the gymnastics and athletics events, resulting in more than double the number of female Olympians than in previous years. The Olympic flame was lit for the first time, and was housed in a tower in the stadium. Athletes from a record 28 different nationalities won gold medals during the Games.

SPORTING HIGHLIGHTS

→ Australian rower Henry Pearce stopped midway through a quarter-final race to allow a line of ducks to cross in front of his boat. He went on to win the race, and, eventually, the gold medal.

→ Percy Williams, of Canada, sprinted to victory in both the men's 100m and 200m races.

ST MORITZ

11–19 FEBRUARY 1928   II OLYMPIC WINTER GAMES

25 Number of nations   **464** Number of athletes
4 Number of sports   **14** Number of events

STAR PROFILE GILLIS GRAFSTRÖM

Gillis Grafström was one of figure skating's greatest innovators. Among his inventions were the spiral, change sit spin, and flying sit spin. He also won more Olympic medals than any figure skater in history. In 1920, the six judges gave Grafström a unanimous victory. In 1924, he edged out Willy Böckl for a second gold medal, and in 1928, another narrow victory over Böckl secured his third.

At St Moritz, the organizers were fortunate enough to be able to use existing sports facilities in a well-established ski resort. Athletes from 25 nations were full of praise for the organization of the Games. For the first time since World War I, German athletes were allowed to compete. As in Chamonix, Norway were the most successful team, winning six gold medals.

SPORTING HIGHLIGHTS

→ Norwegian Sonja Henie caused a sensation by winning the women's figure skating at the age of 15. Her record as the youngest winner of an individual event stood for 74 years.

→ Canada dominated the ice hockey tournament, winning their three matches 11–0, 14–0, and 13–0.

LAKE PLACID

04–15 FEBRUARY 1932   III OLYMPIC WINTER GAMES

Despite the worldwide Depression, the third Winter Olympics went ahead. Unfortunately, they turned out to be a financial disaster for the organizers, who faced a huge loss. Only 252 athletes from 17 nations competed for medals and the credibility of the competitions was further undermined by the fact that more than half of these athletes were from the US or Canada.

SPORTING HIGHLIGHTS

→ The French husband and wife team of Pierre and Andrée Brunet retained the pairs figure skating gold they had captured in 1928.

→ Norwegian skier Johan Gröttumsbraaten became Olympic champion in the Nordic combined and successfully defended his 1928 St. Moritz title.

→ Only four teams competed in the ice hockey competition, so the teams played each other twice to decide the competition. Canada beat the USA team 2–1, and then drew 2–2 to secure overall victory.

17 Number of nations   **252** Number of athletes
4 Number of sports   **14** Number of events

STAR PROFILE EDDIE EAGAN

American Eddie Eagan holds a special place in Olympic history: he is the only person to win gold medals in both summer and winter sports. In 1920, Eagan defeated Sverre Sörsdal of Norway to win the light-heavyweight boxing at the Antwerp Olympics. Twelve years after his victory at the Summer Games, Eagan reappeared at the 1932 Lake Placid Winter Olympics as a member of the victorious four-man bobsleigh team.

LOS ANGELES

30 JULY – 14 AUGUST 1932   GAMES OF THE X OLYMPIAD

37 Number of nations   **1,332** Number of athletes
14 Number of sports   **117** Number of events

STAR PROFILE BOB VAN OSDEL

Duncan McNaughton and Bob Van Osdel were good friends and fellow high jumpers. At the 1932 Los Angeles Olympics, Van Osdel represented the US and McNaughton represented Canada. In the Olympic final, the battle for gold came down to a duel between the two friends. McNaughton cleared the bar at 1.97m to take gold, while Van Osdel missed, taking the silver medal.

Because the 1932 Olympics were held in the middle of the Great Depression and in the comparatively remote city of Los Angeles, half as many athletes took part as had in 1928. Nevertheless, the level of competition was extremely high and 18 world records were either broken or equalled. The 1932 Olympics were the first to last 16 days.

SPORTING HIGHLIGHTS

→ American athlete "Babe" Didrikson won the javelin throw and the 80m hurdles, and took silver in the high jump. She could have won more medals but women were restricted to competing in only three individual track-and-field events.

→ American swimmer Helene Madison won the 100m and 400m freestyle and helped smash the world record in the 4x100m freestyle team relay.

GARMISCH-PARTENKIRCHEN ❄️

06-16 FEBRUARY 1936   IV OLYMPIC WINTER GAMES

28 Number of nations **646** Number of athletes
4 Number of sports **17** Number of events

STAR PROFILE SONJA HENIE

Figure skater Sonja Henie made her Olympic debut at the first Olympic Winter Games in Chamonix in 1924 at the age of 11. Henie won gold medals at both the 1928 and 1932 Olympics. At the 1936 Winter Games, aged 23, she won her third gold medal. A week later, she won her tenth straight world championship, setting a record that still has not been broken.

The 1936 Winter Games were held in the twin Bavarian towns of Garmisch and Partenkirchen. Alpine skiing events were included for the first time, and this led to a major controversy. The IOC declared that ski instructors could not take part in the Olympics because they were professionals. Incensed, the Austrian and Swiss skiers boycotted the events.

SPORTING HIGHLIGHTS

→ Norwegian ski jumper Birger Ruud attempted an unusual double, competing in both the Alpine and ski jumping events. After missing a gate in the slalom he ended up in fourth place, but a week later he won his second consecutive gold medal in the large hill event.

→ Norwegian speed skater Ivar Ballangrud won three gold medals and one silver. This was his seventh medal in three Olympics.

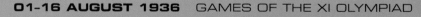

Above (clockwise from top-left); Eddie Eagan, the only man to win gold medals in summer and winter sports; triple gold medallist Sonja Henie; multiple world-record breaker Jesse Owens; Gillis Grafström, one of figure skating's greatest innovators; and medal-winning high jumper Bob Van Osdel.

BERLIN ☀️

01-16 AUGUST 1936   GAMES OF THE XI OLYMPIAD

49 Number of nations **3,963** Number of athletes
19 Number of sports **129** Number of events

STAR PROFILE JESSE OWENS

Jesse Owens assured himself a place in sporting history on 25 May 1935, when he broke five world records and equalled a sixth in the space of 45 minutes. One of these world records, 8.13m (26ft 8in) in the long jump, would last for 25 years. His four gold medals at the 1936 Olympics – in 100m, long jump, 200m, and 4x100m relay – set a world record that would last for 20 years.

The 1936 Berlin Olympics are best remembered for Adolf Hitler's failed attempt to prove his theories of Aryan racial superiority. The most popular hero of the Games was the African-American sprinter and long jumper Jesse Owens, who won four gold medals. The torch relay was introduced, in which a lighted torch is carried from Olympia to the site of the Games.

SPORTING HIGHLIGHTS

→ Rower Jack Beresford of Great Britain set a record by winning his fifth Olympic medal.

→ Thirteen-year-old American diver Marjorie Gestring took gold in the springboard event, becoming the youngest female gold medallist in the history of the Summer Olympics.

ST MORITZ

30 JANUARY – 08 FEBRUARY 1948 V OLYMPIC WINTER GAMES

28 Number of nations
669 Number of athletes (592 men/77 women)
4 Number of sports **22** Number of events

STAR PROFILE BARBARA ANN SCOTT

Barbara Ann Scott was only 11 years old when she won her first national junior title. From 1945–48, she won the North American Figure Skating Championships each year. In 1948, at the Winter Games, she became the first Canadian to win the figure skating gold medal, and was inducted into the Canadian Olympic Hall of Fame. She was awarded the Lou Marsh Trophy as Canada's top athlete of the year in 1945, 1947, and 1948, and was made an Officer of the Order of Canada in 1991.

Did you know that... After a 12-year break, these Winter Games were named the "Games of Renewal". >>> Alpine skiing made its Olympic debut. A few combined events had taken place in 1936, but now there were 3 events for men as well as women.

The 1940 Winter Olympics were scheduled for Sapporo, Japan, but war with China forced the Japanese to admit, in July 1938, that they would be unable to host the Games. Organizational disagreements led the Swiss to withdraw as well, so the Germans volunteered Garmisch-Partenkirchen in July 1939, but four months later the outbreak of World War II forced the cancellation of the Olympics. The first post-war Games were held in St Moritz in 1948, but Germany and Japan were barred from competing. As Switzerland had been neutral during the war, its facilities and infrastructure remained undamaged. However, a shortage of hard currency, combined with restrictions on foreign travel for some nations, meant that many visitors stayed away.

SPORTING HIGHLIGHTS

→ Competing in the slalom, American skier Gretchen Fraser recorded the fastest time in the first round. Despite her second run being delayed by 17 minutes, she skied fast enough to win the gold medal, the first ever by an American skier.

→ Henri Oreiller won the downhill and the Alpine combined, becoming the first Frenchman to win a Winter Olympic title.

→ 19-year-old Canadian figure skater Barbara Ann Scott succeeded Norway's Sonja Henie – winner at the previous three Winter Games – as the women's figure skating gold medallist.

LONDON

29 JULY – 14 AUGUST 1948 GAMES OF THE XIV OLYMPIAD

London was a likely option for the first post-war Summer Olympics because its existing facilities had remained largely intact through the war. In front of King George VI, and more than 80,000 spectators, the XIV Games were opened at the Empire Stadium in Wembley, northwest London. Before the Games, the organizers dropped the idea of building an Olympic village because of the anticipated costs – Britain was, after all, almost bankrupt in the years following World War II. Instead, the athletes stayed in military barracks and colleges around the capital, while rationing meant that many teams had to bring their own food along with them. Not surprisingly, the Games took place without teams from Germany and Japan, while athletes from the Soviet Union did not participate either, since the USSR was not affiliated to the IOC.

59 Number of nations
4,104 Number of athletes (3,714 men/390 women)
17 Number of sports **136** Number of events

STAR PROFILE FRANCINA BLANKERS-KOEN

Francina "Fanny" Blankers-Koen was an outstanding all-round athlete. At the 1948 London Games, she won four gold medals including the 80m hurdles, 100m, and 4x100m relay. She was deprived of more medals by a rule limiting women to three individual events at a time when she also held records in the high jump and long jump. In her career, Blankers-Koen set 16 world records at eight different events, and won five European titles from 1946–50.

Did you know that... The 1948 London Games saw the introduction of blocks to facilitate the start for athletes in sprint races (100m to 400m). >>> This was the first Games to be shown on television.

SPORTING HIGHLIGHTS

→ The 17-year-old American Bob Mathias won the decathlon, becoming the youngest Olympic athlete to win a men's athletics event.

→ Fanny Blankers-Koen of the Netherlands, who made her Olympic debut in 1936, was a 30-year-old mother and world-record holder in six events when she became the star of the London Games.

→ After Hungarian Karoly Takacs' (see p.19) right hand – his pistol hand – was shattered by a grenade, he learnt to shoot with his left hand, winning Olympic gold in the rapid-fire pistol event.

OSLO

14-25 FEBRUARY 1952 VI OLYMPIC WINTER GAMES

30 Number of nations
694 Number of athletes (585 men/109 women)
4 Number of sports **22** Number of events

STAR PROFILE HJALMAR ANDERSEN

Norwegian Hjalmar Andersen was the first man to win three speed skating gold medals at a single Winter Games when, in 1952, he won the 1,500m, 5,000m, and 10,000m in his native Oslo. His winning margins in the 5,000m and 10,000 were the widest in Olympic history. He retired after the 1952 Games but returned in 1954 to win his fourth Norwegian title, having earlier won the World, European, and Norwegian all-round titles from 1950–52.

Did you know that... Oslo hosted the first Winter Olympic torch relay. >>> American Richard "Dick" Button was the first figure skater to perform a double Axel and triple loop in competition. >>> Cross-country skiing for women was introduced.

For the first time, the Winter Olympics were held in a Scandinavian country. The Norwegians received the event with great enthusiasm, and a record number of spectators attended the Games. Before these Games began, the organizers were concerned about Oslo's ability to stage the event; the city did not really have sports facilities that met Olympic standards. However, existing facilities were refurbished and new ones built, well before the opening ceremony. The facilities, as well as the courses, met the high expectations of athletes and officials alike. For the first time since the end of World War II, the German and Japanese teams were allowed to compete. Attracting 150,000 spectators, the ski jump event drew a record attendance that remains unbeaten.

SPORTING HIGHLIGHTS

→ American Dick Button chose to attempt a triple loop, even though no skater had ever performed it in competition. He landed his innovative jump perfectly and the judges were unanimous in voting him the winner.

→ Norwegian Stein Eriksen became the first skier from outside the Alpine countries to win a men's Alpine gold medal.

→ Despite being the oldest competitor, 31-year-old Finn Lydia Wideman won the 10k cross-country pursuit.

HELSINKI

19 JULY – 03 AUGUST 1952 GAMES OF THE XV OLYMPIAD

There was a wonderful atmosphere at the XV Olympics where, to the delight of the crowd, the final torchbearers and cauldron lighters were long-distance stars Paavo Nurmi and Hannes Kolehmainen. For the first time since 1912, athletes from Russia, who were now representing a communist Soviet Union, took part. However, problems arose before the Games when the Soviet team refused to be accommodated alongside athletes from capitalist countries in the Olympic village at Käpyla. Unfortunately Helsinki was overshadowed by the polarization of the two systems; team officials considered every win achieved by "their" athletes as proof of the superiority of their own social system. It was also the first time since the World War II that a (West) German team had participated in a Summer Games. Disagreements over selection criteria had caused East Germany to withdraw.

69 Number of competing nations
4,955 Number of athletes (4,436 men/519 women)
17 Number of sports **149** Number of events

STAR PROFILE KAROLY TAKACS

Karoly Takacs was a member of the Hungarian pistol shooting team in 1938 when, while serving in the army, a faulty grenade exploded in his right hand. Takacs taught himself to shoot with his left hand and returned to competition with great success. In 1952 Takacs defended his Olympic title to become the first repeat winner of the rapid-fire pistol event.

Did you know that... Israel came to the Olympic Games for the first time. >>> The first commemorative coin of the modern Olympic Games was minted. >>> Mixed events took place in the equestrian competitions for the first time.

SPORTING HIGHLIGHTS

→ The great Czech athlete Emil Zatopek became the only person in Olympic history to win the 5,000m, 10,000m, and (his first-ever) marathon.

→ Dane Lis Hartel was one of the first women allowed to compete against men in the equestrian dressage. Despite being paralyzed below the knees because of polio, and needing to be helped on and off her horse, Hartel took silver.

→ American athlete Bob Mathias was the first person to win two successive decathlon titles, winning by an outstanding margin of points, and becoming one of a select few athletes to grace the cover of *Time* magazine.

CORTINA D'AMPEZZO

26 JANUARY – 05 FEBRUARY 1956   VII OLYMPIC WINTER GAMES

32 Number of nations
821 Number of athletes (687 men/134 women)
4 Number of sports **24** Number of events

STAR PROFILE TONI SAILER

Austrian Toni Sailer became the first Alpine skier to win three gold medals. He began by winning the giant slalom by 6.2 seconds, which is still the widest margin of victory in the history of Olympic Alpine skiing. Days later he won the slalom by 4 seconds. The last race was the downhill. Less than 15 minutes before the start, Sailer tightened the straps between his boots and skis, and one of the straps broke. Fortunately the trainer of the Italian team removed his own strap and lent it to the Austrian. Sailer went on to win the race by 3.5 seconds.

Did you know that... The USSR made their Winter Games debut winning the most medals (16). >>> The Olympic Oath was sworn by a female athlete – skier Giuliana Chenal Minuzzo – for the first time in the history of the Games.

The north Italian town of Cortina d'Ampezzo had been earmarked for the 1944 Winter Games, but World War II forced this plan to be abandoned. It was finally given the chance to host the Games in 1956, but a lack of snow cast a shadow over the competition. Such was the concern a few days before the start, that snow had to be transported down the valley from higher snow fields. However, after heavy snowfall on the day of the opening ceremony, much of the imported snow had to be removed. The Games saw the Olympic debut of a pan-German team of 75 athletes. Live television coverage allowed audiences in Central Europe to follow the Games.

SPORTING HIGHLIGHTS

→ American figure skater Teenley Albright took a fall just before the Games, suffering a major injury. Her left skate cut through her right boot, slashed a vein, and severely scraped the bone. However, she still skated well enough at the Games to earn first-place votes from most of the judges.

→ Soviet speed skater Yevgeni Grishin won the 500m and tied first-place in the 1,500m, sharing gold with his compatriot Yuri Mikhailov.

→ Toni Sailer was the first skier to win all three Alpine gold medals.

Below: Soviet gymnast Larisa Latynina was the first female athlete to win nine gold medals (four at Melbourne) and still holds the record for winning the most Olympic medals (18).

MELBOURNE

22 NOVEMBER – 08 DECEMBER 1956 GAMES OF THE XVI OLYMPIAD

72 Number of nations
3,314 Number of athletes (2,938 men/376 women)
17 Number of sports **145** Number of events

STAR PROFILE **DAWN FRASER**

Swimmer Dawn Fraser is an iconic figure in Australian sporting history. An exceptional sportswoman, she won eight Olympic and eight Commonwealth medals. Aged 19, she entered the 1956 Olympic Games and won a gold medal in the 100m freestyle, setting a new World and Olympic record.

Did you know that... The IOC brought together the two Germanys (East and West) in a combined team. **>>>** To avoid the problem of quarantine for horses entering Australia, the equestrian competitions of the Games took place in Stockholm, Sweden.

The first Olympic Games to be held south of the equator posed a particular set of problems. Many athletes from the northern hemisphere did not have sufficient funds to spend much time acclimatizing before the Games, and the later timing of the competition meant that they had to retain peak fitness over a longer period than usual. Because of the high cost of travelling, fewer athletes participated in the Games. The already low number was decreased further when Egypt, Iraq, and Lebanon did not attend because of the Suez crisis; Liechtenstein, the Netherlands, Spain, and Switzerland withdrew in protest at the Soviet invasion of Hungary; and China pulled out because of Taiwan's participation. The competitions themselves also suffered from political tensions. An infamous water polo match between the USSR and Hungary was abandoned due to fighting between some of the players.

SPORTING HIGHLIGHTS

→ With four gold, one silver, and one bronze medal, the Soviet gymnast Larisa Latynina was the Games's most successful competitor.

→ Upon his return to Dundee, Scotland, British boxing gold medallist Dick McTaggart was held aloft by ecstatic fans. As well as winning the lightweight gold medal, he also won the Val Barker Cup for the Games' most stylish boxer.

→ Soviet long-distance runner Vladimir Kuts became a double champion over 5,000m and 10,000m, setting a new Olympic record in the latter event.

SQUAW VALLEY

18–28 FEBRUARY 1960 VIII OLYMPIC WINTER GAMES

When the decision was made in 1955 on the venue for the 1960 Games, the area around Lake Tahoe was completely undeveloped as a winter sports centre. Within four years however, Squaw Valley was ready with sports facilities, infrastructure, and accommodation, for participants as well as over two million visitors. This came about thanks to the organizing committee and financial backing from the states of California and Nevada, together with subsidies from the federal government. Despite this financial backing, they still did not have enough time to build a bobsleigh run, with the result that the International Olympic Committee (IOC) had to cancel all the bobsleigh competitions – the only time this has happened. The opening and closing ceremonies were stage-managed by Walt Disney and it was the first Games to be televised live, reaching millions of viewers worldwide.

30 Number of competing nations
665 Number of athletes (521 men/144 women)
4 Number of sports **27** Number of events

STAR PROFILE **YEVGENY GRISHIN**

At the 1956 Winter Games, Yevgeny Grishin won gold in the 500m speed skating event. Two days later, in the 1,500m, he tied for first place with Yuri Mikhailov, setting a joint world record. At Squaw Valley, Grishin again won the 500m and tied the 1,500m. In 1964 he won silver in the 500m and in 1968 he made his final Olympic appearance, coming fourth and missing a medal by just 0.1 seconds.

Did you know that... The winner of the downhill race wore metal rather than wooden skis – the first Olympic medal to be won on metal skis. **>>>** When Alexander Cushing put forward Squaw Valley's bid to the IOC in 1955 he was the Valley's only inhabitant.

SPORTING HIGHLIGHTS

→ Four years after winning two gold medals, Soviet speed skater Yevgeny Grishin again won gold over 500m, matching his own world record. Then, in the 1,500m, he finished in another tie for first place with Norwegian Roald Aas.

→ Finnish cross-country skier Veikko Hakulinen had already won two gold medals, but his greatest Olympic moment was yet to come. As the anchor of the Finnish relay team, he took off 20 seconds after Norway's Håkon Brusveen, gaining the lead 100 metres from the finish line to win by just a single metre.

ROME

25 AUGUST – 11 SEPTEMBER 1960 GAMES OF THE XVII OLYMPIAD

83 Number of nations
5,338 Number of athletes (4,727 men/611 women)
17 Number of sports **150** Number of events

STAR PROFILE ALADAR GEREVICH

Aladar Gerevich is the only person to win the same Olympic event six times. Indeed, he is the only athlete to earn gold medals at six different Olympics. A specialist in sabre fencing, Gerevich's record might have been even more amazing if World War II had not forced two Olympics to be cancelled. He made his final appearance, at the age of 50, at the Rome Games.

Did you know that... These were the last Games in which South Africa was allowed to participate – until 1992 – because of IOC disapproval at their policy of apartheid (racial segregation). >>> The Games were broadcast by more than 100 television stations.

Rome had been chosen to stage the 1908 Games, but the eruption of Mount Vesuvius in southern Italy had intervened. It was some 52 years later that the Games finally arrived in the Italian capital. The Rome games were broadcast by television to all European countries and were watched by millions. However, the competitions themselves were overshadowed by the rivalry between the US and the USSR. In the final medal table the USSR finished ahead of the US by 43 to 34 gold medals.

SPORTING HIGHLIGHTS

→ Running barefoot, Ethiopian athlete Abebe Bikila (see p.23) did not go unnoticed when he entered the marathon. He refused to be daunted by the condescending remarks and left all his opponents behind to cross the finishing line victorious, near Constantine's triumphal arch.

→ Aged 20, Wilma Rudolph became the first American woman to win three gold athletics medals in one Olympiad: in the 100m, 200m and 4x100m relay. She achieved this extraordinary feat despite suffering from a string of childhood illnesses and recovering from a deformed leg caused by polio.

→ Cassius Marcellus Clay, later known as Muhammad Ali, first gained international prominence by winning the light-heavyweight gold medal. He would later turn professional and embark on a phenomenal career.

INNSBRUCK

29 JANUARY – 09 FEBRUARY 1964 IX OLYMPIC WINTER GAMES

Although the organizers had made all the preparations for the Games that they could, they were unable to influence the weather. Innsbruck's mildest February for 58 years meant that Austrian troops had to transport more than 25,000 tonnes of snow from higher snow fields to the River Inn Valley so that the slopes would be ready for the Alpine skiing competitions. The cross-country skiers, competing further down the valley, found conditions ideal. The schedule included luge tobogganing, where competitors descended an ice run lying face upwards on the toboggan – in 1928 and 1948 there had been skeleton sledding competitions, in which the athletes lay face down – and the bobsleigh competitions returned after their enforced break in Squaw Valley. Meanwhile, new rules were put in place in the ski jump competition.

SPORTING HIGHLIGHTS

→ Russian speed skater Lidiya Skoblikova became the first woman to win all four speed skating events in the same Games.

→ 18-year-old French Alpine skier Marielle Goitschel finished second in the Olympic slalom, beaten only by her older sister.

→ Eugenio Monti, from the Italian bobsleigh team, helped Britons Tony Nash and Robin Dixon win gold when he lent them an axle bolt to replace one that was broken. Monti was given the first De Coubertin Medal for sportsmanship.

36 Number of nations
1,091 Number of athletes (892 men/199 women)
6 Number of sports **34** Number of events

STAR PROFILE KNUT JOHANNESEN

Long-distance skater Knut Johannesen first competed in the 1956 Olympics, winning a silver medal in the 10,000m. At the 1964 Games, fellow Norwegian Per Ivar Moe recorded an excellent time of 7:38.6 for the 5,000m. Johannesen fell three seconds behind Moe, but gradually closed the gap. When he crossed the finish line, the clock read 7:38.7, but it was wrong. His official time of 7:38.4 won him the gold medal.

Did you know that... For the first time in the Winter Games, the flame was lit in Olympia. Since then, it has always been lit there. >>> Britain won its first Winter Olympics gold medal for 12 years in the two-man bobsleigh event.

Above: Despite suffering from polio as a child, US athlete Wilma Rudolph overcame her disability to win three track golds in Tokyo.

TOKYO

10–24 OCTOBER 1964   GAMES OF THE XVIII OLYMPIAD

For the first time, the Olympic Games were hosted in Asia. Japan invested heavily in the most modern sports facilities as well as in improving the infrastructure of a city containing over 10 million people. The extraordinary architectural design of the swimming stadium led to it being described as a "cathedral of sports". Other outstanding new buildings included the judo hall, which was modelled on the architectural style of traditional Japanese temples. The opening ceremony offered a glimpse into how record-breaking the competition would be, when teams from 93 nations (10 more than participated in Rome) paraded into the Meiji Stadium. However, the high standards set by athletes at the Tokyo Games led some critics to warn about exaggerated expectations for the future development of the Olympic disciplines.

SPORTING HIGHLIGHTS

→ Australian swimmer Dawn Fraser (see p.21) won her third successive gold medal in the 100m freestyle. She was the first woman swimmer to win eight medals (four gold and four silver) – over three Olympics.

→ Soviet gymnast Larisa Latynina (see p.20) added six more medals to her tally, becoming the first woman to win nine Olympic gold medals.

→ Deszo Gyarmati won gold with the Hungarian water polo team, thus achieving the (then) unique feat of winning medals at five successive Olympic Games.

93 Number of nations
5,151 Number of athletes (4,473 men/678 women)
19 Number of sports 163 Number of events

STAR PROFILE ABEBE BIKILA

Ethiopian Abebe Bikila's first Olympic marathon was at the 1960 Games in Rome, where he won a gold medal running barefoot. Bikila returned to the Games in 1964, and this time he ran with shoes. Despite having had an appendectomy 40 days earlier, Bikila took a clear lead by the halfway mark and steadily pulled away to win by more than four minutes. His time of 2 hours 12 minutes 11.2 seconds, was a world best for the marathon.

Did you know that... Judo and volleyball were introduced for the first time. >>> American Al Oerter won the discus for the third time despite wearing a neck harness. >>> A cinder running track was used for the last time.

Above: 16-year-old American swimmer Debbie Meyer set new Olympic records in the 200m, 400m, and 800m freestyle events.

GRENOBLE

06–18 FEBRUARY 1968   X OLYMPIC WINTER GAMES

Before the industrial city of Grenoble was able to become a suitable venue for the Winter Games, large amounts of money needed to be invested in the construction of new sports facilities and an improved infrastructure. Even after this money was spent, Grenoble still did not have sufficient sports facilities, so competitions took place in the whole of the surrounding region, and athletes were accommodated in seven Olympic villages. French hero Jean-Claude Killy swept the men's Alpine events, equalling Toni Sailer's achievement, but only after the greatest controversy in the history of the Winter Olympics. This was the also first time that two separate German teams paraded into the stadium. Although united by one flag and a joint anthem, relationships between the two teams soured during the course of the competition.

SPORTING HIGHLIGHTS

→ There was controversy in the women's luge when the three East German entrants, who had finished first, second, and fourth, were disqualified for heating their runners.

→ American figure skater Peggy Fleming easily won the first-place votes of all nine judges. She was the only American winner at the Games.

→ Swedish cross-country skier Toini Gustafsson won both the 5km and 10km races, along with a silver medal in the relay.

37 Number of nations
1,158 Number of athletes (947 men/211 women)
6 Number of sports **35** Number of events

STAR PROFILE JEAN-CLAUDE KILLY

French fans hoped that Jean-Claude Killy would sweep all three Alpine skiing events at Grenoble. He began by winning the downhill and giant slalom. During the slalom, Killy's main rival, Austrian Karl Schranz, claimed that a mysterious man in black crossed his path during this race, causing him to skid to a halt. Given a restart, Schranz beat Killy's time, but a Jury of Appeal later awarded the victory to Killy.

Did you know that... The IOC introduced sex tests for women – British equestrian Princess Anne was the only woman not to have to submit to one. They were discontinued in 1999. >>> Grenoble was the first Winter Olympics to be broadcast in colour.

MEXICO CITY

12-22 OCTOBER 1968   GAMES OF THE XIX OLYMPIAD

112 Number of nations
5,516 Number of athletes (4,735 men/781 women)
20 Number of sports **172** Number of events

STAR PROFILE **DICK FOSBURY**

The 1968 Mexico City Olympics marked the international debut of US high jumper Dick Fosbury and his celebrated "Fosbury flop". Up to that time, jumpers took off from their inside foot and swing their outside foot up and over the bar. Fosbury's innovation was to race up to the bar at great speed and take off from his right (outside) foot. He then twisted his body so that he went over head first with his back to the bar. Fosbury achieved a personal record of 2.24m to take the gold medal.

Did you know that... It was the first Games to use the synthetic Tartan track surface in athletics. >>> Electronic rather than manual timing was used for athletics, cycling, rowing, canoe, swimming, and equestrian competitions.

Mexico City's high altitude – almost 2,240m (7,350ft) above sea level – dominated much of the pre-Games discussion: the consensus being that athletes from lowland countries would be at a disadvantage. However, several weeks of high-altitude training enhanced the performances of many of these athletes. There were violent riots in the run-up to the Games, following complaints about the exorbitant amounts of money being invested in Olympic facilities in contrast to Mexico's own social problems. Controversy also arose over South Africa's participation at these Games and the IOC withdrew its invitation under pressure. Doping controls were introduced for the first time and a Swedish athlete was disqualified for having too much alcohol in his bloodstream.

SPORTING HIGHLIGHTS

→ American Bob Beamon was the favourite in the long jump but he exceeded all expectations. His jump of 8.90m beat the world record by 0.55m.

→ Czech gymnast Vera Caslavska won four gold and two silver medals. These victories were given extra significance by beating the Soviet gymnasts shortly after Soviet tanks had invaded her homeland.

→ American Debbie Meyer became the first woman swimmer to win three individual gold medals at one Olympic Games.

SAPPORO

03-13 FEBRUARY 1972   XI OLYMPIC WINTER GAMES

The 1972 Sapporo Games in Japan were the first Winter Games to be held outside Europe or the Americas. The Japanese government regarded them as a prestigious event, investing enormous sums of money in the construction of new sports facilities. As a result, the Games turned out to be the most extravagant and expensive so far. The subject of amateurism stirred controversy when Karl Schranz was banned for receiving payment from ski product manufacturers, but full-time ice hockey players from the communist nations were allowed to compete. Increased income from television rights helped to offset the Games's increasing costs.

SPORTING HIGHLIGHTS

→ In front of his home crowd, Yukio Kasaya produced the best jump of each of the two rounds to earn the gold medal in the normal hill ski-jumping event. His teammates Konno and Aochi completed a Japanese sweep with silver and bronze.

→ The biggest surprise of the Games was the victory of 21-year-old "Paquito" Fernandez Ochoa of Spain, who won the slalom by a full second. His gold medal was the first to be won by a Spanish athlete in the Winter Olympics.

→ Galina Kulakova of the Soviet Union entered all three cross-country races and finished first in all of them, winning the 5km and 10km and anchoring the relay team to victory.

35 Number of nations
1,006 Number of athletes (801 men/205 women)
6 Number of sports **35** Number of events

STAR PROFILE **ARD SCHENK**

In 1968 Ard Schenk won a silver medal in the 1,500m speed skating. By 1972 Schenk held world records in three of the four Olympic distances. Racing during a snowstorm, Schenk won the 5,000m by 4.57 seconds. In the 500m, he fell after four steps and finished 34th. But Schenk bounced back to win the 1,500m and the 10,000m. Weeks later he became the first skater in 60 years to win all four events at the World Championships.

Did you know that... The Japanese won their first Winter Olympics gold medal. >>> Canada did not send an ice hockey team in protest against the covert professionalism rife in the USSR and Eastern Europe.

MUNICH

26 AUGUST – 11 SEPTEMBER 1972   GAMES OF THE XX OLYMPIAD

121 Number of nations
7,134 Number of athletes (6,075 men/1,059 women)
23 Number of sports **195** Number of events

STAR PROFILE MARK SPITZ

American swimmer Mark Spitz brashly predicted he would win six gold medals at the 1968 Olympics, but ended up winning only two in the relays. At the 1972 Olympics, Spitz tried again. Entering seven events over eight days, he won all seven, setting a new world record in each one. Spitz is the only athlete to win seven gold medals at a single Olympics and he is one of only four to win nine career golds.

Did you know that... Archery and handball were reintroduced to the Olympic programme. >>> Officials took the Olympic Oath for the first time. >>> They were the first Games to have a mascot – Waldi the Dachsund.

The 1972 Munich Games were the largest yet, setting records in all categories, with 195 events and 7,134 athletes from 121 nations. The Games were supposed to celebrate peace, and for the first 10 days all went well. But in the early morning of 5 September, eight Palestinian terrorists broke into the Olympic village, killed two members of the Israeli team, and took nine more hostage. In the ensuing battle, all nine Israeli hostages were killed, along with five of the terrorists, and one policeman. The Olympics were suspended and a memorial service was held in the main stadium. In defiance of the terrorists, the International Olympic Committee ordered the competitions to resume after a pause of 34 hours. All other details about the Munich Games paled in significance.

SPORTING HIGHLIGHTS

→ Finnish distance runner Lasse Viren fell halfway through the 10,000m final, but still set a new world record to win the first of his four career gold medals.

→ The media star of the Munich Games was the petite Soviet gymnast Olga Korbut, whose three gold medals helped establish Soviet dominance in the female gymnastics events and captured the attention of fans worldwide.

→ West German Liselott Linsenhoff, competing in the dressage event, became the first female equestrian to win an individual gold medal.

INNSBRUCK

04–15 FEBRUARY 1976   XII OLYMPIC WINTER GAMES

The 1976 Winter Olympics were awarded to the city of Denver, US, but the people of the state of Colorado voted to prohibit public funds from being used to support the Games. Innsbruck stepped in and hosted the Games only 12 years after hosting its last Winter Olympics. The organizers decided to conduct the medal ceremonies in the ice rink at the end of each evening, rather than after the competition, as the spectators preferred to see the medal ceremonies held "on-the-spot". Arguably the most memorable image of the Games was skier Franz Klammer flying wildly down the downhill course, barely keeping control, on his way to a gold medal.

37 Number of nations
1,123 Number of athletes (892 men/231women)
6 Number of sports **37** Number of events

STAR PROFILE FRANZ KLAMMER

In 1975 Austrian Franz Klammer won eight of the nine World Cup downhill races. When the Olympics came to Innsbruck, Austria, the following year, there was great pressure on Klammer to win the downhill again. Defending Swiss champion Bernhard Russi tore down the hill in a top time of 1:46.06. Klammer fell one-fifth of a second off Russi's pace, but fought back wildly over the last 1,000m of the course, winning by just 0.33 of a second.

SPORTING HIGHLIGHTS

→ German skier Rosi Mittermaier won gold in the downhill, followed three days later by gold in the slalom. She almost won all three Alpine events, but missed out on gold in the giant slalom by 0.12 seconds.

→ Certain figure skating judges did not approve of the style used by Great Britain's John Curry. He emphasized grace and artistic expression over athleticism. During the course of the Games he supplemented his natural elegance with dynamic jumps, and the judges ended up awarding him the highest points total in the history of men's figure skating.

→ The East German luge team won every gold medal; competitors from other countries had to be content with silver or bronze medals.

Did you know that... Two Olympic flames were lit to mark Innsbruck's second time as host of the Games. >>> Ice dancing made its debut. >>> In figure skating, the back flip was successfully attempted for the first and last time – by American Terry Kubicka.

MONTREAL

17 JULY – 01 AUGUST 1976   GAMES OF THE XXI OLYMPIAD

92 Number of nations
6,084 Number of athletes (4,824 men/1,260 women)
21 Number of sports **198** Number of events

STAR PROFILE **NADIA COMANECI**

In 1976 Romania's Nadia Comaneci became the first gymnast in Olympic history to be awarded a perfect score of 10. Comaneci first came to prominence at the 1975 European Championships where she won four gold medals. In the 1976 and 1980 Games she won a total of nine Olympic medals. Following the 1980 Games, natural physical development began to inhibit her performance. Following victory at the 1981 World Student Games, she retired.

Did you know that... The city of Montreal is still repaying debts accrued during the 1976 Olympic Games. >>> Hungarian Miklos Németh became the first child of a gold medallist (in the hammer throw) to win one of his own in the javelin.

The 1976 Montreal Games were marred by the boycott of 22 African nations protesting the fact that despite the New Zealand rugby team touring South Africa in defiance of international sporting sanctions, New Zealand was still allowed to compete. To compound the situation, the host nation suffered an unusually long winter, industrial disputes, and a lack of funds, which made it impossible to finish work on the Olympic facilities in time for the opening ceremony. However, the performances of the athletes did not suffer from the political and national disputes. Despite the problems, the Games were well organized and, following the 1972 terrorist attack in Munich, security was tight.

SPORTING HIGHLIGHTS

→ Nadia Comaneci was the star of the Games. She achieved her first perfect 10 on the uneven parallel bars, and the judges awarded her the maximum mark seven times (see box).

→ With his victory in platform diving, Italian Klaus Dibiasi became the first Olympic diver to win three successive gold medals, and to win medals in four Olympic Games.

→ The US and East Germany dominated the swimming events. Only Great Britain's David Wilkie and the Soviet Union's Marina Koshevaya (both winning their 200m finals in record times) upset the monopoly.

Below: American athlete Edwin Moses burst onto the scene in 1976, winning the 400m hurdles by a record eight metres. 12 years later in Seoul he won bronze.

LAKE PLACID

13-24 FEBRUARY 1980   XIII OLYMPIC WINTER GAMES

37 Number of nations
1,072 Number of athletes (840 men/232 women)
6 Number of sports   **38** Number of events

STAR PROFILE ERIC HEIDEN

As a 17-year-old, American speed skater Eric Heiden competed in the 1976 Winter Games, finishing 7th in the 1,500m and 19th in the 5,000m. He rapidly improved, winning the main title at the World Championships three years running, before achieving a clean sweep of all five speed skating events – from 500m to 10,000m – at the 1980 Games, setting Olympic records in every one. In the 1,500m he hit a rut in the ice and almost fell, but recovered to win by 0.37 seconds.

Did you know that... Artificial snow was used at the Olympics for the first time. >>> President Jimmy Carter threatened a US boycott of the Moscow Summer Olympics in protest at the Soviet Union's invasion of Afghanistan at the end of 1979.

In 1974 the IOC awarded the Winter Games to Lake Placid for the second time. Lake Placid first hosted the Games back in 1932. The organizers had to cope with a lack of snow and with moving enormous crowds to and from a small town of 3,000 inhabitants. People were sometimes forced to wait hours for shuttle buses to take them to venues. Many athletes considered the Olympic village too confined; after the Games it would actually be used as a prison for young offenders. The sports facilities, on the other hand, received high praise despite being some distance apart. Artificial snow was used for the first time, at a cost of $5 million. This was extremely demanding on the athletes, especially when mixed with the newly fallen snow.

SPORTING HIGHLIGHTS

→ Hanni Wenzel won the giant slalom and the slalom, and her nation, Liechtenstein, became the smallest country to produce an Olympic champion.

→ In the biathlon relay, Soviet athlete Aleksandr Tikhonov earned his fourth gold medal. His compatriot Nikolay Zimyatov won three gold medals in the cross-country skiing.

→ The US ice hockey team beat the Soviet team – which had previously won gold at every Games since 1964 – in the medal round, going on to win gold.

Below: The 4-3 "Miracle on Ice" victory over the Soviet Union by a rookie American team is still the best-remembered international ice hockey game in the US today.

MOSCOW

19 JULY – 03 AUGUST 1980   GAMES OF THE XXII OLYMPIAD

80 Number of nations
5,179 Number of athletes (4,064 men/1,115 women)
21 Number of sports **203** Number of events

STAR PROFILE **ALEKSANDR DITYATIN**

Soviet gymnast Aleksandr Dityatin first appeared at the 1976 Olympics, winning a silver medal in the team event. Competing before a home crowd in Moscow, he led the Soviet Union to the team championship and then won the individual all-round title. He also qualified for all six apparatus finals. Dityatin won six medals in one day and is the only athlete in Olympic history to win eight medals at one Games. He was also the first male gymnast to be awarded a perfect score of 10 in an Olympic competition.

Did you know that... The number of participant nations was the lowest since 1956. >>> In the men's coxless pairs rowing, both the gold and silver medal-winning teams were made up of identical twins from East Germany and the USSR.

As a result of the US-led boycott in protest at the Soviet invasion of Afghanistan, only 80 countries were represented at the Moscow Games. Notable absentees included Japan, West Germany, and the US. Western countries have frequently referred to the Moscow Games as being of a low standard, and have raised doubts about the sporting value of the results and medals. Nonetheless, although not of the highest calibre, the Moscow Games were hardly sub-standard: 36 world records, 39 European records, and 73 Olympic records bore testimony to the high level of talent and competition on display.

SPORTING HIGHLIGHTS

→ Soviet swimmer Vladimir Salnikov won three gold medals: in the 400m and 1,500m freestyle, and 4×200m relay. He was also the first to swim 1,500m in a time of less than 15 minutes.

→ British middle-distance runners Steve Ovett and Sebastian Coe faced each other in two memorable duels. In the 800m, Ovett won the gold medal just ahead of his compatriot. Six days later, a determined Coe redeemed himself in the 1,500m, taking gold while Ovett could only manage bronze.

→ By winning the decathlon, Great Britain's Daley Thompson became "king of the athletes", beating home crowd favourite Yuri Kutsenko into second place.

SARAJEVO

08–19 FEBRUARY 1984   XIV OLYMPIC WINTER GAMES

In 1984 the Winter Games was held in the Balkans for the first time, and in a communist country for the first and only time. The people of Sarajevo gained high marks for their hospitality, and there was no indication of the tragic war that would engulf the city a decade later. For the first time, the International Olympic Committee agreed to pay the expenses of one male and one female member from each team. The number of participating nations was greatly increased, up from 37 to 49, although Egypt, the Virgin Islands, Mexico, Monaco, Puerto Rico, and Senegal were represented by only one competitor each.

49 Number of competing nations
1,272 Number of athletes (998 men/274 women)
6 Number of sports **39** Number of events

STAR PROFILE **JAYNE TORVILL AND CHRISTOPHER DEAN**

The 1984 Sarajevo Winter Games was one of the few times that the ice dancing competition was not won by a Soviet couple. Jayne Torvill and Christopher Dean of Great Britain mesmerized the audience with their interpretation of Ravel's "Bolero". The judges awarded them 12 scores of 6.0, including unanimous perfect scores for artistic impression, to give them the gold medal.

SPORTING HIGHLIGHTS

→ Finnish cross-country skier Marja-Liisa Kirvesmiemi-Hämäläinen – the only woman to have competed in six Winter Games between 1976 and 1994 – won all three women's events easily, including the 20km. She added a bronze medal in the 4x7.5km relay.

→ Jure Franko of Yugoslavia won silver in the giant slalom – the only medal for the organizing country.

→ Canadian speed skater Gaétan Boucher won a bronze medal in the 500m and then beat Sergei Khlebnikov in the 1,000m to take his first gold medal. Two days later, he won again in the 1,500m.

→ East Germany's Katarina Witt won her first Olympic figure skating gold medal.

Did you know that... These were the first Games under the presidency of Juan Antonio Samaranch. >>> There was a large increase in the amount charged for television rights. >>> The 20km race was added to women's cross-country skiing.

LOS ANGELES

28 JULY – 12 AUGUST 1984   GAMES OF THE XXIII OLYMPIAD

140 Number of nations
6,829 Number of athletes (5,263 men/1,566 women)
23 Number of sports   **221** Number of events

STAR PROFILE **CARL LEWIS**

American Carl Lewis is one of only four Olympic athletes to win nine gold medals and one of only three to win the same individual event four times. In 1984, Lewis matched Jesse Owens' feat of winning four gold medals with victories in the 100m, the 200m, the long jump and the 4x100m relay. At the Atlanta Games, 12 years after his triumphs in Los Angeles (or, as Lewis put it, "fourteen hairstyles later"), Carl Lewis was still the Olympic long jump champion.

Did you know that... The 14 nations that boycotted these Games accounted for over half the gold medals at the 1976 Olympics. >>> The women's marathon, rhythmic gymnastics, and synchronized swimming made their first appearance.

Although a revenge boycott led by the Soviet Union depleted the field in certain sports, a record 140 nations took part in the first privately funded tournament in Olympic history. More than 30 sponsors together contributed more than $500 million, while other companies funded the building of new sports facilities, in a deal that allowed them to advertise on the admission tickets. The ABC television network paid $225 million for the exclusive television rights, thereby ensuring that most events started in the evenings during prime television time in the US. With these vast amounts of money involved, many critics held the view that what had once been a festival of amateur sport was now a purely commercial spectacle.

SPORTING HIGHLIGHTS

→ American diver Greg Louganis remained unbeaten from the 3m springboard as well as from the 10m platform.

→ Sebastian Coe became the first repeat winner of the men's 1,500m.

→ In the women's 400m hurdles, Nawal El Moutawakel led from start to finish, becoming the first Moroccan athlete to win a gold medal.

→ British decathlete gold medallist Daley Thompson finished just one point off the world record.

CALGARY

13-28 FEBRUARY 1988   XV OLYMPIC WINTER GAMES

Funds for the Calgary Games came from three sources: half the budget was put up by the Canadian government; sponsors, official suppliers, and licensees contributed another $90 million; and the American television network ABC paid $309 million for the broadcasting rights. ABC benefited from the decision to extend the Games to 16 days, including 3 weekends. The consequence for the competitors was that start times for many events were chosen to meet the demands of television advertisers in the US and not for sporting reasons. Although the spectators enjoyed the Calgary Games, many saw them as more of a well-rehearsed show than a series of competitive sporting competitions.

57 Number of nations
1,423 Number of athletes (1,122 men/301 women)
6 Number of sports   **46** Number of events

STAR PROFILE **MATTI NYKÄNEN**

At the 1988 Games, Matti Nykänen of Finland won the normal hill event by a decisive 17 points, and then won the large hill event by 16.5 points. This earned him a place in the record books as the first ski jumper to win two gold medals at the same Olympics. For the first time, a third jumping event – the large hill team event – was added to the programme. Nykänen led the Finnish team to victory and brought his career total to four gold medals and one silver medal.

Did you know that... The speed skating events were held on a covered rink for the first time. >>> Calgary was the first "smoke-free" Olympic Games. >>> Curling appeared on the programme as a demonstration sport.

SPORTING HIGHLIGHTS

→ East German figure skater Katarina Witt won her second consecutive Olympic title.

→ Dutch speed skater Yvonne van Gennip's chances for Olympic victory seemed ruined when she was hospitalized two months before the Games, but she went on to win three gold medals and set two world records.

→ Swedish skier Gunde Svan took his career gold medal total to four.

Above: American diver Greg Louganis was arguably one of the greatest ever; he won two golds in 1988 despite cracking his head open on the springboard.

SEOUL

17 SEPTEMBER – 02 OCTOBER 1988   GAMES OF THE XXIV OLYMPIAD

Happily, the large-scale boycotts of Moscow and Los Angeles did not recur at Seoul. For the first time in 12 years, all leading Olympic nations, except Cuba and Ethiopia, took part in the Olympic Games. Although the drug disqualification of sprinter Ben Johnson became the biggest story of the 1988 Olympics, the Seoul Games were highlighted by numerous exceptional performances and 27 new world records. Once again the Soviet Union (55 gold medals) and East Germany (37) demonstrated their sporting superiority over the Western nations by finishing first and second in the medal table.

159 Number of nations
8,391 Number of athletes (6,197 men/2,194 women)
25 Number of sports **237** Number of events

SPORTING HIGHLIGHTS

→ American swimmer Matt Biondi won seven medals, including five gold. His gold medals came in the 50m and 100m freestyle, and all three relays.

→ Soviet pole-vaulter Serguei Bubka won his first gold medal, clearing 5.90m at the third attempt. Despite being a world record holder and dominating the sport for 14 years (1983–97), it was his only Olympic medal.

→ East German speed skater and cyclist Christa Luding-Rothenburger made Olympic history after becoming the first person to win Summer and Winter Olympic medals in the same year. After winning gold and silver in the speed skating at Calgary, she won silver in the 1,000m sprint cycling.

STAR PROFILE "FLO-JO"

At the 1988 Olympic Trials, American Florence Griffith Joyner ("Flo-Jo") ran the 100m in a stunning 10.49 seconds – beating the previous record by more than a quarter of a second. Her time was faster than the men's 100m record in many countries. Her records for the 100m and 200m look set to last for many years. At the Seoul Games, she ran in both relays, winning a third gold medal as well as a silver. In 1998, at the age of 38, she died in her sleep from an epileptic seizure.

Did you know that... Swedish fencer Kerstin Palm became the first woman to take part in seven Olympics. >>> For the first time, all three medallists in the equestrian dressage were women. >>> Tennis was reintroduced after a break of 64 years.

ALBERTVILLE

08–23 FEBRUARY 1992   XVI OLYMPIC WINTER GAMES

Albertville's successful bid to stage the Winter Olympics had been inspired by the French triple Olympic skiing champion of 1968, Jean-Claude Killy (see p.24), who was chairman of the organizing committee. Killy wanted to stimulate the economic development of the Savoy region. The results of political change in Eastern and Central Europe were clearly noticeable during the nations' parade. Lithuania competed under its own flag for the first time since 1928; likewise, Estonia and Latvia for the first time since 1936. Competitors from other parts of the former Soviet Union formed the Unified Team. For the first time in 28 years, athletes from Germany were reunited in a single team for the Winter Olympics.

64 Number of nations
1,801 Number of athletes (1,313 men/488 women)
7 Number of sports **57** Number of events

STAR PROFILE **ALBERTO TOMBA**

At the 1992 Games, charismatic Italian skier Alberto Tomba "la Bomba" took giant slalom gold to become the first Olympic Alpine skier to win the same event twice. He missed out on a double consecutive gold in the slalom by one place. Tomba was the first Alpine skier to win medals in three different Olympics and he was the first male Alpine skier to win five Olympic medals. In April 2000 he was awarded the Olympic Order.

Did you know that... Speed skiing, curling, ballet, and freestyle aerial skiing were demonstration sports at these Games. >>> Albertville saw Croatia and Slovenia, from the former Yugoslavia, participating for the first time as independent nations.

SPORTING HIGHLIGHTS

→ Freestyle skiing made its debut at the Olympics. The winner of the moguls event was the popular French freestyle skier Edgar Grospiron, who recorded the fastest time and the second best scores for turns and air.

→ Half of Italian cross-country skier Stefania Belmondo's home village (population: 160) turned out to cheer her on. She won gold in the final women's cross-country event, the 30km.

→ Vegard Ulvang of Norway took gold in the men's 30km cross-country race. In the 10km race he competed without wax on his skis for the first time in his career and won again.

BARCELONA

25 JULY – 09 AUGUST 1992   GAMES OF THE XXV OLYMPIAD

169 Number of nations
9,356 Number of athletes (6,652 men/2,704 women)
28 Number of sports **257** Number of events

STAR PROFILE **VITALY SCHERBO**

At the 1992 Games, 20-year-old Vitaly Scherbo of Belarus became the first gymnast to win six gold medals at one Olympics. He began by leading the ex-Soviet Union squad to victory in the team event. Next he put together a superb performance to win the individual all-round competition title. Then, on 2 August, Scherbo took part in the individual apparatus finals, becoming the first person in Olympic history to win four gold medals in one day.

Did you know that... For the first time since 1972, the Games were boycott-free. >>> Yugoslavia was banned from taking part in any team sports. >>> Badminton, women's judo, and baseball were all added to the Olympic programme.

Spanish IOC president Juan Antonio Samaranch brought the Games to his home city of Barcelona, expressing his gratitude to the Games' sponsors at the final celebrations. The IOC received millions of dollars in revenue from the sale of television broadcasting rights, although many athletes complained that the start times of many events were arranged to suit primetime television advertising slots. Teams from a post-apartheid South Africa and a unified Germany were welcomed back onto the world stage. Men's basketball was open to professionals for the first time, allowing the creation of an American "Dream Team", which included Magic Johnson, Michael Jordan, Larry Bird, and Charles Barkley.

SPORTING HIGHLIGHTS

→ Spaniard Fermin Cacho Ruiz was not one of the favourites in the 1,500m. Taking advantage of the fact that the race was run at an unusually slow pace, he started his sprint with half a lap to go and with the crowd behind him, took gold, becoming the first Spanish runner ever to win a gold medal.

→ Great Britain's Linford Christie is the oldest man (32 years) to win Olympic gold in the 100m. He added the World Championship title the following year.

→ In the closely fought women's 100m, Jamaican Merlene Ottey was just 0.06 seconds behind the winner yet still only finished in fifth place.

LILLEHAMMER

12-27 FEBRUARY 1994 XVII OLYMPIC WINTER GAMES

In 1986 the IOC voted to change the schedule of the Olympic Games so that the Summer and Winter Games could be held in different years. This was partly because the television companies could not attract the amount of advertising needed in order to pay for Olympic television broadcasting rights twice a year. From now on, the Winter Games would fall in the same year as football's World Cup finals. To adjust to this new schedule, the Lillehammer Games were held in 1994, the only time that two Games have been staged two years apart. Lillehammer was a small town of 21,000 inhabitants, but within four years the organizers had turned it into a first-rate Olympic site.

67 Number of nations
1,737 Number of athletes (1,215 men/522 women)
6 Number of sports **61** Number of events

STAR PROFILE **BJÖRN DÆHLIE**

Cross-country skier Björn Dæhlie holds several all-time Winter Olympics records. Competing over three Olympics during the 1990s, he is the only winter Olympian to win eight gold medals or twelve medals in total. He is also the only one to win six gold medals in individual events, or nine individual career medals. At the Lillehammer Olympics, Dæhlie won the 10km and combined pursuit races and took silver in the 30km and 4x10km relay.

SPORTING HIGHLIGHTS

→ Norwegian speed skater Johan Olav Koss won three gold medals in front of a lively home crowd, breaking the world record each time.

→ At her fourth Olympics, American Bonnie Blair made history by becoming the first female speed skater to win the 500m three consecutive times.

→ After her first attempt at the slalom, Switzerland's Alpine skier Vreni Schneider was in fifth place. She went on to take gold with a fantastic second run. Schneider also won a silver medal in the combined event and a bronze in the giant slalom.

Did you know that... The Bosnia and Herzegovina bobsleigh team consisted of two Bosnians, a Croat, and a Serb: a great example of Olympic spirit during difficult times. >>> The Games were christened the "White-Green Games" in honour of the environment.

ATLANTA

19 JULY - 04 AUGUST 1996 GAMES OF THE XXVI OLYMPIAD

197 Number of nations
10,318 Number of athletes (6,806 men/3,512 women)
26 Number of sports **271** Number of events

STAR PROFILE **MICHAEL JOHNSON**

American Michael Johnson, with his unique upright running style, was the first man to be ranked world number one at both the 200m and 400m, which he dominated after 1990. By 1996 he had won 54 400m finals and was unbeaten at that distance in seven years. Johnson won the 400m final by the widest margin (10 metres) for 100 years. He also ran a phenomenal 19.32 in the 200m, including the fastest 100m (9.2) ever recorded.

Did you know that... Each team that qualified for the football tournament was allowed to include three professionals, regardless of age or experience. >>> All 197 official National Olympic Committees (NOCs) were represented at the Games for the first time.

The 1996 Atlanta Games were given a poignant start when the cauldron was lit by a visibly shaking Muhammad Ali, by this time suffering from Parkinson's disease. On 27 July, during a concert held in the Centennial Olympic Park, a terrorist bomb killed one person and injured a further 110 people, but the Atlanta Games are best remembered for their sporting achievements, including Michael Johnson's extraordinary 200m and 400m double victory. A record-setting 79 nations won medals, 53 of them winning gold.

SPORTING HIGHLIGHTS

→ French runner Marie-José Pérec won the 200m and 400m, breaking the 400m Olympic record and becoming the first woman to win the 400m at two consecutive Olympics. She is the most successful French female athlete of all time.

→ Russian swimmer Aleksandr Popov won two gold medals in the 50m and 100m freestyle – overtaking American swimmer Gary Hall, Jr on both occasions – and two silver medals in the relays.

→ Naim Suleymanoglu of Turkey became the first weightlifter to win three consecutive Olympic titles.

→ American Michael Johnson's double gold over 200m and 400m was the first for a man in Olympic history.

NAGANO

07-22 FEBRUARY 1998 XVIII OLYMPIC WINTER GAMES

72 Number of nations
2,176 Number of athletes (1,389 men /787 women)
7 Number of sports **68** Number of events

STAR PROFILE HERMANN MAIER

Hermann Maier began representing Austria in 1996. During the downhill race in Nagano, he lost control and took a spectacular fall, flying more than 100 metres through the air. Three days later he won gold in the super-G slalom and then a second gold in the giant slalom.

Did you know that... For the first time, professional hockey players from the USA's NHL participated. >>> A 50% discount on all Olympic tickets was offered to schoolchildren. >>> Official staff uniforms were made from recyclable materials.

The Japanese city of Nagano, 90 minutes by train from Tokyo, was host to the final and biggest Winter Olympics of the 20th century, with 68 events in seven sports being held over a period of 16 days. A criticism of past Winter Games was that the competition sites were too far away from the Olympic village. The Nagano organizers ensured this was not the case by dividing the competition site into six areas, each of them within a 40-km (25-mile) radius of Nagano. As host nation, Japan rode a wave of enthusiasm from excited fans to win more gold medals at Nagano than it had won in the previous 70 years of Winter Games. Germany topped the medal table, followed by Norway and Russia.

SPORTING HIGHLIGHTS

→ Norwegian cross-country skier Björn Daehlie, the most successful male Nordic skier in Olympic history (see box, p.33), won the 10km pursuit and 50km, anchored the Norwegian team to victory in the 4x10km relay, and won silver in the combined pursuit event.

→ Japanese ski jumper Kazuyoshi Funaki won the silver medal in the normal hill event before obtaining perfect style points in the large hill event and taking gold.

→ Italian Deborah Compagnoni repeated her 1994 giant slalom victory and just missed out on gold in the slalom by 0.06 seconds, becoming the first Alpine skier to win gold medals in three separate Olympics.

SYDNEY

15 SEPTEMBER – 01 OCTOBER 2000 GAMES OF THE XXVII OLYMPIAD

The Sydney Games were the largest yet, with 10,651 athletes competing in 300 events. Despite their size, the Games were well organized, renewing faith in the Olympic Movement. Athletes from North and South Korea marched together under the same flag, while four athletes from East Timor (it only became a sovereign state in 2002) were allowed to participate under the Olympic flag as individual athletes. Cathy Freeman, an indigenous Australian, was given the honour of lighting the Olympic flame in the opening ceremony, and repaid the compliment by winning the 400m final in front of an ecstatic home crowd.

199 Number of nations
10,651 Number of athletes (6,582 men/4,069 women)
28 Number of sports **300** Number of events

STAR PROFILE STEVEN REDGRAVE

Steven Redgrave of Great Britain is the only rower to win five consecutive Olympic gold medals. In the Atlanta Games, Redgrave and partner Matthew Pinsent successfully defended their title to win the coxless pairs in their 100th race together. Redgrave won his fifth gold medal in the Sydney Games, at the age of 38, as a member of the coxless fours.

Did you know that... The first Sri Lankan woman to win a medal, Susanthika Jayasinghe, won bronze in the 200m. >>> Vietnam won its first medal since it first began competing in 1952, in women's taekwondo.

SPORTING HIGHLIGHTS

→ After being kept away from competitions for over a year by serious shoulder and back problems, French judo champion David Douillet won his second consecutive Olympic gold by beating Shinichi Shinohara of Japan in an exciting final.

→ 17-year-old Australian swimming sensation Ian Thorpe won his first gold medal in the 400m freestyle by breaking his own world record. He then swam the anchor leg in the 4x100m freestyle to win again. A third gold came from the 4x200m freestyle, and he added a silver medal in the 200m freestyle.

→ German canoeist Birgit Fischer (see p.36) won two golds in the K-2 and K-4 500m to become the first female Olympian to win medals 20 years apart.

SALT LAKE CITY

08-24 FEBRUARY 2002 XIX OLYMPIC WINTER GAMES

The Salt Lake City Games saw the winter programme grow to 78 events, including the skeleton (omitted since 1948) and women's bobsleigh. A record 18 nations won gold, including China and Australia for the first time. Highlights included Norwegian Ole Einar Bjorndalen winning quadruple gold across all biathlon events, Finn Samppa Lajunen winning triple gold across all Nordic combined events, and 20-year-old Swiss Simon Ammann winning both ski jump events. Canada won the men's and women's ice hockey – the men's victory over the US was their first gold for 50 years. By winning silver in the single luge, German Georg Hackl became the first Olympian to win a medal in the same event in five consecutive games.medals.

77 Number of nations
2,399 Number of athletes (1,513 men/886 women)
7 Number of sports **78** Number of events

SPORTING HIGHLIGHTS

→ Returning from knee surgery, Croatian Janica Kostelic became the first woman to win three Alpine gold medals at the same Games: in the combined, slalom, and giant slalom. She also won silver in the super-G.

→ Competing in the women's bobsleigh, American Vonetta Flowers became the first black athlete to win a gold medal at a Winter Games.

→ Australian Steven Bradbury won an unlikely gold in the short track speed skating final when the leading four crashed out on the final bend.

STAR PROFILE KJETIL ANDRÉ AAMODT

Norwegian Kjetil André Aamodt became the first Alpine skier in Olympic history to win seven medals in 2002, with Alpine golds in the super-G and the combined. He also won gold in the super-G in Turin 2006, making him the Alpine skier with the most Olympic titles.

Did you know that... These games saw the introduction of instant video replay in figure skating. >>> Two golds were awarded in pairs figure skating instead of gold and silver. >>> These were the first games under the presidency of Jacques Rogge.

ATHENS

13-29 AUGUST 2004 GAMES OF THE XXVIII OLYMPIAD

In 2004 the Olympic Games returned to Greece, home of both the ancient Olympics and the first modern Olympics. For the first time ever, a record 201 National Olympic Committees (NOCs) participated in the Olympic Games. The overall tally for events on the programme was 301 (one more than in Sydney 2000). The popularity of the Games soared to new heights as 3.9 billion people had access to the television coverage, compared to 3.6 billion for Sydney 2000.

201 Number of nations
11,099 Number of athletes (6,458 men/4,551 women)
28 Number of sports **301** Number of events

SPORTING HIGHLIGHTS

→ Moroccan Hicham El Guerrouj became the first runner since Paavo Nurmi in 1924 to win both the 1,500m and the 5,000m. In the 1,500m, he was passed by Bernard Lagat in the home stretch, but came back to win. In the 5,000m, he came from behind to defeat 10,000m champion Kenenisa Bekele.

→ Turkish weightlifter Nurcan Taylan won the gold medal in the women's 48kg category. She was the first Turkish woman in any sport to win an Olympic championship.

→ Argentina's men's basketball team put an end to the domination of the US's professionals, defeating them 89–81 in the semi-finals. The Argentinians went on to beat Italy 84–69 in the final.

→ German canoeist Birgit Fischer became the youngest and oldest Olympic canoeing gold medallist, winning her gold medals – in K-1 and K-4 500m – 24 years apart, and the first female athlete to win gold in six different Olympics.

STAR PROFILE MICHAEL PHELPS

US Swimmer Michael Phelps won six gold and two bronze medals at Athens. He went on to top that achievement in Beijing, winning a record eight events. Phelps has the perfect physique for a swimmer, with a long torso and arms, short legs, and large, flexible feet. During his training regime, he eats up to 10,000 calories a day – five times a normal adult's intake of food.

Did you know that... Kenya's runners swept the medals in the 3,000m steeplechase, taking gold, silver, and bronze. >>> The marathon followed the same route as in 1896, beginning in Marathon and ending in Athens's Panathenaic Stadium.

TURIN

10-26 FEBRUARY 2006 XX OLYMPIC WINTER GAMES

80 Number of nations
2,508 Number of athletes (1,548 men/960 women)
7 Number of sports **84** Number of events

STAR PROFILE **KATERINA NEUMANNOVA**

Czech cross-country skier Katerina Neumannova first competed in the Games in 1992, but it was not until her third Winter Games that she won her first medals. Because she also competed in the mountain bike event at the 1996 Atlanta Games, the Turin Games were the sixth in which she participated. On 12 February, she won a silver medal in the pursuit. On 24 February, Neumannova won her first gold medal in the 30km race, at the age of 33.

Did you know that... For the first time, live video coverage of the Olympic Games was available on mobile phones. >>> With a population of more than 900,000, Turin became the largest city ever to host the Winter Olympic Games.

A record 2,508 athletes from 80 nations competed at the Turin Winter Games with a record 26 countries taking home medals. The Austrians dominated the Alpine skiing, winning 14 of the 30 medals. South Korea displayed similar success in the short track speed skating, winning 10 of the 24 medals. During the cross-country team sprint, Canadian Sara Renner broke one of her poles. Seeing her struggle, the Norwegian head coach Bjørnar Håkensmoen gave her one of his, which allowed Renner to help her team win silver, and dropped Norway out of the medals.

SPORTING HIGHLIGHTS

→ Philipp Schoch was the favourite to defend his Olympic title in the snowboarding parallel giant slalom, but faced a tough challenger in his older brother, Simon. They both qualified for the final play-off, with Philipp taking his second consecutive gold.

→ The men's ice hockey tournament saw the first all-Scandinavian final as Finland took on Sweden. In the final, Nicklas Lidstrom scored 10 seconds into the final period to give Sweden the lead, and they held on to seal the victory.

→ Local favourite Enrico Fabri won bronze in the 5,000m speed skating, becoming the first Italian to win a medal in this event.

BEIJING

08-24 AUGUST 2008 GAMES OF THE XXIX OLYMPIAD

The 29th Olympiad officially started at eight minutes past eight in the evening on 8 August 2008. Eight is a lucky number in China, and luck certainly held with the weather, as the heavily polluted Chinese capital enjoyed its cleanest air for ten years. The huge building programme for the Olympics included the construction of 12 new venues and a doubling of the capacity of the Beijing underground. The centrepiece was the spectacular 90,000-seater National Stadium, dubbed the "Bird's Nest". Nine new events were held, including BMX cycling, marathon open-water swimming, and the women's 3,000m steeplechase. The medals table was topped by the hosts, who won 51 gold medals.

204 Number of nations
11,196 Number of athletes (6,450 men/4,746 women)
28 Number of sports **302** Number of events

STAR PROFILE **USAIN BOLT**

Jamaican sprinter Usain Bolt broke the world record in three events at Beijing. He won the 100m with a time of 9.69 seconds, and could have run even faster had he not begun celebrating victory 15m from the finish line. Four days later, he took the 200m in 19.30 seconds, breaking Michael Johnson's 12-year-old record. He completed a sprinting clean sweep in the 4x100m relay. Bolt was the first man since fellow-Jamaican Don Quarrie to hold the world record for both the 100 and 200 metres.

A team of 70,000 helped keep the Beijing Games running smoothly. >>> Cuba's Angel Valodia Matos saved his best move until after his taekwondo bout had ended. Angry at his disqualification, Valodia Matos landed a kick right in the referee's face.

SPORTING HIGHLIGHTS

→ Usain Bolt's outstretched arms as he turned to the crowd in the final stages of the 100m final provide the abiding image of the games. Bolt (21) destroyed the field in both the 100 and 200 metres. (see box).

→ Michael Phelps won all eight of the swimming events he entered, breaking Mark Spitz's 36-year-old record for the most gold medals in a single games. He broke the world record in four of his five individual events.

→ Chris Hoy led the way in the velodrome as a dominant British team took seven of the ten indoor cycling gold medals. Hoy, also a seven-time world champion, bagged three golds, the first British athlete to do so since 1908.

VANCOUVER

12-28 FEBRUARY 2010   XXI OLYMPIC WINTER GAMES

The Winter Games continued to grow at Vancouver 2010 with a record number of athletes, events, and nations – including first-timers the Cayman Islands, Colombia, Ghana, Montenegro, Pakistan, and Peru. The opening ceremony was dedicated to 21-year-old Georgian luger Nodar Kumaritashvili, who had died just hours earlier following a crash during training. Chastened by tragedy, public and competitors alike made Vancouver 2010 an explosive, joyous celebration in his memory. Canada put its failure to win a single gold medal in two previous Games as hosts well and truly behind it, setting a record for host-nation success by topping the medals table with 14 golds. Meanwhile, Slovakia and Belarus also won their first golds at a Winter Games.

SPORTING HIGHLIGHTS

→ Norwegian Marit Bjorgen confirmed her status as the most successful female cross-country skier of the modern era. She topped the medals table with three golds, a silver, and a bronze, taking her overall Olympic medal tally to seven.

→ Team Canada capped a record-breaking Winter Games for a host nation by beating neighbours USA in the men's ice hockey. The final gold medal of the Games was won in overtime with a goal from star player Sidney Crosby.

→ Slovenian Petra Majdic won bronze in the cross-country sprint despite breaking five ribs and damaging a lung after falling into a gully. She said of her medal: "Today, this is not a bronze. This is a gold with little diamonds on it".

82 Number of nations
2,536 Number of athletes (1,503 men/1,033 women)
7 Number of sports   **86** Number of events

STAR PROFILE KIM YU-NA

19-year-old South Korean figure skater Kim Yu-Na won her gold medal in breathtaking fashion, scoring a world record 150.86 points for her free skate. Her combined total of 228.56 points was also a new record, beating silver-medal winner Mao Asada of Japan by a massive 23 points. Her routine was acclaimed as "destined to be remembered for as long as Torvill and Dean's famous Bolero in 1984."

Did you know that... With a total of 2.3 million inhabitants, Vancouver became the largest city to host the Winter Games. >>> Environmental measures included real-time tracking and publication of the energy consumption of each Olympic venue.

Below: Norway's Marit Bjorgen edges out Anna Olsson of Sweden to win the cross-country individual sprint final in Vancouver.

LONDON

27 JULY–12 AUGUST 2012   GAMES OF THE XXX OLYMPIAD

204 Number of nations
10,383 Number of athletes (5,814 men/4,569 women)
26 Number of sports   **302** Number of events

STAR PROFILE SHIWEN YE

The 16-year old Chinese swimmer Shiwen Ye announced herself to the world in sensational fashion, winning gold in both the 200m and 400m individual medley. More impressive than the medals themselves were her winning times – she set an Olympic record for the 200m and a world record for the 400m, knocking one second off the previous record. Ye's improved performances were attributed to a 12cm (4.7in) growth spurt she experienced in the two years before the games.

Did you know that... 8,000 people took turns to carry the Olympic torch around Britain, covering an average distance of 300m (328 yards) each. >>> London has now hosted three Olympic Games, more than any other city in the world.

The 2012 London Games saw two breakthroughs in equality for competitors: female athletes participated in every sport on the calendar for the first time and the South African sprinter Oscar Pistorius became the first amputee runner to appear in an Olympics. However, there was also controversy. In the opening round of the badminton women's doubles, four pairs – two from South Korea and one each from China and Indonesia – attempted to secure a favourable draw by playing badly and were disqualified. Perhaps the most memorable aspect of the Games was the opening ceremony, a spectacular history of Britain created by the Oscar-winning film director Danny Boyle.

SPORTING HIGHLIGHTS

→ The American swimmer Michael Phelps (see p.35) won four gold medals, taking his tally of Olympic golds to 18. He retired at the end of the Games, the most successful athlete in Olympic history.

→ For the host nation, the highlight of the Games was undoubtedly Saturday, 4 August, also known as "Super Saturday", the day on which Great Britain secured six gold medals and one silver medal.

→ Usain Bolt repeated his extraordinary feat of 2008 (see p.36), winning gold in the 100m, 200m, and the 4x100m relay. Bolt was thrilled by his achievement, describing himself as "the greatest athlete of all time" and "a living legend".

SOCHI

7–23 FEBRUARY 2014   XXII OLYMPIC WINTER GAMES

The 22nd Winter Games will be held in the Russian city of Sochi, the first Olympic competition to take place in Russia since the break-up of the Soviet Union in 1991. The city is located on the coast of the Black Sea near the Russian-Georgian border and is best known amongst Russians as a summer beach resort. All ice-based events will be held in Sochi itself in purpose-built venues such as the Bolshoy Ice Dome, a 12,000 capacity ice-rink with a design based on the shape of a frozen water droplet. Mountain sports will be held 40km (25 miles) inland at the Rosa Khutor ski resort in the Western Caucasus mountains.

LOOKING AHEAD

→ The Sochi Olympic Park will be located in Sochi itself, on the coast of the Black Sea. It will hold 75,000 spectators at maximum capacity.

→ The 2014 Winter Games will have three mascots – a leopard, a hare, and a polar bear. All of these animals are indigenous to southern Russia.

→ It is estimated that 3.5 billion people worldwide will watch Sochi 2014 on television.

→ Sochi's subtropical climate means it will be the warmest city ever to host a Winter Olympics.

STAR PROFILE VOLOSOZHAR AND TRANKOV

Prior to forming a partnership, the Russian pair figure skaters Tatiana Volosozhar and Maxim Trankov enjoyed moderate success with other partners. Since joining forces in 2010, however, the duo have established themselves as serious contenders. They won gold at the 2012 and 2013 European Figure Skating Championships and in 2013 they were crowned world champions, bettering their consecutive runner-up finishes at the 2010–11 and 2011–12 championships. They will be part of a determined effort by the host nation to top the medal table at the Winter Games in Sochi. Russia recorded a worst-ever finish of 11th at the Vancouver Winter Games in 2010.

Did you know that... The Sochi Winter Games is the most commercially profitable Olympic competition in history, attracting over $1 billion of sponsorship. >>> The city of Sochi sits at the same latitude as the famously balmy city of Nice in France.

Above: The British heptathlete Jessica Ennis was one of six competitors to win gold for the host nation on "Super Saturday" at the 2012 Olympics in London.

RIO DE JANEIRO

rio2016
CANDIDATE CITY

5-21 AUGUST 2016   GAMES OF THE XXXI OLYMPIAD

STAR PROFILE KIRANI JAMES

At the age of 14, Grenada's Kirani James established his reputation as a future star of the track when he ran the 400m in 46.96s, the fastest time ever recorded by an athlete of that age. James confirmed his talent by finishing first at the 2011 World Championships and went on to secure a first ever Olympic medal for Grenada at the London 2012 Games, winning gold in the 400 meters. James will be 23 years old at the 31st Games in Rio, where he will be hoping to defend his gold medal and threaten Michael Johnson's long-standing 400m world record of 43.13s.

Did you know that... The Maracana Stadium has a record high-attendance of 199,854 (before conversion to seated-only), for a World Cup match in 1950. >>> Brazil is the first Portuguese-speaking country to host the Olympic Games.

The 31st Games in Rio de Janeiro will be the first Olympics to take place in South America and the first to be held during the host city's winter. Two new sports have been admitted – rugby sevens (see pp.126–27) and golf (see pp.320–25). Golf has not featured in an Olympic programme since 1904 and several of the sport's top professional players, including Tiger Woods, are expected to compete for medals. Barra da Tijuca, a prosperous area located in the southwest of Rio, will be home to most of the Olympic venues, as well as the athletes' village. Other Rio landmarks will feature in the Games: the iconic Maracana Stadium, with a seated capacity of 80,000, will host the football tournament and the opening and closing ceremonies.

LOOKING AHEAD

→ The Olympic Park in Barra da Tijuca will be built on a former grand prix track and cover an area of more than 300 acres.

→ The 4km (2.5 mile) stretch of the world-famous Copacabana Beach will host the triathlon, open water swimming, and beach volleyball.

→ The logo for the 2016 Olympic Games is based on the shape of Sugarloaf Mountain, a Rio de Janeiro landmark that overlooks Guanabara Bay.

→ The football tournament will take place around Brazil in some of the country's largest cities such as São Paulo and Brasília, the federal capital.

THE PARA ALYMPICS

The Paralympic Games is an Olympiad for athletes with disabilities. Initially conceived as a sports event for World War II veterans with spinal cord injuries, the first major version of the competition was held in Rome in 1960 and featured approximately 400 competitors from 23 nations. Three athletes competed in each event, meaning all of them were guaranteed a medal. At first, the Paralympics was restricted to athletes in a wheelchair but the 1976 Paralympics in Toronto, Canada, was opened up to athletes with a range of disabilities, resulting in competitor numbers rising from approximately 1,000 to 1,600. The first Winter Paralympics was held in Sweden in the same year. Both the Summer and Winter Paralympics now take place in the same year and in the same city as their Olympic equivalents. The Winter Paralympics is a smaller spectacle comprised of six core events – alpine skiing, ice sledge hockey, Nordic skiing, biathlon (skiing and shooting), cross-country skiing, and wheelchair curling.

SPORTING HIGHLIGHTS

→ The 2012 Summer Paralympics in London included 21 sports, many of which also feature on the core Olympic programme – for example, judo, rowing, swimming, and table tennis.

→ Sports appearing only in the Summer Paralympic programme include several disability-specific events such as boccia, a sport similar to bowls, and petanque, contested by wheelchair-bound athletes.

→ The United States is the most successful nation in the history of the Summer Paralympics with a total of 1,939 medals, 697 of them gold, while Germany tops the Winter Paralympic medal table having won a total of 330 medals, including 121 golds.

→ With 55 medals (41 gold, 9 silver, and 5 bronze), the American swimmer Trischa Zorn is the most successful individual in Paralympic history.

Did you know that... "The Paralympics" is short for "the Parallel Games", reflecting founder Sir Ludwig Guttmann's ambition for an elite equivalent to the Olympics for disabled athletes. >>> The youngest Paralympian ever, swimmer Joanne Round, was just 12 when she competed in the 1988 Games in Seoul, South Korea. She won two golds and a silver.

Below: World number one Marie Bochet of France competes in the 2010 Winter Paralympics Downhill Standing ski competition.

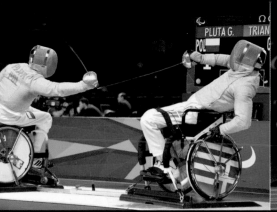

Above: Grzegorz Pluta of Poland attacks Panagiotis Triantafyllou of Greece in the men's sabre wheelchair fencing at the 2012 Paralympics.
Above right: Jonnie Peacock of the UK outstrips Richard Browne of the US and Arnu Fourie of South Africa in the 100m T44 sprint at London 2012.

HOW CLASSIFICATION WORKS

To ensure fair competition, Paralympians are separated into four broad categories – amputee, cerebral palsy, visual impairment or blindness, and spinal injuries or other physical disabilities. Once the athletes have been grouped in this way, a more rigorous process of classification take place: prior to the Games, an expert panel observes every athlete performing a series of sports-specific tasks, enabling them to assess the competitor's ability.

AN EVEN PLAYING FIELD

The focus of these assessments depends on the sport in which the athlete is competing; in equestrian events, for example, there is an emphasis on understanding how the rider's disability affects control of their trunk. A letter-and-number code is used as a shorthand to express the nature of the event and the disabilities of the athletes competing in it. For example, F31–38 designates a field event (F) for Paralympians with conditions that affect the trunk and limbs (31–38), such as cerebral palsy. Certain sports, such as seated volleyball (see below), allow athletes from different categories to compete against each other.

THE CRITERIA

Every sport places different physical demands on the competitors, meaning classification criteria must be tailored to the event in question. The table below outlines how track and field athletes are classified.

TRACK AND FIELD CLASSIFICATION	
CLASS	**CRITERIA**
11–13	Athletes with visual impairments, with 11 signifying the greatest impairment and 13 the least.
20	Athletes with intellectual impairments.
31–38	Athletes with conditions which affect control of the trunk and limbs – a lower number indicates a more severe impairment. Athletsassed 31–34 compete in a seated position.
40	Athletes with short stature i.e. dwarfism.
42–46	Athletes with limb deficiencies, such as amputations. Numbers 42–44 indicate that the legs are affected, while 45–46 involve impairments to the arms.
51–58	Athletes competing in a wheelchair. Athletes in classes 51–54 have no trunk or leg function and varying function of the upper limbs. Athletes in classes 55–58 have increased trunk and leg function.

Below: Competitors at the 2008 and 2012 Paralympics in Beijing and London. Seated volleyball (below left) uses a net roughly 1m (3ft) high; visually impaired athletes run with a guide (below centre); while in swimming (below right), most of the rules are the same as for able-bodied competitions.

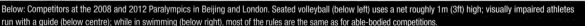

Above left: Tobias Graf of Germany competes in the C123 cycling time trial. Above centre: Japanese ice sledge-hockey player Kazuhiro Takahashi propels himself across the ice with sharpened hockey sticks. Above right: wheelchair rugby is fiercely contested in custom-made reinforced wheelchairs.

ADAPTABLE ATHLETES

Specialized equipment has a major part to play in the Paralympics. Each classification category has its own technological requirements for helping athletes adapt their bodies for elite sport. Wheelchair science is now highly advanced and the top wheelchair basketball teams, for example, benefit from light and manoeuvrable aluminium and carbon-fibre chairs that have been custom-built for each player. In the future, sophisticated technology may make athletes independent of assistants: for example the sighted guides who run with visually-impaired runners may be replaced by headsets equipped with sensors.

Controversy sometimes surrounds the issue of specialized equipment. Developing countries are unable to afford the cutting-edge technology enjoyed by athletes from wealthier nations. The question is increasingly being asked whether prosthetics, such as the carbon-fibre "blades" used by amputees, can actually enhance the performance of a disabled athlete beyond that of able-bodied ones. Prosthetics are limited to bringing the athlete to the stature or ability that they may have possessed without their disability, for example matching blades to original leg length.

STAR PROFILE ORAZIO FAGONE

Orazio Fagone, the speed skater and sledge-hockey player from the Italian island of Sicily, is the only Paralympian to have also won an Olympic medal, a feat he achieved before an accident resulted in him becoming disabled. Fagone began his Olympic career at the Calgary Winter Olympics in Canada in 1988, finishing third in the 1500m and second in the 5000m speed skating demonstration events. Short-track speed skating was ratified as a full Olympic sport at the 1992 Winter Olympics at Albertville in France, and Fagone went on to win gold as part of the Italian men's 5000m relay at the Lillehammer Winter Olympics in Norway in 1994. In 1997, however, Fagone's right leg was amputated after a serious motorcycle crash. He has since competed as a member of the Italian ice sledge-hockey team – the Paralympic equivalent of ice hockey – at two Paralympic Winter Games, in 2006 in Turin, Italy, and in 2010 in Vancouver, Canada.

Some sports appear only in the Paralympics, not in the Olympic Games, such as boccia and goalball. Below left: amputee athlete Josh Vander Vies of Canada throws a boccia ball. Below right: Japan's Akiko Adachi defends the goal, detecting the ball's location by the sound of the bells inside.

THE GREATEST PARALYMPIAN

OCTOBER 1988 – MAY 2007   THE CAREER OF A CHAMPION

Britain's Dame Tanni Grey-Thompson, who retired from competitive sport in May 2007, is one of the world's greatest Paralympians. Born with spina bifida, she was confined to a wheelchair from the age of seven – but this did not hinder her athletic career. She began wheelchair racing at the age of 13 and, during a glittering career, she competed in the widest possible range of disciplines – from 100m to the marathon – achieving great success in all. She held 30 world records, won the London Marathon six times between 1997 and 2002, and in the course of five Paralympics won 16 medals, including 11 golds. She was made a Dame of the British Empire in 2005 in recognition of her achievements in disabled sport and in 2010 she was sworn into the House of Lords as a life peer.

TANNI'S PARALYMPIC ROLL OF HONOUR

YEAR	HOST COUNTRY	MEDALS
2004	ATHENS	2 GOLD
2000	SYDNEY	4 GOLD
1996	ATLANTA	1 GOLD AND 3 SILVER
1992	BARCELONA	4 GOLD AND 1 SILVER
1988	SEOUL	1 BRONZE

OTHER ACHIEVEMENTS

FIRST WOMAN TO BREAK ONE-MINUTE BARRIER FOR 400M

WINNER OF 13 WORLD CHAMPIONSHIP MEDALS

FIRST WOMAN TO BREAK TWO-HOUR BARRIER FOR MARATHON

Below: Tanni Grey-Thompson storms over the line to win the first of her two gold medals at the Summer Paralympics in Athens, in September 2004, determination etched on her face. It is that determination which saw her break 20 world records in a 20-year career at the pinnacle of disabled sport.

THE SPORTS

ATHLETICS

01

TRACK AND FIELD

SPORT OVERVIEW

Track and field, also known as athletics, consists of three types of event: track events (running or walking), field events (jumping or throwing), and combined events, such as the pentathlon, which are a combination of both track and field events. Track and field is at the core of the Olympic movement and featured at the first games at Olympia in 776BCE. The popularity of track and field events wavered during Roman times, but athletics again dominated the first modern Games.

INDOORS AND OUTDOORS

Track and field events are held either indoors (during the winter) or outdoors (in the spring and summer). The majority of events are held at both indoor and outdoor meets, although there are exceptions. Limited space at indoor venues means that throws such as the javelin, hammer, and discus are only contested during the outdoor season. A smaller indoor track also means that the 100m is replaced by the 60m sprint.

MEASURE FOR MEASURE

Accurately measuring time and distance is a crucial part of track and field events. For track events, athletes are timed using sensors linked to cameras, and measured using Fully Automatic Time. For the long jump, triple jump, and throwing events, distances are measured using a certified steel measuring tape.

KEEPING SCORE
Moveable electronic scoreboards are placed around the track, enabling athletes, officials, and spectators to see how much time has elapsed since the start of a race.

PHOTO FINISH
A digital line-scan camera (trained on the finish line and linked to a computerized timing sensor) determines competitor placings. It is accurate to thousandths of a second.

STARTER PISTOL
Track and field events are started by the firing of a starting pistol. The sound of the gun, which contains blank shells, is a signal to the athletes to begin. The gun automatically starts the timers.

NEED2KNOW

→ The word "athlete" comes from the Greek word "athlos", meaning a contest or competition.

→ The first athletics event at the first ancient Olympiad was the "stade" race – a sprint along the full length of the stadium (a distance of approximately 192m/210yd).

→ The order in which track and field events are competed at an official meet is determined by a random draw.

3,000m steeplechase start line
During the steeplechase, athletes must run seven and a half laps, clear 28 hurdles, and leap seven water jumps

Long jump/triple jump
The run-up track must be at at least 40m (131ft) long and the landing pit at least 9m (29ft 6in) long

5,000m start
Athletes run 200m (breaking lanes almost immediately) and then complete 12 laps of the track

200m start line
Slightly staggered starting positions at the beginning of the 200m sprint ensure that all competitors complete the same distance

Discus
The landing area fans out at an angle of just 35 degrees, which limits the danger posed by an errant throw

Water jump
A water jump situated just inside the running track is incorporated into the steeplechase event

Hammer
A wire cage, partly surrounding the throwing circle, protects officials and spectators from any dangerous throws

110m hurdles start line
The men's hurdle event has a start as explosive as the 100m sprint

100m/100m hurdles start line
Competitors must remain in their allocated lanes at all times

TRACK AND FIELD ARENA

A full-size track usually measures 400m in circumference, has six or eight lanes, and encircles a sports pitch that contains specific areas for each field sport. Most tracks have a synthetic rubber or polyurethane surface for year-round use. Indoor tracks are usually only 200m in circumference, have four or six lanes, and have banked turns to accommodate bends that are far tighter than on an outdoor track. Whether competing indoors or outdoors, athletes always race around the track in an anti-clockwise direction. Due to space constraints, indoor field events consist of only the jumps and the shot put.

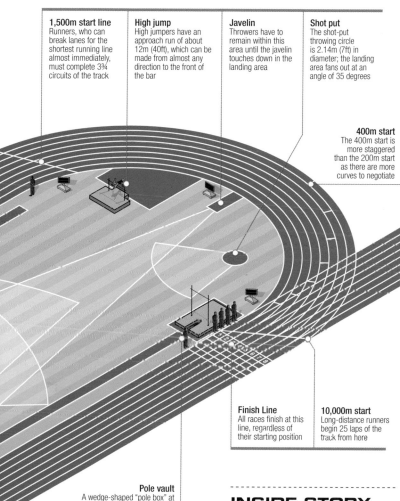

1,500m start line Runners, who can break lanes for the shortest running line almost immediately, must complete 3¾ circuits of the track

High jump High jumpers have an approach run of about 12m (40ft), which can be made from almost any direction to the front of the bar

Javelin Throwers have to remain within this area until the javelin touches down in the landing area

Shot put The shot-put throwing circle is 2.14m (7ft) in diameter; the landing area fans out at an angle of 35 degrees

400m start The 400m start is more staggered than the 200m start as there are more curves to negotiate

Finish Line All races finish at this line, regardless of their starting position

10,000m start Long-distance runners begin 25 laps of the track from here

Pole vault A wedge-shaped "pole box" at the end of the track is sunk to a depth of 20cm (8in)

INSIDE STORY

As well as being fundamental to the Olympic movement, athletics is a glamourous sport that can earn top athletes literally millions of dollars. The IAAF Golden League – an annual event run by the sport's governing body – has a $1 million prize fund up for grabs, with the jackpot being shared between the athletes who win their event at all six meetings during the season (although the award structure varies from season to season). During the 2000/2001 league, the prize money was even replaced by gold bars weighing in at 50kg (110lb).

DRUGS TESTING

The use of performance-enhancing drugs – especially in athletics – never fails to make headline news. In a constant battle to promote fair play, the International Association of Athletics Federations runs a stringent doping control programme to detect improper use of drugs such as anabolic steroids. In 1999, an independent foundation called the World Anti-Doping Agency (WADA) was also set up by the International Olympic Committee.

STAT CENTRAL

OLYMPIC TRACK EVENTS

EVENT	GENDER
100M	M & W
200M	M & W
400M	M & W
100M HURDLES	W
110M HURDLES	M
400M HURDLES	M & W
4 X 100M RELAY	M & W
4 X 400M RELAY	M & W
800M	M & W
1,500M	M & W
3,000M STEEPLECHASE	M & W
5,000M	M & W
10,000M	M & W
MARATHON	M & W
20KM WALK	M & W
50KM WALK	M

OLYMPIC FIELD EVENTS

EVENT	GENDER
DISCUS	M & W
JAVELIN	M & W
HAMMER THROW	M & W
SHOT PUT	M & W
POLE VAULT	M & W
HIGH JUMP	M & W
LONG JUMP	M & W
TRIPLE JUMP	M & W

OLYMPIC COMBINED EVENTS

EVENT	GENDER
DECATHLON	M
HEPTATHLON	W

A STELLA PERFORMANCE

POLISH-BORN ATHLETE STANISLAWA WALASIEWICZ (ALSO KNOWN AS STELLA WALSH) WON GOLD IN THE WOMEN'S 100M AT THE 1932 OLYMPICS IN LOS ANGELES. SHE WENT ON TO SECURE SILVER FOUR YEARS LATER AT THE GAMES IN BERLIN. HOWEVER, AN AUTOPSY CARRIED OUT ON HER BODY – AFTER SHE WAS TRAGICALLY KILLED BY A STRAY BULLET DURING AN ARMED ROBBERY IN A SHOPPING MALL IN 1980 – SHOWED THAT SHE POSSESSED MALE GENITALIA AND BOTH MALE AND FEMALE CHROMOSONES. DESPITE THESE REVELATIONS, STELLA WALSH'S RECORDS STILL STAND.

SPRINTS

EVENT OVERVIEW

At athletics events it is usually the sprints – which are run over 60, 100, 200, and 400 metres – that most firmly grip the spectators' imagination. And it is as if the world stops for the Olympic 100m men's final: there is something mesmerizing – almost primeval – about the competitors exploding out of the blocks, sprinting as fast as is humanly possible, and then streaking across the finishing line a mere ten seconds or so later.

GREATEST RACE?

THE 1996 ATLANTA OLYMPICS MEN'S 100M FINAL IS CONSIDERED ONE OF THE GREATEST SPRINTS EVER. THE FAVOURITE, DONOVAN BAILEY, RECOVERED FROM A POOR START TO WIN THE RACE AND SET A WORLD RECORD OF 9.84 SECONDS.

RUNNING IN LANES

For all the sprints, runners must remain in their starting lane for the duration of the race. At the start of events that involve rounding one or more bends (the 200m and the 400m), the competitors are "staggered" to ensure that each runner travels exactly the same distance.

Body position
To maintain maximum speed, the upper body should be still, upright, and relaxed

Born fast
Sprinters usually have more "fast-twitch" muscle fibres than the average person. This type of muscle fibre provides short bursts of power but fatigues rapidly

No socks
As the foot should have very little room to move inside the shoe, many athletes do not wear socks

Good grip
Lightweight shoes with spikes provide maximum traction

Dressed for speed
Close-fitting, streamlined spandex body suits reduce wind resistance and allow excellent freedom of movement

ATHLETE PROFILE

Sprinters' leg muscles are highly developed to provide explosive power. The upper body is also muscular because, according to the laws of biomechanics, the forces created by the striding legs must be equal and opposite to those created by the swinging arms. Sharp reflexes are needed to react quickly to the starter's gun.

SIDELINES

20 The number of years Jesse Owens of the United States held the 100m world record with his time of 10.3 seconds at the 1936 Olympic Games. Owens is considered one of the finest athletes ever and once defeated a racehorse over 91m (100yd).

53 The number of times Maurice Greene (United States) legally ran the 100m in less than 10 seconds.

33 British athlete Linford Christie's age when he won the 100m at the 1993 World Championships.

0.33 The winning margin, in seconds, achieved by Michael Johnson of the United States in the 200m at the 1991 and the 1995 World Championships. This was the largest difference at this level since Jesse Owen's winning margin of 0.4 in the 200m at the 1936 Olympic Games.

SPRINTING KIT

Sprinters wear an aerodynamically efficient spandex body suit and very light shoes that feature spikes up to 9mm (1/3in) long and a thin sole, which improves the competitor's feel for the track. Starting blocks allow athletes to drive forwards powerfully at the starter's gun and to begin the race in the best position to achieve maximum acceleration.

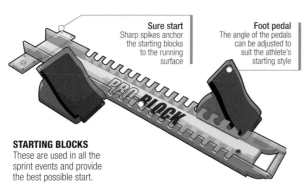

Sure start
Sharp spikes anchor the starting blocks to the running surface

Foot pedal
The angle of the pedals can be adjusted to suit the athlete's starting style

STARTING BLOCKS
These are used in all the sprint events and provide the best possible start.

THE SPRINT DISTANCES

There are four sprint distances. The 60m, which is usually run indoors, favours runners with electrifying speed but not necessarily high endurance. Unofficially defining the "fastest person on Earth", the 100m rewards sprinters who can quickly achieve and then maintain maximum speed. This demands tremendous muscular power and finely honed technique. All the skills of a 100m runner are needed by 200m runners, with the additional ability to manage centrifugal forces when rounding the bend. They must start strongly yet have sufficient energy to finish well. Described as an endurance sprint, the 400m is the most gruelling of all the sprints. Careful pacing of this race is vital because after about 30 seconds of running at near maximum effort, lactic acid builds up in the muscles, making it more difficult and more painful to maintain speed.

FACTORS AFFECTING PERFORMANCE

A sprinter recording fast times will have talent, a powerful physique, good tactical awareness, will have trained hard, and will be in good form – physically and mentally. Other factors that may influence performance include the track type (harder surfaces produce faster times) and climatic conditions, particularly wind speed and direction.

RACE PHASES

A sprint can be divided into four phases: the start (see below), acceleration (the body leans forwards, so that the legs can provide maximum acceleration), stride (full speed has been achieved and is maintained via a relaxed technique, with the body now upright), and finish (the arms are pulled back so that the head and shoulders dip towards the finish line).

Shoulders forward
The shoulders are directly above or a little in front of the hands

Pumping arms
The arms drive hard to propel the athlete forwards quickly

Head down
Watching the track helps the sprinter maintain a low position

THE START
To begin the race with good balance and maximum velocity is the objective.

On your marks
The sprinter crouches on one knee, feet on the pedals of the blocks

Ready position
The fingers form a high bridge, with the hands slightly more than shoulder width apart

Set
At the command of "set", the hips are raised a little higher than the shoulders

Go
On the starter's gun, the sprinter explodes out of the starting blocks

STAT CENTRAL

MEN'S 100M: FASTEST TIMES

TIME	ATHLETE (COUNTRY)
9.58	USAIN BOLT (JAM)
9.69	TYSON GAY (USA)
9.69	YOHAN BLAKE (JAM)
9.72	ASAFA POWELL (JAM)
9.78	NESTA CARTER (JAM)

MEN'S 200M: FASTEST TIMES

TIME	ATHLETE (COUNTRY)
19.19	USAIN BOLT (JAM)
19.26	YOHAN BLAKE (JAM)
19.32	MICHAEL JOHNSON (USA)
19.53	WALTER DIX (USA)
19.58	TYSON GAY (USA)

MEN'S 400M: FASTEST TIMES

TIME	ATHLETE (COUNTRY)
43.18	MICHAEL JOHNSON (USA)
43.29	HARRY (BUTCH) REYNOLDS (USA)
43.45	JEREMY WARINER (USA)
43.50	QUINCY WATTS (USA)
43.75	LASHAWN MERRITT (USA)

WOMEN'S 100M: FASTEST TIMES

TIME	ATHLETE (COUNTRY)
10.49	FLORENCE GRIFFITH JOYNER (USA)
10.64	CARMELITA JETER (USA)
10.65	MARION JONES (USA)
10.70	SHELLY-ANN FRASER-PRICE (JAM)
10.73	CHRISTINE ARRON (FRA)

WOMEN'S 200M: FASTEST TIMES

TIME	ATHLETE (COUNTRY)
21.34	FLORENCE GRIFFITH-JOYNER (USA)
21.62	MARION JONES (USA)
21.64	MERLENE OTTEY (JAM)
21.69	ALLYSON FELIX (USA)
21.71	MARITA KOCH (GER)

WOMEN'S 400M: FASTEST TIMES

TIME	ATHLETE (COUNTRY)
47.60	MARITA KOCH (GER)
47.99	JARMILA KRATOCHVÍLOVÁ (CZE)
48.25	MARIE-JOSÉ PÉREC (FRA)
48.27	OLGA VLADYKINA-BRYZGINA (RUS)
48.59	TAÉÁNA KOCEMBOVÁ (CZE)

→ The relay is a highly tactical race, and teams pay close attention to the order in which the runners race. Usually, the fastest runner (the anchor) is the last to run.

→ The 4x400m became a men's Olympic sport in 1908 (the women's competition followed in 1972). The 4x100m relay first appeared at the Stockholm Games in 1912 (the women's event followed in 1928).

→ The first relay races were held in the US by firemen who ran for charity, passing on a red pennant instead of a baton.

NO TURNING BACK

IN THE 4x400M AT THE 1997 WORLD CHAMPIONSHIPS, THE US TEAM CAME TO GRIEF WHEN TIM MONTGOMERY SET OFF TOO EARLY ON THE SECOND LEG. REALISING HIS MISTAKE, HE TURNED ROUND AND CRASHED INTO ONCOMING TEAMMATE BRIAN LEWIS.

RELAYS

EVENT OVERVIEW

The relay race boasts the competitiveness of a sprint race and the drama of the baton changeovers. Each of the four athletes races one section, or leg, of the race, handing over a baton to the next member of the team within a marked handover zone. The most common relays are the 4x100m and the 4x400m, in both men's and women's disciplines. The men's 4x400m is traditionally the last event of any track meeting. Less common events are the 4x200m, 4x800m, and 4x1600m races.

RUNNING TRACK

Relay races are run on regular running tracks. Due to the difference in the distance run by racers on the inside lane to those in the outer lanes, the racers start at staggered points in both 4x100m and 4x400m competitions. The runner in the inside lane starts on the finish line in both races, while the other runners start from progressively forward positions; the positions are more staggered in the 4x400m. The three handover zones are clearly indicated on the surface of the track.

STAYING COOL
Due to the high speeds involved and the close proximity of other teams, good timing and concentration are required to pass the baton smoothly. This is especially true in the 4x100m which is shown here.

Passing the baton
The incoming runner prepares to pass the baton to the receiver

Steady hands
It's crucial not to drop the baton; in Olympic events the team will be disqualified

Taking the baton
The receiver gets up to speed before putting his hand back, ready for the passer to plant the baton

Baton received
After taking the baton from his teammate, the receiver sets off as fast as possible on his leg of the race

Keep in lane
Runners risk disqualification if they pass the baton outside the handover zone, or stray from their own lane

THE BATON
The baton is a hollow aluminium tube 30cm (12in) long, 4cm (1⅝in) in diameter, and weighing 50g (1¾oz) or more. It is the time of the baton around the track that is measured, not the time of the athlete who carries it.

COMPETITOR PROFILE
4x100m relay runners need to have explosive pace, just as sprinters do. Runners in all distances must be able to time runs efficiently in order to achieve successful changeovers, while 4x400m runners must have the stamina to run the extra distance.

30cm (12in)

BATON K400

Smooth surface
The baton is entirely smooth, so must be handled carefully

Tubular build
The baton is made from a tube of metal, usually aluminium. The hollow construction makes it particularly lightweight

LANE DISCIPLINE

Athletes in the 4x100m remain in their lanes from start to finish, so the handover takes place in the relevant lane. In the 4x400m, runners start in separate lanes but may join the inside lane after the first 100m of the second leg. In the final two handovers, race organisers place the receivers across the finish line according to their teams' placings at the time, with the leading team in the inside lane.

HIGH-SPEED HANDOVER

Unlike the 4x400m handover, where the length of each leg means that the passers are running relatively slowly, the 4x100m handover (see below) is an action-packed phase when passer and receiver are running at high speed. The three run-up and handover zones are staggered around the bends of the track, so that the length of each leg is the same for every team.

STAYING IN THE BOX

The handover zone is 20m in length. The baton must be handed over while both runners are fully inside it and no less than 5m from its end. Second-, third-, and fourth-leg runners begin running in the run-up zone, 10m before the handover zone, in order to pick up speed before the transfer. In 4x100m relays, the speed and timing of the handover is a major factor in determining which team wins.

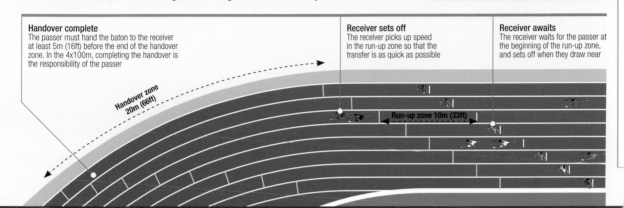

Handover complete
The passer must hand the baton to the receiver at least 5m (16ft) before the end of the handover zone. In the 4x100m, completing the handover is the responsibility of the passer

Receiver sets off
The receiver picks up speed in the run-up zone so that the transfer is as quick as possible

Receiver awaits
The receiver waits for the passer at the beginning of the run-up zone, and sets off when they draw near

Handover zone 20m (66ft)

Run-up zone 10m (33ft)

CHANGING TIMES

The transfer of the baton is the crucial moment in a relay race, and must be handled delicately. In the 4x100m relay the transfer is known as a "blind handoff", as the receiver does not maintain visual contact. The receiver starts to run when the passer reaches a certain point on the track, and the baton-carrier then shouts "stick!" to tell the receiver to hold out a hand. In the 4x400m relay, the receiver jogs forward while looking back at the passer, and holds out a hand for the baton.

UPSWEEP HANDOVER

The baton is passed in an upward movement, a popular method in the 4x100m relay. The receiver must adjust his grip before the next changeover.

DOWNSWEEP HANDOVER

The passer hands the baton to the receiver in a downward movement. This method is popular in the 4x400m relay, and is less risky than the alternative.

Receiver's hand
The receiver's palm faces downwards, ready to take the upsweeping baton

Receiver's hand
The palm faces upwards; the grip will be tightened as soon as contact is felt

Passer's hand
The handover depends on the giver releasing and the receiver clasping at the same time

STAT CENTRAL

MEN'S 4x100M OLYMPIC GOLD

YEAR	COUNTRY
2012	JAMAICA
2008	JAMAICA
2004	GREAT BRITAIN
2000	UNITED STATES

WOMEN'S 4x100M OLYMPIC GOLD

YEAR	COUNTRY
2012	UNITED STATES
2008	RUSSIA
2004	JAMAICA
2000	BAHAMAS

MEN'S 4x400M OLYMPIC GOLD

YEAR	COUNTRY
2012	BAHAMAS
2008	UNITED STATES
2004	UNITED STATES
2000	NIGERIA

WOMEN'S 4x400M OLYMPIC GOLD

YEAR	COUNTRY
2012	UNITED STATES
2008	UNITED STATES
2004	UNITED STATES
2000	UNITED STATES

SIDELINES

300 The length, in metres, of each leg of the earliest recorded relay races, held informally between teams of firemen in the United States in the late 19th century. The batons were red flags. The first official relay race was run in Philadelphia, Pennsylvania, in 1893.

25 The number of Olympic gold medals won by the US athletic team in both men's and women's 4x100m relay, the most of any nation. The US also boasts 13 world titles in the event.

5.4 The number of seconds that have been knocked off the men's 4x100m world record since 1912.

→ Hurdles events are divided into sprint races (110m for men and 100m for women), and the 400m, which is also contested by both men and women.

→ Indoor hurdles are held over shorter distances – typically 60m and 300m. In such events, the distance between the hurdles remains the same as in the outdoor events; there are just fewer of them.

SIDELINES

10 The number of hurdles in an outdoor hurdles race, which remains the same regardless of the distance.

15 The time, in seconds, of the first 110m hurdles world record, set in 1908. The 13-second barrier was broken in 1981.

19 The number of times in the first 24 modern Olympic Games that gold in the men's 110m hurdles was won by an athlete from the US. This overwhelming dominance was challenged in the first two Olympiads of the 21st century.

122 The number of consecutive 400m hurdles races won by Ed Moses between 1977 and 1987.

HURDLES

EVENT OVERVIEW
Always big crowd-pullers, hurdling events are among the most exciting at any athletics meeting. The object of a hurdles race is to jump over a series of gate-like obstacles and reach the finishing line first. There are four main outdoor events: 100m for women and 110m for men (both sprint hurdles), and 400m races for both men and women.

SPRINT HURDLES
In both the 100m and 110m hurdles, the competitors start out of the blocks and run along a straight course, jumping over 10 hurdles along the way. In the men's event, the first hurdle is 13.7m (45ft) from the starting line, and the distance between each hurdle is 9.1m (30ft). After the final hurdle, the runners sprint the remaining 14.4m (47ft 3in) to the finishing line. The first hurdle in the women's event is 13m (42ft 8in) from the blocks. The hurdles are 8.5m (29ft 6in) apart, and the last is positioned 10.5m (34ft 6in) from the finishing line.

ONE-LAP HURDLES
In the 400m hurdles, racers start from the blocks and must leap over 10 hurdles, just like the sprint-distance hurdlers. Racers start from staggered points on the athletics track, according to their lane position. The hurdles are slightly lower in height than their sprint-distance equivalents. The first hurdle is positioned 45m (147ft 7in) from the start, and the distance between each of the following hurdles is 35m (114ft 10in). The last hurdle is 40m (131ft 3in) from the finishing line.

Arms race
The arms play a critical role in counterbalancing the forces that are applied to the torso by the legs as they swing in to and out of the jumps over the hurdles

Low trajectory
It is important that the trailing leg is kept as low as possible. It is better to hit the hurdle with the knee than to lose speed by making an unnecessarily high clearance

ATHLETE PROFILE
Like any other race runners, hurdlers need speed, power, and stamina. Above all, they need to develop quick reflex actions that will help to propel them over a rapid succession of obstacles without a time-wasting loss of rhythm. Hurdlers also need to be flexible (they pay particular attention to hip exercises).

Getting a grip
A plate of small spikes on the sole of the hurdler's shoe provides traction

Material difference
The uprights and bases of the hurdles are made of metal, but the crossbar is wooden

APPARATUS

The height of the hurdles varies from event to event. The sprint events are known as "high" hurdles. Long hurdle races use slightly lower heights. Hurdles must all be L-shaped, and designed to fall over forwards when hit. Adjustable hurdles, in which the height of the crossbar from the ground can be altered, are sometimes used for training.

STAT CENTRAL

MEN'S 110M HURDLES OLYMPIC GOLD

YEAR	ATHLETE (COUNTRY)
2012	ARIES MERRITT (USA)
2008	DAYRON ROBLES (CUB)
2004	JLIU XIANG (CHN)
2000	AÑER GARCIA (CUB)
1996	ALLEN JOHNSON (USA)
1992	MARK MCCOY (CAN)

WOMEN'S 100M HURDLES OLYMPIC GOLD

YEAR	ATHLETE (COUNTRY)
2012	SALLY PEARSON (AUS)
2008	DAWN HARPER (USA)
2004	JOANNA HAYES (USA)
2000	OLGA SHISHIGINA (KAZ)
1996	LUDMILA ENGQUIST (SWE)
1992	VOULA PATOULIDOU (GRE)

MEN'S 400M HURDLES OLYMPIC GOLD

YEAR	ATHLETE (COUNTRY)
2012	FELIX SANCHEZ (DMA)
2008	ANGELO TAYLOR (USA)
2004	FELIX SANCHEZ (DMA)
2000	ANGELO TAYLOR (USA)
1996	DERRICK ADKINS (USA)
1992	KEVIN YOUNG (USA)

WOMEN'S 400M HURDLES OLYMPIC GOLD

YEAR	ATHLETE (COUNTRY)
2012	NATALYA ANTYUKH (RUS)
2008	MELANIE WALKER (JAM)
2004	FANI HALKIA (GRE)
2000	IRINA PRIVALOVA (RUS)
1996	DEON HEMMINGS (JAM)
1992	SALLY GUNNELL (GBR)

Feet
Hurdles must be placed on the track with the feet of the frame on the approach side

Sprint hurdle: men 1.07m (3ft 6in); women 84cm (2ft 9in)

Maximum (both sexes): 1.2m (3ft 11in)

Crossbar
Hitting the bar and knocking over the hurdle is not penalized, but it slows pace

400 hurdle: men 91cm (3ft); women 76cm (2ft 6in)

Maximum (both sexes): 1.2m (3ft 11in)

"HIGH" HURDLES
The highest hurdles (for each sex) are used in the sprint events: the 110m race for men and the 100m for women.

INTERMEDIATE HURDLES
Slightly lower hurdles, height-adjusted according to sex, are used in the longer distance events: the men's and women's 400m races.

TAKE IT IN YOUR STRIDE

Hurdlers do not try to maximize the length of their stride. Their main focus is on the approach to each hurdle, and maintaining a smooth, uninterrupted flow throughout the race: they should never break step for an upcoming hurdle. The other key to success is efficient and economical jumping. To achieve this, competitors "run through" the hurdles – in other words, they simply lift their legs, rather than jump in the conventional sense of the word, and try to stay as close to the track as possible throughout the race. They generally lead with the same leg over every hurdle.

ARMED FOR ACTION

The best hurdlers make full use of their arms to balance their bodies. As they attack the hurdle, they stretch forward, reaching for their lead leg with their opposite hand. This action – which is sometimes referred to as "checking the time" because the runner seems to be looking at the top of his or her wrist – brings the forehead close to the leading knee. The other arm swings backwards in a normal sprint racing action.

CLEARING THE HURDLE
Sprint hurdlers lean their bodies further forward than 400m hurdlers because they need to minimize the height they jump and get their feet back down on the track faster.

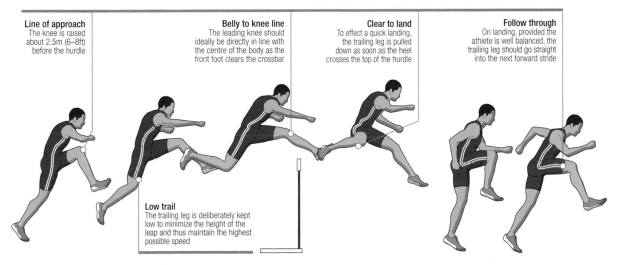

Line of approach
The knee is raised about 2.5m (6–8ft) before the hurdle

Belly to knee line
The leading knee should ideally be directly in line with the centre of the body as the front foot clears the crossbar

Clear to land
To effect a quick landing, the trailing leg is pulled down as soon as the heel crosses the top of the hurdle

Follow through
On landing, provided the athlete is well balanced, the trailing leg should go straight into the next forward stride

Low trail
The trailing leg is deliberately kept low to minimize the height of the leap and thus maintain the highest possible speed

MIDDLE-DISTANCE RUNNING

EVENT OVERVIEW

The most commmon middle-distance events are the 800m and the 1,500m, with steeplechasing also regularly included in athletics competitions. Many athletes run in both events, as the training and physical requirements are similar. Tactics play a part in these races, and are often won or lost in the last few metres. Middle-distance races have always been among the core events of the Olympics and all athletic championships.

ATHLETE PROFILE
Middle-distance athletes need physical and mental staying power. The distances are too long for sprinting, but speed is required for the finish. Tactics are also important.

NEED2KNOW

→ The women's Olympic 800m was first run in 1928, but shock at competitors' exhaustion meant it did not appear again until 1960.

→ Women were finally allowed to run in the 1500m at the Munich Olympics in 1972.

→ Steeplechasing, of varied lengths, has been a men's Olympic event since 1900. It first appeared as a major women's race in the 2005 Helsinki World Championships.

RACING TACTICS

STAYING AT THE BACK IS NOT RECOMMENDED, BUT IN THE 1936 OLYMPICS, JOHN WOODRUFF WAS BOXED IN EARLY IN THE 800M. SLOWING ALMOST TO A STOP, HE LET THE FIELD PASS, AND STILL WON. IN 2004 KELLY HOLMES HAD SUCCESS USING A SIMILAR TACTIC.

Hanging back
While trailing behind can work tactically, there is a risk of being unable to catch up at the end and of being boxed in

In the field
Staying behind the leader allows a runner to choose an acceleration point and pace themselves more easily

Leader
The leader takes the full brunt of the wind resistance and cannot easily tell what is happening behind

THE MAIN EVENTS

In the 800m, runners complete two laps around a standard 400m track. They start from staggered positions along the track and have to stay in their starting lane until the end of the first curve (about 100m). The 800m requires speed and endurance so competitors plan their race and use carefully considered and practised tactics. The 1,500m event consists of three and three-quarter laps around the standard outdoor track and is often called "the metric mile". With an increasingly scientific approach to performance and training, runners have been able to make this race an extended sprint. However, like the 800m, the 1,500m remains very mentally taxing.

BREAKING TO THE INSIDE

Leaving the starting lane after the first curve, called breaking to the inside, allows runners to compete against each other more effectively. Breaking lanes must be done without deliberately obstructing or barging another competitor, although elbow clashing is almost unavoidable.

RUNNING KIT

As for all athletics events, the gear a middle-distance runner wears is chosen with great care. There is an emphasis on lightweight, technical modern materials with little wind resistance and advanced wicking properties. A close, flexible, and comfortable fit are essentials in both the shoes and the clothes.

THE FOOTWEAR

The key features of middle-distance running shoes are their aerodynamic shape, light weight, and spiked soles. Not all have laces.

STEEPLECHASE

Usually 3,000m, the steeplechase includes 35 jumps, seven of which are water jumps. Normally, four barriers are sited around the track, with the water jump – the fifth barrier – at the top of the second turn, either to the inside of lane one or to the outside of the outermost lane. Barriers, which do not fall over if hit, are sited 78m (256ft) apart; runners start jumping them after the first half lap. They must be cleared cleanly by jumping, stepping on and over, or vaulting.

THE WATER JUMP
The water jump combines a barrier and a sloping pool of water. Runners attempt to land as far from the barrier as possible as this is where the water is shallower. Water resistance slows runners down and splashing inhibits freedom of movement and vision.

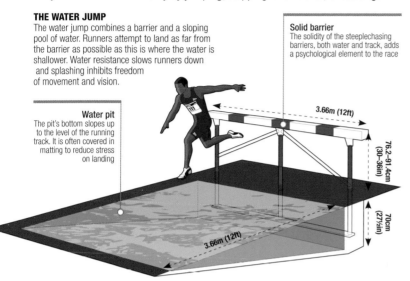

Water pit
The pit's bottom slopes up to the level of the running track. It is often covered in matting to reduce stress on landing

Solid barrier
The solidity of the steeplechasing barriers, both water and track, adds a psychological element to the race

3.66m (12ft)

76.2–91.4cm (30–36in)

70cm (27½in)

3.66m (12ft)

THE FOOTWEAR
Steeplechasing shoes are streamlined, lightweight, and usually have 6–8mm (¼in) pyramid spikes on the sole. Spikes provide extra traction for negotiating the barriers and staying on the track. High-tech mid-sole and ankle cushioning is also provided.

Rubber sole
Flexible, solid rubber outer soles are fitted with nylon spike plates

RUNNING TECHNIQUES

Posture and balance are important in a middle-distance runner. These enable acceleration and maintainance of high speeds. The athlete concentrates on relaxing into the stride, with their arms held close to the body but hanging loosely from the shoulders, allowing them to swing with the body in a down and back movement. In the 800m race, runners aim to complete both laps in more or less the same time. The 1,500m is also run at a steady pace throughout.

TRAINING
Middle-distance runners need both fast and slow twitch muscles, the first for speed, the second for endurance. Interval training, in which fast work is interspersed with short recovery periods, is used to build these, and to increase aerobic and anaerobic fitness. Running at race speeds as well as slower endurance runs are included in training.

STARTING POSITIONS
Runners start without blocks. They stand on the toes of the back foot and the ball of the front foot, opposite arms back and forward respectively.

Body position
To accelerate away at the start, runners lean forward, but they soon straighten their body to run

Feet position
On "go", the back foot drives forward onto the power foot. The arms swing to aid acceleration

STAT CENTRAL

MEN'S BEST 800M TIMES

TIME	ATHLETE (YEAR)
1:40.91	DAVID RUDISHA (2012)
1:41.11	WILSON KIPKETER (1997)
1:41.73	SEBASTIAN COE (1981)
1:41.73	NIJEL AMOS (2012)
1:41.77	JOAQUIM CRUZ (1984)

WOMEN'S BEST 800M TIMES

TIME	ATHLETE (YEAR)
1:53.28	JARMILA KRATOCHVÍLOVÁ (1983)
1:53.43	NADEZHDA OLIZARENKO (1980)
1:54.01	PAMELA JELIMO (2008)
1:54.44	ANA FIDELIA QUIROT (1989)
1:54.81	OLGA MINEYEVA (1980)

MEN'S BEST 1,500M TIMES

TIME	ATHLETE (YEAR)
3:26.00	HICHAM EL GUERROUJ (1998)
3:26.34	BERNARD LAGAT (2001)
3:27.37	NOUREDDINE MORCELI (1995)
3:28.12	NOAH NGENY (2000)
3:28.88	ASBEL KIPROP (2012)
3:28.95	FERMÍN CACHO (1997)

WOMEN'S BEST 1500M TIMES

TIME	ATHLETE (YEAR)
3:50.46	YUNXIA QU (1993)
3:50.98	BO JIANG (1997)
3:51.34	YINGLAI LANG (1997)
3:51.92	JUNXIA WANG (1993)
3:52.47	TATYANA KAZANKINA (1980)
3:53.91	LILI YIN (1997)

SIDELINES

27 The number of times Moroccan Hicham El Guerrouj has run the 1,500m in under 3:30. He also holds the most world titles – four. Briton Steve Cram was first to finish in under 3:30 in 1985.

24 The age of Moses Kiptanui of Kenya when he had already won three steeplechasing world titles (1991, 1993, 1995) and had been the first to finish in under eight minutes – his record is 7:59.18.

1,000,000 The amount in US dollars won by 800m runner Maria Mutola, in 2003. She was the first athlete to win the IAAF Golden League Jackpot outright.

LONG-DISTANCE RUNNING

NEED2KNOW

→ While the men's 5,000m and 10,000m events have featured in the Olympics since 1912, the women's 10,000m and 5,000m runs only debuted in 1988 and 1996 respectively.

→ The marathon is named after the legendary run of the Greek soldier who, in 490BCE, brought news from Marathon to Athens of Greek victory in battle.

→ Marathons in London, New York, Chicago, Hong Kong, and Honolulu each attract more than 30,000 runners.

EVENT OVERVIEW

Long-distance running events include 5,000m and 10,000m races, cross-country running, and marathons. The 5,000 and 10,000m runs and the marathon are Olympic events. The runs take place on a stadium track, while the marathon route is staged around the streets of the host city. Some 5,000 and 10,000m races are held off-road, in which case they are usually known as 5km and 10km runs.

ON THE TRACK

In the 5,000m and 10,000m races, competitors start off lined up across the track, but because the outside curves add extra metres, all runners soon move to the inside lanes to minimize the total distance they have to run. One lap round the track is the equivalent of 400m. Consequently, in a 5,000m event, the athletes must first run 200m and then complete 12 laps of the track. In the 10,000m event, the competitors run 25 times round the track. Both races finish at the same line.

Lightweight shoes
Running shoes help absorb the impact of each stride

Lightweight shorts
The runners wear shorts made of breathable fibre

Cool to run
Loose-fitting, lightweight, sleeveless vests keep runners as cool as possible

ATHLETE PROFILE

Long-distance runners are lighter, more slightly built, and more wiry than the powerhouse sprinters. Stamina and endurance are essential, as is aerobic fitness: it is vital that the heart pumps blood around the body as efficiently as possible to allow more oxygen to reach tired muscles. Success in long-distance running comes not only through peak physical fitness but also through mental endurance and tactical thinking. Competitors are pushed to the limits of body and mind, and need to be able to pace themselves to conserve energy, and to be aware of when to hang back or when to push forward.

HIGH FLYERS

OFTEN DUBBED "THE RUNNING TRIBE", THE KALENJIN PEOPLE OF THE GREAT RIFT VALLEY IN WESTERN KENYA ARE RENOWNED FOR THEIR PROWESS AT LONG-DISTANCE RUNNING. ONE POSSIBLE REASON FOR THEIR CONTINUED INTERNATIONAL SUCCESS IS THE HIGH ALTITUDE AT WHICH THEY LIVE. WITH LESS OXYGEN IN THE ATMOSPHERE AT HIGH ALTITUDES, THE BODY MUST PRODUCE MORE OXYGEN-CARRYING RED BLOOD CELLS. WHEN COMPETING AT SEA LEVEL, THESE EXTRA CELLS PROVIDE A HUGE ADVANTAGE AS THE HEART DOESN'T HAVE TO BEAT AS FAST TO CARRY AN EQUIVALENT AMOUNT OF OXYGEN AROUND THE BODY.

SIDELINES

6,255 The number of runners to cross the finish line at the first-ever London Marathon. The popular annual event was first staged in the city in 1981.

21.1 The length, in kilometres, of a half marathon. Moses Tanui was the first athlete to complete the event in under 60 minutes, setting the record in 1993 in Milan.

8 The number of records broken in a single women's 10,000m race at the 2002 Asian games in Busan. Chinese runner Sun Yingjie won the race, and the first four finishers produced the 3rd, 4th, 5th, and 6th best times ever.

20 Haile Gebrselassie's age when he won his first World Championship gold in the 10,000m. He went on to win another three titles and is one of the most celebrated long-distance runners of all time.

THE GEAR

Whether a race is a city marathon, a track event, or over rough terrain, the athlete's most important piece of equipment is the right pair of shoes. Different types of shoe are designed to provide the appropriate support and control of foot action in different events. Track and cross-country runners need spikes for grip, and for cross-country the shoe must be fairly rigid; for marathon runners, nothing is more vital than shock absorption.

Cushioned heel
A cushioned layer in the heel and sole helps absorb shocks from hard road surfaces

Outer sole
Rubber cleats on the outer sole provide extra grip on rough ground

ROAD SHOE
Marathons are generally raced on roads, often through cities. Marathon runners wear flat running shoes specially designed to absorb the shock of the foot repeatedly striking a hard surface.

OFF-ROAD SHOE
Cross-country runners race on routes that may go through all types of natural terrain. Runners wear shoes with rubber cleats to give them grip on muddy and grassy routes. They are usually less cushioned than road shoes.

CROSS COUNTRY

Cross-country runs take place off-road, over all sorts of terrain, including grass, mud, and even water. There is no fixed length for cross-country running: women's races are generally between 2–8km (1¼–5 miles); men's events may be between 5–15km (3–9 miles). Cross-country running was an Olympic sport until 1924, but was then dropped as it was deemed unsuitable as a summer event. The IAAF organizes the annual World Cross-Country Championships, which are considered the most important competition in the discipline.

TEAM EVENTS
Cross-country running is unusual in that it involves athletes competing both as an individual and as part of a team. Usually it is the first five runners in a team who have their scores put forward to determine the finishing order.

> **SETTING THE PACE**
> One of the most important tactics in long-distance running is the ability to judge pace-setting. Often following a dedicated pacemaker, athletes need to pace themselves exactly. If they run relatively slowly to conserve energy they may not be able to put on a sufficient burst of speed to overtake the front-runners. However, if they run relatively quickly, perhaps assuming an early lead, they may not be able to sustain their advantage, ultimately running out of steam well before the finish line. The most skilful runners can force their opponents to make tactical errors.

MARATHON

Marathons are run on roads over a course 42.2km (26 miles 385yd) long. At the Olympic Games, the race ends in the stadium. The men's marathon is traditionally the last event of the athletics calendar and is sometimes incorporated into the closing ceremony. The marathon was held at the first modern Olympics in Athens in 1896, where the course was only 40km (24 miles 1,496yd) long. The length of subsequent Olympic marathons varied slightly (depending on the established route for each venue) but was set at today's distance during the 1924 Games.

PUBLIC APPEAL
Marathons are popular participation sports, with top athletes competing alongside hundreds or even tens of thousands of amateurs for whom personal triumph means finishing the course rather than winning. Notable events take place annually in cities the world over, including London, New York, Paris, Tokyo, and Boston.

STAT CENTRAL

MEN'S 5,000M OLYMPIC CHAMPIONS

YEAR	GOLD MEDALLIST
2012	MO FARAH (GBR)
2008	KENENISA BEKELE (ETH)
2004	HICHAM EL GUERROUJ (MAR)
2000	MILLON WOLDE (ETH)
1996	VENUSTE NIYONGABO (BDI)
1992	DIETER BAUMANN (GER)
1988	JOHN NGUGI (KEN)

WOMEN'S 5,000M OLYMPIC CHAMPIONS

YEAR	GOLD MEDALLIST
2012	MESERET DEFAR (ETH)
2008	TIRUNESH DIBABA (ETH)
2004	MESERET DEFAR (ETH)

MEN'S 10,000M OLYMPIC CHAMPIONS

YEAR	GOLD MEDALLIST
2012	MO FARAH (GBR)
2008	KENENISA BEKELE (ETH)
2004	KENENISA BEKELE (ETH)
2000	HAILE GEBRSELASSIE (ETH)
1996	HAILE GEBRSELASSIE (ETH)

WOMEN'S 10,000M OLYMPIC CHAMPIONS

YEAR	GOLD MEDALLIST
2012	TIRUNESH DIBABA (ETH)
2008	TIRUNESH DIBABA (ETH)
2004	HUINA XING (CHN)
2000	DERARTU TULU (ETH)
1996	FERNANDA RIBEIRO (POR)

MEN'S MARATHON OLYMPIC CHAMPIONS

YEAR	GOLD MEDALLIST
2012	STEPHEN KIPROTICH (UGA)
2008	SAMMY WANJIRU (KEN)
2004	STEFANO BALDINI (ITA)
2000	GEZAHEGNE ABERA (ETH)
1996	JOSIA THUGWANE (RSA)
1992	HWANG YOUNG-CHO (KOR)
1988	GELINDO BORDIN (ITA)

WOMEN'S MARATHON OLYMPIC CHAMPIONS

YEAR	GOLD MEDALLIST
2012	TIKI GELANA (ETH)
2008	CONSTANTINA TOMESCU (ROU)
2004	MIZUKI NOGUCHI (JPN)
2000	NAOKO TAKAHASHI (JPN)
1996	FATUMA ROBA (ETH)
1992	VALENTINA YEGOROVA (RUS)
1988	ROSA MOTA (POR)

LONG JUMP

EVENT OVERVIEW

The long jump – formerly known as the broad jump – is one of the oldest track-and-field events for men and women. Athletes compete in this technically demanding event to see which of them can leap the greatest distance through the air from a running start. There are five main elements to the long jump: the run up, the last two steps before reaching the take-off board, the take off itself, the technique through the air, and the landing. Over the history of athletics, long jump records have been few and far between. Bob Beamon's long jump world record, set at the 1968 Mexico Olympics, stood for almost 23 years.

NEED2KNOW

→ The long jump was included in the first track and field competitions at Exeter College at Oxford University, England, in 1850.

→ The long jump is one of track-and-field's core events and has been part of every modern Olympic Games.

→ Previously a men-only event, in 1948 the long jump became an Olympic sport for women as well.

ONE GIANT LEAP FOR MANKIND

IN MOST SPORTS, WORLD RECORDS CREEP UP – A CENTIMETRE MORE HERE, 0.01 OF A SECOND LESS THERE. UNTIL 1968, NO ATHLETE HAD JUMPED MORE THAN 8.5M (28FT), BUT AT THAT YEAR'S OLYMPIC GAMES IN MEXICO CITY, AMERICAN BOB BEAMON CLEARED 8.9M (29FT), ALMOST 60CM (2FT) FURTHER THAN THE PREVIOUS BEST. BEAMON'S RECORD STOOD FOR ALMOST 23 YEARS BEFORE FALLING TO ANOTHER US ATHLETE, MIKE POWELL.

SIDELINES

2 The maximum permitted tail wind, in metres per second, for a record long jump to be deemed valid. That is the equivalent of 7.2kph (4.47mph).

4 The number of consecutive Olympic long jump gold medals won by the US athlete Carl Lewis between 1984 and 1996.

22 The average number of run-up strides taken by a top-class male long jumper.

Centre of gravity
For most of the flight phase, long jumpers push their weight backwards to produce upward thrust; then, as they land, they lean forwards to avoid falling back into the pit

Running vest
The vest need not be skintight but must not be so baggy that it billows out behind the athlete

Running shorts
It is important that jumpers' legs can move freely

Cleated shoes
Firm running shoes with running spikes for grip and to withstand the pressure of the take-off stride

ATHLETE PROFILE

One of the keys to success in the long jump is a fast run up, and it is no coincidence that the event's brightest stars are often outstanding 100m and 200m sprinters. Height, though not essential, is also an advantage as the further an athlete can reach, the greater jump distance they will achieve. Most of the leading male long jumpers are 1.85m (6ft 1in) or taller; women tend to be over 1.72m (5ft 8in).

LONG JUMP PIT

The approach runway, made of cinders or synthetic material, should be no less than 40m (131ft) long and is often 45m (147ft 6in). The landing area is a sand-filled pit at least 9m (29ft 6in) long and 2.75m (9ft) wide. Between the two is a 20cm (8in) wide take-off board. To the front of it, judges may place a strip of plasticine, soft earth, or sand, that will show if the jumper's foot was on the ground beyond the take-off limit.

Take-off board
This is set back at least 1m (3ft 3in) from the front of the pit so that judges can tell more easily if the jumper's feet went beyond the forward edge before take off

Landing pit
The pit is filled with sand, then moistened. After every jump the surface is smoothed over with a rake to the same level as the runway

at least 10m (33ft)

RULES AND ATTEMPTS

When attempting a jump, competitors may tread on the take-off board but they must not allow any part of their feet to go over its farthest edge, called the scratch line. If they overstep the scratch line, the jump is invalid. A legal jump is indicated by an official who holds up a white flag; foul jumps are signalled by a red flag. Each contestant has three attempts (known as trials), unless there are fewer than eight competitors, in which case they may each have six jumps. At high level events, athletes must participate in two preliminary knock out rounds; the top eight of whom contest a final. The winner is the athlete with the longest valid jump in the final round; in the event of a tie, the second-best trials are taken into consideration.

FIVE STEPS TO HEAVEN

Five elements of a long jump are crucial: a fast approach, a well measured last two strides, an explosive take off, a long flight, and a well-balanced landing. Since speed in the approach is so important, it is not surprising that many competitive sprinters are also top-level long jumpers. There are three main long jumping techniques: the hitch-kick, the sail, and the hang. There is no "right" or "wrong" technique, and athletes choose the one that suits them best.

MEASUREMENTS

No matter where on the runway the athlete takes off, each valid jump is measured from the front edge of the take-off board to the nearest mark made in the sand by any part of the competitor's body. (That is why the sand in the long jump pit must be completely smoothed after every trial.) Distances are recorded to the nearest centimetre below the actual distance jumped if the distance achieved was not a whole centimetre.

THE FINAL STEP

The take-off board is set into the runway and may have a small hollow beneath to add springiness. The tell-tale strip in front of the board should be replaced every time it is trodden on.

Overstepping the mark
If toe prints are imprinted on the putty-like strip in front of the board, the jump is illegal

20cm (8in)

HITCH-KICK

This technique is the hardest to master, but it is the method most frequently employed by elite jumpers. Also known as "running in the air", the hitch-kick in fact relies on a cycling action to maintain an upright body position. On landing, hitch-kickers touch down feet first and then push their torso forward to prevent losing distance by falling backwards into the pit.

Cycling legs
The legs and arms move in a rapid cycling motion

Explosive take-off
As with all techniques, good lift is crucial at take off

Lean forward
The torso is pushed to shift the centre of gravity forward

SAIL

The sail is the most basic long jump technique. Once airborne, it is important to help force the body through the air by circling the arms. They should first go downward, then backward, upward, and finally forward. On landing, the jumper must attempt to push their body forward so their feet and arms are forced in front of them as far as possible.

Arms up
The arms are stretched as high as possible at take off

Legs forward
At the apex of the jump, the legs start to move forward

Body forward
The body follows the legs into a forward position as the athlete descends

HANG

In this jump, both the arms and the legs are extended upwards to reach a maximum distance from the hips. The limbs are kept "long" until after the jumper has reached the top of the jump, at which point they push the legs forward in readiness for landing. The hang technique is the easiest way to achieve a forward-falling finish, which prevents the jumper falling backwards and losing distance.

Head forward
After take off, the head is brought in front of the arms

Arms back
The arms are thrust backwards

Body shift
To avoid falling back into the sand, the centre of gravity is shifted forwards

STAT CENTRAL

WORLD RECORDS (MEN)		
ATHLETE (COUNTRY)	DISTANCE	YEAR
MIKE POWELL (USA)	8.95m	1991
BOB BEAMON (USA)	8.90m	1968
RALPH BOSTON (USA)	8.35m	1965
RALPH BOSTON (USA)	8.34m	1964
IGOR TER-OVANESYAN (URS)	8.31m	1962

WORLD RECORDS (WOMEN)		
ATHLETE (COUNTRY)	DISTANCE	YEAR
GALINA CHISTYAKOVA (USR)	7.52m	1988
HEIKE DRECHSLER (GDR)	7.45m	1986
HEIKE DRECHSLER (GDR)	7.44m	1985
ANISOARA CUSMIR (ROM)	7.43m	1983
ANISOARA CUSMIR (ROM)	7.27m	1983

ATHLETE PROFILE
Triple jumpers are often also good sprinters, but they can compensate for any lack of pace down the runway by developing power and rhythm. Training focuses on plyometrics (exercises to increase the ability to stretch and contract muscles in quick succession).

Close fit
Vest and shorts are lightweight and close-fitting to lower wind resistance and to ensure that no material will trail the athlete and mark the sand

Athlete ID
Athletes must wear race identification numbers on both sides of the vest. The numbers are usually attached to an athlete's vest with pins

Jumping spikes
Shoes have spikes to help grip on any surface. The soles are specially designed to cushion the impact during the run up and leaps

TRIPLE JUMP

EVENT OVERVIEW

This track-and-field event is also informally known as the hop, step, and jump – a description that perfectly defines the movements of the athletes who compete in this contest. Each athlete runs down a track that is often the same as the one used for the long jump (see pp.60–61). On reaching the take-off board (at full speed), the athlete jumps forwards, lands on the take-off foot, then takes a step on to the other foot, and finally jumps into a sand-filled pit. The competitor who covers the greatest overall distance is declared the winner.

NEED2KNOW

→ The Men's triple jump was a medal event at the first modern Olympics in 1896; there was no women's equivalent for exactly 100 years.

→ Any athlete who walks back through the landing pit after they have made their jump will be disqualified from the competition with immediate effect.

→ Proportionally, the largest phase of the triple jump is the the hop stage (first phase) – about 37 per cent; phase two is about 33 per cent, while the final phase accounts for 30 per cent of the total leap.

→ Elite triple jumpers cover about twice the distance of elite long jumpers. The current long jump record held by Mike Powell is 8.95m (29ft) and the current triple jump record held by Jonathan Edwards is 18.29m (60ft).

HOP, STEP, JUMP

A top-level triple jumper usually takes a run-up of around 40m (130ft). The approach (made at full speed) should be so well judged that the jumper has no need to look down at the board during take off – to do so would compromise the length of the jump. Athletes begin and end the hop on the same foot; as soon as they have landed they launch the other foot into the step, stretching to cover as much ground as possible. For the final jump, the athlete uses the hitch-kick, sail, or hang technique (see p.61) to bring the legs forward for the landing.

Take off
Having sprinted to the take-off board, the jumper pushes forward with the take-off leg and takes one step in mid-air

Stepping
As the jumper lands the hop (on the same leg they took off with), they then stretch the other leg as far as possible to step forward. The legs must not pass each other

HOP

TRACK AND PIT

The take-off board for the triple jump is set much further back than that of the long jump. The adjustment is made so that the athletes can perform the hop and step phases on the cinder or synthetic track before launching the final jump into the landing pit. A strip of plasticine, soft clay, or similar material is usually placed along the leading edge of the take-off board. This leaves a tell-tale impression of the athlete's shoe, so that the officials can detect foul jumps that they may not have noticed with the naked eye. The sand in the landing pit must be level with the track and should be raked completely smooth after every jump is measured. This is so the officials can be sure that any mark made in the sand was left by the athlete who has just made the jump.

EDWARDS: THE UNSURPASSABLE?

JONATHAN EDWARDS WAS THE FIRST ATHLETE TO BREAK THE 18M (59FT) BARRIER, SETTING A NEW WORLD RECORD OF 18.29M (60FT), IN THE PROCESS. IT WAS THE EQUIVALENT OF JUMPING A LITTLE UNDER THE LENGTH OF TWO DOUBLE-DECKER BUSES.

PROMINENT POSITION

The competition area for the triple jump is positioned in front of the grandstand just inside the section of the running track used for sprint events.

Run-up track
Triple jumpers start their approach with a few tentative strides to establish a rhythm. They never go full out along the runway because excess speed will unbalance them

Landing pit
Some competitors miss their intended final destination by applying so much hip swerve during the step phase that they leap off at an angle and land outside the sand

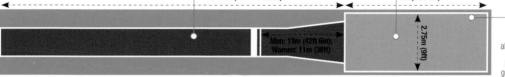

40–45m (131–147ft 6in)

9m (29ft 6in)

Men: 13m (42ft 6in);
Women: 11m (36ft)

2.75m (9ft)

Watering pit
The landing pit is always watered before competitions, so that landing marks do not get filled in too quickly

JUMPING COMPETITIONS

At larger competitions, athletes have to progress through qualifying rounds before being able to compete in the final round, with the possibility of winning a medal of any colour. The athletes have at least three attempts (trials) at a jump. Each jump is measured from the leading edge of the take-off board to the nearest mark in the sand made by any part of the competitor's body. The jump is recorded to the nearest centimetre below the distance cleared. If an athlete is confident that their jump will get them into the next round, or win a medal, they don't have to complete all three trials.

Soft strip
Plasticine, sand, or clay will show illegal impressions

20cm (8in)

RUN UP
One of the most important skills for triple jumpers to master is to judge the approach run up so that the leading foot lands as close as possible to the edge of the take-off board without overstepping the mark and making the jump invalid.

FOUL JUMPS
The officials signal a foul jump by waving a red flag. Most foul jumps occur when the athlete oversteps the take-off board and makes an indent in the soft strip on the take-off board. Sometimes, the jumper will miss the landing pit altogether. A foul may be called if the athlete takes more than the agreed length of time (usually a minute and a half) to complete a jump. Foul jumps may also be called if the jumper lands the hop on the incorrect foot, or if they jump off two feet instead of just one.

STAT CENTRAL

LONGEST TRIPLE JUMPS (MEN)

MARK	ATHLETE (YEAR)
18.29m	JONATHAN EDWARDS (1995)
18.16m	JONATHAN EDWARDS (1995)
18.09m	KENNY HARRISON (1996)
18.01m	JONATHAN EDWARDS (1998)
18.00m	JONATHAN EDWARDS (1995)
17.99m	JONATHAN EDWARDS (1998)
17.99m	KENNY HARRISON (1996)
17.98m	JONATHAN EDWARDS (1995)
17.98m	TEDDY TAMGHO (2010)
17.97m	WILLIE BANKS (1985)
17.96m	CHRISTIAN TAYLOR (2011)
17.93m	KENNY HARRISON (1990)
17.92m	KHRISTO MARKOV (1987)

LONGEST TRIPLE JUMPS (WOMEN)

MARK	ATHLETE (YEAR)
15.50m	INESSA KRAVETS (1995)
15.39m	F. MBANGO ETONE (2008)
15.34m	TATYANA LEBEDEVA (2004)
15.33m	INESSA KRAVETS (1996)
15.33m	TATYANA LEBEDEVA (2004)
15.32m	TATYANA LEBEDEVA (2000)
15.32m	HRYSOPIYÍ DEVETZÍ (2004)
15.30m	F. MBANGO ETONE (2004)
15.29m	YAMILÉ ALDAMA (2003)
15.28m	YAMILÉ ALDAMA (2004)
15.28m	YARGELIS SAVIGNE (2007)
15.27m	YAMILÉ ALDAMA (2003)
15.25m	TATYANA LEBEDEVA (2001)

Jump
The athlete must land on the opposite foot to the take-off foot. To complete the jump, the athlete takes off from the landing foot

The final phase
The jumping technique may be a hang, a hitch-kick, or a sail manoeuvre

Landing the jump
Jumpers land feet-first but throw their body weight forward so that their mark is where they first hit the sand

STEP

JUMP

HIGH JUMP

EVENT OVERVIEW

The high jump is one of the standard track and field events that take place at all athletics meetings. Using only the strength of their bodies, competitors take running jumps to clear a horizontal bar. The high jump is very demanding, both physically and technically, and the progression of the world record shows just how much improvement there has been in the conditioning of athletes and the development of technical innovations.

ATHLETE PROFILE

High jumpers of both sexes are usually above average height: most men are at least 1.85m (6ft 1in) tall; women are usually over 1.75m (5ft 10in). They nearly all have a lean, slim build but have well-developed quadriceps and calf muscles. Speed, flexibility, and good co-ordination are also important. Jumpers often work out on a trampoline to accustom themselves to "controlled" falling.

Close-fitting kit
Vest and shorts or leotard are close-fitting to help keep jumpers clear of the bar

Odd shoes
Jumpers may wear odd shoes: the jump-off foot has a cleated sole, but the other may have a smooth sole; neither sole should be more than 13mm (½in) thick

NEED2KNOW

➡ The high jump has been an Olympic event since the 1896 Olympics in Athens.

➡ The event was revolutionized in the 1960s by the introduction of soft mats that enabled athletes to land on their backs without serious injury.

➡ Almost all modern jumpers use a technique called the Fosbury Flop, after 1968 Olympic champion Dick Fosbury.

SIDELINES

1.94 The height in metres (6ft 4in) of Blanka Vlasic, the tallest world-class woman high jumper. Vlasic, the Croatian record-holder, won gold at the 2009 World Championships.

400 The height in metres (1,312ft) that an adult human would need to jump to emulate the high-jump world record of the common flea.

EQUIPMENT SET-UP

The modern high-jump bar is made of lightweight material, such as reinforced plastic or aluminium, that falls relatively easily if touched by the athlete. It is approximately 4m (13ft) long, round, square, or triangular in cross-section, and rests on two uprights. The measured height of the bar can be adjusted rapidly as a competition progresses. Directly behind the bar is a deep, soft mattress that cushions the jumper's landing.

CUSHIONED LANDING

The landing area is normally made of plastic-covered layers of foam rubber, usually at least 1m (3ft 3in) thick. Old-style sandpits are still sometimes used in school and other junior events, which means that techniques such as the Fosbury Flop – in which jumpers land on their shoulders – are impossible.

COMPACT AREA

The high jump takes up less room than most athletics events. The run-up area – made of asphalt, like a running track – allows for approach runs of about 12m (40ft) from almost any direction. Right-angled approaches to the bar are rare – most jumpers come in from an acute angle.

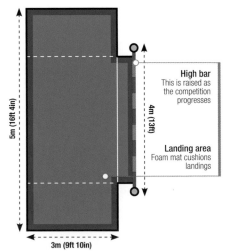

5m (16ft 4in)

High bar
This is raised as the competition progresses

4m (13ft)

Landing area
Foam mat cushions landings

3m (9ft 10in)

RAISING THE BAR

High jumping has few rules and regulations. Competitors can leap off only one foot and must not knock the bar off its supports. Touching the bar is fine, as long as it does not fall – and as long as the jumper does not use any part of his or her body to hold it up.

In competitions, athletes choose the height of their opening jump, which is usually relatively low. As the competition goes on, the bar is raised by increments – usually 3cm or 5cm, but 1cm towards the conclusion of the event.

Once a height has been cleared, competitors may not attempt a lower height. They may pass at any height, even if they have tried but failed to clear the bar already, but as soon as they record three consecutive misses, they are out. The competitor who clears the highest jump wins. Ties are decided on the lowest number of failed attempts.

DOING THE FLOP

TRADITIONALISTS WERE AGHAST WHEN US ATHLETE DICK FOSBURY WON GOLD AT THE 1968 MEXICO OLYMPICS WITH HIS NEW TECHNIQUE. US OLYMPIC COACH PAYTON JORDAN SAID: "KIDS IMITATE CHAMPIONS. IF THEY TRY TO IMITATE FOSBURY, HE WILL WIPE OUT AN ENTIRE GENERATION OF HIGH JUMPERS BECAUSE THEY WILL ALL HAVE BROKEN NECKS".

STAT CENTRAL

MEN'S WORLD RECORD		WOMEN'S WORLD RECORD	
HEIGHT	ATHLETE (YEAR)	HEIGHT	ATHLETE (YEAR)
2.45m	JAVIER SOTOMAYOR (1993)	2.09m	STEFKA KOSTADINOVA (1987)
2.42m	PATRIK SJOBERG (1987)	2.07m	LYUDMILA ANDONOVA (1984)
2.41m	IGOR PAKLIN (1985)	2.05m	TAMARA BYKOVA (1984)
2.40m	RUDOLF POVARNITSYN (1985)	2.03m	ULRIKE MEYFARTH (1983)
2.39m	ZHU JIANHUA (1984)	2.01m	SARA SIMENONI (1978)
2.35m	JACEK WSZOLA (1980)	2.00m	ROSEMARIE ACKERMANN (1977)
2.34m	VLADIMIR JASHTSHENKO (1978)	1.91m	IOLANDA BALAS (1961)
2.28m	VALERIY BRUMEL (1963)	1.77m	CHENG FENG-JUNG (1957)
2.22m	JOHN THOMAS (1960)	1.72m	SHEILA LERWILL (1951)
2.15m	CHARLES DUMAS (1956)	1.71m	FANNY BLANKERS-KOEN (1943)
2.11m	LESTER STEERS (1941)	1.65m	DOROTHY ODAM (1939)
2.06m	WALTER MARTY (1934)	1.55m	PHYLLIS GREEN (1926)
2.00m	GEORGE HORINE (1912)	1.45m	NANCY VOORHEES (1922)

EVOLVING TECHNIQUE

Until the late 1960s the most popular high-jump techniques were the scissors and the Western roll. Using the scissors method, the jumper approached the bar from an angle and threw first the inside leg and then the outside leg over the bar in a scissoring motion, landing on the feet. For the Western roll, the jumper again approached the bar on a diagonal, but used the inner leg for the take-off, while the outer leg was thrust up to lead the body sideways over the bar. The Fosbury Flop, named after American jumper Dick Fosbury, who used it to win Olympic gold, is now almost universal. The last world record breaker not to use Fosbury's method was Vladimir Jashtshenko in 1978.

HIGHER AND HIGHER

Since the end of the 19th century, high jump techniques have evolved rapidly. First sideways, then forwards, then, eventually, backwards, jumpers have been hurling themselves over higher. In less than 100 years (1895–1993), the men's high jump world record rose by nearly 25 per cent.

SCISSORS JUMP

The scissors jump was first used by American Michael F. Sweeney, who took the world record in 1895 with a height of 1.97m (6ft 5½in). The scissors was a popular technique until the late 1960s.

One leg at a time
The leading leg is raised over the bar first, immediately followed by the other leg

WESTERN ROLL

As they reach the high point of their leaps, jumpers rotate their torsos to cross the bar face down. George Horine used the roll to clear 2m (6ft 6¾in) in 1912.

Face down
The jumper must rotate the body as he goes over the bar

THE "FOSBURY FLOP"

A "flopper" takes a curved running approach, then launches herself off the outside foot, head and shoulders first, into a modified scissors jump with her back arching backwards over the bar. By the time the hips pass over the bar, the whole upper body is in descent. As Fosbury explained, a correctly executed Flop involves landing on the shoulders, not the neck.

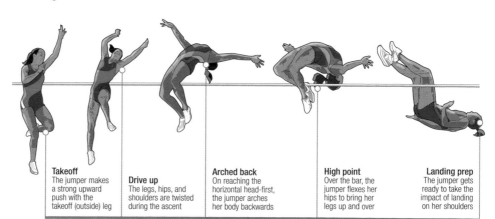

Takeoff
The jumper makes a strong upward push with the takeoff (outside) leg

Drive up
The legs, hips, and shoulders are twisted during the ascent

Arched back
On reaching the horizontal head-first, the jumper arches her body backwards

High point
Over the bar, the jumper flexes her hips to bring her legs up and over

Landing prep
The jumper gets ready to take the impact of landing on her shoulders

POLE VAULT

NEED2KNOW

→ Vaulting with poles was originally a practical method of crossing natural obstacles such as ditches and marshes.

→ The first recorded pole vault competition was held in England in 1812.

→ Broad jumping – a closely related sport in which athletes use a pole to gain distance rather than height – is widely practised but has never become an established event at top-class competitive levels.

→ The men's pole vault has been a medal event at every modern Olympics; the first women's competition was held in Sydney in 2000.

EVENT OVERVIEW

The pole vault is a field event for men and women. Competitors sprint along a runway carrying a long, flexible pole which they plant in a box and use to lever themselves over a crossbar suspended several metres above the ground between two uprights. The height of the crossbar is raised after every round and athletes are eliminated from the competition if they fail three consecutive jump attempts.

Supportive shoes
Vaulters wear running shoes with cleated soles for dependable grip on the runway

Close fitting
Sports vest and running shorts should be close-fitting to reduce the dangers of snagging the pole on the run up and dislodging the crossbar during the jump

No limits
The pole may be any length or diameter, but it must always be round in profile. There is no limit to the pole's flexibility

Fibreglass pole
Wood was most popular until the early 20th century, when it was superseded by bamboo; aluminium was preferred between 1945 and the early 1960s, when fibreglass became the norm

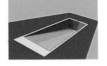

ATHLETE PROFILE
Most leading pole vaulters are tall, but can be any height. They need speed to build up momentum on the runway, explosive power in the legs for the take-off, and great strength in the shoulders, arms, and abdomen to lift themselves up into an upside-down vertical position at the top of the flight phase. Spatial awareness is key to avoiding the crossbar.

EQUIPMENT SET-UP

The pole vault event requires a runway of 40–45m (131–147ft 6in), a pole box, two uprights with pegs, a crossbar, landing mats, and, of course, an athlete with a very long, flexible pole. Officials are on hand to oversee the contest and adjust the height of the crossbar.

IN THE BOX
At the end of the runway is a pole box, into which the vaulter thrusts one end of the pole to gain leverage for the jump. Wedge-shaped and open at the approach end, the box is 1m (3ft 3in) long. It deepens to 20cm (8in) and narrows to 15cm (6in).

Adjustable height
Pegs, positioned on the supports inside the uprights, allow the crossbar to be raised as the competition progresses. The crossbar is 4.5m (14ft 9in) long

Landing mat
Foam rubber no less than 1–1.5m (3–5ft) thick

Starting point
Vaulters sprint down the runway to gain enough speed to propel themselves into the air

White lines
The runway is marked on each edge by a white line. It is not an offence to step over the lines while running

Extra padding
The areas on either side of the pole box are padded in case the athlete falls before completing the jump

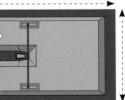

Minimum 5m (16ft 4in)

Minimum 5m (16ft 4in)

40–45m (131–147ft 6in)

RULES OF THE BAR

An opening bar height and a sequence of incremental heights is decided by an event official, and vaulters choose the height at which they wish to enter the competition. Athletes take it in turns to vault. If two or more of them have cleared the bar, the height is increased by the agreed distance, typically 5cm (2in) or 15cm (6in). Vaulters may decline to jump at a certain height and wait to try at a higher one. If at the end of the competition there is a tie on height, the number of failures is taken into consideration. If two or more vaulters have the same number of misses, there may be a sudden-death jump off.

LEARNING TO FLY

Pole vault is a series of phases that, performed perfectly, can produce jumps of more than 6m (19ft 8in) – although only 16 male pole vaulters have ever achieved this. A higher grip on the pole allows more leverage into the swing phase, while whipping the take-off leg through to the vertical position keeps energy in the flight phase, giving the vaulter more height over the crossbar. It doesn't matter if the competitor touches the crossbar during the jump, as long as it stays in position and does not fall. Each phase of the vaulting sequence (below) is crucial to executing a successful jump.

Approach and take off
Vaulters plant the pole in the box at an angle of about 20°; the pole then bows away from them under their weight as they enter the swing phase

Swing and row
The vaulter swings the trailing leg forwards and rows his arms downwards. This helps to bend the pole even more

In flight
Once in the air, vaulters extend their hips and legs to turn themselves upside down as the pole straightens

Clearing the bar
The vaulter pivots his body towards the runway as he pushes himself clear of the crossbar

Fly-away
As the vaulter's descent begins, the pole is released and pushed away so that it does not knock down the crossbar

Run up
Vaulters use the track to build up speed and momentum and are sprinting just before take off. They grasp the pole at one end. At the start they hold the pole up like a lance, then lower it as they near the take-off point

Touch down
The vaulter positions himself to land safely on his back in the middle of the thick landing mats

STAT CENTRAL

MEN'S WORLD RECORD		WOMEN'S WORLD RECORD	
HEIGHT	ATHLETE (YEAR)	HEIGHT	ATHLETE (YEAR)
6.14m	SERGEI BUBKA (1994)	5.06m	YELENA ISINBAYEVA (2009)
5.83m	THIERRY VIGNERON (1983)	4.88m	SVETLANA FEOFANOVA (2004)
5.82m	PIERRE QUINON (1983)	4.87m	YELENA ISINBAYEVA (2004)
5.81m	VLADIMIR POLYAKOV (1981)	4.85m	SVETLANA FEOFANOVA (2004)
5.80m	THIERRY VIGNERON (1981)	4.82m	YELENA ISINBAYEVA (2003)
5.78m	WLADYSLAW KOZAKIEWICZ (1980)	4.81m	STACY DRAGILA (2001)
5.70m	DAVE ROBERTS (1976)	4.60m	EMMA GEORGE (1999)
5.67m	EARL BELL (1976)	4.23m	SUN CAIYUN (1995)
5.65m	DAVE ROBERTS (1975)	4.22m	DANIELA BÁRTOVÁ (1995)
5.63m	BOB SEAGREN (1972)	4.18m	ANDREA MÜLLER (1995)

THE KING OF POLE VAULT

UKRAINIAN SERGEI BUBKA IS INDISPUTABLY THE GREATEST POLE VAULTER OF ALL TIME. HE BROKE 35 WORLD RECORDS DURING HIS CAREER – 17 OUTDOOR AND 18 INDOOR – AND WON SIX CONSECUTIVE WORLD CHAMPIONSHIPS BETWEEN 1983 AND 1997. HE WAS THE FIRST MAN TO CLEAR THE ELUSIVE 6M MARK, A FEAT HE ACHIEVED IN 44 COMPETITIONS, AND REMAINS THE ONLY POLE VAULTER TO HAVE CLEARED OVER 6.10M. OLYMPIC GOLD MEDALS WERE HARDER TO COME BY, HOWEVER; HE WON ONLY ONE, IN THE 1988 OLYMPIC GAMES IN SEOUL.

NEED2KNOW

→ The discus became an Olympic medal event for women at the 1928 Games.

→ The first man to break the 200ft mark was American Al Oerter in 1962.

→ The first woman to throw the discus over 70m (300ft) was Faina Melnik of Russia in 1976.

DISCUS DETAIL

As its name suggests, the discus is disc shaped. It is made mainly of rubber but also has a metallic or wooden rim and core to make up the required weight. The maximum central thickness is 4.4–4.6cm (about 1¾in). The weight and dimensions here are for adult competitions: both may be reduced for junior events.

WOMEN
1kg (2lb 3oz)

MEN
2kg (4lb 7oz)

18.2cm (7in)

22cm (8½in)

TRIALS

Throwers have three attempts, called trials. They must release the discus within the circle and remain there until it has landed; they may leave only from the back half of the circle. The discus must hit the ground within the marked landing sector for the throw to be valid. The length of the throw is measured from the front of the circle to the point at which the discus first lands. Distances are rounded down to the nearest centimetre (or half-inch) below the length of the throw.

CENTRIFUGAL FORCE

The thrower takes up a position at the back of the circle. He or she rests the discus in the throwing hand, then makes one and a half quick, powerful turns on the balls of the feet, like uncoiling a spring, to produce the force to release the discus at shoulder level. As the discus is released off the index or middle finger, it spins clockwise (for a right-handed thrower). Discus throwers welcome a headwind because it helps increase the amount of lift, so lengthening the throw.

Warm up
The throwing arm is taken as far back as possible

PRELIMINARY SWING
The thrower makes two or three swings by rotating the torso. This sets the body into its throwing rhythm and prepares it for the turn.

Spin to win
Bodyweight shifts from foot to foot

TURNING CIRCLE
The thrower spins around one and a half times, from the back of the circle to the front. This move winds up the momentum for the release.

Long reach
The throwing arm is extended behind the thrower

RELEASE
The power in the release comes from an explosion of energy in the body and legs. The discus spins as it is released from the hand.

Foot fault
The feet must remain in the circle for the throw to be good

FOLLOW THROUGH
After releasing the discus, the thrower continues to turn, taking the left leg through almost 360 degrees to avoid overstepping the boundary.

DISCUS

EVENT OVERVIEW

Originally part of the pentathlon in the ancient Olympics, the discus is now one of the standard athletics field events. The aim of the competition is to throw the discus as far as possible.

DISCUS CIRCLE

The discus is thrown from a circle 2.5m (8ft) in diameter. The landing sector is an area fanning out at 35 degrees from the centre of the throwing circle. For safety, a U-shaped cage surrounds the throwing circle. The mouth of the cage is 6m (19ft 8in) wide and sits 7m (23ft) in front of the throwing circle.

Secure grip
The tips of the fingers grip the rim of the discus as the palm rests on top

Smooth soles
Shoes have smooth soles to help the thrower pivot

Sound surface
The surface of the throwing circle must be smooth but not slippery

2.5m (8ft)

ATHLETE PROFILE

Leading discus throwers are big: men average 1.93m (6ft 4in) tall and weigh over 115kg (254lb); most female champions are at least 1.75m (5ft 9in) tall and 93kg (205lb). Although strong shoulders and arms are needed, the power comes from the athlete's legs and torso.

SHOT PUT

SHOT PUT

EVENT OVERVIEW

The shot put is a field event in which athletes compete to see which of them can throw (put) a heavy metal ball (shot) the furthest. Each competitor is allowed to make three attempts. The rules, required skills, and technique of shot put are similar to those of discus (see opposite).

NEED2KNOW

→ The sport is believed to have originated from an ancient form of warfare.

→ Codified in the late 19th century, shot put was one of the men's events at the first modern Olympics in 1896. Women's shot put first became a medal event at the 1948 Olympic Games in London.

Close contact
Shot putters sometimes use chalk on their necks to improve the grip on the shot

ATHLETE PROFILE
Shot putters are often tall and powerfully built: the average male is 1.87m (6ft 2in) tall and weighs 125.6kg (277lb), the average female is over 1.75m (5ft 9in) and 90kg (200lb). The sport requires speed, flexibility, and coordination, as well as strength, so shot putters need to be good all-round athletes.

Competition clothing
Athletes wear vest and shorts. The shorts may be tight fitting to support the thighs

Technical footwear
Smooth soles help the thrower glide or rotate with maximum efficiency

Stop board
This white board, about 10cm (4in) high, marks the front of the throwing circle

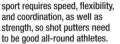

Throwing circle
Set about 2cm (1in) below ground level, the circle has a non-slippery, cement surface

2.1m (7ft)

GLIDE OR SPIN?

The two main styles of shot put delivery are the glide and the spin. In a glide, the athlete faces the rear of the circle and hops backwards while twisting the hips to the front. The feet stay as close to the ground as possible. The spin uses extra rotation to build up momentum.

THE O'BRIEN GLIDE

The spin had its beginnings as an adaption of the glide invented by US champion Parry O'Brien in the 1950s. In the O'Brien Glide, the athlete crouches to face the back of the circle, pushes off powerfully from one leg to rotate the body and face the front, and launches the shot.

THE BARYSHNIKOV ROTATION

This technique (shown below, for a right-handed thrower) was originated in the 1970s by Soviet athlete Aleksandr Baryshnikov. It is very similar to the discus thrower's spin, and makes it easier to maximize the launch speed of the put. Controversial at first, the Baryshnikov Rotation is the style most used by shot putters today.

HEAVY METAL

The shot is usually made of iron or brass, must have a smooth surface, and must not be modified in any way.

WOMEN
4kg (8lb 12oz)

MEN
7.2kg (16lb)

9.5–11cm (3¾–4in)   11–13cm (4–5in)

THE CIRCLE

The landing area is a sector that fans out at 35 degrees from the centre of the throwing circle; its sides are usually no more than 30m (98ft 6in) long.

SHOT PUT LAW

For each of the three shots, the competitor may touch the inside of but not overstep the stop board at the front of the circle. The length of the shot is measured from the front of the circle to the shot's first landing point and recorded to the nearest centimetre or half-inch below the actual length of the throw.

SIDELINES

11 The number of Olympic medals out of a possible 12 won by American male shot putters in the four Summer Games held between 1948 and 1960.

116 The number of consecutive shot put competitions won by Parry O'Brien in the 1950s. He also competed in four Olympic games, winning gold in two of them.

Start position
The thrower comes out of a crouched position, lifting the left leg

Body twist
Weight shifts from right to left side

Energy flow
To keep the power, the left side must stay braced

PUSH OFF
The thrower faces away from the direction of the throw with the shot tucked between neck and shoulder.

SPIN
The thrower spins on the ball of the left foot. The left arm comes forward and points along the trajectory.

THRUST
The athlete releases the shot at the moment of maximum forward velocity, at an angle of about 40 degrees.

NEED2KNOW

→ Finns are particularly successful javelin throwers, tallying a total of 26 Olympic medals, nine of them gold.

→ Despite its long history, javelin throwing was not originally included at the modern Olympics. It made its debut only at the fourth Games in London 1908, when it was a men-only event; women's javelin was introduced in Los Angeles in 1932.

→ For the safety of spectators, the javelin has been redesigned (men's in 1986; women's in 1999) to reduce the distance it can travel.

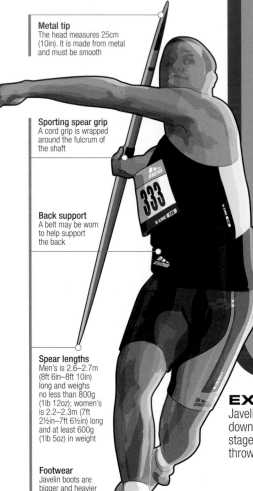

Metal tip
The head measures 25cm (10in). It is made from metal and must be smooth

Sporting spear grip
A cord grip is wrapped around the fulcrum of the shaft

Back support
A belt may be worn to help support the back

Spear lengths
Men's is 2.6–2.7m (8ft 6in–8ft 10in) long and weighs no less than 800g (1lb 12oz); women's is 2.2–2.3m (7ft 2½in–7ft 6½in) long and at least 600g (1lb 5oz) in weight

Footwear
Javelin boots are bigger and heavier than running shoes with front and rear spikes

ATHLETE PROFILE
Strong hips, shoulders, and elbows are key for success, as is speed along the runway. Strength and speed produce the power to throw the javelin long distances.

JAVELIN

EVENT OVERVIEW
Javelin throwing is a field event for men and women. Athletes compete to see which of them can throw a spear-like projectile over the greatest distance. As well as being a sport in its own right, javelin throwing is one of the events included in pentathlon and decathlon competitions.

TARGET AREA
Athletes run up to the throwing line along a synthetic track, 4m (13ft) wide, that may extend across the athletics track. Beyond the line, the landing area is a sector, usually of grass, that fans out at 29 degrees for about 100m (328ft) – the exact size is partly determined by the space available and is partly at the judges' discretion. Sector lines provide a rough guide to the distances thrown.

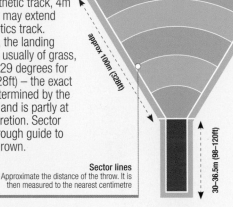

approx 100m (328ft)

30–36.5m (98–120ft)

Sector lines
Approximate the distance of the throw. It is then measured to the nearest centimetre

IN COMPETITION
Athletes get three throws each, unless there are fewer than eight competitors, in which case they throw six times. Once prepared, they have 90 seconds to take their turn. For the throw to be legal, an athlete must stay behind the line at the end of the runway until the javelin lands and the javelin must come down point-first within the landing sector. Throws are measured from the end of the runway to the javelin's first point of contact with the ground. In the event of a tie, the winner is the athlete with the longest second-best throw.

EXECUTING A THROW
Javelins must be held over the shoulder using the cord grip. The athlete accelerates down the runway then, on entering the last few strides, prepares to throw. The final stages of the throwing action are shown below. The athlete must complete his throw without touching or crossing the line at the end of the runway.

LEG CROSSOVER
Near the end of the run up, an athlete crosses his legs in preparation for getting maximum torque on the throw.

DRAW
As his legs untwist, his throwing arm is pulled back; the other is pushed forward to help his aim and follow-through.

LAUNCH
A thrower keeps the javelin behind his shoulders for as long as possible before releasing it.

RELEASE
Stopping suddenly and thrusting the throwing arm forward achieves the greatest possible speed of throw.

HAMMER

EVENT OVERVIEW

The aim of this track-and-field athletics event is to throw the hammer as far as possible from a circle into a marked target area. Although the projectile used is known as a hammer, the term is misleading: it is in fact a heavy metal ball attached by a wire to a handle.

PLAYER PROFILE
Hammer throwers are powerfully built, especially in the arms, shoulders, and torso, which they develop working out with weights and barbells. The outstanding men in the sport weigh on average about 110kg (243lb); the leading women are about 79kg (176lb). Throwers need not be tall, but those who are have a natural advantage.

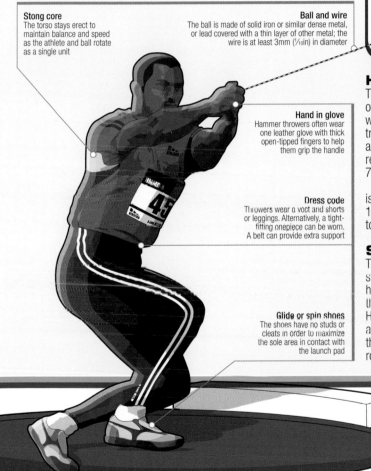

Stong core
The torso stays erect to maintain balance and speed as the athlete and ball rotate as a single unit

Ball and wire
The ball is made of solid iron or similar dense metal, or lead covered with a thin layer of other metal; the wire is at least 3mm (⅛in) in diameter

Hand in glove
Hammer throwers often wear one leather glove with thick open-tipped fingers to help them grip the handle

Dress code
Throwers wear a vest and shorts or leggings. Alternatively, a tight-fitting onepiece can be worn. A belt can provide extra support

Glide or spin shoes
The shoes have no studs or cleats in order to maximize the sole area in contact with the launch pad

2.1m (7ft)

HEAVY HAMMER

The hammer used in men's events is composed of a ball 11–13cm (4⅓–5in) in diameter, a steel wire measuring 1.2m (4ft) in length, and a roughly triangular-shaped handle measuring 13cm (5in) and 10cm (4in) at its widest and longest points respectively. The maximum combined weight is 7.26kg (16lb).

The women's hammer ball is smaller and lighter. It is 9.5–11cm (3½–4⅓in) across and weighs 4kg (8lb 13oz). The wire and handle have similar dimensions to the men's hammer.

SPIN TO WIN

The classic throw consists of four phases. At the start the athlete takes up a stationary position with his or her back to the landing area, then swings the hammer to and fro in a pendulum movement. Having gained momentum, the hammer is raised above the head and whirled in what is known as the windmill sequence. This lasts for two or three rotations before the hammer is released.

CAGED CIRCLE

The throwing area is a concrete circle with a diameter of 2.1m (7ft). In front of the circle, the landing sector fans out at 40 degrees and has sides 80–100m (262–328ft) long. The exact dimensions are determined by the space available.

HAPPY HAMMERING

In most competitions, competitors have three attempts at throwing the hammer, each of which must be completed within 90 seconds of entering the throwing circle. In larger events, there may then be a second round from which all but the eight best performers are eliminated. The finalists get a further three throws each. If two or more athletes tie, the winner is the one with the second-longest throw. For a throw to be valid the competitor must stay within the throwing circle until the hammer has landed in the landing sector. Top male competitors throw the hammer about 85m (276ft); women throw the hammer around 75m (244ft).

HAMMER CAGE
For safety reasons the cage is made of netting capable of stopping a hammer travelling at speed.

Cage
Surrounds throwing area on three sides

Circle
Area from which the hammer is thrown

DECATHLON AND HEPTATHLON

EVENT OVERVIEW

Often seen as the jacks of all trades of athletics, decathletes and heptathletes specialize in being great all-round sportspeople. Their sports comprise 10 (decathlon) or seven (heptathlon) track and field disciplines that are contested over two consecutive days. Men compete in decathlon while women compete in heptathlon. The competitions are a test of endurance and concentration to last the distance, as well as speed, strength, and skill to win the individual events. The decathlon has appeared in the summer Olympic Games since 1912 and the heptathlon since 1984.

NEED2KNOW

→ Decathlon consists of ten track and field events; heptathlon of seven. Male athletes contest decathlon, while female athletes contest heptathlon.

→ Both events have developed from the ancient Greek pentathlon, which featured in the ancient Olympics from around 700 BCE.

→ The sequence of events in decathlon has remained unchanged since 1914.

SIDELINES

14 The number years Jackie Joyner-Kersee held the world hepthalon record of 7,291 points (1988–2002). It is the longest standing hepthalon record, and she is the heptathlete who has gained 7,000 points most often.

9,026 The number of points scored by Czech athlete Roman Sebrle when he broke the world record at Gotzis in Austria in 2001. In doing so he became the first athlete to score more than 9,000 points in a decathlon. In Athens in 2004 he broke the Olympic record, scoring 8,893 points.

17 The age of athlete Bob Mathias when he won Olympic gold in the decathlon at the 1948 Games in London. Despite never having competed in the event prior to 1948, he still holds the record as the youngest Olympic champion in the discipline.

DECATHLON EVENTS
100 METRES
LONG JUMP
SHOT PUT
HIGH JUMP
400 METRES
100 METRES HURDLES
DISCUS
POLE VAULT
JAVELIN
1,500 METRES

HEPTATHLON EVENTS
100 METRES HURDLES
HIGH JUMP
SHOT PUT
200 METRES
LONG JUMP
JAVELIN
800 METRES

DECATHLON

This two-day competition comprises 10 disciplines: 100m, long jump, shot put, high jump, and 400m on day one; 110m hurdles, discus throw, pole vault, javelin throw, and 1500m on day two. Competitors' speed and strength are challenged in the first day's events, while the second day tests their endurance and technical skills.

Athletes must compete in all disciplines in order to be included in the final classification.

HEPTATHLON

The women's seven-discipline competition comprises 100m hurdles, high jump, shot put, and 200m on the first day, and long jump, javelin throw, and 800m on the second day. Originally, female athletes competed in the five-discipline pentathlon, but the javelin throw and 800m race were added in 1981 after the1980 Olympics in Moscow to create the modern event.

COMPETITOR PROFILE

Decathletes and heptathletes need to be great all-rounders, which not only requires speed and mobility but also strength and explosive power. They tend to have lean, athletic physiques, rather than the specific adaptations developed by specialists.

THE BEST EVER

WIDELY REGARDED AS THE WORLD'S BEST-EVER ALL-ROUND ATHLETE, DALEY THOMPSON HOLDS THE RECORD AS THE FIRST PERSON TO WIN OLYMPIC GOLD FOR DECATHLON TWICE, FIRST IN 1980 AND AGAIN IN 1984. HE RETIRED FROM COMPETITION IN 1992 DUE TO INJURY, BUT THAT WAS NOT THE END OF THOMPSON'S SPORTING CAREER. IN THE 1990S HE BECAME A PROFESSIONAL FOOTBALLER, PLAYING FOR MANSFIELD TOWN, AND THEN A FITNESS COACH.

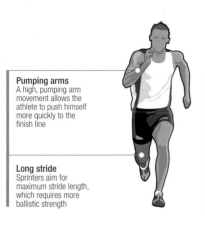

Pumping arms
A high, pumping arm movement allows the athlete to push himself more quickly to the finish line

Long stride
Sprinters aim for maximum stride length, which requires more ballistic strength

SPRINTS
Decathletes and heptathletes compete over different sprint distances. The men have two sprint events, the 100m and 400m, while the women race only over 200m. The maximum number of points on offer for 100m is 1,223.

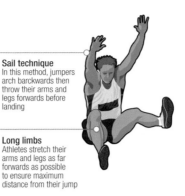

Sail technique
In this method, jumpers arch barckwards then throw their arms and legs forwards before landing

Long limbs
Athletes stretch their arms and legs as far forwards as possible to ensure maximum distance from their jump

LONG JUMP
The second event for men and the fifth for women, the best long jumps rely on speed in the run up, good flight through the air, and a forward landing. The 1,520 points available in this event is the womens' highest single score.

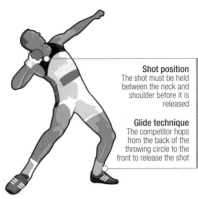

Shot position
The shot must be held between the neck and shoulder before it is released

Glide technique
The competitor hops from the back of the throwing circle to the front to release the shot

SHOT PUT
Athletes have three trials each to score the maximum points on offer: 1,350 for a 23.99m put for men, and 1,500 for a 24.40m throw for women. The shots used are the same as those for the individual competition.

Head and shoulders
The athlete initiates the back arch over the bar with his head and shoulders

Active feet
The athlete must kick his feet up at the end of the jump to ensure they clear the bar

HIGH JUMP
This vertical jump appears on the first day of both the decathlon and heptathlon competitions. The decathletes are chasing a maximum score of 1,392 points, while the women are competing for 1,498 points.

Arm propulsion
The arms provide extra thrust as the athlete jumps the hurdle

Rear leg
An athlete's rear leg must clear the hurdle in order for him or her to keep a smooth fast rhythm along the track

HURDLES
Raced on the first day over 110m in the men's decathlon and on the second day over 100m in the women's heptathlon, the hurdles race carries a maximum score of 1,223 points for men and 1,361 for women.

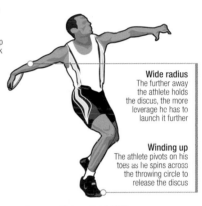

Wide radius
The further away the athlete holds the discus, the more leverage he has to launch it further

Winding up
The athlete pivots on his toes as he spins across the throwing circle to release the discus

DISCUS THROW
The second of the throwing events is contested only in the decathlon competition. There is a maximum of 1,500 points available, but athletes must throw 79.41m to be awarded them.

Take-off
The athlete hangs on to the fibreglass pole as it lifts him up towards the bar

Core strength
The athlete uses his core strength to lift his legs and torso so that he ends up upside down before clearing the bar

POLE VAULT
The second event competed only by decathletes, the pole vault appears on the second day of the competition. Athletes aim to jump heights of 6.49m in order to be awarded the maximum score of 1,396 points.

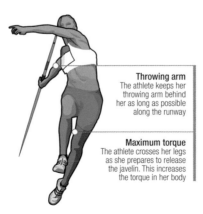

Throwing arm
The athlete keeps her throwing arm behind her as long as possible along the runway

Maximum torque
The athlete crosses her legs as she prepares to release the javelin. This increases the torque in her body

JAVELIN THROW
The final throwing event, the javelin throw features in both men's and women's combined events. Throws of 102.85m for men and 82.63m for women will win the competitors maximum points.

Relaxed stance
Over longer distances athletes keep their arms more relaxed than when sprinting. This helps conserve energy

Long stride
Athletes still aim for a long stride at this distance, keeping contact with the track to a minimum

MIDDLE DISTANCE
The last event of both competitions is the 800m for women and 1,500m for men. Final race positions matter less than who beats whom for the last available points; a maximum of 1,250 for both heptathletes and decathletes.

COMPETITOR PROFILE
Most walkers are tall and lean. In training they work on back, abdominal, and thigh muscles to meet the demands of the walking action. Their feet must be in good condition, and they need a lot of stamina.

COURSES
Most walking races are held on roads. There are judges along the course to ensure that competitors walk in accordance with the rules. Often, walkers do several laps of a circuit so that officials get the chance to observe them several times during the race.

RACE RULES
One foot must be in contact with the ground at all times, and the supporting leg must be straight, not bent at the knee, from the moment the foot touches the ground until the supporting leg passes below the body. Walkers are penalized for illegal techniques, such as "lifting" – having both feet off the ground. Officials report offences to three judges who may show the offender a yellow warning paddle; further violations lead to a red paddle; three red paddles mean disqualification.

SO NEAR AND YET...
AT THE 2000 SYDNEY OLYMPICS, AUSTRALIAN JANE SAVILLE WAS DISQUALIFIED FOR LIFTING JUST 150M (492YD) FROM THE FINISH AS SHE LED THE 20KM RACE. SHE BURST INTO TEARS AND, WHEN ASKED IF THERE WAS ANYTHING SHE NEEDED, REPLIED: "A GUN TO SHOOT MYSELF".

REGULATED WALKING
Race walking is much more demanding than regular walking. Enthusiasts claim that it is even harder than running: it takes a greater toll on the body because the action is less efficient. Walkers swivel and tilt their hips to lengthen their strides and get up as high as possible on the toes of the trailing foot before placing the heel of the leading foot on the ground.

Walking gear
Athletes wear loose-fitting vests, which may be in team colours

Baggy trousers
Shorts tend to be loose to avoid chafing the legs and groin

Silver lining
Socks are not essential with well-fitting shoes, but are sometimes worn to reduce rubbing

Sole control
Shoes have lightweight uppers with thin soles; the heels should be well padded. Shoes wear out quickly and need to be replaced regularly between races

Front foot
Toes raised at about 45° so that heel hits the ground first

Quick step
Trailing leg is raised, but knee kept low for speed

Short stride
Small, quick steps are efficient

Bent knee
The knee is bent once the leg is past the vertical position

CALM ON TOP
The torso is relaxed and upright for balance; the work is done by the arms and legs.

ONE AT A TIME
The lead foot must be grounded before the back foot is lifted: both feet off the ground is running.

WEIGHT AHEAD
In the middle of each stride, the upper body rocks forwards over the front leg.

SWING ALONG
Walkers must swing the arms vigorously to propel themselves forwards.

EVENT OVERVIEW
Race walking bears little relation to what most people know as "ordinary" walking. Athletes look more as if they are trying to stop themselves from running. The technique, requiring short, rapid steps, is difficult to master. Races are a test of the walker's concentration and endurance.

RACE WALKING

ORIENTEERING

EVENT OVERVIEW

Orienteering is a cross-country race in which participants use a map and compass to navigate between checkpoints, or controls, on an unfamiliar route. The winner is the first individual, or team, to reach the finish or, in timed events, whoever has reached the greatest number of checkpoints at the end of an allotted period.

ELEMENT OF SURPRISE

Competitors must not pre-plan a route. They are given a map of the course only when they arrive at a rallying point, which is usually some distance from the starting line. They may all start at the same time or at intervals of one or two minutes.

STAYING ON COURSE

Certain points are marked on an orienteering map, but not the course between them. A triangle marks the start, a double circle marks the finish. Single circles show the control points that competitors must visit. These are marked by red and white or orange and white flags.

Sprint orienteering may take place in city parks and other urban settings. In events held at night, control markers should have cat's eyes or other reflective surfaces, and competitors may wear torches on their heads to help them see.

EQUIPMENT

A map and a compass are essential equipment. Competitors normally sign in at control points, but electronic log-in devices called dibbers are sometimes worn on the fingers. At night, racers carry a whistle to attract attention in emergencies.

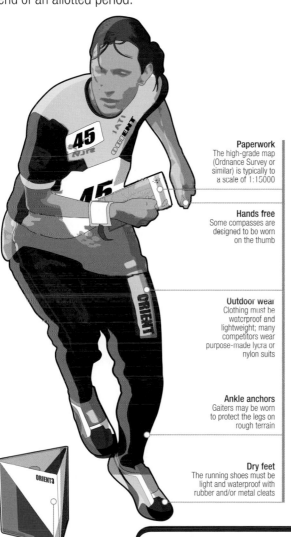

Paperwork
The high-grade map (Ordnance Survey or similar) is typically to a scale of 1:15000

Hands free
Some compasses are designed to be worn on the thumb

Outdoor wear
Clothing must be waterproof and lightweight; many competitors wear purpose-made lycra or nylon suits

Ankle anchors
Gaiters may be worn to protect the legs on rough terrain

Dry feet
The running shoes must be light and waterproof with rubber and/or metal cleats

Course markers
Brightly coloured indicators are located at all control points

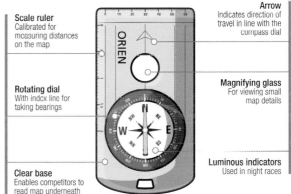

Scale ruler
Calibrated for measuring distances on the map

Rotating dial
With index line for taking bearings

Clear base
Enables competitors to read map underneath

Arrow
Indicates direction of travel in line with the compass dial

Magnifying glass
For viewing small map details

Luminous indicators
Used in night races

LIE OF THE LAND

A straight line is the shortest distance between two points, but it is not necessarily the quickest route. Race organizers often ensure that there are obstacles, such as gulleys and streams, between control points that runners must circumnavigate. Orienteers read the map to assess the landscape and choose a course between points. They use their compass to establish their position and the right direction, perhaps by taking bearings from easily identifiable landmarks.

COMPETITOR PROFILE

Successful orienteers have the stamina and speed of long-distance runners. They need to be able to read a map and compass while on the move and be expert navigators. Orienteers must be ready to use their initiative when confronted with a range of terrains that could include steep, rocky ground or marshes, as well as roads and tracks.

NEED2KNOW

→ At the annual world championships there are four timed events: long (90–100 mins for men; 70–80 mins for women); middle (30–35 mins); and relay (10–12 mins).

→ Most contests are on foot, but some involve the use of mountain bikes or skis.

RACE FORMAT

Most professional triathletes compete in Olympic or Ironman races. The Olympic event consists of a 1,500m (1,640yd) swim, a 40km (25 mile) cycle, and a 10km (6¼ mile) run. The Ironman is the ultimate test of endurance. The race consists of a 3.8km (2½ mile) swim, 180km (112 mile) cycle, and ends with a full marathon (42.2km or 26¼ miles).

SWIM

The swim takes place in a lake, river, or the sea. Swimmers may set off in a large bunch or smaller groups a few seconds apart. Any stroke can be used, but the crawl is the most popular. Wetsuits are compulsory in cold water.

RUN

The run may be a road race or cross country, and the course may be relatively flat or a real up-and-downer. Regular aid stations provide water and energy drinks to sustain the athletes.

BIKE

The cycling phase is a road race that starts and finishes at the transition area. In Olympic races, the pros may cycle in a group and draft in the slipstream of riders ahead. In Ironman events, triathletes must cycle alone.

TRANSITIONS

To keep transitions smooth and efficient, competitors check out the transition area before the race and practice removing wetsuits while running and mounting the bike with cycle shoes attached to the pedals.

Swimming cap
This is worn mainly for identification, but in very cold water an athlete may wear a neoprene cap and bodysuit to reduce heat loss

One-piece suit
Athletes can wear a one-piece suit or a short top and shorts. This outfit can be worn for all three disciplines, thus eliminating the need to change

Timing tags
An electronic chip attached to the ankle enables the accurate timing of all triathletes

Carbon cycle
Pro triathletes use aerodynamic time trial bikes with strong, ultra lightweight carbon fibre frames

ATHLETE PROFILE

Stamina, speed, physical and mental strength, technical ability, and the ability to switch effortlessly from one discipline to the next are all vital. Training typically takes up around 30 hours a week for a professional Ironman triathlete. Pros usually hit peak performances in their late 20s and early 30s.

ALOHA HAWAII

FIRST HELD IN 1978, THE HAWAII IRONMAN WORLD CHAMPIONSHIP IS NOTORIOUS FOR ITS TOUGHNESS. ATHLETES HAVE TO ENDURE HARSH TERRAIN, HIGH WINDS, AND SCORCHING TEMPERATURES.

NEED2KNOW

→ The International Triathlon Union (ITU) organises a series of world championship events annually.

→ The triathlon was first introduced to Olympic competition at Sydney in 2000; there are both men's and women's events.

→ The London Triathlon is the world's biggest event, with more than 8,000 triathletes swimming, cycling, and running the course in Docklands in east London.

→ The World Triathlon Corporation organizes the Ironman Triathlon World Championship. Ironman events in countries around the world offer qualification slots for the big race — Ironman Hawaii.

TRIATHLON

EVENT OVERVIEW

The triathlon is an endurance event that combines three sports in one race — swimming, followed by cycling, and then running. A triathlon is timed from the start of the swim to the end of the run, and the competitors seamlessly switch from one sport to the next in transition zones. Smooth transitions reduce race times, so triathletes often treat the two transitions as a fourth discipline. The standard distance for international triathletes is the Olympic triathlon, but formats vary from short sprints to long-distance Ironman events. Held annually since 1978, Ironman Hawaii is the most prestigious event in the triathlon calendar.

EVENT OVERVIEW

Modern pentathlon is a combination of five events in a day – shooting, fencing, swimming, riding, and running. The sport was the brainchild of Pierre de Coubertin, the founder of the modern Olympics, who believed it to be a measure of the "complete athlete". Men and women are awarded points for their performances in each of the first four events. The points then translate into a time advantage on the run. The overall winner is therefore the first to cross the finish line on the run.

MODERN PENTATHLON

POINTS FOR PRIZES

Generally, the rules governing each event are the same as when they are contested as individual sports. In the showjumping contest, however, the pentathletes draw lots for their horse and have only 20 minutes and up to five trial jumps to get to know their animal. And there is a staggered start for the cross-country run.

ATHLETE PROFILE

Contestants need a very wide range of skills. Older competitors tend to do better in the more technical events of shooting, fencing, and riding. Younger athletes generally excel in swimming and running. Top pentathletes are usually more than 28 years old.

SHOOTING

The shooting takes place on a 10m (33ft) range. Contestants fire 20 shots with a 4.5mm air pistol at a 15.5cm (6in) diameter target with nine rings and a centre circle, which counts the highest. Points are awarded according to how near to the target's centre the contestant's 20 shots hit.

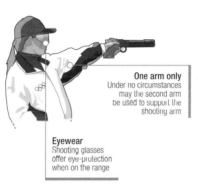

One arm only
Under no circumstances may the second arm be used to support the shooting arm

Eyewear
Shooting glasses offer eye-protection when on the range

FENCING

The fencing competition is held on a standard piste. Competitors fence each other athlete in turn, and bouts last for one minute. The first to land a hit with his or her épée wins the bout. If neither fencer strikes a winning blow, they both lose. Athletes who win 70 per cent of their bouts will be awarded 1,000 points.

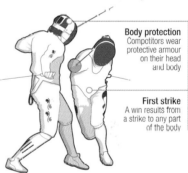

Body protection
Competitors wear protective armour on their head and body

First strike
A win results from a strike to any part of the body

SWIMMING

The swimming competition takes place in a standard Olympic pool. Pentathletes race against the clock – not each other – in a 200m freestyle race. For men, a time of 2 minutes 30 seconds translates into 1,000 competition points, and the equivalent time for women is 2 minutes 40 seconds.

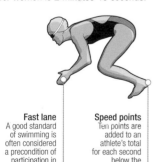

Fast lane
A good standard of swimming is often considered a precondition of participation in a pentathlon

Speed points
Ten points are added to an athlete's total for each second below the benchmark time

RIDING

The showjumping course is between 350–400m (383–437yd) long, with obstacles up to 1.2m (4ft) high. Contestants have 20 minutes to get used to their horse before jumping a 12-obstacle course within a specific time limit. Starting with 1,200 points, riders lose points for faults and slow times.

Horse play
Riding an unfamiliar horse is an unpredictable part of the pentathlon

Up and over
Riders lose 28 points for demolishing a fence

RUNNING

The run takes place on a 3,000m (3,280yd) cross-country course or a road track. The maximum climb of the course is 50m (164ft). The overall leader after the previous event – the riding – starts first, with the others behind in order of their placing. The winner of the running becomes the overall winner.

Running climax
A staggered start provides a nail-biting end to the competition

Points deductions
If an athlete starts before his or her allotted time in the handicap, 40 points are deducted

GYMNASTICS

GYMNASTICS

SPORT OVERVIEW

Gymnastics is a multidiscipline sport in which men and women compete as individuals or in teams. Individuals can compete in single disciplines or as all-rounders. The sport is split into three main sections: artistic gymnastics, rhythmic gymnastics, and trampoline. Rhythmic gymnastics is a discipline for women only. Men's artistic gymnastics consists of six disciplines: floor exercises, pommel, rings, vault, parallel bars, and high bar. Women's artistic gymnastics consists of four disciplines: vault, asymmetric bars, balance beam, and floor exercises.

ON BALANCE

SOVIET GYMNAST OLGA KORBUT SHOT TO FAME AT THE 1972 MUNICH OLYMPICS, BRINGING HER SPORT WITH HER. SHE WAS THE FIRST PERSON TO PERFORM A BACKWARD SOMERSAULT ON A BALANCE BEAM, AND HER EXPLOSIVE, TECHNICAL STYLE REVOLUTIONIZED THE SPORT.

CODE OF POINTS

The official scoring system (the "code of points") was overhauled in 2006 following accusations of inconsistent judging at the 2004 Olympics. However, critics claim the new code rewards technical difficulty at the expense of artistry, and the coveted "perfect ten" is now impossible to attain.

Apparatus scoreboard
This scoreboard gives the marks for the current competitor in that event

Floor exercises
The area for floor exercises and acrobatic gymnastics measures 12m x 12m (39ft 4in x 39ft 4in). Rhythmic gymnasts use a slightly larger area

Raised platform
The apparatus and floor mats are all placed on a raised platform. Only competing gymnasts are permitted on the podium during competitions

Pommel horse
Both the surface of the horse and the surface of the pommels must allow the gymnast to glide over them but must not be slippery

High bar
The 2.4m (7ft 10½in) long horizontal high bar is erected 2.8m (9ft 2in) above the floor.

Asymmetric bars
Featured in women's artistic gymnastics, the asymmetric bars are placed 160cm (63in) apart and have a height difference of 80cm (31in)

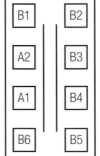

Vault runway
Competitors accelerate along the 25m (82ft) vault runway, which is 1m (39in) wide

JUDGE AND JURY

Top level gymnastics competitions are presided over by an apparatus jury. The jury is divided into an A-jury and a B-jury. The A-jury consists of two judges and the B-jury is made up of six judges. Some disciplines require other officials, such as line judges, for example, for the floor exercises. The A-judges sit in front of the apparatus, where they have a clear view of the gymnast's performance. The B-judges are positioned clockwise around the apparatus from the left of the A-jury.

B1	B2
A2	B3
A1	B4
B6	B5

COMPETITOR PROFILE

Male and female gymnasts come in a variety of shapes and sizes, depending on their area, or areas, of expertise. The men's rings event, for example, requires extraordinary upper-body strength, while women's rhythmic gymnastics relies on flexibility and precise muscle control. Common attributes of all gymnasts are their incredible balance and power – especially remarkable considering the diminutive stature of many top level competitors.

THE GYMNASTICS ARENA

The gymnastics competition arena, also known as the podium, is arranged to allow different competitions to be run at the same time. For example, the men's bars events can run at the same time as the women's balance beam, as they occupy opposite ends of the arena. At large events the competitions may be staged on different days, as was the case at the 2004 Olympics in Athens (where the rhythmic gymnastics competition was run in a different venue entirely).

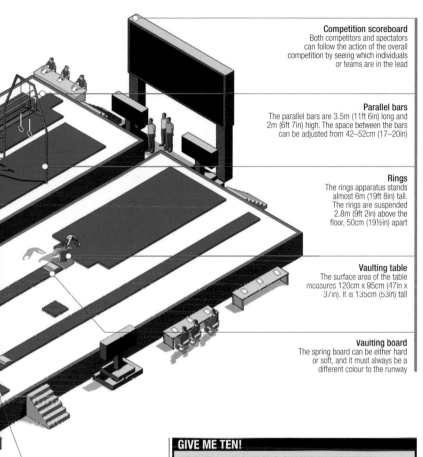

Competition scoreboard
Both competitors and spectators can follow the action of the overall competition by seeing which individuals or teams are in the lead

Parallel bars
The parallel bars are 3.5m (11ft 6in) long and 2m (6ft 7in) high. The space between the bars can be adjusted from 42–52cm (17–20in)

Rings
The rings apparatus stands almost 6m (19ft 8in) tall. The rings are suspended 2.8m (9ft 2in) above the floor, 50cm (19½in) apart

Vaulting table
The surface area of the table measures 120cm x 95cm (47in x 37in). It is 135cm (53in) tall

Vaulting board
The spring board can be either hard or soft, and it must always be a different colour to the runway

Floor mats
Padded floor mats, which are 10cm (4in) thick, are a key safety feature. The mats around the pommel horse, assymetric bars, horizontal bars, and rings are 20cm (8in) for additional protection

GIVE ME TEN!
AT THE 1976 OLYMPIC GAMES IN MONTREAL, ROMANIAN GYMNAST NADIA COMANECI BECAME THE FIRST PERSON TO ACHIEVE A PERFECT SCORE OF TEN – AT THE TENDER AGE OF 14. NOT CONTENT WITH SECURING THE RECORD AS THE YOUNGEST GYMNAST EVER TO DO SO, SHE WENT ON TO WIN FIVE OLYMPIC GOLD MEDALS.

INSIDE STORY

Both as a method of keeping fit and as a form of competition, gymnastics has a long history. The ancient Greeks used to perform the exercises naked. However, the use of clothing and special equipment for each event dates from the 18th century, when Germans developed gymnastics in military training. It soon caught on among civilians, too, and spread to other countries.

GYMNASTICS GOVERNING BODY
A European gymnastics federation was founded in 1881; it became the Fédération Internationale de Gymnastique (FIG) in 1921, when non-European countries were admitted. Gymnastics competitions were featured at the first modern Olympic Games in 1896, and women first competed in 1928.

STAT CENTRAL

MOST OLYMPIC MEDALS

INDIVIDUAL ALL-ROUND MEN

COUNTRY	NUMBER
SOVIET UNION	15
JAPAN	14
FRANCE	8
SWITZERLAND	6
ITALY	5

MEN'S TEAM COMPETITION

COUNTRY	NUMBER
JAPAN	12
SOVIET UNION	9
UNITED STATES	7
FINLAND	6
ITALY	5

INDIVIDUAL ALL-ROUND WOMEN

COUNTRY	NUMBER
SOVIET UNION	18
ROMANIA	11
UNITED STATES	6
RUSSIA	3
CZECHOSLOVAKIA	2

WOMEN'S TEAM COMPETITION

COUNTRY	NUMBER
ROMANIA	12
SOVIET UNION	9
UNITED STATES	7
CZECHOSLOVAKIA	6
HUNGARY	5

GROUP RHYTHMIC GYMNASTICS

COUNTRY	NUMBER
RUSSIA	5
BELARUS	3
BULGARIA	2
ITALY	2
CHINA	1

INDIVIDUAL RHYTHMIC GYMNASTICS

COUNTRY	NUMBER
RUSSIA	7
UKRAINE	4
EUN	2
URS	2
BELARUS	2

→ Of all the disciplines in artistic gymnastics, the floor exercises are considered to offer the best opportunity for the gymnast's personal expression and individuality, particularly in the women's event where dance skills are a core element.

→ Gymnastics has been part of the Olympics since 1896. Floor exercises first appeared in the men's competition in 1936, and in the women's competition in 1952.

→ Some national teams hire choreographers as well as coaches to help gymnasts with their routines.

THE FLOOR

Gymnasts perform floor exercises on a square rubber floor mat. This area is surrounded on all four sides by a clearly marked boundary line. On most floors, the padded area extends for at least one metre (3ft 3in) beyond the perimeter markings to help prevent injuries. Point penalties are incurred if the gymnast steps or falls outside the boundary line.

Panel of judges
Six judges mark the execution of the routine. There are also two technique judges, and one jury resident overseeing all the judges

12m (40ft)

12m (40ft)

The focus of attention
The gymnast performs a solo routine full of tumbling runs, turns, and rolls that he or she has choreographed

Soft and bouncy surface
The mat is made of foam rubber; beneath it is a layer of plywood, which makes the surface bouncy. The gymnast uses the "spring" to give height and/or speed to his or her tumbling runs

FLOOR EXERCISES

EVENT OVERVIEW

Floor exercises are one of the four disciplines in women's artistic gymnastics, and one of six disciplines in the men's event. They are among the most popular gymnastics events, providing spectators with an action-packed display of skill and strength in a confined area. Individual competitors perform choreographed routines on a square floor mat and are scored for both their acrobatic accomplishment and their artistic inventiveness. Competitors are expected to use the whole area of the mat during their routines, and tumbling runs are often performed from one corner of the floor to the diagonally opposite corner.

MEN VERSUS WOMEN

The men's and women's routines are broadly similar, but differ in some important details. Women are expected to demonstrate tumbles, jumps, turns, and dance movements. Men are also expected to show tumbling and jumping skills, but in male competitions there is greater emphasis on strength. In order to display their physical power, male routines normally include presses such as the V-sit position, in which the gymnast takes and holds his whole weight on his hands (see right).

SHEER STRENGTH
This gymnast is performing the V-sit, a move in which the joined legs are raised off the floor and the body is supported by the hands.

Points of symmetry
In poses such as this, gymnasts must keep their feet together and their toes pointed

Strong head
The position of the head is essential in maintaining balance in most gymnastic moves

Muscular strength
Gymnasts must be very strong as well as supple

Short work
Male gymnasts wear shorts for freedom of movement, to stay cool, and so that the judges can see their leg movements

White handedness
Gymnasts often apply chalk to their hands before performing to give them better grip on the floor

TAKING THE FLOOR

Women gymnasts perform floor exercises for a maximum of 90 seconds, to musical accompaniment (the music must be instrumental only). Male gymnasts' routines can last for a maximum of 70 seconds, and are performed without music. Gymnasts must use the whole floor mat, but are penalized for stepping over the white boundary marking. Three or four tumbling runs must feature in the routine, and competitors have to show acrobatic skills combined with strength (men) or dance (women) skills.

PERFECT 10

Floor exercise routines are scored out of 10; obtaining the "perfect 10" is rare. There are two groups of judges: one group scores a routine on its difficulty, the other awards marks for the proficiency of its execution. Each floor exercise routine must feature certain required elements (such as the reverse salto, or backward somersault) and is assigned a variable start value depending to the degree of difficulty. Every element also carries a set value, ranging from A (the easiest) to G. Bonus points may be awarded to competitors who successfully perform all the required elements, at whatever level. However, any slight loss of balance or incorrect body line spotted by the judges will lose marks.

SIDELINES

3 The highest number of successive Olympic gold medals in the floor exercises. The winner was Larisa Latynina in 1956, 1960, and 1964.

5 The length, in years, of the ban received in 2002 by Romanian Olympic double gold medallist Lavinia Milosovici for posing topless in a Japanese fashion magazine.

15 The number of Olympic medals (seven gold, five silver, three bronze) won by Russian gymnast Nikolay Andrianov. Floor exercises brought him two of his golds (at Munich in 1972, and Montreal in 1976), and a bronze in 1980 in Moscow. He held the men's record for most Olympic medals until 2008, when Michael Phelps increased his tally to 22.

IMPRESSING THE JUDGES

A high-scoring floor routine will feature dazzling acrobatic skills, particularly in the tumbling, which includes dynamic combinations of turns, leaps, springs, and somersaults all linked together in a fluid sequence. The required elements in a floor exercise include a turn of 560 degrees, front and back tumbling, and a double salto (somersault). Female gymnasts can end their tumbles in the lunge position (with one foot in front of the other); male gymnasts must land in the stuck position (both feet firmly together).

COSMOPOLITAN RED STAR

SOVIET GYMNAST AND COACH NELLIE KIM WON THE FLOOR EXERCISE GOLD MEDAL AT THE 1976 OLYMPICS FOR THE USSR. SHE IS IN FACT HALF KOREAN AND HALF TATAR, WAS BORN IN TAJIKISTAN, AND TRAINED IN KAZAKHSTAN.

Torso torque
The back handspring is powered by the muscles in the lower back; correct head position is also vital

Star jump
Arms must be raised and lowered together

Angle poise
The lower body and legs appear to be driving down, while the arms stretch upwards and outwards

BACK HANDSPRING
In this move, the gymnast starts from a standing position and leaps backwards on to her hands and then springs off her hands to land upright again. This move is sometimes known as a flic-flac or a flip-flop and often features in tumbling routines.

SPLIT LEAP
The gymnast aims to do the splits in midair, with both legs parallel to the floor; extra points are awarded if the arms mirror the leg movement. The landing should be delicate, and segue seamlessly into the next part of the routine.

HOLD THAT POSE!
While the main object of any floor exercise is a fluent and aesthetically pleasing sequence of moves, there should be moments when the gymnasts strike poses. Even though these last for only an instant, they are scored according to the beauty of their execution.

REVERSE DOUBLE SALTO
A double salto (double somersault) is one of the required elements in the floor exercises. This gymnast is performing her salto in the pike position, with the legs held close to the torso.

Launch and descent
The gymnast stands on her points and stretches her arms above her head, then performs the first back flip

Right angle
As she starts the return to the upright position, her legs are at 90 degrees to her torso

Higher aim
As she launches the first back somersault, the gymnast goes for maximum elevation

Hands down
As she flips again, the gymnast brings her arms down in parallel

Tuck up
Hands clasped behind the knees, the gymnast brings her body round again

Sharper angle
At the apex of the second flip, the gymnast brings her legs up tight to her trunk

Final approach
The hands come down to the outside of the thighs in preparation for the landing

Stuck landing
The gymnast completes the move by standing stock still (no steps allowed), and raising both hands above her head

NEED2KNOW

→ After 50 years of Eastern European domination, modern Olympic bar champions are just as likely to come from the West. At the 2004 Games, Émilie Lepennec of France took gold in the uneven bar, and Italy's Igor Cassina won the high bar event.

→ The outstanding nation at the 2011 World Artistic Gymnastics Championships was China.

HAND GRIPS

To guard against sore and blistered hands, gymnasts working on bars usually wear protective hand grips. These strap round the wrists and have a flexible leather upper section that covers the palm and has sockets through which two or more fingers can pass.

Fingerholes
Hand protectors normally have two or three finger sockets

Wrist straps
The devices are secured around the wrists

Sleek fitting
Men wear leotards and long pants secured under the feet by stirrups. They may use slippers or socks, or perform barefoot

Upper body
In bar work, a gymnast's shoulder muscles bear more of the strain than any other part of the body

Firm grip
Some gymnasts dust powder on their hands to absorb moisture and improve their grip

BAR EVENTS

EVENT OVERVIEW

The three bar disciplines – high bar, parallel bars, and uneven bars – afford spectacular demonstrations of skill, strength, and artistry. The high bar and parallel, or horizontal, bars are used by men only, while events on the uneven bars, also known as the asymmetric bars, are exclusively for women.

AT THE BAR

The bar apparatus stands on a raised floor called the podium; the landing areas are cushioned by shock-absorbing mats. All equipment must conform to specifications laid down by the International Gymnastics Federation. Modern materials have improved the flexibility of apparatus and enhanced performance.

PARALLEL BARS

The parallel bars are made of laminated wood or plastic or a combination of both; they should be moisture-absorbing so that they do not become slippery. The uprights may be made of any weight-bearing material, but are normally iron or steel. The height and width are adjustable for junior events.

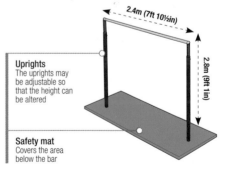

42–52cm (16¼–20½in)
3.5m (11ft 6in)
2m (6ft 6in)

Adjustable
Some parallel bars apparatus may be adjustable

Rubber mat
May be up to 20cm (7½in) thick

HIGH BAR

The apparatus is made of high-tensile steel, and mounted on floor plates to displace the force of the gymnasts' movement. It may also be supported by four tension cables anchored to the floor.

2.4m (7ft 10½in)
2.8m (9ft 1in)

Uprights
The uprights may be adjustable so that the height can be altered

Safety mat
Covers the area below the bar

UNEVEN BARS

The uneven or asymmetric bars are made of wood, plastic, or composite materials. Whatever their composition, the surface of the bars must be absorbent and non-slippery. The frame is of metal or steel. The uprights may be secured with floor-mounted guys.

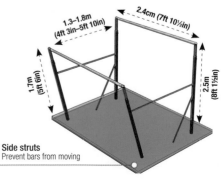

1.3–1.8m (4ft 3in–5ft 10in)
2.4cm (7ft 10½in)
1.7m (5ft 6in)
2.5m (8ft 1½in)

Side struts
Prevent bars from moving

SWINGOMETRY

High bar routines involve various held positions linked by spectacular swings and turns. Parallel bar exercises feature at least 11 skills, including giant swings with a dazzling repertoire of holds and turns, and releases and regrasps. On the uneven bars, gymnasts must show skills from five element groups, including a release and regrasp, and transition moves in which they pass from bar to bar. Gymnasts are expected to swing "fluidly" and to "hold" their handstands.

HIGH BAR

Gymnasts must not touch the bar with their bodies. Routines should include forward and backward swings using continuous movement – over and under the bar – with multiple changes of grip. The bar should be frequently released and regrasped throughout.

Good grip
Release and regrasp moves are an important element of the high bar routine

UNEVEN BARS

After a few preliminary swings to build up momentum, gymnasts perform sequences of movements in both directions above and below the bars. All routines should feature twists and somersaults that can only be executed with alterations of grip. Flight movements between the bars should be as high and as dramatic as possible.

High-flying
The gymnast swings or flies from bar to bar

PARALLEL BARS

On this equipment, gymnasts must combine swinging movements with held positions that display their strength. They must use the whole length of the bars, and move above and below them. Bonus points can be gained by performing somersaults and other particularly difficult moves.

Holding on
The gymnast must perform a "hold" on one bar

PEOPLE POWER

WHEN ALEXEI NEMOV OF RUSSIA SCORED A MODEST 9.725 ON A HIGH BAR ROUTINE AT THE 2004 OLYMPICS IN ATHENS, THE CROWD ERUPTED IN NOISY PROTESTS, FORCING THE JUDGES TO RECONFER. EVENTUALLY THEY UPPED THE MARK TO 9.762, BUT THE UPROAR CONTINUED AND IT TOOK APPEALS FOR CALM FROM NEMOV HIMSELF BEFORE THE EVENT COULD PROCEED.

TAKING PART IN EVENTS

Bar routines are a compulsory part of artistic gymnastics competitions (see pp.80–81), and in international events are performed in a particular order. Men must compete in both the parallel bars and high bar events, following a floor routine, pommel horse, rings, and vault. For women, the bar routine is part of a four-discipline competition which follows the order of: vault, uneven bars, balance beam, and floor exercises. Gymnasts compete both as team members and as individuals.

A MOVE TOO RADICAL

AT THE 1972 OLYMPICS, SOVIET STAR OLGA KORBUT WOWED THE JUDGES BY STANDING ON THE HIGHER UNEVEN BAR, DOING A BACK FLIP, AND CATCHING THE BAR AGAIN. THE SPORT'S WORLD GOVERNING BODY DECIDED THAT THE MOVE WAS TOO DIFFICULT FOR MERE MORTALS, AND PROMPTLY OUTLAWED IT.

SCORING

In all bar events, following the rules of the International Gymnastics Federation, judges award marks in four categories: degree of difficulty, form, technique, and composition. They deduct marks for technical errors, poor body shape, falls, pauses, and "empty" swings that break the sequence of an exercise. At high-profile events, at least four judges are assigned to each type of apparatus.

DISMOUNT WITH FLOURISH

All gymnasts strive to complete their performances with a controlled and acrobatic landing that leaves them on both feet with a perfectly poised body. Taking steps to maintain balance after landing is penalized by deduction of marks. At the end of a high bar routine, gymnasts often dismount with a soaring aerial flourish that involves spectacular flips or twists during the final descent to the mat.

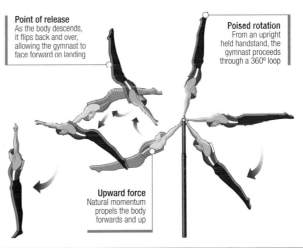

Point of release
As the body descends, it flips back and over, allowing the gymnast to face forward on landing

Poised rotation
From an upright held handstand, the gymnast proceeds through a 360° loop

Upward force
Natural momentum propels the body forwards and up

SIDELINES

1.65 The height in metres (5ft 5in) of Russian Svetlana Khorkina, who had been told that she was too tall to make it as a gymnast.

6 The number of moves in the official Code of Points named after Svetlana Khorkina, asymmetric bars gold medal winner at the 1996 and 2000 Olympics: no other gymnast has ever had so many.

4 The number of artistic gymnastics medals won by Alfred Flatow at the first modern Olympics in 1896. He took gold in the parallel bars, silver in the horizontal bar, and shared another two gold medals with fellow members of the German team that triumphed in the parallel bars and horizontal bar events. No other gymnast has since matched Flatow's amazing achievement.

16.533 The points score of the Dutch gymnast Epke Zonderland when he took the gold medal in the high bar at the 2012 Olympics in London.

0.100 The difference, in points scored, between the gold-medal winner He Kexin of China and fourth-placed Beth Tweddle of Great Britain in the uneven bars final at the 2008 Olympics.

POMMEL HORSE

EVENT OVERVIEW

Gymnasts on the pommel horse perform a fluid sequence of circular and pendulum leg swings without any pauses. They touch the horse and the pommels (handles) only with their hands, which go through complex changes of position. Athletes have to perfect the artistry and technical composition of their routines.

POMMEL PARAMETERS

The performer must make use of every part of the top of the horse, but can touch it only with his hands, "walking" back and forth along it. At least one part of a routine must be performed while holding only one of the handles. Although there is no rule about whether movements should be clockwise or anticlockwise, most gymnasts show moves in both directions. Among the optional elements, the most common are spindles (180-degree turns) and flares, or swinging straddles with legs on either side of the horse.

MARKING CRITERIA

The precise scoring criteria for the horse are altered regularly by the world governing body, the FIG. Whatever the specifics, every competitor starts his routine with a combined score made up of the degree of difficulty (the D-score), which in theory is unlimited, and a score of 10.0 for execution, artistry, and technique (the E-score). The judges deduct marks from the E-score if any part of the apparatus is favoured excessively or omitted altogether. The absence of scissor movements is particularly heavily penalized.

Nice legs
Stirrup tights are worn principally for comfort but also to accentuate the artistic lines of the gymnast's movements

NEED2KNOW

→ The pommel horse is probably the most difficult of the six male artistic gymnastic events. It is the only one in which contestants do not pause or hold a pose during a routine.

→ The pommel horse is still a men-only event at top level, but women also use the apparatus, both recreationally and competitively.

PLASTIC HORSE

Originally a metal frame with a wooden body and a leather cover, the modern pommel horse is typically made of plastic and covered with non-slip synthetic material. The handles may be metal but are commonly plastic. The landing mat on which the pommel horse stands is about 20cm (8in) thick.

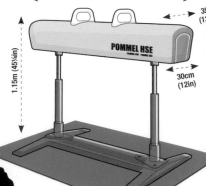

1.6m (63in)

35cm (13¾in)

30cm (12in)

1.15m (45¾in)

POMMEL HSE

Keeping cool
Lightweight cotton is comfortable and doesn't impair movement. A one-piece leotard is sometimes worn instead

Dry grip
Wrist bands prevent sweat from the arms running on to the hands and loosening the grip

12cm (4¾in)

40–45cm (16–18in)

POMMEL HSE
POMMEL HSE POMMEL HSE

Horse sense
Pommels are named for their resemblance to the high front of some horse saddles

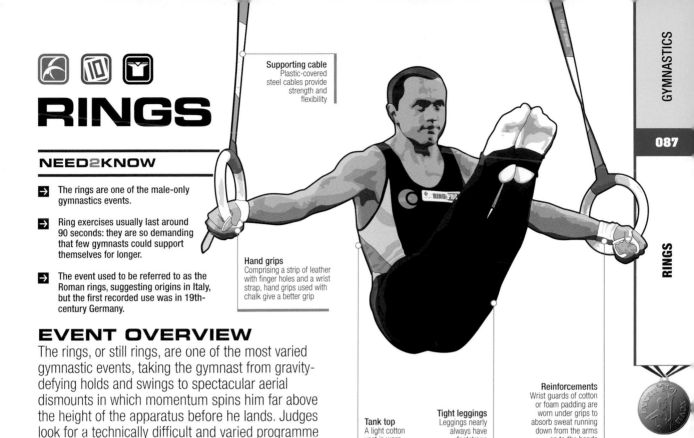

RINGS

NEED2KNOW

→ The rings are one of the male-only gymnastics events.

→ Ring exercises usually last around 90 seconds: they are so demanding that few gymnasts could support themselves for longer.

→ The event used to be referred to as the Roman rings, suggesting origins in Italy, but the first recorded use was in 19th-century Germany.

Supporting cable
Plastic-covered steel cables provide strength and flexibility

Hand grips
Comprising a strip of leather with finger holes and a wrist strap, hand grips used with chalk give a better grip

Tank top
A light cotton vest is worn

Tight leggings
Leggings nearly always have footstraps

Reinforcements
Wrist guards of cotton or foam padding are worn under grips to absorb sweat running down from the arms on to the hands

EVENT OVERVIEW

The rings, or still rings, are one of the most varied gymnastic events, taking the gymnast from gravity-defying holds and swings to spectacular aerial dismounts in which momentum spins him far above the height of the apparatus before he lands. Judges look for a technically difficult and varied programme that is well executed by the gymnast.

IN SUSPENSE

Judges look for a combination of swings and held positions including at least two handstands. One is entered forwards from a position with the arms held at 45 degrees before straightening out, the other exactly the same, but entered backwards. The legs may be held either together or wide apart. There must be at least one front lever hold, with the legs held out at 90 degrees in front of the torso.

SCORING

Judges deduct points for technical mistakes, but also for whatever strikes them as "unaesthetic", such as too much ring and rope movement. Even falling off the rings is not necessarily disastrous as the gymnast can remount the apparatus, and loses only 0.5 of the 10 points on offer.

HANGING RINGS

Two moisture absorbent rings, 18cm (7in) in diameter and 2.8cm (1in) thick, are suspended on ropes or cables from either the ceiling or a free-standing frame. Safety stewards check that they are secure between each round of every competition. A rubber mat about 20cm (8in) thick is placed directly beneath the rings.

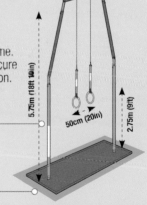

Ring tower
A simple steel frame supports the rings

Landing mat
Soft, thick, and wide enough to cushion even the most flamboyant landing

5.75m (18ft 10in)

50cm (20in)

2.75m (9ft)

A QUESTION OF TENSION

Success on the rings requires maximum tension be kept on the cables at all times. This stops them swinging and keeps the rings as still as possible to offer a solid support for the gymnast. Forwards and backwards swings are performed quickly to limit the time when there is no pressure on the rings.

INVERTED CROSS
The legs are held together, with the arms starting close together and pushing slowly apart. This movement requires great control and strength.

FLAT OUT
A horizontal position should be held for at least two seconds but not disrupt the flow of a routine. The rings and ropes should remain as still as possible.

HANDSTAND PLANCHE MALTESE
After performing a handstand, the legs and body are lowered so they are horizontal to the floor; the arms are held at 45 degrees.

→ The balance beam is traditionally for women only. It is widely believed that men do not compete because of the danger it poses to their genitals, but in fact the distinction is only by tradition.

→ Some of the stunning feats practised on this apparatus are all the more amazing in light of the fact that they are carried out on a surface only 10cm (4in) wide.

BEAM

EVENT OVERVIEW

The beam demands a supreme display of balance. On a perilously narrow bar, gymnasts perform leaps, turns, and flips that most people would find impossible, even on the ground. There is a panel of judges who look for technical and artistic skills, dance elements, leaps, and held poses.

EQUIPMENT SET-UP

Balance beams were traditionally made of polished wood. They still are wooden, but today they are sprung, and covered in suede to make contact softer. The rubber mats beneath the beams should extend as far as possible for safe landings.

Dry skin
Chalk may be applied to hands and feet to reduce risk of sweat causing gymnasts to slip on the beam

Close crop
Hair must be short or tied up tightly: points may be deducted for flopping locks

Colour combinations
Leotards may be of any colour, but are commonly in team or national strip

Barefoot balance
Competitors do not wear any kind of shoes, which would affect the sensitive contact with the beam required for complete control

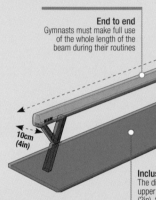

End to end
Gymnasts must make full use of the whole length of the beam during their routines

5m (16ft 5in)

1.25m (4ft 1in)

10cm (4in)

Inclusive height
The distance between the ground and the upper surface of the beam includes 5cm (2in), the thickness of the rubber mat

KEY MOVES

The compulsory elements of the 90-second routine include a 360-degree turn, and a leap with a 180-degree leg split. There must also be an acrobatic sequence with at least two flight sections, during which the gymnast must leave the bar and then return to it in a smooth movement without stumbling or groping for balance.

Head up
Wobbling costs points

DOUBLE LEG LIFT
In this strength element that also requires perfect balance, the gymnast puts her weight on palms and wrists, and brings her knees up to her face.

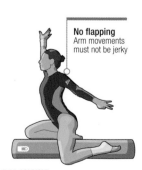

No flapping
Arm movements must not be jerky

BALANCING
Balance elements must be adopted smoothly, and maintained steadily; the pose itself must be shapely and aesthetically pleasing.

Confidence
To somersault on the beam requires lots of confidence

Off beam
The beam exercise often ends with a somersault

SOMERSAULT
Routines may include a step-over somersault, during which the gymnast must keep her head perpendicular to the beam to maintain balance.

STRIKE A BALANCE

Competitors must perform a mixture of compulsory and optional moves. These include acrobatic elements (in which the beam is left altogether), strength elements such as the double leg lift, gymnastic elements (turns, leaps, steps, runs), balance elements (holding, sitting, standing, or lying positions), and dance steps.

Judges look for elegance, flexibility, rhythm, balance, tempo, and self-control. Points are lost for not doing required elements, supporting a leg against the side of the beam, or pausing more than three times.

VAULT

EVENT OVERVIEW

Vaulters take a fast run up of up to 25m (about 82ft) before leaping off a springboard on to their hands on the vault table. They use their momentum to perform different mid-air moves, such as tucks and pikes, before landing squarely on both feet. From take off, a vault takes no more than about two seconds.

FLIGHT PLAN

Speed of approach and power off the springboard generate the height and rotation to perform different styles of vault. Vaults may incorporate moves such as somersaults and pikes, full spins of the body in the air, quarter-turns between the springboard and the table, or running handstands to flip from the floor on to the springboard. The landing is an important part of the vault. The feet should be together, but often one foot is moved forward or to one side and back again for balance.

SCORING

Gymnasts usually take two vaults, one after the other. Two panels of judges mark each vault in two categories: the D-score, for degree of difficulty, and the E-score, for technique, execution, and landing. Judges look for clean take offs and landings, height through the air, and precise movements at each stage.

NEED2KNOW

→ The traditional vaulting horse has given way to the vaulting table to reduce the risk of accidents. The greater surface area is safer for complicated vaults.

→ Vaulting is an event for both sexes; the equipment is largely the same, although the men's vaulting table is 10cm (4in) higher than the women's.

Leotard
Vaulters wear long-sleeved leotards or two-piece spandex outfits

1.2m (3ft 11in)

95cm (3ft 1½in)

S-LINE 114

S-LINE 114

Men: 1.35m (4ft 5in);
Women: 1.25m (4ft 1in)

Hands-on
Both hands must be in contact with the vaulting table

Increased safety
The collar of the vaulting table was introduced to increase athlete safety

Heavy duty
The base of the table is padded and heavily weighted for safety and stability

THE YURCHENKO VAULT

In this vault, the gymnast spins immediately after take off, then does a backward handspring off the table followed by either a tuck or a spectacular double twisting flip in mid-air. The move ends with the compulsory landing: stock-still with both feet together.

SIDELINES

0.031 The number of points by which Spaniard Gervasio Deferr beat his nearest rival, Evgeni Sapronenko of Latvia, to the gold medal at the 2004 Olympics in Athens, Greece. Deferr scored a total of 9.737 out of a maximum possible 10 points.

4 The number of vaulters who have won gold at consecutive Olympics: Nikolai Adrianov (Soviet Union; 1976 and 1980), Yun Lou (China; 1984 and 1988), Gervasio Deferr (Spain; 2000 and 2004), and Vera Caslavska (Czechoslovakia; 1964 and 1968).

THE LAST STRAW FOR THE HORSE

WHAT IS NOW THE VAULTING TABLE USED TO BE THE VAULTING HORSE. THE CHANGE WAS MAINLY MADE FOR SAFETY REASONS, BUT THE CATALYST WAS A MIX-UP AT THE 2000 OLYMPIC GAMES IN SYDNEY, WHERE 18 WOMEN PERFORMED BEFORE SOMEONE NOTICED THAT THE EQUIPMENT WAS SET 5CM (2IN) TOO HIGH.

Tidy hair
Hair must be neat and fastened back from the face

RHYTHMIC GYMNASTICS

Rope trick
Whatever apparatus is used in a routine it must remain in constant motion

All in one
Gymnasts normally wear a leotard or unitard, sometimes with an attached skirt

Precise balance
The gymnast must adopt a variety of poses to show balance and grace

Slippers
Gymnasts perform in special soft slippers, or in bare feet

EVENT OVERVIEW
In this combination of gymnastics and ballet, competitors – either singly or in teams – perform graceful choreographed routines to music while working with different types of hand-held apparatus: club, hoop, ball, rope, and ribbon. The sport is dominated by women, although a few men also compete, especially in Japan.

PERFORMANCE AREA
Known as the platform, this is a carpeted area similar to but slightly larger than that used for gymnastic floor exercises (see pp.82–83). The ceiling must be at least 8m (26ft) and preferably 10m (32ft 6in) above the ground so that the items of apparatus can be thrown as high as possible.

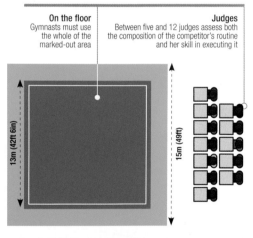

On the floor
Gymnasts must use the whole of the marked-out area

Judges
Between five and 12 judges assess both the composition of the competitor's routine and her skill in executing it

13m (42ft 6in)

15m (49ft)

COMPETITOR PROFILE
As for any gymnastic discipline, competitors must have a strong, flexible body. In addition, rhythmic gymnasts need finely tuned hand–eye coordination for manipulating the apparatus, and an instinctive appreciation of music and rhythm.

"GRACE WITHOUT DANCING"
RHYTHMIC GYMNASTICS HAS ITS ORIGINS IN EXERCISES DEVELOPED IN THE 19TH CENTURY TO PROMOTE SELF-EXPRESSION FOR YOUNG WOMEN – "GRACE WITHOUT DANCING". A KEY FIGURE IN THE EVOLUTION OF THE SPORT WAS U.S. DANCER ISADORA DUNCAN, WHO REJECTED WHAT SHE SAW AS THE RESTRICTIONS OF CLASSICAL BALLET TO CREATE A FREER FORM OF MOVEMENT.

NEED2KNOW

→ Rhythmic gymnastics competitions take place at national and international levels; the discipline has been an Olympic sport since 1984.

→ The world governing body of rhythmic gymnastics is the Fédération International de Gymnastique (FIG), which sets the rules for competitions and also trains judges.

→ Acrobatic movements, such as those used by artistic gymnasts, do not necessarily find favour with rhythmic gymnastic judges, and some movements, such as handsprings, are banned in competitions.

PERFORMING PARAMETERS

Each routine is accompanied by music chosen by the competitor and should last 75–90 seconds for an individual and 135–150 seconds for teams. Gymnasts perform with four out of the five pieces of apparatus – each year, the sport's governing body decides which apparatus is to be excluded.

SITTING IN JUDGEMENT

Although the number of judges may vary, it is never fewer than five. One judge or group of judges takes into account the degree of difficulty in a routine, another considers the choreography and artistry, and a third evaluates how well the routine was executed and how many technical mistakes were made. A judge coordinator oversees the panel and collates the marks, while a chief judge supervises the whole competition and has the last word in any dispute.

SCORING

In individual competitions, the maximum possible score is 20 points for each of the four pieces of apparatus being used, made up of a maximum ten points for execution and a combined maximum of ten points taken as an average of the technical difficulty and artistic marks. In group competitions, the gymnasts' scores are added together to give the team total.

THE APPARATUS

The rules and requirements for using the apparatus are precise, and each piece makes specific physical and intellectual demands. The rope is an explosive, dynamic apparatus that calls for leaps and skipping. The ball is gentler and more lyrical, possibly the easiest piece of apparatus to perform with, while clubs test the gymnast's coordination. With the ribbon, a performer needs grace and dexterity to create dazzling coloured images in the air. Handling the hoop arguably requires the greatest technical skill.

The clubs and balls were originally made of wood, the hoops of rubber, the ropes of hemp, and the ribbons of satin; the modern apparatus is nearly always made of synthetic materials, such as plastics.

DRESS CODE

There are strict costume regulations and competitors can lose points for not adhering to them. An outfit (and apparatus) cannot be coloured gold, silver, or bronze. There are rules regarding the pattern and material of a leotard, and even the cut of the garment's leg or neckline. Marks will be deducted for wearing jewellery, or a non-matching hair band. In a group routine, all the gymnasts must wear identical outfits.

Hand hold
The ribbon is attached to a short stick

Club size
Clubs are 40–50cm (15¾–19¾in) in length

RIBBON
The ribbon, which may be more than 6m (20ft) long, snakes and swirls as the gymnast performs her routine.

CLUBS
To demonstrate dexterity and hand-eye coordination, clubs are swung, spun, tossed, and caught.

Bouncy
The rubber ball is 18–20cm (7–8in) in diameter

On the move
All movements should be balanced

BALL
The gymnast is not allowed to grip the ball but must keep it moving, bouncing it, tossing it, and rolling it around her body and on the floor.

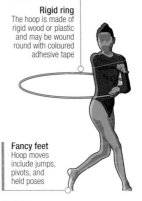

Rigid ring
The hoop is made of rigid wood or plastic and may be wound round with coloured adhesive tape

Fancy feet
Hoop moves include jumps, pivots, and held poses

HOOP
Competition rules require the hoop to be rotated round the body, thrown, caught, and swung. Using the hoop is a difficult skill to master.

INSIDE STORY

By the early 20th century, various forms of exercise to music had combined in the Swedish school of rhythmic gymnastics. Although the sport had been introduced to the United States, it aroused little interest. At first, the only signs of growing popularity were in the former Soviet Union. There, rhythmic gymnastics championships were held from 1948 onwards. The first international competition took place eight years later, but the event was only admitted to the Olympics in 1984 (1996 for group routines). Since then, competitors from Spain, Italy, and Brazil have challenged the traditional dominance of Eastern European countries.

SIDELINES

16 The age at which gymnasts qualify for senior events. Their performing careers are very short. Most rhythmic gymnasts peak in their late teens or early twenties; only a handful continue past the age of 30.

400 The weight in grams of the rhythmic gymnastics ball.

1,500 The monthly salary in US dollars offered in 2007 for a Russian or Ukrainian coach to help develop rhythmic gymastics in Vietnam by teaching schoolgirls.

1 The number of gold, silver, or bronze medals awarded in the All Around group competition at the World Championships – teams include three or four gymnasts, so they just have to share.

9 The record number of victories in the rhythmic gymnastics world team championship, achieved by Bulgaria between 1969 and 1995.

2,000 The estimated number of top-class rhythmic gymnasts in the world today, according to the International Gymnastics Federation.

TRAMPOLINING

SPORT OVERVIEW

Trampolining is a recreational and competitive sport in which individuals perform acrobatics while bouncing on a spring-bound bed. With gymnastic routines full of twists, turns, and elaborate moves reminiscent of diving, the sport is popular in the countries of Europe and the former Soviet Union, as well as the United States, Japan, and China. Trampolinists compete in individual and team events, including synchronized trampolining, double mini-trampolining, and tumble tracking.

Early start
Many trampolinists develop their skills and power while relatively young, often between nine and 14 years of age

Body control
Trampolinists can control the muscle tension in their limbs, shoulders, trunk, and abdomen

Outfit
Competitors usually prefer to wear leotards and trampolining shoes. Men may wear a vest and tight-fitting trousers

NEED2KNOW

→ The trampoline was invented by George Nissen in the United States in the 1930s. He named it after the Spanish word "trampolin", which means diving board.

→ The minimum height of the ceiling in a competition hall is 8m (26.25ft) to allow trampolinists plenty of room to complete their routines safely.

→ During the Second World War the United States Navy Flight School used trampolines to successfully increase the aerial awareness of trainee pilots.

COMPETITOR PROFILE
Regular and intense training keeps trampolinists physically and mentally fit and enables them to develop timing, coordination, and rhythmic movements. The ability to achieve precise balance and body control while rotating through the air leads to increased self-confidence.

THE TRAMPOLINE
Modern trampolines are safe and stable, providing good control in the jumping zone and rebound characteristics that generate the height needed for aerial manouevres. It consists of a flexible jumping bed that is constructed from nylon bands kept under tension by the surrounding springs. A steel frame supports the bed and raises it off the ground.

LEARNING SKILLS
Beginners learn basic skills such as jumping with knees pulled up and landing on their front and back. Intermediate skills include front and back somersaults. Advanced skills include double or triple somersaults and precision moves in fractions, such as one-and-three-quarter back somersaults and somersaults with half twists.

Padding
Around the bed padding protects the trampolinist from injury

Red cross
A red cross 70cm (28in) in diameter marks the centre of the zone

Jumping zone
The jumping zone is 215cm (86in) long and 108cm (43in) wide

2.14m (7ft)

4.28m (14ft)

THE DIVING FOOL

LARRY GRISWOLD WORKED WITH GEORGE NISSEN IN THE EARLY DAYS OF TRAMPOLINES, AND LATER BECAME KNOWN AS THE DIVING FOOL FOR THE ENTERTAINING ACROBATICS, TUMBLING STUNTS, AND CLOWNING TRICKS HE PERFORMED IN A SWIMMING POOL, ON A DIVING BOARD, AND ON TRAMPOLINES.

SIDELINES

18.80 The world record degree of difficulty score for men, recorded by Jason Burnett of Canada at a 2010 World Cup event.

3,333 The current world record for the most consecutive somersaults, achieved by Brian Hudson in September 2003 at the Jumpers rebound centre in Gillingham, UK. The previous record was 3,025.

INTERNATIONAL EVENTS

Individual men and women, as well as teams, compete regularly in international trampolining events such as the annual World Cup and the World Championship, which began in 1964 and alternates every two years with the European Championship and the Pan-Pacific Championship. Trampolining became an Olympic event at Sydney in 2000.

SCORING POINTS

The scoring system judges use at trampolining competitions may vary, but essentially they assess the style and execution of a routine. They look for such aesthetic elements as tidiness of form, consistency of height, and continuity of movement. They also award points when a trampolinist achieves moves that have a certain degree of difficulty.

BODY SHAPES

Trampolining routines consist of a sequence of acrobatic movements in the air, punctuated with contact with the trampoline bed. The aerial movements feature rotations and jumps with three main body shapes – the tuck, straight, and pike – of varying degrees of difficulty. Longitudinal rotations create somersaults, while lateral rotations produce twists. The moves are initiated by taking off and landing manoeuvres on the bed that involve the trampolinist's front, back, feet, or seat.

PUCK

This body shape is a combination of the pike and tuck positions. The puck position is allowed during competitions when performing multi-twisting multiple somersaults.

TUCK

The tuck is a body shape formed when the trampolinist clasps the knees with the hands and pulls them towards the chest. The tuck is often performed at the top of a straight jump.

PIKE

The pike is formed when the trampolinist keeps both legs straight and together, and folds the body towards them, while holding the calf muscles as far down the leg as possible.

STRAIGHT

The straight is formed when the trampolinist keeps the body as straight as possible, with both legs together, while holding the hands and arms along the sides of the body.

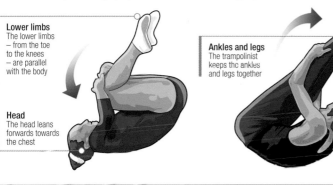

Lower limbs
The lower limbs – from the toe to the knees – are parallel with the body

Head
The head leans forwards towards the chest

Ankles and legs
The trampolinist keeps the ankles and legs together

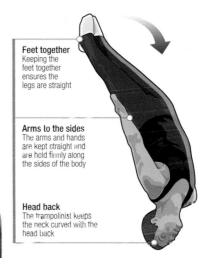

Feet together
Keeping the feet together ensures the legs are straight

Arms to the sides
The arms and hands are kept straight and are held firmly along the sides of the body

Head back
The trampolinist keeps the neck curved with the head back

DOUBLE MINI-TRAMPOLINE

Competitors run up the track, mount the bed and perform two moves that include up to three contacts with the bed. They then dismount on to the landing zone.

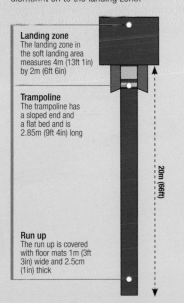

Landing zone
The landing zone in the soft landing area measures 4m (13ft 1in) by 2m (6ft 6in)

Trampoline
The trampoline has a sloped end and a flat bed and is 2.85m (9ft 4in) long

Run up
The run up is covered with floor mats 1m (3ft 3in) wide and 2.5cm (1in) thick

20m (66ft)

TUMBLE TRACK

As competitors run up the track, they perform a routine of eight tumbling elements that are marked for good control, form, and maintenance of tempo. They finish their routine in the landing zone.

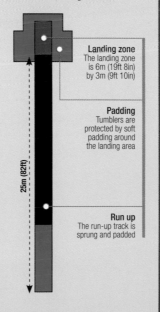

Landing zone
The landing zone is 6m (19ft 8in) by 3m (9ft 10in)

Padding
Tumblers are protected by soft padding around the landing area

Run up
The run-up track is sprung and padded

25m (82ft)

INSIDE STORY

The World Age-Group Games are held in the same year and the same location as the World Championships. A maximum of 80 athletes from each federation affiliated to FIG (see below) are permitted to compete. Some games entertain as many as 800 athletes. Participating athletes are boys and girls who compete in four age groups: 11–12, 13–14, 15–16, and 17–18. They compete in individual trampoline, synchronized trampoline, double mini-trampoline, and tumbling.

GOVERNING BODY
The Fédération Internationale de Gymnastique (FIG) is the world's oldest sports federation. It governs the various sports in competitive gymnastics, including trampolining.

NEED2KNOW

→ The World Championships of Sports Acrobatics have been held annually since the first event, which was organized by the International Federation of Sports Acrobatics (IFSA) in Moscow in 1974. Sports acrobatics featured as a demonstration sport at the 2000 Olympics Games in Sydney.

→ The sport is most popular in Russia and China, but participation has grown in many other countries, including the United States and the UK.

→ Sports acrobatics is also known as acrobatic gymnastics, or acro. It has close links with more conventional gymnastics, and there is increasing crossover between the two disciplines.

Top man
In men's groups, the acrobat who takes up positions at the top of a pyramid is smaller and lighter than other members of the team

Flexible footwear
Shoes should be soft, flexible, and supportive; they are usually white

Middle man
The acrobat at the heart of the balancing act needs both strength and suppleness

Firm base
The biggest and strongest members of the team form the foundation

Lycra clothing
One- or two-piece costume made of Lycra or similar stretchy material

HUMAN PYRAMID
Points are awarded for technique and artistry in this balance routine.

Stabilizer
Takes up position after the middle man has stepped onto the base man

PERFORMANCE ZONE

Acrobats perform on either a rubber mat or a carpeted sprung floor. The judges sit together so that they have the same line of vision and can easily confer.

1 Juries
The decisions of the juries are final

2 Chair of judges' panel
Takes overview and rules on any dispute

3 Difficulty judges
Determine the difficulty value of an exercise

4 Execution judges
Deduct points (from 10.0) for technical shortcomings

5 Artistic judges
Deduct marks (from 5.0) for artistic faults

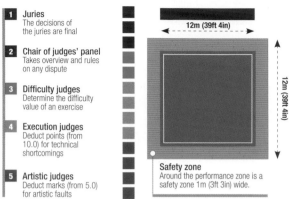

12m (39ft 4in)

12m (39ft 4in)

Safety zone
Around the performance zone is a safety zone 1m (3ft 3in) wide.

PERFORMANCE ROUTINES

Sports acrobatics has five events: men's pairs, women's pairs, mixed pairs, women's triples, and men's quadruples. Competitors perform three routines to show off different skills, each a maximum of 2 minutes 30 seconds long. The routines focus on balance, dynamism, and a combination of both of these, respectively. The sequences need to be highly precise: a panel of officials is watching intently (see above).

ACROBATIC SKILLS

Competitions have three sections, each of which is designed to highlight one aspect of acrobatics and showcase certain key skills of the different members of the pair or team.

BALANCE ROUTINE Teams adopt and hold complex poses, including human pyramids. The positions must be held for three seconds.

DYNAMIC ROUTINE Also known as the tempo routine, this part of the event is more energetic than the balance section. Acrobats throw their partners in somersaults, for example, and carry out technically demanding tumbling at speed.

COMBINED ROUTINE The third routine should be a tour-de-force that combines the skills of the first two parts in a spectacular display.

COMPETITOR PROFILE
Team members usually complement each other: acrobats at the base are tall and strong, while the "flyers" who stand on or spring off them are small and supple. All acrobats have a strong sense of rhythm and so make good dancers.

SPORT OVERVIEW

Sports acrobatics combines the strength, balance, and grace of gymnastics with teamwork and a musical accompaniment. Two or more acrobats perform choreographed sequences of balancing acts, handsprings, somersaults, and tumbles, earning points for execution and artistic impression.

SPORTS ACROBATICS

SPORTS AEROBICS

SPORT OVERVIEW

Aerobics is a fitness programme that became a sport. Gymnasts – alone or in pairs, trios, or groups – execute routines that must show dynamic and static strength, jumping ability, flexibility, and balance.

Regulation clothing
Women wear tights; men wear a one- or two-piece form-fitting costume

OBEYING THE RULES

Accompanied by a vigorous piece of music that they have chosen themselves, gymnasts perform a continuous routine that should last exactly 1 minute 45 seconds. Using the entire performance area and moving rhythmically with the music, they must demonstrate at least eight but no more than 12 compulsory elements, including supports, levers, jumps, leaps, flexibility, and turns. They have to perform at least two elements from push-ups, freefalls, and circles with the legs, and display artistic beauty and originality.

SCORING

Competitors start with 10 points, the maximum possible, and the panel of judges deducts points for errors. For example, they lose 0.2 points for every group element they miss and 1.0 point for performing prohibited moves.

PERFORMANCE AREA

Sports aerobic competitions are held on sprung wooden floors. The performance area measures 7 x 7m (23 x 23ft) for individuals, pairs, and trios. Groups compete on a larger area measuring 10 x 10m (33 x 33ft).

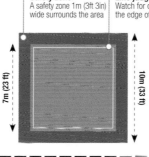

Safety zone A safety zone 1m (3ft 3in) wide surrounds the area
Line judges Watch for overstepping the edge of the mat
7m (23 ft) / 10m (33 ft)

Cusioned footwear Shoes and socks must be white; they should be able to absorb the impact of landing after jumps

COMPETITOR PROFILE

Gymnasts need a high level of cardiovascular capacity. Outstanding performers tend to be loose limbed and can move quickly and elegantly in time to music. They all have superb co-ordination and suppleness.

1 Artistic judges Assess creative originality of programmes
2 Execution judges Mark technical proficiency
3 Difficulty judges Mark performance on strict criteria
4 Time judge Deducts points for programmes that are too long or too short
5 Chair of judges' panel Controls the work of the other judges

FLOOR MOVES

A routine has to include at least one element from each of four groups, demonstrating flexibility and balance, dynamic strength, static strength, and jumping. Competitors also have to present the seven basic steps: march, jog, skip, knee lift, kick, jumping jack, and lunge.

The splits This move demonstrates flexibility

JUMPS The range of leaps and jumps includes scissors, straddles, and splits (above).

Right foot The right leg is held vertically so the foot touches the right hand
Left leg One leg is held still to support the weight of the body
HIGH KICK The hip of the raised leg is flexed up to 180 degrees, while the knee stays straight and the toes pointed.

Holding still One leg is brought forwards, showing strength and suppleness
Arm strength The whole body is held by one arm
THE CAPOEIRA This move demonstrates dynamic strength, an attribute which the judges are looking for.

Out straight The legs are held horizontally
Hands Both hands support the body
STATIC SUPPORT The weight of the body is taken on the hands while the gymnast performs the splits in mid air.

INSIDE STORY

Aerobics became established as a fitness routine during the late 1960s, with its greatest champion being US actress Jane Fonda. At first, aerobics struggled to gain credibility as a sport but gradually achieved acceptance and was eventually recognized by the Fédération Internationale de Gymnastics (FIG) in 1994. The first sports aerobics World Championships were held in Paris, France, in 1995. More than 70 FIG affiliates include aerobics within their gymnastics programme.

WEIGHTLIFTING

→ Weightlifting was a sport at the first modern Olympics in 1896. It reappeared in 1904 and became a regular event for men from 1920. The first women's Olympic competition was held at the 2000 Games in Sydney.

→ Leading athletes can lift more than twice their own bodyweight. In 1988, Belarussian Leonid Taranenko, representing the Soviet Union, made the heaviest clean and jerk of all time, lifting 266kg (586.4lb).

Steel bar
The steel bar is made in different lengths and weights for male and female competitors

Weighty matters
The weights are made of lead. Each is colour-coded according to weight

Lifting gear
The one-piece costume must not obscure the judges' view of knees and elbows

Tight belt
To support back and abdomen; may be no more than 12cm (4¾in) wide

Footwear
Specialized shoes keep the feet flat on the floor and stabilize the lifter

ATHLETE PROFILE
Weightlifters have highly developed neck, shoulder, stomach, and thigh muscles. The effort of lifting weights that are often heavier than the athlete's own body can produce a heart rate of 190 beats per minute (the normal rate is 60–80).

SPORT OVERVIEW
Competitors lift bars, known as barbells, loaded at each end with weights. They are allowed three attempts at any one weight and after each successful lift the weight is increased. The winner is the person who lifts the heaviest weight. There are two distinct weightlifting techniques: the "snatch" and the "clean and jerk".

HEAVY DUTIES
Competitors are divided into categories according to their bodyweight. There are currently eight divisions for men – the lowest is up to 56kg, the highest over 105kg – and seven for women – from below 48kg to over 75kg.
   Athletes take turns to make attempts at each weight. They choose which weight to start with, and the competitor who has opted for the lowest weight lifts first. Anyone who fails at a given weight can either reattempt it or try a heavier barbell later.

LIFTING METHODS
In the snatch lift, athletes must raise the barbell over their heads in a single, steady movement. In the clean and jerk, they must first raise (clean) the barbell from the floor to shoulder level and then, in a separate movement, lift (jerk) the bar until their arms are straight above their heads. Once the lifts are completed, they must hold the barbell steady in the final position, without moving arms and legs, until the referee tells them to put the weight down.

THE SNATCH

1 **Get a grip**
The lifter grips the barbell with hands fairly wide apart, and gathers his strength for the lift

2 **Transit mode**
The lifter straightens his knees and prepares to bend his elbows

3 **Knee thrust**
The knees may be bent again so that the lifter can get all his weight below the barbell

4 **Final push**
The legs are straightened and the weight is controlled over the head

CLEAN AND JERK

1 **Hands on**
The lifter grips the bar and squats in readiness to apply upward movement

2 **Lift off**
The first upward pull is powered mainly by thigh and back muscles, not the legs

3 **Neck brace**
When the barbell reaches neck height, the lifter brings it close to the shoulders

4 **Last push**
Knees are bent to power final upthrust; legs are spread for balance; arms are completely straight

5 **Ending up**
Legs are locked to complete the lift; the position is held until the judges' signal

POWERLIFTING

SPORT OVERVIEW
Powerlifting is the ultimate test of pure strength. This relatively recent sport involves athletes raising weight-loaded bars in three different lifts: the "squat", the "deadlift", and the "bench press". Powerlifting champions are justifiably known as the strongest men and women in the world.

IN COMPETITION
There are four age groups, from over-14s to over-50s. For men there are 11 weight divisions between 52kg and 125+kg; women have ten bands between 44kg and 90+kg. Each event includes all three categories of lift, and competitors are allowed three attempts at each one. The winner is the competitor who lifts the highest combined weight. In the case of a tie, victory goes to the lightest competitor.

ATHLETE PROFILE
The key areas of a powerlifter's strength are the shoulders, chest, arms, back, thighs, and knees. Regardless of muscular build, shorter men and women have an advantage over their taller rivals, as they do not have so far to raise the weights. Lifters work out as a matter of course, and before an event often push themselves to the limit, trying to lift greater weights than they would expect to meet in a competition.

SPOTTERS
In powerlifting contests, officials known as "spotters" may help a competitor to remove the bar from its rack to prepare for a lift. Spotters can also assist in replacing the bar at the completion of the lift, but they must not intervene during the attempt itself.

NEED2KNOW
→ The first world championships were held in 1970 under the auspices of the International Powerlifting Federation (IPF).

→ From small beginnings, powerlifting has become increasingly popular worldwide: the IPF now has more than 100 member states.

Taking the strain
Great strength in the neck muscles contributes to the lifter's stability during sustained holds

Tight one-piece
The tight-fitting costume helps to support the body during lifts

Solid grounding
Shoes have smooth soles to aid balance and weight distribution

Wrist straps
Bandages may be used for support; they must not exceed 10cm (4 in) in total width

Weight discs
These are made of lead, and may be colour-coded for easy recognition

---

Spread out
Legs are spread to distribute the weight over the largest surface area

On the up
Bar starts at 1m (3ft 3in) and is raised in 5-cm (2-in) increments to 1.7m (5ft 5in)

Strong arms
Deadlifts are powered by the biceps and triceps in the upper arms

Chest work
The real work in the bench press lift is done by the chest muscles

SQUAT
The lifter takes the barbell off its rack and squats with the weight on his shoulders and his hips below knee level. He returns to an upright stance, and holds it until told to return the weight to the rack.

DEADLIFT
The competitor raises the barbell from the floor until he is standing upright with a straight back. He holds the position until the judge signals the end of the lift and then replaces the weight, with control, to the ground.

BENCH PRESS
The competitor reclines on a bench. Two "spotters" help him to take the weight from the rack and lower it until it touches the chest. The lifter then pushes the weight back up and holds it, arms locked straight.

TEAM SPORTS

03

FOOTBALL

GAME OVERVIEW

The beauty – and popularity – of football lies in its simplicity: two teams of 11 players each attempt to kick a ball into the opposing team's goal. Compared with more complex team sports such as cricket or rugby, there are fewer rules, and matches are often free-flowing and highly exciting spectacles. Considered the world's most popular sport, football is enthusiastically played and watched by men and women in just about every country on Earth.

Plain shorts
Made of a durable synthetic material, football shorts allow good freedom of movement. While shirts may feature stripes, hoops, or other patterns, the shorts are usually one colour, sometimes with a stripe down the sides

Team colours
Usually made of polyester, a football shirt is light and breathable. All the players on a team (except the goalkeeper) wear the same colours and patterns

Stockings and shinpads
The stockings must completely cover the shinguard, which is now a compulsory part of the player's equipment

Good traction
Studded or cleated football boots provide increased grip on sometimes muddy and slippery surfaces

"KING OF FOOTBALL"

BRAZILIAN LEGEND PELÉ (EDSON ARANTES DO NASCIMENTO) IS PROBABLY THE GREATEST FOOTBALLER OF ALL TIME. HE WAS PART OF THE BRAZILIAN TEAM THAT WON THE 1958, 1962, AND 1970 WORLD CUPS, AND EARNED 91 CAPS AND SCORED 77 GOALS (A NATIONAL RECORD) FOR HIS COUNTRY. WITH EXTRAORDINARY TECHNIQUE, SPEED, DAZZLING CREATIVITY, AND FINISHING, PELÉ WAS THE PERFECT FOOTBALLER.

Standard ball
The dimensions of the ball are specified in the Laws of the Game. If the ball bursts or becomes defective during the course of a match, play is stopped, and the referee requests a replacement ball

PLAYER PROFILE

Footballers are mostly lean and athletic, with excellent ball skills. They are strong and balanced runners, able to quickly and repeatedly change direction. Players combine impressive sprinting skills with the huge reserves of energy required for 90 minutes of almost non-stop running. As football is a contact sport, players – particularly the goalkeeper – require a degree of courage, especially when tackling or competing for a header.

NEED2KNOW

→ Football has been officially known as "association football" since the formation of the Football Association in 1863. "Soccer", as the sport is also known, was originally derived from "association".

→ A football match is played by two teams of 11 players on a rectangular pitch. The game consists of two 45 minute halves separated by a short interval.

→ Other forms of the game include beach football and indoor football (which is also known as "futsal" and is played by two teams of five players over two halves of 20 minutes each).

→ The world governing body of football, Fédération Internationale de Football Association (FIFA), was formed in 1904 and has 208 member nations.

GLOBAL PHENOMENON

ACCORDING TO FIFA'S GLOBAL "BIG COUNT" IN 2006, THERE ARE 265 MILLION MALE AND FEMALE PLAYERS AND FIVE MILLION OFFICIALS. THIS TOTAL OF 270 MILLION PEOPLE ACTIVELY INVOLVED WITH FOOTBALL REPRESENTS ABOUT FOUR PER CENT OF THE WORLD'S POPULATION.

THE PITCH

Football is played on a flat, rectangular grass or artificial turf pitch, the dimensions and markings for which are shown below. The outer extremes of the pitch are delineated by the touch lines and goal lines, and if the ball wholly crosses any of these lines it is out of play (or a goal is scored if the ball crosses the goal line between the goalposts). If part of the ball is on the line, it is still in play. While most matches are played on grass, artificial turf is increasingly employed in countries such as Africa, where conservation of natural resources, especially water, is an acute issue. But whatever the surface, anyone can play social football: all that is needed are two teams, a ball, two makeshift goals, and a flat playing surface – anything from a park or field to a street or beach.

GOAL

This structure consists of two securely anchored vertical goalposts joined along the top by a horizontal crossbar, all of which are white. If a net is attached it must be properly supported and not interfere with the goalkeeper.

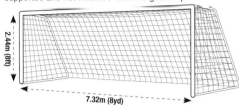

2.44m (8ft)

7.32m (8yd)

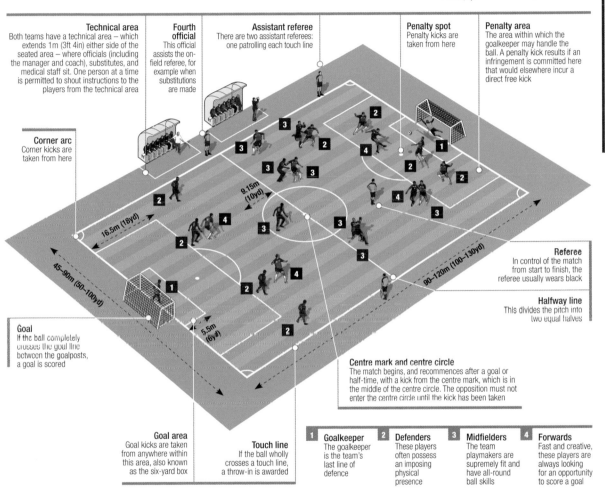

Technical area
Both teams have a technical area – which extends 1m (3ft 4in) either side of the seated area – where officials (including the manager and coach), substitutes, and medical staff sit. One person at a time is permitted to shout instructions to the players from the technical area

Fourth official
This official assists the on-field referee, for example when substitutions are made

Assistant referee
There are two assistant referees: one patrolling each touch line

Penalty spot
Penalty kicks are taken from here

Penalty area
The area within which the goalkeeper may handle the ball. A penalty kick results if an infringement is committed here that would elsewhere incur a direct free kick

Corner arc
Corner kicks are taken from here

9.15m (10yd)

16.5m (18yd)

45–90m (50–100yd)

5.5m (6yd)

90–120m (100–130yd)

Referee
In control of the match from start to finish, the referee usually wears black

Halfway line
This divides the pitch into two equal halves

Goal
If the ball completely crosses the goal line between the goalposts, a goal is scored

Centre mark and centre circle
The match begins, and recommences after a goal or half-time, with a kick from the centre mark, which is in the middle of the centre circle. The opposition must not enter the centre circle until the kick has been taken

Goal area
Goal kicks are taken from anywhere within this area, also known as the six-yard box

Touch line
If the ball wholly crosses a touch line, a throw-in is awarded

1 Goalkeeper
The goalkeeper is the team's last line of defence

2 Defenders
These players often possess an imposing physical presence

3 Midfielders
The team playmakers are supremely fit and have all-round ball skills

4 Forwards
Fast and creative, these players are always looking for an opportunity to score a goal

PLAYER POSITIONS

A football team is divided into forwards, midfielders, defenders, and one goalkeeper. Team members take positions that match their skills and style of play. The main job of the forwards, or strikers, is to score goals (although any player, including the goalkeeper, may score a goal). Strikers have excellent speed, good heading ability, skilful footwork, and an accurate shot. The midfielders provide the link between the defenders and the forwards: their role involves both defensive and attacking play. Defenders assist the goalkeeper in protecting the goal. These players have an effective tackle, a powerful kick, and are good headers of the ball. The goalkeeper, the sole player allowed to handle the ball (but only within the penalty area), has good catching and kicking skills combined with considerable agility and sharp reflexes. Substitutes are permitted during a match, but once substituted a player may not rejoin the game.

BEHIND THE SCENES

Although a team of 11 people plus substitutes takes the field on match-day, leading football clubs rely on the work of dozens of "back-room" staff to get their first team primed and ready. Specialist fitness trainers keep the players in physical condition, while teams of physiotherapists and medics help to keep the players at their best and to recover from injuries. On the technical side, clubs employ a variety of coaches to work with different sections of a team, while at the helm is the manager, the chief tactician, and team selector.

THE GEAR

One of the enduring appeals of the sport is that so little equipment is required. An informal game can therefore be enjoyed by all people, no matter what their means. For an official match, it is compulsory for players to wear a shirt with sleeves, shorts, socks, shinguards, and boots. It is forbidden to wear anything, such as jewellery, that could present a hazard. A player incorrectly attired will be asked to leave the field of play by the referee and may only return when the referee has confirmed that their attire is correct.

MODERN BALL

A match ball has a circumference of 68–70cm (27–28in), weighs 410–450g (14–16oz), and is inflated to a pressure of 600–1,100 g/sq cm (8.5lb/sq in–15.6lb/sq in). Most balls have a covering of synthetic leather panels stitched together (real leather, as used in the past, tends to absorb water and make the ball very heavy). Inside is the air bladder, which is usually made from latex or butyl. Between the bladder and the ball covering is the lining, which is made from polyester or cotton and helps give the ball its strength and bounce.

Valve
The inner bladder includes a valve, which is attached to a pump when inflating the ball

Outer casing
The outer surface consists of hexagonal panels joined by stitching

68–70cm (27–28in)

PLAYING THE GAME

Before the match commences, the two teams take their positions in their respective halves in any one of a multitude of set formations (see p.107). Play begins with the kick-off, whereby the ball is placed on the centre mark and kicked forwards by one of the attackers. Then, very simply, each team attempts to kick the ball into the opposition's goal. The ball may be moved about the pitch using any part of the body except the hands and arms, and the winning team is the one that has scored the most goals after 90 minutes. If at the end of play neither team has scored, or if both teams have scored the same number of goals, the game is a draw. However, in order to find a winner, some competitions allow for "extra time" followed by, if necessary, a penalty shoot-out.

IN ATTACK

The team in possession of the ball and moving forwards is said to be attacking. The ultimate aim of any attacking move is to score a goal, and this can only be achieved if the player with the ball is close enough to the goal to shoot. Attackers must therefore pass or dribble the ball around the pitch, retaining possession and avoiding defenders as they go. In order to outmanoeuvre the defence, attackers off the ball should always be looking for space – areas of the pitch where there are no defenders – to run into, ready to receive a pass.

One-two
Shown here is an attacking move in which a player beats an opponent by passing the ball to a teammate, then receives it back once in a more advanced position

On the move
A one-two relies on anticipation, quick passing, and the player's speed across the ground

PASSING

A well-executed pass consists of three elements: correct weighting (power used), appropriate direction, and good timing. Three parts of the foot can be used when passing: the inside for swift, short passes; the instep for long, powerful passes; or the outside for short, disguised passes on the run.

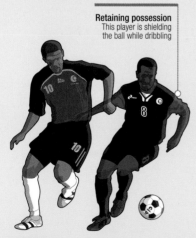

Retaining possession
This player is shielding the ball while dribbling

DRIBBLING
Running with the ball under close control, mostly using the outside and top of the foot, is known as dribbling. The player dribbling should look up often to assess attacking options and defensive dangers.

Curled cross
A well-played cross is an excellent way of beating defences

CROSSING
The cross pass, where the ball is quickly moved from the edge of the pitch to the centre, is used to deliver the ball towards players in attacking positions. Well-hit crosses are very hard to defend against.

Head down
Watching the ball right on to the boot helps ensure an accurate shot

Forceful shot
A powerful swing of the kicking leg enables a strong shot

SHOOTING
As the ball will arrive to the player at a variety of speeds and angles, there are many shooting techniques. However, the most common method is a low, hard shot struck off the instep of the boot.

Studs
In some boots the studs are fixed, but more commonly these are detachable so that the length of stud can be altered to suit different playing conditions. Some modern boots feature moulded blades instead of studs, providing a more stable base

Shinguards
When tackling or being tackled, shinguards provide good lower-leg protection

Gloves
Many modern gloves have removable protective reinforcing inside the fingers

FOOTBALL BOOTS
Footballers need comfortable, lightweight, and durable footwear. On grass, players wear studded boots; on artificial turf, trainers with rubber pimples on the sole provide good grip.

LEG PROTECTION
Guards protect the shins, are made of plastic, rubber, or similar, and must be covered entirely by the socks.

GLOVES
The goalkeeper wears gloves that provide extra grip when catching the ball. The back of the glove is breathable, and a wrist strap gives extra support.

IN DEFENCE
The job of the defending team is to prevent the attackers from scoring and to win back possession so as to mount an attack in return. Defenders can do this by intercepting attacking passes, closing down the space available to the ball carrier and other attackers, close marking of players in the hope of forcing a mistake, and by gaining possession of the ball directly via tackling. Football teams employ defensive strategies to help combat attacking moves. One example is the zone defence system, whereby the defenders are assigned a set area in which to work and mostly move in relation to each other. Another strategy is man-to-man marking, where each defender is assigned a specific attacker to mark.

Diving save
Goalkeepers require great agility and athleticism when protecting the goal

Fingers to the ball
At full stretch, arm extended, the goalkeeper stops the shot

GOALKEEPING
This player saves goals by catching the ball, tipping it over the crossbar or beyond the goalposts, or punching or kicking it away. The goalkeeper then starts the next attack, with a kick or throw.

Battle for possession
The defender launches a feet-first slide towards the ball; he must take the ball and not the player

Quick work
Defenders need fast reflexes to intercept

Defensive pressure
The marker always stays close to the player being marked

TACKLING
Using the feet to take the ball away from a player is known as tackling. The slide tackle (above) can be highly effective, but the defender's timing must be perfect, and there is a risk of conceding a foul.

INTERCEPTION
When a defender intercepts an attacker's pass, this is often the result of the pressure applied by the defending team as a whole, through persistent marking and closing down the available space.

MARKING
When a defender closely shadows the movements of an attacker, this is known as marking. It gives the defender the chance of an interception, and an attacker might not pass to a marked team-mate.

SIDELINES

11 The approximate number in kilometres run by a midfielder during a game. Forwards run about 8km (5 miles), defenders 7km (4 miles), and the goalkeeper about 4km (2½ miles).

42 The age of the oldest player – Roger Milla of Cameroon – to score a goal in a World Cup Finals match.

184 The world record number of international caps, won by Ahmed Hassan of Egypt.

199,854 The number of spectators that turned up to watch the 1950 World Cup match between Brazil and Uruguay at the Estádio Municipal do Maracaná in Rio de Janeiro. This is the highest ever recorded official attendance at a football match.

11 The number of seconds it took Hakan Sukur of Turkey to score against South Korea in the third-place play-off of the 2002 World Cup. Turkey went on to win the game 3–2, and this remains the fastest goal in World Cup history.

1,281 The number of goals Pelé scored in 1,363 games over his 22-year career playing for Brazil, Santos, and the New York Cosmos.

SET PIECES

If the referee stops play for an infringement, or if the ball crosses a touch or goal line, a predetermined, fixed move – such as a corner kick or a throw-in – executed by the attacking team follows. This is called a set piece. As a high percentage of goals come from set pieces, the attacking team will take up positions and adopt patterns of movement designed to produce a goal, while the defending team will do everything in its power to stop this happening. For example, when a free kick is awarded near the goal, the defenders might set up a line of players (called a defensive wall) in front of the kicker to try to block the ball. For a throw-in or corner the attackers look for free space to run into, and the defenders closely mark the attackers.

Correct technique
The player taking the throw-in must release the ball from behind the head using both hands and with both feet on the ground

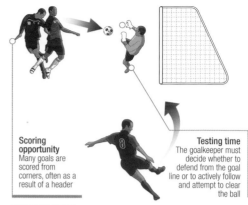

Scoring opportunity
Many goals are scored from corners, often as a result of a header

Testing time
The goalkeeper must decide whether to defend from the goal line or to actively follow and attempt to clear the ball

THROW-IN
When the ball completely crosses the touch line, a throw-in is awarded to the team opposing the player who last touched the ball.

CORNER
When the ball crosses the goal line having last touched a defender, a corner kick is awarded. The kick is taken from the corner arc nearest the point where the ball crossed the line, and a goal may be scored directly.

Curve ball
The kicker will often try to curve the ball around the wall

Target area
The best chance of scoring is to aim high and into a corner

The wall
The goalkeeper takes time over setting a defensive wall to try to prevent the kicker scoring directly

Arms spread
The goalkeeper fills as much of the goal mouth as possible

Ball position
All penalty kicks are taken from the penalty spot

FREE KICK
There are two types of free kick. With a direct free kick – awarded for a more serious offence, such as tripping – the kicker may score a goal directly. For an indirect free kick – given for a less serious offence, such as obstruction – a player other than the one taking the kick must touch the ball before a goal can be scored.

Ball position
The ball is positioned where the infringement occurred

PENALTY KICK
If any of the offences that would normally incur a direct free kick are committed inside the penalty area, a penalty kick is awarded. Until the kick has been taken, the goalkeeper must remain on the goal line. Because a goal is the expected result from a penalty kick, there can be enormous pressure on the kicker, particularly during a penalty shoot-out.

THE OFFICIALS
The referee has full and final authority during a match. This includes enforcing the 17 Laws of the Game (see opposite) and acting as match timekeeper. The referee may play "advantage" by allowing play to continue after an offence if it is felt that to stop play would disadvantage the team offended. A good referee will encourage a free-flowing, good-spirited game.

MISCONDUCT
If a serious breach of the Laws of the Game has occurred, such as showing dissent, the referee may issue either a caution (indicated by a yellow card) or send the player from the field (indicated by a red card). Two yellow cards in the same match automatically incur a red card.

REFEREE SIGNALS
Distinguished from the players by different coloured clothes (often black), the referee blows a whistle to start or stop play and uses a set of five official signals (see right) to indicate decisions made.

DIRECT FREE KICK **INDIRECT FREE KICK** **YELLOW CARD (CAUTION)** **RED CARD (SENDING OFF)** **ADVANTAGE**

ASSISTANTS
The two assistant referees – one on each touch line – officiate in situations where the referee is not in the best position to make a decision. These include offside infringements and which team should be awarded a throw-in.

Flag
This is used to communicate with the referee

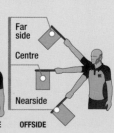

THROW-IN **SUBSTITUTION** **OFFSIDE** **OFFSIDE**

Far side
Centre
Nearside

PLAYING BY THE RULES

In 1863 the first uniform set of rules for football were devised. Today there are 17 Laws of the Game, and these are administered by the Fédération Internationale de Football Association (FIFA). They have been modified over time, with the most recent revision in 2012. The Laws regulate everything from the dimensions of the field of play and the equipment used to the referee's role, fouls, and set pieces.

COMMITTING A FOUL

Law 12 covers fouls and misconduct and the associated sanctions. A direct free kick is awarded if a player kicks, trips, jumps at, charges, strikes, or pushes an opponent with reckless or excessive force; the same is also applied if a player (except the goalkeeper) handles the ball, makes contact with the opponent before the ball during a tackle, or holds or spits at an opponent. An indirect free kick is awarded if a player impedes an opponent, stops the goalkeeper throwing or rolling the ball, or plays in a dangerous way. It is also given for a variety of infringements specific to the goalkeeper; for example if this player takes more than six seconds to release a ball held with the hands.

TACKLING THE PLAYER
If a defender tackles the player rather than the ball, this is a foul. Because it is difficult to play the ball first when tackling from behind, tackles are best made from the front or side. A mis-timed slide tackle (above) can easily result in a foul.

HOLDING
If one player holds another's clothing or person, this is a foul. Referees keep a sharp watch for holding, which is very frustrating for the player held.

DANGEROUS PLAY
This can take many forms but is most commonly associated with a high or reckless tackle, which is dangerous for the player tackled and the tackler.

OBSTRUCTION
If a player is positioned between the ball and an opponent and makes no attempt to play the ball, this is impeding the opponent (obstruction).

TRIPPING
Dangerous and unsporting, tripping constitutes a foul. However, it is sometimes difficult to tell if a player was tripped or fell deliberately.

THE OFFSIDE LAW

Law 11, "Offside", is probably the most controversial and regularly modified rule in football. According to FIFA's *Laws of the Game 2012*, "A player is in an offside position if he is nearer to his opponents' goal line than both the ball and the second last opponent". Or, put another way, if there are not two defenders (one of which will usually be the goalkeeper) between an attacker and the goal line, then the attacker is offside. For offside offences, an indirect free kick is awarded. Although it is not against the Laws to be in an offside position, it is an offence if – when the ball is played by a teammate – a player gains an advantage from being offside or interferes with play or an opponent while offside. A player receiving the ball directly from a goal kick, throw-in, or corner cannot be offside. The Law was introduced to prevent attackers hovering around the goal, which could result in games consisting mostly of long kicks from one end of the pitch to the other – an unappealing proposition for spectators and players.

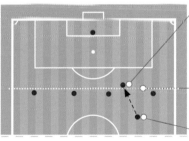

Offside
This is an offside position

No question
Player A is clearly nearer to the goal line than all the defenders except the goalkeeper

Passing forward
Player B has passed the ball to Player A, who is offside

OFFSIDE
In the situation above, Player A is offside, and an indirect free kick would result. This is because when Player B passed the ball (indicated by the arrow), there was only one defender (the goalkeeper) between Player A and the goal line.

"HAND OF GOD"

SOMETIMES A PLAYER INFRINGES A LAW AND GETS AWAY WITH IT. PERHAPS THE MOST FAMOUS INSTANCE WAS DURING THE 1986 WORLD CUP QUARTER-FINAL BETWEEN ARGENTINA AND ENGLAND. JUST INTO THE SECOND HALF, ARGENTINE DIEGO MARADONA FOLLOWED A LOBBED BALL, LEAPT, AND PUNCHED THE BALL INTO THE NET. THE GOAL WAS ALLOWED, AND ARGENTINA WENT ON TO WIN THE GAME (2–1) AND THE TOURNAMENT. MANY YEARS LATER MARADONA ADMITTED THE HAND BALL BUT AT THE TIME CLAIMED THAT IT WAS, "A LITTLE OF THE HAND OF GOD, AND A LITTLE OF THE HEAD OF MARADONA".

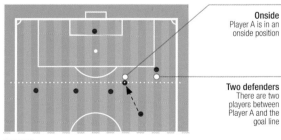

Onside
Player A is in an onside position

Two defenders
There are two players between Player A and the goal line

ONSIDE
In the scenario shown here, Player A is not offside. This is because when Player B passed the ball (indicated by the arrow), there were two players between Player A and the goal line. In-line with the defender is onside.

BALL SKILLS

Footballers must be able to control the ball – mainly with the feet, but also with any other body part except the hands and arms. A team that controls the ball retains possession. Key techniques include kicking and passing (see p.102), close control (including trapping, where the ball is stopped "dead" with the feet, head, chest, or thigh), running with the ball (dribbling, see p.102), shooting (see p.102), tackling (see p.103), and heading. To become a leading player, it is essential that the following skills are mastered.

TRAINING
Footballers train hard and often, and techniques can be practised at team sessions or individually. Good fitness is also essential: an exhausted player is of little use to the team. Fitness training might include sprinting (to develop speed), circuits (for muscular endurance and stamina), weights (strength), and stretching (flexibility).

Landing platform
With arms outstretched to push the chest out, this player has created the largest possible area on which to receive the ball

Good balance
With one foot off the ground, the arms are used for balance

Quick shot
Volleys are commonly used for swift shots at goal

CHESTING
The player's chest can be used to control or even pass the ball. When controlling the ball, the chest "cushions" the ball as it falls; when used to pass, the chest is thrust out to meet the oncoming ball.

THIGH CONTROL
The thigh is used for balls arriving above knee height but too low for the chest. To control the ball, the thigh is lowered slightly before impact to cushion the ball.

VOLLEY
Kicking the ball before it bounces is called a volley. Because the ball is not brought under control prior to being kicked, the direction of the kick is less easy to manage, but the ball is redistributed very quickly.

Firm strike
Headers should come from the centre of the forehead

Shielded ball
Facing away from the defender, the attacker protects the ball

Ball skills
Close control is essential when shielding

HEADING
This is an important skill in football because it gives the player the opportunity to reach a ball too high to be controlled by means other than the head. It is mainly used for passing and shooting at goal.

SHIELDING
When a player in possession is positioned between the ball and a defender, this is known as shielding or "screening". So long as the person in possession is playing the ball, then this is perfectly legal.

HIGH EARNERS
FOR THE WORLD'S BEST PLAYERS THE FINANCIAL REWARDS CAN BE STAGGERING. IN 2012, THE ESTIMATED EARNINGS OF THE HIGHEST-PAID FOOTBALLER (LIONEL MESSI OF BARCELONA) WAS £30 MILLION. TOP ENGLISH PLAYERS CAN EARN MORE THAN 200 TIMES THE AVERAGE WAGE IN THE UNITED KINGDOM. THE RICHEST FOOTBALL CLUB IN THE WORLD IS REAL MADRID, WITH ESTIMATED REVENUES OF OVER £420 MILLION FOR THE 2011–12 SEASON. THESE FIGURES REFLECT FOOTBALL'S STATUS AS THE WORLD'S MOST POPULAR SPORT.

BENDING THE BALL
To curve the ball from right to left (from the player's perspective) using the right foot, the player strikes the bottom half of the right side of the ball with the inside of the boot. To curve the ball from left to right with the right foot, the player strikes the left side of the ball with the outside of the boot. In both cases the foot and leg follow-through in the opposite direction from that of the intended flight path so as to slice across the ball to impart spin on it. This skill is used to curve the ball around defenders when passing, shooting, or when taking a penalty, corner, or free kick.

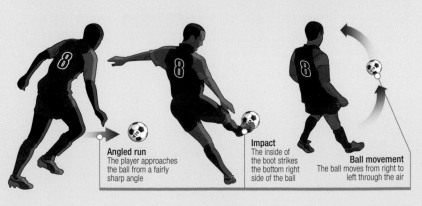

Angled run
The player approaches the ball from a fairly sharp angle

Impact
The inside of the boot strikes the bottom right side of the ball

Ball movement
The ball moves from right to left through the air

FORMATIONS

A team's on-field formation is represented by a set of three or four numbers. For example, 4-4-2 describes four defenders, four midfielders, and two forwards. The numbers always add up to 10 because the goalkeeper is not included in the formation. A team usually starts a match with a formation based on its style of play (see below), but according to the match situation, this might change. If, for example, a team with a lead does not want to risk conceding a goal it might employ a more defensive formation. There are many combinations, and shown here are three common examples.

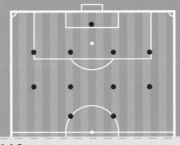

4-4-2
This is probably the most common formation used in football today. The 4-4-2, also known as the "flat back four", is an adaptable system whereby the midfielders work extensively with the defenders and the forwards. Always the workhorses, the midfielders have plenty of running to do in this formation.

3-5-2
In this formation, the left and right midfield players generally take a more attacking role supporting the forwards, while the central midfielder often works closely with the defence, to help resist opposition counter-attacks launched when much of the team is in the opposition's half.

4-3-2-1
Also known as the "Christmas Tree", this formation is a variation of the 4-4-2 (see above) whereby one of the midfielders is pushed forward into an attacking position. This means that in effect there are three forwards, with the centre forward playing slightly in front of the other two.

INSIDE STORY

The earliest known form of football was played in China in the second and third centuries BCE. Football-like games were also played in Ancient Greece and Rome and in other early civilizations. However, the development of football occurred mainly in Britain, over the last thousand years. Early football took many forms, and a "match" was often an anarchic contest between two whole villages. During the nineteenth century the pivotal moment in football's history was reached. Earlier in the century football had become very popular in the public schools. But without standardized rules, some schools favoured a rougher game that included handling and running with the ball while others preferred a game based around dribbling.

FOOTBALL RULES

In 1863 meetings were held to formalize the rules. As part of this process rugby football became a separate sport, and both the Football Association and "association football" – where handling the ball was prohibited – were born. In 1872 the world's first football competition, the FA Cup, was held, and in 1904 the Fédération Internationale de Football Association (FIFA) was founded. Today, FIFA boasts 209 member nations.

INTERNATIONAL COMPETITIONS

Undoubtedly the most significant international competition is the FIFA World Cup, held every four years. With worldwide total viewing figures in the billions, it ranks alongside the Olympic Games as one of the great uniting global sporting events. There are World Cups for men and women. Some of the many other international competitions include: the European Football Championship, Copa América (South America), the African Cup of Nations, and the Asian Cup.

CLUB COMPETITIONS

Many supporters follow club competitions with unparalled fervour. Championships include the Premier League (England), La Liga de Fútbol Profesional (Spain), and Serie A (Italy). Some competitions are played between the top clubs of different nations, such as Copa Libertadores da América (South America) and the Champions League (Europe).

STAT CENTRAL

FIFA WORLD CUP WINNERS

YEAR	WINNER	RUNNER-UP
2010	SPAIN	NETHERLANDS
2006	ITALY	FRANCE
2002	BRAZIL	GERMANY
1998	FRANCE	BRAZIL
1994	BRAZIL	ITALY
1990	WEST GERMANY	ARGENTINA
1986	ARGENTINA	WEST GERMANY
1982	ITALY	WEST GERMANY
1978	ARGENTINA	NETHERLANDS
1974	WEST GERMANY	NETHERLANDS
1970	BRAZIL	ITALY
1966	ENGLAND	WEST GERMANY
1962	BRAZIL	CZECHOSLOVAKIA
1958	BRAZIL	SWEDEN
1954	WEST GERMANY	HUNGARY
1950	URUGUAY	BRAZIL
1938	ITALY	HUNGARY
1934	ITALY	CZECHOSLOVAKIA

EUROPEAN CHAMPIONSHIP WINNERS

YEAR	WINNER	RUNNER-UP
2012	SPAIN	ITALY
2008	SPAIN	GERMANY
2004	GREECE	PORTUGAL
2000	FRANCE	ITALY
1996	GERMANY	CZECH REPUBLIC
1992	DENMARK	GERMANY
1900	NETHERLANDS	USSR
1984	FRANCE	SPAIN
1980	WEST GERMANY	BELGIUM
1976	CZECHOSLOVAKIA	WEST GERMANY
1972	WEST GERMANY	USSR
1968	ITALY	YUGOSLAVIA

COPA AMERICA WINNERS

YEAR	WINNER	RUNNER-UP
2011	URUGUAY	PARAGUAY
2007	BRAZIL	ARGENTINA
2004	BRAZIL	ARGENTINA
2001	COLOMBIA	MEXICO
1999	BRAZIL	URUGUAY
1997	BRAZIL	BOLIVIA
1995	URUGUAY	BRAZIL
1993	ARGENTINA	MEXICO
1991	ARGENTINA	BRAZIL
1989	BRAZIL	URUGUAY
1987	URUGUAY	CHILE
1983	URUGUAY	BRAZIL
1979	PARAGUAY	CHILE
1975	PERU	COLOMBIA
1967	URUGUAY	ARGENTINA
1963	BOLIVIA	PARAGUAY

BASKETBALL

GAME OVERVIEW

Invented in the late 19th century, basketball is a fast-paced, highly technical ball sport, whereby two teams of five players attempt to score points in the opposing side's basket. Most popular in the United States, where the National Basketball Association (NBA) runs the professional game, it also has a strong presence in Europe. Basketball has been an Olympic sport since 1976.

PLAYER PROFILE
Muscular and athletic, basketball players require all-round fitness. Being such a fast-paced game, players need superb stamina allied to agility. Above all, of course, they need to be tall. Players are rarely under 1.8m (6ft) and often as tall as 2.1m (7ft).

Court kit
Players wear loose fitting vest tops and shorts on court, which permit total freedom of movement for the upper and lower body

Wear and tear
In a sport characterized by continual changes of pace and direction, players' knees are highly susceptible to injury

Big air
Modern day basketball boots feature air cushioned soles – which provide both comfort during fast-moving play and leverage for even higher leaps

JAMES A. NAISMITH
NAISMITH WAS NOT JUST THE INVENTOR OF BASKETBALL, HE IS ALSO CREDITED WITH BEING THE FIRST MAN TO INTRODUCE THE HELMET INTO AMERICAN FOOTBALL.

Jumping power
Strong leg muscles are a must in a sport focused on jumping and frequent sprints

NEED2KNOW

→ Basketball was invented in 1891 by a Canadian, James A. Naismith.

→ In the United States, more people play basketball than any other team sport, according to research by the National Goods Association.

→ College basketball is at least the equal of the professional game in terms of popularity in the US – Alaska is the only state that does not have a Division I Men's Basketball programme.

→ Top NBA stars enjoy superstar status and earn prodigious salaries – 13 of the sportspeople in the "Sports Illustrated" 2012 Fortunate 50 (top earners in sport) were NBA stars.

2-point zone
Two points are awarded for any field goal scored from inside the 3-point line

The key
Players on offense can remain in this area for up to three seconds

3-point arc
A player who scores a field goal from anywhere outside this line earns 3 points

Out of bounds
The area outside of the court markings

THE SHOT CLOCK
Introduced to the NBA in 1954 in an effort to speed up play, the shot clock is a 24-second timer. The team in possession must shoot within that time frame. Failure to attempt a shot that hits the rim within this time results in loss of possession. A buzzer sounds, and a red light goes off, when the clock reaches zero.

THE COURT

The basketball court is a rectangular playing surface usually made out of a highly polished hardwood. Courts come in different shapes and sizes. In the National Basketball Association (NBA), the court is 28.5m (94ft) long by 15.2m (50ft) wide. Under International Basketball Federation (FIBA) rules, the court is smaller, measuring 28m (92ft) by 15m (49ft); in US College basketball it is slightly smaller still. Lines mark out the dimensions of the court, three-point line, and free-throw line. The baskets are always 3m (10ft) above the floor and attached to rectangular backboards.

Baseline
Marks the boundary of play at either end of the court

The basket
The scoring hoop, which is 45cm (18in) wide

Backboard
Rectangular in shape and made of reinforced plastic, glass, or fibreglass, this is used to deflect the ball into the basket

15.2m (50ft)

28.6m (94ft)

Free throw line
From where a player takes an unopposed shot at the basket following a shooting foul

Sideline
Line that marks the court on both sides

Jump ball
The referee tosses the ball up between two players who tip it to a teammate to start the game

Mid-court line
The middle of the court, separating both teams' halves

WHO PLAYS WHERE

1 Point guard
Often the fastest player on the team, the point guard organizes the team's attack by calling pre-planned offensive plays, controls the ball, and generates scoring opportunities

2 Shooting guard
Players in this position are often smaller and faster than forwards. This player's job is to score and generate scoring opportunities

3 Small forward
Small forwards are primarily responsible for scoring points, and are often secondary rebounders behind power forwards and centres. Small forwards are prolific scorers

4 Power forward
Though not as physically imposing as power forwards and centres they need to be aggressive rebounders and score most of their points from about 2m (6ft) from the basket

5 Centre
This person is usually the tallest player on the team. They often specialize in blocking opponent's shots and rebounding the ball

FREE-THROW LINE

Because penalties play such a large part in the sport of basketball, the percentage of free throws scored can be the difference between winning and losing a game. Free throws are always worth one point and between one and three throw attempts are awarded to a team, depending on the penalty committed by the opposing team.

SIDELINES

23 The shirt number of former Chicago Bulls star Michael Jordan, widely considered the greatest player of all time. Jordan chose the number out of admiration for his older brother. Larry wore 45, and Michael, believing he had only half his brother's talent, chose 23 (rounded up from 22.5). It was also the shirt number chosen by footballer David Beckham when he signed for Real Madrid in 2003.

38,387 The total number of points accumulated by Kareem Abdul-Jabbar. Although retired since 1989, he remains the NBA's leading all-time points scorer.

100,087,526 The total annual wage bill, in US dollars, of the Los Angeles Lakers NBA team for the 2012–13 season.

2.31 The height, in metres – 7ft 7in – of Manute Bol. The Sudanese centre, who played in the NBA from 1985–1995, is the tallest in the association's history.

30 Circumference of a men's basketball in inches (76cm). The ball is made from eight strips of rubber or leather.

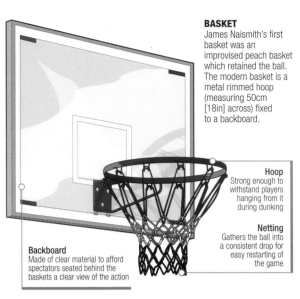

BASKET
James Naismith's first basket was an improvised peach basket which retained the ball. The modern basket is a metal rimmed hoop (measuring 50cm [18in] across) fixed to a backboard.

Hoop
Strong enough to withstand players hanging from it during dunking

Netting
Gathers the ball into a consistent drop for easy restarting of the game

Backboard
Made of clear material to afford spectators seated behind the baskets a clear view of the action

REQUIRED KIT
The beauty of basketball is that you can play almost anywhere, with very little equipment. All that is really required for social play is a ball and two baskets – or one if you play half-court. For tournament and professional play, teams wear regulation vests and shorts bearing their chosen squad number. In a sport where the legs, particularly the ankles and knees, take heavy punishment, boots are carefully chosen for comfort and game-improvement, and some form of muscle and joint support is common. Wrist- and headbands are usual, too.

BALL
The basketball has come a long way since the style first used in the late 19th century. That ball was heavy, with prominent sticthing, and an inconsistent bounce. Today's basketball is made from eight finely stitched pieces of leather filled with air. The men's ball has a radius of 19.3cm (7½in) and a circumference of 76cm (30in). It weighs 600–650g (21–23oz).

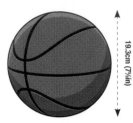

19.3cm (7⅜in)

PLAYING THE GAME
Following the tip-off which starts the match, each team simply aim to score more points that the other via offence and defence. Offence is generated by passing and dribbling (continually bouncing the ball while moving), and when a player feels they are in a position to score they shoot. Basketball is truly an "end-to-end" sport with numerous baskets scored during the course of a game. Often the winning side will have accumulated more than 100 points.

BASKETS, POSSESSION, AND REBOUNDS
If a player is successful in shooting a basket, the team is awarded two or three points depending on the distance from the basket. The game restarts with the opposing team in possession on the baseline underneath their own basket. If a shot is unsuccessful, and it bounces off the rim or backboard, players compete for the "rebound". If the attacking team picks up a rebound they can prepare for another shot, if it is the defending team they attempt to move the ball to the other end of the court to score. Having a centre who is particularly adept at picking up rebounds on defence is a huge advantage, as it inhibits the opposing team's offence. Wilt Chamberlain, who played NBA in the 1960s, is arguably the greatest rebounder of all-time.

OUT OF BOUNDS
The ball is out of bounds when it touches the floor, or any object on, above, or outside of a boundary, or the backboard supports. When the ball goes out of play the clock is stopped. The ball is put back into play by the team that did not not touch it last when it went out of bounds. A player has five seconds to put the ball in play after the referee signals the restart.

TIP-OFF
Also known as the jump-off, this is the short passage of play that starts the game. The opposing players, usually centres, line up in mid-court either side of the referee. To start the game, the referee throws the ball into the air midway between the two players, who jump and attempt to tip it to a team-mate. Having a particularly tall centre, (or a player who can jump particularly well) is an advantage. Gaining possesssion straight form the tip-off affords the offensive team the first opportunity to open the scoring.

Referee
He stands clear of the players after throwing the ball skyward

Size matters
Overall height and the ability to leap vertically from a standing position, are useful attributes at the tip off

Fair play
Players must not impede one another when jumping for the ball

LAWS OF THE COURT

Basketball was born in 1891 with 13 rules covering all the basics of play. Incredibly, the NBA have only 12 main rules today – but each has many clauses and sub-sections. There are subtle rule differences between the game played by the NBA, International Basketball Federation (FIBA), and National Collegiate Athletic Association (NCAA). Games are made up of four 12-minute quarters in the NBA. Teams can have up to 12 players but only five of these can be on the court at a time.

PERSONAL AND TECHNICAL FOULS

The team of a fouled player either receive the ball to pass inbounds, or receive one or more free throws if they are fouled in the act of shooting, depending on whether the shot was successful.

PERSONAL FOUL This is a breach of the rules that concerns illegal personal contact with an opponent including charging, blocking, pushing, holding, and reaching.

TECHNICAL FOUL This is an infraction of the rules usually concerning unsportsmanlike non-contact behaviour, and is generally considered a more serious infraction than a personal foul. Such fouls include profane language by a player or coach, contesting decisions, fighting, time-wasting, and illegal substitutions.

VIOLATIONS

Violations are infractions of the rules governing how the ball can be handled. The ball must stay within the court; the last team to touch the ball before it travels out of bounds forfeits possession. The ball-handler may not move both feet without dribbling, known as travelling, nor may he dribble with both hands or catch the ball in between dribbles, a violation called double-dribbling. A player's hand cannot be under the ball while dribbling; doing so is known as carrying the ball. A team, once having established ball control in the front half of the court, may not return the ball to the backcourt.

TIME LIMITS

There are various limits imposed on regulation play, all of which are designed to promote greater attacking play. The time taken before progressing the ball past halfway (8 seconds in international and NBA, ten seconds in NCAA and high school); before attempting a shot (24 seconds in the NBA, 35 seconds in NCAA); holding the ball while closely guarded (five seconds), and remaining in the restricted area (the lane, or "key") (three seconds), are all monitored by the referee.

SCOREBOARD

With four duplicate sides, some scoreboards keep all members of the crowd informed about the action. A main screen is surrounded by details of timeouts, points, fouls, score, and time remaining.

Big screen
This can offer a direct feed from the live action on the court, or replay action

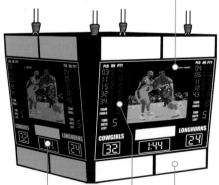

Time and score
The bottom of the scoreboard displays the points total of the two teams and the amount of time left in the quarter or half

Team/player stats
This section shows the total points scored and fouls committed by each player, as well as team fouls and timeouts

Advertising
In the NBA and in college basketball, space around the perimeter of the board is used for advertising

OFFICIALS' SIGNALS

With a myriad of different rules to enforce – it is not just the players but also the coaching staff off-court who can incur penalties – basketball officials need to make split-second decisions and have excellent peripheral vision. Two referees are ably supported by a scorekeeper, timekeeper, and shot clock operator. Referees have a series of established gestures and signals to indicate aspects of play and rule breaches to fellow officials. A selection of these are shown below.

BLOCKING
The referee places clenched fists against the waist to indicate a player illegally impeding another.

CHARGING
An offensive foul that occurs when an attacking player runs into a defender, who has an established position.

TRAVELLING
This rotating motion denotes travelling – essentially moving with the ball (definitions differ) for a period without bouncing it.

JUMP BALL
When two opposing players both have a grip of the ball the referee will hold his arms aloft to signal a jump ball.

2-POINT SCORE
Left arm raised with the index and middle fingers extended, denotes a 2-point basket to the watching scorekeeper.

3-POINT SCORE
Both hands raised with three fingers on each hand extended, indicates a score made from outside the 3-point arc.

TIMEOUT

Timeouts are breaks in the action which can be called by team coaches and players, usually at key points in the game, to discuss tactics and raise player morale. In the NBA, teams are allowed one 20-second timeout per half, and six regular timeouts over the course of the entire game.

STAT CENTRAL

NBA ALL-TIME LEADING POINTS

POINTS	PLAYER
38,387	KAREEM ABDUL-JABBAR
36,928	KARL MALONE
32,292	MICHAEL JORDAN
31,419	WILT CHAMBERLAIN
30,949	KOBE BRYANT
28,255	SHAQUILLE O'NEAL
27,409	MOSES MALONE
27,313	ELVIN HAYES
26,946	HAKEEM OLAJUWON
26,710	OSCAR ROBERTSON

NBA ALL-TIME PLAYOFF POINTS

POINTS	PLAYER
5,987	MICHAEL JORDAN
5,762	KAREEM ABDUL-JABBAR
5,640	KOBE BRYANT
5,250	SHAQUILLE O'NEAL
4,761	KARL MALONE
4,457	JERRY WEST
4,233	TIM DUNCAN
3,897	LARRY BIRD
3,776	JOHN HAVLICEK
3,755	HAKEEM OLAJUWON

NBA ALL-TIME PLAYOFFS PPG

POINTS	PLAYER
33.4	MICHAEL JORDAN
29.1	JERRY WEST
28.5	LEBRON JAMES
27.0	ELGIN BAYLOR
25.9	HAKEEM OLAJUWON
25.9	DIRK NOWITZKI
25.6	KOBE BRYANT
24.7	KARL MALONE
24.3	KAREEM ABDUL-JABBAR
24.3	SHAQUILLE O'NEAL

NBA ALL-TIME PLAYOFF VICTORIES

WINS	TEAM
17	BOSTON CELTICS
11	LOS ANGELES LAKERS
6	CHICAGO BULLS
5	MINNEAPOLIS LAKERS
4	SAN ANTONIO SPURS
3	DETROIT PISTONS
2	PHILADELPHIA 76ERS
2	HOUSTON ROCKETS
2	NEW YORK KNICKS
2	PHILADELPHIA WARRIORS

TECHNIQUES

While height and athleticism are prerequisites for a basketball player, so too are ball handling skills. An ability to pass, dribble, shield the ball from opponents, and above all shoot baskets, is essential and must be mastered for a player to progress. Basketball players will always work as a unit, whether on defence (double-teaming to turn the ball over), or in offence (setting screens to allow a teammate a clear shot). The following techniques are among the most common.

MOVING

Players have unrestricted movement on the court but are prohibited from running while holding the ball. While holding the ball, players can use the pivot foot – one foot set on the ground – while having full mobility with the rest of the body.

Which foot?
The player's position upon receiving the ball determines which becomes the pivot foot

PASSING

When an opponent is positioned to block a normal chest pass, a player can bounce the ball to a teammate instead. This takes longer to complete than the chest pass, but it is also harder for the opposing team to intercept as it is aimed at the court floor.

Firm pass
Bounce passes must be made with conviction and not clearly telegraphed

DRIBBLING

Dribbling is the act of bouncing the ball continuously, and is a requirement for a player taking steps with the ball. When dribbling past an opponent, the dribbler should dribble with the hand farthest from the opponent, making it more difficult for the defensive player to get to the ball. It is therefore important for a player to be able to dribble competently with both hands.

SHOOTING

Shots are commonly made from a standing or jumping position (known as a jump-shot), or as a lay-up shot which requires the player to be in motion towards the basket, and to "lay" the ball in off the backboard. The highest-percentage shot is the crowd-pleasing slam dunk (right), in which the player jumps very high and throws the ball downward through the hoop.

Dunking
The player angles the wrist over the ball and slams it down through the hoop

Getting airborne
Players time their run up to get maximum leverage off their standing foot

LITTLE BIG MAN

MUGGSY BOGUES, FORMER PLAYER FOR THE CHARLOTTE HORNETS, IS THE SHORTEST PLAYER EVER TO PLAY IN THE NBA AT 1.60M (5FT 3IN).

TACTICS

While the object of basketball is simple – to score more points than the opposing team – some of the strategies to achieve this can be increasingly complex as the standard of play rises. Offensive plays usually centre around rapid counterattacks, using a variety of formations to get the ball up court as quickly as possible. Offence is often directed by the team's point guard. Defensive plays require discipline, tracking an opponent stride for stride, and attempting to spoil their work. Timeouts called by the coach will often be used to discuss tactics.

OFFENCE

Teams almost always have several offensive plays planned to ensure their movement is not predictable, including the fast break (right). Plays normally involve planned passes and movement by players without the ball. A quick movement by an offensive player without the ball to gain an advantageous position is called a cut. A legal attempt by an offensive player to stop an opponent from guarding a teammate, is a screen or pick. Screens and cuts are the building blocks of offensive play.

DEFENCE

There are two main defensive strategies: zone defence and man-to-man defence. Zone defence involves players in defensive positions guarding whichever opponent is in their zone, such as the zone press (right). In man-to-man defence, each defensive player guards a specific opponent and tries to prevent him from dribbling, making passes or shots by staying as close to him as possible – invading his "bubble". Defenders always focus on the position of the hands (both their own and the attacker's) and must be adept at spotting a fake pass or shot and stealing.

THE NBA PLAYOFFS

The NBA season starts in November with the regular season, in which teams from the Eastern and Western Conferences compete a gruelling, 82-game schedule. The top eight teams from each Conference qualify for the playoffs which begin in late April. Teams in the playoffs are seeded according to their performace in the regular season. A series of elimination rounds culminates in a best-of-seven series between the victors of both conferences. Known as the NBA Finals, it is held annually in June. The victor in the NBA Finals wins the Larry O'Brien Championship Trophy. With 17 NBA Finals victories, the Boston Celtics are the most successful team in NBA history.

FAST BREAK

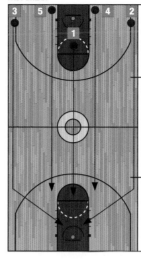

1 Best ball handler
He or she should fill the middle land of the court

2 Shooting guard
Fills the left outside land and runs into court within 30cm (12in) of the sideline

3 Quick forward
Fulfils same role as shooting guard but on other side of court. Too many players fail to do this and the team does not benefit from the spread (floor spacing) needed for a successful primary break

4 Power forward
Also the non-rebounder, trailing the play. He should continue downcourt to follow any attempted shots by players 1, 2, or 3

5 Centre/rebounder
Keeps to his own lane and serves as "safety" in case there is a sudden change of possession

ZONE PRESS

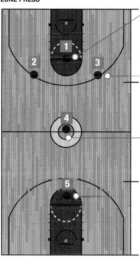

Top-court press
The shooting guard positions himself in the front half of the near foul circle and forces opponents to move. He should be a smaller player with good speed and quick hands. He is limited to lateral movements in the backcourt

Wing men
The wing men, 2 and 3, are taller forward players. The more athletic forward should be placed in the 2 position, as the defensive team should force the attack in his direction

Middle man
The centrefielder should be the quickest player on the team with good court sense and anticipation

Last line of defence
The back man is usually the centre, the biggest man and best rebounder. His primary responsibility is to prevent easy shots by the opposing players

INSIDE STORY

The International Basketball Federation, more commonly known by the French acronym FIBA, is an association of national organizations which governs international competition in basketball. The association was founded in Geneva in 1932, two years after the sport was officially recognized by the International Olympic Committee. Its original name was Fédération Internationale de Basketball Amateur. Eight nations were founding members: Argentina, Czechoslovakia, Greece, Italy, Latvia, Portugal, Romania, and Switzerland. During the 1936 Summer Olympics held in Berlin, the Federation named James Naismith (1861–1939), the founder of basketball, as its Honorary President. FIBA has organized a FIBA World Championship for men since 1950 and a World Championship for Women since 1953. Both events are now held every four years, alternating with the Olympics.

NATIONAL BASKETBALL ASSOCIATION

The NBA is the world's premier men's basketball league. It has 30 teams; 29 in the United States and one in Canada. The league was founded in New York City on 6 June 1946 as the Basketball Association of America (BAA). The league adopted the name National Basketball Association in the autumn of 1949 after merging with the rival National Basketball League. The league's several international and individual team offices are directed out of its head offices located in the Olympic Tower at 645 Fifth Avenue in New York City.

HARLEM GLOBETROTTERS

THE HARLEM GLOBETROTTERS ARE AN EXHIBITION BASKETBALL TEAM AND ONE OF THE WORLD'S MOST FAMOUS SPORTS FRANCHISES. THEY WERE CREATED BY ABE SAPERSTEIN IN 1927 IN CHICAGO. THE TEAM ADOPTED THE NAME HARLEM BECAUSE OF ITS CONNOTATIONS AS A MAJOR AFRICAN-AMERICAN COMMUNITY. OVER THE YEARS THEY HAVE PLAYED MORE THAN 20,000 EXHIBITION GAMES IN 118 COUNTRIES, MOSTLY AGAINST DELIBERATELY INEFFECTIVE OPPONENTS. THEY HAVE WON OVER 98 PER CENT OF THEIR MATCHES.

Oval ball
An official NFL football is 28cm (11in) long, has a 71cm (28in) circumference at its widest point, and weighs 425g (15oz)

Head gear
The helmet and face guard protect the player's head and face from injury

Shoulderpads
Every player suits up with foam-lined plastic shoulderpads

Team colours
Every player wears a jersey in the team colours. The name and number identifies the player and includes NFL and team logos

Tight fit
A combination of nylon and spandex allows the pants to stretch over the bulky leg padding

Padded inserts
Players slip padded inserts under their leggings to protect legs against falls and blows from other players

Lightweight shoes
On grass, players wear shoes with hard plastic cleats, which screw into the soles, but on artificial surfaces, shoes with moulded soles are worn

NEED2KNOW

→ American football is the most popular spectator sport in the United States. Every year, almost half of all Americans tune in to watch the Super Bowl – the NFL championship game.

→ A professional league in Canada plays a version of American football using specific Canadian rules.

→ American football enjoys limited popularity outside of north America. Leagues exist in countries such as Britain, Germany, Japan, and Mexico.

→ The first regular NFL season match to be held outside the United States was staged in Mexico City in 2005. An NFL-record 103,467 people packed the stadium.

GAME OVERVIEW

Jokingly described as "not a contact sport but a collision sport", American football is also known as gridiron football in some countries, and just football in the US. Two teams of eleven players compete during four periods of play (known as quarters) to score points by advancing an oval ball into the opposition's end zone or kicking it through goalposts. The attacking team, or offence, has a series of four attempts, or "downs", to move the ball 10 yards up the pitch. If successful, it is granted a new set of downs. The defence attempts to stop them and win possession of the ball. While huge linemen clash at the line of scrimmage, running backs and lightning-quick receivers provide options for the playmaker, the quarterback. Highly tactical, explosive, and fast, American football is like armoured chess.

PLAYER PROFILE
Since there are so many different positions, each with specific roles and physical demands, there is no typical physical make-up. But most players combine strength and power with outstanding athletic ability, and excellent hand-eye co-ordination is essential. Depending on the position, height ranges from 1.8 to 2m (5ft 11in to 6ft 8in) and weight ranges from 86 to 136kg (190 to 300lb).

AMERICAN FOOTBALL

THE GRIDIRON

A football field is bounded by long sidelines and short end lines, forming a rectangle that measures 120 x 53yd (109 x 49m). The 100yd (91m) between the posts are divided by lines that cross the field every 5yd (4.5m), and are numbered every 10yd (9m). Four rows of hash marks span the length of the field – the outer two mark 1yd (90cm) from the sidelines; the inner, or inbound, two mark the area in which plays must start if the ball goes out of bounds on the previous play. The scoring area (end zone) is bounded by the goal line, the end line, and sidelines. Most fields are covered in grass, but many have an artificial surface.

PLAYERS AND POSITIONS

Every NFL team has a roster of up to 53 players. Only 11 are on the field at any one time, but many are used in the course of a game – some or all of the team may be substituted in the break between plays, if there is enough time. Each player has a specialized role within one of three main playing units: offence, defence, and special teams. Offensive players include the quarterback, offensive linemen, receivers, and running backs. Defensive positions include defensive linemen, linebackers, cornerbacks, and safeties. Positions in the special teams include placekicker, punter, holder, long and short snapper, and punt returner.

ON SAFARI

THE REFEREE AND HIS TEAM OF OFFICIALS ARE SOMETIMES AFFECTIONATELY KNOWN AS "ZEBRAS", DUE TO THEIR BLACK-AND-WHITE STRIPED UNIFORM.

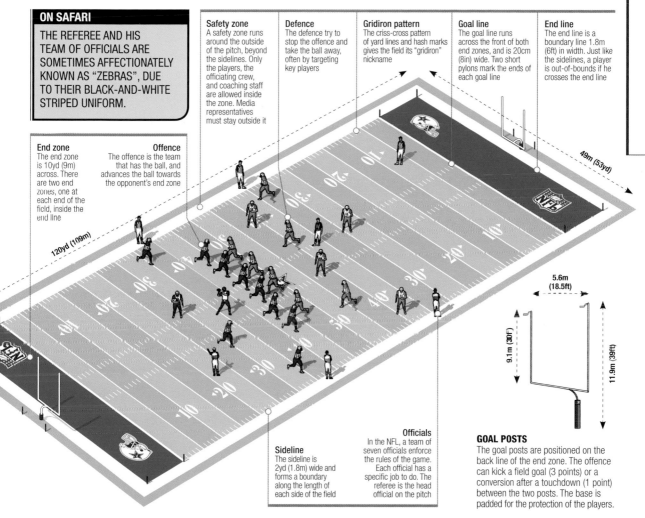

Safety zone
A safety zone runs around the outside of the pitch, beyond the sidelines. Only the players, the officiating crew, and coaching staff are allowed inside the zone. Media representatives must stay outside it

Defence
The defence try to stop the offence and take the ball away, often by targeting key players

Gridiron pattern
The criss-cross pattern of yard lines and hash marks gives the field its "gridiron" nickname

Goal line
The goal line runs across the front of both end zones, and is 20cm (8in) wide. Two short pylons mark the ends of each goal line

End line
The end line is a boundary line 1.8m (6ft) in width. Just like the sidelines, a player is out-of-bounds if he crosses the end line

End zone
The end zone is 10yd (9m) across. There are two end zones, one at each end of the field, inside the end line

Offence
The offence is the team that has the ball, and advances the ball towards the opponent's end zone

120yd (109m)

49m (53yd)

Sideline
The sideline is 2yd (1.8m) wide and forms a boundary along the length of each side of the field

Officials
In the NFL, a team of seven officials enforce the rules of the game. Each official has a specific job to do. The referee is the head official on the pitch

5.6m (18.5ft)

9.1m (30ft)

11.9m (39ft)

GOAL POSTS
The goal posts are positioned on the back line of the end zone. The offence can kick a field goal (3 points) or a conversion after a touchdown (1 point) between the two posts. The base is padded for the protection of the players.

SIDELINES

4,000,000 The estimated cost, in US dollars, to screen a 30-second television advertisement during coverage of the 2013 Super Bowl.

71,024 The attendance at the 2013 Super Bowl at the Mercedes-Benz Superdome in New Orleans, Louisiana, where the Baltimore Ravens defeated the San Francisco 49ers.

200 The NFL record for quarterback sacks – a defensive manoeuvre where the quarterback is tackled behind the line of scrimmage before he releases the ball. Held by Bruce Smith of the Buffalo Bills (1985–99), and the Washington Redskins (2000–03).

48 The record for the most points scored in the Super Bowl throughout a player's career. The record is held by San Francisco 49ers player Jerry Rice, widely acknowledged as one of the greatest wide receivers in NFL history.

PADDED FOR PROTECTION

American football is a full-contact sport. Every part of the body needs to be protected from charging players, or flying hits to the chest or ribs. Spectacular head-clashes are common, but serious injuries are rare. A helmet is the most vital piece of kit, with internal padding, a chin strap, and a mask to protect the face from accidental blows. Most players also wear a mouthguard to shield the teeth from knocks.

The players' body armour is what gives them their "top-heavy" appearance. Hard shoulder pads are worn over soft shock pads, which absorb hard blows. Other pads are used depending on the player's position and as protection against specific injuries. Linemen wear gloves to protect their hands from being trapped between helmets or shoulder pads.

Head and face
The helmet consists of a shell, the face mask, and a chin strap. Air bladders inside the helmet prevent it from slipping. The quarterback's helmet often incorporates a microphone and speaker so he can receive plays and discuss tactics with the coaches

Shoulder and chest
The shoulderpads protect the shoulders and chest area. The outer shell is made from a tough plastic, while the insides are padded with foam to make them more comfortable. The pads are fixed with straps and buckles

Hip protection
Pads for the hips come in various shapes and styles depending on field position. Players carrying an injury may also wear them for extra protection

Thigh pads
Pads for the thighs give extra protection to these high-impact areas

Knee protection
Rigid pads slip into pockets inside the leggings to absorb blows to the knees

PROTECTIVE PADDING
A range of pads can be worn, each of which are designed to protect specific parts of the body.

Neck roll
A foam-padded neck roll sits around the neck and stops the head from jerking back in a tackle

Elastic fit
Elasticated guards fit snugly over the forearm and wrist

Arm guard
Tight-fitting arm guards are worn to cushion the forearms and protect any existing injuries

AIM OF THE GAME

The overall objective is to score more points than the opposition. The main way to do this is by scoring touchdowns, worth six points, by advancing the ball into your opponent's end zone. It can be run over the line or passed to a teammate in the end zone. After a touchdown, the offence can score an extra point by kicking the ball through the uprights, or two points by running or passing the ball into the end zone. A field goal worth three points can be scored by kicking the ball through the uprights. A safety (two points) is awarded if an opponent is tackled or spills the ball in his own end zone and it goes out of play.

KICK OFFS
A kick off starts each half and follows each score. The placekicker boots the ball from the 30-yard line, while his teammates follow it upfield. The opposition's kick returner catches the ball and advances with it; the offensive drive starts where he is tackled. A "touchback" is signalled if the returner catches the ball in his end zone and kneels down (the drive then starts from the offence's 20-yard line). A touchback also occurs if the kick goes beyond the end zone, or if there is a turnover (the ball passing from offence to defence) in the end zone. If a safety is scored, the opposition kick the ball to the scoring team from its 20-yard line.

PENALTIES
Penalties are given for rule violations, and usually consist of moving the ball towards the offending team's end zone, and replaying the down. Some of the most common penalties include:
BLOCK IN BACK An offensive player pushes an opponent in the back.
FACE MASK Grabbing an opponent's face mask.
HOLDING Illegally holding an opponent other than the ball carrier.
INTERFERENCE Illegally obstructing a player attempting to catch a pass.

ENFORCING THE RULES

Officials wear a distinctive uniform consisting of shirts with black-and-white stripes, white trousers, and a black or white hat. The head referee guides six officials with specific duties – the umpire, head linesman, line judge, field judge, side judge, and back judge. An official signals an infringement by throwing a yellow flag. The referee then conveys the decision using a hand signal and an announcement. One referee described the job as "trying to maintain order during a legalized gang brawl involving 80 toughs with a little whistle, a hanky, and a ton of prayer".

INTERFERENCE
A penalty in which a player has interfered with another player during a passing play.

FIRST DOWN
The offence advances 10yd (0.9m) within four downs, so a new series of downs is called.

FALSE START
This is called when a member of the offence moves illegally before the ball is snapped.

OFFSIDE
A defensive player is on the wrong side of the line of scrimmage at the start of play.

HOLDING
A penalty in which a player of either side has illegally held an opponent.

ILLEGAL BALL TOUCH
A penalty in which the ball is illegally touched, kicked, or batted, usually after going out of bounds.

10 YARDS AT A TIME

Territory and possession are the keys to success in American football. The team in possession of the ball is the offence. It has four chances, or "downs", to run or pass the ball 10yd (9m) towards the end zone of the defence. If the offence gains the yards, it gets another four downs in which to advance a further 10yd. The drive continues until the team scores, runs out of time, or loses possession. The offence might not make 10yd in four downs, for example, or there could be a turnover if a pass is intercepted or the ball is fumbled. The two teams then switch roles and play continues.

PLAYING UNITS

The three main playing units in an American football team are the offence, defence, and special teams. Offence and defence are composed of a range of different players in a variety of positions, such as the basic offence and defence formations (see right).

Special teams are the units that do anything that is not regular offence and defence, particularly kicking and returning kicks. They comprise kickers, snappers, ball holders, and returners. The placekicker kicks off and scores points by kicking the ball between the uprights. The punter "punts" the ball back to the opposition if his own team are unlikely to make 10yd. Snappers restart play by passing the ball to a team-mate. Ball holders hold the ball upright when a placekick is taken, and kick returners are catchers and runners who catch kick offs and punts and advance them up the field.

BASIC DEFENCE

The defence aims to stop the offence from gaining yards. Most teams in the NFL use a formation called the 4-3 defence, in which four defensive linemen (two defensive ends and two defensive tackles) line up in front of three linebackers. Two safeties play behind to stop longer passes and runs, while two cornerbacks cover passes to the wide receivers.

POSITIONS:
DE Defensive end **DT** Defensive tackle
LB Linebacker **CB** Cornerback **S** Safety

BASIC OFFENCE

The Standard I Formation is a common attacking offensive using five offensive linemen (two offensive tackles, two guards, and the centre). The "L" refers to the line formed by the quarterback, fullback, and tailback. A tight end sits on one side, with a wide receiver at each end.

POSITIONS:
WR Wide receiver **TE** Tight end **OT** Offensive tackler **G** Guard **C** Centre **QB** Quarterback
FB Fullback **TB** Tailback

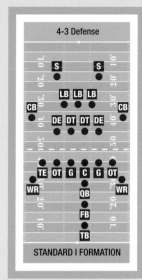

4-3 Defense

STANDARD I FORMATION

PLAYING BY THE BOOK

Strategy is an important part every game of American football. Every team, from the professional NFL sides down to high school teams, has a playbook of plays that have been practised on the training field. Sometimes, teams start a game with five or six plays already decided, after which the coach calls plays to suit the stage of the game.

SPECIAL SKILLS

Each player develops specific skills according to his position. For example, blocking and tackling are important attributes of defensive linemen, a good throwing arm is an obvious requirement for a quarterback, while wide receivers combine lightning acceleration with excellent catching ability. Other players, such as the kicker and punt returner, specialize in one part of the game.

Spiral action
The ball is spun as it is thrown, making it fly straight and true

Laces
The ball is gripped by the laces and thrown point first

THROWING THE BALL
One of the most important duties of a quarterback is to pass the ball to a receiver. Strength and accuracy are vital, as he must be able to throw the ball to a specific player over long distances.

THE SNAP
Each down begins when the centre snaps the ball behind to the quarterback. The quarterback usually stands directly behind the centre. In the shotgun formation, he stands further back to create more space for the pass.

Snapping the ball
The snapper snaps the ball, through his legs, to the quarterback

Ready to play
After taking the snap, the quarterback runs the called play

THE TACKLE
The tackler bends his knees and crouches as the ball carrier approaches. On impact, he accelerates up and through the opponent, generating power by straightening his legs and using his upper body to get the ball carrier to the ground.

Facing up
The tackler braces himself to check the advance of the ball carrier

Play over
The play is over when the tackled player touches the ground with one or both knees, or any other body part other than hands or feet

THE FIELD GOAL
For a field goal attempt, the ball holder stands 6m (7yd) behind the centre, who snaps the ball to him. The holder then catches it and sets it up for the kick. The kicker steps forward and swings his foot through the ball, propelling it between the uprights.

Holding the ball
The holder places the ball upright on its nose, ready for the kick

Kicking for goal
The placekicker boots the ball hard and true, aiming between the goal posts

STAT CENTRAL

SUPER BOWL WINNERS

YEAR	WINNER
2013	BALTIMORE RAVENS
2012	NEW YORK GIANTS
2011	GREEN BAY PACKERS
2010	NEW ORLEANS SAINTS
2009	PITTSBURGH STEELERS
2008	NEW YORK GIANTS
2007	INDIANAPOLIS COLTS
2006	PITTSBURGH STEELERS
2005	NEW ENGLAND PATRIOTS
2004	NEW ENGLAND PATRIOTS
2003	TAMPA BAY BUCCANEERS
2002	NEW ENGLAND PATRIOTS
2001	BALTIMORE RAVENS
2000	ST. LOUIS RAMS
1999	DENVER BRONCOS

NFL ALL-TIME TOUCHDOWNS

NO.	PLAYER
208	JERRY RICE
175	EMMITT SMITH
162	LADAINIAN TOMLINSON
157	RANDY MOSS
156	TERRELL OWENS
145	MARCUS ALLEN
136	MARSHALL FAULK
131	CRIS CARTER
128	MARVIN HARRISON
126	JIM BROWN
125	WALTER PAYTON
116	JOHN RIGGINS
113	LENNY MOORE
112	SHAUN ALEXANDER
109	BARRY SANDERS

NFL ALL-TIME TOUCHDOWN PASSES

NO.	PLAYER
508	BRETT FAVRE
436	PEYTON MANNING
420	DAN MARINO
342	FRAN TARKENTON
334	TOM BRADY
324	DREW BREES
300	JOHN ELWAY
291	WARREN MOON
290	JOHNNY UNITAS
275	VINNY TESTAVERDE
273	JOE MONTANA
261	DAVE KRIEG
255	SONNY JURGENSEN
254	DAN FOUTS
251	DREW BLEDSOE

CLOCK WATCHING

When it comes to offensive play, being aware of how much time is left on the clock is crucial for deciding what set play to follow. Teams do their best to maximize their own chances, while minimizing the risk of the opposition gaining the upper hand. For example, a team down by a few points late in the game will go on the offensive with the objective of stealing the lead, but doing so in such a way as to leave the opposition with less time to score themselves. Communication between players and with the coaching staff is important in order to co-ordinate the team; pauses between each down allow players to re-group, while the coach communicates with the quarterback through an earpiece.

PLAYS

American football is punctuated by a series of set plays during each down. Offensive plays aim to advance the ball towards the opposition's end zone, with the ultimate goal of scoring a touchdown. Defensive plays aim to stop the offence from moving forward, forcing errors that could result in a turnover. Every team uses different positions and formations to deal with specific game situations.

→ Player movement

- - - → Passage of ball

├───┤ Offensive block

● Defensive player positions

● Offensive player positions

TB OFF TACKLE

The tailback off tackle is the most common running play in the offence, and is an excellent method of making small yardage gains. The quarterback hands the ball off to the tailback, who runs through a hole created by the offensive tackle and the tight end. The tailback can also run to the outside of the tight end if the fullback fails to lead block the defensive linebacker.

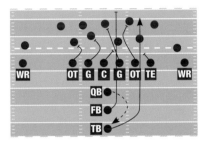

SWEEP

The sweep, or dive, is a highly organised offensive running play in which the tailback takes a pitch from the quarterback and then runs parallel to the line of scrimmage. This gives the fullback and offensive linemen time to block defenders in front of the tailback. Once a gap appears in the defensive line, the tailback turns back upfield and runs straight through it.

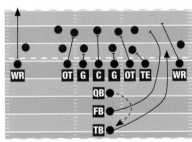

HAIL MARY

The Hail Mary is a passing play in which the quarterback throws a long ball towards a number of receivers who are simultaneously running at the defence's end zone. The play is often used as a last resort by the trailing team at the end of the game. The Hail Mary has relatively little chance for successful completion, but it can force a pass interference penalty from a disorganized defence.

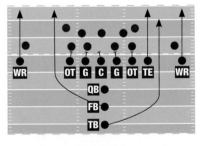

THE BLITZ

Also known as the "quarterback rush", the blitz is a defensive tactic used to combat passing plays. The aim is to put the quarterback under pressure by swamping the offence with defenders. Linebackers or cornerbacks rush the quarterback to disrupt the play. A blitz is a great way to force quarterback errors, but it also leaves receivers open to passes if the offence reads the play.

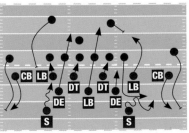

CANADIAN FOOTBALL

Canadian football is essentially the same game as American football, but with a few key differences, as well as many minor rule distinctions. The playing field in Canadian football is generally longer and wider. Each team has 12 players on the pitch at any one time – the extra player in the Canadian game usually occupies a backfield position. And there are three downs to advance the ball 10 yards (9.1m) in Canadian football compared to four in the American game.

SEASONAL DEVELOPMENTS

The timing of the Canadian football season is largely dictated by the extremes of temperature experienced in the northerly latitudes of the host nation. Outdoor stadiums are common, so games must take place once the winter ice and snow have thawed. The professional season starts in June, while the play-offs and season-ending final take place in November.

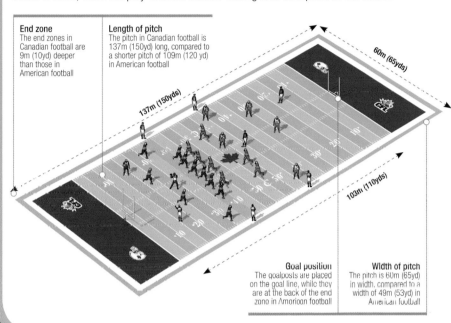

End zone
The end zones in Canadian football are 9m (10yd) deeper than those in American football

Length of pitch
The pitch in Canadian football is 137m (150yd) long, compared to a shorter pitch of 109m (120 yd) in American football

137m (150yds)

60m (65yds)

103m (110yds)

Goal position
The goalposts are placed on the goal line, while they are at the back of the end zone in American football

Width of pitch
The pitch is 60m (65yd) in width, compared to a width of 49m (53yd) in American football

CELEBRATING THE DIFFERENCES
Although the equipment and playing area of Canadian Football may at first glance seem identical to American Football, they are in fact subtly different. The pitch is slightly larger, the goal posts are placed in a different position, and the football carries different markings.

Ball stripes
CFL-sanctioned balls are roughly the same size and weight as those used in the NFL, but they have two white stripes 1in (2.5cm) from each end. NFL balls have no stripes at all

INSIDE STORY

American football grew from rugby football, a game played in England in the early 1800s. By the 1880s, American football and rugby football had grown apart as each sport developed standardized rules. Originally a college sport, American football went professional in the early 1900s, and the National Football League (NFL) was formed in 1920. It became more popular in the 1950s, when TV coverage brought the sport to a national audience. Since the 1990s, football has eclipsed baseball as the most popular spectator sport in the US.

THE SUPER BOWL
The annual Super Bowl is the championship-deciding game of the NFL. Following a play-off series involving 12 teams from the NFL conferences (six from the American Football Conference and six from the National Football Conference), two teams compete for the Vince Lombardi Trophy, named after the coach of the Green Bay Packers, who won the first two Super Bowls in 1967 and 1968. Traditionally, the game takes place on "Super Bowl Sunday" (in late January or early February), and is watched by hundreds of millions of people worldwide.

AMERICAN FOOTBALL AROUND THE WORLD
AMERICAN FOOTBALL ENJOYS LIMITED POPULARITY OUTSIDE THE UNITED STATES AND CANADA. THE NFL NOW STAGES AT LEAST ONE REGULAR-SEASON GAME OUTSIDE THE UNITED STATES EACH YEAR. WEMBLEY STADIUM IN LONDON, ENGLAND, HAS SERVED AS A VENUE FOR MANY OF THESE GAMES. SEVERAL EUROPEAN NATIONS RUN LEAGUES WITH VARYING DEGREES OF SUCCESS. JAPAN HAS THE SUCCESSFUL PRO X-LEAGUE, AND THE SPORT IS ALSO PLAYED IN AUSTRALIA, MEXICO, AND NEW ZEALAND.

NATIONAL FOOTBALL LEAGUE (NFL)
The NFL is the leading pro football league in the United States. It consists of 32 teams in two conferences – the American Football Conference (AFC) and the National Football Conference (NFC). Each team plays 16 games during the regular season. The top six teams from each conference then compete in play-offs that culminate in the annual Super Bowl competition.

CANADIAN FOOTBALL LEAGUE (CFL)
Also known as the Ligue Canadienne de Football (LCF), the CFL was founded in 1958 and consists of eight teams, divided into eastern and western divisions. The teams compete over a 19-week season, at the end of which the top six teams enter play-offs. This culminates in two teams competing in the final for the Grey Cup, the oldest trophy in professional football.

PLAYER PROFILE

Rugby Union is a hard-fought contact sport that requires players to be extremely fit, strong, and physically robust. The contest is particularly tough between the forwards, who are often more than 2m (6ft 6in) tall and weigh in excess of 110kg (17st). They tend to have great upper-body strength and powerful legs, which they use to drive forward. Backs are usually shorter and smaller in frame, and tend to be more nimble and skilful. Ball handling and balance are especially important for the backs, who execute passes, moves, and tackles at high speed. They also need the skill and coolness to kick and catch the ball under considerable pressure.

Head protection
Bandages, soft padding, or scrumcaps are often worn by forwards, whose heads regularly come in contact with other heads, knees, and boots

Oval ball
The focus of every rugby game, the oval-shaped ball is made of four stitched or glued panels of leather or (more recently) synthetic material

Evolving style
Since the mid-1990s, rugby jerseys worn by professional teams have evolved from heavy-duty cotton shirts to hard-to-grab, close-fitting, and light-weight vests made from technologically crafted synthetic materials

Heavy duty
Usually made of heavy-duty cotton, shorts may have the player's number on the leg

Rugby boots
Similar to soccer boots, they have leather uppers and flexible, synthetic soles holding studs or cleats

Leg protection
Beneath the long cotton socks, many players wear shin pads to protect their legs

NEED2KNOW

→ Rugby Union is the most popular form of rugby, followed by rugby league (see pp.128–31).

→ The sport is played in more than 100 countries around the world. It is particularly popular in Britain, Ireland, France, Australia, New Zealand, and South Africa.

→ The inaugural Rugby World Cup, held jointly in New Zealand and Australia in 1987, was won by rugby's most famous team – the New Zealand All Blacks.

→ The Women's Rugby Football Union was set up in Britain in 1983. The first official women's Rugby World Cup was held in 1998.

RUGBY UNION

GAME OVERVIEW

Vividly described as "a hooligans' game played by gentlemen", rugby union is one of the most physically punishing of all ball sports, played under a rigorous rule code. Wearing minimal protection, two teams of 15 players clash to win possession of the oval ball, then advance it towards the opposition's try line. After two halves of 40 minutes each, the winner is the team that has amassed more points by scoring tries – grounding the ball in the opposition's in-goal area – or by kicking conversions, penalty kicks, and drop goals between the uprights and above the crossbar of the opposition's goal posts. The fast pace and great physicality of the game can make it a highly dramatic spectacle.

THE RUGBY PITCH

Rugby union is played on a rectangular grass playing field or
pitch. In professional rugby, the length of the pitch is always
100m (330ft) from try line to try line, but the width of the pitch
and the distance from try line to dead ball line may vary. Each
team defends an in-goal area behind the goal posts defined
by the try line, the dead ball line, and the touchlines. Between
the two try lines, a series of solid and dotted white lines are
marked at regular intervals. These divide the rugby pitch in to
zones, and indicate where restart kicks are taken from, and
where players need to position themselves during set-pieces.

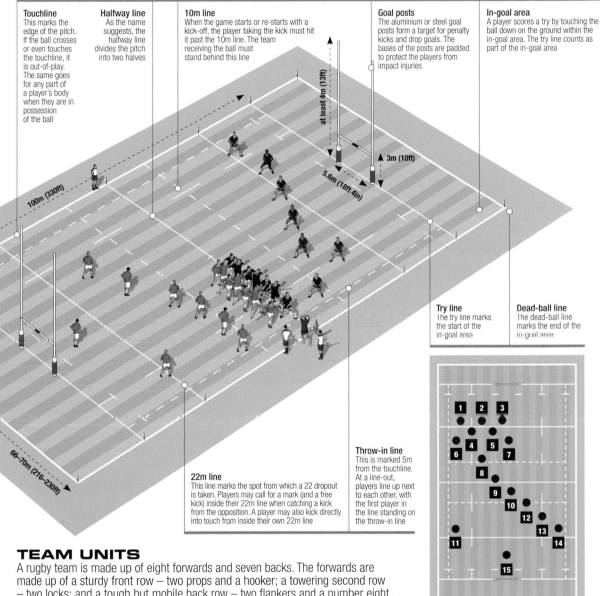

Touchline
This marks the
edge of the pitch.
If the ball crosses
or even touches
the touchline, it
is out-of-play.
The same goes
for any part of
a player's body
when they are in
possession
of the ball

Halfway line
As the name
suggests, the
halfway line
divides the pitch
into two halves

10m line
When the game starts or re-starts with a
kick-off, the player taking the kick must hit
it past the 10m line. The team
receiving the ball must
stand behind this line

Goal posts
The aluminium or steel goal
posts form a target for penalty
kicks and drop goals. The
bases of the posts are padded
to protect the players from
impact injuries

In-goal area
A player scores a try by touching the
ball down on the ground within the
in-goal area. The try line counts as
part of the in-goal area

at least 4m (13ft)

3m (10ft)

5.6m (18ft 4in)

100m (330ft)

66–70m (216–230ft)

Try line
The try line marks
the start of the
in-goal area

Dead-ball line
The dead-ball line
marks the end of the
in-goal area

22m line
This line marks the spot from which a 22 dropout
is taken. Players may call for a mark (and a free
kick) inside their 22m line when catching a kick
from the opposition. A player may also kick directly
into touch from inside their own 22m line

Throw-in line
This is marked 5m
from the touchline.
At a line-out,
players line up next
to each other, with
the first player in
the line standing on
the throw-in line

TEAM UNITS

A rugby team is made up of eight forwards and seven backs. The forwards are
made up of a sturdy front row – two props and a hooker; a towering second row
– two locks; and a tough but mobile back row – two flankers and a number eight.
In the backs, the tenacious scrum half follows the ball and moves it between the
forwards and the backs. The fly half is the team's play maker and pivotal figure. He
calls and initiates moves, and usually does most of the kicking. The two centres are
the defensive heart of the backs and, in attack, look for holes in the opposition's
defences. The wingers and full back are the team's real speed merchants – often
running in tries at the end of backs' moves – but also the last line of defence.

POSITIONS BY NUMBER:
1 Loosehead prop **2** Hooker **3** Tighthead prop
4 Left lock **5** Right lock **6** Left flanker **7** Right
flanker **8** Number eight **9** Scrum half **10** Fly-half
11 Left wing **12** Left centre **13** Right centre
14 Right wing **15** Full back

WHAT THEY WEAR

The traditional rugby kit consists of just a jersey, shorts, socks,
and boots. Although at most levels of the game little has
changed, the professional game has seen quite an advance
in the materials used in making rugby shirts (see p.120).
Similarly, a new approach to injury prevention has seen the
emergence of various body protection systems.

Some forwards wear scrumcaps to avoid "cauliflower ear"
– permanent swelling caused by rubbing of the ears during
scrums – and to provide protection against impacts. Upper-
body padding has evolved more recently and is becoming
increasingly popular.

BODY PROTECTION SYSTEMS

Unlike most sports that involve crunching
physical contact, rugby players traditionally
wore relatively little in the way of protective
clothing. Some professional players now
choose to wear padding around the head,
shoulders, and collar bone.

Scrumcap
Like the other items of padding, the
headguard must meet International
Rugby Board (IRB) standards. It fits
snugly on the head and is kept in
place using a chin strap. Holes keep
the head well ventilated

Universally worn shield
An orthodontic gumshield is
custom-made by a
dentist. Cheaper
versions are
moulded by biting
into a gumshield that
has been softened
in hot water

Body padding
Any padding worn on the
shoulders must be
light and thin enough
to conform to strict
IRB (International Rugby
Board) guidelines. Most
shoulder-pad systems are
made of sections
of ventilated honeycomb-
formed material sewn into
tight-fitting nylon vests worn
under the outer rugby shirt

BALL DIMENSIONS
Although balls used in junior rugby
come in smaller sizes, balls used
in senior rugby must be 28–30cm
(11–12in) long and 58–62cm
(23–24in) at their widest point.

HIGH-CUT BOOTS
Although some rugby boots are made
with high-cut designs, giving extra
ankle protection, many rugby players
prefer to wear low-cut football boots
offering extra mobility.

SCORING POINTS

There are four main ways of scoring in rugby: a try, a
conversion, a penalty goal, and a drop goal. A player
scores a try by grounding the ball in the opposition's
in-goal area. A try is worth five points and earns the
chance of a conversion – a place kick that is worth an
extra two points. A kick at goal as the result of a penalty
is taken just like a conversion, but is worth three points.
Also worth three points, a drop goal can be taken at
any time from anywhere on the pitch, but the player
must drop the ball on the ground just as he kicks it.

PLAYING THE GAME

Teams gain territory by running with the ball in hand,
and passing it between players. Passes must not
go forward, but kicking the ball forward is allowed.
Kicking is a key way to gain territory, often by sending
the ball into touch and setting up a line-out. The main
method of defence is tackling the player with the
ball. Tackles must be made below chest height, and
tackling a player without the ball is forbidden.

SET PIECES

Central to the sport are the set-pieces that restart a game
after a stoppage: restart kicks at the start of each half and
after a score; line-outs when the ball has gone in to touch;
and scrums after infringements such as a forward pass.

Throw in
The hooker throws the ball
towards a teammate in the
line. Coded calls identify
the player who should jump
for the ball, so that the
opposition does not know
who to jump against

Jumper
The tall locks are the common
targets in a line-out. The
props help to lift the jumper.
The flankers and number
eight clean up
and secure
possession

LINE-OUT
The line-out is a jumping contest to secure the ball,
complete with deception, lifting, and precise timing.
Each team may put between two and seven players
in the line.

GROUNDING THE BALL

The grounding of a ball in the opposition's in-goal area is technically more complicated than it might appear. The key rules are that, first, the player must be in bounds, and second, that they must be in control of the ball as they ground it. Players are allowed to slide in to the in-goal area to score a try, but they cannot make a double movement to get the ball on or over the line.

In control
Here, the attacking player grounds the ball with sufficient downward pressure to show he is in full control

PENALTY TRY

A penalty try is awarded for deliberate or repeated foul play, or if a penalty offence prevents the scoring of a probable try. The subsequent conversion is lined up between the posts.

KICKING POINTS

A penalty kick is taken from the place where the offence was committed, or from where the ball lands if a player is obstructed after he punts it. While the kick is being taken, the opposing team cannot encroach within 10m (33ft).

A conversion is taken from any distance in line with the spot where the try was scored. Defenders can start to charge down conversion attempts as soon as the kicker starts to move towards the ball.

Successful kick
The ball must pass between the uprights and above the crossbar to score

HEAD TO HEAD

A scrum is a contest of brute strength and scrummaging technique. The forward pack of each team binds together in formation, and on the order of the referee engages the other pack head-on. On a signal given by the hooker, the scrum half rolls the ball in to the channel between the two teams. The hooker then attempts to secure the ball by heeling it towards the back of the scrum.

Bound on
Back row players must remain bound on until the ball is out of the scrum

Close company
The attentive scrum half of the defending team must not block or interfere with his opposite scrum half until he has taken the ball from the scrum

Put-in
The scrum half must deliver the ball straight down the middle of the channel between the two from rows. A crooked delivery results in a penalty for "feeding"

RUCKING AND MAULING

Rucks and mauls are contests for ball possession during open play. A ruck forms when the player carrying the ball goes to ground. The first players to arrive from either side can bind together over the ball, pushing their opponents back and using their feet to "ruck" the ball back to their side. A maul is similar to a ruck, but the ball carrier remains on their feet, allowing the clump of players to move up and down the field.

Gone to ground
When the ball carrier goes to ground he or she must release the ball or risk conceding a penalty

NO HANDS
Players bound in a ruck may not use their hands to free the ball. If the ball becomes stuck, a scrum is given to the advancing side.

SIDELINES

5,750 The distance in metres that the average professional rugby back covers during a game.

45 The highest number of points scored by a single player in a top-class international test. It was achieved by Simon Culhane of New Zealand during their 145–17 victory over Japan during the 1995 Rugby World Cup.

750,000 The estimated number of people who gathered in London's Trafalgar Square on 9 December 2003 to greet England's World-Cup winning squad.

152 The highest winning margin in an international game. Argentina beat Paraguay by 152–0 in May 2002. Japan won by the same margin in their 155-3 victory over Chinese Taipei in July 2002.

RULES OF RUGBY

The most fundamental rule in rugby is that the ball must not be passed or knocked forward from the hands. The result is a scrum to the opposition. Free kicks are awarded for lesser infringements, such as technical offences, while penalties are awarded against players who become involved in the game while in an offside position, or commit acts of foul play.

STAYING ON SIDE

During open play a player is deemed offside if he or she is in front of a teammate who is carrying the ball. They are liable to concede a penalty if they try to take part in the game before they are back in an onside position. A scrum is awarded against players that are accidentally involved in the game while in an offside position. The offside rule also comes in to play at set-pieces and when mauls and rucks are formed.

PENALTIES AND FOUL PLAY

Many penalties are awarded for fouls at close quarters, such as in a ruck or maul. Players often foul to slow down the speed at which the opposition release the ball into play, or in order to speed up their own ball. Examples of foul play fall into one of four categories: obstruction, unfair play, repeated infringements, and dangerous play and misconduct.

OBSTRUCTION Charging or pushing when players are running for the ball; running in front of a ball carrier; blocking a tackler; blocking the ball; a ball carrier running in to a teammate during a set-piece; obstructing a scrum half during a scrum.

UNFAIR PLAY Time wasting; intentionally throwing or knocking the ball out of play; intentionally infringing any law of the game or playing unfairly.

REPEATED INFRINGEMENTS A player's repeated infringement of any law of the game, whether intentional or not; repeated infringements committed collectively by a team.

DANGEROUS PLAY AND MISCONDUCT Offences include: stamping on or kicking an opponent; tripping an opponent with a leg or foot; early or late tackles; tackling an opponent above shoulder height; tackling a player without the ball; tackling a player with their feet off the ground; intentionally charging a player that has just kicked the ball; dangerous play in a scrum, ruck, or maul; retaliation.

CARD CAUTIONS

As in other sports such as soccer, rugby referees may make use of a card cautioning system. Any player who infringes any part of the foul play law is subject to a verbal warning, then yellow and red cards. If the referee awards a player a yellow card they must spend ten minutes off the pitch, in what has become known as the sin bin, leaving their team short-handed. If the player commits a further cautionable offence once back on the pitch they are awarded a red card, and sent off for the remainder of the match.

"HE IS A FREAK...!"

THE 1995 RUGBY WORLD CUP SAW THE EMERGENCE OF A TRUE RUGBY SUPERSTAR. AFTER JUST TWO CAPS, JONAH LOMU'S INCLUSION IN THE ALL BLACKS SQUAD CAUSED RAISED EYEBROWS. BUT BEFORE LONG HE WAS SWEEPING ASIDE ALL BEFORE HIM. IN THE SEMI-FINAL, IN A DISPLAY OF PURE POWER, LOMU DESTROYED THE ENGLISH BACKS, SCORING FOUR TRIES AND LEAVING THEIR PRIDE AND BODIES DENTED. AFTER THE GAME, THE DEFEATED ENGLAND CAPTAIN WILL CARLING SAID OF LOMU, "HE IS A FREAK, AND THE SOONER HE GOES AWAY, THE BETTER".

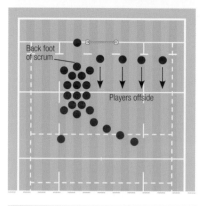

OFFSIDE AT A SCRUM
As in other set-pieces, once a scrum is formed, specific offside rules come into play. Imaginary offside lines run across the pitch 5m behind the rear player in the scrum on each side. Any players, apart from the scrum halves, that cross these lines are deemed offside.

Back foot of scrum

Players offside

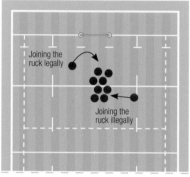

RUCK INFRINGEMENT
Offside rules apply to players joining rucks and mauls. During a ruck or maul a player is deemed offside if he or she enters from the side or from the side of the opposing team. Players may only join the ruck or maul, and bind on to their teammates, from the very back.

Joining the ruck legally

Joining the ruck illegally

TACTICAL APPROACHES

Although the styles of rugby playing have evolved over time, and have even varied in different parts of the world, there are two main tactical approaches to the game of rugby.

KICKING GAME

The first is a forward-dominated, kicking game in which the attacking team secures the ball and keeps it at close quarters, using forward drives and resulting mauls, rucks, and scrums. They also use searching kicks into touch to move upfield and rely on forward muscle to regain the ball in advanced positions. Coupled with a keen blanket defence, this is often an effective approach, resulting in lots of kicks at goal.

15-MAN RUGBY

The second approach is a fast-moving running game in which the team uses speed of movement and ball skills to create space and gain territory. Often referred to as "15-man rugby", this style of play relies on the full integration of mobile forwards and swift backs, and at its best results in an entertaining display of try-scoring action.

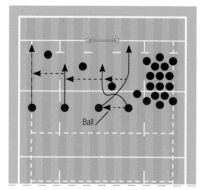

SET MOVES
Both forwards and backs have set moves or plays that they practise in training. The backs' move shown left, known as a loop, involves drawing opposing players out of position to create an overlap that the fast wide players can exploit.

Ball

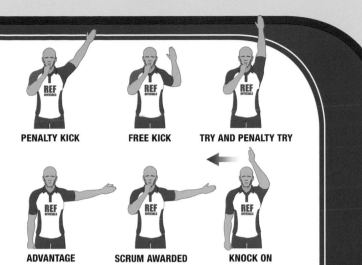

PENALTY KICK   **FREE KICK**   **TRY AND PENALTY TRY**

ADVANTAGE   **SCRUM AWARDED**   **KNOCK ON**

REFEREEING THE GAME

Rugby referees communicate with the players and, by extension, the spectators, through arm and hand gestures. These signals are broken into two tiers: primary signals, which indicate the decision that has been given i.e. a penalty kick, advantage, or free kick; and secondary signals, which communicate why a decision has been made i.e. a knock on, high tackle, or offside. Rugby referees are assisted by touch judges, one positioned on each touchline, whose primary responsibility is to indicate to the referee whether the ball, or a player carrying the ball, has strayed out of bounds.

INSIDE STORY

The apocryphal story of rugby's invention recounts how William Webb Ellis, a pupil at Rugby School in England in the 1820s, picked up the ball in a football match and ran with it. By the end of the century the Rugby Football Union (RFU) and the International Rugby Football Board (IRFB) had been formed to standardize the rules and govern the game. Eventually the RFU joined the IRFB, and in 1995 the IRFB became the International Rugby Board (IRB) as the game entered the professional era. The IRB is made up of more than 100 member and associate member countries.

MAJOR CHAMPIONSHIPS

Staged every four years since 1987, the Rugby World Cup is the sport's leading competition, with 20 countries competing to become world champions. The World Cup features group and knock-out stages, and the winners of the final are awarded the Webb Ellis Cup. Rugby's other international championships, held annually, are the Tri Nations in the southern hemisphere and the Six Nations in the northern hemisphere.

DOWN UNDER

The Tri Nations Series is the annual competition contested by the Southern Hemisphere's rugby superpowers: Australia, New Zealand, and South Africa. The competition is organized as a mini-league, with each team playing the other three times. The overall winning team in the matches between Australia and New Zealand also win a trophy called the Bledisloe Cup.

OLD RIVALRIES

In the Northern Hemisphere, the Six Nations (previously the Five Nations) is the premier European tournament. England, France, Ireland, Italy, Scotland, and Wales play each other once, with home advantage alternating from year to year. Victory in all five games is called a Grand Slam. There is also a women's Six Nations which used to feature Spain and not Italy, but Italy have now replaced Spain.

STAT CENTRAL

RUGBY WORLD CUP WINNERS

YEAR	COUNTRY
2011	NEW ZEALAND
2007	SOUTH AFRICA
2003	ENGLAND
1999	AUSTRALIA
1995	SOUTH AFRICA

MOST FIVE AND SIX NATIONS TITLES

NO. WINS	(SHARED)	COUNTRY
26	(10)	ENGLAND
25	(11)	WALES
17	(8)	FRANCE
14	(8)	SCOTLAND
11	(8)	IRELAND

EUROPEAN (HEINEKEN) CUP WINNERS

YEAR	TEAM	COUNTRY
2012	LEINSTER	IRL
2011	LEINSTER	IRL
2010	TOULOUSE	FRA
2009	LEINSTER	IRL
2008	MUNSTER	IRL
2007	WASPS	ENG
2006	MUNSTER	IRL
2005	TOULOUSE	FRA
2004	WASPS	ENG
2003	TOULOUSE	FRA

HIGHEST POINTS TOTAL IN TESTS

POINTS	PLAYER	TEAM
1385	DAN CARTER	NZL
1246	JONNY WILKINSON	ENG/LIONS
1090	NEIL JENKINS	WAL/LIONS
1083	RONAN O'GARA	IRE/LIONS
1010	DIEGO DOMINGUEZ	ITL/ARG
970	STEPHEN JONES	WAL/LIONS
967	ANDREW MEHRTENS	NZL
911	MICHAEL LYNAGH	AUS
893	PERCY MONTGOMERY	RSA
878	MATT BURKE	AUS

MOST TRIES IN TESTS

TRIES	PLAYER	TEAM
69	DAISUKE OHATA	JPN
64	DAVID CAMPESE	AUS
60	SHANE WILLIAMS	WAL/LIONS
53	HIROTOKI ONOZAWA	JPN
50	RORY UNDERWOOD	ENG
49	DOUG HOWLETT	NZL
47	BRYAN HABANA	RSA
47	BRIAN O'DRISCOLL	IRL/LIONS

RUGBY SEVENS

GAME OVERVIEW

Rugby sevens is a free-flowing and fast variant of rugby union (see pp.120–25), with teams reduced in size from fifteen to seven players. The sport is spectator-friendly, with fewer players and more space resulting in higher-scoring games. The major sevens tournaments tend to be held during the Northern Hemisphere's summer months and the game has historically been regarded as a proving ground for promising players hoping to move into rugby union.

PLAYING THE GAME

Despite the diminished number of players, matches take place on a full-sized rugby union pitch, shifting the emphasis away from attritional forward play and towards quick passing and explosive running. The increased fluidity of the sport places a different set of physical demands on participants, with speed and stamina becoming more important than strength. The team comprises three "forwards" (the two props and the hooker), three "backs" (the fullback, centre, and fly-half), and the scrum-half.

NEED2KNOW

→ Rugby sevens has done much to popularize rugby in Asia. Hong Kong hosts one of the largest and best-attended the Sevens World Series tournaments.

→ Some of rugby union's finest players began their career in rugby sevens. New Zealand international Jonah Lomu and George Gregan, a former captain of Australia, both played international rugby sevens before establishing themselves as prominent figures in the fifteen-a-side version of the game.

PLAYER PROFILE

Rugby sevens is a physically demanding contact sport, and all players must be strong enough to make decisive tackles and fend off opponents. However, set pieces in rugby sevens are scaled down and less frequent than in rugby union, so forwards tend to be quicker, less bulky, and more agile. In addition to covering large amounts of ground quickly, backs must be able to open up opposition teams with creative passing and imaginative running, so game intelligence is just as important as rapid acceleration and physical endurance.

Scrum
Scrums in rugby sevens are formed by three players from each team — with the hooker positioned between the two prop forwards

Hooker
In rugby sevens, hookers have the option of binding under or over the arms of their prop forwards; an overbind is always used in the larger scrums of the 15-man version

Props
Props plant their feet shoulder-width apart and try to get as low as possible

WHAT MAKES RUGBY SEVENS DIFFERENT?

The rugby sevens code is similar to rugby union but, in addition to the reduced number of players, there are other differences: matches consist of two halves of seven minutes each, separated by an interval of one minute; conversions must always be drop kicked rather than place kicked; and all scrums feature only three players per team, rather than eight. Union teams may select seven substitutes and use all of them during a match, while sevens teams are restricted to five substitutes and can make only three changes.

1 Prop
Two props (see below) literally "prop up" the hooker by supporting them in the scrum, and lifting them for catches

2 Hooker
The middle part of the rugby sevens scrum, the hooker attempts to gain possession of the ball, or "hook" it, with their feet

3 Scrum-half
A scrum-half who makes the most of set pieces can be instrumental in deciding the outcome of a match

4 Fly-half
The fly-half usually takes conversions; this requires drop kicking proficiency, as place kicking is not allowed in sevens

5 Centre
The centre is key to a successful sevens team, and must take responsibility for creating scoring opportunities

6 Fullback/winger
In sevens, the fullback/winger must be a productive attacker, as well as a reliable last line of defence

In-goal touch judge
At the highest level of rugby sevens, separate touch judges are responsible for adjudicating goal kicks, so there is a minimum of disruption to the action as a result of disputed goals

100m (330ft)

66–70m (215–230ft)

Goal posts
Drop goals are scored by kicking the ball over the crossbar

Referee
In rugby sevens, referees make advantage decisions as quickly as possible, allowing the game to flow

Touch judge
The touch judge informs the referee whether the ball, or a player carrying the ball, is out of play

Pitch size
Rugby sevens matches are played on a regulation size rugby union pitch

Try line
The "in-goal area" is between the try line and the dead-ball line

Dead-ball line
The dead-ball line marks the end of the in-goal area

THE TOURNAMENTS

The most important sevens competition is the Rugby World Cup Sevens, which has been held in different countries around the world every four years since 1993. Fiji have won the trophy twice, making them the most successful team in the tournament's history. In 2009, Australia won the inaugural women's World Cup Sevens tournament.

Rugby sevens has been chosen for inclusion as an Olympic sport, beginning at the summer Games held in Rio in 2016. Other major competitions include the Commonwealth Games and the IRB Sevens World Series, in which teams compete for points based on their finishing positions at nine tournaments. New Zealand are the outstanding performers, having won 10 out of the 13 Sevens World Series played since 1999, and not lost a single Commonwealth Games match.

SIDELINES

23 The number of tries scored by the Rugby World Cup Sevens all-time leading try scorer, Marika Vunibaka of Fiji.

28 The number of nations participating in the 2013 Hong Kong Sevens, the highest in the tournament's history.

0 The number of nations to have held the Rugby World Cup Sevens and the Rugby World Cup titles simultaneously.

82 The margin of victory achieved by Chinese Taipei over Qatar at the Asian Games in 2006, a record in professional rugby sevens.

GAME OVERVIEW

Regarded as one of the most demanding contact sports in the world, rugby league is played between two teams with 13 players on each side. The object of the sport is to use a ball to score more points than the opposing team over two 40-minute periods. Points are awarded by touching the ball down over the opposition's try line and by kicking the ball over the crossbar. With its roots in the north of England, this fast-paced sport also enjoys popularity in Australia, New Zealand, and the Pacific region.

SIDELINES

40 The percentage of active rugby league supporters who are female.

1,735 The greatest number of points in all competitions in one season was scored by Wigan over 45 matches in 1994–95.

11 The number of tries scored by George West of Hull Kingston Rovers when playing Brookland Rovers in 1905.

40,000 The number of registered rugby league players in the UK, playing for over 450 clubs nationwide.

RUGBY LEAGUE

Head protection
Helmets are especially worn by front-row forwards to protect them in the scrum and are made of lightweight, shatter-resistant plastic

Shirt
Made from a lightweight but strong synthetic material, a player's shirt has to be able to withstand the tugs of opposition players

Tight grip
Fingerless, close-fitting gloves are sometimes worn to give players a better grip of the ball

Shorts
As with rugby shirts, these were traditionally made of strong cotton but are now available in strong synthetic materials

NEED2KNOW

→ New Zealand's victory in the 2005 Tri-Nations Cup was Australia's first test series loss for 27 years.

→ The biggest knockout rugby league competition in the world is the Carnegie Champion Schools tournament held in New Zealand, with over 1,000 schools and 16,000 players taking part.

→ The first Rugby League World Cup was held in France in 1954, with Great Britain, Australia, and New Zealand playing alongside the host nation.

Socks
Part of the team uniform, socks provide some protection for the lower leg

Boots
High cut to provide support for the ankle

PLAYER PROFILE

To succeed in a demanding sport like rugby league requires physical strength, stamina, and speed. Ball-control skills are key, both through kicking and catching, with an ability to handle the ball at pace a vital skill. All-round tactical awareness is essential, particularly for those in positions such as stand off and scrum half.

KICK TO TOUCH

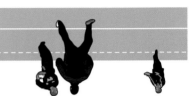

First Bounce
The ball needs to bounce within the field of play

The most important thing to remember when kicking the ball into touch in open play is that the ball must bounce within the field of play before it goes out. The resulting scrum is taken 10m (33ft) in from the point where the ball crosses the line. However, if the ball goes straight out, the scrum-down takes place at the point of the original kick. In both situations the opposite team to that of the kicker puts the ball in at the scrum, so territorial advantage is countered by a loss of ball possession.

THROWING A DUMMY
A player approaches an opponent with a team-mate nearby and just after looking over at him positions the ball in his hands as if he is about to pass it.

SIDE-STEPPING PAST
With the opponent thinking that the ball is going to be passed, his weight shifts over to that side, making it easier for the attacker to run past.

TEAM TACTICS

With the object of the game to score more points than the opposing team, rugby league is about penetrating, attacking play and a solid defence. Both rely on a combination of teamwork and individual skills such as throwing a dummy (making a motion towards passing to a teammate but keeping the ball and running past the opposing player). Kicking into touch is another key tactic, used by an attacking team to gain territorial advantage or by a defending side to relieve pressure on the back line.

INSIDE STORY

Rugby league was born out of the original union game (see pp.120–25) that began in the 1830s. A dispute in 1892 between the Rugby Football Union (RFU) and clubs in the north of England that were paying their players — which went against the amateur spirit of the game — led to the breakaway Northern Rugby Football Union being formed in 1895. The 13-a-side game began in 1906 and the name rugby league was adopted in 1922.

In the UK, the Rugby Football League (RFL) administers the sport. It controls the national leagues, the Super League, the Challenge Cup, and Great Britain's national team.

WORLDWIDE GOVERNING BODY
The Rugby League International Federation (RLIF) is the controlling body in charge of the sport worldwide. It makes decisions on laws and international team rankings.

GOLDEN POINT
If a game is tied at the end of full-time, 10 minutes extra time is played. This period is often called "sudden death", as the first team to score wins the game.

POINTS SYSTEM

The highest number of points (four) is obtained by touching down for a try, but there are a number of other ways that a team can score points. Immediately following a try the scoring team can secure an extra two points if one of its players is able to place-kick the ball over the crossbar between the posts; this is known as a conversion. Drop-kicking the ball over the crossbar from open play is worth one point. Penalties are awarded against a team for numerous offences and one of the options available is to kick for goal as in a conversion, and also with a value of two points.

TRY
A try is deemed valid if the player crossing the try line applies downward pressure on the ball to touch it on the ground. If two players of opposing sides are both holding the ball as it is grounded, the try also counts. It is invalid if a player has any part of his body in touch.

CONVERSION
A conversion can be taken anywhere along a line directly opposite where the try was scored. Touch judges check whether the ball passes over the crossbar and between the posts.

PENALTY
A penalty is given to one team when a player from the opposing team violates the rules, and is taken from the place that the offence occurred. If the infringement happens while the ball is in touch, the penalty is taken 10m (33ft) in from the touchline.

DROP GOAL
The extra point secured by a drop goal can win a match if the two teams are level approaching full-time and the attacking team is still some way from the try line.

SCRUM
A forward pass, knock-on (accidental forward movement of the ball, which then touches the ground), and restart after kick into touch all result in a scrum. This consists of a maximum of six forwards — a front row of two props and a hooker, two second row forwards, and a loose forward slotting in at the back.

Second Row
Front Row
Loose Forward

RUGBY RULES

While most infringements are punished by a penalty or a scrum, some more serious violations will result in a player being sent to an area next to the pitch called the sin bin. He is forced to remain there for ten minutes, thereby putting his team at a disadvantage for that period.

OFFSIDE
A complex rule of the game, offside can take place in open play for a few reasons, one of which is when a player ahead of the one with the ball tries to play the ball. At a penalty kick, a player is offside if he is in front of the kicker.

Defenders

Illegal
Player offside if he tries to affect play

Movement
Player runs with ball

ADVANTAGE
Instead of blowing up for an infringement by one team, a referee can keep a game flowing by giving the other team an advantage. An example is if a player is tackled high but still passes the ball out to a teammate to score.

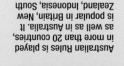

→ Australian Rules is played in more than 20 countries, as well as in Australia. It is popular in Britain, New Zealand, Indonesia, South Africa, Canada, and Japan.

→ The annual Australian Football League (AFL) Grand Final attracts crowds of nearly 100,000, making it the world's best attended domestic club championship event.

→ Women's Australian Rules football has also spread to many countries, such as the US, Britain, New Zealand, Canada, and Papua New Guinea.

AUSTRALIAN FOOTBALL

GAME OVERVIEW

Australian football – known to locals as "Aussie Rules," or "footy," – is an incredibly tough, fast-paced game. Two teams of 22 players (18 on the field, 4 interchangeable) display great courage in their ferocious attack on opponents and the ball, which is passed with incredible accuracy across an oval-shaped pitch. The aim is to score points by kicking the ball through a set of goals, made of four upright posts. After four quarters of 20 minutes each, the team that has amassed the most points wins. Australian football is the most popular winter sport in Australia.

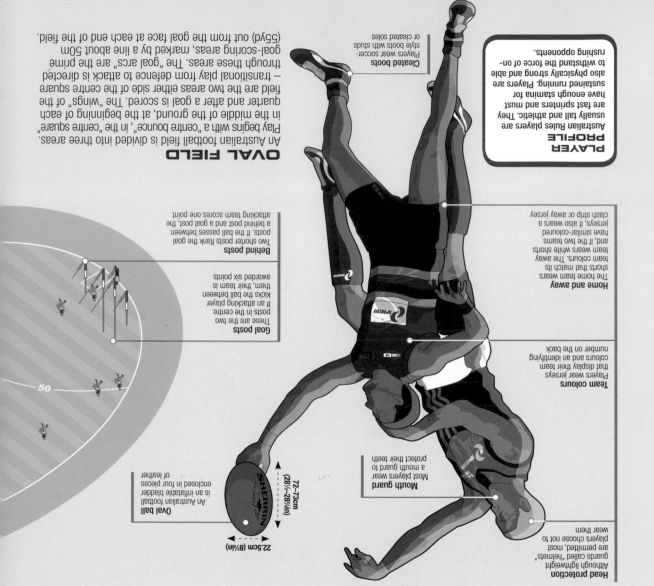

PLAYER PROFILE
Australian Rules players are usually tall and athletic. They are fast sprinters and must have enough stamina for sustained running. Players are also physically strong and able to withstand the force of on-rushing opponents.

Cleated boots
Players wear soccer-style boots with studs or cleated soles.

Home and away
The home team wears shorts that match its team colours. The away team wears white shorts and, if the two teams have similar-coloured jerseys, it also wears a clash strip or away jersey.

Team colours
Players wear jerseys that display their team colours and an identifying number on the back.

Mouth guard
Most players wear a mouth guard to protect their teeth.

Head protection
Although lightweight guards called "helmets" are permitted, most players choose not to wear them.

Oval ball
An Australian football is an inflatable bladder enclosed in four pieces of leather.

72–73cm (28½–28¾in)
22.5cm (8⅞in)

OVAL FIELD

An Australian football field is divided into three areas. Play begins with a "centre bounce", in the "centre square" in the middle of the ground, at the beginning of each quarter and after a goal is scored. The "wings" of the field are the two areas either side of the centre square – transitional play from defence to attack is directed through these areas. The "goal arcs" are the prime goal-scoring areas, marked by a line about 50M (55yd) out from the goal face at each end of the field.

Behind posts
Two shorter posts flank the goal posts. If the ball passes between a behind post and a goal post, the attacking team scores one point.

Goal posts
These are the two posts in the centre. If an attacking player kicks the ball between them, their team is awarded six points.

50

GO THE DISTANCE
On average, an Australian football player will cover close to 13km (8 miles) over the four 20-minute quarters. The majority of this distance is covered by jogging and sprinting. In comparison, a rugby-union player (see pp.120–25) will cover only 6km (almost 4 miles), less than half the distance. Women also play Australian football and, while the tackling rules are sometimes modified, the players need similar stamina.

Boundary umpires
Two umpires police the boundary line. If the ball rolls or bounces out of play, an umpire throws it back in. They also award penalties if it is kicked over the line in the air

Field umpires
Three umpires adjudicate on-field play, covering the centre of the ground, the wings, and both goal arcs

Goal umpires
An umpire stands on each goal line to judge if the ball crosses the line and assess if it is a goal or point

Centre square
Only eight players are permitted inside this area before play starts – the other 28 cannot enter until play has begun

50m line
This is a curved line used to designate the goal arcs at both ends of the ground

Interchange players
Four substitute players are allowed per team, with no limit on the amount of times players can be interchanged

WHO PLAYS WHERE?
Positions are fluid: players go where needed, rather than staying in strict zones. The diagram below shows positions for a team at the start of play. Play starts with a centre bounce, which can only be contested by the ruckman. Offensive players ("forwards") move around the forward area seeking possession of the ball, while defensive players ("defenders") try to negate opposition forwards and create play by running up the field. Midfield players contest the ball in all areas of the ground.

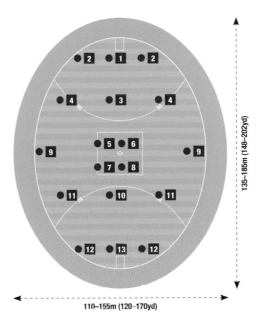

135–185m (148–202yd)

110–155m (120–170yd)

POSITIONS:
1 Full forward 2 Forward pockets 3 Centre half forward 4 Half-torward flanks
5 Ruckman 6 Ruck-rover 7 Rover 8 Centre 9 Wingmen 10 Centre half-back
11 Half-back flanks 12 Back pockets 13 Full back

INTERNATIONAL RULES
Australia and Ireland contested the first official International Rules series in 1998. Mixing elements of Australian and Gaelic football (see pp.174–75), games are fast-paced and infamous for vicious clashes between players (in 2006 the extreme violence led to the cancellation of the 2007 match). To date Australia has won five International Rules matches, Ireland seven, and two matches have resulted in a draw.

SIDELINES
7,146,604 The total number of Australians who attended top-grade AFL games in 2010 – that's roughly equal to one-third of the Australian population.

121,696 The highest ever attendance at a top-grade game. Achieved at the 1970 Grand Final between Carlton and Collingwood, which Carlton won by 10 points.

38,423 The average attendance at an AFL regular season game in 2010 (English Premier League soccer averaged 35,363 in the 2010–11 season).

RULES

The ball may be passed in any direction, using only the feet (a kick), a clenched fist (a handpass), or an open-handed tap. A mark is awarded if a player catches the ball from a kick. That player can take a kick or handpass unimpeded from where they caught the ball. A player can run with the ball, but must bounce it or touch it to the ground every 15m (50ft). A player running with the ball can be put under pressure or tackled, and if tackled must pass or dispose of the ball immediately or risk being penalized. Penalties, known as free kicks, are awarded for infringements such as pushing an opponent in the back, tackling illegally (see opposite), and holding a player who does not have the ball. Finally, a player can be placed on report for striking, tripping, pushing, or kicking another player, and potentially suspended from future games.

SCORING

A goal (six points) is scored only when an attacking player kicks the ball between the goal posts. A behind (one point) is scored when the ball crosses the line between a behind post and the nearer goal post, or is kicked into a goal post. A behind still counts if it comes off a defender's foot, or is knocked over the goal or point line by any other part of a player's body. The total score is the sum of goals and points expressed in two parts: for example, "20.14 (134)" means 20 goals and 14 behinds, a total of 134 points.

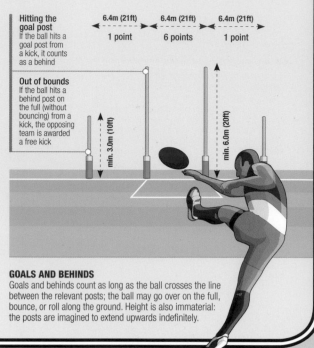

Hitting the goal post If the ball hits a goal post from a kick, it counts as a behind

6.4m (21ft)	6.4m (21ft)	6.4m (21ft)
1 point	6 points	1 point

Out of bounds If the ball hits a behind post on the full (without bouncing) from a kick, the opposing team is awarded a free kick

min. 3.0m (10ft) min. 6.0m (20ft)

GOALS AND BEHINDS

Goals and behinds count as long as the ball crosses the line between the relevant posts; the ball may go over on the full, bounce, or roll along the ground. Height is also immaterial: the posts are imagined to extend upwards indefinitely.

ANTIPODEAN ARTISTRY

Considered a chaotic game to the uninformed, Australian football is in fact a highly skilful affair. Players must win and maintain possession of the ball and advance up the field using strategic passes to teammates. Accurate kicking and passing is the most efficient way of doing this. Players use passes by foot to leading or open players, and quick handpasses, taps, or punches to find an open teammate when in close proximity. Once near goal, players will try to score either from a mark and kick, or by kicking on the run.

MACEDONIAN MARVEL

ONE OF THE MOST SKILFUL PLAYERS EVER WAS PETER DAICOS, OTHERWISE KNOWN AS THE "MACEDONIAN MARVEL". DAICOS WAS RENOWNED FOR HIS AMAZING KICKING SKILLS AND THE ABILITY TO CONSISTENTLY KICK UNLIKELY GOALS FROM ANYWHERE IN THE OFFENSIVE PART OF THE GROUND. DAICOS PLAYED FOR THE COLLINGWOOD MAGPIES DURING THE 1980s AND 1990s.

THE HANDPASS

Almost as common as a kick for passing the ball in today's game, the handpass involves a punch applied with the thumb and index finger of a clenched fist to the pointed end of the ball.

KICKING

There are four main kicks: the drop punt, used in general play; the torpedo, a spiralling rugby-style kick used for extra distance; and the snap and checkside (or "banana") kicks, used to curve the ball.

Shoulder turn The shoulder of the arm that is used to hit the ball is turned back to maximize the length of swing

Ball release A swinging clenched fist is used to punch the end of the ball, propelling it towards a teammate

Guiding the ball The ball is guided towards the foot with the palm of the hand

Ball release The ball leaves the palm dropping point down towards the boot

Spinning ball By striking the ball close to one end, the ball spins end-over-end as it travels through the air

HANDPASSES

This form of delivery is used to move the ball quickly to nearby teammates and for passing in confined space when under pressure. It is a popular move by midfielders to set up play before kicking the ball into the forward line.

DROP PUNT

Due to its consistent spin, the drop punt is accurate and easy to control. Players use the drop punt for passing in general play and for most shots on goal. It has become much more common than the punt kick, which does not spin the ball.

BUMPS AND MARKS

Marking and tackling are the main elements of Australian football that make it such an exciting and tough sport. Players catch the ball running at full speed or by launching themselves fearlessly into the air, often using opponents to propel themselves skyward. The main form of defence is tackling. Players run down or charge opponents who have the ball, hitting them hard to jolt the ball free or wrestling them to the ground to halt their progress.

MARK OF THE CENTURY

Former Geelong player Gary Ablett is considered one of the most exciting players of all time. He kicked more than 100 goals in three consecutive seasons from 1993 to 1995, winning the Coleman Medal for scoring the most goals. Ablett, a high-flying forward, took what is widely touted as "the mark of the century" playing against Collingwood in 1994. He leapt onto his opponent's shoulders and caught the ball with one outstretched hand before crashing to the ground.

MARKING

The mark is the primary method by which players maintain possession. When a ball has been kicked by a player more than 15m (50ft) and is caught by another player, the catching player is awarded a mark. The player can then kick or handpass from that spot without the threat of being tackled or pressured by opposition players.

TACKLING

A player with the ball can be tackled by being held or wrestled to the ground. A tackle must be applied below the shoulders and above the knees, and can be made by more than one player. If a tackled player doesn't dispose of the ball immediately, the opposition is awarded a free kick.

Contesting a mark
Defending players are allowed to punch the ball away from an opponent. Some body contact is permitted in the air, but no holding or hitting of an opponent is allowed

Front position
Players are encouraged to get into front position in a marking contest. It gives them a clear jump at the ball and the chance of receiving a free kick

HIGH FLYERS

Players are allowed to jump on and over each other in attempting to mark a kick. This results in some spectacular leaps and breathtaking marks (called a "screamer" or "spekky"), which are seen as the game's most amazing feat.

Eyes on the ball
A ball that spills free in a contest is fair game for either side

Shoulder action
Players can use their body and shoulders to jostle for position

Standing strong
Good balance and sturdy feet are essential to applying a strong tackle or heavy bump

USING THE HIPS

A player can legally bump an opponent (called a "hip and shoulder") when the ball is within 5m (15ft) of the opponent, as long as the bump is made with the hip or shoulder. Contact to the head is not allowed.

STAT CENTRAL

YEAR	WINNER	RUNNER-UP
	AFL GRAND FINALS	
2012	SYDNEY SWANS 14.7 (91)	HAWTHORN 11.15 (81)
2011	GEELONG CATS 18.11 (119)	COLLINGWOOD MAGPIES 12.9 (81)
2010	COLLINGWOOD MAGPIES 16.12 (108)	ST KILDA SAINTS 7.10 (52)
2009	GEELONG CATS 12.8 (80)	ST KILDA SAINTS 9.14 (68)
2008	HAWTHORN 18.7 (115)	GEELONG CATS 11.23 (89)
2007	GEELONG CATS 8.10 (58)	PORT ADELAIDE 6.8 (44)
2006	WEST COAST EAGLES 12.13 (85)	SYDNEY SWANS 12.12 (84)
2005	SYDNEY SWANS 8.10 (58)	WEST COAST EAGLES 7.12 (54)
2004	PORT ADELAIDE POWER 17.11 (113)	BRISBANE LIONS 10.13 (73)
2003	BRISBANE LIONS 20.14 (134)	COLLINGWOOD MAGPIES 12.12 (84)
2002	BRISBANE LIONS 10.15 (75)	COLLINGWOOD MAGPIES 9.12 (66)
2001	BRISBANE LIONS 15.18 (108)	ESSENDON BOMBERS 12.10 (82)
2000	ESSENDON BOMBERS 19.21 (135)	MELBOURNE DEMONS 11.9 (75)
1999	NORTH MELBOURNE 19.10 (124)	CARLTON BLUES 12.17 (89)
1998	ADELAIDE CROWS 15.15 (105)	NORTH MELBOURNE 8.22 (70)

INSIDE STORY

Australian football was devised in 1857 by sportsman Tom Wills as a fun way for cricketers to keep fit during the winter months. The first recorded match took place in 1858, between Scotch College and Melbourne Grammar School. The first professional league, the Victorian Football League (VFL), was established in 1896, and the following year the league's first games were held. By 1987, the league was flourishing and became national. It was renamed the Australian Football League in 1994. A Rules Committee manages the laws of the game.

AUSTRALIAN FOOTBALL LEAGUE

The AFL Commission is the official governing body of Australian Rules football. It took over national governance of the sport in 1993 and is one of the world's strongest sporting authorities. The AFL Commission is responsible for the administration of the competition and regularly updates the laws of the game, with most changes aimed at making the sport faster and more attractive to supporters.

CRICKET

GAME OVERVIEW

To the uninitiated, cricket can appear an incomprehensible spectacle acted out by eccentrics in long trousers; to millions of devotees the world over, it is the ultimate combination of skill and strategy. Contested by two teams of 11 players, cricket essentially involves a bowler hurling a ball at a batter, who attempts to hit the ball. From this simple premise radiates a multitude of complexities. Once considered genteel, cricket today is as hard-nosed as any professional sport, and the tension that builds over a close five-day Test match is immense.

NEED2KNOW

→ The two international forms of cricket are Test matches (which last five days) and limited-overs games, which are usually 50 overs per side, (although "20/20" cricket allows only 20 overs per innings). Other forms include first-class, club, indoor, and beach cricket.

→ There are over 100 cricket-playing nations, but only the best compete in Tests. Currently the Test-playing nations are: Australia, England, Pakistan, India, Sri Lanka, South Africa, New Zealand, West Indies, Zimbabwe, and Bangladesh.

PLAYER PROFILE
While there is no physical "type" for cricketers, fast bowlers are mostly tall and athletic. Batters require excellent hand-eye coordination and the ability to make rapid decisions. Good fielders are agile and have a strong, accurate throw. All cricketers need fast reactions and the capacity to sustain concentration for long periods.

Tool of the trade
Made of willow and comprising a blade and handle, the bat must not exceed 96cm (38in) in length

Head protection
Seldom worn prior to the 1980s, protective helmets are now commonplace

THE BALL
With a leather exterior and an interior of cork, rubber, and tightly wound string, the cricket ball is extremely hard. Although the red ball is traditional, white balls are regularly used in limited-overs matches.

22.9cm (9in)

Seam
A raised, stitched seam encircles the ball

Gloves
Padded gloves provide good hand protection while not unduly restricting hand and finger movement

Chest protector
Not all batters wear a chest protector, but this piece of equipment is commonly used when fast bowlers are operating. It is worn beneath the shirt and helps prevent bruising and broken ribs

Box
A heart-shaped, hard plastic protector, the box is worn inside the trousers to shield the genital area

Pads
Heavily padded leg guards are worn on both legs, to protect from the ankle to above the knee. Modern pads are compact and lightweight, allowing the batter to play strokes and run freely

THE WICKET
The wicket consists of three wooden stumps and two wooden bails. The bails sit on the stumps in shallow grooves cut along the top of each stump. Two wickets are used in a match – one at either end of the pitch.

Bails
These must be dislodged to affect certain types of dismissal

 22.9cm (9in)

Stumps
Viewed from the front, left to right, the stumps are named: off stump, middle stump, and leg stump. The pointed ends are pushed firmly into the pitch

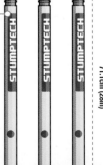

71.1cm (28in)

THE FIELD OF PLAY

Cricket is played on a large, flat oval or circular field with a pitch in the middle. On the field of play there are always two umpires, two batters, and all of the fielding team (the bowler, wicketkeeper, and nine other fielders). The fielding team is organized into positions the captain feels will either prevent run scoring or affect a dismissal (see Modes of Dismissal, p.139). At the end of each over (see Playing the Game, p.138) a new bowler bowls from the opposite end of the pitch, and all the fieldiers and umpires are repositioned accordingly.

PASSIONATE SUPPORTERS

CRICKET FOLLOWERS ARE A FERVENT GROUP – ESPECIALLY THE 90,000 OR MORE THAT ASSEMBLE AT EDEN GARDENS, INDIA, WHERE THE NOISE IS OFTEN SO DEAFENING THAT UMPIRES ARE UNABLE TO DETECT SNICKS.

FIELDING POSITIONS

The image below shows most of the common fielding positions the fielding captain may choose from when a right-handed batter is on strike.

1 Bowler	**12** Silly mid-off
2 Non-striking batter	**13** Mid-off
3 Striking batter	**14** Wide mid-off
4 Wicketkeeper	**15** Leg slip
5 Slips	**16** Short leg
6 Gully	**17** Forward short leg
7 Silly point	**18** Silly mid-on
8 Point	**19** Mid-on
9 Cover point	**20** Wide mid-on
10 Cover	**21** Mid-wicket
11 Extra cover	**22** Square leg

23 Deep square leg	
24 Deep mid-wicket	
25 Long-on	
26 Straight hit	
27 Long-off	
28 Deep extra cover	
29 Deep cover	
30 Sweeper	
31 Backward point	
32 Third man	
33 Fine leg	
34 Long leg	
35 Deep b/w fine leg	
U Umpires	

30-yard circle
This field marking divides the infield from the outfield. In limited-overs cricket, a set number of fielders must remain within this circle for a fixed number of overs

Off side
The half of the field of play further from the on-strike batter's legs when the batter is waiting for the bowler to bowl is known as the off side

Infield
Fielders in the infield possess quick reflexes and must always be alert

On side
The half of the field of play on the same side as the on-strike batter's legs when the batter is waiting for the bowler to bowl is called the on side (or the leg side)

Sightscreens
These moveable structures allow the batter better visibility of the ball

Batter on-striker
All the fielders are positioned relative to the batter about to hit the ball. The batter shown here is right-handed

Outfield
Players with the strongest throw field in the outfield

Boundary
Typically a rope, white line, or set of flags, the boundary defines the outer edge of the field of play

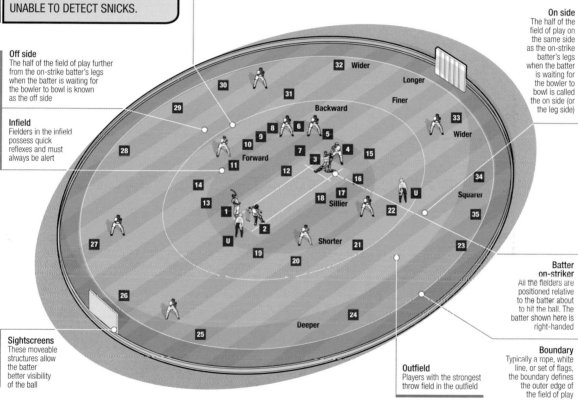

GLOSSARY OF FIELDING TERMS

Cricket uses a number of potentially confusing technical terms, and many of these arise in relation to the field and fielding positions.

STRAIGHT Closer to an imaginary line through the centre of the field of play and in front of the batter.

WIDE Further from an imaginary line through the centre of the field of play and in front of the batter.

FINE Closer to an imaginary line through the centre of the field of play and behind the batter.

SQUARE Further from an imaginary line through the centre of the field of play and behind the batter.

FORWARD In front of the batter's wicket.

BACKWARD Behind the batter's wicket.

SHORT Closer to the batter.

SILLY Very close to the batter.

DEEP Further from the batter.

THE PITCH

The closely mown, even surface at the centre of the field of play is known as the pitch. Moisture content, grass height, soil type, and degree of soil compaction are among the many pitch-related factors that help determine how the ball will travel after it strikes the pitch.

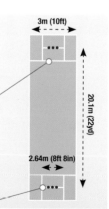

3m (10ft)

20.1m (22yd)

2.64m (8ft 8in)

Popping crease
Unless part of the bowler's front foot is behind this line when the ball is delivered, the umpire will call "no ball"

Bowling crease
The length of a pitch (20.1m/22yd) is the distance between the two bowling creases. A wicket is placed on each of the two bowling creases

THE ASHES

WHEN AUSTRALIA DEFEATED ENGLAND IN 1882, A NEWSPAPER PUBLISHED AN "OBITUARY" FOR ENGLISH CRICKET: "THE BODY WILL BE CREMATED AND THE ASHES TAKEN TO AUSTRALIA". THIS IS THE ORIGIN OF THE REGULARLY COMPETED "ASHES" TEST SERIES, ONE OF SPORT'S GREAT RIVALRIES.

PLAYING THE GAME

Before play begins, the two captains toss a coin to see which side will bat and which side will field. All of the fielding side take their positions, but only two batters are on the field at a time. At the start of play, the batter "on strike" assumes a batting stance (usually with the body side-on to the bowler but the head facing), ready to receive the first bowl. The other batter (the "non-striker") stands at the opposite end of the pitch. The bowler bowls the ball (a "delivery") overarm towards the striker's wicket. If the batter does not hit the ball, the wicketkeeper usually catches it. If the striker hits the ball, the two batters then have the choice whether to run or not. If the batter hits the ball inside the field of play and it then crosses the boundary, this counts as four runs. If the ball is propelled directly over the boundary without bouncing in the field of play, six runs are awarded. After six legal deliveries have been bowled, the umpire calls "over". While the batters attempt to score as many runs as possible, the fielders try to dismiss the batters (see Modes of Dismissal, opposite).

THE END OF AN INNINGS

When a batter is dismissed ("out"), that player leaves the field and the next member of the batting side is "in". When 10 of the 11 members of the batting side are out (there will always be one batter "not out" because batters must operate in pairs), when the allocated time is up, or the set number of overs have been bowled, the innings is complete (see Forms of the Game, below). For the next innings, the batting and fielding sides swap roles.

COMPLETING A RUN

One run is completed if the striker and non-striker can run to the opposite end of the pitch and ground a part of their bat or person behind the popping crease before being "run out" (see Modes of Dismissal, opposite).

Bowling angle
When the bowler's bowling arm is closest to the wicket (as shown here), this is bowling "over the wicket". If the bowling arm is the one further from the wicket, this is bowling "round the wicket"

Umpire
The bowler's end umpire has several things to watch as the ball is delivered, including where the bowler's front foot lands and where the ball pitches

Defending the wicket
The batter defends the wicket by ensuring that the ball does not strike it

Wicketkeeper
In readiness to catch the ball, the wicketkeeper crouches behind the wicket

Batter on strike
This batter attempts to "strike" the ball away from fielders and, if possible, over the boundary

Centre of the pitch
Both batters and bowlers should avoid running on the middle of the pitch, so that it does not become damaged

Non-striker
The batter not facing the delivery must be ready to run and should be part way down the pitch as soon as the ball leaves the bowler's hand

FORMS OF THE GAME

Test cricket – which is played over five days – is the sport's flagship event. Each side has two innings, bowlers may bowl an unlimited number of overs, and to win a Test match is not a straightforward proposition. For example, if the two teams competing are X and Y, for side X to win it must bowl out side Y (by taking all ten wickets) twice. It must do this before side Y can score more than the total runs side X scored. If neither team can do this in five days, the result is a draw. In limited-overs cricket, each side only has one innings – usually limited to 50 overs. The number of overs allocated to each bowler is restricted (10 each in a 50-over game), and wickets lost do not affect the result – simply the team that scores the most runs wins.

TEAM COMPOSITION

A good cricket team has a balance of different types of player. When batting, the side is organized into a batting order. Although there are many variations on a batting order, numbers one to five are usually the specialist batters, number six is often an all-rounder (a highly skilled batter and bowler), the wicketkeeper regularly occupies the number seven position, and numbers eight to eleven are mostly the specialist bowlers.

GAME CONTROL

There are 42 Laws of Cricket, and three umpires uphold these Laws. On the field, one umpire stands at the bowler's end and another at square leg. The on-field umpires may refer close decisions for runouts, stumpings, catches, or boundaries to the third (off-field) umpire, who adjudicates using television replays.

TELEVISION REVOLUTION

TELEVISION TECHNOLOGIES, SUCH AS HAWK-EYE, WHICH TRACKS THE PROJECTED PATH OF THE BALL, HAVE REVOLUTIONIZED THE WAY WE WATCH AND UNDERSTAND CRICKET.

MODES OF DISMISSAL

There are 10 ways in which a batter can be dismissed, although it would be extraordinary if all 10 were seen in a single match. Some dismissals, such as "Timed Out" and "Hit the Ball Twice" are very rare. The most common dismissals are caught (often caught behind by the wicket keeper or slip fielders), LBW, and bowled.

BOWLED When the bowler delivers a ball that breaks the wicket (dislodges at least one bail).

TIMED OUT If the incoming batsman takes more than three minutes to reach the pitch.

CAUGHT If a fielder catches the ball after the batter hits it and before it touches the ground.

HANDLED THE BALL When a batter handles the ball without the consent of the fielding side.

HIT THE BALL TWICE When the batter strikes the ball twice (unless guarding the wicket).

HIT WICKET If the bat or any part of the batter's person breaks the wicket.

LBW When part of the batter intercepts a ball that would have hit the wicket (see below).

OBSTRUCTING THE FIELD If the batter deliberately obstructs or distracts the fielding side.

RUN OUT If the wicket is broken and the bat or the batter is not behind the popping crease.

STUMPED If the wicketkeeper breaks the wicket and the batter is outside the popping crease.

LEG BEFORE WICKET

Law 36 – Leg Before Wicket (LBW) – is perhaps the most complex, controversial, and difficult to judge of all the Laws. This is because there is always an element of subjectivity: would the ball have continued on to hit the wicket?

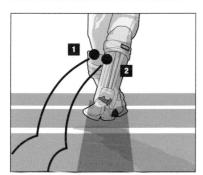

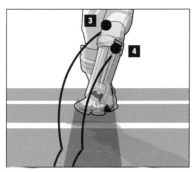

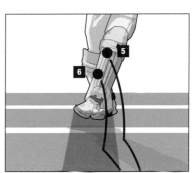

1 Not out or out. The ball has hit the batter's pad outside the wicket to-wicket line on the off side. If playing a shot, the batter is not out. However, if the batter makes no attempt to play the ball, and the umpire is sure that the ball would have hit the wicket, the batter can be given out. This part of the Law was introduced to stop batters protecting their wicket using only their pads.

2 Out. The ball has struck the batter's pad in line with the wicket and would have gone on to hit the wicket. It is of no relevance that the ball pitched outside the line of the off stump.

3 Not out. The ball has hit the batter's pad in line with the wicket, but its projected flight path is such that it would have gone over the top of the wicket.

4 Not out. The ball has hit the pad in line with the wicket, but its projected flight path is such that it would have missed the wicket and continued on a line outside the leg stump.

5 Not out. Although this ball would have continued on to hit the stumps, it has pitched outside the wicket-to-wicket line, on the leg side. The batter can never be out if the ball pitches outside the line of the leg stump, whether playing a shot or not.

6 Out. The ball has not pitched outside the leg stump, has hit the pad in line with the wicket, and would have gone on to hit the wicket.

KEEPING SCORE

The scorer uses numbers and a set of symbols entered in a special cricket scorebook to keep a tally of runs scored and associated statistics. To ensure the scorebook is filled in correctly, an umpire signals to the scorer when any one of a set of particular circumstances arises. The scoreboard provides the specators and players with an ongoing summary of the match situation.

EXTRAS

Runs scored that did not arise from the batter striking the ball are called extras. The most common extras are no balls, byes, leg byes, and wides.

NO BALL When the delivery is deemed illegal, typically if the bowler oversteps the popping crease.

BYE When the batting pair complete a run, but the ball did not touch the bat or the batter. Byes typically arise when the wicketkeeper misfields.

LEG BYE When the batting pair complete a run after the ball struck any part of the batter except the glove or bat.

WIDE When a delivery passes out of the reach of the batter when in a normal batting stance.

UMPIRES' SIGNALS

An umpire will signal if certain events occur, including: if the fielding side conceeds an extra (see below, left); if four or six runs are scored; when the batter is dismissed ("out"); when the ball is not in play (dead ball); and when the batters do not properly complete a run (short run).

NO BALL

LEG BYE

SHORT RUN

OUT

BYE

FOUR RUNS

SIX RUNS

DEAD BALL

WIDE

CRICKET SKILLS

Cricketers must master several skills. Every team member must bat and field, at least four players will be expected to bowl, and there is one specialist wicketkeeper. These disciplines all employ different techniques.

BOWLING

Perhaps more than any other player, the bowler determines how a match progresses. If the bowlers are bowling well, there is often little the batters can do beyond trying not to be dismissed. Broadly speaking there are two types of bowler: pace bowlers (which includes medium-pacers and fast bowlers), who deliver balls at up to 160kph (99mph); and spin bowlers (which includes leg-spinners and off-spinners) who deliver the ball more slowly but have a greater variety of deliveries. Bowlers usually bowl a number of overs (a "spell") from one end of the ground.

PACE BOWLER'S ACTION

To propel the ball at high speed requires great skill and athleticism: pace bowling is less about brute strength and more about rhythm and technique. The illustrations below freeze the three crucial stages in a pace-bowler's action the split-second before the ball is released.

The coil
The bowler is in a side-on position, looking at the batter over the left shoulder and with the ball near the face

Delivery stride
Here the left arm is raised and the body remains upright. The back leg supports the bowler as the front leg extends and points at the batter

Delivery
At release, weight transfers to the front leg

WICKETKEEPING

While the wicketkeeper's primary task is to stop the ball, this player must also take catches and effect run outs and stumpings. For a spin bowler, the wicketkeeper will stand directly behind the stumps; for a pace bowler the wicketkeeper may stand more than 20m (22yd) back.

Special gloves
The large, heavily padded gloves include webbing between the thumb and first finger

Shorter pads
Slightly shorter than batting pads, wicketkeeping pads still provide vital protection for the legs

Stumped
If the batter's foot is not behind the popping crease as the wicketkeeper breaks the wicket, the batter is out, stumped

---

BOWLER'S ROLE

The bowler tries to pitch the ball in an area from which the batter cannot easily score runs and is in danger of being dismissed. This is bowling a "good line and length". The bowler can either attack, in an attempt to take wickets quickly while risking being hit for runs, or bowl defensively, making it difficult for the batter to score. The bowler can also employ several tactical variations, such as changing the line, length, pace, or angle of the delivery.

MOVEMENT

Good bowlers are able to make the ball deviate from its expected "normal" flight path. Pace bowlers do this using swing (movement through the air) and seam (movement off the pitch). A delivery from a spin bowler rotates in the air and then spins away from or into the batter after pitching.

OUT-SWINGER
If the ball moves in the air away from the batter and towards the slips, this is an out-swinger – a very attacking type of delivery.

IN-SWINGER
When the delivery moves through the air towards the batter, it is an in-swinger (and can be difficult to score from).

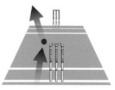
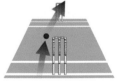

LEG-CUTTER
If a fast delivery moves away from the batter as a result of the way the seam struck the pitch, it is termed a leg-cutter.

OFF-CUTTER
Another pace bowler's weapon, the off-cutter moves off the seam and into the batter, which can result in an LBW decision.

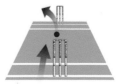
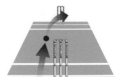

LEG-SPINNER
Similar to the leg-cutter but slower, the leg-spinner moves mainly because of the bowler's wrist action.

OFF-SPINNER
Usually acheived as a result of spin imparted from the bowler's fingers, an off-spinner deviates towards the right-handed batter.

BATTING

The art of batting involves striking the ball with enough technical competence, timing, and placement to score runs (without being dismissed). To achieve this, the batter employs an array of strokes (four of which are illustrated below), each in response to a certain type of delivery. In general, good line and length balls are defended; poor deliveries can be attacked and hit for runs. Balls that pitch closer to the batter are usually played with the weight on the front foot, and balls that land closer to the middle of the pitch are mainly played from the back foot. Most batters try to "build an innings", which usually involves playing more carefully to begin with then accelerating the scoring rate as the game progresses and the player's confidence increases.

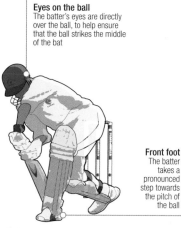

Eyes on the ball
The batter's eyes are directly over the ball, to help ensure that the ball strikes the middle of the bat

Elbow high
A high front elbow facilitates a straight bat, which increases the chances of making clean contact with the ball

Front foot
The batter takes a pronounced step towards the pitch of the ball

Weight back
As this stroke is mostly played to rising deliveries, the weight is on the back foot, which helps direct the ball downwards

FORWARD DEFENSIVE

This stroke is played to a well-pitched-up delivery that the batter feels is too risky to try to hit for runs. The batter should not leave a gap between the bat and the front leg's pad, to avoid being bowled. There is no followthrough: the bat stops level with the pad.

BACKWARD DEFENSIVE

This stoke is often employed to fast, short-pitched deliveries directed at the batter's body, thereby rendering an attacking shot unwise. As with the forward defensive there is no followthrough, and the ball should drop safely just in front of the batter.

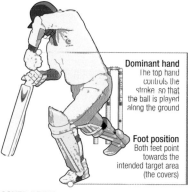

Dominant hand
The top hand controls the stroke, so that the ball is played along the ground

Foot position
Both feet point towards the intended target area (the covers)

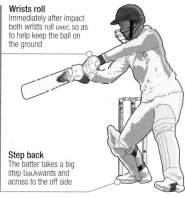

Wrists roll
Immediately after impact both wrists roll over, so as to help keep the ball on the ground

Step back
The batter takes a big step backwards and across to the off side

COVER DRIVE

This attacking, front-foot shot is played to a very full delivery that pitches outside the line of the off stump. Although it can yield many runs, if the ball swings away, a catch behind the wicket may result.

SQUARE CUT

Among the riskiest shots in cricket, this cross-batted stroke (whereby the bat is horizontal) is played to a short-pitched delivery on the off side. The ball should be played into the off side, square of the wicket.

INSIDE STORY

The first official record of a game of "kreckett" was in England, in the 16th century. Early matches were very different from those today, with the bat more like a hockey stick, and the ball delivered underarm. It was not until the 19th century that overarm bowling and equipment such as batting pads were introduced. Today cricket is played in over 100 countries, and there is a men's and a women's World Cup.

ICC

The International Cricket Council (ICC) is the sport's international governing body. Its many tasks include organizing the World Cups.

MCC

The Marylebone Cricket Club (MCC) is based at Lord's (the "home of cricket"), London, and administers the Laws and Spirit of Cricket.

STAT CENTRAL

MOST TEST RUNS

PLAYER	MATCHES	RUNS
SACHIN TENDULKAR	194	15645
RICKY PONTING	168	13378
RAHUL DRAVID	164	13288
JACQUES KALLIS	159	13040
BRIAN LARA	131	11953
ALLAN BORDER	156	11174
STEVE WAUGH	168	10927
SHIVNARINE CHANDERPAUL	146	10696
MAHELA JAYAWARDENE	137	10,674
SUNIL GAVASKAR	125	10122

MOST TEST WICKETS

PLAYER	MATCHES	WICKETS
MUTTIAH MURALITHARAN	133	800
SHANE WARNE	145	708
ANIL KUMBLE	132	619
GLENN MCGRATH	124	563
COURTNEY WALSH	132	519
KAPIL DEV	131	434
RICHARD HADLEE	86	431
SHAUN POLLOCK	108	421
WASIM AKRAM	104	414
HARBHAJAN SINGH	100	408

WORLD CUP WINNERS

YEAR	WINNER
2013 (WOMEN)	AUSTRALIA
2011 (MEN)	INDIA
2009 (WOMEN)	ENGLAND
2007 (MEN)	AUSTRALIA
2005 (WOMEN)	AUSTRALIA
2003 (MEN)	AUSTRALIA
2000 (WOMEN)	NEW ZEALAND
1999 (MEN)	AUSTRALIA
1997 (WOMEN)	AUSTRALIA
1996 (MEN)	SRI LANKA
1993 (WOMEN)	ENGLAND
1992 (MEN)	PAKISTAN
1988 (WOMEN)	AUSTRALIA
1987 (MEN)	AUSTRALIA
1983 (MEN)	INDIA
1982 (WOMEN)	AUSTRALIA
1979 (MEN)	WEST INDIES

BASEBALL

GAME OVERVIEW

Often seen as the defining American sport, baseball is a bat-and-ball game played by two teams of nine players. A game usually lasts for nine innings, during which both teams take turns at bat to score runs by advancing players around four bases. When the fielding team get three players out, they bat. The team with the most runs at the end of the game wins.

FIELD OF DREAMS

The baseball field is divided into infield and outfield. The infield consists of the "diamond", the corners of which are the four bases, and the pitcher's mound. It is bounded by the infield grass line and two foul lines that extend out from home plate and mark the limits within which the ball must be hit. The outfield is all the fair territory between the infield grass line and the outfield fence.

NEED2KNOW

➔ Baseball is a North American adaptation of the British sport of rounders (see p.149). While there is no official birth date for baseball, the first full documentation of a game dates to 1838.

➔ Professional baseball is primarily an American sport, but it has also spread to other countries. There are top-class leagues in China, Japan, South Korea, Taiwan, Cuba, and Venezuela.

Bat attack
The baseball bat can measure anywhere between 63.5cm (25in) and 101.6cm (40in) in length and tapers at the handle. Professional players must use a wooden bat. Aluminium bats may be used in amateur baseball

Batting gloves
Batting gloves enhance the hitter's grip on the bat

BASEBALL IN BOOKS

THE NOVELIST JANE AUSTEN TALKS ABOUT A GAME OF "BASE-BALL" IN HER BOOK *NORTHANGER ABBEY*, WHICH WAS WRITTEN IN 1798. IT IS ONE OF THE EARLIEST WRITTEN REFERENCES TO THE GAME.

PLAYER PROFILE

Baseball is a game of skill, strategy, and athletic ability. Catching, hitting, and throwing all require excellent hand-eye co-ordination. It also helps to have great reflexes when facing the pitcher. Batters have just a fraction of a second to decide whether or not to swing at a pitch. Fitness is another important part of the game, for sprinting between bases and chasing down fast-moving balls in the field. Physical endurance is also crucial as the pros endure a gruelling 162-game regular season.

Head protection
Some pitchers can deliver the ball at 160kph (100mph) and more, so a helmet is essential for a batter's safety

Player identification
Players from all the Major League teams bar the New York Yankees have their names on the back of their jerseys. A number on the front of the jersey also identifies the player

Team strip
Each player wears a strip in the distinctive team colours

Shocking stockings
Two Major League clubs are named for their stocking colour: the Boston Red Sox and the Chicago White Sox

Gripping the dirt
Baseball shoes have metal or plastic cleats on the soles that provide grip when running on dirt

IN THE FIELD

There are nine defensive positions in the field. The pitcher stands on the mound to pitch, and the catcher squats behind home plate to catch the ball. The first baseman, second baseman, third baseman, and the shortstop cover the infield. The left, centre, and right fielders patrol the outfield.

PITCHER'S MOUND

The pitcher's mound is a 5.5m (18ft) dirt circle up to 25.5cm (10in) high. Just behind the centre of the mound is a small pad called the pitcher's rubber. The pitcher must keep one foot touching the rubber during the pitch and so can only take one step back and one forward.

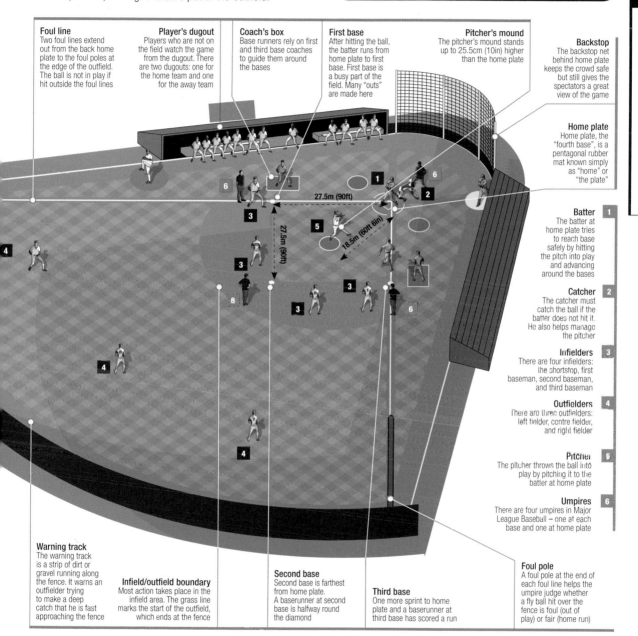

Foul line
Two foul lines extend out from the back home plate to the foul poles at the edge of the outfield. The ball is not in play if hit outside the foul lines

Player's dugout
Players who are not on the field watch the game from the dugout. There are two dugouts: one for the home team and one for the away team

Coach's box
Base runners rely on first and third base coaches to guide them around the bases

First base
After hitting the ball, the batter runs from home plate to first base. First base is a busy part of the field. Many "outs" are made here

Pitcher's mound
The pitcher's mound stands up to 25.5cm (10in) higher than the home plate

Backstop
The backstop net behind home plate keeps the crowd safe but still gives the spectators a great view of the game

Home plate
Home plate, the "fourth base", is a pentagonal rubber mat known simply as "home" or "the plate"

27.5m (90ft)

27.5m (90ft)

18.5m (60ft 6in)

Batter 1
The batter at home plate tries to reach base safely by hitting the pitch into play and advancing around the bases

Catcher 2
The catcher must catch the ball if the batter does not hit it. He also helps manage the pitcher

Infielders 3
There are four infielders: the shortstop, first baseman, second baseman, and third baseman

Outfielders 4
There are three outfielders: left fielder, centre fielder, and right fielder

Pitcher 5
The pitcher throws the ball into play by pitching it to the batter at home plate

Umpires 6
There are four umpires in Major League Baseball – one at each base and one at home plate

Warning track
The warning track is a strip of dirt or gravel running along the fence. It warns an outfielder trying to make a deep catch that he is fast approaching the fence

Infield/outfield boundary
Most action takes place in the infield area. The grass line marks the start of the outfield, which ends at the fence

Second base
Second base is farthest from home plate. A baserunner at second base is halfway round the diamond

Third base
One more sprint to home plate and a baserunner at third base has scored a run

Foul pole
A foul pole at the end of each foul line helps the umpire judge whether a fly ball hit over the fence is foul (out of play) or fair (home run)

SIDELINES

92,706 The highest ever attendance figure for a game in the US was recorded on 6 October 1959, when the LA Dodgers played the Chicago White Sox. The Colorado Rockies hold the record for highest season attendance – 4,483,350 in 1993.

3,562 The record number of games played during a pro career. The record is held by Pete Rose, who played for 24 years.

59 The age of the oldest ever pro, Satchel Paige, who played his last game for the Kansas City Athletics on 25 September 1969.

2,700,000 The price in US dollars for the most expensive piece of baseball memorabilia – the ball that St Louis Cardinals player Mark McGwire hit for record-setting home run number 70 in 1998. Canadian comic book artist and avid baseball fan Todd McFarlane purchased the ball at auction in 1999.

CATCHER'S GEAR

Standing right behind the batter, the catcher is exposed to pitches travelling at up to 160kph (100mph), so his gear is designed for protection. The mask, knee pads, and shin guards are made from hard plastic, and the chest protector is padded to protect the vital organs.

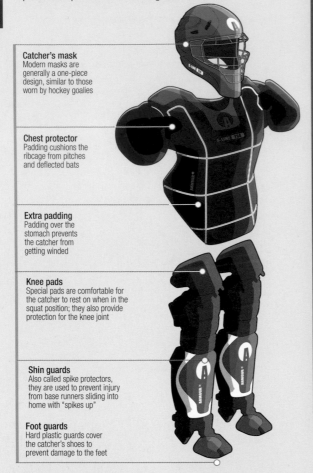

Catcher's mask
Modern masks are generally a one-piece design, similar to those worn by hockey goalies

Chest protector
Padding cushions the ribcage from pitches and deflected bats

Extra padding
Padding over the stomach prevents the catcher from getting winded

Knee pads
Special pads are comfortable for the catcher to rest on when in the squat position; they also provide protection for the knee joint

Shin guards
Also called spike protectors, they are used to prevent injury from base runners sliding into home with "spikes up"

Foot guards
Hard plastic guards cover the catcher's shoes to prevent damage to the feet

INNINGS AND OUT

Baseball is played in segments called innings. During an inning, each team takes a turn in the field and a turn at bat. The visiting team always bats in the first half, called the top half. The home team bats in the second half, called the bottom half. In most leagues, the team with most runs at the end of nine innings wins. If the score is tied at the end of nine innings, the teams play extra innings until one team has a lead at the end of an inning. The most innings played in a Major League game is 25, lasting 8 hours and 6 minutes.

GETTING OUT

Baseball is one of the few team sports in which the defence has the ball. The aim is to get three batters out, which can be achieved in a number of ways. Four are listed here: the umpire calls three strikes against the batter; the batter hits a ball into the air (a fly ball) that is caught by a fielder before it hits the ground in fair territory or foul; a runner who is not standing on a base is tagged by a fielder holding the ball; or a fielder with the ball touches the base to which a runner is forced to go before he gets there.

THE CATCH HE SHOULD HAVE DROPPED

CHICAGO CUBS FAN STEVE BARTMAN WENT INTO HIDING AFTER A 2003 NATIONAL LEAGUE CHAMPIONSHIP GAME AGAINST THE FLORIDA MARLINS. BARTMAN LEANED OVER THE FENCE TO CATCH A BALL – AND PLUCKED IT OUT OF THE HAND OF A CUBS' OUTFIELDER. THE INCIDENT CONTRIBUTED TO THE CUBS' SUBSEQUENT LOSS. BARTMAN BECAME THE SUBJECT OF AN INTERNET HATE CAMPAIGN AFTER THE MARLINS LATER ADVANCED TO THE WORLD SERIES.

VITAL GEAR

The bat and ball are obviously vital to a game of baseball. Other important gear include the fielders' gloves, which help them field the ball.

STITCHED UP
The ball has a core made from rubber and cork. Red cotton yarn is then wound around the core, and the ball is covered with two strips of leather. The leather is then stitched tightly together with more red cotton yarn.

7.5cm (3in)

BAT IN HAND
Made from either wood or metal, the smooth bat tapers from the thickest part, called the barrel, to the handle. Bats typically weigh no more than 1.8kg (4lb).

GLOVES
Leather gloves make it easier for fielders to catch the ball. The size of the gloves depends on the fielding position. Infielder gloves have a size limit of 21.3cm (8½in). The short pockets of infielder gloves make it easier to remove the ball from the glove and throw it quickly.

Padded protection
The gloves of all the fielders are well padded to protect the fingers

Catcher's mitt
The fingerless mitt of the catcher guards the hand and makes it easier to catch pitches

Barrel
The thickest part of the bat is called the barrel and is the part used to hit the ball

Mid-point
The area between the barrel and the handle is the narrowest part of the bat

Tapered handle
The barrel tapers to the handle, which has a rubber or cloth covering to help grip the bat

Safe in hand
The wider "knob" at the end of the handle keeps the bat from sliding out of the batter's hands

up to 7cm (2¾in)

up to 101.6cm (40in)

THREE STRIKES AND YOU'RE OUT

A batter has three attempts to hit a ball pitched into the strike zone above home plate. If he or she swings but misses the ball, the umpire calls a "strike" whether or not the pitch was in the zone. A strike is also called if the batter does not swing at a ball pitched into the strike zone or hits the ball into foul territory. If the batter has two strikes, a foul does not count as the third strike – with one exception. If the batter attempts to hold the bat over the plate, called a bunt, and the ball goes foul on more than two occasions, the batter is out. If the batter swings and hits the ball into fair territory, he or she must try to advance to first base.

THE GROUND-OUT

If a ball is hit on the ground to an infielder, he must field the ball and throw it to first base before the batter reaches the base. If the fielder does so, the batter is out. If the batter reaches base before the throw, he is safe. In the event of a tie, the batter is deemed safe.

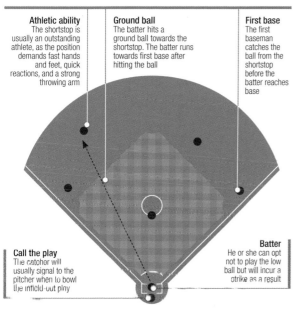

Athletic ability
The shortstop is usually an outstanding athlete, as the position demands fast hands and feet, quick reactions, and a strong throwing arm

Ground ball
The batter hits a ground ball towards the shortstop. The batter runs towards first base after hitting the ball

First base
The first baseman catches the ball from the shortstop before the batter reaches base

Call the play
The catcher will usually signal to the pitcher when to bowl the infield-out play

Batter
He or she can opt not to play the low ball but will incur a strike as a result

STRIKE ZONE

The strike zone is an imaginary window over home plate through which a pitch must pass to count as a strike if the batter does not attempt to hit the ball. The top of the strike zone is the mid-point between the top of the batter's shoulders and the top of his or her trousers. The bottom of the strike zone is level with a point just below the kneecaps. Imaginary lines extending up from the edges of home plate mark the right and left boundaries of the strike zone.

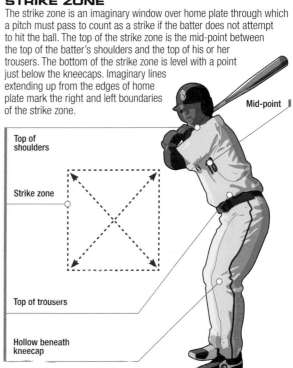

Mid-point

Top of shoulders

Strike zone

Top of trousers

Hollow beneath kneecap

ON-DECK CIRCLES

A circle is marked on either side of home plate. These circles, called on-deck circles, are areas designated for the next batter, who may take practice swings to loosen up before his or her turn at bat.

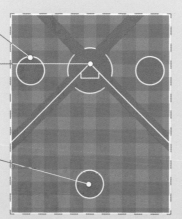

Stepping up to plate
The warm-up circle provides the next batter with a final chance to warm up and observe the pitcher

Home plate
The focus for much of the action on the field

Pitcher's mound
The pitcher's mound lies in the centre of the infield diamond

SHAPE OF THE PLATE

Home plate is a five-sided white slab. It has one long side measuring 42.5cm (17in), two short parallel sides measuring 21.3cm (8½in), and a pointed end, where two 30-cm (12-in) sides meet at right angles.

DESIGNATED HITTER

Traditionally, all members of a baseball team had to be able to take the field. Starting in 1973, however, the American League introduced the designated hitter (DH), a batter who takes the pitcher's turn at bat but does not play a defensive position. The DH allows teams to play a specialized pitcher, who may not be particularly good at batting, or a specialized batter who may be useless in the field, both of whom were liabilities under the old rules. Most Minor League and amateur baseball also allows use of a DH, but the National League prohibits the DH and requires the pitcher to bat.

HITS AND MISSES

Baseball is a game of strategy as well as athletic ability. Strong pitching is vital as it is the most common way to get batters out. The pitchers' ideal situation is a "shutout", where the batting side does not score during the game. Batters do not simply slog. They spend hours studying throwing styles to try and "read" a pitch by watching the movement of the pitcher's arm or the positioning of the catcher's feet.

PITCHING

The type of pitch a pitcher throws depends on how he grips and releases the ball. Major League pitchers usually master at least two or three types of pitch. The catcher calls for a particular type of pitch using hand signals.

Wind up
The pitcher winds up with his back foot on the pitching rubber, often raising the other leg to his chest

Stride
The pitcher plants his front foot firmly and swings the hand holding the ball over his head. A few pitchers, including some of the hardest to hit, pitch sidearm or nearly underarm

Pitch
The pitcher releases the ball towards the batter as his throwing arm reaches its full extent. He throws his entire body weight onto his front foot as he releases the ball

PITCHING STYLES

Pitchers throw a variety of pitches, each of which has a slightly different velocity, trajectory, and/or arm angle. These variations are introduced to confuse the batter in various ways, and ultimately aid the defensive team in getting the batter or baserunners out.

CURVEBALL

The curveball pitch has plenty of topspin, which causes the ball to break, or curve downwards, unexpectedly. A well-placed curveball will drop just before it hits the plate, forcing the hitter to swing above it.

Wrist twist
The wrist is twisted inwards to add spin to the throw

SLIDER

Halfway between a curveball and a fastball, the slider pitch doesn't break as much as the curveball but travels faster, often tricking the hitter into believing it is a straight fastball.

Slider grip
The ball is gripped slightly off centre

FASTBALL

The fastball is the most common pitch in baseball. Some fastballs move or break in flight, some do not – but all of them are delivered at great speed.

Fast fingers
Two fingers are placed over the top of the ball

BATTING

Having warmed up in the on-deck circle, the batter steps up to the plate. He grips the bat firmly around the handle, with hands close together and fingers aligned at the knuckles. Then the chess game begins as the batter and pitcher try to outwit and overpower each other. Batting is often cited as one of the most difficult feats in sport. In fact, if a batter can get a hit in three out of ten pitches faced, giving him a batting average of .300 – pronounced three-hundred – he or she is considered a good hitter. In Major League Baseball, no batter has hit over .400 in a season since Ted Williams in 1941 and no batter has ever hit over .367 in a lifetime.

Stance
A batter at the plate prepares to hit the ball by keeping his legs wide, holding both elbows up, and looking forward

Swing
The batter strides forward into the pitch and rotates his hips to generate power

Follow through
As he follows through, the hitter keeps his head down and completes his swing

SIDELINES

114,000 The highest ever attendance for a baseball match – an exhibition between Australia and an American services team during the 1956 Olympics.

162 The number of baseball games played by every Major League team during the season, which lasts from April to September.

73 The record number of home runs hit by one player during a MLB season. The record is held by Barry Bonds.

SCORING STATS

Baseball aficionados pore over batting, pitching, and fielding averages to rate their heroes, and scorers record all manner of statistics. Batters, for example, are awarded base hits for getting safely on to a base: a single for first base, a double for second, and triple for third.

BASEBALL JARGON

For the uninitiated, baseball may seem to have a language all of its own – in fact there are entire books published on the sport's jargon. The following list of selected terms will help you interpret some of the more common phrases to be heard on the field.

BASES LOADED A situation where there are baserunners on first, second, and third bases.

BEANBALL A pitch deliberately thrown to hit the batter, usually on the head, if he or she does not move out of the way.

DOUBLE A hit in which the batter gets to second base safely.

DOUBLE PLAY When two players from the batting team are put out on the same play.

HOMER A "homer" (or home run) is a hit over the outfield fence that allows the batter to automatically run through all the bases and score a run.

LEFT ON BASE A term used to refer to the total number of baserunners who are left waiting on a base when the third out is called by an umpire.

PINCH HITTER A substitute batter who replaces a weak batter during a critical play (a "pinch").

SHUTOUT When one team prevents the other from scoring.

STOLEN BASE This occurs when a runner successfully advances to the next base.

BASERUNNING

Once the ball is in play, baseball is a contest between the batter's speed of foot and the fielder's speed of throwing. Baserunners can be tagged or forced out when they are not touching a base. They make desperate and spectacular slides to reach a base beneath the fielder's hands, calling for fine judgment from the umpire on the spot.

TAG OUT
The tag out (or simply a "tag") occurs when a fielder holding a live ball touches the baserunner when he or she is not touching a base.

Fair game
A fielder can tag out by touching any part of the base-runner's body

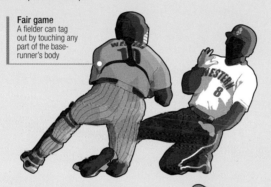

SLIDE
A runner slides into a base to avoid being tagged out or overrunning the base. A runner may slide into base with enough speed to knock over an infielder attempting a tag out or double play.

The Pete Rose
When a runner slides head-first into a base it is known as a "Pete Rose", after the gritty player

INSIDE STORY

The Major Leagues consist of two set leagues – the National League (formed 1876) and the American League (formed 1901). Professional baseball has also become popular in other parts of the world, notably Asia and Latin America. Amateur baseball was an official Olympic sport from 1992, but has been dropped for the 2012 London Games.

INTERNATIONAL BASEBALL FEDERATION (IBAF)
The IBAF is the worldwide governing body for baseball. Founded in 1938, the IBAF manages tournaments such as the World Cup of Baseball and the World Baseball Classic. Despite its international authority, the IBAF has little control over professional baseball in North America.

MAJOR LEAGUE BASEBALL
Major League Baseball is the dominant force behind professional baseball in North America. There are 30 teams in two major leagues: 16 in the older National League and 14 in the American League. Each league has three divisions grouped by geographical location. At the end of the season, the top teams from each league compete in a best-of-seven game series called the World Series to determine the overall champion.

STAT CENTRAL

WORLD SERIES LEADING WINNERS

FRANCHISE	WINS
NEW YORK YANKEES	27
ST. LOUIS CARDINALS	11
OAKLAND ATHLETICS	9
BOSTON RED SOX	7
SAN FRANCISCO GIANTS	7
LOS ANGELES DODGERS	6
CINCINNATI REDS	5
PITTSBURGH PIRATES	5
DETROIT TIGERS	4
ATLANTA BRAVES	3
BALTIMORE ORIOLES	3
CHICAGO WHITE SOX	3
MINNESOTA TWINS	3
CHICAGO CUBS	2
CLEVELAND INDIANS	2
NEW YORK METS	2
FLORIDA MARLINS	2
TORONTO BLUE JAYS	2

WORLD CUP OF BASEBALL

NATION	WINS
CUBA	25
UNITED STATES	4
VENEZUELA	3
COLOMBIA	2
SOUTH KOREA	1
PUERTO RICO	1
DOMINICAN REPUBLIC	1
GREAT BRITAIN	1

TOP MLB CAREER HOMERS

NAME	HRS
BARRY BONDS	762
HANK AARON	755
BABE RUTH	714
WILLIE MAYS	660
ALEX RODRIGUEZ	647
KEN GRIFFEY JR.	630
JIM THOME	612
SAMMY SOSA	609

SOFTBALL

Softball bat
The composite or metal bat is a maximum of 86cm (34in) long

Helmet
Two ear flaps protect the side of the head; a cage to protect the face is optional

Shirts and shorts
Players wear shirts with short sleeves and shorts

Shoes
Shoes may have cleats or spikes, although metal ones are banned

NEED2KNOW

→ The sport that we know today as "softball" is said to have begun indoors in 1887 on Thanksgiving Day in Chicago.

→ One or more on-field umpires monitor the game to make sure the rules are followed.

→ The International Softball Federation (ISF) is the governing body and has more than 120 member countries.

GAME OVERVIEW

Softball is a game in which two teams of nine players take turns to bat and field as they try to score the most runs around four bases laid out on a field of play. A game usually consists of seven innings in which each team bats and fields. Softball has some similarities with baseball, which is also called hard ball.

COMPETITOR PROFILE

Members of a team may display a range of skills. Those with good hand-eye coordination may excel at batting while others can pitch the ball cleverly to deceive the batter. All outfielders know how to catch, pick up, and throw accurately from base to base to stop runners scoring.

FIELDING EQUIPMENT

The catcher standing behind the batter wears a helmet with a face mask and throat protector. Fielders wear a leather glove with webbing between thumb and forefinger to help them catch and field the ball. They may wear sliding shorts to protect their thighs when sliding towards the bases. The stitched white or yellow leather ball is usually either 30cm (12in) or 28cm (11in) in circumference.

FIELD OF PLAY

The softball field features a diamond with three bases and a home plate where the batter stands and tries to hit the ball. To score a run batters run around the diamond, touching the bases and home plate. The outfield can be any size, depending on the space available and the level of play. The outfield fences are furthest back for slow pitch softball because the batters hit the ball further.

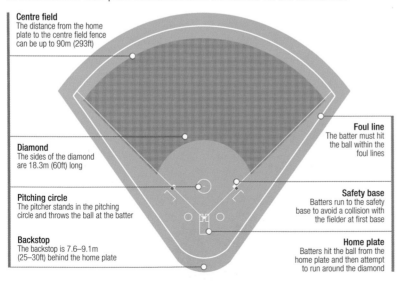

Centre field
The distance from the home plate to the centre field fence can be up to 90m (293ft)

Diamond
The sides of the diamond are 18.3m (60ft) long

Pitching circle
The pitcher stands in the pitching circle and throws the ball at the batter

Backstop
The backstop is 7.6–9.1m (25–30ft) behind the home plate

Foul line
The batter must hit the ball within the foul lines

Safety base
Batters run to the safety base to avoid a collision with the fielder at first base

Home plate
Batters hit the ball from the home plate and then attempt to run around the diamond

GETTING OUT

In each half-inning, the fielding (defensive) team needs to get three of the batting (offensive) team out. A batter may be out in several ways: if three strikes (failure to hit a fair delivery) are called (a strikeout); if a hit ball is caught before bouncing (a flyout); if the batter is touched by the ball or by a glove worn by a fielder holding the ball while the batter is away from a base (tagged); or if a fielder holding the ball touches a base before the batter arrives there (a force out or a force play).

TYPES OF SOFTBALL

Fast pitch, slow pitch, and modified pitch are the three types of softball. Fast-pitch softball favours the pitcher, who, using a windmill motion, delivers the ball underhand as quickly and skillfully as possible, making it hard to hit. Slow pitch softball favours the batter since the ball is lobbed up, making it easier to hit. Modified-pitch softball is like a sloweddown version of fast-pitch softball.

PESÄPALLO

GAME OVERVIEW

Also known as pesis, pesäpallo is Finland's most popular sport. As in baseball, two teams of nine players take turns batting and fielding, and the batting team scores when they advance a player around four bases. When they are batting, teams may also use three extra designated hitters, or jokers.

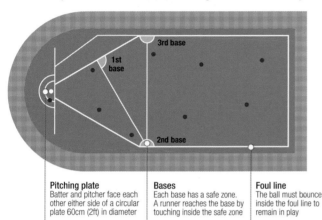

Pitching plate
Batter and pitcher face each other either side of a circular plate 60cm (2ft) in diameter

Bases
Each base has a safe zone. A runner reaches the base by touching inside the safe zone

Foul line
The ball must bounce inside the foul line to remain in play

SCORING

A full game is played over two periods of four innings, with an extra inning if scores are tied. The ball must bounce within the playing area to count as a legal play. Any ball that is hit past the back line is called a strike, so the batter must be careful not to hit the ball too hard. After three strikes a batter is out. If a fielder catches the ball inside the playing area, the batter is "wounded" and cannot bat again in the inning unless the team score. An inning ends when three players are out or all players are either wounded or on a base. The team's plays are directed by a manager, who works out how best to score in this highly tactical game.

FIELD OF PLAY

The game is played on asphalt or other surfaces suitable for running. For men, the field is 92m (302ft) long and 42m (138ft) across. A strip of grass 10m (33ft) wide surrounds it. The bases are laid out in a zigzag, with the distance between each base progressively longer, to a total distance of 126m (413ft). For women, the field is 10 per cent smaller.

NEED2KNOW

→ Pesäpallo was invented in the 1920s by combining the rules of baseball with traditional Finnish games.

→ The pitcher delivers the ball by throwing it up vertically to a height of at least 1m (3ft 3in) above the batter's head. This makes hitting the ball easier than in baseball.

ROUNDERS

GAME OVERVIEW

Rounders is played by two teams of six to 15 players, who take it in turns to bat and field. The team that scores the most rounders at the end of a number of innings is the winner. The game is mainly played in the United Kingdom, Ireland, and Canada. The National Rounders Association (NRA) in the UK and the Gaelic Athletic Association (GAA) in Ireland have developed two sets of rules, although there is some overlap between them and games are played between the two codes.

SCORING

A rounder is scored if a batter hits the ball and runs without stopping around all four posts before the ball can be returned to the bowler. Under NRA rules a half-rounder is scored if the batter hits the ball and reaches second or third base or if he or she runs all the way round without having hit the ball. A penalty half-rounder is scored if the bowler delivers two consecutive no-balls to a batter.

FIELD OF PLAY

Rounders may be played on grass, asphalt, or any surface suitable for running, but not on mixed surfaces. The hitting area and the first three posts form a square with sides of 12m (39ft 5in). The fourth post is 8.5m (27ft 10in) from the third post.

NEED2KNOW

→ Rounders is thought to have originated in Great Britain and Ireland, perhaps as early as the 16th century. It was probably the inspiration for baseball and softball.

→ The game is played by men, women, and children. There may be no more than five men in a mixed team.

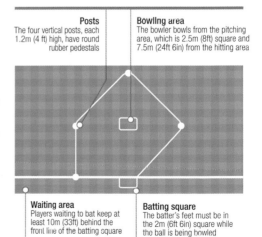

Posts
The four vertical posts, each 1.2m (4 ft) high, have round rubber pedestals

Bowling area
The bowler bowls from the pitching area, which is 2.5m (8ft) square and 7.5m (24ft 6in) from the hitting area

Waiting area
Players waiting to bat keep at least 10m (33ft) behind the front line of the batting square

Batting square
The batter's feet must be in the 2m (6ft 6in) square while the ball is being bowled

NEED2KNOW

→ Originally developed in Canada, ice hockey is played in about 30 countries, principally in North America and Europe.

→ Ice hockey is one of the four major North American professional sports.

→ North America's National Hockey League, known as the NHL, is the sport's premier league.

→ Only six of the 30 NHL franchises are based in Canada, but Canadians outnumber Americans in the league by three to one.

PLAYER PROFILE

Hockey players must think fast, act fast, and be masters of strategy. To reach speeds of up to 40kph (25mph), players must be extremely fit and strong, and to turn and manoeuvre at these speeds they need supreme control of their bodies. The puck can travel at frightening speeds, so to control and pass it or shoot on goal, players need lightning reflexes.

Body armour

The gloves, like the rest of the hockey kit, are geared towards protection – lots of padding is worn to avoid injury during high-speed collisions with other players, the boards, or the puck

Tool of the trade

The main tool of the hockey player's craft, the hockey stick is used both to control and shoot the puck and as a barrier between a player and the opposition

Bladed boots

Hockey skates feature the latest material technology, all sitting on a razor-sharp blade that carves up the ice – and anything else that gets in its way. Skates can cost anything up to £3,000 per pair and are custom-made for the pros

GAME OVERVIEW

Ice hockey, or just "hockey" as it's known in the United States and Canada, is a fast-paced, action-packed sport played on ice. During 60 minutes of regular time, split into three 20-minute periods, two teams of six armoured players try to score by shooting a vulcanized rubber puck into the opposition's goal using their sticks or by deflecting it off their skates. Ice hockey is a dynamic and exciting game to play and watch; it attracts huge television audiences and legions of fanatical supporters.

THE RINK

Hockey rinks are specifically designed for the game. They are rectangular with rounded corners and are surrounded by "the boards" – a wall roughly 1m (3ft 3in) high topped with a shatterproof perspex screen to protect the crowd. There are two standard sizes for hockey rinks; the one used primarily in North America is narrower than that used in Olympic competition and in most other national leagues. At each end of the ice, there is a goal consisting of a metal frame and a cloth net. The ice is about 2cm (¾in) thick and made up of eight to ten thin layers.

Red line
Divides the rink into two zones – one for each team

Neutral zone
Both teams must change players within this zone. Various attack and defence strategies are organized in the neutral zone

23m (75ft)

Face-off circles and spots
The five circles and nine spots indicate where face offs take place

Position lines
Located inside and outside the face-off circles, they indicate where players line up for the face off

Goal line
The puck must be completely over this line for a goal to be scored

GORDIE HOWE HAT TRICK

THE TERM "GORDIE HOWE HAT TRICK", NAMED IN HONOUR OF THE LEGENDARY HOCKEY STAR, IS ASCRIBED TO A PLAYER WHO, IN THE COURSE OF A SINGLE MATCH, SCORES A GOAL, PROVIDES AN ASSIST, AND WINS A FIGHT.

ICE HOCKEY

THE FACE OFF

Each game starts with a face off in the centre circle, and restarts in the same way after every goal that's scored. This is not a moment for the faint-hearted. Two players, one from each team, square up, toe-to-toe, their sticks at the ready, their blades remaining on the ice, poised for action. To start the game, the referee or linesman drops the puck between the two players, then backs out of the way. The players then battle – sticks clashing – to gain possession of the puck and make an assault on the opposition's goal.

WHO PLAYS WHERE?

A team consists of, at most, 22 players, including at least two goaltenders. Six players from each team take the ice at the same time. Usually one of the six is a goalie, who wears heavy-duty protective clothing and positions himself in front of the goal. He is allowed to stop the puck with his hands, body, or stick. His five teammates are divided into three forwards and two defence men. The forward positions – the "glamour" players – are the left wing, right wing, and centre. In defence, lying in wait for the opposition, are the left and right defence.

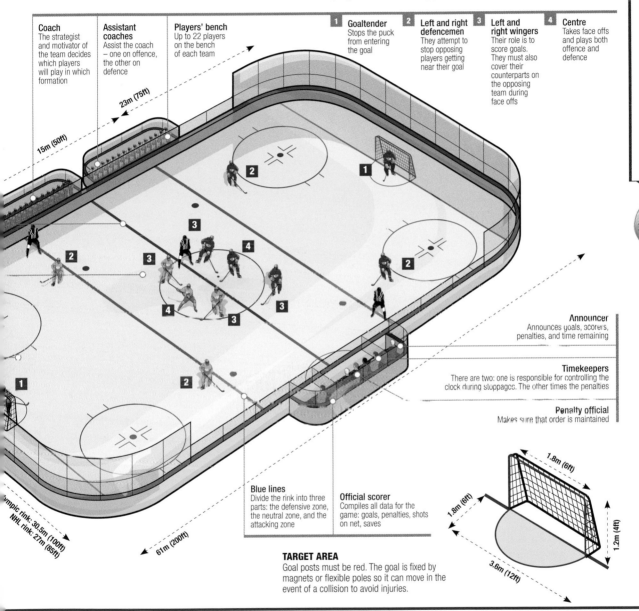

Coach The strategist and motivator of the team decides which players will play in which formation

Assistant coaches Assist the coach – one on offence, the other on defence

Players' bench Up to 22 players on the bench of each team

1 Goaltender Stops the puck from entering the goal

2 Left and right defencemen They attempt to stop opposing players getting near their goal

3 Left and right wingers Their role is to score goals. They must also cover their counterparts on the opposing team during face offs

4 Centre Takes face offs and plays both offence and defence

Announcer Announces goals, scorers, penalties, and time remaining

Timekeepers There are two: one is responsible for controlling the clock during stoppages. The other times the penalties

Penalty official Makes sure that order is maintained

Blue lines Divide the rink into three parts: the defensive zone, the neutral zone, and the attacking zone

Official scorer Compiles all data for the game: goals, penalties, shots on net, saves

TARGET AREA Goal posts must be red. The goal is fixed by magnets or flexible poles so it can move in the event of a collision to avoid injuries.

23m (75ft) · 15m (50ft) · Olympic rink: 30.5m (100ft) · NHL rink: 27m (85ft) · 61m (200ft) · 1.8m (6ft) · 1.8m (6ft) · 1.2m (4ft) · 3.6m (12ft)

SIDELINES

74,544 The largest crowd ever packed into the Spartan Stadium to watch arch rivals Michigan State University and the University of Michigan.

552 The record number of consecutive games played by an NHL hockey goalie, held by Glenn Hall.

35 The record number of professional games without a loss. This record is held by the Philadelphia Flyers (1980).

5 "Five goals, five different ways" is known as a quinella. Mario Lemieux scored the only quinella in NHL history.

1 The number of American-born goaltenders out of the total of 34 enshrined in the Hockey Hall of Fame.

WHAT THEY WEAR

The hard surfaces of the ice and boards, and pucks flying at up to 190kph (120mph) – not to mention other players looking for blood – pose a multitude of safety hazards. Besides ice skates and sticks, hockey players are usually equipped with an array of safety gear to lessen the risk of injury. This includes a helmet, shoulder pads, elbow pads, mouth guard, protective gloves, heavily padded shorts – sometimes known as Breezers – a "jock" athletic protector, shin guards, and sometimes a neck guard. Goaltenders wear masks and much bulkier, specialized equipment designed to protect them from any direct hits from the puck.

"THE GREAT ONE"

NICKNAMED "THE GREAT ONE", WAYNE GRETZKY IS REGARDED AS THE BEST PLAYER OF HIS ERA AND IS ACKNOWLEDGED AS THE GREATEST HOCKEY PLAYER EVER BY SPORTSWRITERS, PLAYERS, COACHES, AND FANS. ALONG WITH HIS MANY AWARDS, RECORDS, AND ACHIEVEMENTS, HE IS THE ONLY PLAYER TO EVER HAVE HAD HIS PLAYING NUMBER, 99, OFFICIALLY RETIRED ACROSS THE ENTIRE NATIONAL HOCKEY LEAGUE.

BODY GUARDS

Ice hockey players are among the best protected sports players – and for good reason. Here is the array of body armour worn by most NHL hockey players.

Face protection
Visors are made of steel bars or mesh, or of transparent reinforced perspex

Upper body
A hybrid of a wetsuit and an NFL player's shoulder pads, this upper-body suit offers great protection and flexibilty

Composite materials
Body padding is made of hi-tech materials that are strong yet breathable

The jock
The groin and pelvis protector is one of the most valued items in the lockers of male hockey players

Thigh guards
Breezers protect the hockey players' best developed and most used muscles

FASTER FOOTWEAR

Hockey boots are made of hardened nylon reinforced with leather around the ankle and heel. A hard toe cap provides protection, and closure is by lace.

Cold comfort
Hockey players spend up to 12 hours a day in their hockey skates, so comfort is high on the list of requirements. Boots are lined with natural, breathable materials such as cotton and silk

Steel blade
The blades on hockey boots are made of hardened steel

HEAD GEAR

Since they were made mandatory in the 1980s, helmets have prevented many a cracked skull. Although wearing a visor is optional, all but the ugliest players use one to protect their pearly whites.

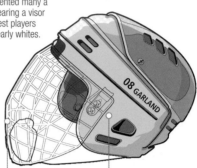

Goalie's visor
Goaltenders wear larger visors that offer more coverage against pucks flying in from all angles

Hard hat
Light but super-strong fibreglass resists the blows of sticks and pucks

GOALIE'S GETUP

The ice hockey goalie inhabits potentially the most vulnerable position in sport. Being bombarded by speeding pucks requires a whole extra level of protection.

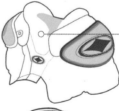

Puck-proof vest
The goalie's vital organs are protected by a vest made of steel mesh and graphite – not quite bulletproof, but almost

Shorts protection
Goalies wear an extra pair of strengthened shorts. Nothing can get in and nothing can escape out

CHOOSE YOUR WEAPON

Hockey players choose their sticks carefully and look after them well. Made of wood reinforced with fibreglass, these flexible lances, 2m (6ft 6in) in length, pack a mighty punch at puck or opponent.

PLAYING BY THE RULES

Shooting the puck into the opposition goal is the aim of the game. Getting it there is a task pretty much unhindered by rules and regulations – fighting is all part of the game – although offside rules do dictate patterns of play.

STAYING ONSIDE

The purpose of the offside rule is to prevent attacking players from goalhanging. The most important offside rule dictates that attacking players must follow the puck into the attacking zone. A player is called offside if both his skates go into the attacking zone before the puck does. The other key offside rules are outlined below.

THE POWERPLAY

The object of a powerplay is to score a goal while the opposing team is playing shorthanded after a penalty has been awarded. Up to two players per side may be penalized, giving a team a possible five-on-three powerplay. The coach will then usually put on his best attacking players to try to push home the advantage. From the face off they try to gain control of the puck and head for the opposition's goal. The players then pass the puck between them until an opening is created and a player gets to take a shot on goal. A powerplay lasts the length of a penalty (two, four, or five minutes) or ends when a goal is scored by either team.

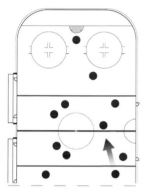

ADVANCING THE PUCK
Players can't pass the puck to a teammate across any two lines. Both skates must be over a line to determine player positions.

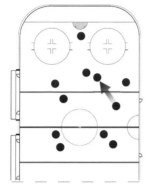

PRECEDING THE PUCK
They can't cross into the attacking zone ahead of the puck and then touch it. Offside is not called if they leave the attacking zone without touching it.

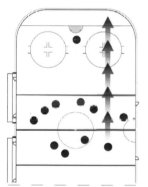

ICING
Icing is called when a player hits the puck across the opponent's goal line from his or her own half, unless it goes into the goal. Icing is legal when a team is shorthanded.

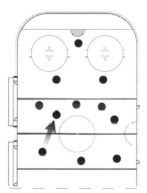

TWO-LINE PASS
The two-line pass (also known as an offside pass) occurs when a player passes the puck from his defending zone to a team-mate across the red centre line.

COMMITTING A FOUL

In men's hockey, players use their hips or shoulders to hit other players if the player has the puck or has just passed it. This is called body-checking and is perfectly legal. However, the following are expressly forbidden and incur penalties:

BOARDING Throwing an opponent violently into the boards.
BUTT-ENDING Jabbing an opponent with the shaft of one's stick.
CHARGING Taking more than two steps towards an opponent before body-checking him.
CLIPPING Throwing one's body below an opponent's knees.
CROSS-CHECKING Hitting an opponent with the shaft of the stick while both hands are on the shaft.
ELBOWING Impeding or striking an opponent with one's elbow.
DELAY OF GAME Failing to keep the puck in motion.
HIGH-STICKING Hitting an opponent above the shoulders.
HOLDING Impeding an opponent with hands or arms.
HOOKING Impeding an opponent with one's stick.
INTERFERENCE Body-checking an opponent who does not have the puck or who has not just passed it.
KNEEING Hitting an opponent with one's knee.
SLASHING Swinging one's stick at an opponent.
SPEARING Jabbing an opponent with the blade of one's stick.
TRIPPING Impeding an opponent around his legs.

OFFICIALS' SIGNALS

There are two categories of officials: on-ice officials are the referees and linesmen that enforce the rules during game play; off-ice officials have an administrative role rather than an enforcement role. The referee will halt the game using a whistle followed by a signal when he spots any of the offences outlined above. The signals used in ice hockey are unique to the game. There are more than a dozen signals used by referees; below are some of the most commonly seen during a game.

DELAYED PENALTY   **HOOKING**   **SLASHING**

GOAL DISALLOWED   **CROSS CHECKING**   **GOAL SCORED**

FISTICUFFS

FIGHTING IN ICE HOCKEY IS A CONTROVERSIAL ASPECT OF THE SPORT. ALTHOUGH IT RESULTS IN A MAJOR PENALTY, PLAYERS WHO ENGAGE IN FIGHTING DO NOT GET EJECTED FROM THE GAME. HOCKEY REMAINS THE ONLY MAJOR PROFESSIONAL SPORT IN NORTH AMERICA NOT TO EJECT PLAYERS FOR FIGHTING. FIGHTS ARE OFTEN SPONTANEOUS KNEE-JERK REACTIONS TO AN ON-ICE INCIDENT DURING A CRUCIAL PART OF A GAME.

STAT CENTRAL

ALL-TIME NHL POINT SCORERS

POINTS	PLAYER
2,857	WAYNE GRETZKY
1,887	MARK MESSIER
1,850	GORDIE HOWE
1,798	RON FRANCIS
1,771	MARCEL DIONNE
1,755	STEVE YZERMAN
1,723	MARIO LEMIEUX
1,658	JAROMIR JAGR
1,641	JOE SAKIC
1,590	PHIL ESPOSITO
1,579	RAY BOURQUE
1,533	MARK RECCHI
1,531	PAUL COFFEY
1,467	STAN MIKITA
1,425	BRYAN TROTTIER

NHL TITLE WINNERS

NO	TEAM
24	MONTREAL CANADIENS
13	TORONTO MAPLE LEAFS
11	DETROIT RED WINGS
6	BOSTON BRUINS
5	EDMONTON OILERS
4	OTTAWA SENATORS
4	NEW YORK RANGERS
4	NEW YORK ISLANDERS
4	CHICAGO BLACKHAWKS
3	PITTSBURGH PENGUINS
3	NEW JERSEY DEVILS
2	MONTREAL MAROONS
2	PHILADELPHIA FLYERS
2	COLORADO AVALANCHE
1	CALGARY FLAMES
1	VICTORIA COUGARS

OLYMPIC MEN'S MEDAL WINNERS

YEAR	GOLD	SILVER	BRONZE
2010	CANADA	USA	FINLAND
2006	SWEDEN	FINLAND	CZECH
2002	CANADA	USA	RUSSIA
1998	CZECH	USSR	FINLAND
1996	SWEDEN	CANADA	FINLAND
1992	USSR	CANADA	CZECH
1988	USSR	FINLAND	SWEDEN
1984	USSR	CZECH	SWEDEN
1980	USA	USSR	SWEDEN
1976	USSR	CZECH	W.GERMANY
1972	USSR	USA	CZECH
1968	USSR	CZECH	CANADA
1964	USSR	SWEDEN	CZECH
1960	USA	CANADA	USSR
1956	USSR	USA	CANADA

PLAYING THE GAME

Ice hockey is a crowd-pleasing, no-nonsense game of attack and defence. When in possession of the puck, players charge up the rink aiming to get into position for a shot on goal. In defence, the players try to intercept the puck and steal it from the opposition by hassling players and blocking their progress up the rink. This high-tempo game relies on players' swift movement across the ice, great passing and shooting techniques, and wily playing strategies.

SLAMMING THE PUCK

Shooting the puck into the net is the aim of every player, and what the crowds pay to see. Shooting techniques are more aggressive versions of those used for passing. There are four basic shots used by ice hockey players.

High stick
The player draws his stick back high

SLAP SHOT
This is the most powerful but least accurate shot. The stick is slapped against the puck with no previous contact.

Shifting weight
The player's weight goes towards his back foot

WRIST SHOT
The blade of the stick starts cupped over the puck, and then straightens as the player transfers his weight from back foot to front foot, before a final flick with the wrist whips the puck up into the air.

SNAP SHOT
The puck is pushed forwards against the stick until at the right moment the pressure is increased and the puck is whipped away.

BACKHAND SHOT
Because of the curve of the stick blade, this is a tricky shot to pull off. It is very hard to defend against because it is difficult to predict in what direction the puck will go.

KEEPING IN CHECK

Hockey is a rough sport, and the players are allowed, under certain circumstances, to smash into each other. When a player is carrying the puck forward, players from the opposing team are allowed to impede his progress by skating into him. This is called checking. They can also check a player who has just received a pass.

PICK A TARGET
Checking is all about anticipation and timing – picking the target, tracking his movement, and approaching at just the right time.

TAKE HIM OUT
The weight and momentum of the attacking player travel through his target, barging him away from the puck.

Attacking the target
Making the shot, the player's weight shifts through the puck and towards the target

Stick swoosh
The force of the hand movement causes the stick to bend, propelling the puck into the air

Top hand
Positioned right at the top of the stick, it creates a pivot against which to push

Bottom hand
Pulls the stick away from the puck then snaps it through towards the target

PULLING THE GOALIE
A team that is losing by a goal or two in the last few minutes of play may decide to "pull" the goalie. This means that they remove the goaltender and replace him or her with an extra attacker with the aim of using the advantage to score a fast goal. However, this tactic is pretty risky, and quite often leads to the opposing team taking advantage of the empty net.

"THE HAMMER"
DAVE "THE HAMMER" SCHULTZ SCORED PLENTY OF GOALS FOR THE PHILADELPHIA FLYERS, BUT MOST OF HIS ACHIEVEMENTS ARE NOW FORGOTTEN. WHAT PEOPLE REMEMBER IS THE TIME HE SPENT IN THE SIN BIN: 259 MINUTES IN HIS ROOKIE YEAR, 348 MINUTES THE FOLLOWING SEASON, AND 405 THE NEXT. HIS CHARGE SHEET IS UNPARALLELED IN NHL HISTORY.

SIDELINES

2,856 The distance, in metres (3,123yd), that the average hockey player covers during an NHL game.

108 The noise level, in decibels, at an Edmonton Oilers match when the team took to the ice.

168 The height, in centimetres (66in), of the Stanley Cup, one of the largest trophies in professional sport.

574,125 The number of registered Canadian hockey players. That's a staggering 1 in 50 of all Canadians.

INSIDE STORY
Ice hockey originated in Canada in the 19th century and soon grew in popularity, spreading to the United States then Europe. The North American-based National Hockey League (NHL) was founded in 1917, and ice hockey was included in the Olympic Games in 1920, and the Winter Games in 1924.

The game has since become one of the most popular spectator sports in the world, and is shown on TV networks all over the globe. Ice hockey is played in more than 30 countries – mostly those with some natural ice cover. It is the official national winter sport of Canada, where the game enjoys immense popularity, and it is also the most popular sport in Finland. The most prominent and successful ice hockey nations are Canada, Czech Republic, Finland, Russia, Slovak Republic, Sweden, and the United States.

GOVERNING BODY
The International Ice Hockey Federation (IIHF) was founded in 1908 and is the worldwide governing body for ice hockey. It is responsible for the management of international ice hockey tournaments, and maintains the IIHF World Ranking. Despite its worldwide authority, the IIHF has little control of hockey in North America.

BEST PLAYERS, TOP LEAGUE
The National Hockey League (NHL) is the world's top league, featuring the world's best players. The league's teams are divided into two conferences, each comprising three divisions.

→ Bandy is an ancestor of ice hockey. The sport resembles both field hockey and soccer – its alternative names include "hockey on ice" and "winter football".

→ The leading bandy-playing nations are Sweden, Norway, Finland, and the Baltic states (Estonia, Latvia, and Lithuania). The game is also popular in parts of Canada, Russia, and the United States.

PLAYER PROFILE

Bandy players must be good ice skaters and, because dribbling with the feet is permitted, many also have the ball skills of top soccer players. They need strong lungs – the round ball travels quicker than a flat puck, so bandy is an even faster game than ice hockey. The matches last longer, too (45 minutes each half, as against ice hockey's three 20-minute periods), and stamina is essential. The strategic complexity of the game means that players also need an instinct for positioning.

BANDY

GAME OVERVIEW

Bandy, or "banty", is a winter sport that is usually played on an outdoor pitch of ice, although there are some indoor rinks. Two teams of 11 players compete over 45-minute halves to hit a small ball into goals at either end of the rink. Players wear skates and wield curved sticks, known as "bandies". They can control the ball with their feet or bodies, but must not use their hands.

The game is fast-moving and high-scoring, averaging seven or eight goals per match. To keep up the tempo, each side can use three substitutes (four in international games), who may come on and off as often as the captain or coach requires. One of bandy's peculiarities – and for some its attraction – is the paucity of rules: there are only 18 in total.

SOCKED BY SOCCER

IN VICTORIAN BRITAIN, IT BRIEFLY SEEMED THAT BANDY MIGHT RIVAL FOOTBALL IN POPULARITY. BOTH SHEFFIELD UNITED AND NOTTINGHAM FOREST FOOTBALL CLUBS BEGAN LIFE PLAYING BOTH SPORTS. BUT BANDY'S POPULARITY FELL SHARPLY IN THE LATE 19TH CENTURY, AS FOOTBALL CONQUERED THE WORLD.

BRIGHT BALL

The ball used for bandy is hard, usually bright orange or red in colour, and approximately the same size as a tennis ball. Traditionally, the outer surface was made of cord, which covered a cork core, but many modern bandy balls are plastic.

Speedy
The ball travels fast when hit

6.5cm (2½in)

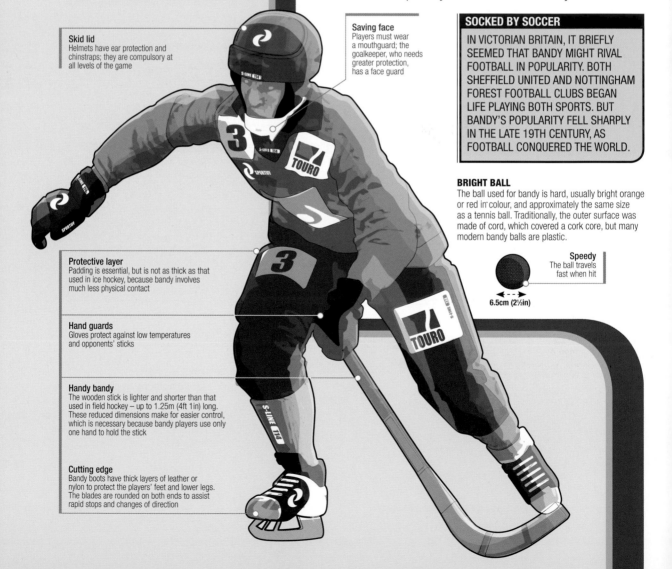

Skid lid
Helmets have ear protection and chinstraps; they are compulsory at all levels of the game

Saving face
Players must wear a mouthguard; the goalkeeper, who needs greater protection, has a face guard

Protective layer
Padding is essential, but is not as thick as that used in ice hockey, because bandy involves much less physical contact

Hand guards
Gloves protect against low temperatures and opponents' sticks

Handy bandy
The wooden stick is lighter and shorter than that used in field hockey – up to 1.25m (4ft 1in) long. These reduced dimensions make for easier control, which is necessary because bandy players use only one hand to hold the stick

Cutting edge
Bandy boots have thick layers of leather or nylon to protect the players' feet and lower legs. The blades are rounded on both ends to assist rapid stops and changes of direction

THE RINK

Bandy was originally played on frozen fields, but now usually takes place on all-weather ice rinks similar in size to soccer pitches. Low wooden fences along the sidelines keep the ball on the pitch. Between matches, the ice is smoothed over by a special motorized vehicle widely known by the name of the leading manufacturer, Zamboni.

1 Goalkeeper
He is permitted to use hands and arms to play the ball, but only within his own penalty area

2 Fullbacks
They guard each flank against attack from the wingers

3 Middle fullback
This player marshals the other defenders from a central point

4 Halfbacks
They are the first line of defence, and the key to getting the ball forward and turning defence into attack

5 Quarterbacks
The strategic generals: their job is to use the ball to create goal-scoring opportunities for the forwards

6 Forwards
Two wingers and a central striker are constantly in motion to receive their teammates' passes

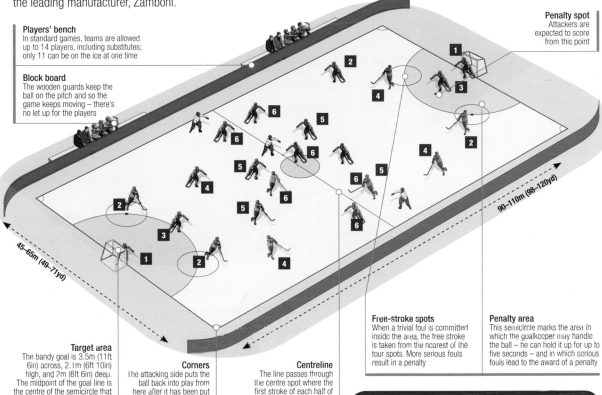

Players' bench
In standard games, teams are allowed up to 14 players, including substitutes; only 11 can be on the ice at one time

Block board
The wooden guards keep the ball on the pitch and so the game keeps moving – there's no let up for the players

Penalty spot
Attackers are expected to score from this point

45–65m (49–71yd)

90–110m (98–120yd)

Free-stroke spots
When a trivial foul is committed inside the area, the free stroke is taken from the nearest of the four spots. More serious fouls result in a penalty

Penalty area
This semicircle marks the area in which the goalkeeper may handle the ball – he can hold it up for up to five seconds – and in which serious fouls lead to the award of a penalty

Target area
The bandy goal is 3.5m (11ft 6in) across, 2.1m (6ft 10in) high, and 2m (6ft 6in) deep. The midpoint of the goal line is the centre of the semicircle that marks the penalty area

Corners
The attacking side puts the ball back into play from here after it has been put out by the defenders

Centreline
The line passes through the centre spot where the first stroke of each half of the game is played

BANDY CANS

Many elements of bandy, such as corners and free strokes, are closely related to soccer (see pp. 100–107). If the ball goes out over the side fence, a stroke in is awarded to the opposition. If the ball goes over the goal line off a defending player, an attacker takes a corner, playing the ball towards the goal. Attackers must be outside the penalty area when the corner is taken; defenders must be on the goal line.

BANDY BANS

Bandy players may not head the ball or control it with their arms or hands; nor can they raise their sticks above head height to control the ball. Although physical contact is allowed, kicking, tripping, pushing, grasping, and slashing are punished by a free stroke or penalty. Players who commit serious or repeated fouls may be sent to a "sin bin" for five or 10 minutes. Free strokes are awarded for fouls. They must be taken within five seconds.

BEST FOOT FORWARD

The best bandy players combine the quick-footed dribbling skills of soccer players with either the kind of spectacular shots familiar from field hockey and ice hockey, or delicate lobs that take out the opponent's midfield defenders. Forwards cover miles during a game as they need to make sure that they're always available for a pass.

STICKLESS WONDERS

Bandy goalkeepers do not have sticks; they catch the ball or block it with their bodies. They wear protective padding on their legs in addition to the clothing worn by outfield players. Having caught the ball, they may hold it for no more than five seconds before throwing or kicking it to an outfield player. When the ball goes out of play behind the goal off an attacker, the goalkeeper restarts the game with the ball in his hand. All other players must be outside the penalty area.

INSIDE STORY

Bandy world championships for men and women have been held in every odd-numbered year since 1957. For the first two decades they were dominated by the Soviet Union, which won the first 11 titles. Since that nation broke up at the end of the 1980s, Russia, one of its former components, has started as favourite in most tournaments, with Sweden as its main challenger.

GOVERNING BANDY

The Federation of International Bandy (FIB) was formed in 1955 in Stockholm, and is still based in Sweden. There are 29 member nations – including India, a nation not usually associated with winter sports.

FIELD HOCKEY

GAME OVERVIEW

Field hockey – often just called "hockey" in countries where ice hockey is not a major sport – is a fast-moving, exciting, and potentially tough game in which two 11-a-side teams of men or women try to hit, push, pass, or dribble a small, hard ball into each other's goal just using J-shaped sticks. The winner is the team with more goals after two 35-minute halves. Gameplay often resembles soccer with sticks – in some countries hockey is the more popular of the two games.

PLAYER PROFILE

Outfield players cover a lot of ground during a match, so they need to be fit, with good stamina but also capable of short sprints. Their training involves demanding leg exercises. They also work hard to perfect their touch – the ability to "feel" the ball through their sticks.

TURKISH DELIGHT

HOLARI IS A UNIQUE FORM OF HOCKEY PLAYED IN TURKEY. THE GOALS AND FIELD OF PLAY ARE SIMILAR TO THOSE IN REGULAR HOCKEY, BUT A WOODEN CYLINDER REPLACES A BALL AND THERE ARE NO CODIFIED RULES AND NO SET TIMES. GAMES MAY START AT DAWN AND GO ON UNTIL THEY ARE TIMED OUT BY SUNSET.

Clothing
Players wear clothing in team colours, made from "breathable" materials that allow rapid evaporation of perspiration. Men wear shirts and shorts, women shirts and skirts

Stick
The crook-shaped head of the stick is flat on the side used to play the ball and rounded on the other. Most sticks are about 95cm (3ft 1in) long

Shin guards
Protection from other sticks and the ball is recommended, but not compulsory

Boots
Sometimes have studs, but now normally have plastic ridges

Ball
The ball is plastic over a cork core. It often has indentations to reduce drag on a wet pitch

"Long" corner
When a defending player puts the ball out of play behind his or her back line, the attacking team restarts the game with a free hit from the 5m line

Umpires
There are two umpires, each meant to control half the field, with the division along an imaginary line running diagonally from corner to corner. In fact, the game is so fast that they have to work closely together and co-operate throughout the pitch

Back line
This is the limit of the pitch at each end. The part of the back line between the posts is known as the goal line

SIDELINES

4 The highest number of World Cups won by a single nation, Pakistan, since the competition began in 1971. Along with India, they dominated hockey in the 1970s.

60 The most goals in international competition in one calendar year, scored by Pakistan's Sohail Abbas in 1999.

143 The number of goals scored by German defender Florian Kunz in only 39 games for his national team in the 1990s. He was World Hockey Player of the Year 2001.

166 The record number of international goals scored by attacking midfielder Alyson Annan in 228 appearances for Australia.

ON THE CARPET

As the name suggests, field hockey was originally played on real grass. Today, though, many top-class matches are played on a type of watered synthetic grass, which is easier to maintain. This speeds up play by providing a flatter surface to help the ball run true. A sand-based pitch is also sometimes used, but it can cause abrasions if players fall over. Synthetic pitches have greatly reduced the likelihood of matches being postponed due to adverse weather conditions.

INDOOR HOCKEY

Developed in the 1950s as a way for hockey enthusiasts to play during the winter, indoor hockey takes place in a sports hall on a small pitch 44m x 22m (145ft x 72ft) between teams of six players. Most elements of the game are like field hockey, but the ball may only be pushed rather than hit, and must stay on the ground except during a shot. Long boards run along the sidelines to keep the ball in play – making the game faster than the outdoor version.

1 Goalkeeper	**2** Fullbacks	**3** Halfbacks	**4** Centre halfback	**5** Inside forwards	**6** Wingers	**7** Centre forward
Inside the circle, the keeper can stop the ball with any part of his or her body, and can kick it, but may not catch it	Their main task is to stop opposing wingers from breaking down the flanks and crossing the ball	They try to control midfield and break up attacks	The fulcrum of the defence; marks the opposing centre forward	Turn defence into attack by feeding the ball to the forwards	Stationed near the sidelines in the attacking half of the field	Hangs close to the goal; main job is to score, but also harries opposing fullbacks

Officials
They check the players' equipment, monitor substitutions, and keep the time and score

Substitutes
Each team can have up to five substitutes. Substitution takes place at any time

Penalty spot
Located 6.4m (21ft) in front of the centre of the goal line

Shooting circle
A semicircle with its centre at the middle of the goal line; radius 14.63m (48ft)

Net
Hangs outside the boards

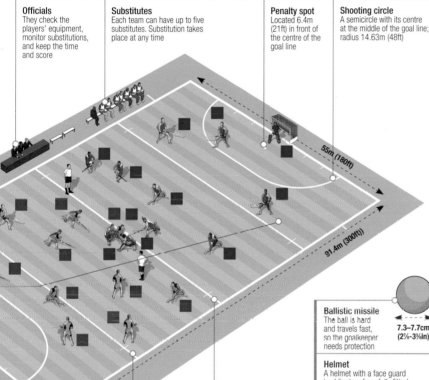

55m (180ft)

91.4m (300ft)

90cm (3ft)

2.1m (7ft)

3.7m (12ft)

GOAL
Along the sides and back of the goal are solid boards 46cm (18in) high and dark coloured on the inner side. These help referees to see and hear if a shot at a penalty corner has risen too high to count. The goal nets are fitted slackly to prevent the ball bouncing back out.

Flag posts
One in each corner; 1.2–1.5m (4–5ft) high and easily bendable to avoid causing injury

23m line
Two, 22.9m (75ft) in from the back line (the pitch was originally measured in imperial units)

Centre line
The opening push off is taken from the midpoint along this central marking

Ballistic missile
The ball is hard and travels fast, so the goalkeeper needs protection

7.3–7.7cm (2⅞–3⅜in)

Helmet
A helmet with a face guard is obligatory for a fully fitted goalkeeper

Body protector
The optional padding covers the arms as well as the torso. The shoulders and elbows are particularly well clad

Hand guard
Protects the hand holding the stick and the free hand

Pads
Goalkeepers' pads are made of springy foam, so a blocked ball bounces a long way

GOALKEEPING GEAR

The hockey rule book makes it compulsory for the goalkeeper to wear a protective helmet, preferably one that completely covers the head and throat. It is permissible for the keeper to remove the helmet to take a penalty stroke. Most goalkeepers also wear full body protection against the speeding ball, including padded shorts, hand protectors, and shin pads.

HOCKEY STROKES

Stopping, controlling, or playing a small ball with a thin stick requires great touch and accuracy. The essential skills range from perfectly timed tackles that stop the ball without touching the player, dribbling by using the stick both forehand and backhand, and smashing the ball at high speeds. In general play the ball must not be raised into the air when hit. However, it can be raised using a scooping or long pushing action of the stick. When the ball is in the air, a player must not play if it is above shoulder height.

SAFETY FIRST

Hockey has many rules, and they change often. Most rules are aimed at making the game safer, but they are highly complex. The ball cannot be hit into the air, for example – unless a player is taking a shot, or unless it is lifted by a scooping motion and does not endanger another player. In the same way, if the ball is in the air, a player may not raise his or her stick above the shoulder to stop it – unless it is to save a shot. When a player brings a high ball under control, opponents must remain 5m (16ft 6in) away until it is on the ground.

PUSH

Less powerful than a drive (see right), the push is used for accuracy over short distances; the stroke is controlled mainly by the wrists. It is an effective stroke in the close quarters of the shooting circle where the attacker has to push the ball accurately between the players defending the goal.

Gentle stroke
The lower hand pushes the stick through the ball

DRIVE

A strong hit along the ground may be either a pass or a shot. The player takes the longest backswing possible before hitting forward. The knees are kept bent to ensure that the ball remains on or close to the playing surface.

Grip
Gripping with both hands at the top of the stick gets more distance from the drive

FLICK

Used mainly from dead ball situations, the flick or scoop is a push with a last-moment turn of the wrists to lift the ball off the ground. The stroke can take defenders out of the game, but will be penalized if the ball endangers an opponent.

Upward lift
A flick of the wrist scoops rather than hits the ball into the air

DRIBBLE

Keeping the ball under close control at the end of the stick involves being able to play both forehand and with the stick reversed, or hooked over the ball, so that the stick is always shielding the ball from a potential tackler.

Protective stance
The head of the stick protects the ball from potential attack as the player moves up the field

Rapid reverse
The stick head flicks back and forth over the ball to keep it under tight control

---

FOULS

Depending on where on the field they occur, fouls are punished by the award of either a free stroke or a penalty hit to the opposition. As most goals are scored through penalty hits, this is an effective way of preventing foul play. These are the main offences:

STICKS Raising the stick above shoulder height.
BACKHANDERS Playing the ball with the rear, rounded surface of the stick.
OBSTRUCTION Tripping, shoving, charging, or striking an opponent.
FEET Deliberately kicking the ball.

CARDS

Umpires may show a player a card for dangerous play or an intentional foul. A green card is issued as an official warning. When umpires show a yellow card, the player is sin-binned for five or more minutes. For persistent fouling or serious offences, a red card is shown and the player is sent off.

PENALTIES

Most goals come from penalty strokes or penalty corners. Penalty corners are awarded against defenders for deliberately playing the ball over their back line; a foul between the 23m line and the circle; or an unintentional foul inside the circle.

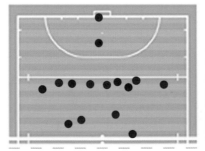

PENALTY STROKE
This is awarded for deliberate fouls by defenders inside the circle or for any foul that prevents a goal. The taker hits the ball from the penalty spot. Only the opposing goalkeeper may defend; all other players must stand behind the 23m line.

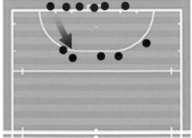

TAKING A PENALTY CORNER
The stroke is taken from the goal line. Teams drill to get the ball as quickly as possible from the corner taker to a team mate on the edge of the shooting circle, who either traps it or plays it to another to slam home before the advancing defence blocks it.

INSIDE STORY

Games similar to hockey were played in Egypt some 4,000 years ago, by the ancient Romans and Greeks and by the Aztecs. The modern game evolved in British schools in the mid-18th century, and hockey became an Olympic sport in 1908 (1980 for women). Until the 1980s, hockey was dominated by the national teams of India and Pakistan, but since then Australia, Germany, and the Netherlands have been the most successful national teams.

GOVERNING BODY

The International Hockey Federation was founded in 1924 to oversee the development of the game. It has 127 member associations in five continents. Based in Lausanne, Switzerland, it organizes the Hockey World Cup, the Women's Hockey World Cup, and is responsible for deciding the rules for the sport.

TACKLING

Players may not make a tackle that will lead to contact with an opponent or use their own bodies to shield the ball. Likewise, the player with the ball cannot use his or her body to push the other player away.

BLOCK TACKLE

This is one of the most commonly used tackles. The defender drops the stick to the floor, thus impeding the attacker's further progress. In a successful tackle, the stick is dropped at the last possible moment.

No swing
The object is not to swing the stick, but to keep it low on the ground

Crossed sticks
The tackler risks hitting the attacker's stick or body before hitting the ball

Defender
Lunges across the attacker towards the ball

REVERSE-SIDE TACKLE

The defender comes from the attacker's left with his stick reversed; the reverse tackle risks giving away a foul because the stick must cross the attacker's body.

STAT CENTRAL

HOCKEY WORLD CUP			
YEAR	WINNER	RUNNER-UP	SCORE
2010	AUSTRALIA	GERMANY	2–1
2006	GERMANY	AUSTRALIA	4–3
2002	GERMANY	AUSTRALIA	2–1
1998	NETHERLANDS	SPAIN	3–2
1994	PAKISTAN	NETHERLANDS	(4–3 PENS) 1–1
1990	NETHERLANDS	PAKISTAN	3–1
1986	AUSTRALIA	ENGLAND	2–1

OPEN-SIDE TACKLE

A defender approaching from the right-hand side potentially has an easier job – he can use his stick the "normal" way around.

Open access
The tackler stands a better chance of taking possession of the ball

Losing control
The attacking player has been forced off the ball

FLOORBALL

GAME OVERVIEW

Often likened to ice hockey without the skates, floorball (also called floor hockey) is a fast-moving game played indoors on a gym floor between two teams of six players. A lightweight plastic ball is used instead of a heavy puck and body-checking is not allowed. This makes the game less physical and more skills-oriented than its ice-based cousin.

NEED2KNOW

➡ Floorball was developed in Scandinavia in the 1970s. The best teams are Finland, Sweden, Switzerland, and Czech Republic.

➡ The sport was officially recognized by the IOC in 2008, and it is hoped that it will make its debut at the 2020 Olympics.

MATCH RULES

A game consists of three 20-minute periods, with extra time and penalties if scores end level. At any one time, five outfield players and one goalie are allowed on the rink, but up to 20 players are allowed in the squad and players may be substituted without stopping play.

LIGHT AND FAST

Outfield players use a lightweight stick with a curved plastic blade to strike a ball that weighs just 23g (1oz). Skilled players may propel the ball at speeds of up to 190kph (120mph). The goalminder does not carry a stick.

Lightweight stick
The stick must weigh no more than 350g (12oz)

Floor ball
The plastic ball has 26 holes in it and may be covered in dimples to make it more aerodynamic

LACROSSE

GAME OVERVIEW

Lacrosse is a fast and furious game in which two teams of ten men or 12 women vie to get a hard ball into the opposition goal. They use crosses – sticks with net pockets – to catch, dribble, tackle, carry, scoop, and throw the ball. The skills of passing the ball huge distances are combined with force: crosses are also used to check opposition sticks and players.

PLAYER PROFILE
Lacrosse players are tough all-rounders: they have the hand–eye co ordination to catch a small ball travelling at speed, the stamina of middle-distance runners, and the physical resilience of rugby players.

PLAYING AREA

Lacrosse is played on grass or artificial turf. The women's pitch is bigger than the men's because female teams have two more players.

1 Goalkeeper
A goalkeeper remains in or near the goal crease (circle) and tries to stop the opposition from scoring

2 Defenders
Three defenders form the penultimate line of protection in front of goal

3 Midfielders
Three midfielders link the defence and attack. They can move up and down the pitch to support either as necessary

4 Attackers
Their job is to score goals. They may not enter the crease around the opposition goal, but their sticks can

Helmet
Men wear helmets with a face mask and chin pad. All players have mouthguards

Shoulder guards
Shoulder guards are compulsory for all players except the goalie

Gloves
All players must wear protective gloves

Arm pads
Men wear arm pads for protection when body checking

Body armour
Many players wear rib protectors; goalies must also wear throat and chest protection

Sound footing
Players usually wear soccer or rugby boots, with studs or cleated soles for grip

NEED2KNOW

→ Lacrosse is most popular in North America, where it originated. It is the official summer sport in Canada, and the fastest-growing sport in the United States.

→ Invented in the 1980s, Intercrosse is a popular non-contact form of the game played by mixed teams of men and women.

PLAYING TIME
Matches vary in length depending on the age and sex of the players. Matches of one hour have four quarters usually with two time outs permitted per half.

End line
Both this and the sideline should be surrounded by a limit line at least 5.5m (18ft) back

Officials
One timekeeper, two penalty timekeepers, a players' bench official, and two scorers

9m (10yd)

18m (20yd)

32m (35yd)

Men: 55m (180ft); women: 60m (197ft)

1.8m (6ft)

1.8m (6ft)

Men: 100m (110yd); women: 110m (120yd)

GOAL CREASE
The goal is made of wood or plastic and the net is always pyramid-shaped. Around the goal is a circle, called the crease, with a diameter of 5.5m (18ft).

Centre line
Four players, including the goalie, stay in the defensive half of the pitch and three in the attacking half

Wing area
Although only marked near the halfway line, this line, 9m (29½ft) in from the sides, is taken to extend the length of the pitch

CUTTING IT DOWN TO SIZE

THE POPULARITY OF LACROSSE HAS INCREASED IN INVERSE PROPORTION TO THE SIZE OF THE PITCH AND THE NUMBER OF PLAYERS. IN ITS ORIGINAL FORM – A TRAINING EXERCISE FOR IROQUOIS WARRIORS KNOWN AS BAGGATAWAY – IT WAS PLAYED ON A PITCH 457M (500YD) LONG BETWEEN TEAMS OF 200-A-SIDE.

LONG AND SHORT OF IT

Crosses come in two sizes: at least half of each team – usually midfielders and attackers – must use short crosses, which are easier to manipulate. Only five players – usually the defenders and always the goalie – can use long crosses.

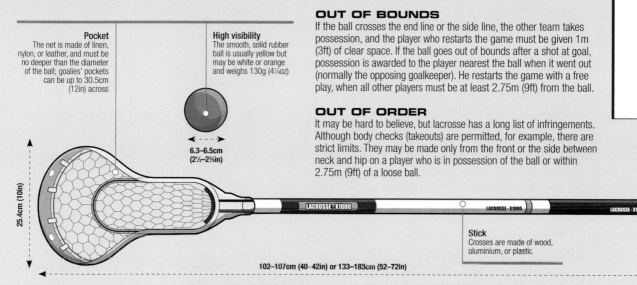

Pocket
The net is made of linen, nylon, or leather, and must be no deeper than the diameter of the ball; goalies' pockets can be up to 30.5cm (12in) across

High visibility
The smooth, solid rubber ball is usually yellow but may be white or orange and weighs 130g (4¼oz)

6.3–6.5cm (2½–2⅝in)

25.4cm (10in)

LACROSSE - X1000   LACROSSE - X1000   LACROSSE - X1000

Stick
Crosses are made of wood, aluminium, or plastic

102–107cm (40–42in) or 133–183cm (52–72in)

STRUCTURED MAYHEM

Lacrosse is one of the fastest of all ball sports, with play switching from end to end in a couple of throws and players barging each other off the ball. The game sometimes looks like a free-for-all – which is why it takes up to three officials to control the match: a referee, an umpire, and a field judge. All three perform the same duties, but the referee can override the others in the case of dispute.

FACE-OFF

The men's game begins with a face-off – one player from each team squats low in the middle of the centre line on either side of the ball. The referee calls "Are you ready? Play", then blows his whistle, and both players try to scoop up and pass the ball. Play is then continuous, except for stoppages for out of bounds or infringements.

OUT OF BOUNDS

If the ball crosses the end line or the side line, the other team takes possession, and the player who restarts the game must be given 1m (3ft) of clear space. If the ball goes out of bounds after a shot at goal, possession is awarded to the player nearest the ball when it went out (normally the opposing goalkeeper). He restarts the game with a free play, when all other players must be at least 2.75m (9ft) from the ball.

OUT OF ORDER

It may be hard to believe, but lacrosse has a long list of infringements. Although body checks (takeouts) are permitted, for example, there are strict limits. They may be made only from the front or the side between neck and hip on a player who is in possession of the ball or within 2.75m (9ft) of a loose ball.

IN CONTROL

The skill of scooping the ball up from the ground is hard to learn, but nothing like as difficult as catching an airborne ball in the pocket of the crosse. Another crucial skill is distribution – the ability to propel the ball over distance to a team-mate running into space.

Passing the ball
The player with the ball tilts the stick head back and with a lever-like forward motion releases the ball

Pocketing the ball
The pouch of the receiver's stick should be facing the thrower. Moving the stick slightly backward cushions the ball preventing rebound

CROSSE MESSAGES

Stick checking is the method used to try to dislodge the ball from the pocket of the player with possession. The defender tries to strike the attacker's stick but may not be successful if the other player has good ball handling technique or uses his body as a shield.

THE WOMEN'S GAME

Women's lacrosse differs from the men's game. The pitch is larger and there are two more players in each team. All women players use the short stick which has a shallower pocket than that of the men's crosses. They wear less protective clothing. Women cannot body check an opponent, nor can they kick the ball. To shoot at goal they must have a clear view of it whereas men can shoot through a group of players.

INSIDE STORY

The first lacrosse Men's World Championship in 1967 had only four entrants: Australia, Canada, England, and the United States. Since then the sport has spread to Japan and Korea, Italy, Finland, Denmark, Argentina, Hong Kong, and Tonga. The 2006 tournament had 21 competing nations: Canada beat the US in the final. The most popular form of the sport in Canada is box lacrosse, or boxla. Played indoors, the game was developed in the 1930s by owners of ice-hockey rinks to make use of their rinks during the close season. The game resembles outdoor lacrosse but there are only six players per team. It is faster as attacking players must pass the ball within 30 seconds.

SIDELINES

9 The number of National Lacrosse League (indoor) teams: six in the United States, and three in Canada.

8 The number of countries playing in the 2011 World Indoor Lacrosse Championship in Prague, Czech Republic: Australia, Canada, England, the Czech Republic, Ireland, Scotland, the United States, and the Canada-based Iroquois Nationals.

NEED2KNOW

→ More than 800 million people across the globe play volleyball at least once a week, leading to claims that it is the most popular sport in the world.

→ The game is particularly popular in eastern and southern Europe, Asia, and North America.

→ Invented in 1895, volleyball became an Olympic sport in 1964.

SIDELINES

8 The maximum number of seconds allowed for a serve; any longer and the ball is given to the opposition.

3 The number of consecutive Olympic gold medals won by the Cuban women's volleyball team; their triumphs came at Barcelona in 1992, Atlanta in 1996, and Sydney in 2000.

0.3 The time, in seconds, typically taken by a volleyball to travel from one baseline to the other when served by a top-class player, a speed of 194kph (121mph).

1,100,000,000 According to the Fédération Internationale de Volleyball (FIVB), the number of people who played or watched the game on one or more occasions in 2006 – one in six of the world's population.

VOLLEYBALL

GAME OVERVIEW

Volleyball is a high-energy sport played between two teams of six players. The object is to score points by hitting a ball over a net so that the opposition cannot return it before it hits the ground. Defensive players dive around the court to get their hands under the ball and push it up towards their teammates in attack, who are ready to leap high to smash it back over the net. At top levels, teams are either all-male or all-female, but volleyball is also a popular recreational sport, played by mixed teams of all ages and abilities.

Headwear
Forehead bands or caps may be worn to keep hair in place or to hold perspiration; hats and jewellery are forbidden

Courting clothes
Players wear lightweight cotton shirts or blouses and shorts or skirts. They may be in team colours and numbered front and rear

PLAYER PROFILE
In its first 100 years volleyball developed from a genteel form of relaxation into a high-energy game requiring great aerobic capacity. Training concentrates on cardiovascular exercise – sprints, long-distance runs, and skipping – but jumping is also important. Dumbbells are used to develop the arm muscles.

Protective kneepads
Often worn to prevent grazes caused by digging (diving to reach the ball before it hits the ground)

Shod or unshod
Players normally wear flat-soled shoes, but may go barefoot with permission

ROTATING PLAYERS
The players usually move round clockwise after every point so that they all serve and take turns in every position. Some teams, however, have a dedicated defender, known as a "libero", who always stays in the back zone and is not allowed to serve.

THE COURT

The playing area is usually made of wood or synthetic material – but the game can be played on any surface that does not cause injuries to diving players. Indoor courts must be flat, but outdoor courts can slope for drainage.

Lines on the court show where players may stand at the start of each point: three defenders in the back zone (including the server, who starts anywhere behind the end line) and three attackers in the front zone close to the net. The standards supporting the net are set 0.9m (3ft) at either side of the sidelines and are sometimes padded to safeguard the players.

KEEPING IT UP

Once the ball is in play, each team has up to three hits to get it back over the net. As long as they do not catch or carry the ball, players can strike it with any part of their bodies, but in practice they usually use an open hand, wrist, or fist. The team that wins the rally wins a point and if not serving wins the right to do so. Matches are usually the best of five sets. In the first four games, the winner is the first to 25 points; in the fifth game, the winner is the first to 15 points. If the score reaches 24–24 or 14–14, respectively, two clear points are needed for victory.

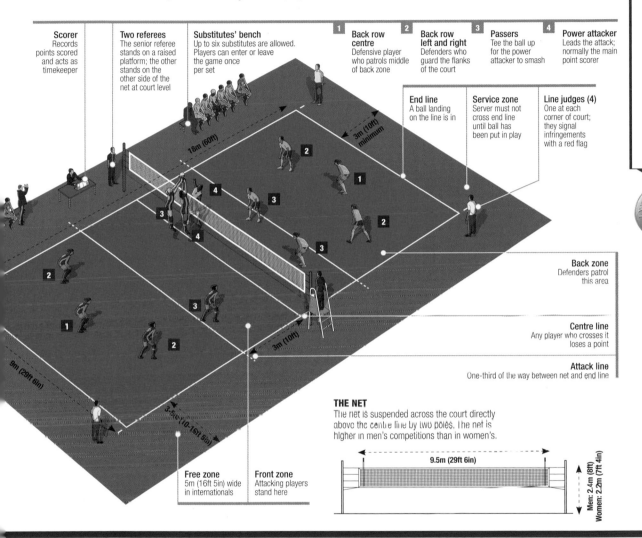

Scorer
Records points scored and acts as timekeeper

Two referees
The senior referee stands on a raised platform; the other stands on the other side of the net at court level

Substitutes' bench
Up to six substitutes are allowed. Players can enter or leave the game once per set

1 Back row centre
Defensive player who patrols middle of back zone

2 Back row left and right
Defenders who guard the flanks of the court

3 Passers
Tee the ball up for the power attacker to smash

4 Power attacker
Leads the attack; normally the main point scorer

End line
A ball landing on the line is in

Service zone
Server must not cross end line until ball has been put in play

Line judges (4)
One at each corner of court; they signal infringements with a red flag

Back zone
Defenders patrol this area

Centre line
Any player who crosses it loses a point

Attack line
One-third of the way between net and end line

18m (60ft)

3m (10ft) minimum

3m (10ft)

9m (29ft 6in)

3.5m (10.15ft 5in)

Free zone
5m (16ft 5in) wide in internationals

Front zone
Attacking players stand here

THE NET

The net is suspended across the court directly above the centre line by two poles. The net is higher in men's competitions than in women's.

9.5m (29ft 6in)

Men: 2.4m (8ft)
Women: 2.2m (7ft 4in)

THE BALL

Volleyballs should be inflated to a pressure that keeps them slightly soft, so that they have some "give". They are then comfortable to play with using the hands.

INFLATED WEIGHT
The match ball should weigh 260–280g (9.17–9.87oz).

22cm (8½in)

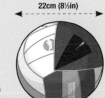

Pump action
Bicycle pumps are commonly used to inflate the volleyball to the requisite pressure and weight

KEEP COOL, DONT GLARE

VOLLEYBALL IS THE ONLY GAME IN THIS BOOK WITH PRECISE RULES ABOUT THE TEMPERATURE AND AMOUNT OF LIGHT REQUIRED FOR PLAY. MATCHES CANNOT START OR CONTINUE IF THE AIR IS COLDER THAN 10°C (50°F). IN WORLD CHAMPIONSHIPS, THE TEMPERATURE MUST BE NO LOWER THAN 16°C (61°F) AND NO HIGHER THAN 25°C (77°F). THE LIGHT ON COURT MUST BE BETWEEN 1000 AND 1500 LUX – ABOUT ONE FIFTH OF WHAT YOU GET ON A CLOUDY DAY – SO THAT PLAYERS DON'T GET DAZZLED.

BASIC SKILLS

Competitive volleyball players master six basic skills: serving, passing, setting, attacking (spike or dink), blocking, and digging.

Hip twist
The front arm and leg are placed ahead of the striking hand to allow a follow-through

Cocking the trigger
The attacker hits the ball at the top of its flight, then swings his arm through 270 degrees

SERVE
The serve is hit either underarm or (usually) overarm; jumping is allowed. Any serve that reaches the opponents' court is valid, even if it touches the net.

ATTACK (SPIKE)
In this spectacular smash, a player jumps above the net and hits the ball hard towards the ground in the other court.

Four hands
Teamwork presents an impenetrable barrier

Against all odds
The attempted spike is intercepted

BLOCK WALL
Blockers crowd the net and stretch above it to return the ball as soon as it has crossed the centre line, before it can do any damage in their court.

Open palms
From this position the attacker can flip the wrists on contact and thus angle the shot

Backhand extremism
Players can stretch further with downturned palms

TIP OR DINK
A light touch by an attack-zone player, using tactical skill rather than strength, sends the ball softly over the net into an unguarded area of the opponents' court.

DIG
Players dive or get down low to stop the ball touching the ground, trying to get enough height on it to allow team-mates to play it.

INSIDE STORY
Volleyball was invented in 1895, and originally named mintonette. The first recorded competitive game was played at Springfield College, Massachusetts, USA, in 1896. The sport's popularity spread from North America in the early 20th century and in 1949 volleyball's first World Championship was held in Prague. The sport was given Olympic status in 1964, although it first featured as part of a demonstration of US sports at the Paris Olympics of 1924.

LARGEST BODY
The Fédération Internationale de Volleyball (FIVB) was founded in 1947 as the sport's governing body. It has 220 affiliated national federations, making it the world's largest international sporting federation.

GAME OVERVIEW

Very similar to standard volleyball, this version of the game is played on sand, on a slightly smaller court, and with a team of only two players. Beach volleyball has been played professionally since the late 1960s and has been an Olympic sport since 1996.

NEED2KNOW

→ The sport was originally a casual form of volleyball played on the seafront at Santa Monica, California.

→ The US, Brazil, and Australia dominate the sport at the highest level.

→ Players wear shorts or swimming costumes on court.

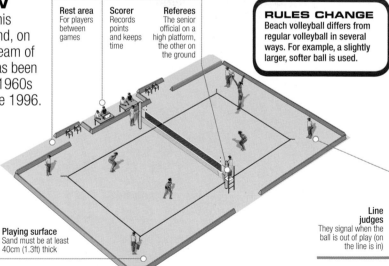

Rest area
For players between games

Scorer
Records points and keeps time

Referees
The senior official on a high platform, the other on the ground

RULES CHANGE
Beach volleyball differs from regular volleyball in several ways. For example, a slightly larger, softer ball is used.

Line judges
They signal when the ball is out of play (on the line is in)

Playing surface
Sand must be at least 40cm (1.3ft) thick

BEACH VOLLEYBALL

FOOTVOLLEY

GAME OVERVIEW

Footvolley began as an informal sport on the beaches of Brazil in the 1960s. The modern game combines the rules of beach volleyball with the skills of the football pitch, as players use any part of their body to play the ball except their hands and arms. Teams of two players may touch the ball alternately three times before it is returned over the net.

Football
The standard ball is a size 5 football

Overhead kick
A winning kick made with both feet off the ground scores two points

Soft landing
For safety, the court is covered in deep sand

NEED2KNOW

→ The net is set at a height of 2.1m (6ft 10in) – lower than a beach volleyball net.

→ Top footballers, such as Ronaldo and Ronaldinho, regularly compete in exhibition footvolley matches in Brazil.

HEAD TO TOE
A point is started by one player kicking the ball into the opponents' court. A team will often return the ball with an attacking header, after one player has set up their partner by controlling the ball on the chest. A "super point", worth two points, is scored by making the winning shot with the foot or leg while both feet are off the ground.

WORLDWIDE APPEAL
Rallies in footvolley tend to be longer than rallies in beach volleyball, and its popularity is spreading. The Pro Footvolley Tour began in 2008 and attracts large crowds. Brazilian football legend Romario is one of the biggest stars.

SEPAK TAKRAW

GAME OVERVIEW

Sometimes known as "kick volleyball", sepak takraw is a spectacular three-a-side game in which a ball is propelled over a high net using any part of the body other than the hands – usually the foot, knee, shoulder, or head. Points are scored by getting the ball to hit the ground in the opposition court. The game combines soccer skills with gymnastics.

NEED2KNOW

→ The game began in Malaysia and Thailand. Sepak means "kick" in Malay; takraw is Thai for "woven ball".

→ Matches are the best of three games up to 15 points. Different sets of three players contest each game.

MATCH PLAY
Play begins with the server standing in the service circle with his or her teammates in the quarter circles. On the other side, one player has to have a foot in the service circle, but the others can stand anywhere. A player in the quarter circle tosses the ball to the server, who sends it over the net. As in volleyball, each side can strike the ball three times before it returns to the opposition half.

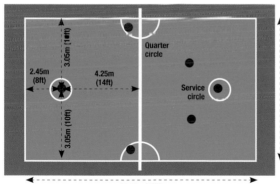

Quarter circle

3.05m (10ft)

2.45m (8ft)   4.25m (14ft)

Service circle

3.05m (10ft)

6.1m (20ft)

13.42m (44ft)

THE COURT
The game is usually played on a badminton doubles court (see pp.192–194) with two circles and semicircles marked to show players' positions for service. The top edge of the net is set at 1.54m (5ft) for men and 1.45m (4ft 9in) for women.

Leg and knee bandages
These prevent grazing from inevitable bumps on the floor

Foot covering
Trainers or similar with smooth soles

LIKE A ROCK-HARD BALL OF WOOL
Traditionally hand-woven to create a rigid sphere, the takraw ball is made of rattan stems or very hard plastic. It weighs approximately 250g.

Dress for comfort
Loose-fitting shorts and shirt or blouse in cotton or (less desirable) nylon; may be in team colours

40cm (1ft 3¾in)

GAME OVERVIEW

Originally conceived as a version of basketball for women, netball rapidly became a sport in its own right and is today enjoyed by millions of dedicated players all over the world. Netball is an exciting, fast-paced game played by two teams of seven players on a rectangular court. The object is to shoot the ball from within the goal circle into a netted hoop more times than the opposition. The players may neither run with nor dribble the ball and are restricted to set zones (determined by their playing position). This means that accurate, often lightning-quick passes and disciplined teamwork are paramount.

NETBALL

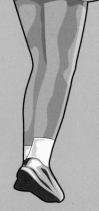

Durable ball
As netball can be played indoors or outdoors, the ball used is durable and waterproof. For matches, either a standard netball or a size five association football ball may be utilized

Shooting
Only two players on each team – the goal shooter and goal attack – are permitted to shoot for goal. To perfect this skill requires good technique and much practice

Player identification
A bib or patch must be worn by players to identify their position. "GA", for example, denotes goal attack. This helps the umpires ensure that the players are within their allocated playing zones

Strong defence
Although players must maintain a distance of 91cm (3ft) from the person with the ball, a defender with outstretched arms, reaching high, makes life difficult for the shooter

Clothing
Today's top level players mostly wear a lightweight, hard-wearing Lycra body suit

Powerful legs
Netball players, particularly when defending or catching the ball, must be able to jump strongly. They must also be able to take-off and accelerate quickly. The leg muscles, therefore, tend to be well developed

NEED2KNOW

→ Netball evolved directly from basketball and was originally known as "women's basketball".

→ Only seven players from each team are permitted on court, but both sides are allowed an additional five substitute players.

→ The World Netball Championships are held every four years. Sixteen teams took part in the 2011 tournament.

→ Although netball is traditionally a women's sport, there are also a number of mixed and men's leagues.

PLAYER PROFILE
Netball players are fast and agile, with high endurance levels. They have sure hands and the mental sharpness to make accurate passes swiftly. Not all players are tall, but height is an advantage, particularly for those attacking or defending the goal. Confident footwork, sharp reflexes, secure balance, and good team play are also important.

Injury danger
Knee and ankle injuries are common. This is because netball requires swift stops, starts, and changes in direction. A good warm-up reduces the risk of injury

1 Goal Shooter GS	**2** Goal Attack GA	**3** Wing Attack WA	**4** Centre C	**5** Wing Defence WD	**6** Goal Defence GD	**7** Goal Keeper GK
The team's primary goal scorer, the goal shooter has an accurate shot. The blue team's goal shooter (below) is restricted to areas A and B	The team's secondary goal scorer, the goal attack also feeds the goal shooter. The blue team's goal attack plays in areas A, B, and C	These players use precise passes to provide possession for the team shooters. The blue team's wing attack is restricted to areas B and C	This player – the team's workhorse – provides the link between attack and defence. The blue team's centre is allowed in all areas except A and E	This player marks the opposition wing attack and tries to intercept passes into the goal circle. The blue team's wing defence is restricted to areas C and D	This player marks the goal attack and works to restrict the opposition's scoring opportunities. The blue team's goal defence plays in areas C, D, and E	The last line of defence, the goal keeper marks the goal shooter and protects the goal. The blue team's goal keeper works in areas D and E

THE COURT

The netball court is divided into three thirds but five areas that help determine where each player may and may not go. At either end of the court is a semi-circular goal circle and a goal post, ring, and net. In the middle is the centre circle, from which play begins. Sprung wooden flooring is the ideal surface for netball, but grass and asphalt are also common.

30.50m (100ft)

15.2m (50ft)

Court markings
All of the lines on court are considered part of the playing area and must measure 5cm (2in) in width

Goal line
The goal line is found at either end of the court. The goal post stands mid-way along the line

Goal circle
Shots at goal may only be taken from the goal circle, a semi-circle with a radius of 4.90m (16ft)

Centre circle
A match begins, and play is resumed after a goal or interval, by a pass from this circle, which has a diameter of 9cm (3ft)

Transverse lines
The lines that divide the court into three equal parts – the centre third and two goal thirds – are known as the transverse lines

PLAYING THE GAME

Play begins with a pass from the centre circle. The team in possession then attempts to pass the ball into their goal circle so that either the goal shooter or goal attack may shoot for goal. After each goal scored, play is restarted with a centre pass. A match is played over four quarters, each of which is 15 minutes long. A team consists of 12 players, but only seven are allowed on court at a time. Unlimited substitutions are permitted between the quarters or during injury breaks.

CONTROLLING THE GAME

Two umpires officiate over infringements of the rules of netball. Major infringements include contact (a player must not come into contact with another if this interferes with play) and obstruction (a player must not be closer than 91cm, 3ft, to the player with the ball). Common minor infringements include: held ball (the player with the ball must pass or shoot within three seconds), offside (players must not move outside their playing zones), and footwork (the player with the ball must not re-ground the first landed foot until the ball is passed). For a minor infringement, the infringed team is awarded a free pass, but may not shoot for goal. Major infringements incur a penalty pass or shot, during the taking of which the offending player stands out of play. Furthermore, if the penalty occurs inside the goal circle, the goal shooter or goal attack may shoot for goal.

Standing still
The players must remain still, arms at their side, until the umpire blows the whistle and tosses up the ball

Umpire's job
The umpire throws the ball from just below the level of the shorter player's shoulders

Face off
The players must be at least 91cm (3ft) apart and each face their goal end

TOSS UP
When two infringements occur simultaneously, or if the umpire is unsure which team last had contact with a ball out of play, a toss up results. The two players adopt positions opposite each other, the umpire – standing between them – tosses the ball into the air, and the players compete for possession.

NETBALL TECHNIQUES

Netball is a fast-moving game in which players must make decisions and precisely execute a variety of techniques in a very short space of time. All players must be able to catch and pass effectively, and the goal shooter and goal attack must also master the art of shooting for goal. All players constantly use solid and decisive footwork throughout the course of a match.

DEFENDING

Sound defence often wins games. It is the job of the defence to gain possession of the ball, which is mainly achieved by pressuring the opposition into making mistakes. Good defenders are determined and persistent, with the ability to predict the flight of, and then intercept, passes.

Good balance
Athletically balanced with just one foot on the ground, this player is effectively pressuring the attacker while obeying the obstruction rule

91cm (3ft)

NO CONTACT

Netball is a non-contact sport, and the rules stipulate that the defender must maintain a distance of at least 91cm (3ft) from the player holding the ball. This makes defending a challenging, but vital, task. Agility, anticipation, and timing are all essential.

FOOTWORK

In a fast-moving game such as netball – where players are required to stop, start, and change directions very quickly – good footwork is essential. Without it a player can easily lose balance and body control, therefore becoming slow and cumbersome on court. In particular, netball's "one-step" rule necessitates specialized footwork skills.

Handling
Sharp, accurate handling is vital. A fumbled catch, or inaccurate pass, can give away possession

Quick thinking
With only three seconds in which to release the ball, the player must swiftly look for other players to pass to or for space into which team-mates could run to receive the pass

Landed foot
The player pivots on the landed foot, which must not drag or slide during the manoeuvre

Stepping foot
The player pushes off and steps with the non-landed foot, and in so doing is able to change the direction of the pass

THE PIVOT

After catching the ball, the player may not re-ground the foot that first touched the ground until they have made a pass. However, the player may step with the other foot any number of times. This is particularly useful when the ball-carrier lands facing one direction but wishes to make a pass in another. The player pivots on the landed foot and steps in the direction of the pass with the other.

SHOOTING

The shooting skills of the goal shooter and goal attack must be finely tuned. In the past the ball was released low, but today it is usually held high, making interception more difficult. The shot is normally taken from a stationary position. The game "freezes" as the player shoots, and attention focuses on the shooter. Steady nerves are essential.

Protecting the ball
The ball is held high to keep it safe from the attentions of the defenders. This allows the shooter to concentrate solely on the target

Bending
The knees are bent before the ball is released

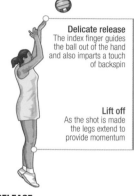

Delicate release
The index finger guides the ball out of the hand and also imparts a touch of backspin

Lift off
As the shot is made the legs extend to provide momentum

PREPARATION

In preparing to shoot for goal, the player stands with the knees slightly bent. The eyes are fixed on the target, and the ball rests on the fingers of the shooting hand.

RELEASE

The ball is released with a flick of the fingers and wrist, so that it travels in a high arc upwards and then down into the goal ring. The knees extend slightly to aid momentum.

PASSING

As players cannot run with or dribble the ball, netball is a passing game. Professional teams can move the ball from one end of the court to the other with impressive speed. Passes fall into two categories: two-handed (which generally give the player more control and are easier to execute) and one-handed (which generate more power).

CHEST PASS

This easily controlled, two-handed pass is useful when a swift, accurate offload is required. It is commonly utilized when passing to a player who is positioned in front of a defender. The chest pass is effective over short or long distances.

SHOULDER PASS

The most frequently used one-handed pass, the shoulder pass is a good option when the player requires a long, direct transfer. It is often employed when defenders wish to clear the ball from their goal third.

BOUNCE PASS

This pass is perfect when the player is "crowded" and is often used by an attacker wishing to outmanoeuvre defenders. The two-handed pass offers disguise, while the one-handed pass allows the player to reach around defenders.

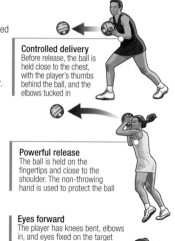

Controlled delivery
Before release, the ball is held close to the chest, with the player's thumbs behind the ball, and the elbows tucked in

Powerful release
The ball is held on the fingertips and close to the shoulder. The non-throwing hand is used to protect the ball

Eyes forward
The player has knees bent, elbows in, and eyes fixed on the target

STRATEGIES

Because the players are restricted to set areas, teamwork is vital: simply to move the ball from end to end the team must cooperate effectively. And with fourteen people on a relatively small court, efficient use of space is also important. Pre-planned strategies are one way in which to work effectively as a team and to best utilize the available court space.

THREE-OPTION ATTACK

This strategy gives the ball-holder (GD) three passing options. First is to pass to a player who has moved into space, in front of the defenders (WD). However, if this becomes unsafe, the second option is to pass to another player who has made a definite move (C). The third choice is a safety option (GK) – often a back pass to allow the attack time to regroup.

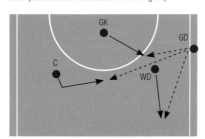

THREE-WAY TIE

THE 1979 WORLD CHAMPIONSHIPS, HELD IN TRINIDAD AND TOBAGO, FAMOUSLY DID NOT FEATURE A FINAL. AS A RESULT, THREE TEAMS – NEW ZEALAND, TRINIDAD AND TOBAGO, AND AUSTRALIA – SHARED THE TITLE.

DEFENSIVE PRESS

Defenders must apply constant pressure, anticipate attackers' movements, and close down the available space. One strategy that achieves all these aims is the defensive press, which involves a group of defenders moving into a specific court area to force an error and secure a turnover. This move can effectively break up free-flowing attacking play.

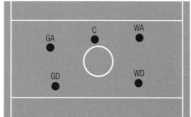

INSIDE STORY

In 1895 "women's basketball" was introduced to England, and it was here that the game was developed. There were no court markings then, and the players wore long skirts and sleeves. In 1901 the first recorded rules of netball were published. Travelling teachers and others propagated netball throughout the British Empire, and the sport became especially popular in New Zealand and Australia. In 1960 the International Federation of Women's Basketball and Netball was founded, and World Championships have been held every four years since 1963.

GOVERNING BODY

The International Netball Federation (INF), which is based in Manchester, England, is the governing body for netball. It is responsible for the rules of netball and claims more than 70 member nations. These countries are organized into five groups, each of which has a Regional Federation, which aids the implementation of INF policies.

KORFBALL

GAME OVERVIEW

Korfball claims to be the world's only truly mixed-gender team sport. It is played between two teams of four male and four female players, who pass a ball between each other by hand, with the ultimate aim of shooting it through the opposition's basket, or "korf". Korfball is played in more than 50 countries and is especially popular in Belgium and the Netherlands, where it originated.

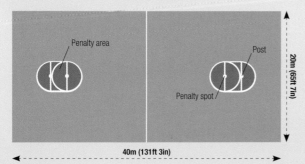

IN THE ZONE

The game is played on a rectangular court divided into two halves, or zones. Each zone features a post, with a korf at the top, surrounded by a shaded penalty area.

NEED2KNOW

→ Korfball was developed in the Netherlands, and the game takes its name from the Dutch word for basket – "korf".

→ Men and women play side by side, although defenders may only oppose players of their own sex.

GAME OF TWO HALVES

A korfball match consists of two halves of 30 minutes. Two men and two women from each team are positioned in each zone, and take up the role of attackers or defenders, depending on whether they are in their own or the opposition's half. Once there have been two goals scored in the game, each player's role reverses – defenders become attackers, and vice versa – and the teams attack the opposite ends.

Defenders may only oppose attackers of their own sex. They "defend" the attacker by standing between them and the korf, with one arm raised to block a shot. As goals may only be scored by an attacker when they are not being defended, they must take a shot before the opponent takes up their position. Taking a shot while being defended results in a free pass to the opposition, while defending an attacker of the opposite sex is a penalty offence.

DUTCH BASKET

Usually made of cane or synthetic material, the korf is fitted to the post, with its top edge positioned 3.5m (11ft 6in) above the ground.

Synthetic korf
This moulded korf is slotted onto the top of the post

Small soft ball
The ball is made of leather or synthetic material; men's diameter 18.5–19cm (7¼–7½in); women's 17–18cm (6¾–7in)

Digital strapping
Players often wear protective bands around their thumbs and fingers to prevent injury while trying to catch fast-moving balls

Sweat bands
These are not compulsory, but they are useful on hot indoor courts

Team strip
Players wear lightweight shirts and shorts or skirts made of cotton or viscose

Light shoes
Any kind of trainer or tennis-type shoe; must not mark the court

PLAYER PROFILE
Handball players must be able to run quickly in short bursts, and be capable of changing direction quickly in order to wrongfoot opponents. These are the skills they practise most often offcourt. Catching ability is also essential, together with a fast and accurate throw.

NEED2KNOW

→ Handball is one of Europe's most popular participation games, with up to 18 million regular players.

→ In Denmark, the sport rivals soccer for popularity with players and spectators.

→ Scores often reach as high as 30–30.

WHO PLAYS WHERE
In addition to the goalkeeper, teams usually comprise two wing players, a centre-left, a centre-right, and two centres, one of whom is primarily defensive, the other the playmaker. The outfielders' roles are fluid, and change according to the state of the game: references to 6–0, 5–1, and 4–2 (the number of attackers is always stated first) relate to the players' positions at a given moment of play, rather than throughout a match. The classic line-up is the 4–2 formation: four attackers and two defenders.

1 Keeper
May touch the ball with any part of the body as long as one foot is in the area

2 Wingers
Tend to operate along the touch lines, but cut inside on demand

3 Outlying centres
One is on the left, the other on the right, but they may alternate

4 Attackers
They focus on the opponents' goal but do not do all the scoring

COURT IN THE ACT
Since demand for handball courts exceeds supply, in many parts of the world the game is played on basketball courts, which are much more numerous. The two games are similar, with the same aim of scoring more goals than the other side. However, with an area of 420sq m (502sq yd), the basketball court is only slightly more than half the size of a dedicated handball arena, which is 800sq m (957sq yd). While organized competitive events are played indoors on designated courts, many informal games of team handball are played outdoors on flat areas of grass, paving, or beach, with a makeshift goal.

REICHS AND WRONGS
HANDBALL MADE ITS OLYMPIC DEBUT IN 1936 IN BERLIN, AT THE INSISTENCE OF ADOLF HITLER, WHO LOVED THE GAME. BECAUSE OF THIS UNHAPPY ASSOCIATION WITH THE NAZI DICTATOR, IT WAS DROPPED AFTER WORLD WAR II, BUT WAS REINTRODUCED AT MUNICH IN 1972.

GAME OVERVIEW
Handball developed in the late 19th century in Germany and Scandinavia. It is a fast and sometimes furious contact sport for men and women in which two teams of seven players (plus up to seven substitutes) bounce and pass a ball towards and ultimately into each other's goal. Players commonly bump into each other – deliberately, as well as accidentally. But they are allowed to do so only with their torsos – any attempt to grab or trip an opponent is a foul.

HANDBALL

Sub lines
The substitutes must sit on the side between these two stub markings

40m (131ft)

20m (65ft 6in)

Goal line
The markings should be 5cm (2in) thick between the outer posts and the corners, and 8cm (3⅓in) thick in the goalmouth

Goalie's restraining line
The keeper must not stand in front of it when facing a 7m throw

ULTIMATE OBJECTIVE
The goalposts and crossbar must be marked with alternating bands in two different colours that contrast with the offcourt surroundings; red and white are most often used.

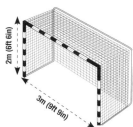

2m (6ft 6in)

3m (9ft 9in)

Seven-metre line
This is 1m (3ft 3in) long, parallel to the goal line, and centred on the middle of it; penalty throws, awarded for serious infringements, are taken from here

Free throw line
This is 9m (10yd) from the centre of the goal line, and runs parallel to it for 3m (9ft 9in) before curving in two 3m-radius circles, each centred on the nearer goalpost. Infringements inside it lead to a direct free throw at goal

Side lines
Anything on the line in handball counts as in play: the ball and the players have to cross it completely to be out

Six-metre line
This marks the outer edge of the goal area. The curves on either side are concentric with those of the free throw line

RIGHTS & WRONGS
Games are normally 30 minutes each way, with ten minutes' extra time and a sudden-death shootout from the seven-metre line if the scores are still level. Play begins with a throw-off – one player stands within 1.5m (5ft) of the centre of the court and passes the ball to a team-mate in the same half of the court. In open play, players normally hold the ball for only three seconds, and take only three steps with it, although there are many local variations to this rule. If the ball goes out of play, it is put back in with a throw-in at the spot where it crossed the line. Penalty throws – awarded for serious infringements, such as tripping – are taken from the seven-metre line; only the goalkeeper may defend them.

MANUAL METHODS
Speed of movement and passing are important, but when both teams are comparably fast, other skills come into play. One of the most important of these is feinting – making opponents think you're going to do one thing, and then, having wrongfooted them, doing another.

Seven o'clock
This angle of bounce helps close control

Two for one
By the time the ball returns to the hand, the player has made two strides

DRIBBLE
The player bounces the ball as he advances, and redirects it at the top of its upward flight with the downturned palm of his hand. Only he knows if he will go left, right, or straight on. (If he takes too many steps, though, possession is given to the other side.)

FIST
One basic passing movement in a punch with the fist clenched in the "thumbs up" position. The leg on the same side as the hand holding the ball is thrust forward, to make room for the swinging arm.

WRIST
The player creates the impression that he is either going to keep hold of the ball or pass to one side, but then, with an upward flick of the wrist, passes it from below his downturned palm in the opposite direction.

OVERHEAD PASS
Made on the run, this move requires the non-throwing arm to be outstretched (for balance and to provide a directional sighter). The left foot hits the ground at the moment the right hand releases the ball.

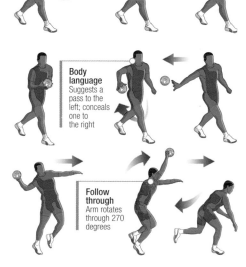

Clear swing
Both arms are held away from the body

Body language
Suggests a pass to the left; conceals one to the right

Follow through
Arm rotates through 270 degrees

→ Gaelic football is an exclusively
amateur game played mainly in
Ireland. It is also popular in Canada,
the United States, and other
countries with large populations
of Irish descent.

→ Matches are played in two 30-
minute halves at club level and
for women, and in two 35-minute
halves at county level.

SIDELINES

36 The highest number of wins
in the annual All-Ireland Gaelic football
competition, first held in 1887. The
holders of the record are County Kerry.

19 The number of counties
(out of 32) that have won the All-Ireland
competition. Two – Armagh and Derry
– have won it once only. An unlucky 13
have yet to lift the trophy.

TROUBLED HISTORY

DURING IRELAND'S TROUBLES,
GAELIC FOOTBALL WAS CLOSELY
LINKED WITH NATIONALISM. ON
21 NOVEMBER 1920, 14 FANS
WERE KILLED WHEN BRITISH
TROOPS OPENED FIRE AT A GAME
AT CROKE PARK, DUBLIN.

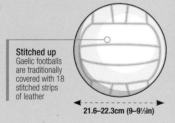

Stitched up
Gaelic footballs
are traditionally
covered with 18
stitched strips
of leather

◄- - - - - - - - - - - - - ►
21.6–22.3cm (9–9⅛in)

OBJECT OF ATTENTION
The ball is rather smaller than a soccer ball,
and thus easier to handle. The permitted
weight range is 450–485g (16–17oz).

PLAYER PROFILE

Gaelic footballers need to be fit,
athletic, muscular, and tough. They
must have good speed and stamina,
a sharp turn of pace, and finely honed
throwing and kicking skills. Players
regularly undertake weight training,
sprints, and long-distance runs.
Preparation for games involves work
on tactics with other members of
the team.

GAELIC FOOTBALL

GAME OVERVIEW

Played by both men and women, Gaelic football is a fast-moving,
physically punishing cross between soccer and rugby. Two teams of
15 players – and up to 15 substitutes, of whom five may be used
– aim to get a round ball under or over the crossbar of their opponents'
H-shaped goal. Players may kick or hand pass the ball to each other.
Once in possession of the ball, they may take no more than four steps
before either bouncing the ball or kicking it into their own hands in an
action known as soloing.

FIELD OF PLAY

The pitch and goals are the same as those used in hurling (see p.176), but some of
the pitch markings for hurling are covered over or disregarded during Gaelic football
matches. Traditionally, the game was played only on grass, but artificial surfaces
were introduced in the second half of the 20th century and are now widespread.

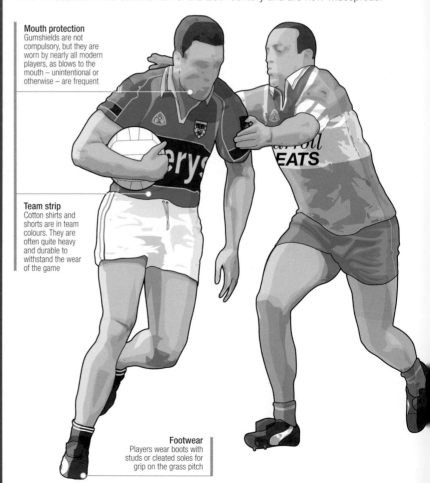

Mouth protection
Gumshields are not
compulsory, but they are
worn by nearly all modern
players, as blows to the
mouth – unintentional or
otherwise – are frequent

Team strip
Cotton shirts and
shorts are in team
colours. They are
often quite heavy
and durable to
withstand the wear
of the game

Footwear
Players wear boots with
studs or cleated soles for
grip on the grass pitch

TELLING SCORES

One point is awarded for putting the ball over the opposition's crossbar between the posts; a shot into the net counts as a goal, worth three points. Scores are recorded in two parts: goals scored then points total. For example, the 2010 All-Ireland Senior Final finished Cork 0–16 Down 0–15.

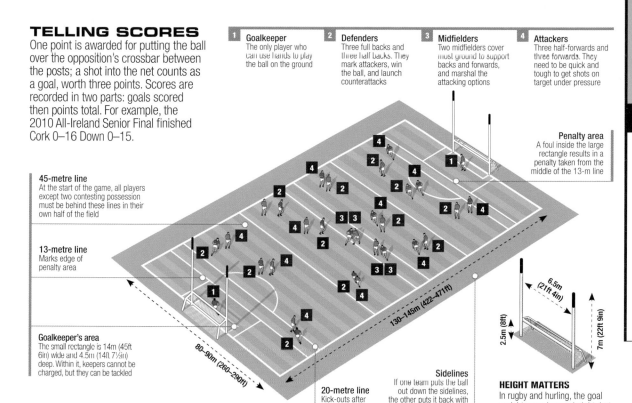

1 Goalkeeper
The only player who can use hands to play the ball on the ground

2 Defenders
Three full backs and three half backs. They mark attackers, win the ball, and launch counterattacks

3 Midfielders
Two midfielders cover most ground to support backs and forwards, and marshal the attacking options

4 Attackers
Three half-forwards and three forwards. They need to be quick and tough to get shots on target under pressure

Penalty area
A foul inside the large rectangle results in a penalty taken from the middle of the 13-m line

45-metre line
At the start of the game, all players except two contesting possession must be behind these lines in their own half of the field

13-metre line
Marks edge of penalty area

Goalkeeper's area
The small rectangle is 14m (45ft 6in) wide and 4.5m (14ft 7½in) deep. Within it, keepers cannot be charged, but they can be tackled

130–145m (422–471ft)

80–90m (260–290ft)

6.5m (21ft 4in)

2.5m (8ft)

7m (22ft 9in)

20-metre line
Kick-outs after scores are taken from this line

Sidelines
If one team puts the ball out down the sidelines, the other puts it back with a kick from the ground or from the hands

HEIGHT MATTERS
In rugby and hurling, the goal uprights may be any height, but Gaelic football rules stipulate the vertical dimensions shown.

THE BALL IN PLAY

Play begins with the referee throwing the ball up the centre of the pitch between two midfielders from each team. After a goal is scored, the keeper restarts play with a place kick from the edge of his or her area. If a defender puts the ball out at the end, an attacker takes a kick from the nearest point on the 45m line.

CROUCH LIFT

Apart from the goalkeeper, no one may play the ball on the ground with the hands. In the crouch lift, the player stoops down and uses a foot to scoop the ball into cupped hands facing backward. The ball can then be pulled up to the body.

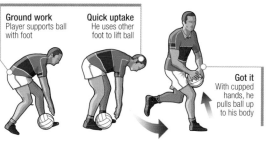

Ground work
Player supports ball with foot

Quick uptake
He uses other foot to lift ball

Got it
With cupped hands, he pulls ball up to his body

HAND PASS

One of the most common passes is to hit the ball with the side of the closed fist, using the knuckle of the thumb; a regular punch with the knuckles or forefingers is forbidden.

Aim and swing
The player eyes the intended target, and draws back his punching arm

Held Low
The ball is held low in the carrying hand

Hand over fist
The carrying hand is withdrawn at the same moment

HANDS AND FEET

Many of the skills are the same as those required in soccer and rugby, but there are three actions in Gaelic football not used in the other sports: crouch lift, hand pass, and solo.

GAINING POSSESSION

The ball may be won by tackling or by using both hands to block a kick.

Foot action
The player in possession goes for a kick…

Hand reaction
… but his opponent thrusts both arms in the path of the ball

SOLOING

A move unique to Gaelic football, soloing is a way of dribbling the ball without committing a foul. Players bounce the ball on the ground then "solo" up to four times, which means dropping the ball onto one foot and kicking it back up into their hands.

INSIDE STORY

Gaelic football is ancient in origin, but was first codified in 1885. It developed in part as Ireland's rejection of the "English" games of soccer and rugby. Today the game is played at club and county levels by male and female teams. The men's county final is broadcast live and attracts crowds of up to 80,000.

GOVERNING BODY

The Gaelic Athletic Association (GAA) was founded in 1884. Its main concerns are with the laws of Gaelic football and hurling.

GAME OVERVIEW

One of the fastest-moving of all team games, hurling is virtually the national sport in Ireland. Second only to soccer in popularity among players and spectators, more than half the country's population watch the annual county hurling competition. The 15-man teams aim to get the ball, or sliotar, into the opposition goal or over the crossbar using a curved stick known as a camán or hurley. Hurling, called iománaíocht or iomáint in Irish, is not quite the free-for-all it may appear: body checks and deliberate obstruction are banned.

HURLING

Headgear
Plastic helmets are compulsory at most levels of the game

Axe-shaped stick
A hurley is made of ash wood and is 70–100cm (27–39in) long

Sliotar
The leather-covered ball is made of cork or composite material; its diameter is 6.5cm (2½in)

Shinpads
Hurlers wear protection against blows to the legs

Football boots
Studded football boots are worn to provide grip on the pitch

PLAYER PROFILE
The game of hurling requires immense stamina, great physical strength, and a wide range of ball skills: the best players are often also good at other moving-ball games, such as soccer, and stationary ball games, such as golf.

GAME PLAY
A game has two halves of 30 minutes each (35 minutes for senior inter-county matches). When knockout matches are drawn, a replay is followed by extra-time of 10 minutes each way. Players use their hurley to pass or shoot, or to dribble the ball by bouncing it off the end of the stick and catching it. They can kick the ball, but they cannot pick it up off the ground, throw it, travel five steps holding it, catch it three times in a row without it touching the ground, or pass it from hand to hand.

OFFICIALS
Hurling has a number of officials: a referee on the pitch, two linesmen who indicate when the sliotar leaves the field of play, and four umpires to assist the referee and linesmen and to signal the scores.

FOULS
Technical infringements and dangerous tackles are punished by a "free"; a player uses his hurley to lift and strike the ball at the point where the offence occurred. If the referee is unsure of the culprit, he stops play and restarts it by throwing the ball between two opponents on the halfway line. A foul inside the large rectangle in front of the goal is punished with a penalty taken from the 20m (66ft) line.

ON THE FIELD
A hurling pitch is the same as the pitch for Gaelic football (see pp.174–175). The two 15-member teams take up set positions on the field of play, although these may change with coaches' tactics. Up to five substitutes are allowed during a match.

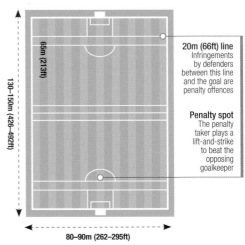

65m (213ft)

130–150m (426–492ft)

20m (66ft) line
Infringements by defenders between this line and the goal are penalty offences

Penalty spot
The penalty taker plays a lift-and-strike to beat the opposing goalkeeper

80–90m (262–295ft)

SCORING
Teams score a point for putting the sliotar over the crossbar and three for a goal (into the net). Scores are recorded in two parts: goals followed by the points total, so a 3-4 score equals 13 points.

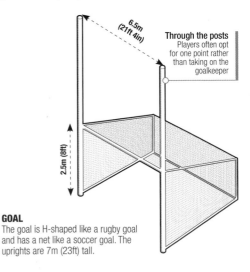

6.5m (21ft 4in)

Through the posts
Players often opt for one point rather than taking on the goalkeeper

2.5m (8ft)

GOAL
The goal is H-shaped like a rugby goal and has a net like a soccer goal. The uprights are 7m (23ft) tall.

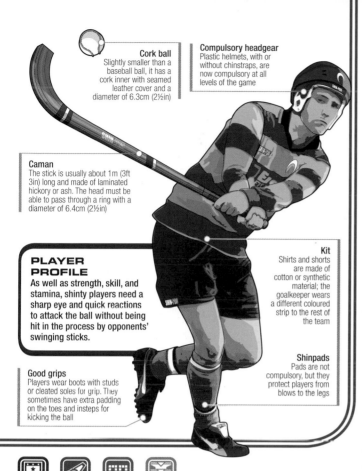

Cork ball
Slightly smaller than a baseball ball, it has a cork inner with seamed leather cover and a diameter of 6.3cm (2½in)

Compulsory headgear
Plastic helmets, with or without chinstraps, are now compulsory at all levels of the game

Caman
The stick is usually about 1m (3ft 3in) long and made of laminated hickory or ash. The head must be able to pass through a ring with a diameter of 6.4cm (2½in)

PLAYER PROFILE
As well as strength, skill, and stamina, shinty players need a sharp eye and quick reactions to attack the ball without being hit in the process by opponents' swinging sticks.

Good grips
Players wear boots with studs or cleated soles for grip. They sometimes have extra padding on the toes and insteps for kicking the ball

Kit
Shirts and shorts are made of cotton or synthetic material; the goalkeeper wears a different coloured strip to the rest of the team

Shinpads
Pads are not compulsory, but they protect players from blows to the legs

SHINTY

ON THE PITCH
The long edge of the pitch is called the sideline and the short edge is called the byline. The main on-field features are a centre circle, two semicircles, and two D-shaped areas around the goal.

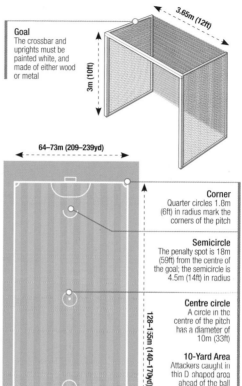

Goal
The crossbar and uprights must be painted white, and made of either wood or metal

3.65m (12ft)

3m (10ft)

64–73m (209–239yd)

Corner
Quarter circles 1.8m (6ft) in radius mark the corners of the pitch

Semicircle
The penalty spot is 18m (59ft) from the centre of the goal; the semicircle is 4.5m (14ft) in radius

Centre circle
A circle in the centre of the pitch has a diameter of 10m (33ft)

10-Yard Area
Attackers caught in this D shaped area ahead of the ball are offside

128–135m (140–170yd)

Goal line

GAME OVERVIEW
Shinty originated in the Highlands of Scotland, where it is known by Gaelic-speakers as camanachd or iomain. Two teams of 12 players (men or women) use hooked or curved sticks, called caman, to hit a ball towards and into each other's goal, or hail. Shinty is a rough and lightning-fast game that resembles field hockey and lacrosse (see pp.158–163). A shinty match is played in two halves; a 12-a-side game lasts 90 minutes, while a six-a-side game lasts 30 minutes.

ORGANIZED CHAOS
Shinty has relatively few rules. To start the game two opposing players cross sticks above their heads and the referee throws the ball into the air above them. Players usually stay in their positions so defence quickly turns to attack. Players can hit the ball while it is in the air, and use both sides of the stick; they can use their sticks to block and tackle opponents. Only the goalkeeper may handle the ball, but may only slap it with the flat of the hand.

INSIDE STORY
Shinty's major competition, the Camanachd Cup, is a knockout tournament that has been held every year since 1896, except during the two World Wars. There is also a league in Scotland, which is divided into North and South sections: the winners play each other in a grand final playoff for the national championship.

CAMANACHD ASSOCIATION
The Camanachd Association was formed as shinty's governing body in 1893. It oversees the game in Scotland and elsewhere, stressing its Celtic traditions, and encouraging indoor versions to bring children into the sport.

NEED2KNOW

→ Shinty is played almost entirely in Scotland. There is one club in England, and a handful in the United States.

→ Traditionally a winter game, in 2003 the shinty clubs of Scotland added a summer season from March to October.

→ Despite the best efforts of the governing body – the Camanachd Association – to codify the game internationally, there are still many local shinty rules.

Dodge ball ball
The ball is a low-pressure bladder, covered by a polyester fabric. Under this is a layer of foam to ensure shape retention and durability. The ball is 25cm (9in) in diameter

Trainers
Any lightweight training shoe that does not leave marks on the court

GAME OVERVIEW
Dodge ball is a thrilling six-a-side mixed, or single sexed ball game, where the object is to get opponents "out" by either hitting an opponent with a ball before it bounces, or by catching a thrown ball cleanly before it bounces. It is prohibited from hitting a player on the head. A game is over if one team's players are "out" or if the game-playing time expires. A match consists of 5–10 rounds. If the number of players on each team is equal, one additional minute of overtime is required. Overtime continues until there is a winner.

DODGE BALL

RUSH RULES
The referee starts play by placing three balls into the dead zone. Only three players can run to collect the balls to begin the game. Players then try to hit opponents, below the shoulders, with the ball to get them out. Play is continuous as each team try to hit opponents, but a player can rejoin the game if a team-mate catches a thrown ball. The ball can be passed three times between team-mates before being thrown, but it must be thrown within five seconds. The winner is the team with the most hits.

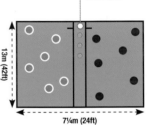

Dead zone
This is 0.6m (2ft) wide in the middle of the court

13m (42ft)

7¼m (24ft)

DOUBLE TEAMING
Dodge ball players are so good at ducking and weaving that cunning teamwork is needed to get them out. Strategies include the targeting of one opponent by a number of players on the other team to get them out.

NEED2KNOW

➡ If teams have the same number of players left in after five minutes, they play one-minute periods of sudden death overtime.

➡ The popularity of the game increased thanks to "Dodgeball: A True Underdog Story", a 2004 film starring Ben Stiller.

TUG OF WAR

EVENT OVERVIEW
In this trial of strength, two teams of eight men or women (and sometimes mixed teams) face each other and pull on opposite ends of a rope. The winner is the side that pulls the other team 4m (13ft), so that a central mark on the rope crosses a marked line. All matches are the best of three pulls.

PULLING TOGETHER
The judge gives three commands: "Pick up the rope"; "Take the strain", and after gesturing clearly that he is about to give the final order: "Pull!" The teams then tug on the rope with all their might, and throw their weight backwards as far as they can. But deliberately sitting on the ground, or failure to return immediately to the pulling position shall result in a caution. Two cautions are given prior to disqualification, however, a team can be disqualified without caution for any offence.

ROPE MARKS
The rope is at least 35m (115ft) in length. At its centre is a red mark. On either side of the rope's midpoint, and 4m (13ft) from it, are two white marks: the event is won by the team that pulls the other's white mark across the centre line on the ground. Another 1m (3ft 3in) towards the ends of the rope in both directions are blue marks: these are the foremost points at which the first pullers can grip the rope.

THE WEIGH-IN
To ensure even contests, tugs of war have strict weight divisions. In men's events, there are normally five categories: up to 560kg (1,234lb), 600kg (1,323lb), 640kg (1,411lb), 680kg (1,500lb), and 720kg (1,587lb) per team; for women the dividing lines are 480kg (1,058lb), 520kg (1,146lb), and 560kg (1,234lb). There is a weigh-in before each contest, and tuggers have their weight stamped on an easily visible part of their bodies – this is to help prevent illicit substitutions in mid-event.

NEED2KNOW

→ The discs used in this sport are made by several manufacturers, but the trade name Frisbee® has become generic, in the same way as "Hoover" is used to describe almost any vacuum cleaner.

→ The main governing body is the World Flying Disc Federation (WFDF). In the United States, the most important organization is the Ultimate Players Association (UPA).

→ Ultimate is most popular in the United States but is also played in more than 40 other countries.

GAME OVERVIEW

Ultimate is a seven-a-side game in which teams float a plastic disc, sometimes known as a Frisbee, to team-mates. A team score a point every time one of them catches the disc inside the end zone that they are attacking – first to 15 points wins. A thrower may pass the disc in any direction to any team-mate. Ultimate is self-refereed and the Spirit of the Game™ guides how players referee the game and how the players conduct themselves.

ULTIMATE

FLICKING RULES

One member of a team throwing the disc to the opposition (called the pull) starts the game. To score a point the disc must be caught in the opponent's end zone. Players must establish a pivot foot when in possession of the disc and can only move the disc by passing it to a team-mate. Failure to release the disc within 10 seconds, an incomplete pass, or interception forfeits possession.

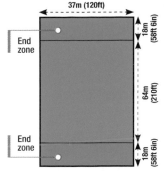

TO HAVE AND HAVE NOT

Since Ultimate is a non-contact sport, the team in possession has a huge advantage. The best that opponents can hope for is to force an error. To do this, they close down the stronger flank of the player with the disc, so that he or she can pass it only from their less favoured side. Below are three basic grips. Most backhands are mirror images played with bent elbows from the opposite side of the chest.

BASIC BACKHAND
This is the default grip for a righthanded player passing the disc from his or her offside flank.

CONTROL FOREHAND
Index and middle fingers make a V-sign; the thumb (hidden) points upwards like a hitchhiker's.

POWER FOREHAND
This is one of the holds used for passes that sacrifice directional control for speed and/or distance.

ARMY AT (TUG OF) WAR

THE TUG OF WAR IS HOTLY CONTESTED IN THE BRITISH ARMY, WHICH FIRST HELD INTERREGIMENTAL CONTESTS IN INDIA IN THE MID-19TH CENTURY, AND SINCE THEN VARIOUS PERIODICAL TRIALS OF STRENGTH AGAINST TEAMS FROM THE ROYAL NAVY AND THE ROYAL AIR FORCE. WHILE YOU MIGHT REASONABLY EXPECT THE CHAMPION ARMY TEAM TO BE MADE UP OF CRACK PARATROOPERS, IN FACT THE PARACHUTE SQUADRON IS ONLY THE SECOND BEST TEAM. PERHAPS SURPRISINGLY, THE TEAMS TO BEAT ARE THE MEDICAL REGIMENTS.

Anchor man
The rope passes alongside the body, diagonally across the back and over the opposite shoulder from rear to front. Only the anchor can hold the rope in this fashion

Bare hands
Pullers must grip the rope with their bare hands. The rope must pass beneath their upper arm

Get a grip
The rope is normally 10cm (4in) in circumference

Extended foot
Puller establishes a foothold with his extended foot before the pull begins

Flush soles
Tuggers wear boots with flush soles and heels. Metal toecaps and toe plates are barred, but metal heel tips are permitted as long as they are flush on the side and bottom

Planted foot
This plays the anchor role; players alternate feet as they draw their opponents backwards

RACKET
SPORTS

TENNIS

GAME OVERVIEW

Tennis in its modern form dates from 1874, when the game was codified by Major Walter Clopton Wingfield. Its basic principles, however, date back to the French jeu de paume (game of the palm), which came to prominence in the 12th and 13th centuries. It is now strictly known as "lawn tennis" to distinguish it from real (royal) tennis, but because the game is played on a variety of surfaces – grass, clay, cement, coated asphalt, carpet – "tennis" is the term most widely used. Both the men's and women's tours are split into different categories. The men's tour comprises four categories: Grand Slams, ATP, Challenger Series, and Futures tournaments.

NEED2KNOW

→ The Open Era of tennis began in 1968, when most world-class tournaments allowed professional players to enter the most prestigious tournaments.

→ The four Grand Slam competitions are the Australian, French, and US Opens, and Wimbledon. They are played on three different surfaces: hard-courts, clay, and grass.

→ Jimmy Connors is the only player to have won the US Open on three different surfaces: grass, clay and hardcourt.

A LOVE GAME

A PLAYER WHO HAS SCORED NO POINTS IN A GAME, OR NO GAME IN A SET IS SAID TO HAVE "LOVE". THIS MAY BE A CORRUPTION OF THE FRENCH WORD "OEUF" MEANING EGG, WHICH DESCRIBES THE SHAPE OF THE ZERO.

Sun protection
Players often play matches during the day in the summer, therefore visors and sunglasses may be worn on court to protect against the sun

Racket grip
The racket handle has eight sides that help the player to find the correct grip

Racket strings
The best players use strings made from animal gut. Synthetic gut strings will offer a combination of good control and durability

Shoes
Good quality shoes should be reinforced at the toe and at the side of the shoe to compensate for the scraping and sliding that occurs during the course of a match. The soles will differ depending upon the court surface

Tennis shorts
Men should always wear shorts, although the length is not specified, and women may also wear shorts, instead of a skirt

Clothing sponsor
Two manufacturer's logos, each not exceeding 12.9sq cm (2sq in), or one logo not exceeding 25.8sq cm (4sq in) are allowed on the front of the shirt

PLAYER PROFILE

Tennis players need high levels of energy and stamina. Play should be continuous – other than in exceptional circumstances, there should be no more than 90 seconds between games – and matches can last for up to four hours. They also need excellent hand-eye coordination to hit the ball well, strong powers of concentration, the ability to adapt to different court surfaces, and have the nerve to either close out a game or to hang in there when the game is going badly.

THE COURT

Although a tennis court is made of materials ranging from concrete, which is a fast-playing surface, to clay, which plays slower, its dimensions are invariable. Most courts are laid out for both singles and doubles, as shown on the opposite page. Some, however, are marked only for singles. Before the start of play, the officials or players must satisfy themselves that the net is the correct height and that its tension is acceptable. Many courts have now been fitted with electronic devices and large television screens to determine line calls and net calls, which increases the level of spectator involvement in matches.

SIDELINES

17 Unseeded outsider Boris Becker, aged 17 years, seven months, became the youngest ever Wimbledon champion. Becker was also the first German ever to win the title, and the first unseeded player to do so.

59 The number of Grand Slam titles won by Martina Navratilova during her career. Her titles were made up of 18 Singles, 31 Doubles, and 10 Mixed Doubles titles.

1337 The number of matches won by Jimmy Connors of the United States between 1972 and 1993, more than any other player in modern times. Of these victories, 109 were in title-winning finals.

156 The fastest serve recognized by the ATP – 251kph (156mph) – was delivered by Ivo Karlovic, while playing a Davis Cup match against Germany in March 2011.

665 The duration in minutes of the longest ever top-rank match, more than twice as long as the previous record. John Isner (USA) beat Nicolas Mahut (France) 6-4, 3-6, 6-7, 7-6, 70-68 over three days at Wimbledon in 2010.

81 The number of consecutive matches that Rafael Nadal won on clay between April 2005 and May 2007. Nadal's 81-match winning streak was an all-surface record.

Singles sideline
This line defines the singles court. Some courts are only marked with singles lines

Umpire's chair
The chair is raised off the ground for a better view of the court, and stands in between the player's chairs

Service line
The serve must land between the net and this line

Back court
This is the area between the service line and the baseline

Centre mark
This short mark protruding beyond the middle of the service line is an extension of the centre line; the server must stand to the right of it when serving into the deuce court (as shown), and to the left of it when serving into the advantage court

Court surround
No dimensions are stipulated in the rules, but there must always be sufficient space around the lined playing area for players to return wide-angled shots

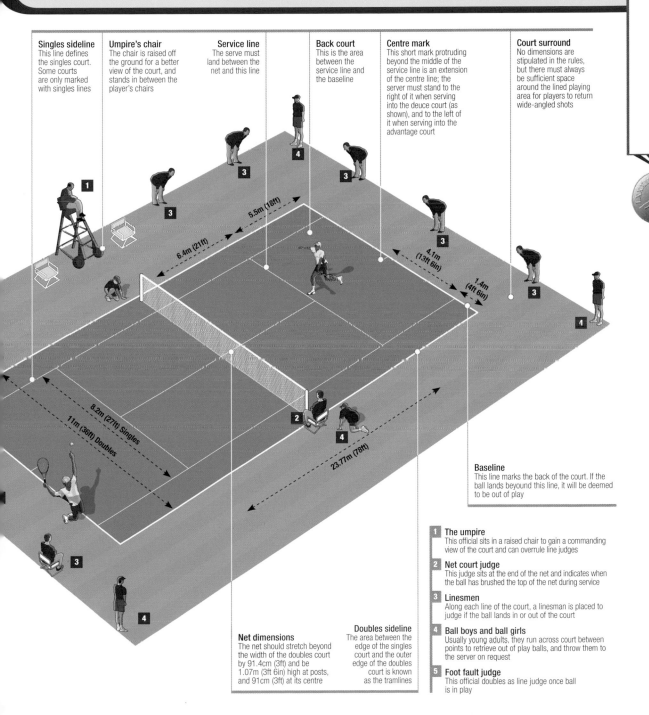

Baseline
This line marks the back of the court. If the ball lands beyound this line, it will be deemed to be out of play

1 The umpire
This official sits in a raised chair to gain a commanding view of the court and can overrule line judges

2 Net court judge
This judge sits at the end of the net and indicates when the ball has brushed the top of the net during service

3 Linesmen
Along each line of the court, a linesman is placed to judge if the ball lands in or out of the court

4 Ball boys and ball girls
Usually young adults, they run across court between points to retrieve out of play balls, and throw them to the server on request

5 Foot fault judge
This official doubles as line judge once ball is in play

Net dimensions
The net should stretch beyond the width of the doubles court by 91.4cm (3ft) and be 1.07m (3ft 6in) high at posts, and 91cm (3ft) at its centre

Doubles sideline
The area between the edge of the singles court and the outer edge of the doubles court is known as the tramlines

TENNIS ESSENTIALS

The International Tennis Federation (ITF) rules on which balls can be used for competiton, and on which surface they can be used. There are three different ball specifications. Type 1 is a fast ball, and must be used on a slow court; the Type 2 is a medium-paced ball, and is used on a medium- to fast-paced court; and the Type 3 ball is slow, and will be used on a fast paced court. The altitude also determines the choice of ball. The specifications of the tennis racket are also governed by the ITF, therefore manufacturers must produce rackets to a maximum length, width, and thickness. They must also be free of any device that can change the shape or physical property of the racket during a rally.

TENNIS BALL

Certain specifications must be met before a ball will be judged legal by the ITC. The ball shall have an outer surface of a fabric cover that should be white or yellow in colour. The ball's weight and size, will also be manufactured to a required specification. During a match the balls are replaced with new ones after an agreed odd number of games, usually after five, and then after seven.

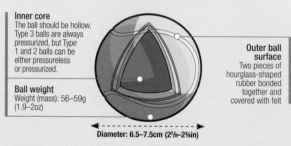

Inner core
The ball should be hollow. Type 3 balls are always pressurized, but Type 1 and 2 balls can be either pressureless or pressurized.

Ball weight
Weight (mass): 56–59g (1.9–2oz)

Outer ball surface
Two pieces of hourglass-shaped rubber bonded together and covered with felt

Diameter: 6.5–7.5cm (2⅝–2¾in)

THE RACKET

Whereas the ITF can govern the overall size of the racket, it cannot determine its construction. Tennis racket frames have changed a lot in recent years, as stiffer carbon materials have replaced wood and metal. Carbon rackets generate a lot of power because they are not flexible, so choosing the right strings and stringing tension is crucial to aid ball control.

PLAYING THE GAME

Before a match, a coin is tossed and the winner chooses whether to serve or receive first, and the end that they want to start the match from. Players stand on opposite sides of the net; the server (the player who puts the ball in to play) begins the rally by hitting the ball over the net, in to the service court directly opposite, from the right of the centre line, and from behind the baseline. The server plays the ball from alternate sides of the centre line throughout the game, starting from the right. The receiver may stand anywhere on their own side of the net, but may not return the ball before it has bounced. After the ball is served, play continues until one player hits the ball out of play.

POINTS

Each player starts with "love" (zero); one point is called "15"; two points are "30", three points are "40". 40-all is known as "deuce". After deuce, the player who wins the next point is said to have "advantage"; if they win the next point, the game is over. If they don't, the score goes back to "deuce". At this point, the game will only be won when one player has won two successive points, the "advantage" point, and the "game" point. Players change ends at the end of every odd-numbered game.

WINNING A SET

Matches are the best of three or five sets. (Women only ever play the best of three sets.) The first player to win six games wins the set, but if the games go to 5-all, the set is extended to see if a two-game margin can be achieved (7-5, for example). If, however, the score reaches six games apiece, the tie-break system might come into operation.

TIE-BREAK

During a tie-break game, points are scored "0" to "7". The first player to win seven points, provided there is a margin of two points, wins the game and set. The player whose turn it is to serve, serves the first point, and the following two points are served by the opponent.

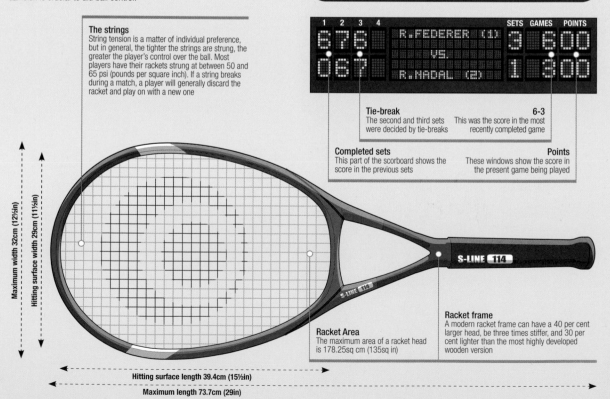

The strings
String tension is a matter of individual preference, but in general, the tighter the strings are strung, the greater the player's control over the ball. Most players have their rackets strung at between 50 and 65 psi (pounds per square inch). If a string breaks during a match, a player will generally discard the racket and play on with a new one

Tie-break
The second and third sets were decided by tie-breaks

6-3
This was the score in the most recently completed game

Completed sets
This part of the scoreboard shows the score in the previous sets

Points
These windows show the score in the present game being played

Maximum width 32cm (12½in)

Hitting surface width 29cm (11½in)

Racket Area
The maximum area of a racket head is 178.25sq cm (135sq in)

Racket frame
A modern racket frame can have a 40 per cent larger head, be three times stiffer, and 30 per cent lighter than the most highly developed wooden version

S-LINE 114

Hitting surface length 39.4cm (15½in)

Maximum length 73.7cm (29in)

TENNIS TECHNIQUES

The most important and most used shots in modern tennis are the serve, and the forehand and backhand, otherwise known as groundstrokes. Until these strokes are mastered the player will struggle to win points and compete in matches. The serve starts every point in a match, and a good server is considered to have an advantage. This is partly because this player has two chances to get the ball in to play, and partly because the opponent doesn't necessarily know where the ball will go. Groundstrokes are the basic shots you make once the point has begun and are usually played from near the baseline and after the ball has bounced. They can be played with different types of spin; topspin and slice being the most used.

SLICE BACKHAND

The backhand can be played with either topspin or slice (backspin). Hitting sliced backhands is most effective when playing matches on fast courts, were the ball skids through at speed. It is also used when playing defensive shots on the run, or where the ball is above shoulder height.

Making contact
The player swings the racket out to the side using a high to low motion to impart backspin, while remaining sideways-on

Following through
The racket makes a down-to-up U-shaped motion, with the racquet face facing upwards

Shot preparation
The player should turn sideways-on, with the racket arm slightly bent, by turning the shoulders while making the backswing. Holding the racket with the free hand helps to turn the shoulders. The player should raise the racket higher than the ball

THE FOREHAND

The forehand is the most used shot in tennis, and the one that most poeple learn first. This major groundstroke, for both the beginner and the advanced player, will allow a player to control a rally from the back of the court. The shot is usually hit with topspin, but backspin, and sidespin can both be applied to the ball.

THE SERVE

A good serve will help the player win there service games easily, so the more force there is behind it, the better. Practise it as much as possible for consistency.

The ball toss
Tossing the ball upwards, the player's arm is extended as much as possible. The shoulders are sideways on before the swing is started

Hitting the ball
The player raises the racket and starts to swing it. Then, while bending the knees, drops the racket behind the back. The player pushes up with the legs and rolls the right shoulder forward to hit the ball

Wrist action
The player snaps the wrist down to generate ball speed

Starting position
Standing sideways behind the baseline, the player's feet are shoulder-width apart

Finishing position
The player lands on the inside leg, and should not over-balance

On the move
The player moves forward to play the low forehand, while making a half-turn sideways, and beginning the backswing. The circular swinging action is made by rotating the shoulders

Racket speed
The player ensures the racket is below the level of the ball, swinging the racket from a low to a high position, and accelerating the racket. The player lifts the racket when contact has been made, to control the ball

Shifting the weight forward
The player bends the knees to hit the ball at the highest point. When swing upwards, the player's bodyweight is transfered to the front leg to get power into the swing

THE LOB

The lob – a shot that goes high in the air – may be defensively or aggressively played. Offensive lobs are hit with topspin from around the baseline. The more topspin the player is able to get on the ball, the faster the ball will drop in to the court, which means the player can hit a deeper lob. Volleying players often close in after hitting their first volley, and this is an ideal time to use the lob. Defensive lobs are usually hit with backspin or very little spin, as they are used when the ball is low, or wide, when little or no topspin is possible.

JUST A GAME

ON 30 APRIL 1993 MONICA SELES WAS STABBED BY GUNTHER PARCHE WHILE SEATED DURING A CHANGEOVER. WHY DID HE DO THIS? PARCHE WANTED TO INJURE SELES SO THAT HIS IDOL, STEFFI GRAF, COULD REGAIN TOP SPOT IN THE WORLD RANKINGS.

SMASHING TIME

A smash is an aggressive volley played overhead. It is often a response to a lob that has failed to clear the player's head. A smash requires good footwork to ensure that the ball is played down into the opponent's court; any error of judgement may result in an air shot (missing the ball altogether) or a wild hit out of court.

LOB SCENARIO

Player A has advanced to the net but has played the ball too short. Because of this Player B has two options. He can either play a passing shot, or he can play a lob. It is best, whenever possible, to play the lob over the opponent's backhand side, as it produces the weaker shot if attempted. When in control of the rally, hide the intention to lob until the last possible moment as this will put the opponent on the back foot in future exchanges.

Hitting the lob
Player B plays an offensive lob with topspin to control the ball, and to keep the ball in court

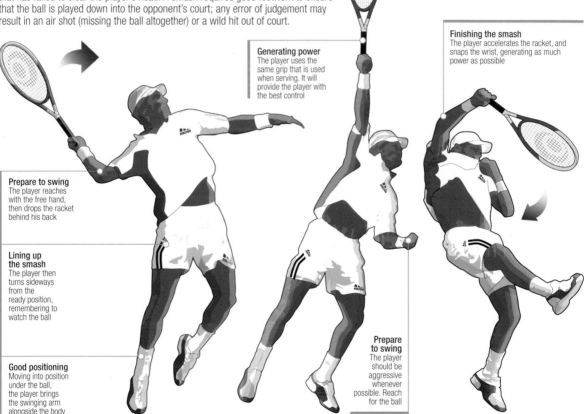

Generating power
The player uses the same grip that is used when serving. It will provide the player with the best control

Finishing the smash
The player accelerates the racket, and snaps the wrist, generating as much power as possible

Prepare to swing
The player reaches with the free hand, then drops the racket behind his back

Lining up the smash
The player then turns sideways from the ready position, remembering to watch the ball

Good positioning
Moving into position under the ball, the player brings the swinging arm alongside the body

Prepare to swing
The player should be aggressive whenever possible. Reach for the ball

SIDELINES

14 Serena and Venus Williams have both won the US Open title without losing a set. To achieve this feat they won 14 sets without conceding one, from the first round to the final. This has happened only 24 times in the history of the Open.

8 The number of left-handed players to have won a Wimbledon singles title during the Open era – the most recent being Petra Kvitová in 2011.

210 The record for the fastest serve by a woman is held by Sabine Lisicki, who achieved a speed of 210kph (130.5mph) in 2009.

EXHIBITION MATCHES

On 2 May 2007 at the Palma Arena, Majorca, Rafael Nadal, the king of clay, played grass champion Roger Federer on a half-clay half-grass court in an exhibition match dubbed "the battle of the surfaces". Playing on a court that cost $15,000,000 to construct, the Spaniard Nadal prevailed 7-5, 4-6, 7-6 (12-10). The organisers had to lay a brand new surface on the grass side of the court a few days before the event because an infestation of worms made the original turf unusable. During the match, the changeovers were extended to two minutes to give the players a chance to change their footwear for each surface.

COURT SURFACES

The governing body of tennis, the ITF (International Tennis Federation) has identified three different categories of court surface. The categories are based on the speed of the ball after the bounce; the amount of spin on the ball after contact with the surface; the height of the bounce, and the level of traction the court gives the player. Category 1 courts are slow paced: Category 2 surfaces are medium, or medium-fast paced hard-courts, and Category 3 courts are fast-paced surfaces.

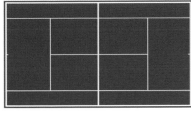

CLAY COURT: CATEGORY 1
Examples include most clay courts. Rallies on this surface tend to last a long time, as the speed of the ball after the bounce is relatively slow. Players can also slide on clay, increasing their reach.

HARD-COURT (DECOTURF): CATEGORY 2
This surface has the same characteristics as the Rebound Ace court. Its top surface uses a different type of sand. Aggressive groundstoke play is the most dominant style of play on category 2 surfaces.

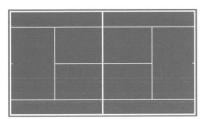

HARD-COURT (REBOUND ACE): CATEGORY 2
These are hard-courts, which are concrete or asphalt coated with synthetic rubber. The top layer is reinforced acrylic paint mixed with sand. The ball bounces true, to a medium height.

GRASS COURT: CATEGORY 3
Natural grass and artificial turf surfaces fall into this category and are characterized by their low, skidding, and often irregular, bounce. Players look to finish points as soon as possible.

TENNIS TECHNOLOGY

Electronic review technology, a high-speed multi-camera system which tracks the trajectory of a moving ball, was first used in a grand slam during the 2006 US Open at Flushing Meadow. Its success has led other grand slams adopting this system, with both the Australian Open, and Wimbledon first using the system in 2007. At the US and Australian Opens, each player is allowed to make two challenges per set and one during a tie-break. If proved right the player retains their quota of challenges.

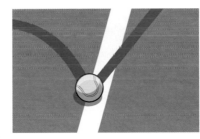

HAWK-EYE
An instant replay of the contested point is shown on large screens allowing both the players and the crowd to see whether the ball was judged in or out by review technology, Hawk-Eye.

INSIDE STORY

The most common view is that it was a crude courtyard ball game invented by 11th or 12th century French monks. The name tennis is said to come from the French word "tenez", from the verb tenir meaning "to take". It means, "take this", which the monks would yell as they served the ball with their hand.

INTERNATIONAL FEDERATION
The International Tennis Federation (ITF) is the rulemaker and governing body of world tennis. Its membership comprises more than 200 national associations.

PLAYER'S ASSOCIATION
The Association of Tennis Professionals (ATP) was formed in 1972 to protect the interests of male professional tennis players. The Women's Tennis Association (WTA) launched in 1973.

STAT CENTRAL

GRAND SLAM SINGLES WINNERS (MEN)

NAME	WON/LOST
ROGER FEDERER (SUI)	17/7
PETE SAMPRAS (USA)	14/4
ROY EMERSON (AUS)	12/3
ROD LAVER (AUS)	11/6
BJORN BORG (SWE)	11/5
RAFAEL NADAL (ESP)	11/5
BILL TILDEN (USA)	10/5
IVAN LENDL (CZE/USA)	8/11
KEN ROSEWALL (AUS)	8/8

GRAND SLAM SINGLES WINNERS (WOMEN)

NAME	WON/LOST
MARGARET SMITH COURT (AUS)	24/5
STEFFI GRAF (GER)	22/9
HELEN WILLS MOODY (USA)	19/3
CHRIS EVERT (USA)	18/16
MARTINA NAVRATILOVA (CZE/USA)	18/14
SERENA WILLIAMS (USA)	15/4
BILLIE JEAN KING (USA)	12/6
MONICA SELES (YUG/USA)	9/4
MAUREEN CONNOLLY BRINKER (USA)	9/0

MEN'S GRAND SLAM WINNERS

PLAYER (COUNTRY)	YEAR
ROD LAVER (AUS)	1962, 1969
DON BUDGE (USA)	1938

WOMEN'S GRAND SLAM WINNERS

PLAYER (COUNTRY)	YEAR
STEFFI GRAF (GER)	1988
MARGARET SMITH COURT (AUS)	1970
MAUREEN CONNOLLY BRINKER (USA)	1953

ATP PRIZE MONEY LEADERS ($)

NAME	CAREER EARNINGS
ROGER FEDERER (SUI)	$76,583,434
RAFAEL NADAL (ESP)	$50,190,237
NOVAK DJOKOVIC (SRB)	$48,246,016
PETE SAMPRAS (USA)	$43,280,489
ANDRE AGASSI (USA)	$31,152,975
ANDY MURRAY (GBR)	$26,214,181
BORIS BECKER (GER)	$25,080,956
YEVGENY KAFELNIKOV (RUS)	$23,883,797
IVAN LENDL (USA)	$21,262,417
ANDY RODDICK (USA)	$20,637,390
STEFAN EDBERG (GER)	$20,630,941
GORAN IVANISEVIC (CRO)	$19,878,007
LLEYTON HEWITT (AUS)	$19,425,179
MICHAEL CHANG (USA)	$19,145,632
DAVID FERRER (SPA)	$17,705,519

PLAYER PROFILE

Real tennis requires many of the same skills needed to play lawn tennis, although the service depends much more on spin and placement than raw power. The real tennis court is hard, and as many shots involve "digging" low-bouncing balls, the game's greatest physical demands are on the legs and knees.

Court clothing
Cotton dress or polo shirts and shorts or skirts; some clubs require players to wear white

THE COURT

No two real tennis courts are the same, but they all have certain features in common. The playing area is enclosed by four walls and a ceiling. Three of the walls have sloping roofs, known as penthouses. There is a service end and a receiving, or "hazard", end. The wall on the server's left has various windows, which are both viewing galleries and openings into which the ball can be played. The wall behind the server has a similar window that is both a viewing point for spectators and the "dedans", into which the receiver tries to drive shots beyond the server in order to gain the serve. On the receiver's side of the net are a buttress, known as a "tambour", and a grille.

Match ball
The ball has a yellow or white covering of hand-sewn felt around a core of cork wrapped in fabric tape, and has a diameter of 6.4cm (2½in). It is heavier and less bouncy than a lawn tennis ball

Real racket
This is made of wood and has very tight strings. The head is angled slightly to one side to make it possible to play shots off the floor or in the corners. Its overall length is about 70cm (27in)

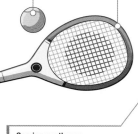

Winning gallery
Any shot from the service end into these windows is a winner

Service penthouse
The server must send the ball along this roof to the hazard end

Service end
Spectators viewing through the dedans behind the server are protected by a net

Floor chase line
Lines painted on the playing floor are used to measure where the ball drops during a "chase", when players strive to gain the service end

9.8m (32ft)

NEED2KNOW

→ There are only about 50 courts in the world, so real tennis is one of the most exclusive of all sports.

→ Professionals compete in annual real tennis Grand Slam events – the Australian, British, French, and US Opens – and a biennial World Championship.

→ The outstanding player in the history of real tennis is Robert Fahey of Australia, who won his eleventh world title in 2012, four more than Pierre Etchebaster of France who won eight titles between 1928 and 1952.

GAME OVERVIEW

The precursor of modern lawn tennis (see pp.182–87), real tennis is an indoor racket sport played by two people (singles) or two teams of two (doubles). The object is to hit the ball over a central net so that it cannot be returned. With a history going back hundreds of years, the game reached the height of its popularity in the 16th and 17th centuries. Although real tennis now has an elitist image, any tennis club with a real tennis court will welcome members who wish to have a go. Many leading real tennis professionals were formerly lawn tennis players.

REAL TENNIS

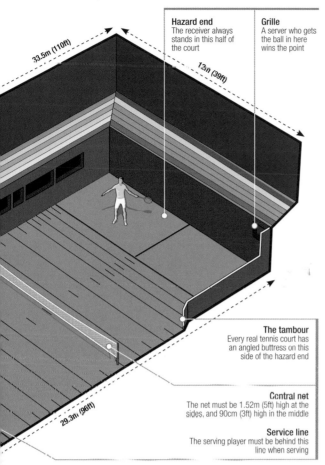

Hazard end
The receiver always stands in this half of the court

Grille
A server who gets the ball in here wins the point

33.5m (110ft)

12m (39ft)

29.3m (96ft)

The tambour
Every real tennis court has an angled buttress on this side of the hazard end

Central net
The net must be 1.52m (5ft) high at the sides, and 90cm (3ft) high in the middle

Service line
The serving player must be behind this line when serving

CHASING THE GAME

The server (usually chosen by spinning a racket) plays from one end of the court only. In a service, the ball must bounce at least once on the lefthand penthouse on the receiver's side of the court (the hazard end).

Service does not alternate between the players as in lawn tennis; the receiver has to gain the right to serve. It takes four points to win a game, and six games to win a set (even if the score reaches five-all: there is no tiebreaker). Matches are the best of three or five sets.

The server has two areas in which to place the ball to win a point. These are the winning gallery and the grille. The receiver has a large area, called the "dedans", behind the server, into which he or she can hit a clean winner.

Players do not automatically lose a rally if the ball bounces twice in their half of the court. Instead, the score remains the same, but the players change ends and replay the rally. The player who originally failed to get to the ball then has to try and send a shot that bounces twice further back from the net than the first missed shot. This part of the game is known as a "chase" if it results from the server's failure to return the ball, and a "hazard chase" if it stems from the receiver's error.

Measurement of distance is aided by the lines drawn 90cm (36in) apart from side to side of the court.

LOOKING FOR ANGLES

Spin is a major feature of real tennis – because of it, some of the slowest shots can be the hardest to return. However, the main aim of the game is to produce forcing strokes off or into the court's architectural features. A shot onto or off the tambour is often hard to reach because the ball rebounds off it unpredictably. Strokes played into the "nick" (the corner of the floor and the wall) and aggressive drives into the dedans, the winning gallery, or the grille are unreturnable.

SOFT TENNIS

GAME OVERVIEW

This is a form of regular lawn tennis that can be played on indoor or outdoor courts. What makes it different is the soft, squishy ball, which means that the game is characterized by long rallies rather than by powerhouse shots.

NEED2KNOW

➡ The game's greatest strongholds are in Japan and Taiwan, but its appeal is spreading among people who have tired of serve-and-volley "big gun" tennis.

➡ Due to its popularity in Asia, soft tennis has been an official sport at the Asian Games since 1994.

RULE RÉSUMÉ

Serves can be underarm or overarm; scoring in games is the same as in lawn tennis. Singles matches are the best of seven games, doubles the best of nine. Tiebreaks come into operation at 3–3 and 4–4. Grunting is expressly forbidden!

Any racket you like
The surface must be the same on both sides, but apart from that, almost anything goes. Rackets can be any shape or size, be made of any material, and weigh as much or as little as players want; the strings are similarly unrestricted, as long as they do not make the ball fly off completely unpredictably

Ball requirements
Should be made of rubber, filled with air, and be 6.6cm (2½in) in diameter. The International Soft Tennis Federation stipulates that the balls should be "white in principle", but in practice they are often yellow, and sometimes red

TABLE TENNIS

GAME OVERVIEW

Also known as ping-pong, table tennis is a fast-moving and physically demanding racket game. Men and women play as individuals or in pairs. Players win points by hitting a lightweight ball over a net so that their opponents either cannot return it or are forced into an error. Most matches are short and sharp, and the rules have ways of dealing with games that go on too long.

PLAYER PROFILE

Table tennis players need fast reactions, exceptional hand-eye coordination, and strong and flexible leg muscles. They need to be able to move quickly over short distances, and to change direction in an instant. They must take particular care of their shoulders, lower backs, and knees: these are the areas that are most commonly injured. Away from the table, players typically practise with jumping sessions, squats, short sprints, and at least three 20-minute runs per week.

TABLE TERRAIN

Tables are made of Masonite or a similar manufactured hardwood, and layered with a smooth, low-friction coating. They are usually dark green, but may be dark blue or black. The net extends 15.25cm (6in) beyond the edge of the table on both sides. The centre line indicates where the service must land in doubles: it should bounce in the right-hand courts of both server and receiver (in singles, it can land anywhere on the table).

PLAYING A MATCH

Matches are the best of five or seven games. Each game is won by the first side to reach 11 points or, from 10-10, two clear points. Play begins when one player serves the ball by throwing it up at least as high as the net and then striking it with the bat. The ball must be thrown from an open palm to rule out finger spin. The ball must bounce twice – once on each side of the net – before being returned by the other player. Thereafter, in open play, the ball may bounce only once per shot, on the receiver's side of the net.

If the ball touches the net during a service but then lands on the receiver's side, a let is played, and the server serves again. A player serves for two points, after which it is the opponent's turn. Players swap ends after each game.

15.25cm (6in)

2.75m (9ft)

1.5m (5ft)

76cm (2ft 6in)

101

Leaving no trace
A player's shoes must have soles that do not mark the floor surface

THAT WAY WE CAN ALL GO HOME

THE FINAL OF THE 1936 SWAYTHLING CUP – THE MEN'S TEAM TABLE TENNIS WORLD CHAMPIONSHIP – WAS BETWEEN HUNGARY AND AUSTRIA, AND THE MATCH DEVELOPED INTO A MARATHON THAT LASTED FOR THREE DAYS. IN ORDER TO PREVENT FURTHER STALEMATES, WHICH RISKED KILLING THE GAME AS A SPECTATOR SPORT, THE LAWMAKERS BROUGHT IN WHAT IS KNOWN AS THE EXPEDITE RULE: IF A GAME GOES ON FOR LONGER THAN 10 MINUTES, SERVERS THEN LOSE POINTS IF THEY CANNOT BEAT THEIR OPPONENTS IN FEWER THAN 13 SHOTS FOLLOWING EACH SERVICE.

TABLE MANNERS

It is legal to hit the ball around the side of the net to land on the opponent's side. Volleying is not allowed: the ball has to touch the table. A player who touches the playing surface with his or her free hand during a rally loses the point.

In doubles matches, players strike the ball in turn – no one may make two consecutive shots. As a result, doubles players must switch positions quickly so that the next receiver is standing in front of the centre line. That location gives the player the best chance of hitting the ball, whichever side of the table it lands on.

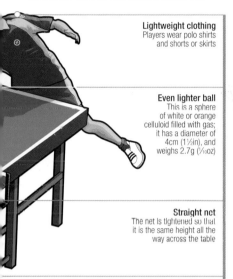

Lightweight clothing
Players wear polo shirts and shorts or skirts

Even lighter ball
This is a sphere of white or orange celluloid filled with gas; it has a diameter of 4cm (1½in), and weighs 2.7g (⅒oz)

Straight net
The net is tightened so that it is the same height all the way across the table

On the edge
A ball touching any part of the top of the table, including the white edges, is "in"

SPEED RESTRICTIONS
One form of table tennis aims to slow the game down. The "hardbat" game is seen as a return to classic table tennis. Sponge-faced bats are not permitted, making it harder to spin the ball. Instead players concentrate on ways to draw their opponents out of position before they can hit a winner.

INSIDE STORY

The game was inspired by 19th-century lawn tennis players, who in bad weather practised indoors using cigar-box lids as bats, the rounded tops of champagne corks as balls, and a row of books for a net. This early game had a number of names, including whiff-whaff.

INTERNATIONAL TABLE TENNIS FEDERATION
This was founded in 1926 by Austria, England, Germany, and Hungary. It now has 217 member organizations.

GETTING TO GRIPS WITH IT

There are many ways of holding a table tennis bat, but most grips fall into one of two categories: the orthodox or shakehand grip and the penholder. There is also a V-grip, in which the blade is held between the index and middle fingers.

WOODEN BAT
Also known as a racket, the bat has a blade that is made mainly of five-ply wood. It may be any weight or size, and the shape may be square, oval, or round. The rubber coverings on both sides must be no more than 4mm (⅕in) thick.

FRONT VIEW

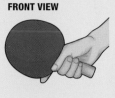

BACK VIEW

Rubber surface
Uniquely, the front and back of the bat may be of different thickness and texture – smooth or dimpled. Opposite sides must have different colours

SHAKE HAND GRIP
This is the most natural, and hence the most popular, way of holding a table tennis bat.

PENHOLDER GRIP
The handle is clasped between thumb and forefinger in the same way as holding a pen.

SHOTS AND SPINS

Strength of shot plays an important role in table tennis, but the key in the modern game is spin. The ball is so light that almost anyone can make it rotate in the air and so bounce in an unpredictable way on the receiver's side; the skill is to conceal the amount and type of spin used.

BACKSPIN
Backspin is applied by hitting through and under the ball with the lower part of the bat angled ahead of the upper section. The aim is to make the ball slow down and "die" (bounce as little as possible) on contact with the table.

Arc of stroke
The shot is played with a downward slashing motion

FOREHAND SMASH
This is one of the most devastating shots in any player's armoury, in which the ball is hit at high speed. As well as adding topspin, the player can conceal in which direction the ball will travel by flicking his wrist to direct the ball across the table.

Top up
The upper edge of the bat is angled forwards

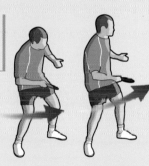

BACKHAND TOPSPIN
The basic technique is the reverse of the backspin shot: the bat is slanted so that the top is further ahead of the player than the bottom. Topspin stops the ball rising too high into the air. Instead it dips quickly onto the receiver's side and has a low bounce, making it harder to return.

The lowdown
Grounded heels and bent knees help the player to keep the shot low

BADMINTON

GAME OVERVIEW

Badminton is a game for singles and doubles. Players win points by hitting a conical shuttlecock over a high net so that it lands on the other side of the court before the opposition can return it. The shuttlecock's lightness and aerodynamic shape means that badminton can be a game of great delicacy, or sudden bursts of power featuring spectacular smashes.

PLAYER PROFILE
A top badminton player covers about 1.6km (1 mile) per game, so strong thigh and calf muscles are essential. Sprinting is a key element of training. Another essential skill is footwork: athletes practise sudden changes of direction and sharp acceleration over short distances. The shuttle moves through the air quite differently from a ball, so strokeplay is unlike that of any other racket sport. It can only be improved by playing the game.

What a racket
Pro-level rackets are made from carbon fibre composite, which is stiff, stong, and light, weighing as little as 75g (2½oz). Modern strings are usually synthetic

THE COURT
The surface of a badminton court consists of a sprung, often plywood, floor beneath a vinyl covering or strips of treated hardwood. The surface is marked with lines that define the playing areas for both singles and doubles games. The shuttle travels very fast but not very far, so the playing area is compact and suitable for venues with limited space.

Light clothing
Lightweight cotton shirts and shorts or skirts keep the players cool

All in the legs
Covering the court and leaping for high shots requires powerful thigh muscles

Supporting role
Bandages are often worn to support the knees, which can jar as a player lands and turns on the court

Leave no trace
Badminton players wear non-marking rubber-soled shoes and almost always have socks to prevent blisters

NEED2KNOW

→ After football, badminton is the second-most popular participation sport in the world. It is particularly popular in Malaysia and Indonesia.

→ With the shuttlecock travelling at up to 332kph (206mph), badminton is the fastest racket game in the world.

SIDELINES

16 The number of goose feathers on an Olympic shuttlecock.

332 The highest recorded speed in kph (206mph) of a shuttlecock during a competitive match.

13.5 The average number of shots per rally in a game of badminton. Tennis rallies are comparatively short, with an average of 3.4 shots per rally.

42 The percentage of badminton gold medals won by China – for men's and women's singles and doubles, and mixed doubles – since the sport became an Olympic event in 1992.

JIANZI

GAME OVERVIEW

Jianzi, or shuttlecock, is played indoors and outdoors by individuals, pairs, or teams of men and women who propel a jianzi or chapteh (shuttle) to each other using any part of their body but their arms or hands. Points are won for successful passes and lost for letting the shuttle touch the ground.

ANY AREA

Some forms of jianzi are played on badminton courts, and competitors have to get the chapteh over the net every time they play it. In other versions there is a line instead of a net. It is also possible to play without a defined playing area. Such casual games, which resemble soccer keepy-uppy, are a familiar sight in parks in many Asian countries, where they are a popular form of exercise for all ages.

TEAM GAME

In individual matches, players may have two successive hits of the chapteh. In the team game, each side has a total of four hits. Teams may contain any number of players but usually have six, of whom three are on the court at any one time; the others are substitutes. The winning score is usually 21 points.

FANCY FOOTWORK

Players can do anything with the chapteh except touch it with their hands or arms, but in matches they mainly use their feet. A player usually takes a first touch to bring the shuttle under control, and a second to pass to a team-mate or hit it back over the net. They most often use their insteps but might also flick the shuttle up with the tops of their toes or slam it over the net with the sole of the foot in a "snake kick". Receivers sometimes block the chapteh at the net with their chest, playing it down on to the floor on the opponent's side to win a point.

Jianzi wear
The normal gear is lightweight (usually cotton) shirts and shorts or skirts in uniform colour or colours if the match is between two or more teams

Sensitive footwear
Players wear flat-soled shoes with very thin uppers so they can "feel" the chapteh

Flying feather
The jianzi or chapteh is made from feathers that are attached to a plastic or rubber disc base

PLAYER PROFILE

Excellence at jianzi requires the skills of a juggler – with the feet. High levels of coordination, as well as muscular and aerobic fitness are essential, as is the ability to make long stretches. Top-grade players work out on weights and do circuit training and flexibility exercises as a matter of routine. But jianzi gameplay can only really be improved by hours of practice or actual competition: not even a badminton shuttlecock has the same shape and aerodynamic peculiarities of the chapteh.

INSIDE STORY

Originally from ancient China, jianzi has spread across the world. The leading playing nations are China and Vietnam, but the sport is growing in Europe, especially Finland, France, Germany, Greece, Hungary, the Netherlands, Romania, and Serbia.

GOVERNING BODY

Taking the anglicized name for the sport, the International Shuttlecock Federation (ISF) was founded in 1999 in Vietnam and now has 19 members. The ISF staged the first world championships in Hungary in 2000, where Vietnam took most of the medals. The Shuttlecock Federation of Europe was founded in 2003, and the first European Cup was contested that year in Germany.

Feather ball
In Europe, players may use a badminton shuttlecock rather than a chapteh

LEOPARD HEAD

The first touch is all important. When the chapteh drops from height, players may use a knee to knock it into the air – a move known as the leopard head – to get the right height for a kicked return.

Joint strength
Many people use jianzi for improving aerobic fitness and flexibility

SITTING TIGER

Playing the chapteh with the instep requires great flexibility and balance. Players practise repeatedly knocking the chapteh up with first one foot and then the other – a basic technique that underlies much match play.

PLAYER PROFILE
Squash players need good hand-eye coordination and high levels of fitness. Strong, healthy knees are essential for sudden stops and changes of direction. Squash is good for cardiovascular exercise, but is notoriously hazardous for players with a heart condition.

Colour-coded ball
Squash balls are available in a variety of speeds, indicated by a small coloured dot

Loose-fitting shirt
A loose-fitting, lightweight cotton shirt (which can be of any colour) is worn

Cotton shorts
Players wear lightweight cotton shorts, similar to those worn by tennis players

Quality socks
It is important to wear a pair of good-quality, well-fitting socks to prevent rubbing and blisters

Squash shoes
Specially designed squash shoes have heels and grips that aid performance, help protect against injury, and don't leave any marks on the court

Eye guards
Lightweight glasses or goggles are recommended to protect players' eyes from injury

Open-collared shirt
For greater freedom of movement on the court, an open-necked shirt is necessary

Lightweight racket
Advanced players prefer lightweight rackets that allow them to "feel" each shot

SQUASH

GAME OVERVIEW

Squash is normally a game for two players, although doubles matches are contested on larger courts. Matches are the best of three or, at international level, five games. A player wins a game by being the first to score either nine points or 11 points, depending on which scoring system – points or rally – is being played. Opponents take it in turns to hit the ball, which may touch the ground only once between each stroke. The ball may hit the side and back walls below the out lines, and must bounce off the front wall above a metal strip known as the tin. Because of the small size of the squash court, players often get in each other's way during matches: collisions can happen and lets are commonplace.

NEED2KNOW

➡ Squash – or squash rackets, as it was originally known – was first played at Harrow school, England, in the early 1800s and derived from an earlier game, called rackets.

➡ Squash is played by more than 150 nations. There are approximately 125,000 courts worldwide, and at the start of the 21st century their number was increasing by 2,000 a year.

➡ Most of the big names in squash have come from relatively few countries: Egypt, Pakistan, Great Britain, Australia, New Zealand, France, and Malaysia.

SIDELINES

17 The number of times Jahangir Khan of Pakistan beat the same opponent – Australian Chris Dittmar – in the finals of major world squash tournaments. The run began in 1987 and Khan, who retired in 2001, is regarded as one of the greatest squash players of all time.

281 The speed in kph (175mph) of the highest recorded speed of the ball off the racket. It was achieved by the Australian Cameron Pilley in 2011.

700–1,000 The number of calories a player can expend during a game of squash, which is one of the healthiest sports.

2,666 The highest number of strokes recorded in a single squash rally. The exchange – which took place in 2004 in Jersey, Channel Islands, Great Britain – was a deliberate bid for a world record, rather than part of a competitive game. It ended when the players reached the previously agreed 60-minute time limit: there was no winner, and they could have played on...

COURT PROCEDURE

The diagram below shows the standard dimensions for a singles squash court. At the highest level, clear-sided courts are used to allow for better TV broadcasting. The ball may be bounced off any of the walls below the out-of-court lines, including the back wall. The tin is marked with a metal strip: the noise made when a ball hits it tells the players (and officials, if there are any) that the shot is not "up".

PREMATCH PREPARATIONS

Before any match, the players warm up themselves and, just as importantly, the ball for five minutes by stroking the ball to each other. The players swap sides after exactly two and a half minutes. If there is a referee, he or she will call "half time", and then "time" when the full five minutes have elapsed. The referee carefully observes the warm-up session, and may intervene if he or she decides that one player is denying the other adequate practice by dominating the court.

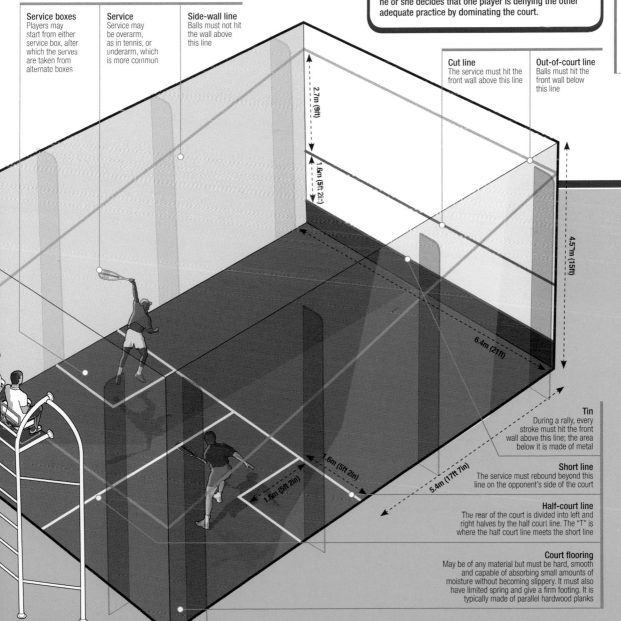

Service boxes
Players may start from either service box, after which the serves are taken from alternate boxes

Service
Service may be overarm, as in tennis, or underarm, which is more common

Side-wall line
Balls must not hit the wall above this line

Cut line
The service must hit the front wall above this line

Out-of-court line
Balls must hit the front wall below this line

2.7m (9ft)

1.6m (5ft 2in)

4.5m (15ft)

6.4m (21ft)

1.6m (5ft 2in)

1.6m (5ft 2in)

5.4m (17ft 7in)

Tin
During a rally, every stroke must hit the front wall above this line; the area below it is made of metal

Short line
The service must rebound beyond this line on the opponent's side of the court

Half-court line
The rear of the court is divided into left and right halves by the half court line. The "T" is where the half court line meets the short line

Court flooring
May be of any material but must be hard, smooth and capable of absorbing small amounts of moisture without becoming slippery. It must also have limited spring and give a firm footing. It is typically made of parallel hardwood planks

KEY EQUIPMENT

Most squash rackets are made of graphite with the addition of a small amount of another material, such as Kevlar or titanium, which makes them stiff, light, strong, and powerful. String tension is an important factor in producing a good on-court performance. Generally, harder hitters have their rackets strung more tightly than lighter hitters. String width, or gauge can also vary. Thin strings are more powerful than thick strings as they stretch more and launch the ball further. Beginners should use a fast ball with plenty of bounce, while professional players use much slower balls.

EYE PROTECTION
During rallies, squash players risk being hit by their opponent's racket or the ball; many facial injuries are sustained in this way. The World Squash Federation recommends that all players wear appropriate eye guards at every level of the game. Eye protection is essential if a player has a history of medical problems with their eyes, or has had surgery. Few professionals wear eye protection, however, although eye guards are now compulsory in the doubles game and for juniors.

21.5cm (8½in)

68.6cm (27in)

Frame depth
The frame can measure between 7mm (¼in) and 26mm (1in)

Strung area
The strung area measures a maximum of 500sq cm (77½sq in)

Racket grip
Grips can be made of towelling, leather or synthetic materials

RACKET
Originally made of laminated wood, modern rackets are made of graphite and have two layers of synthetic string woven in a uniform pattern. The strings may be animal gut (which can add more spin to a shot) but are more commonly made of nylon. A racket should weigh no more than 225g (9oz).

BALL SPEED
A coloured dot indicates the level of bounce and speed of a squash ball. The standard competition ball is the yellow.

- Double yellow – extra super slow
- Yellow – super slow
- Green or white – slow
- Red – medium
- Blue – fast

RUBBER BALL
The ball is formed of two hollow hemispheres of rubber compound glued together.

Hollow ball
Air inside the ball expands as it warms up, increasing the level of bounce

4cm (1½in)

SERVING

The right to serve first is determined by a "racket spin". The server continues to serve until he or she loses a rally, after which the opponent takes service and the procedure continues. Part of the server's foot must be completely inside the service box (not touching the box lines) and in contact with the floor when the ball is put in to play. The ball must hit the front wall between the cut line and the out-of-court line and then bounce on the floor in the opposite half of the court beyond the short line. If a serve fails to satisfy these criteria, service immediately passes to the other player.

At the start of each game or after service has passed to an opponent, the server may begin play from either service box. Serves then alternate between the two boxes, regardless of which player is serving, except when a let has been called, in which case the ball is hit back in to play from the same box as the previous serve. If the players are unsure of which box to serve from, the marker (the referee's assistant) announces the correct box.

RALLYING
Alternate players must hit the ball against the front wall between the out-of-court line and the tin. It may be deflected off any of the other three walls, but may hit the floor only once per stroke to remain in play. The ceiling of the court is out of bounds.

DOMINATING THE "T"
A game of squash revolves around the "T", the point at which the half-court line and the short line meet. The player who dominates the "T" also dominates the game as they are in the best possible position to place winning shots and are perfectly balanced to go in any direction to return their opponent's shots.

USING THE WALLS

During a rally the striker may play off one or more of the three walls to deceive the opponent through rapid changes of angle or to draw them to the forecourt. With the opponent in a weak position at the front, the attacker may try to win the point with a hard drive in to the vacant back court. Alternatively, a ball played to hug the wall is extremely awkward to return.

STRAIGHT DRIVE
The straight drive or "rail" is one of the most effective shots in the game. The first bounce should land on the front wall above the service line, followed by a second bounce off the back wall near the floor. If left, the ball will drop in to the "nick" between the back wall and the floor – virtually impossible to retrieve. A good drive has length (to reach the back court) and is tight to the wall.

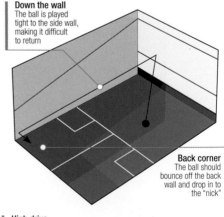

Down the wall
The ball is played tight to the side wall, making it difficult to return

Back corner
The ball should bounce off the back wall and drop in to the "nick"

FORECOURT SHOT
Squash players aim to draw their opponents away from the "T" at the centre of the court, the most advantageous position. In this diagram, for example, a drive played high on to the side wall near the corner loses most of its power on making contact with the wall, falls on to the front wall and then drops away into the forecourt. The chasing player has to run and fetch to keep the rally alive.

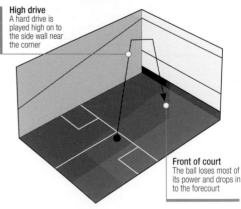

High drive
A hard drive is played high on to the side wall near the corner

Front of court
The ball loses most of its power and drops in to the forecourt

SCORING SYSTEM

Points are won at the end of a rally of "good" balls, which occurs either when one player fails to return the opponent's shot or plays a "bad" ball. A good ball is one that reaches the front wall below the out line and above the tin before touching the floor. Bad balls include those that bounce twice on the floor, hit the tin or hit the wall above the out-of court-lines.

POINT-A-RALLY (PARS) SYSTEM

In the point-a-rally or PARS system, either the server or receiver may score a point at the end of each rally. The winner of each game is the first to 11 points. However, when the score reaches 10-all the game must be won by two clear points. The rally system is used in international and doubles matches, and also in the men's professional singles tour.

POINT SYSTEM

Only the server can score in the point system, and the winner of each game is normally the first player to reach nine points. An exception is made when the score reaches eight-all for the first time. In this situation, the receiver may choose to continue that game to nine or 10 points. The former is known as "set one"; the latter is called "set two".

PLAYING A LET

A let is played when one player obstructs another during a rally. If the striker hits their opponent with the ball before it reaches the front wall, or the striker's racket hits the opponent, play is paused and the referee decides whether the ball would have been good. If the referee decides it would have been good, or if the opponent deliberately intercepted the ball, the stroke is awarded to the striker. If the ball would not have been good, the stroke is awarded to the player who was hit.

STAT CENTRAL

MEN'S WORLD OPEN CHAMPIONS

YEAR	PLAYER (COUNTRY)
2012	RAMY ASHOUR (EGY)
2011	NICK MATTHEW (ENG)
2010	NICK MATTHEW (ENG)
2009	AMR SHABANA (EGY)
2008	RAMY ASHOUR (EGY)
2007	AMR SHABANA (EGY)
2006	DAVID PALMER (AUS)
2005	AMR SHABANA (EGY)

WOMEN'S WORLD OPEN CHAMPIONS

YEAR	PLAYER (COUNTRY)
2012	NICOL DAVID (MYS)
2011	NICOL DAVID (MYS)
2010	NICOL DAVID (MYS)
2009	NICOL DAVID (MYS)
2008	NICOL DAVID (MYS)
2007	RACHAEL GRINHAM (AUS)
2006	NICOL DAVID (MYS)

MEN'S BRITISH OPEN CHAMPIONS

YEAR	PLAYER (COUNTRY)
2012	NICK MATTHEW (ENG)
2011	NO COMPETITION
2010	NO COMPETITION
2009	NICK MATTHEW (ENG)
2008	DAVID PALMER (AUS)
2007	GRÉGORY GAULTIER (FRA)
2006	NICK MATTHEW (ENG)

WOMEN'S BRITISH OPEN CHAMPIONS

YEAR	PLAYER (COUNTRY)
2012	NICOL DAVID (MYS)
2011	NO COMPETITION
2010	NO COMPETITION
2009	RACHAEL GRINHAM (AUS)
2008	NICOL DAVID (MYS)
2007	RACHAEL GRINHAM (AUS)
2006	NICOL DAVID (MYS)
2005	NICOL DAVID (MYS)

OFFENSIVE SHOTS

The volley (hitting the ball before it bounces on the floor) is a key attacking shot that allows a player to interrupt the rhythm of play. A lob that sails over an opponent's head and drops in to the back corner is an equally effective offensive shot.

DEFENSIVE SHOTS

The drop shot, which can be played from anywhere on the court, will force an opponent that is dominating the "T" out of position. The "boast" (a shot played with pace against a side wall first) may be necessary to retrieve a ball played in to the back corner.

FOREHAND GROUND STROKE
The forehand is a versatile stroke that is vital for both offensive and defensive play. The stroke allows a player to hit both hard drives and delicate drop shots with accuracy.

Backswing
Keeping the racket back and the arm high on the backswing adds power to the shot

Strike
Swinging the racket through a smooth curve helps ensure the shot is accurate

Follow-through
A proper follow-through means the player is in control of the ball throughout the shot

INSIDE STORY

Squash has its origins in the UK and the British Open Championships was one of the first major squash tournaments. Prior to the creation of the World Open, it was effectively considered to be the world championships. The first women's contest was held in 1922 and the men's in 1930. It is still highly regarded by many on the circuit despite its lower prize money. The World Open Championships has been held since the 1970s, and is contested annually by the world's best men and women.

GOVERNING BODY

The World Squash Federation (WSF) has more than 100 member nations. It organizes the sport's world championships for men, women, boys, girls, and masters (over 35s) at individual and team levels in singles and doubles. The men's professional game is governed by the Professional Squash Association (PSA) and the women's by the Women's International Squash Players Association (WISPA).

AND KHAN TAKES IT...

BETWEEN 1951 AND 1997 THE WORLD CHAMPIONSHIP WAS WON 30 TIMES BY PLAYERS FROM A SINGLE VILLAGE IN PAKISTAN. THE VICTORS WERE NOT ALL RELATED, BUT WERE ALL NAMED KHAN: AZAM, HASHIM, JAHANGIR, JANSHER, MOHIBULLAH, AND ROSHAN.

→ Most sports evolve, but racquetball was invented in 1950 by Joe Sobek, an American handball player who was dissatisfied with the range of indoor games then on offer.

→ Racquetball caught on fast because it could be played on the handball courts that already existed in most US high schools and colleges.

→ Confusingly, "racketball" is not just an alternative spelling, it is a completely different game played on a squash court with a smaller and less bouncy ball.

RACQUETBALL

GAME OVERVIEW

Racquetball is a fast game played on indoor or outdoor courts by two, three, or four players. It is a combination of handball and squash (see pp.196–99) with several exciting features that are all its own. At the start of the 21st century, there were 8.5 million racquetball players worldwide.

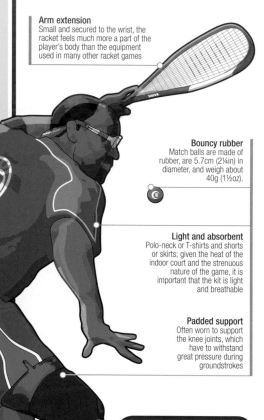

Arm extension
Small and secured to the wrist, the racket feels much more a part of the player's body than the equipment used in many other racket games

Bouncy rubber
Match balls are made of rubber, are 5.7cm (2¼in) in diameter, and weigh about 40g (1½oz).

Light and absorbent
Polo-neck or T-shirts and shorts or skirts; given the heat of the indoor court and the strenuous nature of the game, it is important that the kit is light and breathable

Padded support
Often worn to support the knee joints, which have to withstand great pressure during groundstrokes

Non-marking
The trainers worn are similar to those used in other court sports; they must not mark the surface

GAME PLAY

Players take turns to hit a ball against a wall. Only the server scores points, and only if they serve an ace or win a rally. A rally is won when the opposition cannot stop the ball hitting the floor twice or cannot return it so that it touches the front wall before the floor. The receiver wins the serve by winning the rally.

The server must stand in the service zone, bounce the ball on the floor once, then hit it directly on to the front wall, making it rebound and touch the floor beyond the short line without touching a side wall. In rallies, the ball may hit the side walls or the roof as long as it also hits the front wall and bounces only once between opponents' strokes.

THE GEAR

The racket and ball are similar to those used in squash, but larger. The game is fast-paced and furious and players often wear protective safety goggles.

LIGHT FRAME
Modern rackets are often constructed with a light graphite-titanium composite frame and weigh only about 184g (6½oz).

PLAYER PROFILE
For top players, a strong heart and physical fitness are vital to sustain the necessary stamina and speed across the court. One of the main reasons for the popularity of racquetball is that almost anyone can play it, and the nature of the sport means it is a good way of keeping fit.

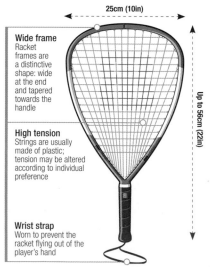

25cm (10in)

Up to 56cm (22in)

Wide frame
Racket frames are a distinctive shape: wide at the end and tapered towards the handle

High tension
Strings are usually made of plastic; tension may be altered according to individual preference

Wrist strap
Worn to prevent the racket flying out of the player's hand

COURTSHIP

Apart from the top of the back wall, all surfaces are in play, including the ceiling. The floor surface is usually made of planks of polished wood or similar material. The back wall (and sometimes the side walls) is made of transparent perspex. The court is a confined space that retains heat and may quickly render players in need of refreshment.

POINT FOR POINT

Professionals play the best of five games, the winning player or team being the first to 11 points with a two-point margin of victory. Amateurs play two games, with the winning player being the first to 15 points. If each player wins one game, a tiebreaker is required. It is not necessary to win by two clear points in amateur racquetball. In addition to singles and doubles, three-player variants include "ironman" (two against one) and "cutthroat", in which players take it in turns to oppose the other two.

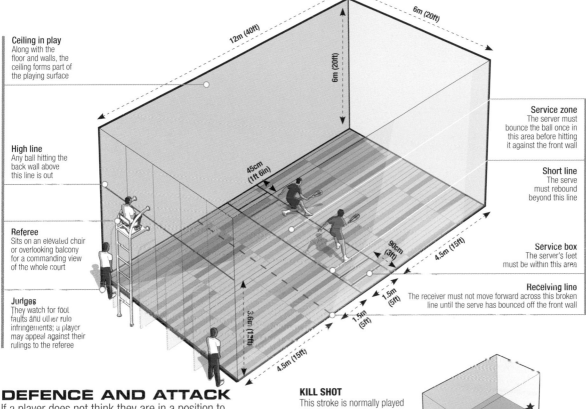

Ceiling in play
Along with the floor and walls, the ceiling forms part of the playing surface

High line
Any ball hitting the back wall above this line is out

Referee
Sits on an elevated chair or overlooking balcony for a commanding view of the whole court

Judges
They watch for foot faults and other rule infringements; a player may appeal against their rulings to the referee

Service zone
The server must bounce the ball once in this area before hitting it against the front wall

Short line
The serve must rebound beyond this line

Service box
The server's feet must be within this area

Receiving line
The receiver must not move forward across this broken line until the serve has bounced off the front wall

12m (40ft)
6m (20ft)
6m (20ft)
45cm (1ft 6in)
90cm (3ft)
4.5m (15ft)
1.5m (5ft)
1.5m (5ft)
3.6m (12ft)
4.5m (15ft)

DEFENCE AND ATTACK

If a player does not think they are in a position to finish a rally, they may play a defensive shot to lure their opponent away from the centre of the court. If successful, they can go for the kill with their next shot. Some of the key rally strokes are as follows:

CEILING SHOT
Since the roof is in bounds, players often take advantage of it. This stroke aims to make the ball bounce for the second time in the back court.

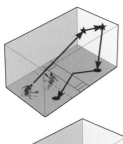

DOWN THE LINE PASS
A player standing near the side wall sends a forcing shot back past him even closer to the side of the court. The strokemaker must be careful not to obstruct the opponent.

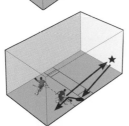

KILL SHOT
This stroke is normally played with bent knees when the ball is already close to the ground; the idea is to keep it as low as possible when it hits the front wall.

PINCH SHOT
This is the name for any stroke that hits the side wall first, then the front wall, and "dies" near the side wall on the opposite side of the court. The aim is to get the ball to bounce twice before it reaches the flanks.

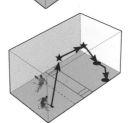

INSIDE STORY

The International Racquetball Federation organizes World Championships every two years, with competitors from more than 40 countries. The IRF regularly updates the world rankings.

GOVERNING BODIES
Professional racquetball is run by two separate organizations for men and women: the International Racquetball Tournament (IRT), and the Women's Professional Racquetball Association (WPRA).

ETON FIVES

GAME OVERVIEW

This little-known ball game is played by two teams of two men or women on an unusual court that is enclosed on three sides, and is about 15cm (6in) higher at the front than the back. The players can strike the ball only with their hands or wrists and must hit the ball "up" against the front wall to stay in a rally. The ball can only bounce once before each hit.

NEED2KNOW

→ The game originated at Eton College and spread to other private schools in England, but it is now played by only a few thousand athletes.

→ Although there are a few courts in Europe, Eton fives is played mainly in Britain and in Nigeria, where a version of the game flourishes in the northern states and there are at least 30 courts.

Cutter's partner
This player hits the ball if his or her partner cannot reach it

Server's partner
This player tries to return any shots that the server misses

Column
It is difficult to return a shot that hits one of the columns

Buttress
At the base of this feature on the front court side is a niche (the "hole"). If the ball goes into the hole it is virtually unplayable

Server
The server throws the ball so that it bounces off the front and right walls, landing roughly in the middle of the lower court

"Up"
The area above the upper ledge on the front wall is known as "up"

Blackguard line
This vertical black line is about 75cm (30in) from the right wall. Cutters returning service play the ball to the right of the line

Key step
Vertical, and about 12cm (6in) high

Cutter
This player can choose when to return a serve and can leave any number of serves unhit. Should he or she decide to return it, the ball will be smashed hard against the right wall and the front wall to the right of the blackguard line and above the ledge

SCORING

Matches are the best of five games and each game is won by the first pair to reach 12 points. Only the serving pair can score. Points are won if the ball hits the ground more than once, hits the front wall under the line or ledge, or leaves the court completely.

A STRANGE CONVERSION

THE ORGAN ROOM AT THE OPERA HOUSE IN GLYNDEBOURNE, EAST SUSSEX, IS NOW ONE OF ENGLAND'S GRANDEST SITTING ROOMS. STRANGELY, IT BEGAN LIFE AS AN ETON FIVES COURT BEFORE CONVERSION TO A MORE SEDATE USE.

THE COURT

The Eton-fives court is based on an area of the chapel at Eton College where the game was first played. Every court differs slightly, but a number of features are universal. A step divides the court into front and back sections. The court is enclosed on three sides by irregular walls. There is a buttress on the left of the court where the upper and lower courts meet, brick columns either side of the open end, and a ledge on all three sides. These features ensure that, after hitting a wall, the ball's trajectory is almost impossible to predict. The home team, however, are usually at an advantage as they are familiar with the court's unique elements.

Hard ball
The ball is a little larger than a golf ball and is made of rubber and cork. It loses little of its pace when bouncing off the walls and floor of the court.

Soft gloves
Padded leather gloves protect the hands. Reversed rough leather on the palm side gives added grip. Inner gloves absorb sweat and give further protection.

RACKETS

NEED2KNOW

→ First played as an improvised prison-yard game, rackets gained respectability when it became a public school sport in the 1800s.

→ English players have dominated world racket championships for nearly 200 years.

SCORING

Only the server can score. He or she must play the ball from the service box to strike the front wall above the service line and rebound into the service court. Players returning service must hit the ball before it bounces twice; shots must strike the front wall above the play line. A missed shot either gains a point for the server or results in a change of service. The first side to reach 15 points wins the game.

GAME OVERVIEW

Rackets is a fast and furious indoor sport, very similar to squash (see pp.196–99) but using a harder ball, and wooden rackets. Both singles and doubles are played.

THE COURT

The court is enclosed, with front and side walls 9m (30ft) high and a back wall half that height. The surfaces of both walls and floor are hard and smooth. There is a fixed wooden board on the front wall, the upper edge of which is the play line, 68cm (2ft 3in) from the floor. Another line, 3m (9ft 6in) from the floor, is the service line.

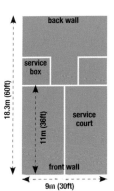

Heavy ball The ball is heavy for its size. Only 2.5cm (1in) in diameter (about the size of a golfball) it weighs 28g (1oz)

Wooden racket This averages 76cm (27in) in length and weighs 255g (9oz). It is strung with catgut

Shorts and shirt Clothing is loose-fitting to allow free movement

Court diagram labels: back wall, service box, service court, front wall, 18.3m (60ft), 11m (36ft), 9m (30ft)

NEED2KNOW

→ Paddleball originated in the United States, where it is still most popular.

→ The governing body of one-wall paddleball is the United States Paddleball Association.

 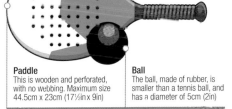

Paddle This is wooden and perforated, with no webbing. Maximum size 44.5cm x 23cm (17½in x 9in)

Ball The ball, made of rubber, is smaller than a tennis ball, and has a diameter of 5cm (2in)

PADDLEPOINTS

For a 15-point game, two one-minute time-outs are allowed; 21-point and 25 point games, allow three one-minute breathers. Tournament committees allow substitutes in some competitions. Unusually in a racket sport, a player can switch the paddle from hand to hand during a game.

PADDLEBALL

GAME OVERVIEW

Players hit a ball against the wall or walls of a court with a paddle, while their opponents attempt to hit it on the rebound. There are one-, three-, and four-wall games, both singles and doubles. In one- and three-wall games play is to 11, 15, 21, or 25 points. Four-wall is a 21-point game.

RULES OF SERVICE

The server must remain inside the service zone, between the short and service lines. A serve is illegal if the ball hits the floor before crossing the short line, or if it rebounds from the front wall and hits two or more walls before striking the floor. The server loses the right to serve if he or she makes two illegal serves in a row.

THE COURTS

The most popular version of paddleball is played on a court 6.1m (20ft) wide and 10.3m (34ft) long, with a single wall, 4.9m (16ft) high, topped with a fence. The short line, 4.9m (16ft) from the wall, defines the front court. The long line, 5.4m (18ft) behind the short line, defines the back court. The front court of a three-wall court has side walls 3.7–4.9m (12–16 ft) high. A four-wall court has a ceiling, front and side walls 6.1m (20ft high) and a back wall at least 3.7m (12ft) high.

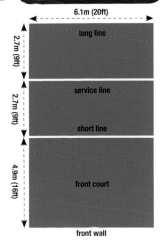

Court diagram labels: 6.1m (20ft), long line, 2.7m (9ft), service line, 2.7m (9ft), short line, 4.9m (16ft), front court, front wall

ONE-WALL COURT The server must not cross either the service line or the short line. Served balls should hit the wall and rebound to land in the receiving area, which is between the short and long lines.

→ Often regarded as a Basque and Catalan sport, pelota is also played in other parts of France and Spain, as well as in Argentina, Ireland, Italy, and Mexico.

→ In its native Spain and France, pelota is known as "jai alai", which is the Basque for "happy festival".

→ A ball that is well hit by a highly skilled pelota player may reach speeds of 300kph (188mph).

PELOTA

GAME OVERVIEW

This is the fastest ball game in the world. Standard pelota, known as "cesta punta", is a game for two players, but other versions can be played as doubles. Using bizarrely shaped rackets-cum-baskets, which are strapped to their wrists, players aim to sling a ball against a wall in such a way that their opponents cannot return it before it bounces twice. There are numerous variants, including a bare-handed game, "pelota a mano", that may be single combat or two against one. The form known as "frontenis" is played with tennis rackets with reinforced strings; "xare" also uses tennis rackets, but with loosened strings; "leather paleta" and "pala corta" are played with solid wooden bats.

Cesta
The racket is made of plaited willow twigs mounted on a curved arm of chestnut or ash

On hand
The glove is attached to the cesta and held in place on the player's wrist by a strap (cinta)

Pelota
The ball is hard, with a latex core wrapped in wool and an outer casing of two leather strips sewn together

5cm (2in)

Safety lid
The helmet is vital safety wear. No pelotari (player) would be seen alive for long without one

PLAYER PROFILE
Pelota players need to be wealthy (or at least have sponsorship) just to afford the rackets, which are handmade and often last less than a single match. The arms, legs, and back must all be in good condition, but the critical area is the hip, which is heavily involved in every stroke. Old players often suffer from arthritis in the hip joints.

Waistband ribbon
May be coloured to denote the player's team or status

Court dress
Players wear polo shirts and trousers: shorts are not generally considered suitable attire

Leave no trace
Running shoes with non-marking soles allow quick movement and prevent damage to the court

DYNAMIC ACTION
The cesta punta player (pelotari) catches the speeding ball, or pelota, with his cesta. Once the ball is safely snared, he will draw back his throwing arm, then whip it forward again, launching the pelota towards the front wall of the court at blistering speed.

PLAYING PELOTA
The score required to win a match can be anything between 25 and 50 points. In doubles, both teams can score, regardless of whether they have the serve. At the start of each point, the server throws the ball in to play with the cesta from behind the service line; a legal serve must go straight on to the front wall above the low horizontal metal strip, and land on the floor in the area between lines 4 and 7. The side and back walls may be used only once the ball is in play. Rallies continue until the ball goes out or is not returned. If one player obstructs another, a let is normally played unless it is clear what would have happened.

ONE TO WATCH
One of the sport's most important requirements is that rallies should be continuous, and the judges keep a close eye on every stroke to ensure that they are all one fluid movement. If it looks as if the player has cradled the pelota in the cesta — even for a moment — he or she loses the point.

GAME FOR A FLUTTER
IN PELOTA DE GOMA, THE BALL IS PRESSURIZED AND FILLED WITH GAS, MAKING IT EVEN QUICKER THROUGH THE AIR THAN THE STANDARD PELOTA. THE GAME IS SO FAST THAT IT'S HARD TO APPRECIATE WITHOUT SLOW-MOTION REPLAYS, BUT DESPITE THIS IT'S STILL A BIG CROWD-PULLER AND ONE OF THE MOST WAGERED SPORTS IN SPAIN.

COURTING RITUAL

Most variants of pelota are played on indoor courts known as frontons. The overall length may vary, but the marked areas are always in proportion. The front, back, and lefthand walls are parts of the playing area. The flooring (cancha) is made of polished cement, but beyond the sideline the surface changes to wood, so that any ball that lands on it makes a recognizably different sound. To the right, a glass or perspex panel covers the whole wall area: behind it is seating for spectators.

WALLCRAFT

Some players overpower their opponents by force of stroke, but most rely on subtle and deceptive spin. Among the most effective shots are the chula, in which the ball lands in the join between the back wall and the floor, and the carom, which hits side wall, front wall, and then floor, falling away towards the righthand screen. The dejada is a drop shot that hits the front wall just above the foul line. The arrimada is a forcing drive that goes as close as possible to the side wall and is thus almost unplayable.

Service line
The server (left) must put the pelota in to play from behind this mark

Back court players
Note how in doubles the non-server covers the right of the court, leaving the left to his team-mate

FRONTONS

There are three standard courts. Frontenis and pelota de goma are played on a 30m (98ft) court; pelota a mano and leather pelota are contested on a 36m (118ft) fronton; and cesta punta is a game for a court that measures 54m (177ft) in length.

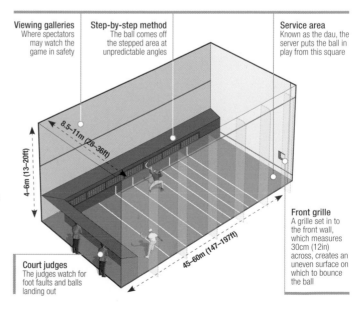

Pasa line
Marked with the number 7 on the wall; any serve must hit the frontis and then bounce before it reaches this mark

Falta line
Marked with the number 4 on the wall; any serve must bounce beyond this mark

Front court players
They try to intercept the pelota during rallies

10m (33ft)

9–11.5m (29ft 6in–37ft 9in)

30–54m (98–177ft)

3.5m (11ft 6in)

Metal strip
This extends across the front wall and is 60cm–100cm (2ft–3ft 3in) in height

Frontis
The front wall of the court is made of granite

TRINQUET COURT

The most unusual pelota court is called the trinquet, and this gives a whole new meaning to the term "spectator sport". The steps on the side are part of the playing area, but members of the audience can sit on them at their own risk. (There are also upstairs viewing galleries for those who value their safety.) Players make use of these areas during a game because a ball that hits the steps or a spectator will bounce in an unpredictable way, making it more difficult for the opposition to return.

KNOWING THE ROPE

In the traditional Valencian trinquet game known as "pelota vasca", opponents face each other on either side of a rope hung across the middle of the fronton. Other variant forms of pelota contested on a trinquet are played off the front wall, using cestas or gloved hands. These include leather and rubbers pelota, pelota a mano, and xare. The ball – known as "pilota de vaqueta" ("little cow ball") – is 4.2cm (1¾in) in diameter.

Viewing galleries
Where spectators may watch the game in safety

Step-by-step method
The ball comes off the stepped area at unpredictable angles

Service area
Known as the dau, the server puts the ball in play from this square

Court judges
The judges watch for foot faults and balls landing out

Front grille
A grille set in to the front wall, which measures 30cm (12in) across, creates an uneven surface on which to bounce the ball

8.5–11m (28–36ft)

4–6m (13–20ft)

45–60m (147–197ft)

COMBAT SPORTS

05

BOXING

SPORT OVERVIEW

Boxing is a sport of great skill and physical toughness. Two combatants endeavour to punch one other to score points from the judges or referee, while avoiding being hit themselves. Almost all area of the head and body above the waist are designated scoring areas. Contests are won on points or by knockout. There is a major disparity between the amateur and professional ranks in boxing. Leading professional fighters are among the biggest earners in world sport.

FIGHTER PROFILE
Boxer require good upper body strength – particularly a strong punch – and a high resilience to being hit (a "good chin"). Boxing is a really tough aerobic workout so fighters need to display a fanatical training ethic and great stamina. Speed, agility, and quick reflexes are beneficial, particularly for those fighting at lower weight levels.

Bob and weave
Head movement is vitally important for fighters; it is more difficult for opponents to hit a moving target

Trunks
Cotton shorts have padded waistbands to provide some protection from low body shots

Fist protection
Fighters' hands are wrapped in bandages before being fitted into padded gloves

Solid base
Boxing shoes provide comfort, ankle support, and above all grip on the ring floor

SIDELINES

120 The total amount, in millions of US dollars, generated from pay-per-view sales of the world title fight between Oscar de la Hoya and Floyd Mayweather Jr. in May 2007.

135,132 The highest live attendance for a boxing contest – Tony Zale versus Billy Pryor in August 1941.

45 The age of George Foreman when he regained the world heavyweight title – knocking out Michael Moorer for the IBF and WBA titles in November 1994. Foreman had first won the world heavyweight title in 1973.

242 Number of fights fought by American featherweight Willie Pep during a 26-year career (1940–66).

NEED2KNOW

→ Modern boxing was first codified in 1867 by a set of 12 rules written by John Graham Chambers and endorsed by the 9th Marquis of Queensberry.

→ Amateur boxing differs in various ways from the professional arm of the sport.

THE RING

The name boxing "ring" is an atavism that dates from when contests were fought in a roughly drawn circle on the ground. A modern boxing ring is set on a raised platform. It is square, with a post at each corner to which four parallel rows of ropes are attached with a turnbuckle. Each side of a standard ring is 4.88–7.32m (16–25ft) between the ropes, with another 60cm (2ft) outside known as the apron. The platform is 90–120cm (3–4ft) from the ground with the posts rising around 1.5m (5ft).

Rope-a-dope
Ropes are about 2.5cm (1in) in diameter and held up on posts at heights of 45cm, 75cm, 110cm, and 140cm (18in, 30in, 42in, and 54in)

Hit the deck
The ring floor has about 2.5cm (1in) of padding covered by stretched canvas. The canvas commonly features advertising from the promoter or sponsors

Referee
The referee is assisted by three judges and a timekeeper, but only he can stop the contest

4.8–7.3m (16–25ft)

4.8–7.3m (16–25ft)

Cornermen
Each boxer has a trainer, a second (assistant trainer), and cuts man at their disposal during the break between rounds

Top judgement
Three judges work with the referee to score the bout

Neutral corner
Each fighter is allocated an opposite corner to which he retreats at the end of each round. The other two corners are designated neutral. Boxers are sent to a neutral corner after a knockdown or following a rule breach that requires intervention from the referee

FIGHTING GEAR

Boxers wear shorts, boxing shoes, and padded gloves which come in two sizes – 227g (8oz) and 283g (10oz) – depending on the weight of the boxer. Mouth guards are compulsory and groin guards optional in professional boxing. In amateur bouts fighters additionally wear headguards and vests and have larger, softer gloves. This is the only equipment fighters wear and use in the ring, but in training boxers additonally use free weights, punchbags, skipping ropes, speed balls, and other items to hone themselves into fighting shape.

AMBLING ALP

ITALIAN BOXER PRIMO CARNERA, HEAVYWEIGHT CHAMPION IN 1933, WAS A GIANT OF A MAN – STANDING 197CM (6FT 5IN) TALL AND WEIGHING 125KG (276LB). HE HAD A PRODIGIOUS APPETITE. FOR BREAKFAST, IT IS CLAIMED HE ATE 19 PIECES OF TOAST, 14 EGGS, A LOAF OF BREAD, HALF A POUND OF VIRGINIA HAM, A QUART OF ORANGE JUICE, AND TWO QUARTS OF MILK.

GROIN GUARD
Protects fighters' groins from injuries resulting from illegal low blows.

MOUTH GUARD
Plastic gumshields guard the top teeth from being knocked out.

GLOVE
Gloves are specially padded to protect only the wearer.

Cushions blows
Usually made of leather with a foam interior

Side holes
The headwear does not fully cover ears to enable fighters to hear referee's instructions

HEAD GUARD
Worn for amateur contests and professional sparring only, they offer protection but limit peripheral vision.

LAWS OF THE FIGHT GAME

The basic rules of boxing are that two fighters of a similar weight, under the supervision of a referee, attempt to strike one another above the waist with clenched fists with the intention of scoring more points than the opponent (to win rounds) or knocking the opponent to the canvas for a period of 10 seconds. Blows to the back of the head or kidneys are illegal, as are blows with the open, laced part of the gloves. Beyond that, rules differ between the amateur and professional arms of the sport.

AMATEUR

Amateur fighters wear shorts, vests, and shoes. For protection they wear a gumshield, groin guard, and leather headguard. Contests are held over three two-minute rounds. Points are scored for every legal punch landed with the knuckle portion of the glove (painted white) and the totals run for the whole fight, not for individual rounds.

PROFESSIONAL

Pro fighters, in contrast, fight stripped to the waist and without headguards. Contests are much longer, too – world championship fights consist of ten three-minute rounds, with a one-minute break in between. Individual rounds are scored out of ten by a panel of three judges. The fighter that wins the round is awarded ten points, the loser nine. If a round is particularly one-sided – a knockdown occurs – the scores are given as 10/8. Points are deducted by the referee for indiscretions.

THE COUNT
Following a knockdown, the referee first escorts the aggressor to a neutral corner and then starts counting to ten. The prostrate fighter has ten seconds to both regain his feet and present himself in an acceptable condition to continue or the fight is over.

STAT CENTRAL

TOP WEIGHTS (10.oz GLOVES)

TITLE	WEIGHT
HEAVYWEIGHT	91+kg (201+lb)
CRUISERWEIGHT	80–90.5kg (176–200lb)
LT. HEAVYWEIGHT	76.5–79kg (169–175lb)
SPR. MIDDLEWEIGHT	73–76kg (161–168lb)
MIDDLEWEIGHT	70–72.5kg (155–160lb)
SPR. WELTERWEIGHT	67–70kg (148–154lb)

LOWER WEIGHTS (8.oz GLOVES)

TITLE	WEIGHT
WELTERWEIGHT	64–66.5kg (141–147lb)
SPR. LIGHTWEIGHT	61.5–63.5kg (136–140lb)
SPR. FEATHERWEIGHT	57.5–59kg (127–130lb)
FEATHERWEIGHT	56–57kg (123–126lb)
SPR. BANTAMWEIGHT	54–55kg (119–122lb)
BANTAMWEIGHT	52.5–53.5kg (116–118lb)
SPR. FLYWEIGHT	51–52kg (113–115lb)
FLYWEIGHT	49–51kg (109–112lb)

RING CRAFT

Basic boxing training centres around physical fitness, speed of movement, throwing jabs, and footwork. Good punches can only be thrown from a solid base. The techniques of throwing different punches are taught later. Top boxers work with their trainers for weeks at a time leading up to championship fights, working on their overall conditioning and on a fighting style tailored to their upcoming opponent. They will practise key punches and spar with fighters of a similar build and fighting style to their opponent in an attempt to gain some advantage.

ON THE ATTACK

Boxers must show aggression and throw punches in order to win fights, so attacks – either as single punches or more usually two or three punch combinations – are essential. In order to launch a flurry of punches the boxer must first contain their opponent – a moving target is hard to strike. Therefore good quick footwork, with the intention of cutting off the ring and trapping the opponent in a corner, is important.

SOUTHPAW
A boxer's stance and method of fighting is either described as orthodox (left arm and foot forward) or southpaw (right arm and foot forward). A southpaw is usually someone who is left-handed, using their right hand for jabs and their left for power punches and hooks. Some particularly dextrous fighters are able to switch between styles during bouts. Because most fighters are orthodox, a southpaw opponent can be a tricky proposition, requiring an altered set of tactics.

Perfect punch
A fully extended arm makes for a textbook jab

Feel the pain
Hooks to the body greatly weaken a fighter's resilience

Block
This straight has been blocked by a good defence

Knockout
A tight defence is sometimes no equal to an uppercut

JAB
The staple punch of any boxer, a stiff jab keeps an opponent at bay and sets up attacks. Jabs are usually the first punch in any combination.

HOOK
Hooks are delivered to the side of the head or body. Because of the angle of delivery the receiving fighter will often not see a hook coming.

STRAIGHT
Thrown with the "second" arm (right arm for orthodox boxers) the straight has a greater distance to travel, leaving the aggressor open to a counter-punch.

UPPERCUT
The most devastating punch in boxing, the uppercut is delivered from a crouching position onto the opponent's chin from below with great force.

IN DEFENCE

The ability to avoid being hit, something the great Muhammad Ali was a master at, is probably more important than landing your own punches. The sheer speed of movement of some fighters can make them difficult to hit. However, the best means of repelling an attack is by covering up the head and body with the arms and hands with elbows tucked into the waist.

COMBINATIONS

A series of punches thrown in quick succession with both hands and from different angles is far more likely to achieve results than single shots, however hard they are thrown. These attacks often cause the opponent to lower or raise his guard, enabling the oncoming boxer to score hits in unprotected areas. A typical sequence might start with a 1-2 combination to the head. When the opponent raises his hands to defend, this is an opportunity to sidestep and throw hooks to the body to finish off.

Angled attack
The cross strikes the opponent at an angle

CROSS
Thrown with the "second" hand, the cross punch is delivered right-to-left or left-to-right across the opponent's head or body.

TYPES OF FIGHTER

The style of fighting that a boxer chooses will be designed around his physical stature and strengths and weaknesses. For instance, former heavyweight champion Mike Tyson had a bullying, forward style, and a fearsome punch. Floyd Mayweather Jr's style, in contrast, is about grace and poise. He is often able to outclass opponents with guile rather than brute force.

OUT-FIGHTER

Boxers who fight at a distance are usually tall men with a long reach. They do not need to get close to an opponent to inflict damage and will resist all attempts to be drawn into a brawl. Top out-fighters, such as former heavyweight champion Lennox Lewis, typically have a strong jab, too.

IN-FIGHTER

Conversely, in-fighters are often shorter in height and with a short reach. As they cannot win contests from distance, they use their lower centre of gravity to muscle in close, spoiling the work of their opponent and inflicting their own damaging punches. A fight between two in-fighters is always dramatic as neither will back down.

BRAWLER

Also known as the "slugger", or "one puncher", the brawler often stands for everything that's most brutal in the sport. Sluggers tend to lack finesse in the ring, but make up for it in raw power, often able to knock almost any opponent out with a single punch. This makes them exciting to watch.

ROPE-A-DOPE

A phrase coined by Muhammad Ali, the rope-a-dope is the technique of willingly lying on the ropes in a tight defensive stance and inviting the opponent to throw punches until they tire. Although considered a sin in boxing circles, Ali used this style to great effect on several occasions, most notably during the Rumble in the Jungle in Zaire in 1974. Reigning champion George Foreman threw hundreds of punches at his apparently helpless opponent before, in the eighth round, Ali came off the ropes and knocked out a visibly exhausted Foreman.

INSIDE STORY

Amateur boxing has been governed around the world since 1946 by the Association Internationale de Boxe Amateur (AIBA). They oversee the rules and regulations of the sport, govern boxing at the Olympic Games, and have organized a world championship since 1974. The professional sport is marred by disagreement and corruption at governing level. A series of governing bodies recognize their own world champions at different weights. It is rare in modern professional boxing for a fighter to be acknowledged as an undisputed world champion.

PROFESSIONAL GOVERNING BODIES

In the complex world of professional boxing there are currently more than 10 organizations who purport to be world governing bodies. The four most credible are as follows: The World Boxing Association (WBA) dates from 1921 and is the longest-standing professional governing body, but did not have global coverage. In 1963, the World Boxing Council (WBC) was created in the interests of achieving the first truly international body to control the sport. In 1983, the International Boxing Federation (IBF) – formerly the United States Boxing Association – was formed by breakaway members of the WBA. It is based in New Jersey. Then, in 1988, the World Boxing Organization (WBO) was created in Puerto Rico by further disillusioned members of the WBA.

STAT CENTRAL

MOST CONSECUTIVE TITLE DEFENCES

NAME	DEFENCES/CLASS
JOE LOUIS	25 (HEAVYWEIGHT)
RICARDO LOPEZ	21 (STRAWWEIGHT)
HENRY ARMSTRONG	19 (WELTERWEIGHT)
EUSEBIO PEDROZA	19 (FEATHERWEIGHT)
KHAOSAI GALAXY	19 (JR. BANTAMWEIGHT)
WILFREDO GOMEZ	17 (JR. FEATHERWEIGHT)
MYUNG WOO YUH	17 (JR. FLYWEIGHT)
ORLANDO CANIZALES	16 (BANTAMWEIGHT)
BOB FOSTER	14 (LT. HEAVYWEIGHT)
CARLOS MONZON	14 (MIDDLEWEIGHT)

OLYMPIC HEAVYWEIGHT GOLDS

YEAR	NAME	COUNTRY
2012	OLEKSANDR USYK	UKR
2008	RAKHIM CHAKKHIEV	RUS
2004	ODLANIER SOLIS FONTE	CUB
2000	FELIX SAVON	CUB
1996	FELIX SAVON	CUB
1992	FELIX SAVON	CUB
1988	RAY MERCER	USA
1984	HENRY TILLMAN	USA
1980	TEOFILO STEVENSON	CUB
1976	TEOFILO STEVENSON	CUB

MOST CAREER FIGHTS

NAME	WEIGHT	FIGHTS
LEN WICKWAR	LT. HEAVY	463
JACK BRITTON	WELTER	350
JOHNNY DUNDEE	FEATHER	333
BILLY BIRD	WELTER	318
GEORGE MARSDEN	N/A	311
MAXIE ROSENBLOOM	LT. HEAVY	299
HARRY GREB	MIDDLE	298
YOUNG STRIBLING	LT. HEAVY	286
BATTLING LEVINSKY	LT. HEAVY	282
TED (KID) LEWIS	WELTER	279

BIRTH NAMES OF SOME GREATS

BIRTH NAME	FIGHTING NAME
WALKER SMITH	SUGAR RAY ROBINSON
ANTHONY ZESKI	TONY ZALE
ROCCO BARBELLA	ROCKY GRAZIANO
ARNOLD CREAM	JERSEY JOE WALCOTT
JOSEPH BARROW	JOE LOUIS
ROCCO MARCHEGIANO	ROCKY MARCIANO
GERARDO GONZALEZ	KID GAVILAN
JUDAH BERGMAN	JACKIE (KID) BERG
WILLIAM GUIGLERMO PAPALEO	WILLIE PEP
ELIGIO SARDINIAS MONTALBO	KID CHOCOLATE
ARCHIBALD LEEWRIGHT	ARCHIE MOORE
RICHARD IHETU	DICK TIGER

Face mask
Fencers wear a mask that covers the head and neck. The face is protected by a fine-mesh metallic grille, and the neck is covered by a fabric bib

Protective jacket
Competitors wear a padded long-sleeved cotton jacket and, for added safety, a protective undergarment, or plastron, on the sword-arm side

White breeches
Fencers traditionally wear white cotton knee-length breeches. The legs are not padded

Hand guard
A metal guard at the sword's hilt protects the fencer's fingers from injury

Flexible blade
The shape and stiffness of the blade depends on the weapon

Socks
The fencer wears black or white knee-length socks

Shoes
Nimble footwork is a key fencing skill, and competitors wear light, flat-soled trainers with a good grip

ATHLETE PROFILE
Speed, fast responses, agility, and quick footwork are important skills for fencing champions, who tend to be lightly built and lithe. Poise, balance, and hand–eye co-ordination are also necessary attributes. Mental skills are as crucial as physical ones: concentration, quick thinking, and tactical ability are all important.

NEED2KNOW

→ The term "fencing" derives from the word "defence", which is a hangover from the time when sword-fighting was a vital skill on the battlefield.

→ There are three types of fencing distinguished by the type of sword used in contests: the foil, the épée, and the sabre.

→ Fencing is primarily a European tradition. It was particularly associated with France and Italy, which is why so many fencing terms still in use are French.

SIDELINES

25 Number of fencers competing in the 1896 Olympic Games. Fencing is one of only four sports to have appeared in every modern Olympic Games.

5 Fencing is one of the five modern pentathlon events in the Olympics, along with shooting, swimming, showjumping, and running.

13 Number of Olympic medals (including six gold) won by Italy's Edoardo Mangiarotti. He holds the record for winning the most fencing medals.

7 Number of hours a Masters Championship bout lasted in New York in the 1930s – after which bouts were limited to 30 minutes. Today, a bout lasts for just three minutes.

FENCING

SPORT OVERVIEW
Fencing matches consist of bouts between two opponents armed with lightweight, blunt-tipped swords. Points are scored by hitting target areas on the opponent's body with the tip of the weapon. The target areas are determined by the type of weapon being used. Modern fencing developed from the centuries-old tradition of sword-fighting in warfare. Swordplay as a sport rather than as a means of survival developed during the 16th century. Fencing featured in the first modern Olympic Games of 1896 and has appeared ever since.

"DISONISCHENKO"
DURING THE 1976 OLYMPICS (AT THE HEIGHT OF THE COLD WAR) SCANDAL ROCKED THE GAMES. BORIS ONISCHENKO OF THE USSR WAS COMPETING AGAINST BRITAIN'S JIM FOX. FOX SUSPECTED FOUL PLAY AND IT WAS DISCOVERED THAT ONISCHENKO'S ÉPÉE HAD BEEN RIGGED, ALLOWING HIM TO FALSELY RECORD HITS. DUBBED "DISONISCHENKO" BY THE PRESS, HE WAS DISQUALIFIED, ALONG WITH THE WHOLE SOVIET PENTATHLON TEAM.

ON THE PISTE

Fencing bouts are conducted on a narrow, raised platform known as a piste. There is a runback, or extension, at either end of the fighting area of the piste. The height of the platform may vary; the piste is raised to allow spectators a better view of the contest. The fighting area is covered with non-slip conductive mesh, which neutralizes any floor touches.

Referee and judges
Bouts are overseen by a referee, assisted by floor judges (standing on either side of the piste) who check whether the fencer is making touches out of bounds

Electrical scoring apparatus
Fencers wear conductive plastrons wired up to a cord. This registers when a successful touch has been landed by the opponent, and is rigged up to electrical scoring equipment to automatically display points won by each fencer

Timer and recorder
They keep the time for each bout and record the scores

1.5-2m (5-6½ft)

14m (46ft)

On-guard lines
Competitors start each bout standing behind their respective on-guard lines, about 2m (6½ft) behind the centre line. After each hit, they resume this position

Warning line
This indicates to the fencer that he or she is 2m (6½ft) away from the end of the piste

Rear line
A fighter will be penalized for stepping over this line

Centre line
This line indicates the centre of the piste

CHOOSE YOUR WEAPON

There are three different weapons used in fencing: the foil (the sword with which novices usually learn how to fence), the épée, and the sabre. Each has its own associated scoring zone on the opponent's body, and is played to a unique set of rules. Elite fencers usually prefer to specialize in one of these disciplines rather than attempt to master all three.

ELECTRONIC SCORING

An electronic scoring system was first used for épée events at the 1936 Olympic Games in Berlin. A spring-loaded button at the tip of the sword is depressed with each hit, activating an electric scoring light. As the whole body is a target in épée, a reliable scoring system was relatively easy to introduce. It wasn't until the 1956 Olympics in Melbourne that an electric system was first used for foil. It required the use of an electric jacket to cover the target areas, enabling the device to differentiate between "on-target" and "off-target" hits.

FOIL
A lightweight weapon with a flexible blade, the foil has a push button at its tip that must be depressed with a pressure of at least 500g (1.1lb) to register a hit.

ÉPÉE
The épée is heavier and stiffer than the foil, requiring a pressure of 750g (1.6lb) on the push-button to register a hit. The whole body is a valid target.

SABRE
With the sabre, points can be scored using the edge of the blade as well as the tip. There is no push-button: for safety, the sharp point is folded back.

GRIPS
The grip is where the fencer holds the weapon. There are four main types: French, Italian, Spanish, and pistol. The French grip (shown here) is popular with both novices and advanced fencers.

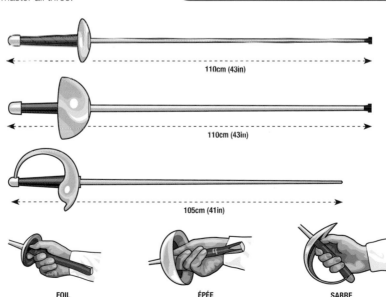

110cm (43in)

110cm (43in)

105cm (41in)

FOIL   ÉPÉE   SABRE

THE RULES OF COMBAT

A fencing match consists of three three-minute bouts with one minute's rest between each bout. The winner is the first competitor to score 15 points, or whoever has the higher score at the end of regulation time. A competitor scores a point by making a legitimate touch to a target area on the opponent's body. Each of the three disciplines within fencing has its own associated target area. If a fencer steps behind the rear limit of his or her side of the piste, the opponent is awarded a point. At Olympic events, there are no preliminary rounds, only elimination contests.

FENCING TERMS

Fencing was a popular pursuit in France, Italy, and Spain, and many of the technical terms are French:

ATTACK AU FER An attack on the opponent's blade.

CORPS À CORPS Literally translated as "body to body", this is when two fencers come into bodily contact (an illegal move).

COUP SEC A meeting of blades that is both crisp and firm (literally, a "dry" blow).

DÉROBEMENT An evasive slide off an opponent's blade.

DESSOUS The low line.

DESSUS The high line.

FINALÉ The last part of an offensive action.

JOUR An opening into which an attack can be launched.

REPARTÉE Making repeated jabbing motions with the sword arm.

TOUCHÉ A touch with the weapon.

BASIC TARGET AREAS

The torso is the main target area (and the only target area in foil fencing). For assault purposes, the torso is divided into four quarters: areas on the upper half are known as the high lines; those on the lower half are called the low lines.

INSIDE AND OUTSIDE LINES

The four quarters of the torso can also be described as inside and outside lines. The two quarters of the target area facing the palm side of the sword hand are known as the inside lines. The two quarters facing the back of the sword hand are referred to as the outside lines.

HIGH LINES

The two quarters of the high lines are each divided into two further areas. Quarte and sixte touches (four and six) are made with the sword hand in supination (nails up). Tierce and quinte (three and five) are made with the sword hand in pronation (nails down).

ALL WHITE ON THE NIGHT
The uniform worn during a fencing bout is traditionally white (although the International Fencing Federation now permits the use of other light colours). It is thought that the outfit of white jacket and breeches is a throwback to the days before electronic scoring systems: the blade would often be covered in soot or ink so that a touch would show up clearly on the opponent's jacket.

FOIL

Foil fighting offers the smallest target area, concentrated on the opponent's torso. The electronic scoring system will only register a hit landed in this area.

ÉPÉE

In épée fighting, a touch can be registered anywhere on the body. However, most attacks are made on the closest part of the competitor, such as the hand, arm, or front foot.

SABRE

The whole of the upper body is a target area in sabre fighting, including the arms and the head. Sabre fencing is lightning fast and usually consists of attacks and feints (false attacks).

Torso target
The torso and "V" of the groin are the only target areas for foil

Access all areas
A valid hit is scored anywhere on the opponent's body

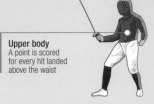

Upper body
A point is scored for every hit landed above the waist

THE EIGHT TARGET AREAS

The four quarters of the torso are each divided into two sections. These sections are known as: prime, seconde, tierce, quarte, quinte, sixte, septime, and octave (this means simply one to eight).

1 Prime
The first target area – on the low line

2 Seconde
The second target area – on the low line

3 Tierce
The third target area – on the high line

4 Quarte
The fourth target area – on the high line

5 Quinte
The fifth target area – on the high line

6 Sixte
The sixth target area – on the high line

7 Septime
The seventh target area – on the low line

8 Octave
The eighth target area – on the low line

ON GUARD

Fencing matches begin with the fencers taking up their positions behind their respective on guard lines. The referee signals the start of a bout by shouting "on guard!". Play is athletic and fast (making an electronic scoring system a necessity), consisting of a series of attacks, parries, and ripostes (counterattacks). In foil and sabre fencing, a "right of way" rule determines who receives the point if both players land a hit simultaneously. This generally means the attacking player wins the point. In épée, both players receive a point.

THE SALUTE

Fencing is a sport that takes its tradition seriously, and players adhere to a strict code of courtesy, etiquette, and honour. An important part of this is the ritual of the salute. The opponents salute each other before the bout by standing with their weapons held vertically in front of their faces. They also salute the referees and spectators. After the bout, the opponents will salute each other again, and shake hands.

ATTACK AND PARRY

Fencing techniques focus on scoring successful touches on the legitimate target areas of the opponent's body. Attacking and defending moves are of equal importance in contests, and a skilful fencer can parry an attack to turn it into an opportunity to launch a counterattack. In contrast to the dramatic gestures and daring attacks often seen in swashbuckling movies, small, precise movements are generally required to land (or avoid) a hit – a surreptitious attack is more difficult to anticipate than a dramatic one.

ATTACK

An attack involves extending the sword arm towards the opponent. The arm is extended from the shoulder completely straight, and the attack is made in one fluid movement. A lunge forward will add force to the attack.

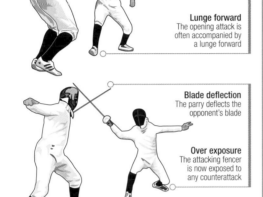

In position
The "on guard" position is the starting point for both offensive and defensive moves

Lunge forward
The opening attack is often accompanied by a lunge forward

PARRY

The parry is a defensive action. This move is designed to deflect or block the opponent's weapon from its intended attacking course. Parries are named after the target position at which they take place, such as a "quarte" parry.

Blade deflection
The parry deflects the opponent's blade

Over exposure
The attacking fencer is now exposed to any counterattack

RIPOSTE

The riposte is the counterattacking follow-up to the parry. Once the opponent's weapon is deflected by the parry, this leaves a space open for the defender to go on the attack in turn. The riposte can be made directly after the parry or can be delayed.

Counterattack
Here, the riposte results in a successful hit

Balancing act
The unarmed arm helps maintain balance

INSIDE STORY

Fencing evolved from a form of combat practised by the ancient Egyptians and Romans, although the current rules and regulations are loosely based on the conventions developed in Europe in the 18th and 19th centuries. Fencing's governing body is the Fédération International d'Escrime (FIE), which was established in Paris in 1913 to standardize the rules that made international fencing tournaments possible. The FIE organizes World Championships that take place every year apart from Olympic years. Fencing has been an Olympic sport since the first modern Olympics in 1896, with the women's event first appearing in 1924.

FIE

Founded in 1913 and with headquarters in Lausanne, Switzerland, the Fédération International d'Escrime (International Fencing Federation) is the organization responsible for setting the rules and regulations for international contests. There are currently 147 affiliated national fencing federations.

FOILED AGAIN

TENSIONS RAN SO HIGH AT THE 1924 OLYMPICS THAT AN ACTUAL DUEL WAS FOUGHT BETWEEN SPARRING COMPETITORS. AFTER JUST TWO MINUTES, BLOOD WAS DRAWN – AND HONOUR RESTORED.

STAT CENTRAL

OLYMPIC MEN'S FOIL CHAMPIONS

YEAR	NAME	COUNTRY
2012	LEI SHENG	(CHN)
2008	BENJAMIN KLEIBRINK	(GER)
2004	BRICE GUYART	(FRA)
2000	KIM YOUNG-HO	(KOR)
1996	ALESSANDRO PUCCINI	(ITA)

OLYMPIC WOMEN'S FOIL CHAMPIONS

YEAR	NAME	COUNTRY
2012	ELISA DI FRANCISCA	(ITA)
2008	VALENTINA VEZZALI	(ITA)
2004	VALENTINA VEZZALI	(ITA)
2000	VALENTINA VEZZALI	(ITA)
1996	LAURA BADEA	(ROM)

OLYMPIC MEN'S ÉPÉE CHAMPIONS

YEAR	NAME	COUNTRY
2012	RUBEN LIMARDO	(VEN)
2008	MATTEO TAGLIARIOL	(SUI)
2004	MARCEL FISCHER	(SUI)
2000	PAVEL KOLOBKOV	(RUS)
1996	ALEKSANDR BEKETOV	(RUS)

OLYMPIC WOMEN'S ÉPÉE CHAMPIONS

YEAR	NAME	COUNTRY
2012	YANA SHEMYAKINA	(UKR)
2008	BRITTA HEIDEMANN	(GER)
2004	TIMEA NAGY	(HUN)
2000	TIMEA NAGY	(HUN)
1996	LAURA FLESSEL	(FRA)

OLYMPIC MEN'S SABRE CHAMPIONS

YEAR	NAME	COUNTRY
2012	ARON SZILAGYI	(HUN)
2008	ZHONG MAN	(CHI)
2004	ALDO MONTANO	(ITA)
2000	MIHAI CLAUDIU COVALIU	(ROM)
1996	STANISLAV POZDNIAKOV	(RUS)

OLYMPIC WOMEN'S SABRE CHAMPIONS

YEAR	NAME	COUNTRY
2012	KIM JIYON	(KOR)
2008	MARIEL ZAGUNIS	(USA)
2004	MARIEL ZAGUNIS	(USA)
2000	COMPETITION NOT HELD	
1996	COMPETITION NOT HELD	

NEED2KNOW

→ Freestyle sparring, or randori, is the best way to learn the techniques and tactics of judo. This form of training is considered to be the most effective way to improve muscle strength and cardiovascular fitness, speed up reaction time, and hone the skills needed to resist an opponent's attack.

→ Strangulation and choking are some of the most effective techniques in judo. Strangulation cuts off the blood supply to the brain at the carotid arteries at the sides of the neck, while choking blocks the passage of air at the front of the neck. Both may render an opponent unconscious in seconds.

→ The Kodokan Judo Institute in Tokyo, Japan, is the spiritual home of judo. It was founded by Jigoro Kano (1860–1938), creator of judo, in 1882.

Jacket
In international competitions, the judoka wears a blue or white jacket, called a uwagi, made from heavyweight cotton. The size and fit must conform to the sport's regulations

JUDO

SPORT OVERVIEW
Judo developed in the 19th century from the teachings of Jigoro Kano of Japan. Based on the centuries-old techniques of jujitsu, this unarmed combat sport forbids any form of punching or kicking. Instead, the aim is to score an ippon – the equivalent of a knockout punch – by throwing an opponent to the ground, pinning an opponent down, or forcing a submission using an armlock or choke.

FIELD OF PLAY
The size of the competition area conforms to the rules of the International Judo Federation (IJF). The floor is covered with protective mats called tatami, which usually measure 2 x 1m (6ft 6in x 3ft) and cushion the impact of throws. Traditionally, tatami are made from pressed straw, but pressed foam is more common today. Most competitions take place within a contest area that measures 8 x 8m (26 x 26ft), although an area up to 10 x 10m (33 x 33ft) is allowed. IJF rules also require a safety area of 3m (10ft). The contest area and safety area are together known as the field of play.

Referee
The referee stands within the contest area and shouts "Hajime!" to start the fight. The referee judges the fight and signals his scores to the scorers. If there is a dispute, the referee will consult with the two corner judges to come to a decision

Belt
The belt is 3m (10ft) long, and the colour indicates the judoka's rank

Identifying colours
In competition, the colour of the tatami that make up the contest area is different from those that make up the safety area. Any colour combination can be used

PLAYER PROFILE
Anyone can practise judo. There are different weight classes, so there are no size restrictions, and it is open to both sexes. Strength is vital, but agility is equally important.

Safety Area
The safety area is a 3m (10ft) wide border that encloses the danger area. The safety area is not completely out of bounds. A judoka may throw his or her opponent into the safety area and still score points if a step is taken into the safety area after the throw. But an automatic penalty is given if a judoka intentionally steps out of the competition area

SIDELINES

67 The official number of throws in Kodokan judo.

77 The age of Jigora Kano when he died in 1938.

3 Judoka ranked at 10th dan in 2013, worldwide.

7 The number of judo weight categories in the Olympics.

200 The number of national federations affiliated to the sport's official governing body, the International Judo Federation.

10 The average number of seconds it takes a person to fall unconscious when placed in a chokehold.

Legwear
The legwear, called zubon, are made from a light canvas-style fabric, with double stitching and knee patches

BELT SYSTEM

The colour of a judoka's belt corresponds to his or her rank within the kyu-dan grading system. Traditionally, there are six student grades, or kyu. In western judo, they have the following belt colours: sixth kyu (white), fifth kyu (yellow), fourth kyu (orange), third kyu (green), second kyu (blue), and first kyu (brown). Some countries have extra kyu and belt colours. In Japan judoka usually wear a white belt up to the rank of first kyu. The belt colours of the 12 advanced grades are much more consistent. The belt for the first five dan is black. Judoka from sixth dan to eighth dan wear belts with alternating white and red (or black) panels. Solid red (or black) belts are accorded to judoka up to eleventh dan. Twelfth dan has a wider version of the simple white belt of a beginner.

SCOREBOARD

The scoreboard displays the stopclock and the points and penalties accumulated by each judoka during the fight. Judo has four scores (see p.218), which are shown at the top of the scoreboard below (from left to right): "I" for ippon, "W" stands for waza-ari, "Y" stands for yuko, and "K" stands for koka. Judo has two penalties, which are shown by the red light next to the letters in the centre of the scoreboard. "H" stands for hansokumake (immediate disqualification), and "S" stands for shido. If a judoka is awarded four shidos, the result is a hansokumake and the judoka is disqualified.

Timers
There are two timekeepers. One records the time for the contest. The other specializes in "osaekomi", the referee's command to begin timing a hold

Scorers
The scorer and contest recorder keep a written record of the score and the overall course of each fight

White
The judoka in white scored an ippon to win the match. The scoreboard shows three penalties (shido) against white

Stopclock
The time limit for international competition is five minutes for men and four minutes for women

Blue
The judoka in blue scored three kokas, two yukos and one waza-ari. There is one shido against blue

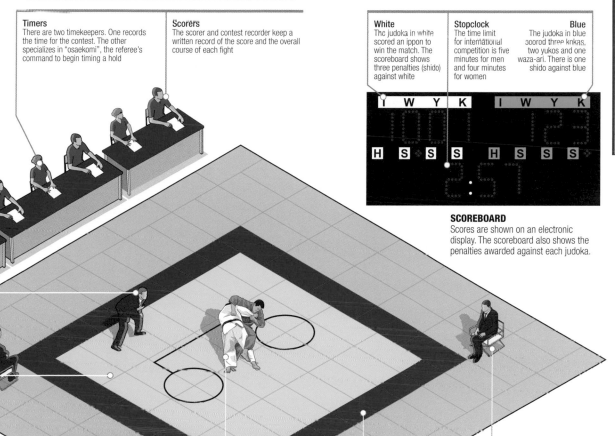

SCOREBOARD
Scores are shown on an electronic display. The scoreboard also shows the penalties awarded against each judoka.

Corner judge (2)
Two corner judges sit at opposite corners of the contest area. Their main responsibility is to check that the fight remains within the contest area. If the referee disputes a call, all three officials vote to decide on the outcome

THE GENTLE WAY

JUDO IS JAPANESE FOR "GENTLE WAY", AND REFERS TO THE AIM OF TURNING AN OPPONENT'S STRENGTH TO YOUR OWN ADVANTAGE. THE GOAL OF A JUDOKA IS TO UPSET THE OPPONENT'S BALANCE AND MOMENTUM TO ACHIEVE FORCEFUL THROWS WITH MINIMUM EFFORT.

Judoka
In competition, the first judoka called to fight wears a blue judogi. His or her opponent wears a white judogi. At the beginning and end of the contest, each contestant stands on the mark that corresponds to the colour of his or her gi and bows as a sign of respect. Both contestants return to their marks if the referee shouts "Matte!" during a fight

Danger Zone
The danger zone is a border 1m (3ft) wide that encloses the contest area. The danger zone forms part of the contest area, but there is a penalty for spending too long in this part of the competition area. Red tatami are used to make up the danger zone. In 2006, a trial rule change did away with the danger zone. The IJF made the rule change permanent in 2007

BASIC JUDO GRIP

The basic judo grip is the sleeve and lapel grip. This involves gripping the lapel of the opponent's uwagi with the right hand and using the left hand to grip the opponent's right sleeve under the elbow. The basic grip is an excellent starting point for throws.

Gripping the lapel
The lapel is used in a number of moves to get hold of the opponent

Elbow grip
The judoka grips their opponent's right sleeve under the elbow

RULES OF ENGAGEMENT

Judo is governed by the rules of the International Judo Federation (IJF). Recent rule books show a trend toward a more dynamic style of judo – a defensive style is heavily penalized.

IPPON, WAZA-ARI, YOKO, KOKA

There are four scores in a judo contest. A judoka can win the fight outright by scoring an ippon or by scoring two waza-aris, which counts as an ippon. Lesser scores include the yoko and koka. If the time limit passes before an ippon is scored, the number of lesser scores are taken into consideration.

PENALTIES

Judoka are expected to fight fairly and in the spirit of the sport. Foul play is heavily penalized. The four levels of punishment are: first shido (known simply as shido), second shido (chui), third shido (keikoku), and hansokumake (disqualification). Penalties are cumulative and result in the next higher penalty.

ATTACKING OPTIONS

There are two main phases of combat in judo. During the standing phase (tachi-waza), the aim is to throw your opponent on to their back using control, force, and speed. During the ground phase (ne-waza), the aim is to pin your opponent on to the ground or force a submission.

THROWS

A judoka uses a variety of throwing techniques (nage-waza) to force an opponent onto the ground. A judoka can score an ippon and win the fight outright by executing a powerful and controlled throw to force the opponent onto his or her back. In competition, however, judoka are evenly matched so a throw will usually score a koka, yuko, or waza-ari.

O-GOSHI

The o-goshi is one of the traditional throws developed by judo's founding father, Jigoro Kano (1860–1938). It is classified as a hip-throwing technique, or koshi-waza. A hip throw uses the hip as a pivot point to throw the opponent to the floor. There are several types of hip throws. O-goshi is one of the first throws a judoka will learn.

Pivot point
The hip is the pivot point for the throw

Floor contact
The opponent is thrown off balance once contact with the floor is lost

IPPON SEOINAGE

The ippon seoinage is the most common throw encountered in elite judo competition. It is classified as a hand-throwing technique, or te-waza. Ippon seoinage involves throwing an opponent over the shoulder and onto the floor. It has been likened to throwing a sack of rice over the shoulder.

Sack of rice
Gripping the elbow sleeve, the opponent is thrown over the shoulder and then forced to the floor

Flexible knees
The thrower's knees are bent and flexible to add momentum to the throw

TOMOE NAGE

Some throwing techniques, called sacrifice throws, or sutemi-waza, are dangerous to execute because the thrower is positioned on the ground. One of these is the tomoe nage, or circle throw, which uses a foot planted on the stomach or thigh to throw the opponent over the head or shoulders.

High flying
The opponent is launched in to the air over the thrower, who is on the floor

Foot to stomach
The thrower plants their foot into the opponent's stomach as leverage for the throw

OSOTO GARI

The osoto gari is another of the original judo throws used by Jigoro Kano. It is classified as a foot-throwing technique, or ashi-waza. This type of throw involves using one of the legs to sweep away one of the opponent's legs. An effective osoto gari pinpoints the load-bearing leg so that the opponent falls over.

Getting a grip
The thrower grasps the sleeve at the elbow and the jacket

Leg sweep
The opponent's leg is swept up, throwing them off balance

SIDELINES

7 The number of points awarded for throwing an opponent on their back without control and force.

2 The number of main phases of combat: the standing (tachi-waza) and the ground (ne-waza) phase.

4 The number of phases in throwing technique: off-balancing; body positioning; execution; and finish.

25 The number of seconds an opponent must be held or pinned down to the floor in order to win a match.

STAT CENTRAL

OLYMPIC WEIGHT CATEGORIES

FEMALE	MALE
+78kg (+172lb)	+100kg (+220lb)
78kg (172lb)	100kg (220lb)
70kg (154lb)	90kg (198lb)
63kg (139lb)	81kg (179lb)
57kg (126lb)	73kg (161lb)
52kg (114lb)	66kg (146lb)
48kg (106lb)	60kg (132lb)

MEN'S HEAVYWEIGHT OLYMPIC CHAMPIONS

YEAR	WINNER (NATIONALITY)
2012	TEDDY RINER (FRA)
2008	SATOSHI ISHII (JAP)
2004	KEIJI SUZUKI (JAP)
2000	DAVID DOUILLET (FRA)
1996	DAVID DOUILLET (FRA)
1992	DAVID KHAKALESHVILI (EUN)
1988	HITOSHI SAITO (JAP)
1984	HITOSHI SAITO (JAP)
1980	ANGELO PARISI (FRA)
1976	SERGEI NOVIKOV (USSR)
1972	WILLEM RUSKA (NED)

WOMEN'S HEAVYWEIGHT OLYMPIC CHAMPIONS

YEAR	WINNER (NATIONALITY)
2012	IDALYS OTIZ (CUB)
2008	TONG WEN (CHI)
2004	MAKI TSUKARA (JAP)
2000	HUA YUAN (CHI)

PINS

A pinning hold (osaekomi-waza) is a grappling technique that aims to hold the opponent on the ground. Osaekomi, in which both shoulders touch the ground for more than 25 seconds, results in an ippon. For holds of shorter duratons, a judoka may score a waza-ari (20–24 seconds), yoko (15–19 seconds), or koka (10–14 seconds).

SAMURAI SPORT

JUDO IS DERIVED PARTLY FROM JUJITSU, THE HAND-TO-HAND COMBAT TECHNIQUE USED BY SAMURAI WARRIORS. IT IS THE ONLY OLYMPIC SPORT WHERE SUBMISSION HOLDS ALLOW PARTICIPANTS TO CHOKE AN OPPONENT.

Round the neck
The judoka wraps his arm around the opponent's neck

Hip to chest
The judoka's hip is against his opponent's chest

Secure hold
One hand holds the neck

Grip the belt
The other hand passes through legs and grips the belt

KESA GATAME
Many judo throws end with kesa gatame in the ground phase, since the basic judo grip already has one hand on the opponent's lapel and one hand near the opponent's elbow.

YOKO-SHIHO GATAME
This osaekomi holds the opponent's neck and leg while laying on their chest. One hand wraps round the neck and grips the lapel. The other passes through the legs and grips the belt at the back.

SUBMISSIONS

A submission is achieved through a joint lock (kansetsu-waza) or strangulation (shime-waza). For reasons of safety, arm locks are the only kansetsu-waza allowed in competition. Strangulations are equally dangerous, and the use of shime-waza is usually restricted to age and rank in competitive judo.

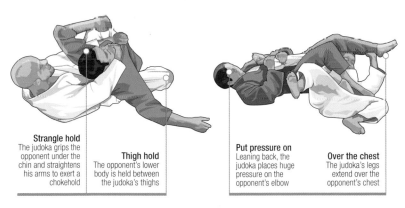

Strangle hold
The judoka grips the opponent under the chin and straightens his arms to exert a chokehold

Thigh hold
The opponent's lower body is held between the judoka's thighs

Put pressure on
Leaning back, the judoka places huge pressure on the opponent's elbow

Over the chest
The judoka's legs extend over the opponent's chest

OKURI-ERI-JIME
The judoka slides one hand under the opponent's armpit and grips the opposite lapel. At the same time the judoka wraps the other arm around the neck and slides the hand up the free lapel.

JUJI GATAME
A powerful joint lock, here the legs end up across the opponent's chest, the arm locked between the thighs. The arm is held with the wrist to the chest. Leaning back places huge pressure on the elbow.

INSIDE STORY

Judo was first seen at the Olympics in the 1964 Tokyo Games. It was not included at the 1968 Mexico City Olympics, but Judo has been a regular Olympic sport for men since the 1972 Munich Games. Women's judo was included as a demonstration sport in the 1988 Seoul Olympics and became an official Olympic event at the 1992 Barcelona Games. World Championships for men, women, and juniors are held every two years.

GOVERNING BODY
The International Judo Federation (IJF) is the world's governing body for judo. Founded in 1951, the IJF comprises five unions representing Africa, Asia, the Americas, Europe, and Oceania.

→ Wrestlers are known formally as sumotoris, informally as rikishi.

→ From the first bout in Japan in 453CE until the 1990s, sumo wrestling was a men-only sport, but the International Sumo Federation (IFS) now actively encourages female participation.

→ The elaborate ceremonies surrounding a sumo contest are derived from Shinto religious practices: the pre-fight sprinkling of salt on the dohyo, for example, is to ward off evil spirits.

SUMO

SPORT OVERVIEW

Sumo wrestlers attempt to throw their opponent out of the ring or off balance so that he or she has to touch the ground with a part of the body other than the feet. Many matches last no longer than a few seconds, but the techniques, tactics, and rituals are endlessly fascinating to millions. Sumo probably originated in China in the 3rd century BCE, but was practised almost exclusively in Japan until the 20th century, when its popularity spread worldwide.

Four corners
The four corners may be decorated to symbolize the seasons of the year

Gable roof
The structure resembles a Shinto shrine; Rikishi always enter from east or west

In suspense
The tsuriyane is hung from the roof on ropes, wires, or poles

TSURIYANE CANOPY
The overhead structure above the dais on which the combat takes place is known as a "tsuriyane" (canopy). It traditionally resembles the roof of a Shinto shrine, but in some modern arenas it may be no more than a sheet of perspex.

COMBAT ZONE

Sumo bouts are played on a dohyo, a raised square platform within which a circular combat area is marked. The area is regarded as sacred to the spirits of the Shinto religion. A new dohyo is built for every major tournament. The edges of the circle are sprinkled with sand to help the referee see when a wrestler touches the perimeter.

Chon-mage
Japanese term for the sumo topknot and hair slicked with oil. The hair is tied to denote rank: the greater the wrestler, the more complex the knot

Mawashi
This thick belt is made of a band of silk about 10m (32ft) long, wound repeatedly around the wrestler's midriff, and secured between his legs

Raised leg
This ritual pre-combat gesture is a show of strength

Judges
Four judges are positioned around the dohyo. The gyoji refers to them if he cannot decide a winner himself

Combat area
A circular clay surface is covered with sand; it is set on a raised platform 34–60cm (13–24in) above the ground

Gyoji
The Japanese term for referee. He wears a samurai kimono and a hat similar to that worn by medieval Shinto priests. He also carries the battle fan of Japanese generals

5.7m (18ft 9in)

PLAYER PROFILE
Sumo wrestlers must weigh more than 69kg (154lb), and be over 1.7m (5ft 7in) tall. Although many of the most famous exponents are huge men with enormous torsos and low centres of gravity, small and skilful combatants can often overcome much bigger opponents.

Sagari
Decorative silk tassels adorn the lower edge of the mawashi

Step to raised dais
This feature enables the referee and the wrestlers to mount the dohyo elegantly

Parallel lines
Combatants square up behind these marks before the intial clinch

Water
For refreshment before the bout and at breaks during it

WINNING A BOUT

At the start of a bout, each wrestler claps his hands to show that he is not holding anything. Once battle commences, the first wrestler to go down is the loser but, if both wrestlers fall simultaneously, the referee or the judges may award the bout to either fighter if, in their view, the other had no chance of winning. Punching, kicking, choking, going for the eyes or stomach, pulling hair, and hitting below the belt are all prohibited and punishable by disqualification.

SUMO STYLES

There are two main styles of sumo wrestling: oshi-zumo and yotsu-zumo. In the former, also known as "fighting apart", the aim is to push the opponent out of the ring, often by using his own weight to his disadvantage. In yotsu-zumo, the objective is to get hold of the opponent's belt, and then carry him out or throw him down. Specific techniques are shown below.

RANKING SYSTEM

Sumo wrestlers have a strict pecking order: their rankings rise in victory and fall in defeat. The exceptions are those in the highest echelon, the yokozuna, who generally retire rather than decline. Juryo wrestlers and those ranked above are entitled to wear kesho mawashi (ceremonial silk aprons).

YOKOZUNA The highest level a sumo wrestler can achieve; there are usually no more than two at any one time, and there have been fewer than 70 in the entire history of the sport.
OZEKI The honorary title given to any winner of 33 bouts over three consecutive tournaments.
SEKIWAKE Usually between three and five per tournament.
KOMUSUBI Again, usually three to five per tournament.
MAEGASHIRA The lowest elite echelon; usually number about 120.
JURYO A group of 28 wrestlers of approximately equal ability.
MAKUSHITA Apprentices who are learning from the grade above them; there are usually about 120 of them.

Handling charge
Grab the mawashi and start moving

YORIKI
This move involves seizing the opponent's belt and attempting to march him out of the ring.

Low grip
Attacker grasps bottom of belt

UWATENAGE
Gripping the mawashi, the sumotori pulls his opponent down while turning his own upper body.

Ground force
Heavy pressure to prevent recovery

YORITAOSHI
The frontal crush-out: the opponent is driven backwards and collapses under the force of the attack.

Shoo off
The push is best aimed at the rump

OKURIDASHI
The rear push-out: wrestlers often become victims of this move after an attack of their own has gone wrong.

Turning tables
The right arm turns defence into attack

HATAKIKOMI
As one wrestler charges, the other sidesteps and slaps the opponent's back or arm, pushing him over.

Flip over
The aim is to force a fall within the circle

OKURITAOSHI
The rear push-down: the wrestler attacks from behind and forces the opponent to the ground.

Upper hand
The thrust is at the face and upper body

OSHIDASHI
Frontal push-out: the attacker shoves the opponent out of the ring without gripping the mawashi.

Top to bottom
The attacker pushes in order to get the opponent back on to his heels

TSUKIDASHI
The attacker drives his opponent out of the ring with a rhythmic thrusting motion.

SIDELINES

284 The weight, in kilograms, of Konishiki, the heaviest wrestler in sumo history. Born in Hawaii in 1963, he became an ozeki in 1987. He became famous worldwide under the byname "The Dump Truck".

700 The approximate number of full-time professional sumo wrestlers across the six divisions. Most are Japanese, although several other nationalities are also represented.

34,000,000 The annual fight money, in Japanese Yen, earned by leading sumotori (about US$284,000). Some sumo stars supplement these basic earnings by sponsoring commercial products and making personal appearances.

INSIDE STORY

In the modern sport of sumo wrestling the most prestigious events are the Grand Sumo tournaments. Six of them are held each year – three in Tokyo, and one each in Osaka, Nagoya, and Fukuoka. Each of the tournaments lasts 15 days and is watched by millions of television viewers. Wrestlers may be promoted or demoted from one rank to another as a result of their performances at these events. From its historical stronghold in Japan, sumo wrestling spread to many other parts of the world during the second half of the 20th century: it is now firmly established in 76 other countries, including the United States and 24 European nations.

INTERNATIONAL SUMO FEDERATION
The world governing body is still based in Tokyo, and most of the administrators are Japanese.

WRESTLING

NEED2KNOW

→ Wrestling is enjoyed around the world, and is particularly popular in the United States, southeastern Europe, and West and Central Asia.

→ As well as Greco-Roman and freestyle wrestling many local forms exist, such as glima in Iceland, kushti in Iran, schwingen in Switzerland, yagli in Turkey, and sombo (see p.238) in Russia.

→ A women's freestyle world championship was introduced in 1987.

EVENT OVERVIEW

Wrestling is a combat sport in which players try to grapple their opponents to the ground using a variety of holds. It demands concentration and strategy, in addition to strength. The two main variations are freestyle, the more popular form, and Greco-Roman wrestling. Women's wrestling is also popular in some countries, such as the United States.

COMPETITOR PROFILE

Wrestlers must be physically strong and quick on their feet. Training involves weights and distance running to build up strength and stamina. Wrestlers also spend long periods rehearsing moves with sparring partners.

Colour coded
Wrestlers wear singlets; in each bout, one contestant wears red, the other blue

Ankle support
Rubber-soled boots come up over the ankles to help prevent twists and sprains

Skull cap
A head guard is not compulsory, but many wrestlers wear them to reduce the risk of damage to ear lobes during close encounters

Knee guards
Knee guards give support to the joints, which take a lot of pressure, and prevent grazing

COMBAT AREA

The wrestling area must be marked as shown. The surface, made of rubber, should be raised no more than 1.1m (3ft 7in) above the floor. In opposite corners are red and blue triangles that mark the wrestlers' bases at the start of the bout. Matches are observed by a referee, who joins the wrestlers on the mat, so that he can study every move at close quarters. On the sidelines sit a judge and a third official known as the mat chairman: they may stop the bout if they notice an infringement that the referee has missed.

MARKING TIME

In freestyle wrestling, a pin (fall) ends a match. It must be held for about a second to score – the time it takes the referee to count "21, 22", which he does in French ("vingt-et-un, vingt-deux"). A wrestler with a six-point lead is awarded that period of the bout.

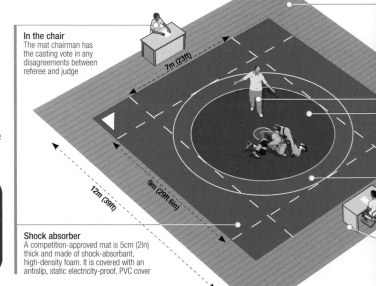

In the chair
The mat chairman has the casting vote in any disagreements between referee and judge

7m (23ft)

9m (29ft 6in)

12m (39ft)

Shock absorber
A competition-approved mat is 5cm (2in) thick and made of shock-absorbant, high-density foam. It is covered with an antislip, static electricity-proof, PVC cover

RULES OF ENGAGEMENT

Bouts are divided into two three-minute periods, with a third period – known as the clinch – to settle ties. If a wrestler pins both his opponent's shoulders to the ground, he wins outright. More often the bout goes to the wrestler with the higher score. Points – from one to five, according to the move – are awarded by the officials for throws and getting an opponent to the floor, particularly in the "danger position", with his back close to the mat, from where a pin may be easily possible.

GETTING A GRIP

In Greco-Roman wrestling only the upper body is involved: the legs may never hold or be held. Freestyle is more of an "anything goes" event: even crotch holds are permitted.

STARTING POSITIONS

The players are called from their corners by the referee, who checks that their clothing has no sharp attachments and that their fingernails are not too long. They then salute each other and shake hands before the start of the bout.

FREESTYLE TAKEDOWN

Although the arms play a significant role in freestyle wrestling, both during and after the initial grapple, leg holds normally predominate. Most of a bout is fought out with both players on the mat. The double-leg takedown is a common way to get an opponent down.

Close fit
The key is to keep the chest close to the opponent

Constrictor
The attacker may also use his or her arms to hold down the opponent's legs

ATTACK
The wrestler begins the move by going down on one knee as he advances towards his opponent.

GRASP
He then drops on to both knees, and grabs the opponent's legs behind the knees for leverage.

TWIST
Maintaining his grip, the attacker then twists and begins to get his legs around those of the other wrestler.

DROP
The attacker keeps hold of the opponent after he hits the floor and should be in the better position.

GRECO-ROMAN GRAPPLE

There are two categories of Greco-Roman hold: standing holds and mat holds. Among the most spectacular moves is the shoulder throw, shown here, which requires strength, timing, and the agility to get out of the way of the other wrestler as he or she falls.

  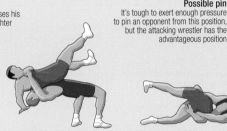 

Tight grip
If the attacker loses his grip the other fighter may turn on him

Possible pin
It's tough to exert enough pressure to pin an opponent from this position, but the attacking wrestler has the advantageous position

START
Approaching from the flank, the attacker grabs his opponent around the chest.

LIFT-OFF
Having gained a hold, the attacker lifts the other wrestler up, using his thighs and back.

PITCH
Keeping his feet on the floor, the attacker leans back and pulls the opponent over.

LAND LOCK
The attacker maintains his chest hold until the other wrestler is doubled up on the mat.

Protection area
The bout is stopped if a wrestler touches this zone with any part of his body

Wristy ref
The referee wears a red cuff on one arm and a blue cuff on the other; he shows points awarded to each wrestler by raising fingers on the appropriate hand

Wrestling area
The bout begins with the wrestlers facing each other on opposite sides of the inner circle

Passivity zone
A 1m (3ft 3in) circle warns wrestlers that they are near the edge of the wrestling zone. They can fight here, but not begin moves

Judge
The judge records the scores he awards and also those signalled by the referee

INSIDE STORY

Wrestling has been a medal sport at every modern Olympic Games since 1896. Women first competed at the Olympics in 2004. Professional wrestling emerged in the United States in the early 20th century. The eventual result was the creation in 1963 of what became the World Wrestling Federation, or WWF (now World Wrestling Entertainment, WWE). The WWF oversaw the 1980s' and 1990s' heyday of events such as Wrestlemania, theatrical star-studded bouts that owed as much to entertainment as to sport.

GOVERNING BODY

The Fédération Internationale des Luttes Associées (FILA) was founded in Sweden shortly before the opening of the Stockholm Olympics in 1912. In 1946 it relocated to France. In 1965 it moved to its current home in Lausanne, Switzerland. The organization currently has 174 affiliated national federations.

STAT CENTRAL

WEIGHT DIVISIONS (MEN)

DIVISION	WEIGHT/MAX. WEIGHT
SUPER HEAVYWEIGHT	96–120kg (211–264lb)
HEAVYWEIGHT	96kg (211lb)
MIDDLEWEIGHT	84kg (185lb)
WELTERWEIGHT	74kg (163lb)
LIGHTWEIGHT	66kg (145lb)
BANTAMWEIGHT	60kg (132lb)
FLYWEIGHT	50–55kg (121lb)

TV TIMES

THE 1970S AND 80S SAW BRITISH WRESTLING AT ITS PEAK, WITH MILLIONS TUNING IN EVERY SATURDAY.

- → Karate is the most widely practised of all the Oriental martial arts. There are more than 70 different styles.

- → Karate and kickboxing are quite closely related and for many years the same governing bodies oversaw both sports.

- → Karate began in Okinawa in the 17th century. Funakoshi Gichin, who created the Shotokan style in the 20th century, is considered the father of modern karate.

SPORT OVERVIEW

Karate is a Japanese martial art that literally means "empty hand". Derived from Chinese combat techniques karate uses the arms, hands, elbows, knees, feet, and head. Its key tenets are self-defence, physical fitness, and spiritual awareness, which karate practitioners, known as karateka, traditionally use for self-development. As pupils, they learn the basic techniques of breathing, kicking, punching, and blocking, and the various stances that provide a platform for stability or mobility. Karate's three main elements are kata (a series of moves), kumite (sparring with a partner), and kobodo (weapons forms). In the 1970s and 1980s, karate became competitive and eventually evolved into a sport with world championships.

KARATE

Foot strikes
Kicks should strike the opponent using the ball of the foot or the instep. First extending the knee and then snapping through the lower leg generates extra power

Loose fit
The uniform must be light and loose fitting to give a full range of movement, including high kicks and low sweeps

Eye contact
As a sign of respect for their opponent, karateka never take their eye off their rival, even when bowing before the contest begins

Coloured belt
The colour of the karateka's belt indicates the level of proficiency he or she has reached

FIGHTER PROFILE
Karateka are toned, athletic individuals with strong upper bodies and leg muscles. For kumite, karateka require a relatively high pain threshold. All leading karateka must have a high level of self-discipline and live their life according to the karate code (dojo kun).

Balancing act
Achieving good balance is fundamental to all martial arts. If a karateka's stance is poor and not well rooted he or she will be easy to knock down or throw

SIDELINES

178 The number of competitors taking part in the 1st World Championships held in Tokyo in 1970. The competitors at the 2012 World Championships in Paris, France, numbered more than 1,000.

15 The number of cement slabs broken by Bruce Haynes, an 8th-dan black belt and champion of tamashiwari. This karate art literally means "trial by wood" but has become the art of breaking objects with a single blow from a bare hand.

50,000,000
The estimated total number of individual members belonging to clubs, associations and groups affiliated to the World Karate Federation (WKF).

SUPERFOOT
BILL "SUPERFOOT" WALLACE WAS ONE OF THE WORLD'S LEADING EXPONENTS OF KARATE AND KICKBOXING IN THE 1970S, WINNING 23 CONSECUTIVE FIGHTS BETWEEN 1974 AND 1980. WALLACE FOCUSED ON BUILDING MUSCLE IN HIS LEFT LEG AFTER A JUDO INJURY TO HIS RIGHT KNEE. HIS NICKNAME DERIVED FROM THE PRODIGIOUS POWER OF HIS LEFT LEG AND THE SPEED WITH WHICH HE COULD STRIKE. DURING TRIALS THIS WAS CLOCKED AT 90KPH (60MPH).

AREA OF COMBAT

Kumite (sparring) matches are held on a square mat surrounded by a number of officials who ensure the contestants do not break the rules and are awarded the points for displaying the correct techniques. The karate rules of etiquette and respect are followed: for example, contestants bow to each other before the start of a bout by bending forwards from the waist but always keeping alert and looking ahead.

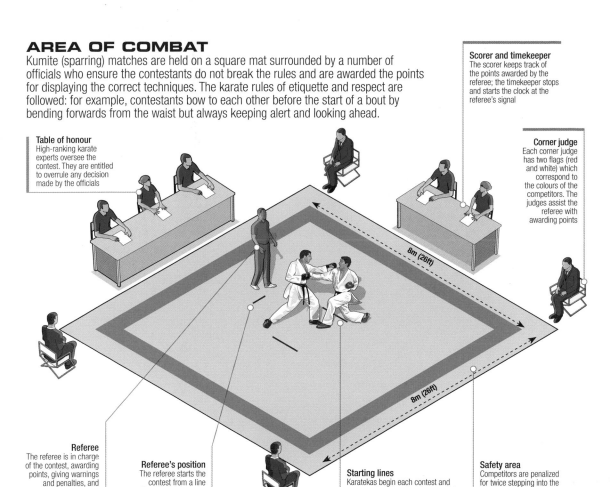

Scorer and timekeeper
The scorer keeps track of the points awarded by the referee; the timekeeper stops and starts the clock at the referee's signal

Table of honour
High-ranking karate experts oversee the contest. They are entitled to overrule any decision made by the officials

Corner judge
Each corner judge has two flags (red and white) which correspond to the colours of the competitors. The judges assist the referee with awarding points

8m (26ft)

8m (26ft)

Referee
The referee is in charge of the contest, awarding points, giving warnings and penalties, and signalling the start and end of each bout

Referee's position
The referee starts the contest from a line 2m (6ft 6in) from the centre of the mat

Starting lines
Karatekas begin each contest and resume after a break at two parallel lines, 3m (10ft) apart

Safety area
Competitors are penalized for twice stepping into the 2m (6ft 6in)-wide safety area around the mat

KARATE KIT

A karateka wears a white uniform, or gi, made up of a jacket, trousers, and belt (see p.224). Like the judo uniform, the karate gi is cut from a canvas-style cloth which can stand up to a considerable amount of wear and does not restrict the mobility of the karateka. The gi may be light, medium, or heavy. Karateka usually wear protective gear — men wear an athletic cup to protect their groin and women use a bust protector. Other kit, such as padded mitts, gloves, shin guards, foot protectors, shoes, and gumshields may also be permitted.

Karate gloves
Some kumite competitions allow the use of gloves with closed finger design for semi-contact sparring

Karate shoes
Beginners and intermediates may benefit from using soft footwear that provide good purchase with the floor

COLOURED BELTS

Levels of proficiency in karate are normally indicated by the colour of the karateka's belt, or obi. Several elements in the student's abilities are evaluated when progressing from one grade to the next, including knowledge and mastery of techniques, as well as kata and kumite. The higher the grade, the more extensive the requirements. The number and colour of gradings vary between karate styles, but white is always the most basic grading and brown the highest kyu (pupil). Black belt is the highest karate grade. Upon attaining black, the pupil becomes a dan (master), although there are up to 10 levels of dan.

Black	1st–10th Dan
Brown	1st Kyu
Blue	2nd Kyu
Green	3rd Kyu
Red	4th Kyu
Yellow	5th Kyu
White	9th–6th Kyu

THE KARATE CODE
Karate has a dojo kun, a set of guidelines which karetekas follow in their everyday lives and in the room, or dojo, in which karate is taught. This karate code can be summarized by five commands; Seek perfection of character; Be faithful; Endeavour; Respect others; Refrain from violent behaviour.

KARATE STYLES

The Federation of All Japan Karate-do Organizations recognizes four main karate styles – Goju-ryu, Shito-ryu, Shotokan, and Wado-ryu – although there are more than 70 different styles, including Shorin-ryu, Uechi-ryu, and Kyokushinkai. Styles that do not belong to one of these schools are not considered to be illegitimate. Most schools are affiliated with or heavily influenced by one or more of these traditional styles.

SHOTOKAN

Shotokan is a school of karate, developed from various martial arts by master Gichin Funakoshi (1868–1957). Techniques in kata are characterized by long, deep stances which provide stable, powerful movements and also help strengthen the legs. Strength and power are demonstrated instead of slower, more flowing motions.

WADO-RYU

After receiving tutelage from Funakoshi and other Okinawan masters, Hironori Ohtsuka set off to merge Shindo Yoshin Ryu with Okinawan karate and formed Wado-ryu. The name is translated literally as "harmony".

SHITO-RYU

This was developed in 1931 by Kenwa Mabuni. It is a combination style, which attempts to unite the diverse roots of karate.

GOJU-RYU

Using a combination of hard and soft techniques, this style's specialty is close-quarters combat. Major emphasis is given to correct breathing and body conditioning.

RULES OF CONTACT

In kumite, the level of contact varies according to the style and the standard of the karatekas. All techniques must be controlled and executed without excessive force, especially to the head and neck. Attacks to the throat, groin, temples, spine, instep, and back of the head are not allowed and the referee may award penalties for any foul.

KUMITE

Kumite matches are usually organized by age, gender, weight, and experience. Each bout is three minutes long for men and two minutes for women and juniors. Two competitors stand on the starting lines on the mat, bow to each other, and at the referee's signal begin fighting. Kumite bouts feature punching, kicking, knee/elbow strikes, open handed techniques, locks, throws, and also grappling (see right). Karateka issue a loud kiai, or "spirit shout", as they execute a technique. A perfectly delivered strike, or throw receives an ippon, or point. If the strike is slightly flawed, the judge may award a waza-ari, or half point.

NEVER ATTACK FIRST

GICHIN FUNAKOSHI, THE FOUNDER OF SHOTOKAN KARATE, BELIEVED THAT KARATE WAS A FORM OF DEFENCE ONLY. HE DECLARED THAT "THERE IS NO FIRST ATTACK IN KARATE" BECAUSE IT IS AN ART OF DEFENDING IN WHICH THE ATTACKER ALWAYS LOSES.

SCORING CRITERIA

Scoring in kumite depends on the personal assessment of the referee, who needs to evaluate whether a particular move was delivered from the right distance as well as being perfect in form, timing, and attitude. The referee also decides if a technique would have been effective in a real combat.

REFEREE SIGNALS

During a bout the referee may use various hand signals as a way of communicating to the karateka and the judges. These include signals for starting, stopping, and resuming the contest, as well as for points awarded, techniques executed simultaneously, fouls committed, and warnings for excessive contact.

AWARDING A POINT
A referee signals that a point (ippon) has been awarded by placing a hand on the opposite shoulder and extending the arm downwards at 45 degrees on the side of the scorer.

KATA

In kata, a competitor executes a series of choreographed combat techniques, such as kicks, blocks, punches, and strikes (see right), against an imaginary opponent. Officials evaluate competence by various criteria – precision, breathing, strength, coordination, rhythm, balance, concentration, and comprehension of movement. As well as individual events, pairs of karateka demonstrate synchronized movements.

Toes back
The toes are pulled back so the kick is made with the ball of the foot

FRONT KICK
In this front kick (Mae geri) the right leg lifts and the foot kicks forwards. The right hand stays on the hip, with the elbow in.

Knuckles out
The knuckles of the right fist face out; the left fist is under the right elbow with the knuckles uppermost

BACK FIST BLOCK
The back fist block (Uraken gamae) in the front stance position ends with the right fist forwards at chest height.

From the hip
The right fist is punched from the hip and, with knuckles facing out, ends in line with the chest

REVERSE PUNCH
In the reverse punch (Gyaku zuki) in the front stance position one fist punches forwards as the other goes back to the hip.

PUNCH TO MID
A key characteristic of punching in karate is the art of rotating the wrist so the palms go from facing upwards at the start of the punch, to facing downwards at impact.

Maximum impact
Wearing gloves lessens the power of the strike, which would usually be with the knuckles of the index and middle fingers

SIDE KICK
The side kick (Yoko Geri) is one of the most powerful karate kicks, especially when aimed at the ribs or solar plexus. Either the side or the heel of the foot can be used in the kick.

Counter punch
A kick to the middle, if properly evaded, can be efficiently countered with a punch to the opponent's midriff

BACK KICK
The back kick (Ushiro Geri) can be used when facing an attack from the rear. A variation of this is to spin around to attack an opponent who is in front – a spinning back kick.

Heel first
The strike when performing the back kick should be made with the heel of the foot, with the toes pointing downwards

KICK TO HEAD
As the knee comes up it is twisted sideways and thrust forwards at the opponent. At the same time, the body is rotated on the supporting leg.

Leg grab
The high kick, unless executed very quickly, is prone to a retaliatory leg grab, as shown here

Fists together
The fists are held together with the knuckles facing outwards and the thumbs at the top

Open palm
The palm of the right hand is open, the left fist is kept on the left hip, and the breath is slowly and strongly exhaled

DOUBLE PUNCH
The double punch (Heiko tate zuki) in the front stance position has both fists forwards and the arms fully extended at chest height.

KNIFE HAND BLOCK
This hand block (Tate shuko uke) is performed in the rooted stance position and the open right hand is pushed slowly forwards at shoulder height.

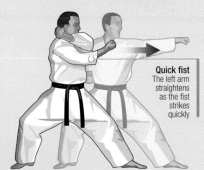

Quick fist
The left arm straightens as the fist strikes quickly

Fists aloft
The right fist is at eye level, the left in front of the forehead; the knuckles of both hands face backwards

ARM STRIKE
In the back stance the crossed arm strike with the right fist (Ura zuki) moves to the side fist strike with the left fist (Mawashi tettsui uchi).

DOUBLE-HANDED BLOCK
This block (Jodan haiwan uke) in the back stance position starts with both fists beside the left hip and ends with both arms raised and forming a rectangle.

INSIDE STORY
The World Karate Federation (WKF) organizes the World Karate Championship every two years. Individual mens' events are held in kumite at various weights (60kg, 65kg, 70kg, 75kg, 80kg, and +80kg) and in kata. Individual women's events are held in kumite at various weights (53kg, 60kg, and +60kg) and kata. There are also men's and women's team events in both kumite and kata. In addition, the World Union of Karate-do Organizations (WUKO) organizes a World Karate Championships for seniors (between 18 and 35 years of age) and veterans (36 and over), and the World Children, Cadets and Juniors Karate Championships.

WKF
The World Karate Federation was formed in 1990. It is the largest international governing body of sport karate with over 180 member countries and is the only one recognized by the International Olympic Committee.

KUNG FU: TAOLU

NEED2KNOW

→ In China, kung fu is generally known by the term "wushu" and is the country's national sport. Wushu literally means "military arts" or "martial arts".

→ The International Wushu Federation (IWUF) is the governing body for competition taolu as well as the full-contact sport of sanshou (see pp.230–31).

→ The types of taolu seen in competition are known as "external" forms. "internal" forms of taolu are meditative and reflective. Taijiquan (tai chi) is a well-known type.

COMPETITOR PROFILE
Taolu competitors need to demonstrate gymnastic prowess and aesthetic flare. Many positions are carried out with the performer in very low squats, which require considerable stamina and leg strength. Speed, grace, flexibility, and balance are key attributes. In individual competition performers choreograph their own routines, so need artistic inventiveness as well.

Skilled swordsman
Competitors need great mastery of taolu to wield weapons such as the jian in routines

Soft shoes
Lightweight, soft leather shoes are worn during competition

EVENT OVERVIEW

The Chinese art of taolu (forms) was born in 1958 with the establishment of the All-China Wushu Federation. It is a style of kung fu in which competitors perform choreographed routines comprised of basic movements (stances, kicks, punches, balances, jumps, sweeps, and throws) on a padded mat. Performances are judged for artistic merit, much like ice-skating routines or rhythmic gymnastics. Some categories of taolu are performed without weapons (so-called "empty-hand" styles) and some with weapons. Most categories are for solo performers, but some are for pairs or groups.

TAOLU ON FILM

HOLLYWOOD ACTOR JET LI, STAR OF "ROMEO MUST DIE", IS THE WORLD'S MOST FAMOUS TAOLU PRACTITIONER. HE WON THE NATIONAL WUSHU CHAMPION OF CHINA TITLE FIVE TIMES.

THE FIELD OF PLAY

Taolu competitors perform on a padded mat much like that on which gymnasts perform floor exercises. Performances by individual competitors take place on a mat measuring 14 x 8m (46 x 26ft 3in). The edge of the mat is marked out by a white border 5cm (2in) wide. The mat is surrounded by a 2m (6ft 6in) safety area. Events for pairs or groups of performers are carried out on a larger mat, 16 x 14m (52ft 6in x 46ft), which is surrounded by a 1m (3ft) safety area. The competition area is often set on a raised platform that is 50–60cm (1ft 6in–2ft) high.

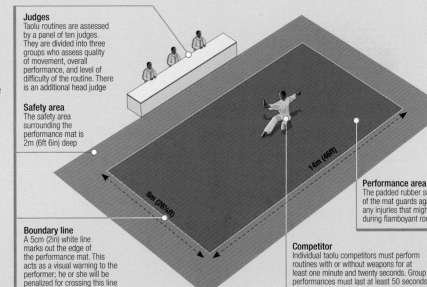

Judges
Taolu routines are assessed by a panel of ten judges. They are divided into three groups who assess quality of movement, overall performance, and level of difficulty of the routine. There is an additional head judge

Safety area
The safety area surrounding the performance mat is 2m (6ft 6in) deep

Boundary line
A 5cm (2in) white line marks out the edge of the performance mat. This acts as a visual warning to the performer; he or she will be penalized for crossing this line during their routine

14m (46ft)

8m (26¼ft)

Performance area
The padded rubber surface of the mat guards against any injuries that might occur during flamboyant routines

Competitor
Individual taolu competitors must perform routines with or without weapons for at least one minute and twenty seconds. Group performances must last at least 50 seconds

THE WEAPONS

Many of the forms of taolu focus on showing off the dexterity with which the performer handles one of a number of traditional weapons. Choreographed contests between two performers also take place.

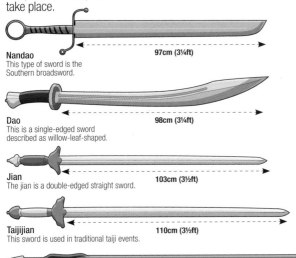

Nandao
This type of sword is the Southern broadsword.

97cm (3¼ft)

Dao
This is a single-edged sword described as willow-leaf-shaped.

98cm (3¼ft)

Jian
The jian is a double-edged straight sword.

103cm (3½ft)

Taijijian
This sword is used in traditional taiji events.

110cm (3½ft)

180cm (6ft)

210cm (7ft)

PERFORMING TAOLU

The main taolu events for individuals and groups, performed with and without weapons, are explained below:

CHANGQUAN Long fist; a type of "empty-handed" solo contest derived from northern Shaolin boxing.

NANQUAN Southern fist; solo contest derived from southern boxing.

TAIJIQUAN Shadow boxing; form of "empty-handed" solo contest.

DAOSHU Routine performed with a broadsword

JIANSHU Performance with double-edged sword

NANDAOSHU Southern-style broadsword

TAIJIJIANSHU Taiji sword

QIANGSHU Spear

GUNSHU Staff or cudgel

NANGUNSHU Southern-style staff or cudgel routine. This event was created in 1992.

DUILIAN Choreographed routines for two performers; these may be performed with or without weapons.

JITI Choreographed routines performed by a group, often to music.

Quiang
The qiang is a type of spear made of wax wood. This weapon is often practised in conjunction with the jian (sword)

Gun
The gun is a type of staff or cudgel made of wax wood. This is often practised along with the nandao (the broadsword)

OTHER WEAPONS

Taolu routines are sometimes performed with more exotic and esoteric weapons than those illustrated, including a three-sectioned staff, a rope dart, and a nine-sectioned whip.

SCORING SYSTEM

Each individual taolu performer starts their routine with ten points. Five of these points are allocated to quality of movement, three for overall performance, and two for the degree of difficulty of the routine. Each error – whether a divergence from the routine, a stumble or poor technique – is penalized by the deduction of a point. Group performers are also scored on a 10-point system, split equally between quality of movement and overall performance.

TAOLU TECHNIQUES

Taolu contestants are awarded points for performing moves and manoeuvres to a regulated standard; these might include somersaults, kicks, jumps and balances. Competitions are either in the form of set compulsory routines that all contestants perform, or individually choreographed routines. Changquan is considered to be the foundation of taolu and is often the first taolu form that new practitioners learn. Some fundamental changquan stances are described below.

INSIDE STORY

The governing body of taolu is the International Wushu Federation (IWUF), which was set up in China in 1990. IWUF is currently campaigning to have wushu (both sanshou and taolu) recognized as an official Olympic sport.

CHINESE WUSHU ASSOCIATION

The Chinese Wushu Association was set up in 1958. It is one of 148 national associations under the aegis of the IWUF, and is influential because of the art's Chinese origins.

Posture
The head and torso are kept in perfect vertical alignment during this stance

Balance
Arm arches over the head to offer counterbalance during the stance

Finger point
The hand points forward

Endurance
This provides great strengthening for the back and leg muscles

SEATED STANCE
Also known as the Sitting stance (or chi bu). One thigh is wrapped over the other. The front foot is flat on the floor, while the ball of the back foot is in contact with the floor.

CROUCH STANCE
In Chinese this is the pu bu, also known as the Drop or Arrow stance. This is a very low squat in which the crouching thigh of the back foot is in contact with the calf.

HORSE STANCE
Also known as the Horse riding stance (ma bu in Chinese). The tops of the thighs are parallel to the floor, and the knees are turned outwards while the feet point forwards.

KUNG FU: SANSHOU

Head protector
Since blows to the head are allowed, fighters wear head guards for safety

Chest protector
The torso is protected by a padded nylon chest shield

SPORT OVERVIEW
Sanshou is a Chinese martial art that resembles kickboxing (see pp.236–37). Bouts feature two fighters who score points by landing blows on their opponent or knocking them out. Unlike taolu (see pp.228–29), sanshou is never practised with weapons.

COMBAT AREA
Sanshou matches take place on a square raised platform called a lei tai, surrounded by padded mats. The lei tai was traditionally 1.5m (5ft) above ground level, but lower heights are now more common. It is legitimate to try to force or throw an opponent off the platform. Fighters are penalized if any part of their body crosses the boundary line, which forms a square 1m (3ft 3in) inside the edge of the platform.

Timekeeper and recorder
The recorder keeps a note of all points and penalties awarded. The timekeeper times each round and bangs a gong to announce the end of a round

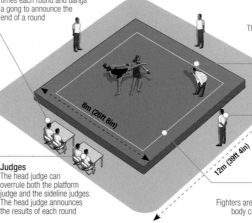

Lei tai judge
The platform judge supervises the fight. He shouts "kaishi!" to start a round, and "ting!" to end one

8m (26ft 8in)

12m (39ft 4in)

Sideline judge
There may be three or five of these. Their job is to signal if one of the combatants crosses the boundary line

Judges
The head judge can overrule both the platform judge and the sideline judges. The head judge announces the results of each round

Boundary line
Fighters are penalized if any part of their body crosses this line during a bout

NEED2KNOW

→ Sanshou (which translates as "loose hands") was developed by the Chinese army after the Korean War (1950–1953) to improve soldiers' hand-to-hand combat skills.

→ Sanshou is not so much a sport as a way of life that demands self-discipline on and off the lei tai.

SIDELINES

12 The number of fighters who were banned from the National Chinese lei tai tournament at Nanking in 1928 for fear of killing other competitors. Lei tai combat was the ancestor of modern sanshou.

92 The number of Chinese provinces represented by martial arts masters to discuss the new fighting style which would become sanshou.

50 The number of participants at the 2012 Sanshou World Cup, which was held in the Chinese city of Wuyishan. The competition is separated into 18 different categories, with 11 categories for male fighters and seven for women.

10,000 The prize money, in Chinese Yuan, awarded to the winner of the 2006 World Cup in Xi'an. That's equivalent to US$1,200: Sanshou may be a way of life, but it is not a good way to earn a living.

SANSHOU CAN DO

Competitors fight in one of ten weight categories. Matches consist of a maximum of three two-minute rounds with one minute's rest in between (if a fighter wins the first two rounds, he wins outright, and the third round is not competed). Points can be scored by landing blows with the fists or the feet to the opponent's torso or head, by kicks to the thigh, by knockout, or by making the opponent fall over. Double points are awarded if a fighter makes the opponent fall over while remaining standing himself. Leg sweeps, flying jumps, and grappling are all legitimate moves. Three points are also awarded if the opponent falls off the lei tai.

ILLEGAL MOVES

Blows may not be made with the knees or the elbows or by headbutting. Fighters cannot hit opponents in the back of the head, the neck, or the groin. Punches are not allowed below the belt, although blows with the feet can be made to the opponent's upper leg. Groundfighting is not allowed.

METHODOLOGY

Sanshou fighting features many of the tactics and techniques used in other kickboxing-style martial arts, such as punches and kicks, but with the addition of throws and sweeps.

THE KICKING CRAFT

There are several dramatic ways of getting an opponent to the floor. These include the flying scissor-kick, in which one fighter jumps at his opponent, wraps his legs on either side of the opponent's waist, and knocks him to the ground. Leg sweeps are also an effective way of telling an opponent, as shown right. They also allow the fighter to keep his head and torso out of his opponent's reach.

Evasive techniques are also important; combatants must be on their toes at all times other than when they are actually kicking. A sanshou fighter is never more vulnerable than when he just launched an attack into thin air.

COLOUR-CODED

During bouts sanshou fighters wear boxing-style vests and shorts. Boxing gloves soften hard blows from the fist but fighters are bare-footed, affording no protection from kicks. One contestant wears black clothing and the other wears red so the judges can easily distinguish between them. Combatants also wear gum shields or mouth guards.

BLOW SOFTENERS

Combatants protect their fists with standard boxing gloves strapped around the wrists.

Hard-wearing leather
Gloves are made of an outer layer of leather, stitched with nylon thread, and padded with high-density polyurethane

COMBAT ARMOUR

Sanshou is a high-impact, often violent sport, so fighters are obliged to wear protection for the chest, head, hands, groin, and mouth.

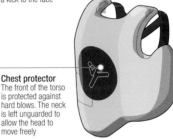

Gum shield
A mouth guard reduces the risk of damage from a kick to the face

Chest protector
The front of the torso is protected against hard blows. The neck is left unguarded to allow the head to move freely

Groin protector
Blows to the groin are forbidden but groin guards are still essential

Head sway
This fighter's attempt to get his head out of the way is futile because his feet are flat on the mat

Heel spin
As the kick follows through, this leg moves clockwise

BACK SWEEP KICK

The fighter rotates on his front foot so his back faces his opponent. His back leg sweeps up to his opponent making contact at chest height with the back of the leg. Unless the opponent anticipates this attack he will be knocked off balance.

Point of contact
This flailing kick found its target below the opponent's knee

Upright stance
The standing knee and leg are locked to act as a pivot for the swing

HOOKED-LEG KICK

In this attacking move, the fighter balances on his left foot, extends his back leg behind him and sweeps it round in a circular movement, kicking his opponent's front leg from under him and knocking him off balance.

INSIDE STORY

Sanshou's governing body, the International Wushu Federation (IWUF), was established in 1990. It organizes the World Championships of Wushu (covering both sanshou and taolu) every two years. First held in 1991 in Beijing, the championships circled the globe (stopping at, among other places, Baltimore, Hanoi, Rome, and Yerevan), before returning to the Chinese capital in 2007. The first Sanshou World Cup was held in Shanghai in 2002 and is now organized in alternate years to the World Championships of Wushu.

GOVERNING BODY

The International Wushu Federation was recognized by the International Olympic Committee (IOC) in 2002, but the sport has yet to make its debut as an Olympic event. The headquarters of the IWUF are in Beijing. The IWUF has 148 member nations around the world.

JU-JITSU

SPORT OVERVIEW

Ju-jitsu is an ancient Japanese martial art whose popularity has spread worldwide and developed in to different forms. The two versions currently sanctioned by the JJIF, the world governing body, are the fighting system and the duo system. The object of the former is to score points. This can be done by striking the opponent, and – after knocking them off balance and on to the mat – forcing a submission. In the duo system, fighters spar in a range of prearranged moves.

COMPETITOR PROFILE

Fighters, known as jutsukas, must be quick, have excellent balance and strength, especially in the grip. Joints need to be as flexible as possible, both to deliver attacks and – since blows are mostly directed at the shoulders, elbows, and knees – to take them. Technical ability is crucial for performing moves.

COMBAT AREA

The whole of the combat zone, including the warning area, is known as the competition area. It is usually 10m (32ft 6in) square, although some national and international tournaments take place on smaller fighting areas measuring 6m (19ft 6in) square. In major competitions, the surface is made of traditional woven straw mats, known as tatami.

NEED2KNOW

→ Ju-jitsu comes from two Japanese words: "ju" means "gentleness", and "jitsu" is "art".

→ As the sport spread across the world, teachers developed their own schools, known as "ryu".

→ Ju-jitsu is based on a range of Indian and Chinese fighting techniques more than 2,000 years old. It is the forerunner of both judo and aikido.

Hand and foot protectors
Fighters must wear protection for the hands and feet: usually fingerless mittens and socks

Cotton gi
Known as a gi, the outfit comprises a loose-fitting cotton jacket and trousers. Women jutsukas wear a plain white teeshirt or leotard underneath the gi; male jutsukas are naked beneath it so that opponents cannot grab their undergarments

Coloured belt
One jutsuka wears a red belt, the other a blue one, to indicate their respective corners. Belts must pass twice around the body and leave 15cm (6in) on either side of the knot

Long trousers
Trousers cover at least half the shin bone; must not be rolled up

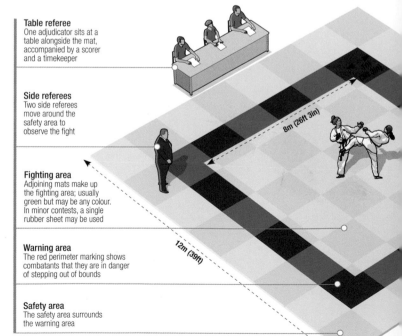

Table referee
One adjudicator sits at a table alongside the mat, accompanied by a scorer and a timekeeper

Side referees
Two side referees move around the safety area to observe the fight

Fighting area
Adjoining mats make up the fighting area; usually green but may be any colour. In minor contests, a single rubber sheet may be used

Warning area
The red perimeter marking shows combatants that they are in danger of stepping out of bounds

Safety area
The safety area surrounds the warning area

8m (26ft 3in)

12m (39ft)

RULES OF ENGAGEMENT

The requirements for victory in ju-jitsu vary according to the ryu, or school, being followed. In IJJF competitions there are two sets of rules, one for the fighting system, and one for duo.

FIGHTING SYSTEM

The winner is the jutsuka who first scores an ippon (point) in each of the three phases of a fight: a clean punch or kick in the striking phase; a clean takedown in the throwing phase; and a submission in the groundwork phase.

DUO SYSTEM

Before the jutsukas enter each stage of the contest, the referee calls out a number that corresponds to one of 20 authorized moves. One jutsuka attacks, and the other defends. For example, the attacker may be called on to attempt a stranglehold, while the defender is given the objective of countering with a throw (avoiding the attack is not enough). Marks are awarded for technique and speed.

DUO THROW

Under the duo system, when the referee calls the number that corresponds to the shoulder throw, the designated attacker moves in from behind and puts his arm around the opponent's neck. That the defender counterattacks is not in doubt; what counts is the way he does it.

Mat referee
The mat referee observes from close quarters and awards points

1m
(3ft 3in)

POINTED MANOEUVRES

Ju-jitsu originated as a philosophy and a way of life; it has only comparatively recently become a sport. Hence, many of the point-scoring techniques have been contrived so that they can be judged by set criteria.

FIGHTING PHASES

Under the fighting system, an ippon can be scored in a variety of ways in each of the three phases of combat. Ju-jitsu is classed as a martial art, but injuring the opponent has no part of it. Jutsukas who have gained an advantage need not – indeed, must not – drive it home; they have already proved their point and scored their ippon.

STRIKE PHASE
The jutsuka on the left aims to land a foot or hand on the body of the opponent, who takes evasive measures and aims to turn defence into counterattack.

Striking moment
The standing leg must be braced, with the foot firmly grounded on the mat for balance during the strike

THROWING PHASE
The attacker attempts to put one arm over the opponent's shoulder and the other around his torso, and swivels his own upper body to push him across his thigh and onto the mat.

Role reversal
The jutsuka on top may appear to be in control, but he is about to be thrown on to the mat

GROUNDWORK PHASE
One jutsuka puts the other in an armlock; when the latter can stand the pain no longer, he or she will tap on the mat with the free hand to indicate submission.

Double jeopardy
The assailant uses both hands to twist the opponent's arm to the limit

Engagement
The jutsukas allow each other to take up the starting position; they do not have to fight to reach it

Push and pull
The defender on the left bends his knees; when he straightens them again he will lift the attacker off the mat

Pivotal moment
Having lifted the opponent off the mat, the defender bends forwards to complete the throw; note how he keeps hold of the other fighter's arm throughout the move

Happy landings
The ability to land gracefully and without injury is every bit as important in ju jitsu as the art of throwing

INSIDE STORY

At the start of the 21st century, ju-jitsu's biggest growth area was in Brazil, where there are three types of contest: sport ju-jitsu, in which no strikes are allowed; submission wrestling, which is much the same as the sports variety apart from the fact that the fighters wear shorts rather than the conventional gi; and, most popular of all, vale tudo contests (straight fights with few rules).

INTERNATIONAL JU-JITSU FEDERATION

The JJIF was founded in 1987 and grew from the European Ju-Jitsu Federation, which itself was founded in 1977. The JJIF controls every aspect of the study and teaching of all styles of the sport, and divides them into two broad categories: koryu (classical) and goshin (modern).

→ The word "Taekwondo" is variously translated as "the way of hand and foot" or "the way of kicking and striking".

→ Taekwondo originated in Korea, where it remains the national martial art. In other parts of the world, it is also popular as a form of exercise.

TAEKWONDO

SPORT OVERVIEW

Taekwondo is a spectacular combat sport between two men or women who score points by striking their opponent, often with a rapid combination of kicks – including jumping or flying kicks – and punches. The fighter with the greater number of points at the end of the timed bout is the winner, unless one is knocked down for a count of ten.

PLAYER PROFILE

Taekwondo athletes are light, lithe, fast-moving, and strong. Agility and flexibility are important attributes, as high kicks are a key tactic: kicks to the opponent's face score more highly than blows to the torso. Quick responses are essential for effective defence.

Doctor on call
A medical doctor can administer treatment to competitors and ensures they are fit to continue a contest, or stop the contest if not

Recorder
The recorder keeps a record of the points and penalties awarded to each competitor by the judges and times the contests

Referee
The referee starts and ends each bout, supervises the match, and indicates fouls

11m (35ft 9in)

Waist bands
A coloured belt knotted around the waist indicates the fighter's rank

Dobok
The uniform is a light and loose white jacket and trousers

SIDELINES

4 The number of weight divisions into which both male and female combatants are divided in the Olympic Games: flyweight, lightweight, middleweight, and heavyweight.

8 The number of medals – out of a possible 16 – won by South Korea at the first two Olympics – Sydney 2000 and Athens 2004 – in which taekwondo was a competitive sport. The tally is made up of five gold, one silver, and two bronze.

10 The number of student ranks, from 10th (beginner) to first. Ranks are known as dans.

204 The number of member nations in the World Taekwondo Federation.

Coaches' position
The fighters' coaches watch the bout from opposite sides of the competition area

Judges
Four lineside judges observe the combat to award points for legitimate blows and deduct points for penalties. Two or more judges must register a point for it to be recorded to a competitor

Alert Line
An alert line warns competitors that they are near the edge of the mat

COMPETITION AREA

Contests take place on a square rubber mat at least 2cm (1in) thick. The competition area may be raised by 50–60cm (19½–23½in), with a shallow slope (around 30 degrees) to floor level. The officials take up position around the outside of the competition area.

COMPULSORY CLOTHING

Fighters wear full protective clothing when they take up position on the mat. To make each combatant distinct, one wears blue and one wears red markings on the chest guard or helmet, or on hand and foot protectors if they are worn. Only the chest guard is worn over the loose-fitting white uniform.

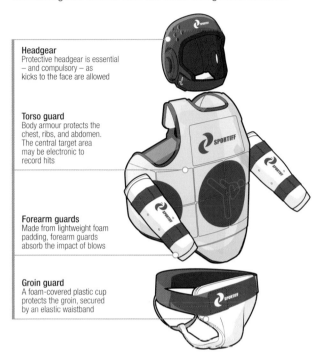

Headgear
Protective headgear is essential – and compulsory – as kicks to the face are allowed

Torso guard
Body armour protects the chest, ribs, and abdomen. The central target area may be electronic to record hits

Forearm guards
Made from lightweight foam padding, forearm guards absorb the impact of blows

Groin guard
A foam-covered plastic cup protects the groin, secured by an elastic waistband

ESSENTIAL VOCABULARY

Taekwondo retains its Korean origins in much of the language associated with the sport. Referees begin bouts by shouting "Shi-jak!" ("Start") and end bouts by shouting "Keu-man" ("Stop"). Combatants often scream "Kiai!" (which means "working with ki") when delivering a blow to their opponent; the shout releases energy (ki) and helps them to strike a blow with greater strength and force. As with boxing, a knockout is concluded by the referee counting to ten – announced by the referee declaring "Yeol" (the Korean word for "ten").

SCORING POINTS

Points are earned by landing blows on the opponent or, in sparring competitions, by stopping blows 2cm (1in) from an opponent. A blow to the torso with the hand or foot earns one point, a kick to the neck or head earns two, and knocking the opponent down earns three. Under World Taekwondo Federation rules, if a fighter reaches 12 points or gets 7 points ahead, he or she wins the match. A match can also be won by knockout. Points are deducted for fouls such as hitting below the belt, hitting the back, and hitting behind the head. In the case of a tie, a sudden-death bout is played.

HAIR-RAISING ROOTS

TAEKWONDO EVOLVED SOME 2,000 YEARS AGO FROM A NUMBER OF KOREAN MARTIAL ARTS. ONE FIGHTING TECHNIQUE, AT A TIME WHEN IT WAS FASHIONABLE FOR MEN TO WEAR A LONG PONYTAIL, WAS TO TIE A SHARP COMB OR METAL WEIGHT TO THE END OF THE PLAIT AND SWING IT TO STRIKE AN OPPONENT IN THE EYES.

KICKING OUT

Taekwondo places more emphasis on kicks than most martial arts, and takes advantage of the legs' ability to deliver blows with more force and from a greater distance than punches. Two of the most effective kicks are the hook kick and the side kick (below).

Parallel lines
The leading arm and leg are parallel to each other

Rock solid
The feet are firmly planted on the mat

STARTING POSE
The fighter is in regular defensive pose, with his hands raised to block any attack.

INTO MOTION
The fighter raises his knee to hip level and keeps his hands raised.

First footing
The standing foot pivots the body forwards

Leg thrust
The attacker twists the leg outwards

WIND-UP
The fighter pivots to face forwards to come into an attacking position.

SIDE KICK
The leg is fully extended to the side, and the hip twisted for extra power.

STRAIGHT PUNCH

In the straight punch-pull combination, the nonstriking hand is kept low with the fist palm upwards as the striking hand quickly punches straight with the fist palm down.

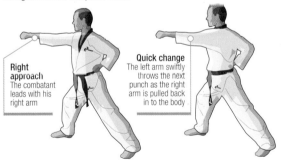

Right approach
The combatant leads with his right arm

Quick change
The left arm swiftly throws the next punch as the right arm is pulled back in to the body

INSIDE STORY

Taekwondo was internationalized by US troops returning home after the Korean War in the early 1950s. Korean lobbying led to the founding in 1973 of the World Taekwondo Federation (WTF) as the sport's governing body. The first world championships were held the same year. Taekwondo became an Olympic sport in 2000.

GOVERNING BODY
The World Taekwondo Federation was recognized by the International Olympic Committee in 1980 and today has 204 member nations around the world.

KICKBOXING

→ Kickboxing is a professional sport for both men and women. Top bouts draw huge audiences in Southeast Asia and Japan, where kickboxers enjoy superstar status.

→ In the West, kickboxing has become a popular form of exercise, due to its high fitness demands and challenging moves.

→ The rules of kickboxing are complicated by the fact that there is no one governing body, but a number of rival organizations.

SPORT OVERVIEW

Kickboxing is a fast-moving combat sport that combines boxing techniques with kicks derived from martial arts, mainly karate. Although it resembles traditional Thai boxing and Full Contact (see box opposite) it was developed by martial arts exponents in the United States in the 1970s. Professional bouts are up to 12 rounds long, and each round lasts two minutes. Fights are decided by knockout or, more usually, by points scored for blows landed on the opponent.

FIGHTER PROFILE

Kickboxers need the strength, speed, resilience, and endurance of boxers, combined with the agility and flexibility required to execute the extended high kicks. A high level of resistance to pain is necessary, particularly when competing under rules that allow kicks to the fighters' legs.

Referee
The referee stands in the ring with the fighters, starting and ending each bout and overseeing the contest

Starting positions
The fighters line up on two white lines, marked 1m (3ft) from the centre of the ring on opposite sides

Corner team
Each fighter has a trainer, who discusses tactics, and two seconds, who tend to injuries, between rounds

Timekeeper
He times each bout, ringing a bell to start and end each round

Scorekeeper
Seated alongside the third judge for convenience, he records all points and penalties scored

Hand protection
Kickboxers fight in standard boxing gloves

Exposed target
No padding is worn to the torso, and this area of the body is a major target

Baggies
Loose boxing-style shorts give the legs freedom of movement

Foam boots
In Full Contact kickboxing padded foam protectors are permitted for the feet and shins

Strength
During training fighters work extensively on building leg muscles

THE RING

Originally fought on mats, modern kickboxing contests now take place in standard boxing (see pp.209–211) rings – sprung canvas squares enclosed on all four sides by four ropes. The bottom rope must be a minimum of 33cm (13in) above the canvas floor; the top rope no more than 1.32m (4ft 4in).

BOXING BEAUTY

TRAINED AS A MONK, NONG TOOM BECAME ONE OF THAILAND'S LEADING KICKBOXERS – AND THE MOST NOTORIOUS. HE WAS A MAKE-UP WEARING TRANSSEXUAL, WHO FOUGHT TO EARN CASH FOR A SEX CHANGE, WHICH HE HAD IN 1999. HIS STORY WAS TOLD IN THE 2005 MOVIE "BEAUTIFUL BOXER".

KICKBOXING, FULL CONTACT, AND MUAY THAI

The pure form of kickboxing is often confused with Thai boxing (Muay Thai) and the European sport of Full Contact. All are closely related and it is important to understand the key differences. Fighters in all three sports wear mouthguards, gloves, and groin protection.

• In kickboxing, combatants are permitted to punch according to the rules of professional boxing – i.e. no blows below the belt – and kick to any part of the body.

• In Full Contact, fighters wear long trousers and T-shirts, protective foam boots, and optional shin pads and headguards. Normal boxing rules apply, but fighters are prohibited from kicking below the waist.

• Muay Thai is the oldest and most violent form of "kickboxing". The rules regarding punching and kicking are more relaxed, and fighters are permitted to strike using their hands, shins, elbows, and knees.

Doctor
Medical assistance on hand in case of head injuries

Scorekeeper
Seated with the third judge, he records all points and penalties scored

8m (26ft)

Judges
Each fighter is assigned a judge who monitors the number of kicks and punches

PROTECTIVE GEAR

Most protective equipment is mandatory for Full Contact combat. Shin guards and footpads are not allowed in Oriental, Muay Thai, and sanshou bouts but are optional, or even recommended, in other forms of the sport – and certainly for amateur bouts.

Helmet
Protects the vulnerable temples and head from blows or punches

Shin guards
In Full Contact, shin guards offer protection from illegal kicks

Foot pads
Cushions the impact of kicks for both fighters

SCORING SYSTEM

Contests are won either through knockouts or accumulation of points. In some contests winners are decided based on the number of rounds won, not overall points. The scoring areas are the front, back, and side of the head; the front and side of the body; and all areas of the leg. Points are awarded as follows: One point is awarded for all successful punches. Footsweeps and kicks to the body also score one point. Two points are awarded for a kick to the head. A jumpkick that lands on the body is awarded two points, and one that connects with the head is awarded three points.

FIGHTING STYLES

Kickboxers can target the opponent's torso and head with punches such as jabs, hooks, crosses, and uppercuts. There is also a variety of kicks, including front and side kicks and the swinging roundhouse kick. A roundhouse kick is one in which the fighter swings his or her leg in a circular motion to gain momentum for a blow to the opponent's lower leg, torso, or head. There is very little difference between the punching styles of kickboxing and traditional boxing – indeed, many fighters move between one or other discipline. A well-executed punch is often less destructive than a kick, however, owing to the padded gloves used.

KNEE STRIKE
Low kicks to the leg are often most effective, as they slow the opponent down and prevent him or her from preparing a retaliatory kick. Low kicks (excluding sweeps) are not permitted in Full Contact.

No advance
A low kick to the knee stalls any forward movement by the opponent

MID-LEVEL KICK
A mid-level kick is aimed at the mid section of the opponent's body. When performed with speed and power such kicks can bruise or even damage the opponent's ribs.

Soft spot
The attacker aims to connect with the opponent's unprotected ribs

AIM HIGH
High kicks to the head are potentially the most risky, as they leave the attacker most open to counter-attack, but are spectacular – and can potentially win a bout with a single blow.

Knockout
The attacker swings his leg high, aiming for the opponent's head

INSIDE STORY

The first governing body associated with kickboxing when the sport emerged in the 1970s was the Professional Karate Association (PKA). Today the governance of the sport is fragmented, with several different organizations each hosting regular events and world championships. The World Kickboxing Association (WKA), which was established in the late 1970s and has over 40 member nations, is the best known of this group of rival federations.

SOMBO

238

NEED2KNOW

→ Sombo was developed in the Soviet Union in the 1920s when Joseph Stalin wanted his army to improve its hand-to-hand combat skills. Military leaders combined disciplines including karate and judo with traditional wrestling styles from Armenia, Georgia, Moldova, Mongolia, and Russia.

→ The International Amateur Sambo Federation (FIAS) is the sport's governing body. Sambo is an acronym that stands for "self-defence without a weapon".

FIGHTER PROFILE

Strength and resilience are essential. Fighters need endurance to withstand attacks, together with the fighting spirit and tactical awareness to overcome their opponents. Speed and agility are also important qualities that help combatants to outmanoeuvre the opposition.

SPORT OVERVIEW

Sombo is a Russian combat discipline featuring many wrestling techniques, such as throws, pins, and locks. There are two types of sombo (which is also known as sambo): sport sombo and combat sombo. Sport sombo includes many moves, such as leg locks, that are illegal in judo. Combat sombo also includes punches and kicks.

SCORING SOMBO

Sombo matches usually last five minutes and are supervised by a centre referee (who gestures when points have been awarded), a mat judge, and a mat chairman. Points are awarded for hold downs: a fighter who holds his opponent's back to the mat for ten seconds gains two points and for 20 seconds gains four points. Whoever is first to achieve a 12-point margin wins the match.

OUTRIGHT VICTORY

A fighter can win outright without the necessary points margin if he can throw his opponent on to his back while remaining standing. He also wins outright by forcing his opponent into a successful submission hold. This kind involves getting the opponent in an arm or leg lock while on the floor. Choke holds and holds to feet and hands are illegal. When the grip is so strong and the opponent can no longer stand the pain, he calls out or hits the mat, prompting the referee to end the match.

Top layer
This is a cotton karate-style jacket known as a kurtki. Gripping and pulling on the opponent's jacket is a legitimate move

Bare legs
Fighters wear shorts so that judges see clearly what they are doing with their legs, and thus monitor the risk of injury from potentially crippling leg locks

Supple boots
Fighters wear light, supple boots with a good grip

Leg lock
This fighter is executing a leg lock and stretching his opponent's Achilles heel

Out of the loop
The victim cannot use his right leg to resist because of the pressure on his left thigh

FIELD OF COMBAT

Sombo contests take place on a circular area in the middle of a hexagonal or square mat. The bout begins in the inner circle, marked with a white boundary line. This is where sombo fighters begin their bout. Around the mat is the protection area, which is coloured pale blue. This is padded to help prevent injury if a fighter is thrown out of the main wrestling area.

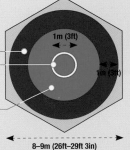

Passivity zone
This red ring warns fighters of the mat's edge

Inner ring
The action starts here

Action area
Most of the fight take place in this ring

1m (3ft)

1m (3ft)

8–9m (26ft–29ft 3in)

THE BEST POLICY?

VASILI OSHCHEPKOV'S DECLARATION THAT HE HAD BEEN INSPIRED TO DEVELOP SOMBO BY JIGARO KANO, THE JAPANESE FOUNDER OF JUDO, ANGERED STALIN, WHO WANTED THE SOVIET UNION TO BE THE SOURCE OF EVERYTHING GOOD IN THE WORLD. OSHCHEPKOV PAID FOR HIS HONESTY WITH HIS LIFE.

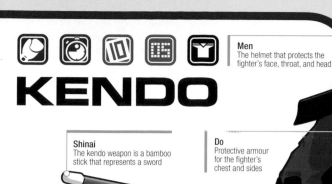

KENDO

Men
The helmet that protects the fighter's face, throat, and head

Shinai
The kendo weapon is a bamboo stick that represents a sword

Do
Protective armour for the fighter's chest and sides

SPORT OVERVIEW

Kendo is a Japanese martial art in which ritual, philosophy, and etiquette are as important as fighting skills. The sport is based on an ancient form of Japanese sword-fighting called kenjutsu. Modern kendo fighters use a bamboo stick known as a shinai rather than a real sword. Bouts feature two contenders, clothed head to foot in distinctive black gear, who aim to strike each other with their shinai.

CAN DO'S

Kendo matches last for five minutes and whoever is the first to score two points wins. An extra three minutes may be played if there is no outright winner after the first five minutes – then whoever scores the first point wins. A point is scored by making a cut to one of seven permitted areas (see below) with the top third of the shinai, or by a thrust to the throat with the tip. Usually, one chief referee and two sub-referees score the match – a point is logged when at least two of them signal that a clean hit has been made.

FIGHTER PROFILE

Kendo fighters train their minds as well as their bodies: mental discipline is as important as physical fitness, and calmness and concentration are vital. The cuts and thrusts require precision and skill to execute, and fighters need quick reactions to defend themselves from attack.

Men
A cut can be made to the top centre of the opponent's head

Hidari-Men
Cuts are allowed to the left side of the head

Migi-Men
A fighter can make a cut to the right side of the head

Chudan tsuki
A thrust can be made with the tip of the shinai to the opponent's throat

Hidari-Do
A cut can be made to the left side of the body

Migi-Do
A cut can be made to the right side of the body

Hidari-Kote
A fighter can make a cut to the left wrist

Kote
A cut can be made to the right wrist

LEGITIMATE TARGETS

There are eight legitimate areas for a kendo fighter to cut or strike an opponent with the shinai: three on the head, one on the throat, two on either wrist, and the final two are on any part of the two sides of the body.

ON THE SQUARE

Kendo contests, known as shiai, are fought on a wooden floor in a court known as a shiajo that has a cross marked in the centre. Fighters must remain on the shiajo during a contest. Traditional etiquette is observed, and fighters bow to one another at the beginning and end of the match.

BREACHING THE DEFENCE

A key offensive technique is to draw the opponent out of position with a feint, then land a blow on one of the other target areas thus exposed. When landing a blow, the fighter calls out the part of the body he has struck; for example, "do!" for the side. Fighters shout "kiai!" before launching an attack to try to intimidate their opponent.

Attempting a men
One fighter aims his shinai at his opponent's headguard

Scoring a do
The opponent strikes the armour on the side of the body, and scores a do

WATER SPORTS

Hi-tech swimsuit
Swimsuit technology is now tightly regulated by FINA, with limits on fabric width, weave, and buoyancy

Swimming cap
Long-haired swimmers usually wear a cap, but it is not compulsory to do so

Body shaven
Some swimmers remove as much of their bodily hair as possible in order to prevent it slowing them down in the water; however, this is a fashion, not a requirement or a necessity

COMPETITOR PROFILE
The arms and legs must be strong, as endurance is essential for both sprinters and long-distance swimmers. Swimmers are recognisable by the shape of their upper bodies, which develop broad shoulders and taper to narrow waists and hips.

Plastic goggles
Goggles can be worn to reduce irritation caused by chemicals in the pool water. They must fit tightly to be effective

Modest swimwear
Swimming costumes must be tasteful, discreet, and – above all – never transparent when dry or wet

Ear plugs
They are not essential, but ear plugs are used by competitors who find water in the ears uncomfortable

NEED2KNOW

→ There are four main competitive swimming styles: backstroke, breaststroke, butterfly, and freestyle.

→ There are currently 34 officially recognised Olympic swimming race events, 17 for each sex.

→ Olympic Games competitions, before 1908, included a variety of unusual events such as underwater swimming, 200m obstacle swimming, and the plunge, for vertical distance.

SIDELINES

20.91 The number of seconds it took Brazilian freestyle swimmer César Cielo to achieve a world record for completing one length of a 50m (164ft) pool on 18 December 2009.

8 The number of gold medals won by American swimmer Michael Phelps at the 2008 Olympic Games in Beijing.

15 Age at which Australian Ian Thorpe, nicknamed "Thorpedo", became the youngest ever individual World Champion, in 1998.

24.51 The time in seconds it took China's Jingye Le to swim 50m, the first female to break 25 seconds for this distance.

SWIMMING

SPORT OVERVIEW

No matter what the distance – and the length of events varies from 50m (164ft) to 1,500m (1,640yd) – the object of any swimming race is to complete the course in the shortest possible time. Each race requires a particular stroke, or combination of four swimming styles: breaststroke, backstroke, butterfly, and freestyle. There are both individual and team races; the team races see four swimmers from each country compete against each other, and they usually take place at the end of a meeting.

THE POOL

The pools used in top-class competitions are 50m (164ft) long, and 25m (82ft) wide. They are divided into eight lanes, each 2.75m (9ft) in width; there is an extra 40cm (1ft 3in) of water outside lanes one and eight. The water is a uniform 1.8m (6ft) deep throughout. When lanes are used, the colour of the lane ropes is two green ropes for lanes one and eight; four blue ropes for lanes two, three, six, and seven; and three yellow ropes for lanes four and five. The floats extending for a distance of 5m (16ft 6in) from each end of the pool are red, and at the 15m (49ft) mark from each end of the wall of the pool the floats are different in colour from the surrounding floats.

In other events, such as diving, pools with sloping bottoms may be used, as long as they are no less than 1.2m (4ft) deep at the start, and at least 1m (3½ft) deep at the other end; they may be divided into as many as ten lanes, each about 2m (7ft) across.

IN THE SWIM

There are several different swimming styles and the rules of competition are tailored to take account of each discipline. However, the configuration of the pool, starting and finishing regulations, and the way in which races are timed and judged are common to all types of races, and rules for international events are laid down by the Fédération Internationale de Natation Amateur (FINA), the world governing body for the sport.

START BLOCK

For many competitive events, each swimmer mounts a start block, which is a small platform situated on the end of the pool, above the racing lane. When the start of a race is signalled, swimmers dive from the start block into their lane and begin swimming.

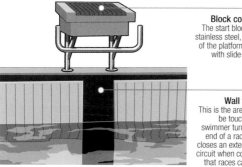

Block construction
The start block is built of stainless steel, and the top of the platform is covered with slide-free rubber

Wall touch pad
This is the area that must be touched when a swimmer turns, or at the end of a race. Pressure closes an external electric circuit when contacted, so that races can be timed

WHAT THEY WEAR

Traditional-style swimming costumes have largely been replaced by hi-tech swimwear. Suits fit tightly and reduce drag, although regulations were tightened by FINA in 2010 amid fears that the suits lent athletes an unfair advantage.

SWIMSUIT DESIGN

The full-body skinsuits used to great effect at the 2000 and 2004 Olympics were limited to leg and torso coverage only for Beijing 2008, then banned altogether from 2010.

Hi-tech material
Modern bodysuits are made of a combination of materials, including Nylon, Spandex, and Lycra®

Strict regulations
FINA rules state that women's suits must not cover the neck, shoulders, or knees, while men's suits must leave knees and navel bare

GOGGLES

Anti-fog, scratch-resistant lenses in a flexible PVC frame are an essential aid for improving the visibility of competition

No leaks
Some goggles have silicone seals for improved waterproofing

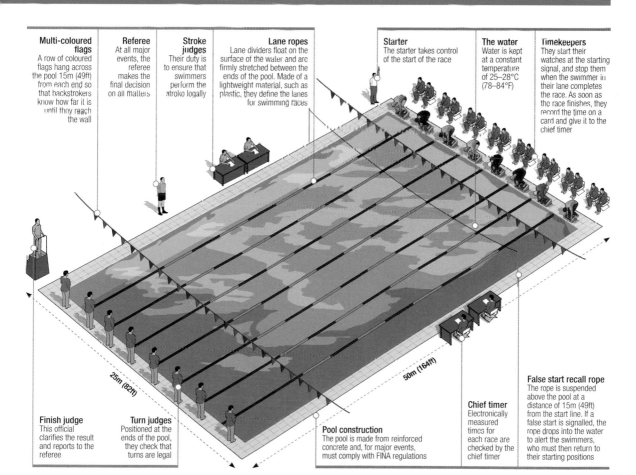

Multi-coloured flags
A row of coloured flags hang across the pool 15m (49ft) from each end so that backstrokers know how far it is until they reach the wall

Referee
At all major events, the referee makes the final decision on all matters

Stroke judges
Their duty is to ensure that swimmers perform the stroke legally

Lane ropes
Lane dividers float on the surface of the water and are firmly stretched between the ends of the pool. Made of a lightweight material, such as plastic, they define the lanes for swimming races

Starter
The starter takes control of the start of the race

The water
Water is kept at a constant temperature of 25–28°C (78–84°F)

Timekeepers
They start their watches at the starting signal, and stop them when the swimmer in their lane completes the race. As soon as the race finishes, they record the time on a card and give it to the chief timer

25m (82ft)

50m (164ft)

Finish judge
This official clarifies the result and reports to the referee

Turn judges
Positioned at the ends of the pool, they check that turns are legal

Pool construction
The pool is made from reinforced concrete and, for major events, must comply with FINA regulations

Chief timer
Electronically measured times for each race are checked by the chief timer

False start recall rope
The rope is suspended above the pool at a distance of 15m (49ft) from the start line. If a false start is signalled, the rope drops into the water to alert the swimmers, who must then return to their starting positions

STAT CENTRAL

LONG COURSE WORLD RECORDS (MEN)

EVENT SWIMMER	TIME
50M FREESTYLE CÉSAR CIELO	20:91
100M FREESTYLE CÉSAR CIELO	46:91
200M FREESTYLE PAUL BIEDERMANN	1:42:00
400M FREESTYLE PAUL BIEDERMANN	3:40:07
800M FREESTYLE ZHANG LIN	7:32:12
1500M FREESTYLE SUN YANG	14:31:02
100M BACKSTROKE AARON PEIRSOL	51:94
200M BACKSTROKE AARON PEIRSOL	1:51:92
100M BREASTSTROKE CAMERON VAN DER BURGH	58:46
200M BREASTSTROKE AKIHIRO YAMAGUCHI	2:07:01
100M BUTTERFLY MICHAEL PHELPS	49:82
200M BUTTERFLY MICHAEL PHELPS	1:51:51

LONG COURSE WORLD RECORDS (WOMEN)

EVENT SWIMMER	TIME
50M FREESTYLE BRITTA STEFFEN	23:73
100M FREESTYLE BRITTA STEFFEN	52:07
200M FREESTYLE FEDERICA PELLEGRINI	1:52:98
400M FREESTYLE FEDERICA PELLEGRINI	3:59:15
800M FREESTYLE REBECCA ADLINGTON	8:14:10
1500M FREESTYLE KATE KIEGLER	15:42:54
100M BACKSTROKE GEMMA SPOFFORTH	58:12
200M BACKSTROKE MISSY FRANKLIN	2:04:06
100M BREASTSTROKE JESSICA HARDY	1:04:45
200M BREASTSTROKE REBECCA SONI	2:19:59
100M BUTTERFLY DANA VOLLMER	55:98
200M BUTTERFLY LIU ZIGE	2:01:81

RACE STARTS

The start of competition races is governed by an official starter, who is responsible to the event referee. Once the referee gives permission for an event to start, the starter assumes authority to begin the race. At the starter's first signal, swimmers take up their starting positions. For a backstroke event, this is in the water; for other races, the competitors mount their starting blocks and face down their respective lanes.

RACE TIMING

In major swim meets, such as the World Championships and the Olympics, races are electronically timed to the nearest one-hundredth of a second. Electronic touch pads are affixed to the walls of the pool at the end of each lane. Their upper edge must be at least 30cm (12in) above the water level. Touch pads are linked to an electronic timing system and respond to the slightest pressure from the swimmer at the end of the race. Individual timekeepers are also used and each one takes the time of the swimmers in the lane assigned them. After the race they record the times on a card which is passed to the chief timekeeper.

FALSE STARTS

These occur when a swimmer attempts to begin a race before the official signal to do so. Fédération Internationale de Natation Amateur (FINA) rules state that anyone causing a false start will be disqualified. When a false start happens, the starter gives a second signal (identical to the start signal), and the false start rope also falls into the pool to alert the swimmers.

Diving in
The start block is a non-slip platform

STARTING FROM THE BLOCKS

Apart from backstroke, competitive events begin from the starting blocks. When the starting signal sounds, swimmers dive from their block into the water to begin swimming. A block is usually 50cm x 50cm (20in x 20in), and stands 50–75cm (20–30in) above the water. Blocks have a maximum downslope of 10 degrees from back to front.

STARTING IN THE POOL

Backstroke and medley relay events begin with each swimmer in the pool gripping the starting block. Swimmers brace their legs against the pool wall. When the start signal is given, they use the leverage to push backwards and begin racing.

QUICK TURNS

A vital part of any race is the turn, which takes place when a swimmer reaches the end of the pool and needs to begin another length in the quickest possible time. A smooth turning technique can shave vital seconds from a competitor's overall event time. Each swim stroke requires a slightly different turning method. In butterfly and breaststroke, the swimmer has to touch the pool wall with both hands when turning. In freestyle and backstroke events, the swimmer is allowed to turn using just the feet, without touching the pool wall with the hands.

THE TUMBLE TURN

The rapid tumble turn (right) is used in freestyle and backstroke events. Swimmers racing backstroke events are allowed to turn on to their front (while gliding only) just before executing the turn. As with the start of the race, swimmers are only allowed to be underwater for 15m (49 ft) before breaking the surface and using the event stroke.

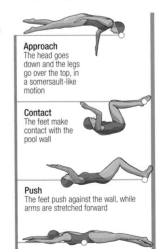

Approach
The head goes down and the legs go over the top, in a somersault-like motion

Contact
The feet make contact with the pool wall

Push
The feet push against the wall, while arms are stretched forward

Twist
The swimmer twists into a downward-facing position when racing freestyle, or remains on their back for the backstroke

SWIMMING STROKES

Swimming styles have developed from basic principles. To achieve maximum speed, the torso and legs should be kept parallel to the surface of the water, to reduce the amount of drag acting on the swimmer. The arms and hands should extend in front of the head as much as possible. A longer stroke generates more forward thrust, as the arm spends more time moving through the water.

SEVEN UP

AT THE 2007 LONG COURSE CHAMPIONSHIPS IN MELBOURNE, AMERICAN MICHAEL PHELPS PROVED HIS DOMINANCE IN THE SPORT BY WINNING SEVEN GOLD MEDALS, FOUR OF THEM IN NEW WORLD RECORD TIMES.

BREASTSTROKE

To execute the breaststroke good coordination is needed. The arm movements must be made simultaneously, as should the leg movements. The arm cycle comes first, and is followed by a kick, then a brief glide. The event starts with the swimmer diving from the blocks.

Forward start
After the dive, the swimmer shrugs the shoulders up, with elbows turned out and the palms of the hands facing outward at an angle of 30–45 degrees to the forearms

Beginning the stoke
The swimmer pushes her hands, palm first, back and down in a full circle. She breathes in as she finishes the circle, lifting her face out of the water

Finishing the stroke
She puts her face back in the water, stretches her arms forward, and kicks, bending her knees and lifting her feet up. She turns her feet, pushing them back in a circular motion

BACKSTROKE

Also known as the back crawl, the swimmer counts the number of strokes to work out when he will reach the end of the pool. The swimmer remains close to the surface of the water. The race begins in the pool, not on top of the block (see opposite).

Backward start
The swimmer puts one arm in the water, little finger first, in a straight line above his shoulder. He keeps the arm straight all of the time it is out of the water

Beginning the stroke
Once the swimmer's hand is in the water, he pushes it down and towards his feet, slightly bending the elbow. He kicks his legs in an up-and-down motion from the knee

Finishing the stroke
He keeps pushing his hand towards his feet until his elbow is straight. Then he lifts his arm out of the water, back to its original position

FRONT CRAWL

The fastest swimming stroke, the front crawl (also known as freestyle) requires the swimmer to move face-down through the water, breathing after every two or three strokes by turning the head up through the surface. Movements should be as smooth as possible, and the legs should kick continuously.

Forward start
The swimmer puts her hand into the water in front of her head and stretches it forwards as far as it will go

Beginning the stroke
She increases her speed by bending her elbow and pushing her hand towards her feet, until it reaches the top of her leg

Finishing the stroke
The kicking legs remain submerged, while the swimmer lifts alternate arms forwards and pulls them back through the water

BUTTERFLY

This stroke requires a high degree of stamina and strength, particularly in the upper body. The arms must break the surface, then power back down through the water. It can be hard getting the right order: kick as the hands go in; kick again as the hands come out; when the arms are near the thighs, lift up the torso and breathe.

Forward start
Diving from the starting block, the swimmer begins dolphin kicks with the legs when submerged

Beginning the stroke
He puts his hands in the water in front of his shoulders and pulls them towards his feet. The arms keep moving throughout the stroke

Finishing the stroke
When the hands reach the thighs, he lifts them out of the water, breathes, then throws them back to the start, kicking as his arms go in and come out of the water

MEDLEY

The medley relay involves individuals or teams of four, each member swimming at least 50m (164ft), before handing over to a teammate. A different stroke is used for each "leg" of the race, in a prescribed order.

Backstroke
The medley relay begins in the pool, with the backstroke

Breaststroke
The second leg of the race is the breaststroke

Butterfly
The third part of the race is swum using the butterfly

Freestyle
The final leg is swum using any other recognised stroke

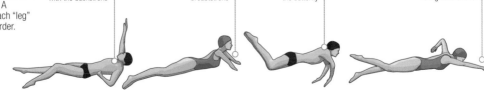

INSIDE STORY

Representations of swimmers date from the Stone Age, but competitive swimming began in Europe around 1800 and modern styles have evolved since that time. Swimming events were included in the first modern Summer Olympic games in Athens, Greece, in 1896. Women were not eligible to compete until the Stockholm games of 1912.

INTERNATIONAL BODY

The international governing body for swimming is the Fédération Internationale de Natation Amateur (FINA), established in 1908. FINA oversees and runs all world championship and Olympic events, as well as diving, water polo, open water marathon and synchronised swimming events.

ATHLETE PROFILE

Divers are supple yet strong enough to hold or alter their position in mid-air. Legs, arms, and joints must be in peak condition. Divers often emerge at the top level between about 14 and 16 years of age.

THE POOL

Diving events take place from platforms and springboards in a diving pool or swimming pool. The length and breadth of the pool are variable: some competitions are held in the deep end of regular pools. The platforms and springboards have non-slip surfaces and are reached by suitable stairs, not ladders. The minimum depth of water beneath a 10m platform is 3.5m (11ft 6in). For other platforms and springboards, it should be at least 1.8m (6ft) deep.

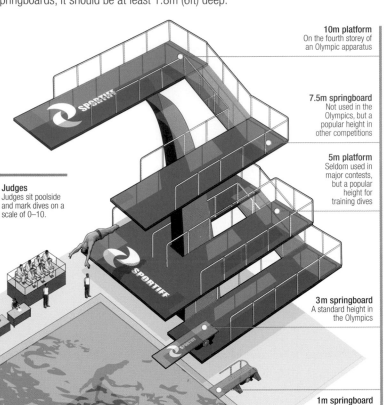

10m platform
On the fourth storey of an Olympic apparatus

7.5m springboard
Not used in the Olympics, but a popular height in other competitions

5m platform
Seldom used in major contests, but a popular height for training dives

Judges
Judges sit poolside and mark dives on a scale of 0–10.

3m springboard
A standard height in the Olympics

1m springboard
The 1m board is bouncier than its higher counterpart, so divers usually execute a high jump to get maximum momentum into the air

Water jets
Water is sprayed across the surface to ease the force of a diver's impact

Water dressing
Divers wear a one-piece swimsuit that must not be transparent, even when wet

Shaping up
Judges award marks for the lines formed by the diver's body during the descent: the more shapely the silhouette, the higher the score

Arm shape
The hands and arms are brought together above the head in a single, sweeping, symmetrical motion: any failure incurs a point penalty

SPORT OVERVIEW

Diving is the art of jumping acrobatically into the water of a swimming or diving pool from platforms or springboards of different heights. Competitors are judged on the degree of difficulty of their dives and the technical proficiency with which they execute them.

DIVING

SIDELINES

3 The number of consecutive Olympic diving gold medals – a record – won by Klaus Dibiasi, an Austrian-born Italian, who won the 10m platform diving events at Tokyo in 1968, Munich in 1972, and Montreal in 1976.

13 The age of China's Fu Mingxia when she became the youngest ever champion in the women's 10m platform event at the 1992 Olympics. Four years later she took gold in both 10m and 3m dives.

5 The number of World Championship competitions won by American diver Greg Louganis. He also won Olympic golds in 1984 and 1988 in the 3m springboard and 10m platform events.

70 The number of Olympic medals won by US male divers between 1904 and 2012. The total includes 13 golds in the 10m platform and 15 golds in the 3m springboard. The United States has been the world's leading diving nation but they were eclipsed by China at the 2012 Games, winning one gold medal in comparison to China's six.

KEEPING SCORE

Divers are allowed a certain number of attempts per round, usually six for men and five for women. Every dive must feature various elements, such as somersaults and twists: the exact requirements are notified by the organizers before the competition. Contestants are marked not only on the way they perform these compulsory moves but also on the way they hit the water: top marks are awarded to splashless entries, known as "rips".

SCORING

There are seven judges in Olympic and world events, five in most other competitions. Each judge awards every dive a mark out of 10: 3 for take off, 3 for flight, and 3 for entry (they award the 10th point at their discretion). After logging the scores they eliminate the highest and lowest and multiply the remainder by a previously agreed degree of difficulty (DD) factor to determine the final score for the dive.

BOARD MANOEUVRES

There are 91 officially recognized platform dives and 70 springboard dives. They are divided into six groups: forward, backward, reverse, inward, twist, and handspring (or armstand). Handsprings are permitted only from the 10m platform; all other dives must be launched by the feet.

SYNCHRONICITY

In synchronized competitions, two teammates jump simultaneously from platforms or springboards of the same height and try to perform either exactly the same dive or two different dives that complement or mirror one another. One peculiarity of this event is that divers who have jumped badly may score highly – as long as they both made the same mistakes. Synchronized diving became an Olympic event in 2000.

TUCK

In the perfect tuck, the body is compact and bent at the hips, with the knees bent and held together. The diver tucks the calves against the backs of the thighs, holding them in position with the hands clasped on the shins. The feet are close together and the toes are pointed throughout the movement. In a tuck dive that contains a twist, the diver needs to clearly show the tuck position.

Foetal position
Straight backs incur penalties so divers aim for a kind of foetal position

PIKE

In a pike, both legs are straight, with the body bent at the hips, the feet together, and the toes pointed. The position of the arms is at the diver's discretion – the arms may be clasped around the back of the knees or the calves, as shown, or held out at the sides. If a pike dive contains a twist, it is important for the diver to clearly show the pike position in order to avoid the judges deducting points.

Joint to joint
When clasping the calves the elbows touch the knees

STRAIGHT

Also known as the layout, the straight dive calls for an absolutely rigid and fully stretched body, with straight legs, feet together and pointed toes; the arms may be stretched above the head or held tight against the side of the body. If a straight dive contains a twist, the twist must not be initiated from the platform or springboard.

Human torpedo
The whole body is as stiff as a board

PLUNGE FOR DISTANCE

IN THIS ONE-TIME-ONLY OLYMPIC EVENT, HELD IN 1904 IN ST LOUIS, COMPETITORS MADE STANDING DIVES FROM THE POOLSIDE TO SEE HOW FAR THEY COULD GO UNDER WATER. THEY WERE NOT ALLOWED TO MOVE THEIR BODIES IN THE WATER AND HAD TO RELY ON THEIR PRE-ENTRY MOMENTUM. GOLD WENT TO WILLIAM DICKEY OF THE UNITED STATES, WHO DESCENDED FOR OVER 19.05M (62FT 6IN).

FORWARD TWO-AND-A-HALF SOMERSAULTS WITH TUCK

One of the most popular and spectacular dives, this demanding move packs the maximum of athleticism into a total flight time of less than two seconds.

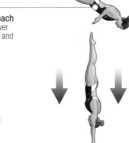

Take off
The launch must be upwards to create enough time and space for the full movement

Tuck up
The diver must be fully tucked before her head first points directly downwards

Revolution number one
By the time the diver's head returns to the upright position, she has held the tuck through a 180-degree spin

One complete cycle
As the diver's head points directly downwards she has completed one somersault

The second somersault
After the second somersault, the diver will prepare for the final half-somersault

Moment of release
The diver unclasps her legs and holds her thighs in readiness to adopt the entry position

Line-up and final approach
One last half turn as the diver straightens the whole body and points the toes

Perpendicular entry
Divers aim for a 90-degree angle and lose points for deviations

➡️ Early forms of water polo were played in England and Scotland in the 1800s. The earliest was based on rugby and was notoriously violent and lawless.

➡️ Water polo first appeared at the Olympics in 1900. The men's event has taken place at every Olympics since 1908. The women's event was introduced in 2000.

➡️ Water polo is popular in the US and Europe, particularly Hungary, Italy, and Spain.

SIDELINES

20 The number of goals shared by Croatia and Serbia in the final of the men's World Cup in Oradea, Romania, in 2010. The Serbia team won the game 13-7.

7 The number of gold medals shared by the women's teams of the United States, Italy, and Hungary in World Championships.

WATER POLO

GAME OVERVIEW

Water polo is a water-based sport played by two teams of seven players (six outfield players and one goalkeeper). The object of the sport is to propel the ball into the opposing team's goal; each goal scores one point, and the winning team is the one with the highest number of goals. Matches are made up of four quarters lasting seven minutes each; two three-minute phases of extra time may be played if necessary. Water polo is a particularly challenging and fiercely competitive sport; the action is fast and fouls are very common, particularly underwater – referees have to be extra alert to spot them all. The sport has been likened to a mixture of swimming, volleyball, rugby, and wrestling.

THE POLO POOL

The dimensions of a water polo pool vary according to the level at which the match is being played, but most are between 20m x 10m (65ft 6in x 32ft 9in) and 30m x 20m (98ft 6in x 65ft 6in). For the Olympics, the water must be at least 1.8m (5ft 9in) deep. Conventional swimming pools may be used, but their shallow ends are not ideal, since outfield players are not allowed to touch the bottom. The playing area is marked by buoys or painted lines on the bottom of the pool (or both), and comprises a white goal line, red two-metre line, and yellow five-metre lines on either side of a white midline.

Ear protectors
The caps feature ear protectors that are designed to keep out water while allowing the players to hear their team-mates and the referees

Swimming cap
Competitors wear swimming caps in team colours; the home team wear dark-coloured caps and the away team light-coloured caps. Each cap has a number to designate the player's position

GOAL AREA
The goals are either attached to the side of the pool or fixed in place with cables. A limp net encloses the entire goal area. The goalkeeper guards the goal area by trying to deflect or catch the ball, but must be careful not to knock the posts or crossbar – the goal is relatively flimsy and can be moved by hand.

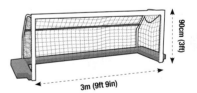

90cm (3ft)

3m (9ft 9in)

PLAYER PROFILE
Players need strong swimming skills, including the ability to sprint. Accurate ball-handling is essential; this is particularly difficult as throws are made while treading water and the player must propel his or her body out of the water. Players need to be strong to tackle opponents and withstand attacks. Team skills and strategic thinking are also key.

WHO PLAYS WHERE?

The goalkeepers are not allowed to move over the midline in to the other half of the pool. The outfield players can move anywhere in the pool and play both offence and defence, depending on which team is attacking. The centre forward, who leads the attack, takes up a position directly in front of the opponent's goal. The other five outfield players are known as perimeter players. At the highest level of competition, the perimeter players tend not to keep to one position, exchanging roles with their team-mates as the situation demands.

STARTING PLAY

Water polo matches are divided into four quarters. Each quarter begins with the two teams lined up on opposite sides of the pool, on their respective goal line. The referee blows a whistle to indicate the start of the quarter, and then drops the ball on to the midline. The players sprint towards the ball and whoever reaches it first wins possession. That team now takes the offence. Whenever a team takes possession of a ball, they have 30 seconds in which to shoot at goal or surrender possession – a shot clock starts counting down the time.

First winger
The two wingers are offensive players positioned on the two-metre line

Second winger
The second winger sets up attacks on the other side of the pool

First driver
The drivers' role is to move the ball into a goal-scoring position. The drivers position themselves either side of the centre forward

Second driver
The second driver backs up the first driver to set up goal-scoring chances

Point man
In offence, the point man directs offensive moves. In defence, he marks the opposing centre forward

Centre forward
The centre forward is usually positioned in front of the opponent's goal, between the two-metre and five-metre lines

Goalkeeper
Defends the goal area and deflects opponents' attacks on the goal

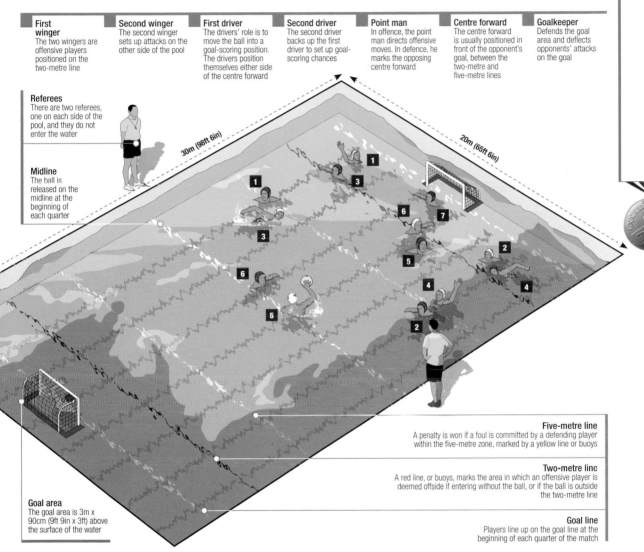

Referees
There are two referees, one on each side of the pool, and they do not enter the water

Midline
The ball is released on the midline at the beginning of each quarter

30m (98ft 6in)

20m (65ft 6in)

Goal area
The goal area is 3m x 90cm (9ft 9in x 3ft) above the surface of the water

Five-metre line
A penalty is won if a foul is committed by a defending player within the five-metre zone, marked by a yellow line or buoys

Two-metre line
A red line, or buoys, marks the area in which an offensive player is deemed offside if entering without the ball, or if the ball is outside the two-metre line

Goal line
Players line up on the goal line at the beginning of each quarter of the match

POLO ORIGINS?

THE ORIGIN OF THE USE OF THE WORD "POLO" IS CONTESTED. IT COULD DERIVE FROM AN EARLY VARIANT, WHERE PLAYERS RODE FLOATING BARRELS, SIMULATING HORSES, OR IT COULD COME FROM THE BALTI WORD FOR EARLY INDIA-RUBBER BALLS.

WET GEAR

All competitors must wear swimsuits and coloured, numbered caps, which are important for identifying players. Players are not allowed to apply grease or oil to any part of the body, for any reason.

FLOATING BALL

The ball must be spherical, and has a waterproof rubber outer, an air chamber, and a self-closing valve. Competition balls weigh 400–450g (14–15oz) and are usually yellow. Balls for men's matches are larger than those used in women's matches.

21.6–22.6cm (8½–9in)

LIGHT AND TIGHT

Shorts and swimsuits must be tight-fitting but allow ease of movement through the water. Items that may cause injury are not permitted.

No see-throughs
Only non-transparent one-piece or two-piece swimsuits are allowed

POOL RULES

Matches consist of four quarters of seven minutes, with a two-minute break between each quarter. Each team is allowed a timeout of two minutes during each match. In case of a draw, two further three-minute sessions are played, followed, if necessary, by three minutes decided by a golden goal.

Field players may touch the ball with only one hand and cannot use their fists to hit the ball. They must not touch the bottom or side of the pool.

Goalkeepers may handle the ball with both hands, may hit the ball with their fists, and may touch the bottom of the pool. However, they are not allowed past the halfway line. Players cannot push the ball underwater when being tackled, or push or hold an opponent unless that player is holding the ball. If an attacker's shot goes out of play at the end of the pool, the game is restarted by the defence. If the defence touched the ball last, the attacking side is awarded a free throw from the two-metre line.

SCORING

A goal is counted if the whole of the ball crosses the line between the goal posts and the crossbar. Although goals can be scored with any part of the body other than the fist, in practice they nearly all come from attacking throws.

FROM DEFENCE TO ATTACK

As well as preventing the opposing team from scoring, the goalkeeper has a key part to play in launching team-members on the offensive. Accurate passing is a vital skill.

Two hands good
The goalkeeper is the only player permitted to catch the ball with both hands

Red head
Goalkeepers wear a red cap to make them easily identifiable

Touch and go
The defender keeps an eye on the goalkeeper and the ball as she swims out of her team's goal area to make herself available for a pass

WATER SKILLS

Outstanding swimming skills and stamina are essential for water polo players, who may swim 3–5km (1¾–3 miles) during a typical match. There is a lot of physical contact, and resilience is needed to withstand robust opposition challenges. Players must be constantly aware of their surroundings – the rapidly changing range of opportunities and threats in every part of the pool. That is why water polo features some swimming styles that look different from those employed in swimming races. Players always swim with their heads out of the water to observe the action, and a type of backstroke where the player is almost upright in the water is frequently used. Swimming is combined with ball-handling skills to shoot goals or advance the ball to teammates, as discussed below.

TREADING WATER

Outfield players cannot touch the bottom or the side of the pool; shots and passes must be made while treading water. To power their shots, players propel their bodies out of the water; some can lift themselves out to thigh level. The popular "eggbeater" method of treading water involves rotating the legs rather than using a scissor kick to maintain a constant position.

SHOOTING

There are several ways to shoot. The lob is a high, arching overhead shot, often taken from an angle either side of the goal. The skip shot involves bouncing the ball off the water with enough force to propel it into the goal. The power shot is made by a player propelling his or her body out of the water and throwing the ball at the goal. The diagram below shows an attacker through on goal feinting to shoot in one direction and then, having made the keeper dive, throwing the ball into the unguarded other side of the goal.

DRIBBLING

Players can advance the ball up the pool by swimming while pushing the ball in front of them. They must neither hold the ball while pushing nor push it beneath the surface of the water as they advance. Any player attempting to dribble the ball will almost certainly be challenged, and he or she will need to fend off tackles from the opposing side. Here, the attacker has jinked his way through the last line of defence to create a shooting opportunity in an advanced position. A pass to that position would have been offside.

PASSING

All but the simplest passes require great skill, as the ball must be thrown and caught accurately with one hand only. A dry pass is a high-speed pass made to an outfield player without the ball touching the water. A wet pass is made by bouncing the ball off the surface of the water to an attacking teammate. In the diagram below, the player in possession has several passing options, including the simple one to the player on his immediate right, and a more ambitious through ball for a team mate swimming quickly into space.

The attacker may shoot right or left

If the keeper dives right, the attacker shoots right

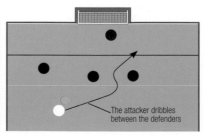
The attacker dribbles between the defenders

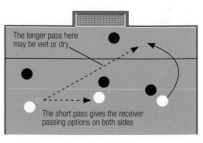
The longer pass here may be wet or dry

The short pass gives the receiver passing options on both sides

EXCLUSIONS

Players are excluded from the game if they commit major fouls, and are sent to a specially demarcated penalty area for a maximum of 20 seconds. Major fouls include sinking a player (holding him or her underwater); interfering with a free throw; pulling back on a player; holding on to an offensive player; or intentionally coming into contact with a defensive player. An excluded player can be substituted with another player.

BLOOD IN THE WATER

HUNGARY BEAT THE SOVIET UNION 4–0 IN A FAMOUS GRUDGE MATCH SHORTLY AFTER THE RED ARMY HAD SUPPRESSED THE 1956 HUNGARIAN UPRISING. IN THE POOL, VERBAL ABUSE SOON TURNED TO PHYSICAL VIOLENCE. THE WORST OF THE NUMEROUS PUNCHES THAT WERE TRADED THROUGHOUT THE MATCH FORCED HUNGARY'S ERVIN ZÁDOR TO LEAVE THE POOL WITH BLOOD GUSHING FROM BELOW HIS EYE.

POLO SPEAK

The following are some of the most commonly used specialist terms that relate to water polo tactics and techniques:

DRIVER An attacking player, usually a fast swimmer, whose main duty is to advance the ball into a goal-scoring position.

HOLE GUARD A defensive player who takes position in front of his or her goal and marks the centre forward.

HOLE MAN Alternative term for a centre forward; also called a hole set.

PRESS DEFENCE A form of man-marking; the defence plays very tight to the attackers in an effort to prevent or impede their passing or driving movements.

PUMP FAKING When a player gets in position to shoot but stops halfway, causing the defending keeper to commit too early to block the shot, thus leaving the goal at the attacker's mercy.

STALLING Failure to shoot within 30 seconds of gaining possession, which is penalized by a free throw to the opposition.

SWIM-OFF The sprint for the ball in the centre of the field of play that starts each quarter of the match.

STAT CENTRAL

OLYMPIC CHAMPIONS

YEAR	TEAM
2012	CROATIA (MEN)
2012	UNITED STATES (WOMEN)
2008	HUNGARY (MEN)
2008	NETHERLANDS (WOMEN)
2004	HUNGARY (MEN)
2004	ITALY (WOMEN)
2000	HUNGARY (MEN)
2000	AUSTRALIA (WOMEN)
1996	SPAIN
1992	ITALY
1988	YUGOSLAVIA
1984	YUGOSLAVIA
1980	SOVIET UNION
1976	HUNGARY
1972	SOVIET UNION
1968	YUGOSLAVIA
1964	HUNGARY
1960	ITALY
1956	HUNGARY

TEAM FORMATIONS

Defence positions in water polo can either be man-to-man or zone-based. The most common formation is a 3-3 formation, with two lines of three players. The 4-2 formation is a useful attacking formation when the opposing team has a player excluded (they are sent off for 20 seconds for a major foul), while the 1-4 is a formation used when the defending team is a man down.

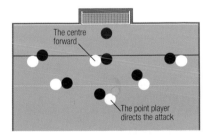

STANDARD "UMBRELLA" ATTACK
The standard "umbrella" attack is an offensive formation adopted by high-level teams. The point man sits at the apex of the umbrella, while the centre forward sits inside it, in front of the goal.

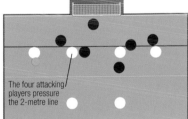

4-2 ATTACK (6 ON 5)
If one team has a player excluded, the opposing team will press the advantage by playing in the 4-2 formation. Four players are placed on the 2-metre line and two on the 5-metre line.

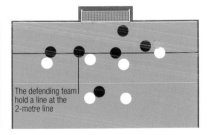

1-4 DEFENCE
When playing with one player down, the defending team will often adopt the 1-4 defence, with four players positioned on the 2-metre line and one on the 5-metre line.

SIDELINES

9 The number of Olympic gold medals won by Hungary, the most successful water polo team in the history of the modern Olympic Games. The second-most successful nation – with gold medals in 1900, 1908, 1912, and 1920 – is Great Britain. Italy has won a total of five gold medals at the Water Polo World Championship, making it the most successful nation since the event began in 1973.

14 The total number of nations that participated in the men's and women's water polo events in the 2012 Olympics.

13 The highest number of goals scored by an individual player in an international. This was achieved by Debbie Handley, playing for Australia against Canada at the 1982 World Championships. Australia won 16-10.

INSIDE STORY

Apart from the Olympics, the main international competitions are the World Water Polo League, which has been contested in July and August each year since 2002, and the World Championships, which has taken place every two years since 2001. Both contests are organised by the Fédération International de Natation (FINA), the world ruling body for aquatic sports.

NEED2KNOW

→ Originally known as water ballet, the sport began in Canada in the 1920s. It spread to the United States in the early 1930s, where a display at the 1934 Chicago World's Fair drew rave reviews.

→ Synchronised swimming has been an Olympic sport since 1984; the two medal events are altered from time to time, but most recently have been for duets and teams of eight.

BODY SHAPE

Maintaining a pleasing body shape is the most important requirement in both the artistic and free sections of any synchronised swimming event. There are heavy penalties for any visible unsteadiness in the water. Teams must ensure that all their movements are made in unison or are complementary, and are performed in perfect time to their chosen music.

BARRACUDA (A BIG PIKE)
This move begins with a bottom-first downward thrust with the legs together and pointing straight up; this position must be maintained while the trunk is straightened below the surface.

PLATFORM POSITION
One person is supported at or above the surface by the rest of the team. They must all rise and descend once, with the person being lifted rising head first.

SYNCHRONISED SWIMMING

SPORT OVERVIEW

This pool sport is a unique combination of dance, swimming, and gymnastics. Competitors perform graceful movements to a musical accompaniment while out of their depth in water. Judges award them marks out of ten for technical merit and artistic effect. The term "synchronised" implies multiple participants and most contests involve teams of two or more, however, there are individual competitions.

TECHNICAL MERIT

Both team and solo events consist of a technical routine and a free routine, each performed to music within a time limit. In the technical routine, swimmers perform specific moves in a set order, including boosts, rockets, thrusts, and twirls. In the free routine, there are no restrictions on music or choreography. Judges of each routine look for a high degree of difficulty and risk, flawless execution, innovative choreography, pool coverage, patterns, perfect synchronisation with one another and with the music, and a seemingly effortless performance.

SWIMMER PROFILE
Besides demanding strength, endurance, flexibility, grace and artistry, it also requires exceptional breath control, as routines can last up to five minutes. Good musical sense is necessary to keep time with the beat of the music.

Underwater love
An underwater speaker lets the swimmers hear the music clearly while underwater, helping them achieve the split-second timing critical to synchronised swimming

Perfect hair
Gelatine keeps the hair in place. Make-up brings out the features

Keeping the water out
A nose clip prevents water from entering the nose, allowing the swimmers to remain underwater for long periods

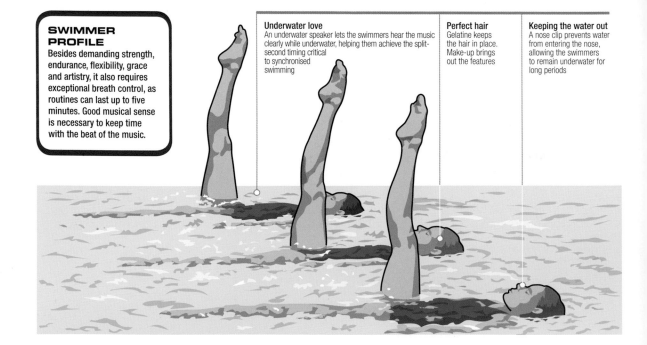

UNDERWATER SPORTS

EVENT OVERVIEW

The three most popular underwater team activities are hockey, rugby, and soccer. They have fewer players than their on-land counterparts, and since nearly all the action takes place beneath the surface, these strenuous subaqua sports are naturally not big spectator attractions. However, they have an enthusiastic and growing band of participants in Australia, Europe, and North America, and many scuba divers use the games as a form of recreation-cum-training.

I LOVE WATER HOCKEY

A fast moving game played competitively by some and for fun by others, often as a means of keeping fit for another underwater pursuit. It is a non-contact sport in which size and strength are not important, so it is often played at local level by mixed teams.

Agile and fast
As manoeuvrability and speed are important, softer, free diving fins are often used

Ear protection
A blow to the ear can easily burst an eardrum, so ear protectors are required in tournament games

Touch or no touch?
The wooden hockey stick must not be more than 35cm (14in) long, including the handle

Rapid breathing
A large bore snorkel allows faster intake of air, reducing time spent at the surface

Safety gear
Players must wear a diving mask, a cap, and at least one reinforced glove

Deep puck
The puck must be 80mm (2⅝in) in diameter, 30mm (1in) thick and weigh 1.3kg (3lb)

UNDERWATER HOCKEY

Matches are contested between two teams of six players who are chosen from a squad of 12. Matches are 33 minutes long, each half lasting for 15 minutes, with a three minute break when the teams change ends. The object of the game is to outscore the opposing team. A goal is scored by hitting a puck into a 3m x 25cm (9ft 10in x 10in) wide goal using a plain white or black wooden or plywood stick. Players take turns at being under the water. If there is no winner at full time, a period of overtime (two 5-minute periods) will be played. If there is still no winner, the team who scores the next goal is declared the winner.

UNDERWATER RUGBY

Usually played with a round, rather than an oval-shaped 25cm (10in) ball, this six-a-side game for men and women is known as rugby because opponents may be grabbed and tackled as long as they are in possession of the ball. A tackled player must release the ball, which is filled with dissolved salt, when tackled. The goals are metal buckets 40cm (16in) in diameter, situated on each end of the floor of the pool. A foul is called if the ball leaves the water.

UNDERWATER FOOTBALL

A five-a-side game somewhat misleadingly named as players may use their hands. The object is to propel a sand-filled ball into the opposition goal. To score, the ball must be placed in the goal area of the gutter at the side of the pool in such a way that the ball rests for a moment while still in the scorers grasp. A match is 10 minutes each way, with a three-minute halftime interval. If the match is drawn, an extra ten minutes is played to determine the winner.

PLAYING TOGETHER

NOT VERY MANY PEOPLE PLAY UNDERWATER RUGBY, SO BECAUSE OF THIS IT IS OFTEN PLAYED IN MIXED MALE-FEMALE TEAMS.

INSIDE STORY

Underwater hockey emerged in the 1950s, and was followed 20 years later by soccer and rugby. The 2006 Underwater Hockey World Championships were contested by 17 nations. The first world underwater rugby championship was held in Germany in 1980.

GOVERNING BODY
World tournaments are run by the Confédération Mondiale des Activités Subaquatiques (CMAS), which was established in 1959.

→ There were 11 classes of boat selected for the 2008 Olympics.

→ At the 2012 Olympics, six male classes (Sailboard, Laser, 470, Star, Finn, 49er) and four female classes (Sailboard, Laser, 470, and Yngling) were selected.

→ At the 2008 Olympics, three classes (Finn, 49er, and Tornado) were open to either sex. Open classes were discontinued for 2012.

COMPETITOR PROFILE
For racing sailors, physical fitness and strength are important, but mental skills and attitude are the key to success. Upper-body strength is needed for hoisting and trimming (adjusting) sails, plus leg strength to move around the boat quickly, and a strong trunk to hike or lean out. Quick thinking and fast reaction time are essential, as racing is all about tactics and using the ever-shifting elements to maximum advantage. Racing can start young: children race tiny dinghies, many Olympic athletes are in their mid twenties, and round-the-world racers are often much older than sportsmen competing at international levels in other sports.

SIDELINES

1851 The year in which the yacht America challenged English boats to race around the Isle of Wight, England, for a trophy that has since become known as the America's Cup.

67 The age of the oldest competitor to date in the Velux 5 Oceans Single-Handed Race (Sir Robin Knox-Johnson).

16 The VHF Radio channel dedicated for use in an emergency at sea, to request help from coastguard or other vessels.

1,852 The number of metres (6,076ft) in a nautical mile – a standardization of the measurement of 1' (minute) of latitude.

5,000 The number of sailors competing in the annual Kiel Week regatta, in northern Germany, in 2,000 boats.

BUILT FOR SPEED
Boats raced in the Olympics are small, with between one and three crew members. A typical Olympic boat will have a large sail area for such a small, light boat, and a planing hull, which allows it to skim over the water and minimizes drag.

Physical agility The crew hikes out as far as possible, using a trapeze, to balance the weight of the wind in the sails. Quick reflexes are needed to react to wind shifts and avoid a dunking

Luffing the mainsail The luff (front edge) of the mainsail should not flutter, or speed will be reduced

The slot A slot between mainsail and jib, with sides as parallel as possible, gives a clean wind flow over both sails

Avoiding a flutter The leech (back edge) of the jib should not flutter, or speed will be reduced

Steering The helm steers as steady a course as possible, and controls the mainsail, working with the wind

Foresail The crew adjusts the foresail to work efficiently with the mainsail

Smooth sailing Keeping the hull level in the water maximizes hydrodynamics and is the fastest way to sail

SAILING

SPORT OVERVIEW
Sailing has been described unjustly as akin to standing under a power shower ripping up money while someone is throwing buckets of cold water at you. It is an exhilarating and demanding sport, both physically and mentally. There are many different types of racing, governed by strict international rules as well as local regulations. Racing may take place on lakes or coastal bays and estuaries, round courses defined by temporary marks; in coastal waters, using fixed navigational marks to define the course; or far offshore across entire oceans. Sailors may race single-handed, in a small crew, or in a crew of 20 or more athletes.

WHERE THEY RACE

Offshore races usually follow a route delineated by fixed navigational buoys. Shorter coastal and inland races have temporary race marks laid, in such a way as to provide the best test of sailing ability for the conditions of the day.

OLYMPIC COURSES

Racing is based on short events of 30–75 minutes. A classic Olympic course has a distance of 1.6km (1 mile) between race marks, which are set to provide a variety of different sailing angles (see p.260). Beating (sailing towards the wind, or windward) provides the best test of ability, and the windward leg is the most important part of the course. On an Olympic course, such as the triangle course below, the windward leg will be sailed twice, and there will be at least one leg downwind (sailing away from the wind). Reaching (sailing between 45 and 135 degrees to the wind) is the easiest and fastest point of sailing, and usually there will be one reaching leg in each direction relative to the wind. The Start line is ideally set square (at right angles) to the wind, to provide a fair, unbiased start for all the boats (see p.259).

WINDWARD/LEEWARD COURSE

The emphasis of this course is on direct upwind and downwind sailing, provided by several laps of two separate marks at the downwind end of the course.

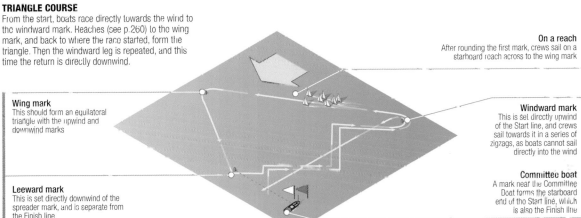

Spreader mark
Reaching round this takes the downwind boats away from those beating to windward

Windward mark
Crews beat up to this mark, which also forms the port end of the Finish line for the final lap

Start line
The line between this buoy and the Committee Boat is ideally set at right angles to the wind

Leeward mark
This is set directly downwind of the spreader mark

Committee boat
A small mark near the Committee Boat is the starboard end of the Start line

Second committee boat
This can be used to set a Finish line at the windward end of the course

TRIANGLE COURSE

From the start, boats race directly towards the wind to the windward mark. Reaches (see p.260) to the wing mark, and back to where the race started, form the triangle. Then the windward leg is repeated, and this time the return is directly downwind.

On a reach
After rounding the first mark, crews sail on a starboard reach across to the wing mark

Wing mark
This should form an equilateral triangle with the upwind and downwind marks

Windward mark
This is set directly upwind of the Start line, and crews sail towards it in a series of zigzags, as boats cannot sail directly into the wind

Leeward mark
This is set directly downwind of the spreader mark, and is separate from the Finish line

Committee boat
A mark near the Committee Boat forms the starboard end of the Start line, which is also the Finish line

OCEAN RACING

Ocean racing is the pinnacle of yachting challenges, the ultimate test of both boats and sailors. These races are long, often lasting many months, and gruelling, taking competitors far from the shelter of home waters.

All ocean races are held under the Racing Rules of the International Sailing Federation (ISAF). Some are raced single-handed, testing the endurance of a single yachtsman or woman. They face extreme loneliness and tough challenges, but most do endure and are recognized for their skill and resilience in adversity. Other races are sailed with a large crew, where the skill of the skipper is in leading a team that can work and live together at close quarters through storms and calms. Interestingly, it is often the calms that produce severe psychological difficulty; the phenomenon of drifting aimlessly through the ocean, far off the planned course because there is no wind to drive the boat, creates frustrations that many sailors find difficult to deal with.

Ocean racers must be resourceful. They must know how to achieve the best sailing speeds from their boats, and be able to navigate safely through unmarked oceans. They must also deal with breakages of equipment that occur in stressful conditions, improvising repairs to complex equipment with only the most basic of materials or tools to hand.

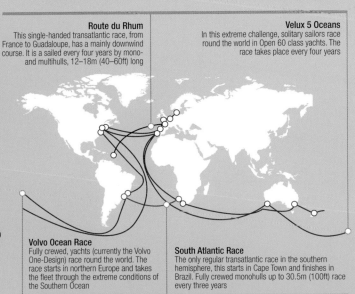

Route du Rhum
This single-handed transatlantic race, from France to Guadaloupe, has a mainly downwind course. It is sailed every four years by mono- and multihulls, 12–18m (40–60ft) long

Velux 5 Oceans
In this extreme challenge, solitary sailors race round the world in Open 60 class yachts. The race takes place every four years

Volvo Ocean Race
Fully crewed, yachts (currently the Volvo One-Design) race round the world. The race starts in northern Europe and takes the fleet through the extreme conditions of the Southern Ocean

South Atlantic Race
The only regular transatlantic race in the southern hemisphere, this starts in Cape Town and finishes in Brazil. Fully crewed monohulls up to 30.5m (100ft) race every three years

WHAT THEY RACE

Boats of all sizes may have one hull (monohulls), or two or three parallel hulls (multihulls). A boat with two hulls is a catamaran, while a boat with three hulls is a trimaran. Racing boats have a large sail area for the size of boat, and underwater foils (the fins and rudder) to minimize leeward drift (the sideways force of the wind). Designers constantly strive to find ways to construct boats in ever lighter materials, and are always looking for ways to improve the balance between speed and safety.

OLYMPIC CLASSES

Boats sailed for Olympic events are measured to precise formulae, so that craft in any one class are as nearly identical as possible. The test is then of the athlete's skill, not that of the boat-builder. Classes are chosen by the International Sailing Federation (ISAF), and occasionally changes are made to the list, to reflect developments in boat design and greater athleticism of sailors.

The Laser, Laser Radial, and 470 dinghies are very popular, and commonly sailed in club racing throughout the world, both inland and in coastal waters. The Tornado catamaran, high-performance 49er skiff, and the Yngling and Star keelboats are less commonly seen outside elite racing circle. The Tornado was not selected for the 2012 Olympics.

GETTING THE EDGE
Racers work hard to find ways to "tune" or "tweak" their boats to achieve a technical edge over competitors. The measurement rules are strict, so everyone is using the same equipment, but even quite small adjustments to rigging or sails might produce a tiny advantage that could lead to a big medal.

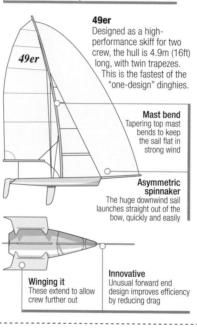

LASER
This 4.2m (14ft) monohull dinghy is popular worldwide. It is simply designed, mainly for single-handed sailing, with basic rigging.

Sleeved sail
The single sail has a "sleeve" that slides over the mast

Control lines
All controls must be rope, with no high-tensile strength materials such as Kevlar

Within the rules
Design is governed by class standards

Unstayed mast
A slot in the deck supports the tall mast, which fits into it

49er
Designed as a high-performance skiff for two crew, the hull is 4.9m (16ft) long, with twin trapezes. This is the fastest of the "one-design" dinghies.

Mast bend
Tapering top mast bends to keep the sail flat in strong wind

Asymmetric spinnaker
The huge downwind sail launches straight out of the bow, quickly and easily

Winging it
These extend to allow crew further out

Innovative
Unusual forward end design improves efficiency by reducing drag

470
The single hull is 4.7m (15.4ft) long, designed for a crew of two. A trapeze helps crew keep the planing hull level in the water.

Stayed mast
The mast is supported by stainless steel wire rigging

"Bermuda" rig
Conventional mainsail and jib give a large sail area, with a spinnaker for downwind sailing

Adjustable foils
As on all dinghies, the rudder and centreboard can be raised as required

Self-buoyant
The lightweight hull includes integral buoyancy tanks

TORNADO
A 6.1m (20ft) catamaran sailed by a crew of two, the Tornado is capable of speeds above 30 knots (56kph/35mph), and 18 knots (33kph/20mph) upwind.

Large sails
Large mainsail and jib are augmented by a spinnaker for downwind sailing

Fast tack
A self-tacking jib makes for quick direction changes

Adjusting mast
A rotating mast improves aerodynamics and sail shape

Flying high
The Tornado is typically sailed with one hull "flying" (out of the water)

OCEAN RACERS

Some ocean racing events are open to any type of boat, often grouped into classes of different-sized yachts handicapped according to criteria such as weight and sail area. Other events are for "one-design" classes.

Yacht designers are constantly searching for ways to combine lightweight materials such as carbon fibre with the strength needed to deal with huge forces and potentially heavy seas. Those boats destined for round-the-world racing are extremely robust, yet also sleek and hydrodynamic. They have strong mechanisms for handling huge sails, and up-to-date electronic navigation and communications equipment – safety is a serious consideration in this dangerous sport. There also has to be some living accommodation; the crew must be able to sleep and eat in order to maintain their ability to perform under arduous conditions, but space and weight are at a premium so there are no frills and crew will be expected to "hot bunk" (alternate in bunks) to save space.

Mast
The mast extends 31.5m (103ft) above the waterline

Sail power
The mainsail is 186sq m (223sq yd) and the spinnaker 500sq m (598sq yd)

Light and fast
The yacht weighs 12,500–14,000kg (12.3–13.8 tons), yet is capable of great speeds

Canting keel
The 7,000kg (6.9 ton) ballast bulb on the keel is rotated to increase stability and power

OCEAN RACER (VOLVO 70)
This 21.3m (70ft) monohull yacht was designed for the 2005–6 Volvo Ocean Race. A core crew of nine sails the boat (11 for an all-female crew), with 11 different sails (excluding storm sails) to choose from.

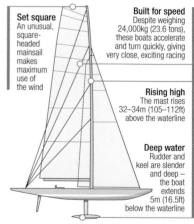

Set square
An unusual, square-headed mainsail makes maximum use of the wind

Built for speed
Despite weighing 24,000kg (23.6 tons), these boats accelerate and turn quickly, giving very close, exciting racing

Rising high
The mast rises 32–34m (105–112ft) above the waterline

Deep water
Rudder and keel are slender and deep – the boat extends 5m (16.5ft) below the waterline

AMERICA'S CUP CLASS
This is a design-restricted class that is newly developed for each series of challenges. The boats are 24m (79ft) long and only 4.1m (13.5ft) wide. A crew of 17 is stipulated, with an optional 18th non-racing crew.

PARTS OF A BOAT

All sailing boats consist of a hull; a rig with spars such as mast and boom; sails; and underwater foils for steerage and to resist leeway (sideways drift). Fittings and control systems vary enormously in size and complexity, but are recognizable from boat to boat. Many sailing boats are at least partially decked.

KEELBOAT

A keelboat falls midway between a dinghy and a yacht – larger than most dinghies but with a ballasted keel or centreplate instead of the dinghy's adjustable centreboard. Keelboats are considerably more stable than dinghies and less likely to capsize. Below decks accommodation is usually either absent or rather cramped, but an open cockpit may have room for several crew.

Mainsail
Most racing boats have a triangular mainsail, extending right up to the top of the mast

Mainsheet
A rope-and-pulley system attached to the main boom is used to control the mainsail

Sheets to the wind
The ropes used to control the sails are known as sheets

On course
In smaller keelboats and dinghies, the rudder is controlled via the tiller in the cockpit; larger yachts use a wheel

Steerage
Turning the rudder from one side to another changes the direction of the boat

Spinnaker
The bellying downwind sail is set on a spinnaker pole. Modern asymmetric spinnakers are set off a bowsprit

Foresail
A standard foresail is a jib that reaches from the bow (front) of the boat back to the mast. A larger foresail, which overlaps the mainsail and sweeps the deck, is known as a genoa

Strong spars
Mast and booms may be made of aluminium, fibre-reinforced plastic, or lightweight modern composites reinforced with carbon fibre

Boom
While the mast supports the sails vertically, the boom supports the mainsail laterally

Halyards
Ropes used to raise and lower the sails are called halyards and are usually fastened close to the mast

Keel
The keel resists drift caused by pressure of wind on the sails, turning this sideways pressure into forward motion. A ballasted (weighted) keel makes capsize unlikely

WHAT THEY WEAR

Keeping warm, comfortable, and dry is part of safety on the water. Specialist fabrics and purpose-designed clothing are an important part of successful racing.

DINGHY
Buoyancy aids must be worn by all racing dinghy crews, and wetsuits are worn by most racers. There is a choice between a full suit – covering from neck, to wrist, to ankle – and a shortie, which leaves lower legs and arms bare.

Buoyancy aid
Helps flotation without impeding swimming – essential in a craft liable to capsize

Wetsuit
Tight-fitting neoprene traps a layer of water against the skin, where it warms quickly

Sailing gloves
With or without finger-ends, gloves with reinforced palms protect hands from rope-burn and aid grip on the ropes

Dinghy shoes
Wetsuit shoes keep feet warm, and grip the side decks firmly and safely

Lifejacket
An inflatable lifejacket is worn folded flat, to be inflated only if the wearer falls into the water. It is designed to turn the wearer face up in the water

Dungarees
Chest-high waterproof trousers, which can also be worn over warm fleece layers, are heavily reinforced at seat and knees

Jacket
A wind- and waterproof jacket with tightly fitting cuffs is essential. A high collar helps keep the wind and water out

OFFSHORE/OCEAN
There are times when a yacht crew can strip to shorts and T-shirts in the sunshine, but foul-weather clothing is usually essential. Clothing systems are based on layering for warmth, with the top layer as waterproof as possible.

Full gloves
Waterproof gloves protect from the elements and from rope-burn, while also giving better grip

Yachting boots
Knee-high boots with soft rubber, non-slip soles are worn underneath the trousers

RACING RULES

All yacht and dinghy racing is governed by rules established by the International Sailing Federation (ISAF), with local rules applying if circumstances demand. The rules are complex and, to race successfully, competitors must know them all in detail, and be able to apply them tactically.

TACTICAL RACING

Sail racing is about tactics. To the uninitiated, some of the manoeuvres undertaken during racing may look like sharp practice; but when both helms know the rules thoroughly, each should use the rules to the fullest extent possible in order to gain an advantage. This is most noticeable to spectators in match racing – such as the America's Cup races – where two evenly matched yachts race boat-for-boat over a short course.

The Race Committee is not responsible for making sure that rules are not infringed. Sometimes it is possible to have referee boats out on the water, watching all competitors, especially at the turning marks. Otherwise, one boat can "protest" another for infringing rules, by raising a red flag. If the protest is disputed, the Protest Committee will take evidence from both boats after the race, to adjudicate.

WINNING ISN'T EVERYTHING

RACING RULES STATE: "A BOAT OR COMPETITOR SHALL GIVE ALL POSSIBLE HELP TO ANY PERSON OR VESSEL IN DANGER". IN 2006, SAILORS IN THE VELUX 5 OCEANS RACE (SINGLE-HANDED) RAN INTO SEVERE STORMS. ALEX THOMSON'S YACHT *HUGO BOSS* LOST HER KEEL AND HE WAS FORCED TO TAKE TO HIS LIFERAFT. MIKE GOLDING IN *ECOVER* WAS SEVERAL HOURS AHEAD, IN SECOND PLACE, BUT TURNED BACK TO RESCUE HIS FRIEND. "THAT IS THE GAME", HE WROTE. "THAT IS WHAT WE DO". SOON AFTER, *ECOVER*'S MAST BROKE AND SHE TOO WAS FORCED OUT OF THE RACE.

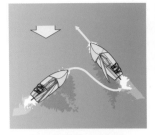

STARBOARD RIGHT OF WAY
If two boats are approaching each other on opposite tacks, the boat on port tack (with the wind coming from the left side of the boat) must always keep clear of the boat on starboard tack (with the wind coming from the right side of the boat).

WINDWARD BOAT KEEPS CLEAR
When two boats are on the same tack (both have the wind on the same side of the boat), the windward boat (the one closest to the side the wind is coming from) must keep clear of the other boat.

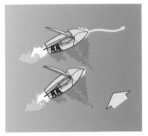

OVERTAKING BOAT KEEPS CLEAR
A boat overtaking another on the same tack must keep clear until the masts are level. The boat being overtaken can "luff" (sail closer to the direction the wind is coming from) to force the overtaking boat off course, but only until their masts are level.

OVERLAP AT A MARK
When two boats are on the same tack at a mark, the outside boat must give the boat overlapping her on the inside room to round or pass the mark without touching it, including room to tack or gybe if necessary.

TACTICS AND TACKS

The course shown on the right is a standard Olympic course, involving all points of sailing (see p.260). Racing requires not just technical skill but also clever use of tactics to exploit any advantage possible and to disadvantage the opposition.

BEATING TO WIN

Sailing directly into the wind requires a zigzag course, known as "beating". Each time the boat changes course so that the wind passes across the bow (front) of the boat, it is said to "tack" (see p.260). If the wind comes from the side of the boat, the sails are not hauled in so tightly, and the boat is said to be "reaching". With the wind directly behind, the boat is "running". A turn so that the wind passes across the stern (back) of the boat is called a "gybe" (see p.260).

STRATEGIC STARTS
Approaching the Start line, starboard tack is the safest tack since it confers right of way. A skilled helm (helmsperson) may judge there is room to approach the line and cross it on port tack before meeting a starboard tack boat. If that judgment is wrong, the port tack boat can be forced early over the line by a boat approaching fast on starboard tack. The penalty for that infringement is a detour round the end of the Start line and back over it from the correct side – behind most of the fleet.

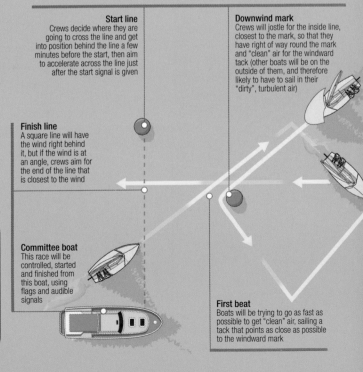

Start line
Crews decide where they are going to cross the line and get into position behind the line a few minutes before the start, then aim to accelerate across the line just after the start signal is given

Downwind mark
Crews will jostle for the inside line, closest to the mark, so that they have right of way round the mark and "clean" air for the windward tack (other boats will be on the outside of them, and therefore likely to have to sail in their "dirty", turbulent air)

Finish line
A square line will have the wind right behind it, but if the wind is at an angle, crews aim for the end of the line that is closest to the wind

Committee boat
This race will be controlled, started and finished from this boat, using flags and audible signals

First beat
Boats will be trying to go as fast as possible to get "clean" air, sailing a tack that points as close as possible to the windward mark

ON THE START

Sail races are usually set to start directly into the wind. A Race Committee Boat marks the Start line, anchoring in the starting area, and a mark buoy is laid close to it. An outer distance mark is then anchored in position to make a line that is directly at right angles to the wind (in shifting winds this line may have to be laid and relaid several times). The first mark is then laid directly upwind, at right angles to the Start line. If several classes are racing, scheduled so that starts are spread over time, the wind may shift so that the line is no longer square to the wind. This can give an advantage to boats starting at one end of the line or the other – yet another tactical element to add to the skippers' calculations.

COUNTDOWN

Each class racing is identified by a separate code flag. An audible signal is given each time a flag is hoisted or lowered. The class flag is raised five minutes before the start; the preparatory signal (P) at four minutes. The preparatory signal is then lowered one minute before the start; the class flag at the point of go. Referees check that no boat is over the line at the Start; if a boat is over, the Committee will signal that the boat is over and it must return via the outer distance mark and start again; an "over" boat that does not restart will be disqualified.

PORT-END BIAS
If the wind shifts so that the outer distance mark lies at less than 90 degrees to the wind, boats at the port (left-hand) end of the line will have a shorter distance to sail to the first mark. This creates crowding at that end of the line, as boats jockey for position.

SQUARE LINE – NO BIAS
With a Start line that is properly square to the wind, boats should be evenly spread along its length, giving all an equal distance to sail to the first mark.

STARBOARD-END BIAS
If the wind shifts so that the outer distance lies at more than 90 degrees to the wind, boats at the starboard (right-hand) end of the line will have the shorter distance to sail to the first mark. With the extra obstruction caused by the Committee Boat, this can become a tricky Start.

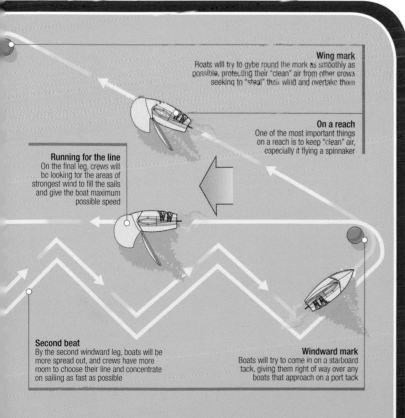

Wing mark
Boats will try to gybe round the mark as smoothly as possible, protecting their "clean" air from other crews seeking to "steal" their wind and overtake them

On a reach
One of the most important things on a reach is to keep "clean" air, especially it flying a spinnaker

Running for the line
On the final leg, crews will be looking for the areas of strongest wind to fill the sails and give the boat maximum possible speed

Second beat
By the second windward leg, boats will be more spread out, and crews have more room to choose their line and concentrate on sailing as fast as possible

Windward mark
Boats will try to come in on a starboard tack, giving them right of way over any boats that approach on a port tack

FLAGS

Races are controlled by visual signals, supported by audible signals. Internationally recognized racing signals use maritime code flags. Audible signals are also given – such as gun, whistle, or hooter, but it is the visual signal that counts for timing.

ANSWERING PENNANT
Race is postponed (numeral signals tell how long the postponement will last).

ANSWERING PENNANT OVER "A" FLAG
No more racing today.

"N" FLAG
Race is abandoned.

"P" FLAG
Preparatory signal (four minutes before Start); competitors are now under Racing Rules.

"X" FLAG
Indicates that there are boats over the Start line at the start gun.

FIRST SUBSTITUTE
General recall due to several yachts infringing the Start line – too many to identify individuals.

"S" FLAG
The course has been shortened.

"C" FLAG
The position of the next mark has been changed.

"L" FLAG
Come within hailing distance.

"M" FLAG
An object displaying this signal is replacing a missing mark.

"R" FLAG
Sail the course in the reverse direction to the sailing instructions.

BLUE FLAG
This Race Committee Boat is on station on the Finish line.

SAILING TECHNIQUES

Sailing is all about using the wind to best advantage, to gain speed and reach a specified destination. This involves the set of the sails, and the hydrodynamics of the hull in the water. It all starts with boat design; but how the sails are adjusted, and how the boat is balanced by the crew, are the techniques that sailors must learn.

POINTS OF SAIL

Each time a boat alters its angle to the wind, the set of the sails must be altered. In a dinghy, the crew's weight must be adjusted to trim the balance of the boat fore and aft, and from side to side. Each different point of sailing has a technical name.

PORT OR STARBOARD?
If the wind is coming over the starboard (right) side of the boat, the boat is on a starboard tack. If the wind is coming over the other side, the boat is on a port tack.

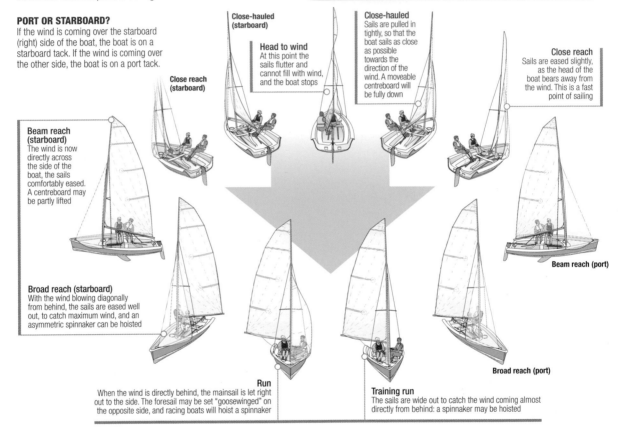

Close-hauled (starboard)

Head to wind
At this point the sails flutter and cannot fill with wind, and the boat stops

Close-hauled
Sails are pulled in tightly, so that the boat sails as close as possible towards the direction of the wind. A moveable centreboard will be fully down

Close reach
Sails are eased slightly, as the head of the boat bears away from the wind. This is a fast point of sailing

Close reach (starboard)

Beam reach (starboard)
The wind is now directly across the side of the boat, the sails comfortably eased. A centreboard may be partly lifted

Beam reach (port)

Broad reach (starboard)
With the wind blowing diagonally from behind, the sails are eased well out, to catch maximum wind, and an asymmetric spinnaker can be hoisted

Broad reach (port)

Run
When the wind is directly behind, the mainsail is let right out to the side. The foresail may be set "goosewinged" on the opposite side, and racing boats will hoist a spinnaker

Training run
The sails are wide out to catch the wind coming almost directly from behind: a spinnaker may be hoisted

TURNING THE BOAT
To change the direction of the boat, both sails and rudder need to be adjusted. Sails provide most of the power: pulling in the mainsail ("luffing") turns the boat towards the wind; letting it out turns it away from the wind. At the same time, the tiller or wheel is turned to move the rudder, and the jib is adjusted to work efficiently with the new mainsail position. If the boat is racing, tacking and gybing are critical manoeuvres that need to be carried out with complete crew coordination. Lack of precision can cost vital seconds, and crews will spend hours practising tacking and gybing to ensure the turns are as quick as possible.

TACKING
If the wind direction across the bow is changed, the sails "tack" to the other side of the boat. To change tack, the crew pull in both sails and adjust the rudder. As the boat moves through the head-to-wind position and onto the new tack, the sails flip onto the other side of the boat. The idea is to do this as quickly and smoothly as possible, without losing any forward momentum.

GYBING
Changing direction with wind crossing behind the boat is less easy to control than a tack: on a broad reach or run the sails will be far out to one side. To "gybe" the sails, they are first brought in as far as possible without altering course, then, as the tiller or wheel is turned hard, the boom and mainsail gybe across the boat on to the new side. Sails are adjusted quickly to keep the boat sailing smoothly.

HEELING AND HIKING OUT

The force of the wind on sails naturally makes a boat heel over to one side, but it sails faster if level in the water. In a dinghy or small keelboat, the crew balance the tendency to heel by moving their weight towards, and then beyond, the outer edge of the hull. In conventional dinghies, this means sitting on the gunwale (the side of the boat), tucking toes under the toe straps for grip, and leaning backwards over the water. This effect can be enhanced by use of a trapeze – the crew hooks on to a wire attached to the upper mast, and stands on the gunwale to lean out over the water. Some modern, extreme boats such as the 49ers have wings that extend dramatically the distance the crew can hike out.

HIKING OUT

If the crew use their weight to counter-balance the heeling power of the wind in the sails, they can harness that power to drive the boat forwards faster rather than letting the wind simply push the boat over sideways.

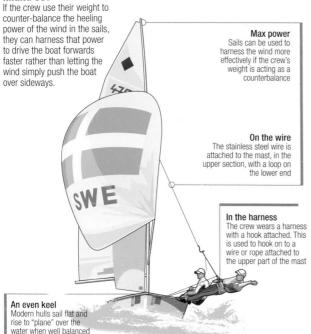

Max power
Sails can be used to harness the wind more effectively if the crew's weight is acting as a counterbalance

On the wire
The stainless steel wire is attached to the mast, in the upper section, with a loop on the lower end

In the harness
The crew wears a harness with a hook attached. This is used to hook on to a wire or rope attached to the upper part of the mast

An even keel
Modern hulls sail flat and rise to "plane" over the water when well balanced

ON THE RAIL

Modern yachts carry huge sails. Although the yachts are ballasted and self-righting, weight distribution is still important, and crew will often be seen lined down the windward side deck (on the "rail"). This contributes towards levelling the angle of heel, enabling the helm to steer the desired course without reducing the amount of sail – thus giving more speed.

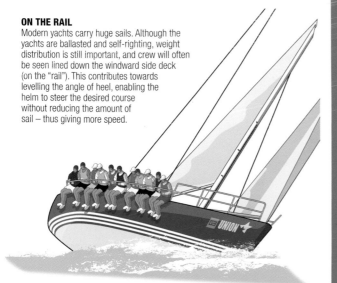

STAT CENTRAL

ROUND THE WORLD (ONE-HANDED/VELUX 5 OCEANS)

YEAR	BOAT/SAILOR	COUNTRY
2010–11	LE PINGOUIN	
	BRAD VAN LIEW	USA
2006–07	CHEMINEES POUJOULAT	
	BERNARD STAMM	SUI
2002	BOBST GROUP ARMOR LUX	
	BERNARD STAMM	SUI
1998–99	FILA	
	GIOVANNI SOLDINI	ITA

AROUND THE WORLD (CREWED/VOLVO OCEAN RACE*)

YEAR	BOAT/SKIPPER	COUNTRY
2011–12	GROUPAMA 4	
	FRANCK CAMMAS (FRA)	FRA
2008–09	ERICSSON 4	
	TORBEN GRAEL (BRZ)	SWE
2005–06	ABN AMRO ONE	
	MIKE SANDERSON (NZL)	NED
2001–02	ILLBRUCK CHALLENGE	
	JOHN KOSTECKI (USA)	GER
1997–98	EF LANGUAGE	
	PAUL CAYARD (USA)	SWE

*FORMERLY WHITBREAD AROUND THE WORLD RACE

OLYMPIC GAMES LONDON 2012

COUNTRY	GOLD	SILVER	BRONZE	TOTAL
GBR	1	4	0	5
AUS	3	1	0	4
NED	1	1	1	3
ESP	2	0	0	2
NZL	1	0	1	2

INSIDE STORY

The International Sailing Federation (ISAF) is descended from an organization dating back to 1907, when the International Yacht Racing Union (IYRU) was formed in Paris, France. Yachting authorities were included from France, Austria-Hungary, Holland and Belgium, Finland, Denmark, Germany, Great Britain, Italy, Norway, Sweden, Switzerland, and Spain. They devised a code for measuring racing yachts, and rules for racing in Europe. In 1929 the North American Yacht Racing Union aligned their rules with Europe, and in 1960 a worldwide code was adopted. The IYRU became the ISAF in 1996. Some of the rules devised in 1907 are still in use today.

SIDELINES

6,000 The average number of calories consumed each day by an Olympic oarsman to give him enough energy to complete his training programme.

5:19 The current Olympic record time, in minutes and seconds, set by the USA heavyweight men's eight in the 2004 Athens Games.

68 The number of nations that participated in the 2011 World Rowing Championships.

135 The number of national federations affiliated to rowing's governing body, the International Rowing Federation (FISA).

10,000 The average distance rowed each year (in kilometres, equivalent to more than 6,200 miles) by an Olympic oarsman during training.

ROWING

EVENT OVERVIEW

Rowing can be described as hurtling backwards as fast as possible in an unstable craft while ignoring burning lungs and screaming muscles. One of the few athletic disciplines that actually involves all of the body's major muscle groups, rowing demands high fitness and power levels for racing. Many different disciplines have evolved within the sport – heavyweight or lightweight events, for example, and sprints or long-distance races – for both individuals and for teams of up to eight crew.

"SHOOT ME"

ONE OF THE MOST SUCCESSFUL OLYMPIC ATHLETES EVER IS BRITISH ROWER SIR STEVEN REDGRAVE – THE ONLY ATHLETE EVER TO HAVE WON FIVE CONSECUTIVE OLYMPIC GOLD MEDALS IN AN ENDURANCE EVENT. IMMEDIATELY AFTER HIS FOURTH WIN, IN ATLANTA IN 1996, REDGRAVE FAMOUSLY GASPED "IF YOU EVER SEE ME NEAR A BOAT AGAIN, YOU HAVE MY PERMISSION TO SHOOT ME". HIS RETIREMENT DIDN'T LAST LONG, HOWEVER, AND HE WENT ON TO WIN A FIFTH GOLD MEDAL IN SYDNEY IN 2000.

ATHLETE PROFILE

Rowing demands a challenging blend of strength, stamina, balance, technical skill, and mental discipline. Rowers have some of the highest power outputs of athletes in any sport, and racing 2,000m (1 mile 427yd) requires the power of a sprinter together with the physical and mental endurance to keep going while the muscles are burning with lactic acid – and while maintaining balance, rhythm and technical control. It helps to be tall, since long arms and legs provide the advantage of a long stroke through the water; many top male rowers are nearing 2m (6ft 7in) and many of the top women are over 1.8m (6ft).

Bowside
A rower whose oars extend from the right (starboard) side of the boat is called a bowsider

Strokeside
If the oar extends out on the left (port) side of the boat, the rower is a strokesider

S-LINE 114

The oar
A modern oar is usually hollow carbon with a rubber handle and a flat blade or spoon at the other end

Rowlock
Also called an oarlock, and fastened by a bar called a gate, the rowlock holds the oar as it rotates through each stroke

Rigger
Bolted to the shell, the rigger is a frame, usually aluminium or steel, that supports the rowlock

Tight fit
Rowers wear a tight-fitting onepiece, also known as a unisuit, zootsuit or all-in-one, reflecting their club or national colours

Tough shell
A rowing boat is called a shell and is typically made of lightweight carbon fibre and plastic

RACE FORMATS

There are many different types of rowing race, reflecting the sport's long history. In addition to standard 2,000m races, there are time-trial events called head races, long-distance events such as the Tour du Léman, and regattas over non-Olympic distances. In the UK there are also bumps races that involve a pursuit to "bump" the boat in front, while stake-racing is an American event that involves a race to a marker some distance away and back to the starting point.

COASTAL AND OCEAN ROWING
Although not included in the Olympic programme, there are many coastal and ocean rowing events. FISA organizes the World Rowing Coastal Challenge as a championship event for international crews, and there are many other cross-ocean races and coastal regattas worldwide.

OLYMPIC RACES
The Olympic course is competed over a straight course. Crews race in six lanes and compete in a series of heats and repechages (the "second chance" for crews facing elimination) to reach the final. The first three crews in each semi-final race in the "A" final for places 1–6 and the last three crews in each semi-final compete in the "B" final for places 7–12.

Finish tower
On the first floor sit the three race judges, while below them sit the official time-keepers and administrators

Red zones
The first and last 100m of each lane are marked by red buoys

Finish line
The finish line is marked by a board on one side of the course with a black line down it: this is aligned with a wire in the finish tower

Lining up
The aligner aligns the bows of each boat with a line on a board on the far side of the course, ready for the starter to start the race

Course markers
Every 250m there is a marker to tell the rowers how far they have left to the finish line

Lanes
Each lane is 12.5–13.5m (41–44ft) wide

Lane markers
Small white or yellow buoys mark the boundaries of each lane at 10m-intervals: there may also be larger red buoys at each 250m-mark

2000m (2,187yd)

Lane numbers
Each boat carries a number on its bow corresponding to the lane in which it is racing

Ready to go
Race officials hold the sterns of each boat in position ready for the race to start: some courses also have starter shoe mechanisms that hold the bows in place and drop down below the water-line automatically as the race starts

Start pontoon
These adjust to accommodate the different lengths of the various classes of boat racing, to ensure they all align with the start line correctly

2,000M RACES
The Olympics, World Cup, and World Championships are all rowed over a distance of 2,000m (2,187yd). There are 14 different events in the Olympics and the World Cup, eight for men and, since 1976, when women's events were introduced, six for women. World Cup events are held every year. Every year except an Olympic year sees the staging of a World Championship, which has 22 events, including 13 for men and 9 for women. Adaptive rowing events, for rowers with physical disabilities, were first incorporated into the World Championships programme for 2002 and the Beijing Paralympic Games for 2008.

LIGHTWEIGHT ROWING
Rowing is unusual in that it is one of the few non-combat sports to have a special weight category for lightweights. This allows countries with "less statuesque" people to participate in the sport. For men, the crew average must be 70kg (154⅓lb), with no individual crewmember weighing more than 72.5kg (159⅘lb); for women, the crew average is limited to 57kg (125lb), with an individual maximum of 59kg (130lb) per crewmember. Lightweight events were first included in the World Championships in 1974 for men and 1985 for women, and were added into the Olympic programme in 1996.

HEAD RACES
An alternative to side-by-side racing, a head race is essentially a time trial and can involve hundreds of crews setting off in procession, seconds after each other, and chasing each other down the course. The oldest, founded in 1926, is the Head of the River Race on the Thames in London, UK, and the largest is the Head of the Charles in Boston, US, which is the largest two-day rowing event in the world.

OTHER RACES
Over time various other events have established themselves in the rowing calendar. First held in 1829, the Oxford and Cambridge Boat Race is contested annually by the two English universities over a course of 6,779m (4 miles 374yd) on the Thames in London, UK. Yale and Harvard universities have been having a similar annual battle since 1852 in New London, Connecticut, US. There are many other variations on university races and on regattas over distances other than 2,000m, such as Henley Royal Regatta. Established in 1839, this unique and prestigious international event races crews side-by-side two abreast down a course that is 2,112m (1 mile 550yd) long. In 1988 the first Henley Women's Regatta was held, and in 1993 Henley Royal Regatta introduced its first event for women, for single sculls. This has since been followed by events for eights and quads.

ONE OAR OR TWO?

The difference between rowing and sculling lies in the number and size of the oars used – the shells used are the same, just rigged differently to accommodate the respective number of oars.

ROWING

Competing in combinations from a pair through to an eight, rowers have one blade each. Many rowers have one preferred side, just as most people have a preferred writing hand.

SCULLING

Scullers have two oars, one in each hand. Although octuples (eight scullers in a boat) do exist, most sculling events are for combinations from a single through to a quad (containing four scullers).

EVENTS

The classification system used to describe rowing events uses a mixture of characters:

L OR LT The event is for lightweights.

J The event is for under-19s.

B The event is for under-23s.

M The event is for men.

W The event is for women.

1 The number of athletes in the boat; the number will be either 1, 2, 4, or 8.

X The event is for scullers.

+ OR – Signifies whether a cox is or is not present.

So, for example, LM4x denotes a lightweight men's quad, while W8+ is a heavyweight women's eight. There are further classifications to denote experience or handicap levels, but these vary from country to country and are not used for international competition. Additional age classifications also exist for Masters (veteran) events.

BOATS AND BLADES

Rowing equipment is expensive and usually owned and maintained by rowing clubs or squads, although many scullers own their own single scull. For racing, rowers usually wear a one-piece suit in club or national colours. This garment is designed to be tight-fitting to avoid snagging on the boat or blades during the race. Additional layers of breathable clothing may be worn depending on the weather conditions.

SHELLS

Traditional wooden rowing boats have been largely replaced by boats made from modern materials such as carbon fibre and fibreglass. The shell has a long, narrow shape to cut through the water with minimum drag. The length conforms to the rules of FISA and varies according to the class (see below for minimum requirements). The shells range from 59.7cm to 62.2cm (23½ to 24⅛in) wide. A small fin or skeg is fitted to the hull for stability, and a small rudder will be attached to all classes of boat except single and double sculls.

STEERING

Most racing shells have rudders not much larger than a credit card, and these are connected to rudder wires that feed back into the boat. If the boat is coxed, the coxswain will control the rudder (see box below): if not, the rower or sculler nearest to the bow (the front of the boat) will usually control the steering via a moveable footplate to which the rudder wires have been attached. He or she may have to look round to check the direction of the boat at regular intervals, depending on how straight the course is.

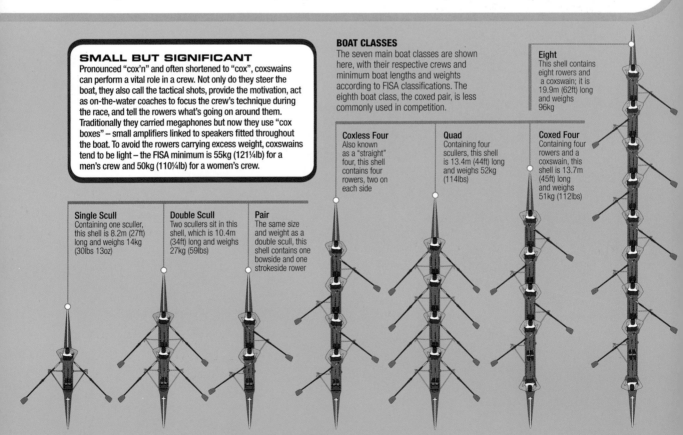

SMALL BUT SIGNIFICANT

Pronounced "cox'n" and often shortened to "cox", coxswains can perform a vital role in a crew. Not only do they steer the boat, they also call the tactical shots, provide the motivation, act as on-the-water coaches to focus the crew's technique during the race, and tell the rowers what's going on around them. Traditionally they carried megaphones but now they use "cox boxes" – small amplifiers linked to speakers fitted throughout the boat. To avoid the rowers carrying excess weight, coxswains tend to be light – the FISA minimum is 55kg (121¼lb) for a men's crew and 50kg (110¼lb) for a women's crew.

BOAT CLASSES

The seven main boat classes are shown here, with their respective crews and minimum boat lengths and weights according to FISA classifications. The eighth boat class, the coxed pair, is less commonly used in competition.

Eight
This shell contains eight rowers and a coxswain; it is 19.9m (62ft) long and weighs 96kg

Coxless Four
Also known as a "straight" four, this shell contains four rowers, two on each side

Quad
Containing four scullers, this shell is 13.4m (44ft) long and weighs 52kg (114lbs)

Coxed Four
Containing four rowers and a coxswain, this shell is 13.7m (45ft) long and weighs 51kg (112lbs)

Single Scull
Containing one sculler, this shell is 8.2m (27ft) long and weighs 14kg (30lbs 13oz)

Double Scull
Two scullers sit in this shell, which is 10.4m (34ft) long and weighs 27kg (59lbs)

Pair
The same size and weight as a double scull, this shell contains one bowside and one strokeside rower

IN THE BOAT
Much of the equipment used for rowing and sculling is exactly the same, although the riggers and oars for sculling are smaller than those for rowing. There is no restriction on blade size or shape, but both oars and riggers are usually designed to be lightweight and very strong. The internal mechanisms within the boat, such as the seats and feet, are identical.

OARS
Modern oars are usually made of hollow carbon fibre. Lengths given are averages, as many designs have adjustable shaft lengths.

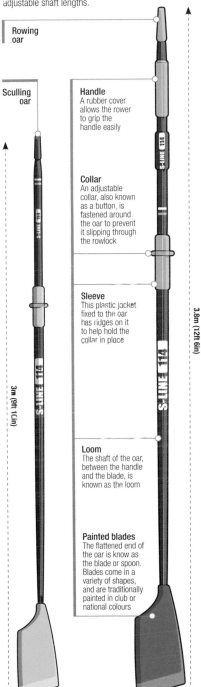

Rowing oar

Sculling oar

Handle
A rubber cover allows the rower to grip the handle easily

Collar
An adjustable collar, also known as a button, is fastened around the oar to prevent it slipping through the rowlock

Sleeve
This plastic jacket fixed to the oar has ridges on it to help hold the collar in place

Loom
The shaft of the oar, between the handle and the blade, is known as the loom

Painted blades
The flattened end of the oar is know as the blade or spoon. Blades come in a variety of shapes, and are traditionally painted in club or national colours

3m (9ft 10in)

3.8m (12ft 6in)

BOAT BASICS
Rowing shells are light, quite fragile, and built in different weights and strengths to suit a crew's size and weight. They are quite unstable without their oars in place.

Bowball
Every boat must have a rubber bowball secured to its bow. The bows of the boat would otherwise be very sharp, so bowballs can prevent any nasty spearings if a collision occurs

Canvas
The narrowing sections of the boat between the crew area and the bow or stern are named after the material historically used to cover them. Crews that win by just over 1m (3ft) are said to "win by a canvas"

Sliding seat
The seat is mounted on wheels that roll back and forth on rails (slides) fixed to the shell. The sliding seat allows the rower to use the legs to drive the oar through the water

Fixed feet
Shoes are bolted to an adjustable footplate within the boat. Fixing the feet provides the rower with a strong platform from which to push the legs and drive the oar through the water. Shoes have quick-release Velcro straps in case the boat capsizes

Built for speed
A modern shell is made from lightweight materials such as carbon fibre, and shaped to cut through the water. It has to be as light as possible, yet strong enough to support the crew

8.2m (27ft)

ROWING RULES
Within each country there is a national governing body with its own rules for rowing and sculling events. Although these rules vary slightly, they all exist to ensure that races run safely and fairly. Each national governing body is a member of the International Rowing Federation (Fédération Internationale des Sociétés d'Aviron; FISA), which is the world governing body for the sport.

RACES AND REGATTAS
Regattas take place under the supervision of a committee of race officials headed by a chairman. Before a crew takes to the water, officials check that the crew and the boat conform with the rules of the sport. At the start of the race, each crew lines up in lane and are held in place either by an electronic mechanism called a starter shoe or by an official, while the aligner checks that all the boats are lined up properly. A loud beep or gun may be used to start a race, the starter may call "Go", or a "traffic light" system may be used. At this point the boats are released and the race gets under way. In the event of a false start, a bell is rung and the starter waves a red flag to recall crews. Crews are allowed one false start only before being disqualified.

An umpire follows each race down the course to ensure that there are no steering infringements, for which crews can be disqualified. A hooter sounds as each boat crosses the finish line, and the umpire raises a white flag at the end of a race to confirm that it has been completed properly. The winner is the boat whose bow is deemed to touch the finish line first. Three photo-finish judges adjudicate if the race is too close to call. A jury of at least three officials, appointed by the race umpire before a race, resolves any formal protests arising out of competition.

CATCHING A CRAB

THE ROWER'S ULTIMATE NIGHTMARE IS CATCHING A CRAB – NOTHING TO DO WITH THE CLAWS OF CRUSTACEANS, BUT STILL VERY PAINFUL. CRABS ARE CAUSED BY THE BLADE ENTERING THE WATER AT THE WRONG ANGLE, WHICH SLICES THE BLADE DOWN AND CAUSES THE OAR HANDLE TO SHOOT UPWARDS OR BACKWARDS FAST – SOMETIMES FAST ENOUGH TO CATAPULT A ROWER OUT OF THE BOAT OR CAPSIZE IT. AND THAT'S IF THE ROWER'S LUCKY – IF HE OR SHE IS UNLUCKY, THE HANDLE JUST SLAMS THROUGH THEIR RIBS INSTEAD.

THE ROWING STROKE

Although rowing may look like an upper-body sport, the power in a rowing stroke comes from the legs. Rowers sit facing backwards (towards the stern), holding an oar or oars, and propel the boat forwards by pushing with the legs. The technique is fundamentally the same for both rowing and sculling, and involves four key phases (see below) – the secret is to flow smoothly from one phase to the other. Good rowing looks graceful and effortless, but this belies the tremendous power and physical demands required. Applying the necessary power smoothly enough to avoid acting as a brake on the boat, while also maintaining balance and keeping in time with the crew, is a task that requires great technical skill and many hours of practice.

INDOOR ROWING

Most indoor rowing takes place on an ergometer (often shortened to "ergo" or "erg"), which is a land-based machine designed to simulate the experience of rowing. The ergo is a useful training tool and allows coaches to test a rower's performance and power output. It can be a factor in making crew selections, although performance on the ergo does not always equate directly with performance on the water, where technique and balance also play a critical factor. Indoor rowing has also become a competitive sport in its own right. There are numerous local and national competitions worldwide, with hundreds of thousands of participants, and an annual world championship event, called the CRASH-B Sprints, which is held in Boston, Massachusetts, US.

TAKING THE CATCH

The rower leans forward with knees compressed so that the shins are vertical. With arms outstretched for maximum "reach", the rower places the oar blades vertically ("squared") in the water and starts to push with the legs against the footplate.

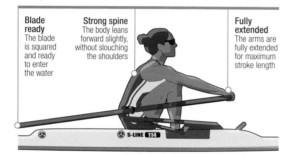

Blade ready
The blade is squared and ready to enter the water

Strong spine
The body leans forward slightly, without slouching the shoulders

Fully extended
The arms are fully extended for maximum stroke length

THE DRIVE PHASE

As the legs engage and start to power the blades through the water, the seat slides backwards. The rower uses the momentum gained through the leg drive to draw the blade handles towards the body and leans back slightly to optimize the stroke length.

Opening up
During the leg drive, the body opens up and the arms draw the oar in towards the body

Power supply
The legs provide propulsion for the drive phase

THE EXTRACTION

Also known as the finish or the release, for this phase the rower pushes down on the handle of the oars to lift the blades out of the water. Once the oars are clear of the water, the rower rotates the handle to "feather" or position the blades parallel to the water, which cuts down on air resistance.

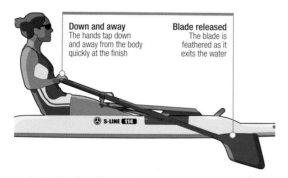

Down and away
The hands tap down and away from the body quickly at the finish

Blade released
The blade is feathered as it exits the water

RECOVERY TIME

The rower begins by stretching the hands forward beyond the knees, with the blades initially still parallel to the surface of the water. The body then rocks forwards to be ready in the catch position, while the hands are rotating the oar handles to square the blade and the legs are compressing to bring the body forward for the next catch.

Coming forward
As the oar handle is pushed forwards, the blade is squared ready for the next catch

SIDELINES

250,000
The number of spectators lining the banks of the Thames each year to watch The Boat Race between Oxford and Cambridge.

7,500 The number of competitors competing in the annual Head of the Charles race in Boston, US.

11.68 The lung capacity in litres of British rower Peter Reed (equivalent to 20½ pints and more than double that of the average person).

0.08 The margin of victory in seconds over the Canadian boat when British rower Matthew Pinsent took his fourth consecutive Olympic gold in the men's coxless four in the 2004 Athens Olympics. Pinsent's team mates were James Cracknell, Ed Coode, and Steve Williams.

RACING TO WIN

Rowers talk in terms of "rating" – the number of strokes a crew completes in a minute. At the start of a race the stroke rate will be high – upwards of 50 for a men's eight – as the boat sprints away. During this phase the rowers are working hard and building up lactic acid in their muscles. Once the boat is up to speed, the crew settle into their race pace and the rate steadies out – around 38–40 for a men's eight. At tactical points in the race, or to counter threats from the opposition, there may be a call for a "power ten" on the legs or an "up two" of the rating. Approaching the finish, crews wind up for another sprint and the stroke rate rises again – 46 or more is not uncommon – and the rowers' muscles and lungs will be burning even more than they did at the start. A high rate does not always guarantee speed, however: a good technical crew may go faster than a less able crew rowing at a higher rate.

TEAM WORK

Aside from the single scull, rowing requires a high level of team work. One rower cannot pull a crew to victory alone; it takes the whole crew to win. Bladework and timing must be synchronized, body positions and movements must be coordinated. Crews are numbered from the bow through to the stern, with Bow first, then Two, Three, etc through to Seven and finally Stroke.

8 Stroke
A good technical rower who sets the pace and rhythm for the crew

7 Seven
Supports Stroke and transmits the rhythm and cadence to the rest of the crew

6 Six
Leads the "engine room" of the middle four crew-members; helps keep rhythm and length in the water

5 Five
Backs up six in supplying power to back up the stern pair and transmitting rhythm

4 Four
Lynchpin of the engine room, Four connects the crewmembers in the bows to the action in the stern

3 Three
Provides power and keeps bow pair in touch with the rhythm in the boat

2 Two
Leads bow pair; a technical rower who has quick bladework and can anticipate each stroke

1 Bow
First over the finish line: another technical rower who, with Two, helps to balance the boat

Coxswain
Steers the boat and calls the tactics (see box, p.264)

STAT CENTRAL

WORLD BEST TIMES (MEN)

CLASS	CREW	TIME	YEAR
M1X	NEW ZEALAND (M. Drysdale)	6:33.35	2009
M2–	NEW ZEALAND (H. Bond, E. Murray)	6:08.50	2012
M2X	FRANCE (J.-B. Macquet, A. Hardy)	6:03.25	2006
M4–	GREAT BRITAIN (A. Triggs-Hodge, T. James, P. Reed, A. Gregory)	5:37.86	2012
M4+	GERMANY (J. Dederding, A. Weyrauch, B. Rabe, M. Ungemach, A. Eichholz)	5:58.96	1991
M4X	RUSSIA (V. Ryabcev, A. Svirin, N. Morgachev, S. Fedorovtsev)	5:33.15	2012
M8+	CANADA (G. Bergen, D. Csima, R. Gibson, C. McCabe, M. Howard, A. Byrnes, J. Brown, W. Crothers, B. Price)	5:19.35	2012

WORLD BEST TIMES (WOMEN)

CLASS	CREW	TIME	YEAR
W1X	BULGARIA (R. Neykova)	7:07.71	2002
W2–	ROMANIA (G. Andrunache, V. Susanu)	6:53.80	2002
W2X	NEW ZEALAND (G. Evers-Swindell, C. Evers-Swindell)	6:38.78	2002
W4–	AUSTRALIA (R. Selby Smith, J. Lutz, A. Bradley, K. Hornsey)	6:25.35	2006
W4X	GERMANY (J. Richter, C. Baer, T. Manker, S. Schiller)	6:09.38	2012
W8+	USA (E. Lofgren, Z. Francia, J. Redman, A. Polk, M. Musnicki, T. Ritzel, C. Lind, C. Davies, M. Whipple)	5:54.17	2012

INSIDE STORY

"Modern" competitive rowing probably began between the watermen of the Thames in London, but had spread to Europe and North America by the late 18th century. In the UK, The Boat Race, between Oxford and Cambridge universities, was first held in 1829, followed by the first annual regatta at Henley in 1839. In the US, Yale and Harvard established their own intercollegiate race in 1852, and by 1892 the sport's popularity ensured its inclusion in the 1896 Athens Games, although bad weather prevented the Olympic debut until the 1900 Paris Games. Women's events were first introduced in the 1976 Montreal Games, and lightweight rowing has been an Olympic sport since the 1996 Games in Atlanta.

INTERNATIONAL ROWING FEDERATION

The International Rowing Federation (Fédération Internationale des Sociétés d'Aviron; FISA) is the world governing body for rowing. FISA organizes international regattas such as the Olympics, the World Championships, and the Rowing World Cup. Founded in 1892, it is the oldest international sports federation in the Olympic movement.

KAYAKING

SPORT OVERVIEW

From the adrenaline-fuelled excitement of the white-water slalom to the sheer speed and lung-busting effort of the flat-water sprint, kayaking is a sport of supreme athletic ability and technical skill. In the Olympics, there are individual, paired, and four-person flat-water sprints over various distances, as well as the dramatic white-water slalom. In this individual race against the clock, each competitor paddles around a series of gates, in assigned order and direction, without touching any part of the gate. In addition to the Olympic events, marathon and wild-water races are contested at international level. There is even a ball sport, confusingly called canoe polo, played in kayaks.

COMPETITOR PROFILE
Flat-water kayak events demand a high degree of aerobic fitness and muscular stamina. Competitors must maintain excellent technique under pressure. Technical ability is more important in slalom races, but strength, power, and aerobic endurance are still essential.

NEED2KNOW

- Kayaking differs from canoeing in that competitors paddle from a seated position and use a double-bladed paddle.

- Especially popular in North America and Europe, kayaking is governed by the International Canoe Federation (ICF).

- The Olympic Games are the highest level of competition. The ICF World Championships are also highly prized.

- Flat-water and slalom races require different techniques, and some of the gear used is unique to each event.

ON THE COURSE
Olympic flat-water events take place over 200m (218yd), 500m (542yd), or 1,000m (1,083yd) of calm water. The straight course is marked into nine lanes (see right), each of which is 9m (29ft 3in) wide. Slalom events take place on the rapids of natural rivers or purpose-built waterways. The course varies in length but always includes between 18 and 25 gates (pairs of poles) suspended above the surface of the water. Each gate has a number that indicates the route of the course. Competitors must negotiate at least six of the gates upstream.

SAFETY FIRST
Kayaking gear is designed with safety in mind. Perhaps the most important safety equipment is the personal flotation device, which keeps a kayaker afloat in the water. Equally important, however, are wetsuits and drysuits, which guard against hypothermia in cold water.

Propulsion
High-level competitors use a double-bladed paddle made from a lightweight carbon-epoxy laminate

Gripping the paddle
Many competitors use paddle grips to provide a better grip for more efficient paddling

Head protection
The helmet is made from reinforced plastic, fibre glass, or super-light carbon. Compulsory in the slalom, the helmet protects the head from impacts against rocks or gates

Staying afloat
A personal flotation device (PFD) is an essential piece of paddling gear. Lightweight and comfortable, the foam-filled PFD keeps the competitor afloat after capsize

Staying dry
Outer shells made from synthetic fabrics are waterproof and windproof yet allow sweat to escape from the inside

Power paddle
Kayakers need fantastic upper body strength to power through the water – the more forceful their paddling, the faster they will travel

Spray skirt
A neoprene spray skirt fits around the waist and stretches around the cockpit of the kayak to form a water-tight seal

FLAT-WATER BASIN
Depending on the facilities at a particular competition, the flat-water basin may be used to host canoe and kayak races of all distances as well as all the rowing events. The basin is usually sheltered from the wind and has no current. The sides of the basin are designed to absorb waves rather than reflect them.

Keeping in line
An aligner lies on each lane of the starting jetty to ensure each kayak starts from the same position

90m (295¼ft)

1,000m (1,083yd)

Scoreboard
Displays the names of the competitors, their nationality, lane number, race time, and final position

Finish line
Finish line judges manually record the finish time of each competitor to back up the electronic systems

On-course judges
Two judges follow the race in motorboats and use red flags to signal infringements to the chief race official

White buoys
White buoys mark the lanes for most of their length. Red buoys mark the last 200m (217yd)

Starting line
An official at the starting line gives the starting signal and checks with the alignment judge to rule on false starts

SHUNYI SUCCESS
THE SHUNYI ROWING-CANOEING PARK WAS ONE OF THE FIRST OLYMPIC VENUES TO BE COMPLETED FOR THE 2008 BEIJING GAMES. IT IS THE BIGGEST OF ALL THE OLYMPIC VENUES IN BEIJING, SPANNING AN AREA OF 1.62SQ KM (0.63SQ MILES).

Control tower
The control tower is home to the chief race official and the race announcer, who relays race information over a tannoy system

Grandstands
Spectators watch the race from either side of the course

FLAT KAYAK CLASSES
In flat-water Olympic races, there are three different kayak classes: K1, K2, and K4. The letter "K" stands for "kayak", and the number represents the number of competitors in the boat. In the Olympic K1 and K2 classes, men race over 200m (218yd) and 1,000m (1,083yd). In the Olympic K4 class, men compete over 1,000m (1,083yd). Women race over 200m (218yd) in the WK1 class (the letter "W" stands for "women") and over 500m (542yd) in all three classes. The specifications of the single, double, and four-person kayaks are listed below.

	K1 SINGLE	K2 DOUBLE	K4 FOUR-PERSON
LENGTH	5.2m (17ft)	6.5m (21ft 3in)	11m (36ft)
BEAM	51cm (1ft 10in)	55cm (1ft 11in)	60cm (2ft 1in)
WEIGHT	12kg (26lb 6oz)	18kg (39lb 10oz)	30kg (66lb)

JOHN MACGREGOR AND ROB ROY
MANY PADDLERS DATE THE BEGINNING OF RECREATIONAL SEA KAYAKING TO JOHN MACGREGOR'S FAMOUS ADVENTURES IN THE SECOND HALF OF THE 19TH CENTURY. MACGREGOR COMMISSIONED A KAYAK OF CEDAR AND OAK, WHICH HE CHRISTENED "ROB ROY" AFTER THE FAMOUS SCOTTISH OUTLAW TO WHOM HE WAS RELATED, AND TRAVELLED AROUND EUROPE AND THE MIDDLE EAST. HIS BOOK *A THOUSAND MILES IN THE ROB ROY CANOE* BECAME AN INTERNATIONAL BESTSELLER.

WHITE-WATER SLALOM
The white-water slalom is a technical and demanding race in which competitors guide their kayaks through a series of numbered gates over challenging rapids (see p.272). In the Olympics, there are single slalom kayak events for men (K1) and women (WK1). Each competitor has two attempts on the course. The final result is based either on the faster of the two runs or the total time for both runs, plus any time penalties.

GATE PENALTIES
There are between 18 and 25 gates on a typical Olympic course. Officials hand out time penalties for touching or missing gates or taking them in the wrong direction.

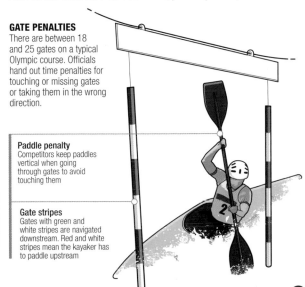

Paddle penalty
Competitors keep paddles vertical when going through gates to avoid touching them

Gate stripes
Gates with green and white stripes are navigated downstream. Red and white stripes mean the kayaker has to paddle upstream

COMPETITION CLOTHING

Competitors' clothing is made from the latest synthetic materials. The aim is to keep warm, dry, and comfortable, but the clothing also incorporates some vital safety features, such as the combined dry top and spray skirt, which stops water from entering the cockpit of the kayak and prevents it from sinking.

WARM AND DRY
The vest and trunks are made from lightweight anti-microbial fabrics. These undergarments act as base layers, keeping competitors warm, dry, and free from infection.

Water resistant
A waterproof dry top combines with the spray skirt to prevent water from entering the cockpit of the kayak

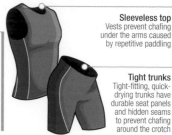

Sleeveless top
Vests prevent chafing under the arms caused by repetitive paddling

Tight trunks
Tight-fitting, quick-drying trunks have durable seat panels and hidden seams to prevent chafing around the crotch

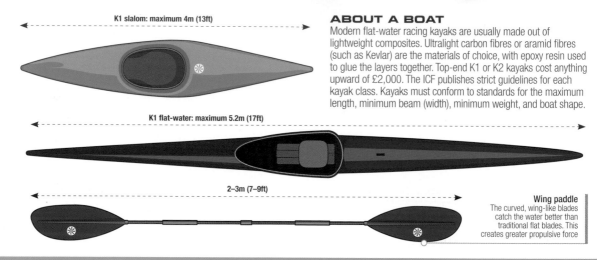

K1 slalom: maximum 4m (13ft)

K1 flat-water: maximum 5.2m (17ft)

2–3m (7–9ft)

ABOUT A BOAT
Modern flat-water racing kayaks are usually made out of lightweight composites. Ultralight carbon fibres or aramid fibres (such as Kevlar) are the materials of choice, with epoxy resin used to glue the layers together. Top-end K1 or K2 kayaks cost anything upward of £2,000. The ICF publishes strict guidelines for each kayak class. Kayaks must conform to standards for the maximum length, minimum beam (width), minimum weight, and boat shape.

Wing paddle
The curved, wing-like blades catch the water better than traditional flat blades. This creates greater propulsive force

PADDLING SKILLS
The body is the driving force behind all the key paddling strokes. Beginners often try to power the stroke with the arms, resulting in rapid fatigue and poor technique. Experienced kayakers use the body as the engine, the arms as the transmission, and the blades as the wheels. Another common mistake for novices is to grip the shaft tightly with both hands. An experienced kayaker grips the shaft securely with the control hand only. The shaft should be able to rotate freely in the other hand.

PADDLING
Every stroke in kayaking involves pulling against the water with the control hand and letting the other hand relax and push the stroke through. The stroke is done with both arms held comfortably in front of the body. A left pull starts by cocking the wrist of the left hand down to turn the pulling blade into position. After the pull, the left hand relaxes and rotates the shaft into position for the right pull.

FORWARD SWEEP
The forward sweep is a control stroke used to spin the kayak in a stationary position or to make a turn when moving forward. It is both a propulsive stroke and a turning stroke, so it is the best way of turning without losing momentum. The stroke is powered by a solid catch at the same time as rotating the upper body.

STARTING THE SWEEP
The forward sweep begins in the same position as the basic forward stroke. The kayaker plants the blade in the water and then rotates his or her upper body toward the stern. The kayaker then pushes the legs in the direction of the new course.

SWEEP TO STERN
The kayaker sweeps the paddle through an arc extending about 1m (3ft) from the boat, at the same time rotating his or her upper body as the blade moves to the stern. Most of the power is produced as the paddle sweeps between the hip and the stern.

BODY BALANCE
At the end of the sweep, the kayaker's body faces toward the side of the turn, with the shaft of the paddle over the water and parallel to the kayak. Before starting the next stroke, the kayaker edges his or her body back into the centre of the kayak.

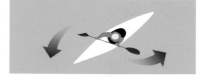

CATCH
The basic paddling stroke starts with the catch, when the driving paddle enters water.

Plant the paddle
The kayaker plants the paddle firmly in the water

BRACE
The brace steadies the kayak in preparation for the main propulsive phase of the stroke.

Body rotation
Upper body and paddle rotate to one side ready for the stroke

OTHER KAYAK SPORTS

Flat-water and white-water slalom are the only kayak events contested at the Olympic Games, but there are many other competitive races and sports held at international level. Wild-water is a race against the clock along a white-water section of a river. Marathon races are long-distance races on natural bodies of water. And canoe polo is a ball sport played by two teams of five players in kayaks.

WILD-WATER

Unlike the slalom events, there are no gates to consider in wild-water; the simple aim is to complete the course in the fastest time possible. There are two types of events. Sprint events are frenetic dashes over 500–750m (542–820yd). Classic races take place over a longer distance, usually 6–10km (4–6 miles). The kayaks used for wild-water racing are longer and narrower than those used for flat-water racing.

MARATHON

ICF rules set the minimum distance for marathon races as 20km (12½ miles) for men and 15km (9½ miles) for women. At the World Cup and World Championships races usually cover up to 40km (25 miles) and include obstacles such as rocks and shallows. Many marathon races are extreme endurance events, often held over hundreds of kilometres and taking many hours to complete.

CANOE POLO

Described as a cross between water polo and kayaking, the object of canoe polo is to score more goals than your opponent in two ten-minute halves. The game is usually played in an indoor swimming pool. Enjoyed competitively in many countries throughout the world, the pinnacle is the World Championships, which is held every two years.

SIDELINES

6.5 The cost in millions of US dollars to construct the Penrith Whitewater Stadium for slalom canoe-kayak events at the 2000 Olympic Games in Sydney, Australia.

44:56 The record in hours and minutes to complete the solo 740km (460 mile) Yukon River Quest. The record is held by American Carter Johnson.

77 The number of Olympic medals won by Hungary in canoe-kayak events, making it the most successful nation in the sport.

SURFSKI RACING

SURFSKIS ARE LONG, NARROW KAYAKS USED FOR LIVESAVING IN SURFING HOTSPOTS AROUND THE WORLD, ESPECIALLY AUSTRALIA, NEW ZEALAND, SOUTH AFRICA, AND CALIFORNIA AND HAWAII IN THE UNITED STATES. MANY LIFEGUARDS COMPETE IN SURFSKI RACES ORGANIZED BY THE INTERNATIONAL LIFESAVING FEDERATION (ILF). THERE ARE MANY DIFFERENT EVENTS, FROM SHORT SPRINTS TO LONG-DISTANCE "IRONMAN" SURFSKI EVENTS.

ESKIMO ROLL

The Eskimo, or sweep, roll is a technique that involves a flicking hip motion and use of the paddle to right a capsized kayak. The hip flick is the key step in a kayak roll. It involves jerking the lower body to one side so that the kayak begins to return to an upright position. The Eskimo roll is one of the easiest techniques to master. Other roll styles suit different kayaks. An example is the hand roll, which is performed without a paddle.

INSIDE STORY

Competitive kayaking first came about in the 19th century, when people began to race over set distances. Flat-water racing became an official Olympic sport in the 1936 Berlin Games. White-water slalom is a more recent addition to the Olympic calendar, becoming a regular event since the 1992 Barcelona Games.

INTERNATIONAL CANOE FEDERATION

The International Canoe Federation (ICF) is the ruling body for all canoe and kayak events held at international level, including the Olympic flat-water and slalom races. It is also responsible for dragon boat racing and ocean kayaking. The ICF was founded in Stockholm in 1946 to replace the International Repräsentantschaft für Kanusport (IRK). It is now based in Lausanne, Switzerland.

SIT-UP START
To do an Eskimo roll to the left, the kayaker does a "sit-up" to the right side and pushes his hands up and out of the water so the forearms press against the side of the kayak.

FLICKING THE HIP
Keeping the head near to the water's surface, the kayaker then sweeps his body and paddle away from the side of the kayak. The hip flick begins at the same time as the sweep.

FLIPPING OVER
The hip flick continues until the kayak flips all the way over to an upright position. The kayaker straightens his back to recover and begin paddling again.

Hip flick A flick of the hips starts to flip the kayak over

STROKE
Propulsion is achieved as the blade sweeps through the water.

Held aloft The paddle is almost vertical as the kayak is propelled forwards

TRANSITION
The transition of strokes from side to side should be as smooth as possible.

Side swap As soon as the blade emerges, the catch starts on the other side

SPORT OVERVIEW

Canoeing is a strenuous water sport for men and women, competing either singly or as a pair. Competitors race to complete the course in the quickest time, and use a single-bladed paddle to propel the craft through the water. There are two competitive disciplines – slalom and flatwater canoeing. Staged on fast-flowing water, slalom events involve competitors negotiating a series of gates, while flatwater racing takes place on calm water with competitors racing side-by-side. Unlike kayakers, canoeists usually paddle from a kneeling position.

NEED2KNOW

→ A popular worldwide sport, canoeing is governed by the International Canoe Federation (ICF), based in Switzerland.

→ Developed by the indigenous peoples of the Americas, craft are sometimes referred to as Indian or Canadian canoes.

→ Competitors from 88 nations competed in 37 events at the 39th ICF Canoe Sprint World Championships in Hungary in 2011.

CANOEING

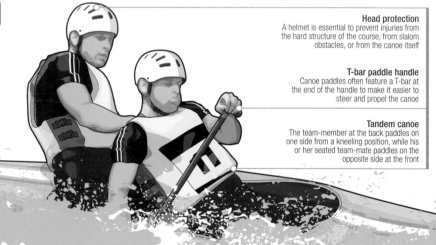

Head protection
A helmet is essential to prevent injuries from the hard structure of the course, from slalom obstacles, or from the canoe itself

T-bar paddle handle
Canoe paddles often feature a T-bar at the end of the handle to make it easier to steer and propel the canoe

Tandem canoe
The team-member at the back paddles on one side from a kneeling position, while his or her seated team-mate paddles on the opposite side at the front

COMPETITOR PROFILE

Competitive canoeists tend to develop a very high level of physical flexibility, strength, and stamina, as the repetitions involved in the aerobic activity of paddling make use of all the muscles in the upper body – abdominals, arms, shoulders, back, and chest – as well as those in the legs.

THE SLALOM COURSE

Slalom events are staged on natural stretches of water, such as fast-flowing rivers, or on purpose-built courses that recreate the effects of fast-moving currents. In each case, the course is approximately 400m (1,300ft) long. Suspended above the water are gates (pairs of poles) that define the route. Green and white striped gates must be negotiated in a downstream direction, while at least six red and white striped gates require the canoeist to paddle upstream. Slalom courses are also used for kayaking (see pp.268–71).

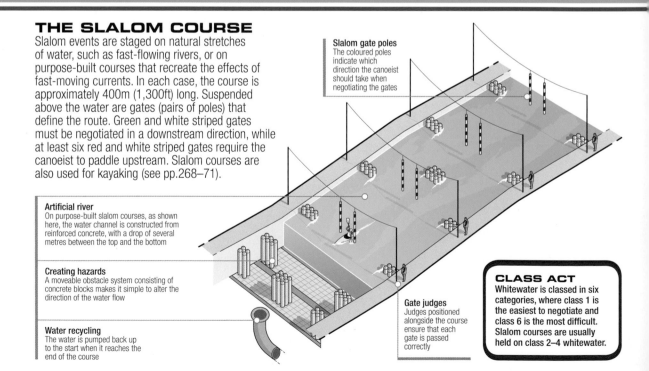

Slalom gate poles
The coloured poles indicate which direction the canoeist should take when negotiating the gates

Artificial river
On purpose-built slalom courses, as shown here, the water channel is constructed from reinforced concrete, with a drop of several metres between the top and the bottom

Creating hazards
A moveable obstacle system consisting of concrete blocks makes it simple to alter the direction of the water flow

Water recycling
The water is pumped back up to the start when it reaches the end of the course

Gate judges
Judges positioned alongside the course ensure that each gate is passed correctly

CLASS ACT
Whitewater is classed in six categories, where class 1 is the easiest to negotiate and class 6 is the most difficult. Slalom courses are usually held on class 2–4 whitewater.

SPEED AND SAFETY

Racing or sprint canoes are long and narrow to facilitate high speeds. Slalom canoes are shorter and are fitted with a spraydeck – a waterproof apron worn around the canoeist that stretches over the rim of the canoe cockpit to prevent water from entering the boat.

Protective helmet
A lightweight yet tough and rigid outer shell covers an inner foam lining to provide maximum protection and comfort

Paddle top
A fully waterproof cagoule, which allows the canoeist complete freedom of movement, is made from a specialist lightweight rubber material

Flexible spraydeck
The cagoule is combined with a rubber spraydeck that stretches over the canoe cockpit to form a watertight seal

Buoyancy vest
To help a canoeist remain afloat in case of a capsize, a foam-filled vest is a useful piece of safety kit, particularly on fast-flowing watercourses, such as white-water rivers

Lightweight paddle
Many modern canoe paddles consist of a durable polypropylene blade mounted on an aluminium shaft

Solo slalom canoe 3.6m (12ft 1in)

Team racing canoe 4.9m (16ft)

TOUGH HULL
Canoe hulls, which need to be lightweight yet impact-resistant, are constructed from materials such as fibreglass, Kevlar, polyethylene plastic, or ultralight carbon fibre.

SLALOM RACING

The object of canoe slalom racing is to negotiate a rapid-flowing natural or artificial river course measuring around 400m (1,300ft) in length. The course is defined by 18–25 gates, and the competitor must finish the course, without making any faults, in the shortest possible time. Each competitor's run is accurately timed, with a time penalty of two seconds added for touching a gate. An international competition consists of two runs, and the times are added together to give the overall time.

RACING ON FLATWATER

ICF-recognized flatwater canoe race competitions take place over clearly defined, unobstructed courses. Competitors race alongside each other, often in lanes, along courses ranging from 200m (650ft) to 1,000m (3,250ft) in length. A minimum of three boats are required for each race, and the winner is the first canoe to completely cross the finish line. As in slalom canoeing, separate events are held for men and women.

EXTREME PADDLING

AS WELL AS SLALOM AND FLATWATER RACING, CANOEING HAS MANY OTHER DISCIPLINES. IN PLAYBOATING (OR RODEO), FOR EXAMPLE, COMPETITORS EARN POINTS BY PERFORMING STUNTS AND TRICKS, WHILE EXTREME AND WHITEWATER RACING INVOLVES NEGOTIATING DIFFERENT GRADES OF WHITEWATER.

POWERING UP
To gain the optimum power from each stroke, the flatwater canoeist braces his or her body by kneeling on one knee with the other leg thrust forward. From this position, the paddle is driven swiftly into the water, with the canoeist leaning into the paddle and using their full body strength to pull against the paddle handle.

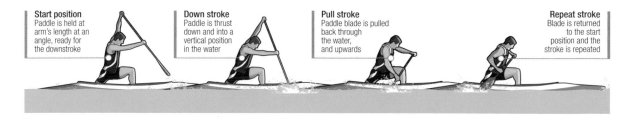

Start position
Paddle is held at arm's length at an angle, ready for the downstroke

Down stroke
Paddle is thrust down and into a vertical position in the water

Pull stroke
Paddle blade is pulled back through the water, and upwards

Repeat stroke
Blade is returned to the start position and the stroke is repeated

DRAGON BOAT RACING

NEED2KNOW

→ Most dragon boats can carry crews of 20 paddlers, although these boats are often raced with just 18 paddlers.

→ The largest boats, called swan boats, carry about 50 people. They are largely ceremonial and seldom raced. Smaller phoenix boats are raced with 10 paddlers.

→ Competitive events are held over a range of distances, between 200m (217yd) sprints and marathons of 50km (31¼miles).

SPORT OVERVIEW

Originally based on Chinese customs, dragon boat races have been taking place for more than two thousand years, and today elite crews race each other all over the world. With up to seven brightly decorated dragon boats taking part, the races make an impressive spectacle.

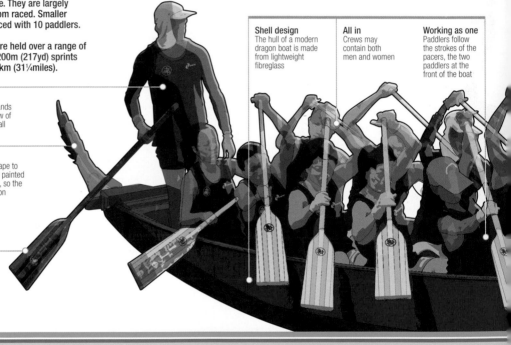

In control
The steerer, or helmsman, stands in the stern; with the best view of the water ahead, he has overall command of the boat

Stern look
The stern has a traditional shape to symbolize a dragon's tail; it is painted in the same style as the head, so the whole boat resembles a dragon

Steering oar
The helmsman has a long oar that trails behind the boat; he pull the handle towards him to go right, and pushes it away to go left

Shell design
The hull of a modern dragon boat is made from lightweight fibreglass

All in
Crews may contain both men and women

Working as one
Paddlers follow the strokes of the pacers, the two paddlers at the front of the boat

ON THE HEAD

Races, especially sprints, may be very close. In the days before photo finishes, crews had an elegant solution to determine the winner, one which is still widely used today. As the boat approaches the finish, an extra crew member – the flag puller, or catcher – climbs onto the dragon's head and reaches forwards. The finish line is marked by flags in each lane, and whichever crew's puller grabs a flag first is the winner. Boats with large heads to accommodate pullers originate from Taiwan.

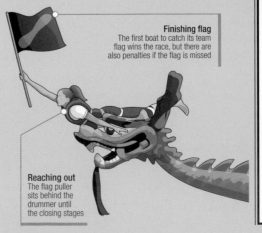

Finishing flag
The first boat to catch its team flag wins the race, but there are also penalties if the flag is missed

Reaching out
The flag puller sits behind the drummer until the closing stages

TRADITIONAL ORIGIN

ACCORDING TO ANCIENT CHINESE LEGEND, DRAGON BOAT RACING COMMEMORATES THE DEATH OF QU YUAN, A FAMOUS POET AND KING'S MINISTER OF THE 3RD CENTURY B.C.E. QU YUAN COMMITTED SUICIDE IN PROTEST AGAINST CORRUPT RULERS BY JUMPING INTO A RIVER. VILLAGERS ROWED OUT TO SAVE HIM BUT WERE TOO LATE. THEY STAYED IN THE WATER, HOWEVER, AND BEAT DRUMS AND SPLASHED THE WATER TO KEEP FISH AND EVIL SPIRITS AWAY FROM HIS BODY. THE RACES COMMEMORATE THEIR UNSUCCESSFUL RESCUE ATTEMPT.

EQUIPMENT
The boats and equipment used in modern dragon racing are produced using the latest technology and materials, but must still conform to a set of traditional standards.

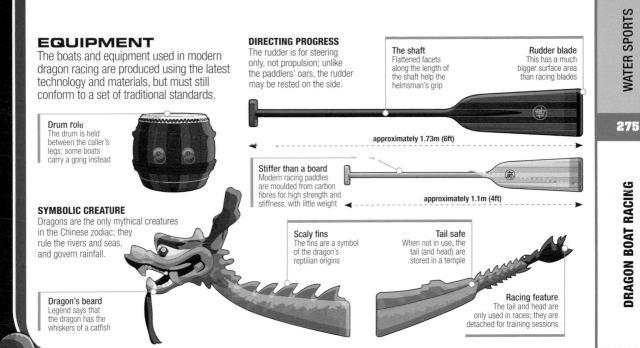

Drum role
The drum is held between the caller's legs; some boats carry a gong instead

DIRECTING PROGRESS
The rudder is for steering only, not propulsion; unlike the paddlers' oars, the rudder may be rested on the side.

The shaft
Flattened facets along the length of the shaft help the helmsman's grip

Rudder blade
This has a much bigger surface area than racing blades

approximately 1.73m (6ft)

Stiffer than a board
Modern racing paddles are moulded from carbon fibres for high strength and stiffness, with little weight

approximately 1.1m (4ft)

SYMBOLIC CREATURE
Dragons are the only mythical creatures in the Chinese zodiac; they rule the rivers and seas, and govern rainfall.

Scaly fins
The fins are a symbol of the dragon's reptilian origins

Tail safe
When not in use, the tail (and head) are stored in a temple

Dragon's beard
Legend says that the dragon has the whiskers of a catfish

Racing feature
The tail and head are only used in races; they are detached for training sessions

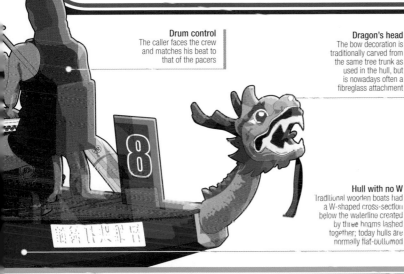

Drum control
The caller faces the crew and matches his beat to that of the pacers

Dragon's head
The bow decoration is traditionally carved from the same tree trunk as used in the hull, but is nowadays often a fibreglass attachment

Hull with no W
Traditional wooden boats had a W-shaped cross-section below the waterline created by three beams lashed together; today hulls are normally flat-bottomed

SYMBOLIC SPORT
In China, dragon boat races are held on May 5th, the so-called Double Fifth – the fifth day of the fifth month. The races mark the beginning of the rice planting season, and by celebrating the spirit of the dragon – the ruler of water – the racers hope that rain will come to flood the fields. Before a boat can be raced, its dragon head is "awoken" by a priest or another dignitary, who paints red dots on the bulging eyes.

Today, the safety of crews is taken seriously, but in ancient times racers that fell in and were drowned were thought to have been sacrificed to the dragon spirit – a sign of a good harvest to come.

STROKE-PULLING
A crew must paddle in time to move at top speed. Even small discrepancies in timing slow the boat. It is hard for people in the stern to see the paddles of the pacers in the bow; that is why the caller's beat is so important. Paddle blades hitting the water a fraction of a second after the ones in front is called "caterpillaring" because the paddles resemble a many-legged animal. The drummer must match the pace of the paddlers, rather than the other way round.

The largest paddlers sit amidships to keep the boat balanced and to be the powerhouse that drives the boat along. A paddle may be any length between 104cm (41in) and 129cm (51in). Taller crew members have longer paddles.

TAKE THE A-FRAME
At the moment of entry into the water, the paddle and the paddler's upper body should form the shape of the letter A. There should be no splashing, because splashing is inefficient and wastes energy.

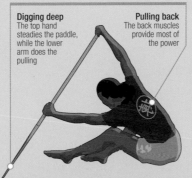

Digging deep
The top hand steadies the paddle, while the lower arm does the pulling

Pulling back
The back muscles provide most of the power

INSIDE STORY
The sport became popular outside of China in the late 1980s, at first in Canada and the west coast of the United States. The sport has since spread to Australia and Europe. The annual international Hong Kong races have been held since the mid-1970s, and a World Nations Championship has been held every two years since 1995. In the even-numbered years there is a world championship for the top club crews.

INTERNATIONAL DRAGON BOAT FEDERATION (IDBF)
The IDBF currently has more than 70 member nations, including Britain, Denmark, Germany, Italy, South Africa, and Switzerland.

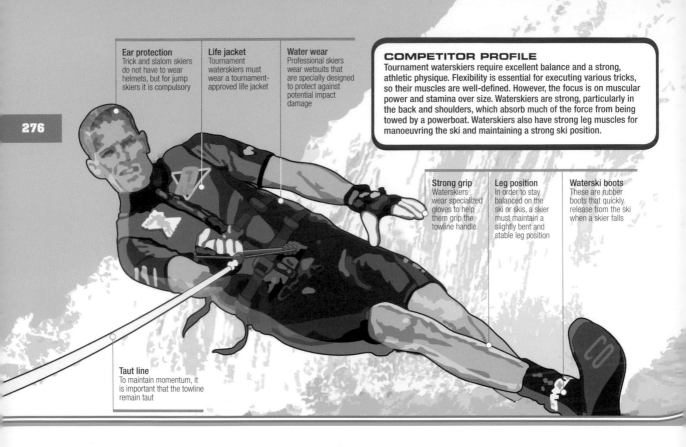

Ear protection
Trick and slalom skiers do not have to wear helmets, but for jump skiers it is compulsory

Life jacket
Tournament waterskiers must wear a tournament-approved life jacket

Water wear
Professional skiers wear wetsuits that are specially designed to protect against potential impact damage

COMPETITOR PROFILE
Tournament waterskiers require excellent balance and a strong, athletic physique. Flexibility is essential for executing various tricks, so their muscles are well-defined. However, the focus is on muscular power and stamina over size. Waterskiers are strong, particularly in the back and shoulders, which absorb much of the force from being towed by a powerboat. Waterskiers also have strong leg muscles for manoeuvring the ski and maintaining a strong ski position.

Strong grip
Waterskiers wear specialized gloves to help them grip the towline handle

Leg position
In order to stay balanced on the ski or skis, a skier must maintain a slightly bent and stable leg position

Waterski boots
These are rubber boots that quickly release from the ski when a skier falls

Taut line
To maintain momentum, it is important that the towline remain taut

WATERSKIING

SPORT OVERVIEW

Waterskiing is a high-speed, adrenaline-fuelled water sport. Skiers demonstrate impressive agility and balance in executing jumps, turns, and acrobatic manoeuvres while being towed at great speeds behind a powerboat. Tournament waterskiing consists of three events: slalom, ski jump, and trick skiing. There are winners in each event, as well as men's overall and women's overall tournament champions. There are also professional tournaments for other waterskiing sports, such as wakeboarding, barefoot skiing, ski racing, and show skiing.

NEED2KNOW

→ Tournament waterskiing is popular all over the world. It is particularly popular in Australia, Canada, Ireland, France, New Zealand, and the United States.

→ Waterskiing is not currently an Olympic sport and has never been. The closest it has come to acceptance was at the 1972 Olympic Games in Munich, where it was a demonstration event. To date there are no plans for the sport to be added to the Olympic programme.

WATER COURSES

Tournament events can be conducted on almost any stretch of still water and are mostly held on lakes or rivers. If courses overlap, buoys from the unused course must be removed.

SLALOM

The slalom course is 259m (283yd) in length and consists of six small rubber buoys that a skier must successfully round. The start and finish gates are also marked by buoys that are different in colour from the course buoys. The distance from the entry gate to the first buoy is 29m (95ft), as is the distance from the sixth buoy to the finish gate. The distance between each successive course buoy is 47m (154ft). The line the powerboat must take runs straight from entry to finish gate and is marked by six pairs of buoys spaced 2.5m (8ft) apart. A turning buoy is placed 140–180m (153–197yd) beyond the start and finish gates, which boat and skier must round to continue the run.

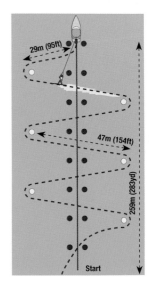

29m (95ft)

47m (154ft)

259m (283yd)

Start

THE GEAR

Water skis were first made of wood, but modern skis are far more advanced. Most skis consist of a fibreglass or carbon fibre base, a fin secured to the bottom of the ski to make turning easier, and a foot binding that holds the skier's boot.

JUMP SKIS
Long and wide towards the back of the ski, jump skis have raised front edges that allow for entry on to the ramp.

Jump fins
Jump skis have short, wide tailfins, suited to sliding on the hard surface of a jump ramp

TRICK SKI
Wide and flat, the trick ski has a smooth bottom and no fins, making it easier to turn and slide on the water's surface.

Bindings
Trick skis can have one or two foot bindings

SLALOM SKI
Designed for making sharp turns at high speed, slalom skis have a tapered tail and concave underside.

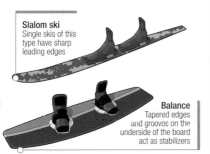

Slalom ski
Single skis of this type have sharp leading edges

WAKEBOARD
This is a wide board with a concave base, which helps the skier achieve greater height jumping off the wake.

Balance
Tapered edges and grooves on the underside of the board act as stabilizers

TOWLINES
Two lines are used in a tournament, measuring 23m (75ft) and 18.5m (61ft) respectively. The longer line is used for jump skiing; the shorter line for slalom. There should be no movement between the rope and the handle when the towline is in use.

Towline material
Towlines are made of a single-braided plastic material that must meet tournament specifications

Grip
A non-slip rubber or similar surface must be used for the handle

SAFETY GEAR
Protective equipment is important to competition skiers. They expose themselves to serious injury when reaching extreme speeds and dizzying heights, and in executing awkward manoeuvres.

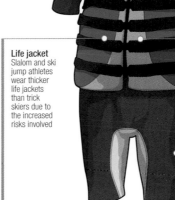

Helmet
Waterski helmets have thick ear padding to protect against eardrum perforations caused by high-speed falls

Life jacket
Slalom and ski jump athletes wear thicker life jackets than trick skiers due to the increased risks involved

Stomach protection
Waterski wetsuits are lined with padding in the abdominal area. This protects the ribs and internal organs from damage caused by high-speed impact with the water

Wetsuits
Waterski wetsuits are made of neoprene, a synthetic rubber that is flexible and allows exceptional freedom of movement

Boot buckles
Lock down buckles increase the responsiveness of the skis

Boots
Waterskiing boots are made from waterproof rubber and have strong ankle support

JUMPING
The jump course is 180m (197yd) in length, from the start buoy to the front edge of the jump ramp. The ramp is made of wood or fibreglass and has either a waxed surface or is equipped with a watering system that ensures the surface is always wet. The ramp surface is also required to be completely flat. It can range from 6.4–6.8m (21–22ft) in length and 3.7–4.3m (12–14ft) in width. In tournament jump skiing, a skier has a choice of two heights for the ramp: for men, either 1.65m (5ft) or 1.80m (6ft), and for women, either 1.50m (5ft) or 1.65m (5ft 4in). Beyond the ramp, the water is marked with measurement buoys, which judges use as a guide for measuring the skier's jump.

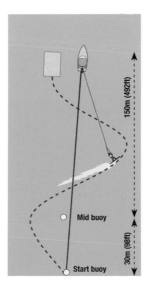

150m (492ft)

30m (98ft)

Mid buoy

Start buoy

WATER INTO GUINNESS
RALPH HILDEBRAND AND DAVE PHILLIPS WATERSKIED 2,152KM (1,337 MILES) NON-STOP AROUND INDIAN ARM, AN INLET OF THE PACIFIC OCEAN IN CANADA. IT TOOK THE CANADIANS 56 HOURS 35 MINUTES AND 3 SECONDS TO ACCOMPLISH, WHICH GAVE THEM THE WORLD RECORD FOR THE LONGEST WATERSKIING MARATHON.

RAMP COLOUR
The sides of the jump ramp are different in colour from the ramp surface, so that a fast-moving skier can easily differentiate between the different surfaces.

Starting the jump
The front of the ramp is below the level of the water

1.5–1.8m (5–6ft)

3.7–4.3m (12–14ft)

28°–50° (45° recommended)

6.4–6.8m (21–22ft)

TOURNAMENT COMPETITION

Standard competitions involve three events: slalom, jump skiing, and trick skiing. Each event consists of a preliminary elimination round and a final round. In slalom, the winner is the skier who rounds the most buoys using the shortest towline in the final round. In jump skiing, the skier who jumps the furthest distance in the final round is declared the winner. In trick skiing, the skier who scores the most number of points in either of two 20-second passes in the final round is the winner. The overall tournament champion is awarded to the skier who accumulates the best overall score across the three disciplines. A skier's overall score is determined by summing the points attributed to their best performance in each discipline, which are calculated using a predetermined formula.

SLALOM

The skier is towed through the slalom course and must pass around the outside of all six buoys and proceed through the finish gate, make a turn and return through the course in a similar fashion until a buoy or gate is missed. A skier is allowed three attempts in the preliminary round and three again if competing in the final round. The length of the towline is reduced for each run, making it harder for a skier to get from buoy to buoy. To round a buoy, the skier must ride outside or partially outside the buoy. Riding over or partially inside the buoy does not score. A run is concluded once the skier misses a buoy or misses an entry or finish gate.

BOAT SPEEDS

The slalom and jump events both have predetermined boat speeds. For men's slalom it is 58kph (36mph) and for women's slalom it is 55kph (34mph). In the jump event, the maximum speed allowed for men is 57kph (35mph) and for women it is 54kph (34mph). In trick skiing, there are no predetermined boat speeds.

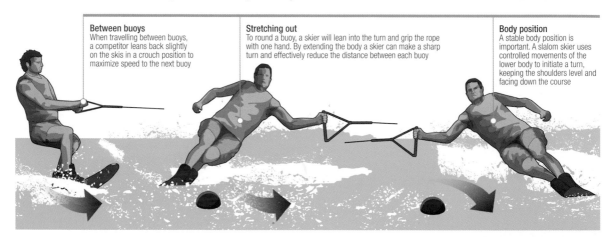

Between buoys
When travelling between buoys, a competitor leans back slightly on the skis in a crouch position to maximize speed to the next buoy

Stretching out
To round a buoy, a skier will lean into the turn and grip the rope with one hand. By extending the body a skier can make a sharp turn and effectively reduce the distance between each buoy

Body position
A stable body position is important. A slalom skier uses controlled movements of the lower body to initiate a turn, keeping the shoulders level and facing down the course

SKI JUMP

Towed behind a powerboat at a fixed speed, the skier cuts a deliberate path across the course to achieve maximum speed on to the ramp. The path takes the form of an "S" shape (see p.277), known as a "double-wake cut", with the skier cutting across the wake of the boat to create a slingshot effect. This method can increase approach speed up to 100kph (66mph). The skier is then slung from the ramp high into the air for many metres, holding the body rigid to reduce wind resistance. For the jump to be scored as complete, the skier must land and ski away without falling.

CRACK THE WHIP

ALFREDO MENDOZA DEVELOPED THE MODERN SKI JUMP APPROACH IN 1951. THE DOUBLE-WAKE CUT, OR "CRACK THE WHIP" AS IT WAS KNOWN THEN, HELPED MENDOZA WIN MANY WORLD TITLES DURING THE 1950S.

Aggressive approach
Approaching the ramp, the skier crouches low and cuts aggressively across the wake to increase speed

Ramp position
Skiers must maintain a crouch and launch themselves from the ramp's edge with expert timing for increased distance

Flight position
The skier positions the skis in a V-style formation, because it is aerodynamically efficient and helps to increase jump distance

Raised edges
Nearing the ramp, the skier will raise the front edges of the skis

Flight path
The skier launches to create a steeper angle than the incline of the ramp

TRICK SKIING

The trick ski course is 175m (191yd) in length. The skier is towed behind a powerboat at a constant speed of their choice, usually about 29kph (18mph). The skier is allowed two 20-second passes to complete as many tricks as possible, which must be submitted to the judges prior to starting the competition. A skier can use one or two skis, with each option suited to different types of tricks. A trick is any action completed by the skier that is specified in the tournament trick rules. Points are awarded for any successful trick according to its degree of difficulty and the accuracy of its execution. The degree of difficulty is calculated according to pre-set scores attributed to different elements of a trick.

TRICK TECHNIQUES

A trick skier's run will involve various combinations of flips, turns, spins, and holds. The highest scoring tricks usually combine the greatest number of spins and flips. A spin is known as a "wake-turn" (when executed in mid-air crossing the wake) or "water-turn" (when executed on the water surface). A skier will rotate anywhere through 180 degrees to 900 degrees during a spin. A "step-over" involves the skier jumping over the towline and is often combined with a spin or spins. Variations of both forward and back flips are used, which must involve the tail of the ski passing directly above the skier's head.

TOEHOLD

One of the more awkward tricks is the "toehold". A special harness is used to secure the skier's foot to the towline handle. The competitor then proceeds to execute combinations of step-overs, jumps, and spins, with the foot secured to the handle. This trick requires exceptional balance and although not as breathtaking as a flip, it is still very difficult.

Do the twist In order to execute a spin, skiers create momentum by rotating their upper body

No touching Once in the toe harness, a skier cannot intentionally touch the ski with the harnessed foot

WAKE FLIP

One of the most exciting tricks is the "wake flip". A skier uses the wake created by the powerboat as a ramp from which to launch into the air. While airborne, the skier flips forwards or backwards and lands upright on the water. During the flip, the skier will also incorporate twists or spins and is capable of rotating through 720 degrees.

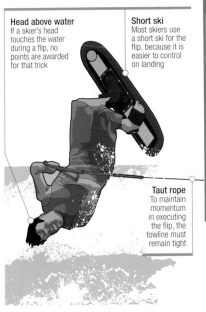

Head above water If a skier's head touches the water during a flip, no points are awarded for that trick

Short ski Most skiers use a short ski for the flip, because it is easier to control on landing

Taut rope To maintain momentum in executing the flip, the towline must remain tight

OTHER WATERSKI SPORTS

One of the main attractions of waterskiing is its variety. It is also one of the few sports in which exhibitions are every bit as exciting as competitions. A number of new waterskiing sports have their own international tournaments and are rapidly gaining the popularity of traditional waterskiing events.

BAREFOOT SKIING

The three main competitions in barefoot skiing tournaments are similar to those in tournament waterskiing. In the trick event, competitors have two passes (each of 15 seconds) in which to execute as many tricks as possible. In barefoot slalom, the objective is to cross the powerboat's wake as many times as possible in the 15-second time limit. In the jump event, the goal is to jump the furthest distance, with top professionals capable of clearing 27m (88ft).

SKI RACING

This is the fastest form of waterskiing. It is held over long set-courses: the longest distance covered by an event being 140km (87 miles). Skiers race each other at high speed, and are capable of reaching 190kph (118mph). Professionals use a long, single ski because it is easier to control. The skier holds and is harnessed to a towline to reduce strain on the arms.

WAKEBOARDING

This event is almost identical to trick skiing, except that the skier uses a long, wide board. Competitors are allowed a two-pass run over a set course, which varies in length between 305m (1,000ft) and 427m (1,400ft).

Board style The wakeboard platform is short and broad, with front and rear fins

Speed limit With top speeds of no more than 25–37kph (16–23mph), wakeboarders move across the water more slowly than conventional waterskiers

SHOW SKIING

Teams have one hour to perform "acts" of their own design, which are often themed. These acts can involve activities such as a "ballet line", a team ski-jump, and a "final pyramid", in which all team members create a human pyramid while skiing. Multiple boats are often involved in acts, and the backing music and the skill of the powerboat drivers is also considered in the scoring, which is assessed by five judges.

INSIDE STORY

The invention of waterskiing is widely credited to Ralph Samuelson. In 1922, Samuelson first tried skiing on the Mississippi River on two curved staves detached from a wooden barrel. He fastened the staves to his feet using two leather straps and his brother Ben pulled him along using a window sash as a towrope. Samuelson later fashioned water skis out of two lengths of wood.

GOVERNING BODY

The International Water Ski Federation is the sport's governing body, which sets the official rules for events. Founded in 1946, it was originally known as the World Water Ski Union. It later organized the first World Championship in 1949, which have since been held every two years.

WINDSURFING

SPORT OVERVIEW

Windsurfing is both a high-speed and acrobatic water sport. Competitors sail or race a board powered by a single sail across an inland lake or the open sea. When professional windsurfers aren't reaching speeds of up to 80kph (50mph) they are performing gravity-defying tricks, such as jumps, spins, and loops. There are a number of professional disciplines, some of which focus on speed and technical skill, while others focus on tricks and style.

NEED2KNOW

→ The popularity of windsurfing peaked in the 1980s. In 1984, it was introduced as an Olympic sport called sailboarding.

→ Indoor windsurfing is a popular event. In 1991, the first indoor race was held in Paris. Sailors race in a 75m (246ft) pool with 25 fans set up to create wind.

→ The first professional windsurfing World Cup tour involving multiple events in various countries was established in 1983.

COMPETITOR PROFILE

Windsurfing is a very physical sport. Studies have shown that Olympic windsurfers are as fit as Olympic rowers and cross-country skiers. Competitors must be extremely strong through the chest and shoulders to control the sail in strong winds and must have powerful leg muscles for manoeuvring the board on rough open water. Stamina is also crucial for extended periods of racing in difficult conditions.

PLANING

The term given to how a windsurf board skims across the water surface is "planing". In winds of 28–46kph (17–29mph), the windsurfer is lifted on to the water surface and can reach significantly faster speeds because it is no longer breaking through the water.

Extra strength
Sails are reinforced with "battens" to make the sail more taught and therefore stable in strong winds

WINDSURFER DESIGN
The basic premise of the windsurfer has not altered much since it was first patented by Jim Drake and Hoyle Schweitzer of the United States in 1970.

Luff tube
The luff is the leading edge of the sail, which houses the mast in a sleeve called the luff tube

Sail size
Small sails catch less wind and are easier to manoeuvre. Large sails catch more wind and are good for high-speed sailing

Leech
This is the rear edge of the sail. A loose leech makes the sail easier to handle in high winds, and a tight leech keeps power in the sail in light winds

Sail material
This is made from a lightweight polyester composite material and is reinforced with a light but strong Kevlar mesh

Sail types
There are two types of sail: the camber-induced sail and the rotational sail. Camber-induced sails create greater speed and stability. Rotational sails are easier to handle and manoeuvre

Wishbone boom
The boom is the steering mechanism for a windsurfer. It is attached to the mast and supports the sailor

Seat harness
The sailor is attached to the boom with a harness, which provides stability and lower back support

Board weight
At the top level, race and wave boards can weigh as little as 5–7kg (11–15lb)

COMPETITION

The main competition divisions of windsurfing each focus on differing elements, such as speed, technical skill, tricks, and style.

WAVE AND FREESTYLE

Wave and Freestyle competitions are the high-flying, acrobatic divisions of windsurfing. In Wave performance, sailors perform jumps and tricks in a pre-determined area of surf and are judged on how well they execute tricks and ride waves. Freestyle competitions involve timed runs on a set area of open water, where sailors perform jumps and tricks for which they are judged and awarded points.

SLALOM

Slalom courses follow a figure of eight pattern and are raced primarily downwind. Races can be started afloat or ashore and competitors race together. The course is on open water and marked by buoys, which sailors must follow and "gybe" or "tack" (see p.283) around in completing the course. An event will normally constitute a number of heats (maximum of 15), using either elimination rounds or an aggregate points system to find a winner.

SPEED SAILING

There are two forms of speed sailing. The first involves sailors racing separately on a 500m (1,641ft) course. A sailor's best two speeds from a two-hour heat are averaged and the sailor with the best average speed wins. The second format is based on record attempts. Sailors wait for favourable winds to attempt to break the current speed sailing record of 90kph (56mph).

OLYMPIC AND FORMULA

In both Olympic and Formula competition, sailors race as one fleet (a fleet can be as many as 120 windsurfers) around a set course marked by buoys. A competition has two to three races per day, which are usually 60 minutes in duration. Races are held on a "windward/leeward" course (meaning it contains mainly upwind and downwind sections) or a trapezoid-shaped course (see below). In Olympic competition, sailors must use identical windsurfers. In Formula competition, sailors' boards and sails can differ slightly in size, but must still be certified Formula-class windsurfers.

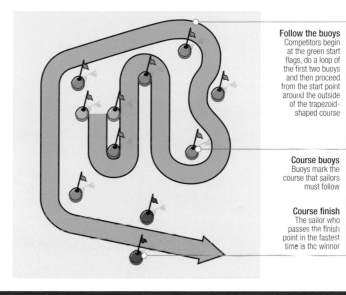

Follow the buoys
Competitors begin at the green start flags, do a loop of the first two buoys and then proceed from the start point around the outside of the trapezoid-shaped course

Course buoys
Buoys mark the course that sailors must follow

Course finish
The sailor who passes the finish point in the fastest time is the winner

---

WINDSURFERS

Windsurfers come in various shapes and sizes. The type of windsurfing being practised will determine what style of windsurfer is needed. Some sailors choose to wear wetsuits, especially in colder conditions, and competitors are responsible for wearing life jackets suitable for racing. Head protection is advised but not mandatory.

BOARDS

Board sizes are measured by volume in litres. A beginner's board will typically measure 150–250 litres (33–55gal). Professional boards are much lighter; for example, a Freestyle board measures 80–110 litres (18–24gal), which makes them harder to control but faster and easier to manoeuvre. Professional boards are fragile, consisting of a polystyrene foam core and reinforced with a composite casing of carbon fibre, Kevlar, and fibreglass.

SAILS

The size and shape of a sail will give it particular performance characteristics. Larger sails catch more wind, so are better in light wind conditions, while smaller sails are used in strong wind conditions.

OLYMPIC

All competitors must use a windsurfer made to identical specifications. All competitors must use a board that weighs no less than 15.45kg (34lb). Formula-class boards are similar in size.

Uniform sail
Men use sails measuring 9.5sq m (102sq ft). Women use sails that measure 8.5sq m (91sq ft)

One design
All competitors use a NeilPryde RS:X board

2.9m (9ft 4in)

Footstraps
Footstraps on both sides of the board secure the sailor when sailing

SLALOM

The board and sail used for Slalom are designed to maximize speed and planing ability. A slalom sail is usually shorter than an Olympic sail but has more battens, making the sail taught and therefore faster.

Rigid sail
Standard slalom sails are taught and measure from 4.5sq m (48sq ft) to 10sq m (108sq ft)

Wide board
The board measures 63.5cm (25in) in width

2.4–2.5m (7ft 8in–8ft 2in)

Wide tail
The wider tail provides greater stability on the water

FREESTYLE

Manoeuvring and jumping are the key features of Freestyle windsurfing. Boards are therefore short in length and weigh only 5–7kg (11–15lb). Wave performance windsurfers have similar dimensions.

Sporty and light
Freestyle sails are small, measuring from 4.5sq m (48sq ft) to 6.5sq m (70sq ft)

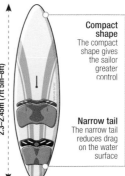

Compact shape
The compact shape gives the sailor greater control

2.3–2.45m (7ft 5in–8ft)

Narrow tail
The narrow tail reduces drag on the water surface

STAT CENTRAL

MEN'S OLYMPIC MEDALLISTS

2012	LONDON
GOLD	DORIAN VAN RIJSSELBERGHE (NED)
SILVER	NICK DEMPSEY (GBR)
BRONZE	PRZEMYSLAW MIARCZYNSKI (POL)

2008	BEIJING
GOLD	TOM ASHLEY (NZL)
SILVER	JULIEN BONTEMPS (FRA)
BRONZE	SHAHAR ZUBARI (ISR)

2004	ATHENS
GOLD	GAL FRIDMAN (ISR)
SILVER	NIKOLAOS KAKLAMANAKIS (GRE)
BRONZE	NICK DEMPSEY (GBR)

WOMEN'S OLYMPIC MEDALLISTS

2012	LONDON
GOLD	MARINA ALABAU NEIRA (SPA)
SILVER	TUULI PETAJA (FIN)
BRONZE	ZOFIA NOCETI-KLEPACKA (POL)

2008	BEIJING
GOLD	YIN JIAN (CHN)
SILVER	ALESSANDRA SENSINI (ITA)
BRONZE	BRYONY SHAW (GBR)

2004	ATHENS
GOLD	FAUSTINE MERRET (FRA)
SILVER	YIN JIAN (CHN)
BRONZE	ALESSANDRA SENSINI (ITA)

SIDELINES

8,120 The greatest distance covered in kilometres on a windsurfer. Flavio Jardim and Diogo Guerreiro travelled from Chui to Oiapaque in Brazil, from May 2004 to July 2005.

4 The number of consecutive world titles won by Finian Maynard in speed windsurfing. Maynard was world champion from 1998 to 2001.

13 The age at which Robby Naish of the United States won his first world championship. Naish went on to claim another 22 world titles over the next 16 years in various divisions.

45.83 The speed, in knots, (83kph or 52.72mph), of the 500m world speed record in the women's division. This was set by Zara Davis of Britain in 2012 at Walvis Bay, Namibia.

COMPETITION REGULATIONS

Competitions for all disciplines are governed by strict regulations, primarily about who has right of way over whom. When windsurfers are on the same "tack" (turning), a windsurfer who is positioned downwind has right of way over a windsurfer who is positioned upwind. When on opposite tacks, a windsurfer on a "port tack" (wind blowing from the left side of the board) must give way to a windsurfer on a "starboard tack" (wind blowing from the right side of the board). In general, turning windsurfers must keep clear of those not turning. In racing competitions, if a windsurfer is on the inside line when rounding a buoy, they have right of way over a windsurfer on the outside line. In trick events, windsurfers coming into shore must give way to those going out. In Wave performance, if two windsurfers share a wave, the first board completely on the wave sailing shoreward has possession.

SCORING

In Slalom and racing events, points are awarded according to placement in a pre-determined number of heats. In trick events, a panel of judges awards points for tricks executed in each run, based on the style and successful execution of the manoeuvres. The winner of a heat scores 0.7 of a point, the sailor in second place two points, and so on. Scores are aggregated at the end of an event and the competitor with the lowest score wins. In speed sailing, the average speed from a sailor's best two runs determines their placement. The sailor with the best average speed wins.

WIND CONDITIONS
A wind speed range of 11–65kph (7–40mph) is best for windsurf racing and trick events, with a minimum wind speed of 11kph (7mph) required for most disciplines. Ideal wind conditions for racing allow sailing along or back towards the shore for the benefit of spectators.

AIRBORNE ACROBATICS

Freestyle and Wave performance are the crowd pleasers of windsurfing. Accomplished sailors perform stunts and tricks in dizzying combinations with apparent grace and ease. In sailing out over the waves, windsurfers execute various loops and jumps and when returning to shore on a wave will display a number of spins and turns. A panel of three to five judges awards points based on the style, variety, and quality of a performance.

BACK LOOP

There are three classic loops – forward, backward, and push loops. Of these the back loop is a notoriously difficult move to execute successfully: while initiating the take-off is relatively simple, a clean, nose-first landing is another matter. Speed, timing, and correct body and board position are fundamental. Performed by professionals, the back loop looks smooth and effortless and is a high point-scorer.

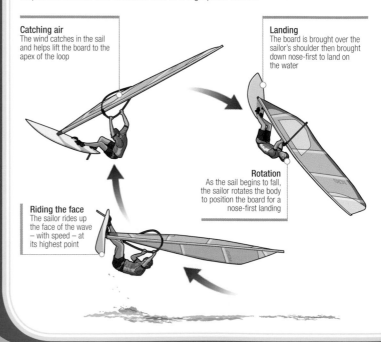

Catching air
The wind catches in the sail and helps lift the board to the apex of the loop

Landing
The board is brought over the sailor's shoulder then brought down nose-first to land on the water

Rotation
As the sail begins to fall, the sailor rotates the body to position the board for a nose-first landing

Riding the face
The sailor rides up the face of the wave – with speed – at its highest point

SAILING TECHNIQUES

In windsurfing, the sail catches the wind to create lift, which raises the board and allows it to plane across the water's surface. The stronger the wind, the faster the board can move. A key windsurfing technique is "sheeting", which is angling the sail to increase or decrease the amount of wind in the sail, and thus control the speed of the board. "Sheeting in" (holding the sail close to the body) increases power by catching more wind. "Sheeting out" (holding the sail away from the body) decreases power by catching less wind. Another key technique only allowed in certain disciplines is "pumping": in light winds, sailors repeatedly pull the sail towards the body to create wind, which can induce planing and increase speed.

ADVANCED MANOEUVRES

There are a variety of manoeuvres available to a windsurfer, with the full repertoire mainly used by Freestyle and Wave windsurfers. Many manoeuvres have unusual names, such as the "Vulcan", "Flaka", and "Spock". The Vulcan, also called the "Air-Gybe", is one of the most direct methods of switching direction. It involves launching the board off a small wave or swell and swinging it with the feet into the opposite direction. The Flaka is an aerial spin through 360 degrees executed by jumping the board off a wave or swell into the wind. The Spock again involves launching off the water and landing on the nose of the board while spinning the sail. This causes the windsurfer to pivot, creating an eye-catching spin. Professionals also use variations of these moves that are more difficult to execute.

BREAKING THE BARRIER

THE 50-KNOT BARRIER HAS LONG BEEN THE HOLY GRAIL OF WINDSURFING SPEED RECORDS. FASTER SPEEDS HAVE BEEN SET IN RECENT YEARS BY WINDSURFING ALONG SPECIALLY CONSTRUCTED 500M COURSES RATHER THAN THE TRADITIONAL NAUTICAL MILE (1.852KM OR 1.51 MILES). IN 2012, FRENCHMAN ANTOINE ALBEAU, SURFING ON THE LUDERITZ CANAL IN NAMIBIA, REACHED A SPEED OF 52.05 KNOTS (96KPH OR 60MPH). KITESURFERS ARE ABLE TO REACH FASTER SPEEDS DUE TO THEIR SMALLER, LIGHTER EQUIPMENT, AND THAT RECORD STANDS AT 55.65 KNOTS (103KPH OR 64MPH).

INSIDE STORY

The first windsurfer patent was granted in the US in 1970, to Jim Drake and Hoyle Schweitzer, widely seen as the founders of modern-day windsurfing. However, windsurfing was practised earlier by ingenious amateurs. In the 1940s, a young Australian boy built crude windsurfers out of iron canoes that he equipped with sails and booms made from split bamboo. He successfully sailed these on a river in Perth and is recognized as the first individual to sail a windsurfer.

GOVERNING BODIES

The International Windsurfing Association (IWA) and the Professional Windsurfers Association (PWA) are the main governing bodies of the sport. Many professional windsurfing events are organized and sanctioned by these bodies, which are also responsible for making new rules, and providing support and services for windsurfers worldwide.

KITEBOARDING

EVENT OVERVIEW

Kiteboarding fuses elements of surfing and parasailing to create an extreme sport in which competitors use a large kite to steer a board across water, performing tricks and jumps as they do so. The sport has gradually increased in popularity since the late 1990s and in 2012, after a high-profile campaign, the Olympic Committee agreed to include it in the official programme for the 2016 Games, as a replacement for windsurfing. However, later in the same year they reversed their decision.

STYLES

There are a number of kiteboarding styles but the most popular competitive disciplines are freestyle, wave riding, course racing, and slalom. In freestyle, competitors perform tricks such as spins and jumps and are awarded points for their efforts by a panel of judges. Wave riding is a crossover between kiteboarding and competitive surfing, with boarders attempting to execute complicated manoeuvres on breaking waves. In course racing, competitors navigate a route in the shortest time possible, while slalom racing involves multiple competitors racing along a figure-of-eight course.

NEED2KNOW

→ Major kiteboarding competitions, along with the development of the rules of the sport, are overseen by the International Kiteboarding Association.

→ The optimum wind speed for kiteboarding is 15–25mph (25–40kph).

→ In 2012, the number of kiteboarders worldwide was estimated at 1.5 million.

→ Most of the Earth's prevailing winds are westerlies, so many of the best surfing areas are on western coasts, such as those of California, USA, and Cornwall, England.

→ The world championship circuit, organized by the Association of Surfing Professionals, takes place in top venues in Australia, South Africa, Hawaii, Tahiti, and Fiji.

→ In competitions at all levels there are separate events for men and women.

SURFING

SPORT OVERVIEW

Exhilarating for both participants and spectators, the object of competition surfing is to ride breaking waves for as long as possible, performing tricks and manoeuvres to impress a panel of judges. The most familiar form of surfing involves standing on either a short or a long board. Variations include bodyboarding, bodysurfing, kneeboarding, surf-skiing, kite surfing, and windsurfing (see pp.280–83). The most spectacular category is tow-in surfing, in which the boarder is hauled by a boat on to waves so big and powerful that they could not be caught any other way.

COMPETITOR PROFILE

Wiping out (falling off the board) in big waves can be dangerous, so most surfers are outstanding swimmers. Professional surfers have excellent all-round fitness and a fine sense of balance. The ability to pick the best waves for the best rides is gained partly from local knowledge and partly from experience. Training on dry land involves gym repetitions on the muscles of the legs and abdomen.

Water wear
Surfing wetsuits have permeable middle layers that let in water, which is then warmed by the heat of the surfer's body and provides them with insulation from the cold outside

Lifeline
A leash links the board to the surfer's ankle so the two are not separated

Board basics
Traditionally wooden but now made of fibreglass and polystyrene, most boards weigh less than 1kg (2.2lb)

Surf stabilizers
Fins on the rear underside of the board help to stabilize it on the wave

STAT CENTRAL

ASP WORLD CHAMPIONS: MEN

YEAR	NAME (COUNTRY)
2012	JOEL PARKINSON (AUS)
2011	KELLY SLATER (USA)
2010	KELLY SLATER (USA)
2009	MICK FANNING (AUS)
2008	KELLY SLATER (USA)

ASP WORLD CHAMPIONS: WOMEN

YEAR	NAME (COUNTRY)
2012	STEPHANIE GILMORE (AUS)
2011	CARISSA MOORE (HAW)
2010	STEPHANIE GILMORE (AUS)
2009	STEPHANIE GILMORE (AUS)
2008	STEPHANIE GILMORE (AUS)

THE BOARD

There are two main types of surfboard: the longboard and shortboard. Pro surfers use shortboards for international competitions, although there is still a longboard category in the International Surfing Association (ISA) world championships.

LONGBOARD
The heavy longboard provides greater stability than the shortboard but is harder to turn. For this reason, longboards are often used by beginners.

Minimum 2.75m (9ft)

55cm (1ft 9in)

SHORTBOARD
The shortboard is light and streamlined to allow for tight turns. A wax covering or non-slip pads on the surface of the board gives the surfer better grip.

1.8m (6ft)

46cm (1ft 6in)

Non-slip
Pads or wax aid traction

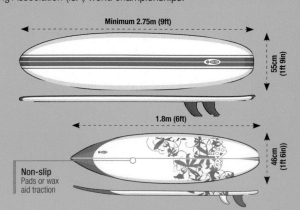

BREAKER RULES

Surfers take to the water either two or four at a time and ride the waves several times in heats of 20 minutes. The regulations may vary from event to event, but in general the best two, three, or five rides are marked by a panel of five or six judges according to the following criteria: choice of wave (the harder the better); position on wave (the crest is best); time on wave; and quality of manoeuvre. In a four-surfer heat, the top two progress to the next round.

BOARDING PROCEDURES

There are two basic ways of addressing any wave: forehand, in which the surfer faces the wave, and backhand, where the surfer has his or her back to it. Getting the board position right is important, but it's what the surfer does while riding the wave that counts for points and prizes. Two of the fundamental surfing techniques are outlined below.

A SURFEIT OF SURFERS

IN 2003 IN CORNWALL, ENGLAND, A TEAM OF 12 MEN AND TWO WOMEN SURFED THEIR WAY INTO THE GUINNESS BOOK OF RECORDS BY RIDING THE WORLD'S BIGGEST BOARD, AN 11M (37FT) MONSTER WEIGHING 180KG (400LB).

CUT-BACK

This is a turn from the top to the bottom of a breaking wave and back up again. The surfer rides to the crest of the wave, transfers their weight on to the heels, and leans back, twisting the upper body into the turn. At the bottom of the wave, the surfer swings back on to the wave again.

PUSH BACK
The surfer rides up to the crest of a breaking wave and pushes back on the heels.

TURN AWAY
Twisting the upper body, the surfer turns into the wave as the board hits the foam.

SPEEDING UP
The surfer relies on the power of his turn to pick up speed for the remount.

THE RE-MOUNT
The surfer pushes down on the back of the board to re-mount the crest of the wave.

FLOATER

The floater is a tricky manoeuvre that a surfer uses to ride up on to the lip of a breaking wave and then "float" back down with the foam on to the clean face of the wave. The surfer's biggest challenge is making a good landing as the board hits the wave face.

BREAKING WAVE
The surfer rides up the face of the wave to approach the breaking section.

OVER THE LIP
Instead of turning, the surfer continues to ride up on to the lip of the wave as it peels away.

SKIMMING THE FOAM
The surfer hovers on the foam, arms outstretched, as the wave breaks below the board.

FINAL ASCENT
As the board drops down on to the wave face, the surfer bends the knees to absorb the impact.

SURF SLANG

Surfing has its own language, much of which originated in the United States. Here are just a few surfing terms you might encounter when reading about the sport:
BARREL (OR TUBE) The ultimate wave-riding experience – a wave that curls over as it breaks, leaving a hollow tube through which the surfer rides.
CRUNCHER Any big, hard wave that is almost impossible to ride.
GLASSHOUSE The space inside a barrel or tube.
GOOFY FOOTER Someone who rides the surfboard with the right foot forward. Left foot forward is the normal stance.
HANG FIVE (OR TEN) To place one (or both) sets of toes over the front of the board when riding a wave.
NATURAL FOOTER Someone who rides the surfboard with the left foot forward. Also known as a regular footer.
SOUP Foam, or whitewater, from a broken wave.

INSIDE STORY

Surfing was commonplace among Pacific Islanders for thousands of years before Europeans got wind of it from Captain James Cook, who observed the practice when he visited Hawaii in 1778. Although the main surfing centres are still located in the Pacific, the sport is now also popular in other parts of the world, including Brazil, Costa Rica, South Africa, Australia, France, Ireland, Jamaica, and Spain.

ASSOCIATION OF SURFING PROFESSIONALS

The Association of Surfing Professionals now runs the highest level of competition worldwide, the ASP World Tour.

SIDELINES

23.7 The height in metres of the tallest wave to be ridden. Garrett McNamara achieved this feat in 2011 in Nazaré, Portugal, where a deep underwater canyon creates unusually large waves.

64 The time in minutes for the longest ride on a single wave. The record belongs to Steve King, who in February 2013 surfed the Kampar River in Sumatra, Indonesia, for 20.6km (12.8 miles).

WINTER SPORTS

07

NEED2KNOW

→ The early form of skiing is known as Telemark after the Norwegian mountains where it was developed in the 1870. Telemark boots are bound to the ski at the toe only, making it easier to lift the foot and the ski when crossing flat areas.

→ The first downhill race using alpine skis and boots was held in 1921 in Switzerland. In 1930, the downhill and slalom disciplines were recognized as official sports. They have been Olympic events since 1936.

→ The word "slalom" comes from the Norwegian for "gentle slope". Alpine skiers learn slalom skills first before attempting downhills.

THE COURSES

There are no set lengths for alpine-ski courses; the more famous ones have been used for decades and have remained largely unchanged in that time. Speed-event courses are designed to test competitors with a mixture of steep drops, sharp turns and flat stretches. Slalom races are held on less challenging slopes, and the courses follow a much straighter route down the mountain. All courses are clearly marked with coloured gates, through which every racer must travel. Men's races are held over longer distances and contain more gates than women's competitions.

Hand in glove
Gloves keep the hands warm and must not reach past the elbow; they are not a compulsory piece of racing equipment, but few skiers race without them

Number check
All racers must wear a standard polyester bib that displays each competitor's race number

Second skin
Racers wear skin-tight suits to cut down on air resistance that might slow them down; the suits may be padded on the shins and around the shoulders

Point and stick
Ski poles are used to help maintain balance during tight turns when the skier's body weight is shifted from side to side

SPORT OVERVIEW

Alpine skiing is an exhilarating sport of speed and skill. Millions of amateur skiers get a taste of the excitement every winter at the world's many ski resorts, but few of them compete in organised races. There are five official types of alpine-ski competitions. Two of the disciplines – downhill and super giant slalom – focus on speed. Slalom and giant slalom are more technical events, in which a competitor's skill will win the day. The fifth "combined" event tests both speed and technique.

ALPINE SKIING

DEADLY SLOPE

THE FASTEST AND MOST DANGEROUS DOWNHILL RACE IS HELD ON THE HAHNENKAMM, NEAR KITZBÜHEL, AUSTRIA. THE EVENT HAS BEEN RUN THERE SINCE 1931, WITH COMPETITORS REACHING SPEEDS OF 150KPH (93MPH). SKIERS RACE ON A RUN CALLED THE STREIF, WHICH BEGINS WITH THE MOUSETRAP, A 50-M (164-FT) JUMP THAT HAS PROVED FATAL ON SEVERAL OCCASIONS.

OPEN AND CLOSED

Alpine-ski courses are set out on managed slopes, or pistes, using pairs of coloured flags called gates. The gates are most widely spread on the downhill courses, and placed closest together for slalom races. A gate composed of flags positioned side-by-side is called an "open" gate. A "closed" gate has one flag positioned in front of the other. Open gates show the direction that the competitor must follow down the piste, while closed gates are used to force racers to turn across the fall line – the natural line of descent.

AT THE PIPS
A competitor passes though an electronic gate to start the timer and enter the course. Two beeps followed by a higher-pitched tone signal each racer to begin.

Letting it slide
The course is prepared by spraying it with salt and water to melt the top of the snow and create a layer of ice, which ensures racers achieve top speeds

At the summit
Downhill and super giant slalom courses start near the top of the mountain

Clear off
Most races are run on pistes ordinarily occupied by tourists; however, the steepest slopes are reserved just for races

Cutting up
Icy courses are best because they do not degrade quickly, although rutting occurs at sharp bends

In the net
Stretches of the course with high drops at the side are lined with netting to stop racers from falling; pads cover solid objects that might cause injuries

Big drop
The longest courses are 5km (3 miles) and descend up to 1,000m (3,281ft) for men's races

Doing the splits
The time taken to complete half the course shows spectators whether a racer is likely to finish in the fastest time so far

BEND NOT BREAK
The first slalom courses were marked with bamboo poles. In the 1980s these stiff sticks were replaced with "breakaway" gates, which are flexible plastic poles that have a hinge at the base.

THIS IS THE END
The finish line is marked by a giant gate. Often competitors can see their course time displayed on a large screen as they approach the finish.

Flat out
The lower section of a course might be a lot flatter than higher up; racers have to ensure they arrive on flats at top speed so they do not lose momentum

Watch out
Spectators line the route cheering racers on by ringing large cow bells

WINNING WAYS

Alpine skiing events are time trials in which racers battle against the clock to complete the course in the shortest time. Downhill racers are allowed to practise on the course (to find the best racing line) in the three days prior to the contest. However, slalomists would cause too much damage to the pistes during practice, so they are limited to a one-hour course inspection before the race.

SIDELINES

70 The maximum number of gates on a men's giant slalom course; 56 is the minimum number. A women's competition has between 46 and 58 gates.

1 The minimum number of minutes it must take to complete a downhill race. Any less than that and the course must be lengthened.

0.01 The fraction of a second to which races are timed.

120 The average speed in kilometres per hour of a downhill skier.

800 The maximum vertical drop – the difference in metres between the altitudes of the start and finish – of a women's downhill race.

PISTE-WEAR

Alpine skiers wear as little as possible to make themselves aerodynamic. Loose clothing creates drag, which slows the racer down. However, a racing suit must conform to a minimum air permeability – in other words, it must not be treated to make it airtight and so offer less resistance to the air.

Racers are allowed to protect parts of the body with pads. The pads must not alter the natural shape of the competitor's body in a way that might reduce drag. For example, skiers may wear back protectors. These are heavily controlled and monitored for creating any aerodynamic advantage.

SKI BOOTS
Alpine ski boots are made from stiff plastic; they are close fitting and hold the feet tightly to create a very sturdy connection between the legs and the skis. The foot is unable to move inside, but the lower leg can bend forwards.

Soft touch
The lower leg is surrounded by thick padding

Clunk click
The buckles should not be tightened too much in case the circulation is restricted

Stiff upper
Top alpine skiers have the stiffest boots; beginners wear more flexible footwear

Chunky heel
The thick sole is attached to the ski

Ski clips
These secure the boot to the foot

HELMET
Every competitor in an alpine-ski race must wear a crash helmet. These must cover the head and ears only; spoilers or fins are forbidden.

In place
The helmet is kept in place by a padded chin-strap

Hit me again
The protective shell is designed to withstand several impacts without needing to be replaced

Strap to it
The hand passes though the strap from below; the strap is held between the palm and handle

Nice curves
Downhill skiers use curved poles that tuck in behind the body and minimize drag

Lightweight
Poles are made from aluminium tubes

Basket
A plastic basket stops the pole sinking into the snow

GOGGLES
Well-fitting ski goggles are essential for protecting the eyes from the elements. Certain lenses also help improve visibility in low-light conditions.

Snug fit
A wide band keeps the goggles firmly in place

Tinted shield
The colour of the goggle lenses cuts out glare and keeps snow out of the eyes

POLES
Ski poles are used to balance the skier and help them shift their weight. The length of a pole depends on the height of the skier: with the knees slightly bent, the pole should reach just above the elbow.

IT'S ANCIENT HISTORY
THE WORLD'S OLDEST SKI IS APPROXIMATELY 4,500 YEARS OLD. REMAINS OF THE WOODEN RELIC WERE FOUND IN A SWEDISH BOG. SKIING IS THOUGHT TO HAVE BEEN INVENTED BY THE ANCESTORS OF THE SAMI PEOPLE FROM LAPLAND.

SKIS AND BINDINGS
Each alpine-ski event demands a certain type of ski. An alpine ski has a particular shape. When viewed from the side it has a slight arch, or camber, at the centre – a shape that focuses the skier's weight towards the tips of the skis. Modern skis also have a side cut – both edges of the ski curve inwards from each end making the ski narrowest near the central point. The curved edge cuts, or carves, into the snow easily making turning faster.

GIANT SLALOM
The skis used in giant and super giant slalom races are hybrids of slalom and downhill skis. They are longer to produce speed, but have medium-depth side cuts to make turning easier.

DOWNHILL
Long and wide skis produce the fastest speeds because they glide over the surface of the snow better. However, wide skis are hard to steer. Downhill skis have a small side cut to aid turning.

SLALOM
The shortest alpine skis are used in slalom races, where competitors sacrifice speed for manoeuvrability. The side cuts are deeper than on other skis so the ski cuts into the piste and bends into turns.

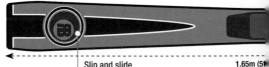

Slip and slide
The underside of the ski is coated with wax to keep it slippy

1.65m (5

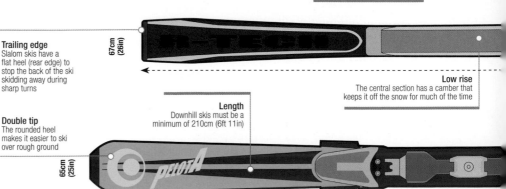

Trailing edge
Slalom skis have a flat heel (rear edge) to stop the back of the ski skidding away during sharp turns

67cm (26in)

Low rise
The central section has a camber that keeps it off the snow for much of the time

Length
Downhill skis must be a minimum of 210cm (6ft 11in)

Double tip
The rounded heel makes it easier to ski over rough ground

65cm (25in)

2.15m (7ft)

MASTERING THE SLOPES

Every alpine-ski discipline requires a different set of skills. The speed events are decided by a single timed run. Mistakes from the leaders and lucky runs from unknowns often turn the leader boards on their heads. Technical racers make two runs, both on the same day, and the times are added to determine each racer's finishing place. Competitors in the combined event are placed according to the combined time of a downhill and slalom run. The super giant slalom requires a unique set of skills. Like in a downhill race, competitors have just one run to show what they can do. However, as in other slalom events, practice on the course is forbidden: a super-G course is run once, and once only.

RUNNING ORDER

A competitor's starting position can have an effect on the race. During a downhill in snowy conditions, early racers are slowed by the fresh snow and may be beaten by late starters. Starting first in a slalom is an advantage, because the course has yet to be rutted by previous runs.

The 15 highest-ranking entrants race first. Their starting positions are allocated by a draw. Any remaining racers start according to their world ranking. In the second run of slalom races, the 15 fastest from the first run race in reverse order.

DOWNHILL

Courses are generally 2.5–5km (1.5–3 miles), and must take more than a minute to complete – most take about two. There are limits on steepness: men's courses must not drop more than 1,000m (3,280ft), while women's courses drop less than 700m (2,300ft).

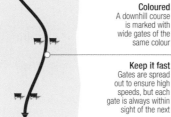

Coloured
A downhill course is marked with wide gates of the same colour

Keep it fast
Gates are spread out to ensure high speeds, but each gate is always within sight of the next

GIANT SLALOM

The longest technical event, a giant slalom course is filled with twists and turns, but unlike in a slalom race, every giant-slalom gate does not require a change in direction. The number of turns is about 13 per cent of the course's vertical drop in metres.

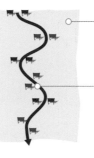

Top to bottom
Giant slalom courses have a vertical drop of about 300m (984ft)

Mix match
Giant slaloms have an equal mixture of open and closed gates

SUPER-G

This is the newest alpine skiing discipline; it was introduced in 1982. Super-G, as it is known, merges the concepts of downhill and giant slalom. A downhill course is marked with giant-slalom gates, but these are widely spaced so races are run at near-downhill speeds.

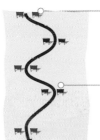

Colour changes
Slalom courses are always marked with gates of alternating colours

Show the way
A super-G course has mainly open gates

SLALOM

Although it is the safest discipline, slalom is also regarded as the most technically challenging alpine-ski event. Every course has combinations of gates to test the skill of the competitors, including delay gates, which direct racers across, rather than down, the slope.

Racing line
The horizontal offset between gates is lowest in slalom creating a direct root down the mountain

Drop
The average vertical drop between each gate is 9m (30ft)

Thin out
Slalom skis are the narrowest of all alpine skis

Carving edge
A deep side cut makes the ski turn more efficiently

Staying wide
The front (and back) of the ski is wide to maintain stability

Heel toe
The toe (and heel) is locked to the ski by the binding

Quick release
A lever is pushed down to release the boot

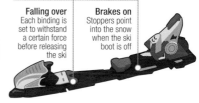

In the middle
Bindings are attached to the ski just behind the central point

Cut out
Giant slalom skis have a small side cut

Making a point
Slalom skis have pointed tips at the front to stop them digging into snow

Falling over
Each binding is set to withstand a certain force before releasing the ski

Brakes on
Stoppers point into the snow when the ski boot is off

1.85m (6ft)

Speed above all
The wide ski spreads the skier's weight and ensures high speeds

In the round
The tips are low and rounded to make the ski aerodynamic

Twister
Turning a screw adjusts the bindings to fit different-sized boots

Integrated
Alpine racing skis are sold with bindings already attached

STAT CENTRAL

OLYMPIC MEDALS (OVERALL)

MEDALS	COUNTRY
105	AUSTRIA
56	SWITZERLAND
43	FRANCE
39	UNITED STATES
28	ITALY
26	NORWAY
23	GERMANY
16	SWEDEN
10	CANADA
9	CROATIA
9	WEST GERMANY
5	UNITED TEAM OF GERMANY
5	SLOVENIA
2	SPAIN
2	LUXEMBOURG

WOMEN'S OLYMPIC GOLD MEDALS

YEAR	DOWNHILL	G. SLALOM	SLALOM
2010	USA	GER	GER
2006	AUT	USA	SWE
2002	FRA	CRO	CRO
1998	GER	ITA	GER
1994	GER	ITA	SUI
1992	CAN	SWE	AUT
1988	GDR	SUI	SUI
1984	ITA	USA	ITA
1980	AUT	LIE	LIE
1976	GDR	CAN	GDR
1972	SUI	SUI	USA
1968	AUT	CAN	FRA
1964	AUT	FRA	FRA
1960	GDR	SUI	CAN
1956	SUI	GDR	SUI

MEN'S OLYMPIC GOLD MEDALS

YEAR	DOWNHILL	G. SLALOM	SLALOM
2010	SUI	SUI	ITA
2006	FRA	AUT	AUT
2002	AUT	AUT	FRA
1998	FRA	AUT	NOR
1994	USA	GER	AUT
1992	AUT	ITA	NOR
1988	SUI	ITA	ITA
1984	USA	SUI	USA
1980	AUT	SWE	SWE
1976	AUT	SUI	ITA
1972	SUI	ITA	ESP
1968	FRA	FRA	FRA
1964	AUT	FRA	AUT
1960	FRA	SUI	AUT
1956	AUT	AUT	AUT

RACING TECHNIQUES

It takes several years to learn how to ski to a high standard. Most world-class alpine skiers will have begun to ski before they even went to school. A very few top skiers have been winners in several events. For example, the Swiss star Pirmin Zurbriggen won medals in the downhill, super-G, giant slalom and the combined competition in the 1980s. However, most alpine skiers concentrate on speed or technical disciplines.

TURNING

For those who have not been on skis, making turns looks complicated. It certainly takes practice to be able to do it at racing speeds, but thanks to the shape of modern skis, turning has never been easier. The latest technique is to make so-called carving turns: For example, a racer shifts his weight onto the left ski, making its outside edge cut into the slope. The ski bends to match the shape of the slope, as the ski rotates to the left.

DOWNHILL
In speed events, turning is kept to a minimum because it slows the racer. When adjustments are needed to stay on the racing line, racers rely on their strength and balance to stay on their feet.

Shifting shape
The skier leans his weight onto the lower ski

Close call
The turn must follow the racing line; too wide or too tight will cost time

Sign posts
Downhill gates are often placed at natural bends in the course

Bend down
The racer stays as low as possible during the turn to maintain speed

Straight up
The crouching skier makes his skis parallel to get up to full speed again

SLALOM
Racers are forced to make turns through slalom gates. Top slalomists make turns very close to the gates, so their route is as straight, and short, as possible. The racers are allowed to push the gate poles out of the way, using techniques called blocks.

Rapid gates
Modern slalom gates have a hinge at the base so they bend out of the racer's path

Cross over
Top slalomists aim the body behind the pole while the skis pass in front; this is known as cross-blocking

Outside-clear
Junior racers might use their outside arm to clear the gate

On guard
Slalomists are allowed to wear stiff protectors on the forearm to prevent injuries

Inside-clear
The simplest block is to push the gate away using the inside forearm

Up and down
Slalom racers bob up and down to shift their weight between turns; they make up to 60 turns in a race

JUMPING

Slalom racers rarely leave the ground; however, faster races often involve competitors making jumps. Downhill skiers, travelling faster than motorway traffic, fly up to 80m (260ft) in a single jump. A jump at this speed requires a lot of skill to prevent serious injury. Racers who fall on landing also rely on their equipment: the bindings release the skis, and the smooth racing suit allows them to continue sliding and to slow down gradually and safely.

Up and away
Downhill jumps, or airs, result when the racer reaches a steep drop

Tuck for landing
The heel, or back, of the ski will land first, and the racer absorbs the shock with his knees while crouching down into a high-speed tuck position

Skid lid
Although jumpers are rarely more than a few metres above the ground, their speed makes helmets essential

Don't dangle
At first the skis drop down and begin to point upward

Keep it down
The racer does not push off as he leaves the ground; the jump needs to be long but not high

Push forward
As the jump continues the skier must keep his weight forward so he is ready for landing

Straighten out
The racer must keep the skis level and pointing downward to reduce drag and ensure he travels in a straight line

WORLD BEATER

PERHAPS THE GREATEST SKIER OF ALL TIME IS JANICA KOSTELIC, A CROATIAN ALL-ROUNDER WITH FOUR OLYMPIC GOLDS. IN THE 2006 SEASON, KOSTELIC (BORN 1982) WON RACES IN ALL FIVE ALPINE-SKI DISCIPLINES. SHE WON WORLD CHAMPIONSHIPS IN SLALOM AND THE COMBINED EVENT IN BOTH 2003 AND 2005. IN 2005 SHE ALSO ADDED THE DOWNHILL TITLE.

SUPER SPEED

The friction between skis and snow is only small and the biggest limiter to a racer's speed are their turns and air resistance, or drag. Skiers reduce drag by making the forward surface area that is exposed to the oncoming wind as small as possible by adopting a tuck position.

Head down
The head is hunched under the shoulders, but the racer still needs to be able to see!

Wrap around
The poles bend in behind the body, so the baskets stay hidden from the front

Fold over
The upper body folds down onto the thighs

Out in front
The hands are held in front of the face with the palms facing inward

Making a point
With the hands and arms, the bent knees form a forward point that cuts through the air

Flatten out
The ankles must keep the skis flat so the edges do not cut into the snow and slow the skier

Shin up
The body weight is held forward on the shins

FASTER THAN FALLING

Downhill racers are not the fastest skiers in the world; that honour goes to the speed skiers. This sport is outside the rules of normal alpine skiing: speed skis are longer and wider than racing designs, and skiers wear lightweight foam fins on the limbs and helmet to create a more aerodynamic shape. Speed skiers make straight runs down 1-km (3,280-ft) courses. Their speed is recorded halfway down, leaving the lower slope for slowing down safely. The current world record is held by Italian Simon Origone who reached 251.4kph (156.2mph) in April 2006. That is even faster than the terminal velocity of a skydiver (193kph; 120mph).

INSIDE STORY

The first recorded ski race was held in Tromsø, Norway, in 1843. By the late 19th century competitions were being held across Europe and North America. These early skiers were using Telemark equipment. Downhill races using alpine skis and according to modern rules have been held since 1921; the first slalom was in 1922. In 1936 Alpine skiing became part of the Olympic programme for the first time. Giant slalom became a standard event in 1950; super giant slalom was introduced in 1982.

GOVERNING BODY
The Fédération Internationale de Ski (FIS; International Ski Federation) is the governing body of all ski competitions, including speed skiing, Nordic skiing (such as ski jumping and cross-country), snowboarding and freestyle (acrobatics) as well as alpine skiing. The FIS was founded in 1924. It is based in Switzerland and has 111 national members.

SIDELINES

3.65 The number of people who are injured while skiing each day per every 1,000 skiers.

328 The number of skiers who have achieved speeds of 200kph (124mph) or more, generally achieved on high-altitude courses.

40 The minimum number of seconds left between the starts of downhill competitors.

FREESTYLE SKIING

SPORT OVERVIEW

The two main types of freestyle skiing are moguls and aerial, while a third variety, acro, is practised on a more limited basis. Moguls involves skiing down a steep slope covered with "moguls" (small bumps) and jumping off two ramps, while aerial involves jumping off a ramp and performing twists and spins in mid-air. Acro (not an Olympic sport) is a combination of gymnastics and dance, performed on a gentle slope.

KITTED OUT
Competitors in each of the three disciplines use similar gear. Acro skiers, and the mogul skier shown here, have the full complement of waterproof and insulated clothing, poles for balance, twin-tip skis, helmet, and goggles. Aerial skiers wear the same clothing and skis, but don't use poles.

Protective helmet
A helmet is vital for freestyle skiing, giving warmth and extra protection for the head

Waterproof jacket
Insulated, waterproof jackets are worn to stay warm

Ski poles
Poles are crucial for turning and propelling the skier. Acro poles must not exceed the skier's height, and mogul poles are usually 60cm (2ft) shorter than the athlete

Ski bindings
Standard ski bindings are used to attach the boots to the skis

Twin-tip skis
Freestyle skiers use flexible skis with smooth undersides and raised tips at both ends

THREE-PISTE SUITE

Moguls, aerials, and acro are sufficiently distinct disciplines to each require a dedicated course. Mogul courses are the steepest of the three, with a constant incline for the whole slope. The aerial slope has four stages, each at different gradients – the inrun, table, landing zone, and finish area. The acro course is a single slope at a constant gradient.

HOT DOGGING

A SKIING TREND DUBBED "HOT DOGGING" BROUGHT FREESTYLE SKIING TO A NEW AUDIENCE IN THE LATE 1960s. INSPIRED BY THE MOVES AND STYLE OF SKATEBOARDERS, AMERICAN SKIERS BEGAN TO EXPERIMENT WITH JUMPS AND TRICKS ON THE SLOPES, AND ADOPTED THE TERM TO DESCRIBE THE SHOWBOATING STYLE THAT EVOLVED.

MOUNTAIN MOLEHILLS
The mogul slope has a constant gradient of 24–32 degrees. Skiers negotiate the moguls at high speed, before jumping off ramps called kickers to perform aerial manoeuvres.

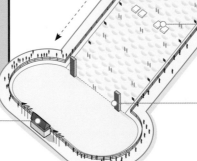

Starting position
The competitor starts here and descends the piste between the control gates. In dual moguls, two skiers descend at the same time

Control gates
Contestants pass between control gates 8–15m (26–49ft) apart

Judges' stand
Each run is scored by seven judges, who sit in a stand in the finish area

25m (82ft)

200–270m (218–295yd)

Mogul mounds
The moguls are placed about 3.5m (11½ft) apart

Kicker ramps
There are two rows of ramps, made from ice, called kickers. Skiers take off from these to perform aerial twists, turns, and somersaults.

Finish line
The run ends when the skier goes through a photoelectric cell between two uprights

NEED2KNOW

→ The first appearance of freestyle skiing was in the 1930s in Norway, when skiers began to perform acrobatics during alpine and cross-country training.

→ Freestyle skiing is one of the most dynamic forms of skiing – the ethos is very much on individual creativity and expression. It has much in common with snowboarding, particularly in clothing and techniques.

→ Moguls and aerial are both Olympic sports. Acro was a demonstration sport in 1988 and 1992, but has not been adopted fully.

SIDELINES

3 The maximum number of backflips permitted in an aerial competition. Up to five twists may also be added, in order to win as many points as possible for "form".

18 The height in metres (59ft) that top aerial freestylers rise above the slope after lifting off from a kicker. Jumps in mogul contests are smaller in size.

98 The vertical drop, in metres (321ft), of the Sauze d'Oulx mogul run, which was used for the Turin Winter Olympics. Fresh snow for the moguls was produced artificially from rainwater.

4 The total number of freestyle skiing medals won by the United States at the 2010 Winter Olympics. Although this was the highest national total in the competition, Canada won two gold medals in comparison to the United States' one.

SKIER PROFILE

Each freestyle discipline has its own demands, but they all require physical endurance and technical ability. Some freestylists work out by bouncing on trampolines while wearing skis, and in the absence of snow during the off-season, aerial skiers practise on artificial ramps that end in swimming pools or lakes.

SKI BOOTS

Made from plastic, ski boots are incredibly stiff with high sides to support the ankles, to ensure that the feet are secured firmly to the skis.

Ski clips
The boots are closed and secured by a number of clips

STYLISH GEAR

Headgear and clothing are the same in all three forms of freestyle. Acro skis are shorter and more flexible than their mogul and aerial equivalents.

PLASTIC HELMET

Helmets are nearly always worn, and are compulsory for aerial skiers. Made from plastic, they are held in position with a chinstrap.

Padded fit
Helmets come with padding on the inside for a comfy fit

SKI GOGGLES

Goggles are worn to protect the eyes from the glare of the sun, and also to prevent snow from getting in the eyes.

Elastic strap
The goggles are secured with an elastic strap

SKI LENGTHS

Moguls and aerial skis have specific maximum lengths. Acro skis may be no more than 80 per cent of the skier's height.

Ski bindings
The bindings secure the skier's boot onto the ski

Men: up to 1.9m (6ft 3in);
Women: up to 1.8m (5ft 11in)

Flexible ski
The ski's profile is curved, which makes it more flexible

AERIAL SLOPE

On the aerial course, the takeoff slope (known as the "inrun") descends at an angle of 20 to 25 degrees, then flattens out at the takeoff area (known as the "table").The landing zone is built at an angle of 37 degrees, while the finish area is completely flat.

Table
The table is completely flat to allow skiers to accurately gauge the angle of the kickers

64–74m (210–243ft)

30m (98ft)

Judges' stand
The judges sit on a raised platform that gives a good view of the jump

Knoll
The transition from the table to the landing zone is known as the knoll, and is marked with a line

Landing zone
The slope in the landing zone is scattered with wood shavings to give the skiers a clear view of the ground

Finish area
There are no size regulations for the finish area; it is usually built as large as possible

Inrun
The length of the inrun varies according to the angle of the slope

Marker flags
Flags are placed to help competitors judge their progress down the inrun

Sculpted kickers
Kickers are individually sculpted from snow and have no artificial infrastructure at all. Once built, they must be maintained at the same temperature throughout the event

Boundary wall
The finish area is enclosed by fencing to keep spectators out

MOGUL MAGIC

The aim of moguls is to get down the course as fast as possible, while winning points awarded by seven judges for the overall style and technique of the descent, and for compulsory elements, such as jumps. There are three scoring elements: the quality of turns around the moguls, manoeuvres made in the jumps, and the overall speed of the descent.

BUMPY RIDE

Skiers can go straight over the moguls, but this takes longer than twisting and turning around them. Bumps are absorbed by bending the knees.

Pole position
As the skier prepares to turn right, he or she pivots on the right pole and shifts his or her weight to the right

BACK SCRATCHING

The back scratcher is a move performed in mid-air just after a jump, in combination with one or two other positions. The skis must stay parallel with each other.

Lifted high
The poles must be lifted high and wide, to avoid striking the skis or legs

Pointing back
The skis are pointed down at the ground and the trailing ends "scratch the back"

SPREAD EAGLED

The spread eagle is a popular mid-air move. The skier launches off a kicker and spreads both arms and legs as wide as possible.

KNEE-TO-SHOW BASIS

IN 1994, CANADA'S JEAN-LUC BRASSARD WORE BRIGHTLY COLOURED KNEEPADS TO ENSURE THE JUDGES MISSED NONE OF HIS TRICKS ON THE MOGUL SLOPE. HE TOOK GOLD – AND NOW EVERYONE WEARS THE PADS.

ACRO AFFAIR

Acro skiers perform a 90-second choreographed routine of flips and spins, set to a musical accompaniment chosen by the competitor. The manoeuvres fall into one of three categories: spins, leverage moves, and somersaults.

FORWARD SOMERSAULT

The forward somersault is a key acro move. It can be augmented by holding the upside-down position on the poles before returning to the ground.

Swing into line
In the penultimate phase of the somersault, the skier brings the trailing ski as close as possible to the first ski

Tripod moment
As the skier flips, he or she is supported on both poles and the trailing ski, which is implanted upright in the ground

Over and out
After landing on both skis, the skier returns to the upright position and continues down the slope

Pushing off
The skier pushes back on the ski that, later in the manoeuvre, will be raised above the head first

Braced for action
Both poles are pushed into the snow together, ahead of the skis

THE ACRO SLOPE

Acro skiers perform their moves on a slope with a gradient of approximately 24 degrees. The slope must be as smooth as possible – the winter sports equivalent of a bowling green. Competitors use the whole available area, beginning their routines almost as soon as they have left the start line, and ending right at the finish.

Judges' stand
Seven judges observe from a stand alongside the middle section of the piste

Coloured edgings
A coloured line marks the edge of the skiing area

Finishing line
The skier goes through a photoelectric cell between the uprights

150m (164yd)

25m (82ft)

Warning flags
Flags give a clear indication of the extent of the performance area

Smooth piste
In complete contrast with the moguls slope, the descent is smooth, with no bumps

Starting position
Skiers begin their performance close to the start, to fit as many manoeuvres into their routine as possible

MOGUL MOVES

The highlights of each mogul run are the jumps and manoeuvres that are carried out at the two kickers. Competitors build up as much speed as possible before they get to the jumps. Most skiers attempt either a sequence of up to three individual moves, such as the back scratcher and spread eagle, or a single jump involving multiple twists.

540 DEGREE AERIAL TURN
This impressive manoeuvre consists of one-and-a-half horizontal rotations, performed in mid-air.

Touchdown
The knees are bent to absorb the impact; on landing, the skier pushes off down the slope

Revolution
After completing two-thirds of the move, the skier twists again for the final half-circle

No waving
The skis must stay together throughout the spin; the judges penalize deviations in either the horizontal or vertical plane

Takeoff
At the lip of the jump, the skier starts to spin by turning head and shoulders to the right; the rest of the body will follow

AERIAL ACTION

In aerial events, each skier has two jumps, which are scored by seven judges. Five judges score the takeoff, length, height, and form of the jump, while the other two score the landing. The total is multiplied by a degree of difficulty (DD), to give the total score.

DOUBLE FULL-FULL-FULL
This jump involves three "full" somersaults, with two horizontal twists on the first somersault and one on each of the other two. Three is the maximum number of somersaults permitted in competitive aerials.

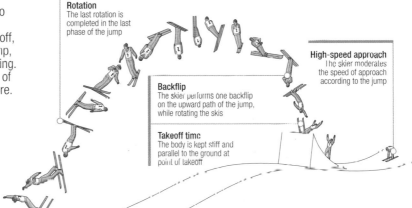

Rotation
The last rotation is completed in the last phase of the jump

High-speed approach
The skier moderates the speed of approach according to the jump

Backflip
The skier performs one backflip on the upward path of the jump, while rotating the skis

Takeoff time
The body is kept stiff and parallel to the ground at point of takeoff

Parallel lines
The skis must be kept parallel on landing, and the knees are bent to absorb the impact

STAT CENTRAL

OLYMPIC CHAMPIONS: MEN'S MOGULS

YEAR	NAME	COUNTRY
2010	GUILBAUT COLAS	(FRA)
2006	DALE BEGG-SMITH	(AUS)
2002	JANNE LAHTELA	(FIN)
1998	JONNY MOSELEY	(USA)
1994	JEAN-LUC BRASSARD	(CAN)

OLYMPIC CHAMPIONS: WOMEN'S MOGULS

YEAR	NAME	COUNTRY
2010	HANNAH KEARNEY	(USA)
2006	JENNIFER HEIL	(CAN)
2002	KARI TRAA	(NOR)
1998	TAE SATOYA	(JPN)
1994	STINE LISE HATTESTAD	(NOR)

OLYMPIC CHAMPIONS: MEN'S AERIAL

YEAR	NAME	COUNTRY
2010	ALEXEI GRISHIN	(BLR)
2006	XIAOPENG HAN	(CHN)
2002	VALENTA, ALES	(CZE)
1998	ERIC BERGOUST	(USA)
1994	ANDREAS SCHÖNBÄCHLER	(SUI)

OLYMPIC CHAMPIONS: WOMEN'S AERIAL

YEAR	NAME	COUNTRY
2010	LYDIA LASSILA	(AUS)
2006	EVELYNE LEU	(SUI)
2002	ALISA CAMPLIN	(AUS)
1998	NIKKI STONE	(USA)
1994	LINA CHERYASOVA	(UZB)

INSIDE STORY

The first freestyle skiing World Cup was held in 1981; the inaugural World Championship followed four years later. Moguls first featured in the Winter Olympics in 1992; aerials joined the Games in 1994. Acro ski is still unrecognized by the International Olympic Committee (IOC), although it was a demonstration sport at the 1988 and 1992 Olympics.

GOVERNING BODY
The Fédération Internationale de Ski (FIS) currently has 111 member nations.

NEED2KNOW

→ Snowboard Cross, in which four boarders race each other downhill through a series of obstacles, was introduced at the Turin Winter Olympics in 2006.

→ In "Big Air", riders jump off a 18m (60ft) ramp, then spin and flip for 30m (100ft).

→ Craig Kelly, the "godfather of freeriding", won four World Championships and three US Championships. He was killed in an avalanche in January 2003.

SPORT OVERVIEW

Developed in the United States in the 1960s, snowboarding combines the skills required for skiing, skateboarding, and surfing. Snowboarders race down snow slopes on a ski-like board to which their feet are attached, and perform stunts. Snowboarding has been a Winter Olympic sport since 1998.

RACING AND TRICK RIDING

Snowboarding has a variety of different elements, including downhill riding and racing, mogul techniques, tricks performed in half- and quarter-pipes, and powder riding, when boarders use a surfing technique to carve tracks through deep, loose snow. Racing, known as alpine snowboarding, uses skills similar to downhill ski racing; competitors race against the clock on a giant slalom course. Parallel giant slalom consists of two boarders racing against each other on parallel courses.

EXTREME SNOWBOARDING

Done on near-vertical (45 degrees plus) mountain slopes with cliffs, deep snow, chutes, and trees, extreme snowboarding is not for the faint-hearted. Competitions include racing and freestyle events that involve courses of up to 1,220m (1,334yd) with many natural obstacles. Entrants are judged on factors such as time and style.

RIDER PROFILE

Daring, self-confidence, and a sense of adventure are prerequisites for a snowboarder. Competitive riders need to be fit and flexible, with strong muscles. They train in a similar way to skiers. As with any snow sport, balance, coordination, and quick reactions are also vital. A flair for putting on a performance is an important quality for freestylers.

Helmet
A safety helmet to minimize head injuries is a must on the snow slopes

Sweatshirt
Lightweight, warm, and breathable, a sweatshirt makes a comfortable outer- or under-layer

Gloves
Mitts or gloves have palm and finger reinforcement and are waterproof. They are usually lined with fleece or synthetic material for warmth

Goggles
Goggles protect the eyes against snowblindness. They also prevent snow getting in the eyes, which can cause temporary vision loss, dangerous at high speeds

Upper body
Body armour is designed to protect the shoulders, elbows, and spine. Dense, high-impact foam padding is used, with neoprene for flexibility

Wrist guard
In the event of a fall, wrist guards reduce the likelihood of sprains or breaks

Lower body
Padded trousers and knee protection reduce damage from knocks and falls. Wicking material draws away sweat and keeps the wearer warm

Footwork
Control largely depends on boots and bindings

Regular or goofy?
Some riders keep the left foot leading on the board (regular), others favour the right foot (goofy). It is a matter of what feels comfortable

Stance
The feet are commonly placed a little more than shoulder-width apart. A narrower stance gives more control for turning on the piste, and a wider one is more stable for freestyle boarding

SIMON DUMONT

DUMONT SMASHED THE WORLD QUARTER-PIPE RECORD ON 11 APRIL 2008. THE 21-YEAR-OLD AMERICAN BOARDER JUMPED 10.8M (35FT 6IN), EXACTLY 1M (3FT 3IN) HIGHER THAN THE PREVIOUS RECORD.

SNOWBOARDING

HALF-PIPE

A half-pipe is a specially constructed, U-shaped, sloping, tubular arena with curved walls and a flat bottom in which snowboarders can perform acrobatic tricks. Half-pipes originated in skateboarding parks.

HOW IS IT DONE?

Snowboarders descend one wall of the U to get up speed; this enables them to ascend the opposite wall and reach the lip, from where they launch themselves into the air and perform moves and tricks. The further up the pipe they start, the more jumps they can do down the length. Half-pipe riders need excellent edge and turning control. They need to be able to go backwards (a manoeuvre called a fakie) as well.

COMPETITIONS

Most half-pipe competitions have five judges, each responsible for a different area. Scores are given for tricks such as spins and flips, technical merit, landing, and the height a rider attains in jumps.

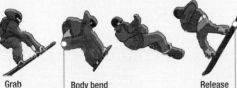

Jumps
An experienced rider can jump to a height of up to 0m (20ft 3in) above the flat floor of the half-pipe. This gives plenty of "air" to perform a series of impressive tricks

Platform or deck
A flat edge runs around the edge of the half-pipe. This oroatoo tho lip (top odgo) whoro riders jump off

Entry ramp
Snowboarders enter the half-pipe via the ramp, which helps them to get up speed beforehand

50–100m (164–328ft)

End to end
Snowboarders must travel the whole length of the pipe, from the entry ramp to the exit

13–18m (42–59ft)

Vertical (vert)
The upper section of the wall is vertical. The right-angled lip links the verts with the plaform or deck

Transition (trannie)
This is the curved area between the floor and the vertical wall (vert)

TECHNIQUES

In a half-pipe a boarder employs a variety of techniques, such as a rolling edge (ascending on one board edge and descending on the other) and making a slide turn (on the snow or ice) or jump turn (in the air) at the top of the vertical.

ALLEY OOP

This half-pipe trick involves an uphill turn through 180 degrees in the air. The rider needs to be travelling at speed to achieve enough height in the air and the board must be flat on take off.

Grab
In the air, the rider grabs the toe edge of the board to start the turn

Body bend
The body turns to the front of the board. The rider draws his knees up to his body

Release
As he approaches the half-pipe lip, he releases the grab and lands flat to ride away

INDY GRAB

To make an indy grab the rider needs plenty of "air" at the lip. He draws his knees up, using his trailing hand to grab the board between the bindings, and extends his leading arm.

Upside down
Being upside down is a way of life for a talented freestyle snowboarder. Grabs assist mid-air stability during complicated tricks

Straight leg
Once the rider has made the grab, he straightens the leading leg as far as possible

Leading arm
The leading arm provides a counterbalance

BOARDS, BOOTS, AND BINDINGS

For freestyle, the board is comparatively short and flexible with a symmetrical nose and tail; the boots are soft. For alpine events, boards are longer, narrow, and rigid, with a distinct front and back; the boots have a hard outer shell.

Snug fit
Boots should fit closely round the ankles and the rider's heels should not be able to lift

Highback
A moulded support sits behind the ankle and extends up the calf

SNOWBOARD
Snowboards have a light, strong, and flexible wood core with fibreglass lamination. The base is made of a porous plastic saturated with wax for a smooth, fast run, and is patterned to channel snow and water.

BOOTS
Freestylers use flexible boots of soft synthetic leather (as shown here). Alpine riders' boots have a rigid shell.

BINDINGS
These hold the feet on the board and do not release automatically. Bindings can be adjusted for a perfect fit.

Curve
The edges are symmetrically curved. Curves assist turning. The shorter the radius, the tighter the turn

Edges
A steel edge allows the board to "grab" the snow on turns

INSIDE STORY

The first crude snowboards were made in the 1950s by surfers and skaters who wanted to try a new sport. In 1965 Sherman Poppen bolted two skis together to make a "snurfer", a hybrid board that came somewhere between a skateboard and a toboggan. Jake Burton Carpenter started making fibreglass snowboards in 1979, and added bolted-on bindings for more control. Steel edges arrived in the 1980s, as did highback bindings. Snowboarding became a Winter Olympic sport in 1998.

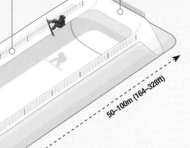

CROSS-COUNTRY SKIING

NEED2KNOW

→ Cross-country skiing has long been a favoured winter sport in northern Europe and Canada. Its popularity is growing in the USA and other countries with winter snow cover.

→ The sport is on the programmes of the Winter Olympics, the FIS World Cup, and the Nordic World Ski Championships.

→ There are 12 cross-country skiing competitions at the Winter Olympics, six for men and six for women.

SPORT OVERVIEW

Cross-country skiing is probably one of the most demanding winter sports. Competitive cross country is divided into classic and freestyle events, and races are run against the clock over distances ranging from 400m (¼ mile) sprints to 50km (31 mile) marathons or longer. In classic competitions, skiers use a "walking" stride on prepared parallel tracks cut through the snow. The faster freestyle events are run on smooth trails and require a technique similar to that used in skating.

COMPETITOR PROFILE
A cross-country skier needs aerobic fitness, muscular strength, good balance, and both physical and mental stamina. Athletes train and develop their technical skills on snow in winter, and follow an arduous regime of cycling, running, and roller skiing in summer to stay in peak condition.

UP, DOWN, AND ROUND

Cross-country circuits vary enormously, but international competition guidelines recommend that a course contains uphill, downhill, and undulating terrain in roughly equal measure. The uphill section should have a gradient of 9–18 per cent. For sprints, the difference between the lowest and highest points should not exceed 30m (98ft). For races of 15km and more, the difference should not be greater than 200m (218yd). However, Norway's Birkebeiner race involves more uphill than downhill.

THE "NANNESTAD EXPRESS"
NORWEGIAN SKIER BJORN DAEHLIE HAS WON MORE WINTER OLYMPIC MEDALS THAN ANYONE ELSE. FAMED FOR HIS SPEED, DAEHLIE WON HIS EIGHT GOLDS AND FOUR SILVERS FROM 1992 TO 1998. IN 1994 HIS RELAY TEAM MISSED GOLD BY 0.4 SECONDS – AFTER A RACE OF 40KM (25 MILES).

Head cosy
A ski hat keeps the head warm, and non-fogging eyewear reduces sun glare without impairing vision

Poles apart
Skiers carry two poles made of lightweight material such as graphite or aluminium. Classic poles (seen here) are shorter than those used in freestyle

Competition bibs
Skiers wear their start numbers on their chest and back; numbers may also appear on the leg closest to the camera at the finish line

Handcover
Cross-country gloves are lightweight, thermal, and windproof

Ski suit
A body-hugging Lycra suit allows unrestricted, streamlined movement

Ankle support
The boots used for freestyle cross-country skiing are relatively rigid and give more ankle support than classic-style boots

Fixed toe
The binding secures only the toe of the boot to the ski. The heel remains free

Slippery stuff
A variety of waxes can be applied to the underside of skis to improve either grip or speed, according to the event

"Skinny" skis
Cross-country skis are typically narrower than those used by Alpine skiers. The length is determined by the height of the individual skier

THE RIGHT GEAR

The equipment used in cross-country skiing is not interchangeable between the styles. Because of differences in technique and speeds, and also in the type of tracks used in races, classic skiers and freestyle skiers do not have the same requirements when it comes to getting on the gear.

FREESTYLE SKIS

These skis measure 1.7–2m (5ft 7in–6ft 6in) in length and are 4.5–5cm (about 2in) wide. The upward curve of the tips is not so pronounced as that of classic skis.

Hi-tech
Racing skis are made of carbon fibre and other cutting edge materials

maximum 2m (6ft 6in)

CLASSIC SKIS

Longer than freestyle skis, classic skis are designed to spread the weight of the racer more evenly. The length of skis for classic events is 1.95–2.3m (6ft 5in–7ft 6in).

Wax to win
Glide wax is used on the undersurface of the ski to reduce friction

maximum 2.3m (7ft 6in)

Ankle angles
Flexible boots allow for maximum strides

Hard case
Boots support the joints that do most work

CLASSIC BOOT

The classic boot is relatively flexible and similar to a running shoe, allowing for plenty of ankle movement.

FREESTYLE BOOT

The freestyle boot is more rigid and gives greater support to the ankle than the classic ski boot.

POLES

Freestyle ski poles should reach up to the mouth or chin. Poles used for classic cross country should come up to the armpits when the skier is standing.

TRAIL RULES

In any competition, racers are penalized if they obstruct other skiers, make a false start, or wax, scrape, or clean their skis during a race.

Competitors in non-sprint classical races may be penalized for failing to allow a faster skier to overtake them at the first request, unless they are in the marked zone at the end of the course. Skiers may also be disqualified for using non-classical techniques.

However, there is one style of race when both classical and freestyle techniques can be used legitimately. This is the double pursuit race, which consists of two courses, one requiring classical-style skiing, and the other freestyle. Between the courses the competitors must stop in order to switch over their skis and poles. Meanwhile, the clock keeps going, and the first skier across the finish line wins.

Light and strong
The graphite and Kevlar shaft tapers to the bottom

Getting a grip
A plastic web or disc, called a basket, gives more purchase and prevents the pole from plunging too deeply into the snow

GETTING ALONG

Classic skiers use several techniques, including diagonal stride, double poling, and herringbone (for climbing hills). Freestylers use these traditional techniques, but they angle their ski edges like ice skaters.

DIAGONAL STRIDE

This technique is the workhorse of classic cross country. The skis must remain parallel and in the tracks, apart from in marked areas.

Gliding off
The skier glides one leg forward. He leans his body forward and plants a pole in the snow on the same side as the leading leg

Pulling forwards
The skier pulls on the pole to move forwards

Switching sides
The pole is pulled out of the snow, and the skier pushes forward with the other leg

Gathering pace
Alternating between left ski and pole and right ski and pole, the skier gathers pace

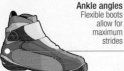

DOUBLE POLING

The skier plants both poles in the snow at the same time and gives a strong thrust to move both skis forward together.

Big push
The skier bends forward to start the push. He remains bent until the push is complete

SKATING STEPS

In this freestyle technique, the skier pushes out and forwards, driving the inner edge of the ski into the snow. The technique can be used only on firm snow, but is faster than diagonal strides.

INSIDE STORY

Cross-country skiing was probably first practised by Nordic peoples hundreds, if not thousands, of years ago. It was the most efficient way for hunting communities to move long distances in winter as they tracked herds of elk. Cross-country skiing was recognized as a sport in Norway by the 18th century. Men's cross-country skiing was included in the first Winter Olympics in 1924, but women's events did not make an appearance there until 1952.

GOVERNING BODY: FIS

The Fédération Internationale de Ski (International Ski Federation) was founded on 2 February 1924 during the first Olympic Games in Chamonix, France, with 14 member nations. Today, 111 National Ski Associations comprise the membership of FIS.

SLOPESTYLE

GAME OVERVIEW

Pioneered by snowboarders, slopestyle is an expressive and spectacular winter sport in which participants navigate a downhill course littered with obstacles such as rails and jumps while they attempt to pull off a range of tricks. Scores are awarded for staying upright for the duration of the course and for the most complex and ambitious tricks executed successfully. Slopestyle snowboarding and skiing have both been added to the official programme for the Winter Games in Sochi in 2014 (see p.39). The organizers hope the sport will attract younger spectators to the Games.

NEED2KNOW

→ The American Shaun White is probably the finest snowboarder in the history of slopestyle, with five Winter X Games gold medals in the event.

→ Canada's Kaya Turski is one of the most successful athletes in the history of slopestyle skiing – she has won four Winter X Games gold medals.

→ There is no standardized course format for slopestyle skiing and snowboarding; a unique course is designed for each event.

Helmet
Slopestyle carries a high level of risk, so protective headgear is an essential piece of equipment

Upper body
Dense foam body armour is worn to protect the arms, spine, and chest from high-impact falls

Wrists
Frequent wrist injuries mean many snowboarders wear guards

Legs
High-impact landings place stress on the knee joints of skiers and snowboarders

COMPETITOR PROFILE
Slopestyle requires the same basic attributes as other ski and snowboarding sports – strong core and leg muscles, good balance and coordination, and quick reactions. Points are awarded for more ambitious tricks, but deducted for poor execution and falls.

THE KIT

Apart from a slight adjustment to their bindings, snowboarders do not require any special equipment to participate in slopestyle events. Skiers on the other hand must use freestyle skis (also known as twin-tip skis) to cope with the demands of the sport.

FREESTYLE SKIS

The tips of freestyle skis curve up at both the back and the front, allowing the user to land or take off on the front or back of the ski. They are also more flexible than alpine or speed skis.

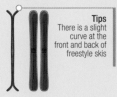

Tips
There is a slight curve at the front and back of freestyle skis

BOOTS

Slopestyle skiers use freestyle boots and position them towards the centre of the ski rather than the rear. This makes it easier to manipulate the ski in mid-air.

Comfort
The lining of freestyle boots provides increased comfort for the foot and ankle

BINDINGS

Skiers and snowboarders in slopestyle events will usually set a softer binding, allowing for greater flexibility on impact when landing a jump.

Highback
Slopestyle boarders use a binding with a soft highback and minimal forward lean

THE COURSE

The basic elements of a slopestyle course are the same for both skiers and snowboarders and consist of a downhill run containing a series of obstacles and challenges such as jumps and rails.

THE COMPETITIONS

Currently, the most high-profile slopestyle competition in the world takes place at the Winter X Games, an annual competition for winter action sports organized by the American broadcaster ESPN. The competition has taken place annually since 1997 and has been held in Aspen, Colorado, since 2002.

HOW IS IT DONE?

Contestants descend the course at speed, attempting to make the most of the obstacles. They are judged on the skill and difficulty level of their tricks, how smoothly they move from one trick to the next, and the overall impression of their run as a whole.

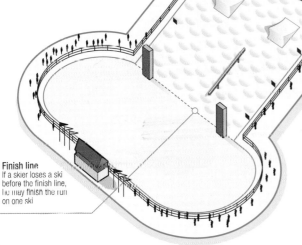

Rail
Narrow features, these can be straight or kinked to provide an extra challenge

Kicker
Simple jumps built from or covered in snow

Wall
Almost vertical sides force competitors to skim or spin on the wall at steep angles

Table
Tables come in numerous shapes, such as curved concave or convex "rainbows"

Finish line
If a skier loses a ski before the finish line, he may finish the run on one ski

SCORING

Slopestyle skiing and snowboarding are judged in the same way. Competitions normally take place over two rounds, with a panel of judges awarding contestants a score for each round. In some tournaments, the judges are allocated a specific aspect of the performance – tricks or overall impression – to mark. The resulting scores are then combined. The marks given for overall impression reflect the skill with which participants move from one trick to another and the sculpting of the overall routine. Each contestant's best score over the two rounds is then ranked against the other competitors' best scores.

TECHNIQUES

In slopestyle, a creative combination of jumps, stunts, and tricks is required to achieve a high score from the judges. Each obstacle on the course is suited to a specific type of trick: ramps are used for spins (rotating 360° in mid-air), flips (performing a front or backwards somersault in mid-air), and grabs (grabbing the skis or board while in mid-air). Rails are used for grinding, where the boarder or skier jumps in the air and slides a part of the skis or board along the rail. Most basic tricks have several more complex variations.

50-50

A 50-50 is a trick taken from skateboarding, in which a snowboarder grinds (rides) along the length of a straight or kinked rail. The rider must gather sufficient speed before attempting to mount the rail.

MUTE GRAB

The mute grab requires the skier to become airborne off a ramp before crossing the skis and grabbing hold of one. The mute grab can be varied by grabbing the ski behind the boot, rather than in front of it.

Popping
As the rider approaches the rail, he flexes his knees and pops the board into the air and onto the rail

Balancing
The boarder rides along the rail with his shoulders positioned over the centre of the board

Dismounting
As the rider leaves the rail he flexes his knees, bracing for the landing

Creating the shape
Once airborne, the skier crosses the skis to create the shape of an 'X'

Grabbing
The skier grabs the inside of the top ski in front of the boot

Preparing to land
The skis are released and straightened and the knees flexed for landing

304

NEED2KNOW

→ The average jump takes eight to twelve seconds, of which only two or three seconds are spent in flight.

→ The most successful jumpers have been from Scandinavia and Japan.

→ A proposal for women to compete in the 2010 Winter Olympics was rejected because too few female athletes from too few countries participate in the sport.

→ Jumping was the most popular skiing spectator sport until downhill skiing took over after World War II.

ATHLETE PROFILE

Ski jumpers must have nerves of steel and a head for heights. The top athletes start jumping from around the age of five, gradually building up confidence by jumping from higher hills. Once the basic skills have been honed, jumpers perfect each part of the jump by training on smaller hills. Endurance is vital, and most of the top ski jumpers include cross-training to build up cardiovascular fitness.

THE EAGLE HAS LANDED

EDDIE "THE EAGLE" EDWARDS ACHIEVED FAME AT THE 1988 WINTER OLYMPICS IN CALGARY, CANADA, FOR SKI JUMPING SO POORLY. ALTHOUGH THE BRITISH PLASTERER FINISHED LAST, SPECTATORS WARMED TO HIS PERSONALITY AND PASSION, TURNING EDWARDS INTO A MEDIA SENSATION.

SIDELINES

246.5 The distance in metres of the world record mark set by Johan Remen Evensen of Norway in 2011.

5 The number of medals won by the most successful Olympic ski jumper – Matti Nykänen of Finland, who has won 4 golds and 1 silver.

50,000 The average number of spectators that gather to watch the annual Holmenkollen ski-jumping competition in Norway.

SKI JUMPING

SPORT OVERVIEW

Ski jumping is a spectacular sport that involves skiing down a steep ramp, taking off, jumping as far as possible, and then landing smoothly without falling over. Its best practitioners hold their near-horizontal pose – and their nerve – as they soar through the air until bringing their skis down at the last second, to a cacophony of cheers and cow bells. Skiers in this popular and predominantly male winter sport compete not only for the longest distance jumped, but also for the style of their take-off, flight, and landing.

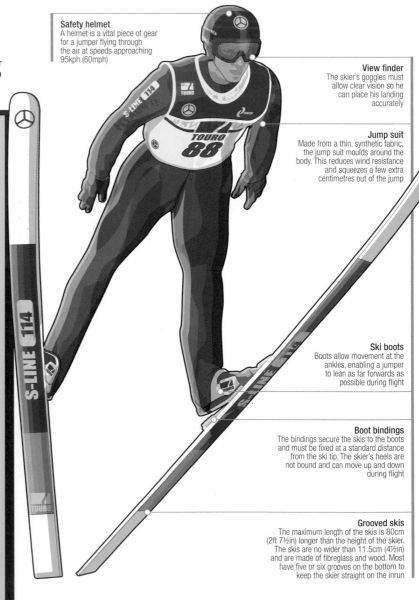

Safety helmet
A helmet is a vital piece of gear for a jumper flying through the air at speeds approaching 95kph (60mph)

View finder
The skier's goggles must allow clear vision so he can place his landing accurately

Jump suit
Made from a thin, synthetic fabric, the jump suit moulds around the body. This reduces wind resistance and squeezes a few extra centimetres out of the jump

Ski boots
Boots allow movement at the ankles, enabling a jumper to lean as far forwards as possible during flight

Boot bindings
The bindings secure the skis to the boots and must be fixed at a standard distance from the ski tip. The skier's heels are not bound and can move up and down during flight

Grooved skis
The maximum length of the skis is 80cm (2ft 7½in) longer than the height of the skier. The skis are no wider than 11.5cm (4½in) and are made of fibreglass and wood. Most have five or six grooves on the bottom to keep the skier straight on the inrun

EVENTS ON THE HILL

Competitors start from a jumping ramp on to two types of ski-jumping hill. A K90 hill measures 90m (295ft) from the take-off table to the recommended landing point, or K point. A K120 hill measures 120m (131yd). Competitions usually have two jumps in three events: an individual K90 jump, an individual K120 jump, and a team competition on the K120 hill.

FARTHER AND FARTHER

Changing techniques have enabled jumpers to fly farther and farther. At first, jumps were only about 45m (148ft). In the 1920s, jumpers flew 100m (110yd) with the Kongsberger technique – they leaned forwards, bodies bent at the hip, arms extended, and their skis parallel. In the 1950s, Swiss skier Andreas Daescher brought the arms in towards the body to squeeze out an extra few metres. In 1985, Jan Boklöv of Sweden pioneered the flying V technique (below) – the skier holds the tips of the skis apart in a V-shape, thereby gaining both extra lift and stability.

Jumping ramp
Skiers wait at the starting gate for the signal to jump, then they push off and quickly gain momentum

Accelerating down
Skiers tuck themselves into an aerodynamic crouch and accelerate down the inrun towards the take-off table

Inrun
The surface of the jumping ramp is called the inrun. It is covered with hard-packed snow during the winter or an artificial surface in summer

Take-off table
The take-off table at the end of the inrun has a gradient of 11 per cent to provide sufficient lift for the jump

Norm point
The norm point, or P point, is marked in blue and indicates where the curve of the hill ends and the steepest part of the slope begins

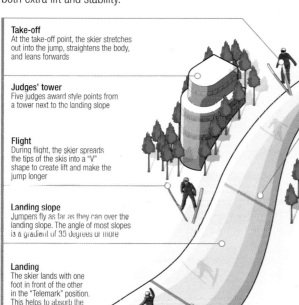

Take-off
At the take-off point, the skier stretches out into the jump, straightens the body, and leans forwards

Judges' tower
Five judges award style points from a tower next to the landing slope

Flight
During flight, the skier spreads the tips of the skis into a "V" shape to create lift and make the jump longer

Landing slope
Jumpers fly as far as they can over the landing slope. The angle of most slopes is a gradient of 35 degrees or more

Landing
The skier lands with one foot in front of the other in the "Telemark" position. This helps to absorb the shock of the landing

Outrun
The outrun provides a safe, gently sloping area in which the skier can come to a controlled stop after the jump

K point
The K point is the lower control point. Skiers use the K point as the target distance for a safe landing. Judges award extra points for jumps that exceed the K point

FOUR HILLS

THE PRESTIGIOUS FOUR HILLS TOURNAMENT, PART OF THE ANNUAL SKI JUMPING WORLD CUP, IS CONTESTED ON TWO HILLS IN AUSTRIA AND TWO IN GERMANY. JANNE AHONEN OF FINLAND IS THE ONLY SKIER TO HAVE WON THE TOURNAMENT FIVE TIMES.

SCORING

Judges score for distance and style. A skier who jumps to the K point is given 60 points. Two points per metre are added or deducted on K90 hills for longer or shorter jumps, 1.8 points for K120 hills. Five judges also award up to 20 points each for style: good body position during take-off, flight, and landing; steady skis in flight. The distance score and middle three style scores are combined to give the jump an overall score. The skier with the highest score for two jumps wins.

INSIDE STORY

Once a local event held at Norwegian winter carnivals, ski jumping has spread throughout Europe and North America to become one of the most popular events in the winter sporting calendar. Ski jumping was recognized as an official sport in 1892, when brave competitors contested the King's Cup at Holmenkollen, Norway. It remains one of the Winter Olympics' most coveted prizes.

AN OLYMPIC SPORT

Ski jumping has been an Olympic sport since the first Winter Games were held in Chamonix, France, in 1924. Although Finland tops the Olympic medal table, with ten golds, Norway has won more medals in total: 29 compared to Finland's 22.

RECORDS GALORE

During the 2005 World Cup Finals held in Planica, Slovenia, several jumpers broke the world ski jumping record of 231m (253yd), set by Finland's Matti Hautamäki. Bjoern Romaeren from Norway set the new world record with 239m (261yd), with Hautamäki achieving the second best jump of 235.5m (257yd). Another of Romaeren's jumps reached 234.5m (256yd).

NEED2KNOW

→ Nordic combined has been on the Olympic programme since the first Winter Games were held at Chamonix, France in 1924.

→ The individual event consists of two jumps from K90 and a 15km (9¼ mile) cross-country race. Competitors in the sprint make one jump from K120 and ski a 7.5km (4½ mile) cross-country race.

→ In the team event, each member of a team of four jumps twice from K90 and skis 5km (3 miles) of a 20km (12 mile) relay.

COMPETITOR PROFILE

Nordic combined athletes need courage for the jumps, and stamina and strength in cross-country races. Both disciplines are technically demanding. Competitors spend as much training time working on their technique as they do on maintaining cardiovascular fitness.

Bodysuit
Competitors wear skintight bodysuits made from thin, synthetic fabrics

Ski poles
Long, straight ski poles help the skier push hard against the snow to maintain momentum

Free heels
Bindings hold the boots to the ski at the toes, leaving the heels free to "skate" across the snow

SKI JUMPING

The jump has four main phases: inrun, take-off, flight, and landing (see also pp.304–305). The jumper approaches the take-off table with their body crouched and arms behind their back. On take-off, they straighten their body and lean forward, spreading the skis in a V-shape to create lift. At the end of the jump, they land with knees bent and one foot in front of the other, "telemark" fashion.

Start and inrun
The jumper leaves the starting gate and accelerates to about 96kph (60mph)

Take-off table
The jumper launches in to the air from the take-off table

JUMPING HILLS
There are two jumping hills, which differ only in size. The smaller hill is also known as K90 because the horizontal distance between the take-off table and the K point – the par landing point – is 90m (295ft). The take-off table of the larger hill, K120, is 120m (131yd) from the K point.

Hill height
Hills vary in height but are all daunting for novices

K point
The jumpers aim for the K point or beyond. Extra points are awarded for jumps that exceed the K point

OUTRUN

K POINT

Judging tower
A panel of five judges watches each jump and awards points from a tower next to the landing slope

Outrun
The jumper comes to a controlled stop in the outrun and braking area

JUDGING THE JUMPS

For each jump, points are given for distance achieved and overall technique. Jumps that reach the K point are worth 60 points. The score is increased for longer jumps and deducted for shorter ones. The five judges may also award between 0 and 20 for technique, and the middle three results are taken into consideration in the final score.

Skis
Cross-country skis measure up to 2m (6ft 6in) long and have curved tips. Competitors wax the skis to help them slide easily over the snow

NORDIC COMBINED

SPORT OVERVIEW

Nordic combined is a one-day winter competitive sport that combines ski jumping with cross-country skiing. Ski jumping usually takes place first, followed by cross-country. Athletes take part in individual, sprint, and team events. There are Olympic, World Cup, and World Championship Nordic combined events, and currently all these are for men only.

CROSS COUNTRY

The cross-country starting order is decided by the results of the previous days' jumping competition, with points being converted into seconds. Most competitors race using the "skating" style, sliding each leg forward with the ski angled so its inside edge drives back against the snow. Weight is transferred entirely from one ski to the other as the skier moves. In this way, they can achieve speeds of up to 30kph (16mph). The first past the post in the cross country is the overall winner.

BIATHLON

SPORT OVERVIEW

Biathlon as a winter sport combines cross-country skiing with rifle shooting. The sport has a military origin in 18th-century Scandinavia, when accurate shooting and fast skiing were vital for soldiers patrolling the long border between Norway and Sweden. There are individual, sprint, relay, pursuit, and mass-start events. All involve racing in laps around an undulating course and firing at targets in a shooting range.

THE COMPETITION

Competitors usually start at timed intervals and ski in "skating"-style against the clock, stopping to shoot at the targets. When shooting, they alternate between standing and prone (lying down) positions. Missing a target is penalized (see below). The distance of the race and number of shooting phases depends on the event.

RACE TYPES

The main event is the individual race, which is 20km (12 miles) for men and 15km (9 miles) for women, including four shooting phases. The sprint is 10km (6 miles) for men, or 7.5km (4½ miles) for women, with two shooting phases. In the relay, four biathletes each ski 7.5 or 6km (4½ or 3¾ miles), and shoot twice. The pursuit is a 12.5 or 10km (7½ or 6¼ mile) race with four shooting phases.

SHOOTING RANGE

The shooting range is positioned near the start/finish line. A typical range consists of up to 30 lanes, numbered from right to left. There may be two distinct areas: left for standing shooting, right for prone shooting.

Standing up
The second and last shooting stages of the individual event are shot from a standing position

On the mat
Nonslip mats give a secure footing. For standing shots, both skis must stay on the mat

Wind flags
Rows of flags help biathletes assess the speed and direction of the wind

2.5–3m (8–10ft)

50m (164ft)

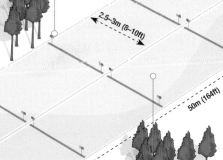

Target area
Each target has five plates fixed in a straight row

Bank or backstop
The targets are usually placed on a bank or slope to minimize any danger from stray bullets

Lying down
In the individual competition, the first and third shooting stages are shot from a prone position

Posture
When prone, the biathlete may lean on their elbows, but their wrists must not touch the ground

Downrange
The area that is in front of the firing line

OFF TARGET

Before they start to shoot, competitors must come to a complete stop and drop both ski poles. They may slow down just before the shooting phase to bring their heart-rate down, which helps achieve accuracy. Penalties are awarded for missing a target. In the individual event, there is a time penalty of one minute for each target missed. In other events, competitors must ski a 150m (164yd) penalty loop for every target missed. For elite athletes, this typically adds up to about 30 seconds on the overall race time.

NEED2KNOW

→ Biathlon became an Olympic event for men in 1960, and for women in 1992. There are also World Championships, first held in Austria in 1958, and a World Cup.

→ Skis must be at least 4cm (2½in) shorter than the height of the skier, while the length of the poles must not exceed the biathlete's height.

→ In the summer biathlon, skiing is replaced with cross-country running.

TARGETS
The black targets, which work electronically or mechanically, turn white when hit. They are very small, being 11.5cm (4½in) wide for standing shooting and 4.5cm (1¾in) wide for prone shooting.

STANDING TARGETS   **PRONE TARGETS**

COMPETITOR PROFILE

Two main features of a biathlete are excellent marksmanship and a high degree of cardiovascular fitness. They must also have good concentration to be able to swap from the fast effort of skiing to the calm focused work of shooting.

SHOOTING GEAR

Competitors carry 3.5kg (7lb 8oz) small-bore rifles on their backs. These fire .22 (5.6mm) ammunition and are loaded manually or have a five-bullet magazine.

NEED2KNOW

→ The name bobsled comes from early racers bobbing their heads to try to increase their speed at the start.

→ Four-man bobsleds can reach speeds of up to 160kph (100mph).

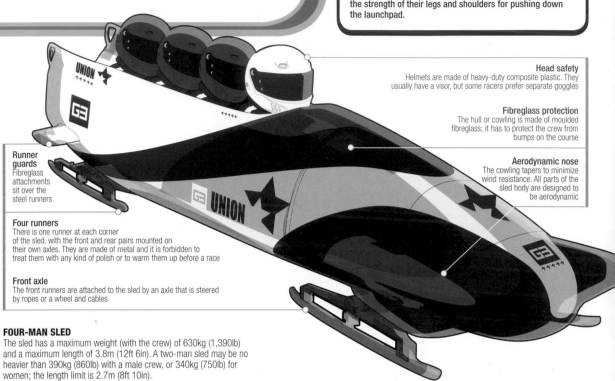

Head safety
Helmets are made of heavy-duty composite plastic. They usually have a visor, but some racers prefer separate goggles

Fibreglass protection
The hull or cowling is made of moulded fibreglass; it has to protect the crew from bumps on the course

Aerodynamic nose
The cowling tapers to minimize wind resistance. All parts of the sled body are designed to be aerodynamic

Runner guards
Fibreglass attachments sit over the steel runners

Four runners
There is one runner at each corner of the sled, with the front and rear pairs mounted on their own axles. They are made of metal and it is forbidden to treat them with any kind of polish or to warm them up before a race

Front axle
The front runners are attached to the sled by an axle that is steered by ropes or a wheel and cables

FOUR-MAN SLED
The sled has a maximum weight (with the crew) of 630kg (1,390lb) and a maximum length of 3.8m (12ft 6in). A two-man sled may be no heavier than 390kg (860lb) with a male crew, or 340kg (750lb) for women; the length limit is 2.7m (8ft 10in).

BOBSLEDDING

SPORT OVERVIEW

Bobsledding (or bobsleighing) is one of the fastest winter sports. Teams of two men or women or four men make timed runs down steep, twisting ice tracks in steerable sleds. After a push-off by the whole team, it is the driver's responsibility to steer the best line to complete the course in the fastest time over a number of runs.

The sport is not for the faint-hearted: crews regularly undergo up to five times the force of gravity on the banked curves. Bobsled crashes are spectacular and potentially dangerous. The shell of the sled protects the crew, who wear compulsory safety helmets and one-piece suits.

SIDELINES

6 The number of Winter Olympics competed in by bobsledder Carl-Erik Eriksson of Sweden between 1964 and 1984 – the first athlete to do so. Gerda Weissensteiner of Italy also featured in six Winter Oympics, competing twice in the bobsleigh and four times in the luge.

48 The age in years of Jay O'Brien when he became the oldest-ever winner in the four-man event, taking gold for the United States in the 1932 Winter Olympics at Lake Placid.

30,000 The approximate minimum cost in US dollars of a four-man Olympic-quality bobsled.

30 The number of Olympic bobsledding medals won by Switzerland between 1932 and 2010 (nine gold, ten silver, eleven bronze) – more than any other country.

5 The G force to which bobsledding crews may be subjected for up to two seconds as their sled corners a bend at speed.

THE COURSE

Bobsled runs are made of U-shaped concrete half-pipes covered with artificial ice. They are at least 1,200–1,300m (1,300–1,400yd) long and should have at least 15 curves. At the Winter Olympics the refrigerated track is shared with competitions for luge and skeleton. The angle of descent is 8–15 per cent.

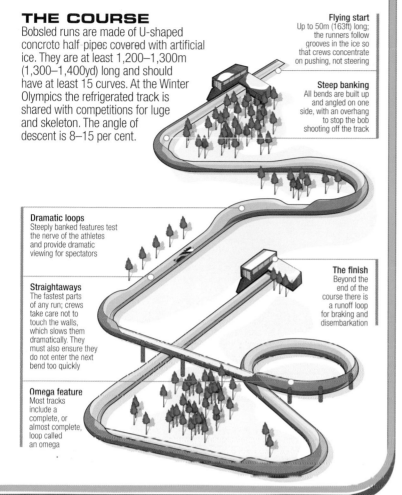

Flying start
Up to 50m (163ft) long; the runners follow grooves in the ice so that crews concentrate on pushing, not steering

Steep banking
All bends are built up and angled on one side, with an overhang to stop the bob shooting off the track

Dramatic loops
Steeply banked features test the nerve of the athletes and provide dramatic viewing for spectators

Straightaways
The fastest parts of any run; crews take care not to touch the walls, which slows them dramatically. They must also ensure they do not enter the next bend too quickly

Omega feature
Most tracks include a complete, or almost complete, loop called an omega

The finish
Beyond the end of the course there is a runoff loop for braking and disembarkation

TRACK TALK

A seeding system decides the order of racing. Teams that have performed better in the previous competitions get the advantage of racing early in the first round, before the track is cut up by other sleds. In the second round, the order is reversed: the team with the best first descent has the last run. The race is timed from the start line until the nose of the sled breaks a light beam at the finish. Weights can be added to bring the sled up to the combined weight for sled and crew. There is also a minumum combined weight of sled and crew.

SERIES OF RUNS

In Olympic and World two-man events, each crew makes four runs down the course over two days; women also make four runs over two days. Other major competitions are held over two runs. Olympic and World four-man events have four heats over two days.

CHILLED OUT

IT HAS LONG BEEN TAKEN FOR GRANTED THAT BOBSLEDDING IS BEST DONE BY COUNTRIES WITH SNOW AND MOUNTAINS. THE 1988 WINTER OLYMPICS IN CALGARY, CANADA, CHANGED THE GAME BY INCLUDING TEAMS FROM "HOT" COUNTRIES INCLUDING AUSTRALIA, MEXICO, AND, MOST NOTABLY, JAMAICA. THE WEST INDIAN TEAM'S STORY WAS MADE INTO A 1993 MOVIE CALLED *COOL RUNNINGS* STARRING JOHN CANDY.

PUSHING OFF

A fast start is key, so bobsleigh athletes all wear specially designed spiked shoes to provide traction on ice. Every crew member helps push the pod using retractable handles. The driver jumps on first, followed in a four-man crew by the two middlemen; the brakeman always gets in last. Top crews aim to complete the push-off in about five seconds.

Brakeman
Watches the course ahead and controls the speed of the bob

Driver
Responsible for steering the best line

ROCK AND SLIDE
After taking up their positions, the team members rock the sled and then push off down the launch pad.

Last in
If any member of the crew fails to get on board, the team is disqualified

FINAL PUSH
The brakeman jumps in after the driver and other members of the crew are in position; he or she must climb on board within 50m (163ft).

Full speed ahead
The driver has a perfect view of the course

ALL ABOARD
The driver steers the sled; the brakeman slows it after the finish line by moving a rear-mounted handle that lowers a line of metal teeth into the ice.

INSIDE STORY

Bobsledding was invented in the late 19th century, when Swiss tobogganers added a steering mechanism to a sled and gained control of direction. The first bobsled club was founded in Switzerland in 1897. For its first decades, the sport was largely a diversion enjoyed by the rich upper class who raced at Europe's leading alpine resorts. It took on a more competitive form in the 1950s and 1960s. The Olympics and World Championships were the leading bobsledding competitions until the mid-1980s, when the World Cup was introduced. This is a very demanding competition, in which teams race throughout the season on a variety of tracks in different countries.

GOVERNING BODY
Fédération Internationale de Bobsleigh et de Tobogganing (FIBT) was founded in 1923, a year before four-man sledding became an Olympic sport. The first two-man medal events were held in 1932. Bobsledding for women made its debut at the 2002 Games in Salt Lake City, USA.

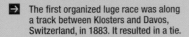

→ The International Luge Federation (FIL), based in Germany, is responsible for the sport worldwide.

→ The first organized luge race was along a track between Klosters and Davos, Switzerland, in 1883. It resulted in a tie.

→ Germany has had more Olympic luge champions than any other country. Georg Hackl won gold in three successive tournaments: 1992, 1994, and 1998. He also won the World Championships in 1989, 1990, and 1997.

ATHLETE PROFILE
Luge racers are physically sturdy and need to withstand G forces and great stresses, particularly on their neck, abdomen, chest, and feet. They are psychologically tough, and have sharp reflexes that enable them to control the runners of their luge.

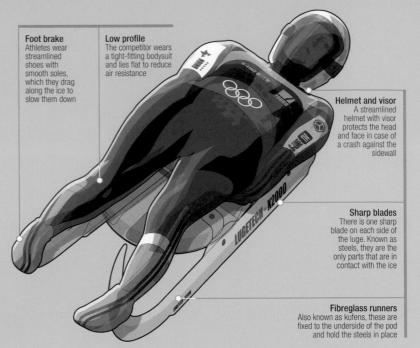

Foot brake
Athletes wear streamlined shoes with smooth soles, which they drag along the ice to slow them down

Low profile
The competitor wears a tight-fitting bodysuit and lies flat to reduce air resistance

Helmet and visor
A streamlined helmet with visor protects the head and face in case of a crash against the sidewall

Sharp blades
There is one sharp blade on each side of the luge. Known as steels, they are the only parts that are in contact with the ice

Fibreglass runners
Also known as kufens, these are fixed to the underside of the pod and hold the steels in place

A MEGA-SLIDE
Luge tracks are mostly artificial with a 2.5cm (1in) thick covering of ice. They measure between 1,000m (1,100yds) and 1,300m (1,420yds) for men's singles and between 800m (875yds) and 1,050m (1,150yds) for women's and doubles events. The tracks feature left and right turns, S-curves, 180-degree bends, and hairpins. Typically, the average gradient over this distance may be eight per cent. Sidewalls, which are also covered with a thin coating of ice, keep the luges on course as they bank around corners at hair-raising speeds. Popular in some countries in Central Europe and North America, natural tracks are created during winter on winding roads covered with ice. They have no sidewalls or artificial banks.

LUGE

SPORT OVERVIEW
Luge athletes contest the fastest sport on ice as, lying feet first on their back on a fibreglass sled, they twist and turn down a track at breathtaking speeds of more than 135kph (85mph). In races against the clock, men compete in singles and doubles and women in singles. These events are held in competitions such as the World Championships and the Winter Olympics.

Start houses
Men's singles races begin at the upper start house, while doubles and women's races begin at the lower start house

Finish cells
A luge run triggers photo cells at the start and finish and is timed to the nearest millisecond

Labyrinth
Fast bends in quick succession form a labyrinth. The force acting on a luge racer around a bend may be four times the force of gravity

Straight
Courses also have straight sections

Omega
The course must have a 180-degree bend, called an omega

FIBREGLASS POD
The luge, which is French for sled, is a fibreglass pod of variable length attached to two runners on steel blades. The luge in singles events weighs no more than 23kg (51lb); the doubles' luge is longer and cannot exceed 27kg (60lb).

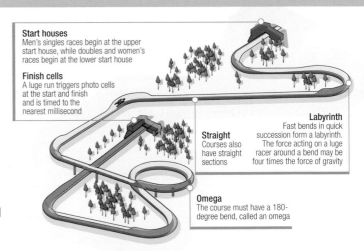

Moulded pod
The length of a singles' luge is 1.45m (4ft 9in) on average

Steering bows
The athlete places his or her legs outside the steering bows

MOVING AND STEERING
To start a run, the racer sits on the luge and slides back and forth while holding on to handles either side of the track. After a powerful push, the racer paddles the ice with spiked gloves and then lies back and steers by either applying leg pressure to the steering bows or by shifting the body weight with a movement of the head or shoulders. The race winner is usually the fastest over four (singles) or two (doubles) runs.

SPORT OVERVIEW

Although the top speeds achieved by skeleton racers are slightly slower than luge competitors, in some ways the sport requires even more courage, because athletes travel headfirst. Skeleton events for men and women are held at World Championships and at the Winter Olympics.

SKELETON

NEED2KNOW

→ The first competitive skeleton race was organized between the Swiss towns of St Moritz and Celerina in 1884. The winner received a bottle of champagne.

→ Olympic skeleton events – men's singles and women's singles – are timed to 0.01 seconds. There are four runs over two days, and the fastest aggregate time wins.

→ The Fédération Internationale de Bobsleigh et de Tobogganing (FIBT) is the governing body for skeleton. It organizes the World Skeleton Championship.

FAST AND STEEP

Skeleton events are run on the same tracks as bobsleigh competitions. Male and female athletes compete on the same course and over the same distance. The track is fast and steep – it must be at least 1,200m (1,312yd) long, with total vertical drops that average around 116m (127yd).

SPEED SADDLE

The athlete lies on the steel frame and saddle, and the sled moves along on runners. The base-plate is made of fibreglass or steel, and the runners are steel. The skeleton weighs a maximum of 43kg (95lb) for men and 35kg (77lb) for women.

ATHLETE PROFILE
Razor-sharp reflexes are essential for a skeleton racer. Since the push phase is so important, competitors need strong legs and ability to sprint. They also need a strong responsive body core that shifts their weight from one side to the other while steering the skeleton.

Weight restriction
The combined weight of the skeleton and athlete must not exceed 115kg (254lb) for men and 92kg (203lb) for women, or the maximum weight of the sled has to be reduced

Head protection
A helmet and visor are compulsory

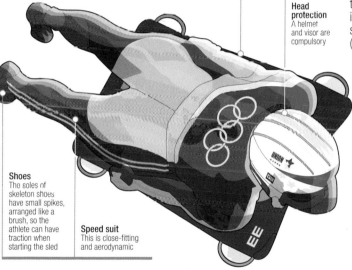

Shoes
The soles of skeleton shoes have small spikes, arranged like a brush, so the athlete can have traction when starting the sled

Speed suit
This is close-fitting and aerodynamic

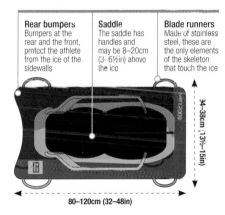

Rear bumpers
Bumpers at the rear and the front, protect the athlete from the ice of the sidewalls

Saddle
The saddle has handles and may be 8–20cm (3–6½in) above the ice

Blade runners
Made of stainless steel, these are the only elements of the skeleton that touch the ice

34–38cm (13½–15in)

80–120cm (32–48in)

GETTING A WINNING START

To stand any chance of a fast time, the athlete needs a quick running start. This is called the push phase and is typically 25–40m (82–131ft) long.

Crouch and run
The athlete crouches down and prepares to push and run

RUN!
At the start, the competitor runs as fast as he or she can, holding the handles and pushing the skeleton along the ice.

RACING RULES

There are two key skeleton rules. First, athletes cannot warm the runners of their sled to make them run faster. At the start of the race the runners must be within 4°C of the reference runner, which is exposed to the air for an hour beforehand. Second, the contestant must cross the finish line on the skeleton for the run to be valid.

Body control
Tremendous arm strength is needed to control the transition from take off on the ice to landing on the skeleton

JUMP!
The athlete leaps up from the track and forwards on to the skeleton. If this move is not carried out precisely, he or she will probably lose control of the sled.

Streamlined position
Arms are tucked in close to the body to reduce wind resistance

FLOP!
The racer lands headfirst and belly down on the skeleton with the arms pulled in tightly against the side of the body for the most aerodynamic profile.

NEED2KNOW

→ Skaters can achieve speeds of 65kph (40mph) on the long track. On the short track, the top speed is around 50kph (30mph).

→ Long-track skating is particularly popular in Scandinavia, Eastern Europe, the Netherlands, the United States, Canada, and Japan.

→ Short-track skating is a newer sport. It has attracted many competitors from traditional non-skating nations, such as South Korea and Australia.

SPEED SKATING

SPORT OVERVIEW

Speed skating is a spectacular sport in which male or female athletes race on skates around an oval ice track, alternating between powerful, rhythmic gliding on straights and demanding cornering around the bends. On the long track, skaters race in pairs over various distances – from 500m to 10km – against the clock. Short-track events involve up to six skaters racing on a circuit with no lane markings, and crashes are common. There is also a short-track relay event for teams of four.

COMPETITOR PROFILE

Speed skaters are powerful and agile, with explosive power at the start. Short-track skating is technically demanding, and requires courage as skaters hurtle around tight curves at high speed. Aerobic endurance is more important on long-track skating.

Bodysuit
The long-track skater wears a skin-tight bodysuit, with a hood and loops for the thumbs to minimize drag

Leg power
Skaters develop strength in their legs, particularly the thighs, by running, heavy weight sessions, and endless circuits of the skating rink

Skates
These are attached to ankle-high boots

WHEN GOD SMILES DOWN

STEPHEN BRADBURY BECAME AUSTRALIA'S (AND THE ENTIRE SOUTHERN HEMISPHERE'S) FIRST WINTER OLYMPIC CHAMPION IN THE 1,000M SHORT TRACK AT THE 2002 GAMES IN SALT LAKE CITY. TRAILING NEAR THE END OF THE FINAL, HE WATCHED THE OTHER FOUR COMPETITORS CRASH OUT IN FRONT OF HIM AND SAILED PAST TO CLAIM GOLD. "GOD SMILES ON YOU SOME DAYS", HE NOTED.

THE RINKS

The long-track rink is a 400m (437yd) oval; short-track courses are 111.12m (121½yd) long. Long-track lanes are marked with painted lines and movable blocks of rubber or wood. The blocks are 50cm (1ft 8in) apart for the first and last 15m (49ft) of the track, and 1m (3ft 3in) apart elsewhere.

LONG TRACK

There are two racing lanes on the long track. Skaters switch between the lanes every lap. Depending on the event, competitors start from different parts of the circuit.

Starting lines
Different events have different starting points: (left to right) 3,000/5,000m; 1,000m; 1,500m

Straightaway
A long track has two fast straightaways

Finish line
For all but the 1,000m

Crossing straight
Every lap, the skaters change lanes in the crossing straight so that they both cover the same distance during the race

Finish line
For 1,000m races

Warm-up lane
Skaters prepare for the race in the inside "warm-up" lane. During an event, the referee controls the race from this lane

500m start
This short event begins here

Blocks
A skater can touch the blocks marking the lanes but must not obstruct his or her opponent or alter the course

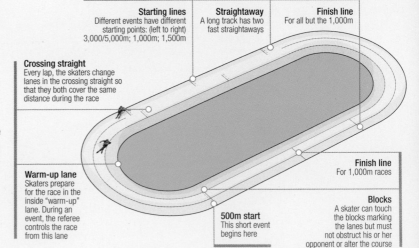

ALL ROUNDERS
The "all-round" is the name given to a combination of long-track races held over 500m, 1,500m, 3,000m, and 10,000m. The times for each race are converted into points using a set scale. The skater with the fewest points wins the overall competition. Although the "all-round" is popular, it has been included in the Olympics only once (in the men's games in 1924) because skaters tend to specialize at particular distances.

GEARED FOR SPEED
On the short track, skaters' skin-tight bodysuits are lined with Kevlar – also used in bullet-proof vests – for protection from slashing blades. Skaters also wear helmets and guards on their neck, shins, and knees. Gloves with coated fingertips are also essential, where skaters place their hands on the ice to stay upright in rapid turns. The profile of the bottom of a speed skate's blade is flat, unlike the concave shape of a figure skating blade.

SKATE DIFFERENCES
The blade of the short-track skate is long and thin. It is positioned diagonally across the sole, and curves to help with cornering. On the long track, skaters wear clap skates. The long, straight blade is centred on the sole and hinged at the toe.

Clap skate hinge
The blade of the clap skate detaches from the heel at the end of each stride. This increases the time the blade is in contact with the ice

42cm (17in)

SKATING THE RULES
Skaters can touch the blocks marking the turns, but may not skate inside them. Physical contact is part and parcel of the short track, but on the long track, interfering with an opponent or skating out of lane leads to disqualification.

TRACK TECHNIQUES
Short-track skaters use small running steps to gain speed at the start. In the basic body position on the straight, the short-track skater leans the body forward, bends the knees, and swings the arms to maintain momentum. Approaching a corner, the skater crouches very low and leans in to the turn, often touching the ice with the inside hand. Crossover steps make cornering easier.

On the long track, skaters make long, gliding strokes on the straightaway, and keep one arm behind their backs to reduce drag. Crossover steps are used to negotiate corners.

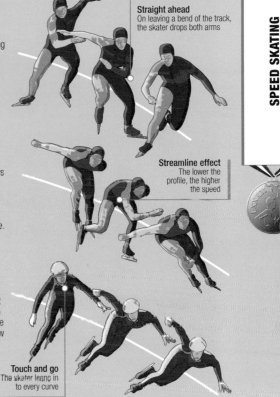

BALANCING ACT
This sequence shows how a skater who is negotiating a bend compensates for having one foot off the ice by extending the arms onto the same side of the body.

Straight ahead
On leaving a bend of the track, the skater drops both arms

IN FULL CRY
When accelerating down the straightaways of a long track, the skater bends and crouches to lower the centre of gravity and reduce wind resistance.

Streamline effect
The lower the profile, the higher the speed

PASSING CONTACT
The corners on the short track are so tight that the hand closer to the inside of the course may come down so low that it scrapes the ice: no penalty is incurred for this, it is just a touching moment.

Touch and go
The skater leans in to every curve

SHORT TRACK
The short track is usually set up on an ice rink. The track has no lanes, and skaters jostle for position on the 111.12m circuit.

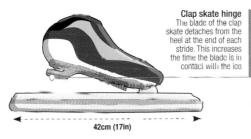

Blocks
Rubber, wood, or plastic blocks mark the shape of the track at each end of the oval

Start
For 500 and 1,500m events

26.7m (29¼yd)

radius 8m (8¾yd)

28.85m (31½yd)

Start and finish line
The 1,000m, 3,000m, and 5,000m races start here; all races

LAP COUNT
The number of laps per event is as follows:
500M – 4½ laps   **1,000M** – 9 laps
1,500M – 13½ laps   **3,000M** – 27 laps
5,000M – 45 laps

INSIDE STORY
Competitive speed skating began on frozen canals and lakes in 19th-century Europe. The International Skating Union (ISU), founded in 1892, formalized the rules. Short-track skating began in North America in the early 20th century.

INTERNATIONAL SKATING UNION (ISU)
The ISU was founded in 1892 in the Netherlands and is the oldest governing body of any winter sport. The ISU was originally a federation of 15 European countries until Canada joined in 1894.

NEED2KNOW

→ Figure skating is popular worldwide, but particularly in North America, Europe, and the former Soviet states.

→ Figure skating competitions are contested between individual male and female skaters and mixed pairs. There is also a competition for synchronized skating and ice dance.

→ Many of the outstanding moves in skating are named after the skaters who first made them famous. For example, the Axel jump is named after Norwegian skater Axel Paulsen, who first performed it in 1882.

COMPETITOR PROFILE
Top figure skaters must have the flexibility of a gymnast, the poise of a dancer, and the balance of a speed skater to perform breathtaking combinations of spins, leaps, lifts, and spirals. Hours of meticulous drilling and training are necessary to perfect these incredible skills. Perhaps even more so than gymnasts, figure skaters need finely honed positional sense so that they know exactly where they are at any given moment in the air or on the ice.

Costume decoration
Nondetachable decoration can be worn, and outfits can reflect the style of the music

Competition clothing
Outfits allow free movement, but competitors must be modestly dressed

Ankle bracing
Skating boots are custom-made for each foot. Extra support is added to brace the ankles and the interior is reinforced with stiff leather

Technical specialists
The technical specialist and assistant technical specialist determine which elements the skater has – or hasn't – performed

Judges
A panel of 12 judges marks the skaters on technical ability and performance

Referee
A referee sits with the panel of judges to oversee all elements of a competition

Spin speed
A skater can speed up or slow down her spin by moving her free leg inwards (accelerate) or outwards (decelerate)

GET YER SKATES ON
The structure of the boot gives the skater support and control, but allows enough flexibility to perform the moves. The blade is 4mm (1/8in) thick and has two edges, inner and outer, and a serrated toe pick on the tip.

Wide tongue
A wide, padded tongue aids a skater's stability and increases their flexibility

FIGURE SKATING

SPORT OVERVIEW
Both technical and beautiful, figure skating is a whirl of leaps, spins, and spirals. Single skaters or pairs of skaters perform prescribed movements on the ice in front of a panel of judges, who give them marks for technical ability and artistic interpretation. Figure skaters compete in a short programme of required elements that tests their technical skills, and an original free skate programme that permits them to demonstrate artistic expression. Figure skating became an official sport of the Olympic Winter Games in 1924.

BARBARA ANN SCOTT
IN 1942, CANADIAN BARBARA ANN SCOTT BECAME THE FIRST FEMALE SKATER TO LAND A DOUBLE LUTZ IN COMPETITION. SHE WAS ONLY 13 AT THE TIME.

THE ICE RINK

The temperature of the ice is an important factor: it is maintained at -5.5ºC (22ºF), which is 3.5ºC (6ºF) warmer than an ice hockey rink. Colder ice is harder and slower, whereas warmer ice is faster and offers more glide and softer landings. At major competitions, such as the Winter Olympics and ISU championships, referees, judges, and other officials sit outside the rink. At lower levels, officials often sit on the ice.

Covering the ice
A skater's routine must cover the entire surface of the ice. Marks are deducted if the full area is not used or if competitors perform the majority of their routine in front of the judges' bench

Surface area
The ice rink has a surface area of up to 1,800m sq (19,375ft sq) and contains as much as 54m cu (1,907ft cu) of ice

Entrance and exit
Skaters enter and leave the ice through gaps in the rink wall

26–30m (85–98ft 6in)

56–60m (183ft 6in–197ft)

Surface depth
The ice measures 2 to 3cm (1–1½in) in depth

SKATING ON THIN ICE

Figure skaters perform two programmes – short and free skate – and need to fulfil certain elements in each. Eight prescribed elements are required for the technical short programme, which can include a double Axel jump, flying sit spin, combinations of double and triple jumps, and, for pairs, spirals and throws. The second part of the competition, the free skate programme, requires a balance of elements that cover the full rink area, including jumps, spins, spirals, and step sequences. Pairs are required to perform moves simultaneously, either in parallel or symmetrically. For maximum marks, skaters must link the elements together with difficult connecting steps in different holds and positions.

SCORING

The ISU Judging System was introduced in 2004 after a scandal hit the headlines during the 2002 Winter Olympics in Salt Lake City, Utah. The judging of the figure skating competition was alleged to have been not entirely objective. In the new system, the judges' individual marks are not revealed

ISU JUDGING SYSTEM

Every element is given a scale of value that determines how many points it is worth; a grade of execution from –3 to +3 is then applied to that value, depending on how well the element is performed. In major competitions, the marks of only seven judges determine a skater's final score. Nine judges from the panel of 12 are selected at random by a computer. The highest and the lowest marks are then deleted and the scores of the remaining seven judges are averaged to leave the "trimmed mean", which is added to the base value for the final score.

TECH TALK

Knowing what commentators are talking about helps to understand the intricacies of a skating routine and the sheer physical skill of the skaters on the ice:

TOE JUMP When the skater uses the toe pick of the blade to launch themselves into the air in, for example, a flip, Lutz, or toe loop.
EDGE JUMP When the skater uses a particular edge of the blade of one boot to take off, for example, in Axel, loop, and Salchow jumps.
SPIN A move in which the skater pirouettes on the spot on the ice. In combination spins, the skater changes foot and position while maintaining the speed of the spin.
LIFT A technique of pairs skating in which the man lifts his partner, often overhead, and sometimes throws her in the air.
FOOTWORK Step sequences that move the skater across the ice to link set moves while showing off their skills.

SIDELINES

60 The temperature in ºC of the water that is sprayed on the ice rink by a machine called a Zamboni to create a smooth surface. The hot water melts the top rough layer of ice to create a smooth new layer.

11 The number of Olympic golds won by Soviet and Russian pairs skaters since 1908.

160,000 The fine in US dollars disgraced American figure skater Tonya Harding paid in March 1994 for her involvement in an attack on fellow American figure skater Nancy Kerrigan at a practice session for the US Figure Skating Championships. Harding won the competition while Kerrigan withdrew due to the injury. Harding was later stripped of her title.

2 The number of gold medals awarded in the 2002 Winter Olympics pairs figure skating competition. A judging scandal resulted in both the Russian and Canadian pairs winning gold.

PERFORMING PERFECTION

Perfect execution of the technical elements in the skating programmes ensure high scores. Not only do the elements have to be performed flawlessly, they also have to be performed at speed, in complex flowing combinations, and, in the free skate programmes, with individual artistic expression.

SYNCHRONIZED SKATING

A skating spectacular, synchronized skating involves teams of 16 skaters (usually all women, although mixed teams are allowed) performing as single, coordinated units. Skaters need flawless skills in speed and footwork, as well as in jumps, turns, and lifts. In competition, teams perform a technical short programme, including lines, circles, and other complex formations, and a creative free programme, allowing competitors freedom of expression.

JUMPS

For the spectator, dazzling jump sequences are the mark of a great skater. At the top level of competition men perform triple or quadruple rotation jumps, while women perform triples. Jumps can be driven from the toe or the edge of the blade and performed singly or in combinations.

Backward landing
The skater lands backwards on his right foot after rotating through the air

Axel jump
The skater takes off forwards from the front outside edge of the blade on his left foot

SPINS

Speed and control are the keys to successful, point-winning spins. The speed of the spin dictates the number of rotations the skater performs (the more the better). The ability to spin on one spot shows mastery of the technique, while looking effortless shows total control throughout the spin.

Spinning splits
The skater raises his right leg behind him as he spins

Biellmann spin
The skater arches his back and catches his right foot by the blade

SPIRALS

Spirals are flamboyant and rather dangerous looking moves performed by pairs in both the short and free skate programmes. At least one full revolution must be made.

Inside, outside
The death spiral can be performed backward outside or backward inside. This means that the pair skate on the rear outside or rear inside edge of the blade

Flat out
The man holds his partner with the same arm as his skating foot and spins her round as she leans back towards the ice, aiming to bring her back parallel and her head as close to the ice as possible

Death spiral
The man is the pivot of the spiral

Perfect harmony
The pair must work in complete synchronicity

INSIDE STORY

Figure skating competitions have been held since the 1880s and the first World Championship, for men, was held in 1896. The women's first World Championship was held in 1906. The event first appeared at the Summer Olympics in 1908, but has since become the longest standing Winter Olympic sport.

INTERNATIONAL SKATING UNION (ISU)

The ISU was founded in 1892 in the Netherlands and is the oldest governing body of any winter sport. It was originally a federation of 15 European countries until Canada joined in 1894, and today it has 57 member countries. During its history, the ISU has seen all its disciplines become official Winter Olympic sports.

ICE DANCING

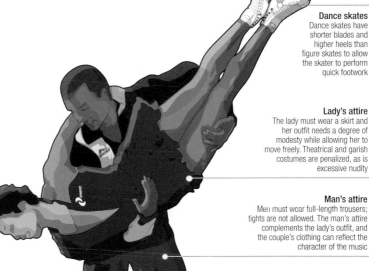

Dance skates
Dance skates have shorter blades and higher heels than figure skates to allow the skater to perform quick footwork

Lady's attire
The lady must wear a skirt and her outfit needs a degree of modesty while allowing her to move freely. Theatrical and garish costumes are penalized, as is excessive nudity

Man's attire
Men must wear full-length trousers; tights are not allowed. The man's attire complements the lady's outfit, and the couple's clothing can reflect the character of the music

NEED2KNOW

→ Couples skate the compulsory and original dances in traditional closed dance holds, such as the Kilian, waltz, or foxtrot positions, for the majority of the routine. In the free dance, holds are much more open and couples are therefore encouraged to be creative.

→ Ice dancing is popular in Europe and has strong roots in the UK. In more recent years the sport has been dominated by former Soviet-bloc countries.

→ The first Olympic ice dance champions were Ludmilla Pakhomova and Alexander Gorshkov of Russia, in 1976.

SPORT OVERVIEW

Ice dancing is a couples' event with three phases of competition at the highest level – the compulsory dance, the original dance, and the free dance – and is often likened to ballroom dancing on ice. The free dance allows couples to show off their creativity. Ice dancing is sometimes competed as a group event with two competing couples on the ice together. The first world championships were held in 1952, but ice dancing did not become a Winter Olympic sport until 1976, at Innsbruck in Austria.

TORVILL AND DEAN

GREAT BRITAIN'S JAYNE TORVILL AND CHRISTOPHER DEAN BECAME HOUSEHOLD NAMES AT THE 1984 WINTER OLYMPICS, WOWING JUDGES TO BECOME THE HIGHEST-SCORING ICE DANCERS OF ALL TIME. THEY SCORED 12 PERFECT SIXES FOR THEIR PERFORMANCE.

RULES OF ENGAGEMENT

In ice dance competitions, couples must stay close together on the ice, keeping a constant distance between them. The man must lead and the lady must follow. They are judged on how well they perform set moves as a unit and how well they interpret the music in each dance. Points are awarded for the level of difficulty of an element and the quality of its execution. Points are deducted for illegal moves or elements, or wrong interpretation and expression of the musical rhythm.

COMPETITION

Ice dancing is contested in three phases. The compulsory dance is chosen by the ISU and couples are required to skate prescribed patterns to set musical rhythms and tempos. For the original dance, the couple use their own choreography, including some required elements, and music, but the dance rhythm is selected by the ISU and the couple must dance to the strong beat rather than the weak (less obvious) beat. The free dance allows couples to choose their own music and choreography, although they must include some required elements, and express their artistic skills through their interpretation of the music. Originality is rewarded by the judges. The free dance lasts for four minutes, plus or minus ten seconds.

BALANCING ACT

The main technique ice dancers need to learn is balance. This is especially important for the man, whose job it is to lift the woman. A close second is endurance, because ice dancers need to skate at speeds comparable to those of speed skaters. Coordination is key, because delivering perfect footwork in a ballroom clinch is no mean feat.

DANCING BY NUMBERS

Ice dancers use patterns and step charts to learn and perfect a dance before performing it in competition. The pattern of the Westminster Waltz is shown here as a diagram, with the numbers indicating different step sequences. The rink is divided into quarters by long and short axes; the curved line – the passage of the dance – is the continuous axis, which must not cross the long axis.

The Westminster Waltz is characterized by stateliness, elegance, and dignity, and the couple tries to convey this to the judges as they perform two sequences.

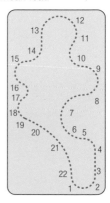

TARGET SPORTS

NEED2KNOW

→ St Andrews golf course in Scotland, where the sport has been played since 1574, is known as the Home of Golf.

320

→ Tiger Woods was the sport's undisputed world number one for a record 281 consecutive weeks from 2005–10.

→ A game of fractions, with a very fine line separating a good shot from a very poor one, golf has a reputation for being both devilishly difficult and highly addictive.

GOLF

GAME OVERVIEW

Golf is an individual sport in which players strike a ball with metal clubs around a course of nine, or more commonly 18, holes in the fewest shots possible. Each hole starts on a teeing ground and ends on a green which contains a small, circular hole in the ground into which the ball must be sunk. Golfers carry with them up to 14 clubs which are capable of hitting the ball different distances on a variety of trajectories, and use whichever of them is most appropriate for each shot.

THE COURSE

Course length (usually measured in yards) varies greatly – anything from 1,300yd (1,190m) for a par-3 nine-hole course to more than 7,000yd (6,400m) for some of the more brutal 18-hole courses, particularly in the US. These figures do not take into account the distances between the green and the teeing ground of the next hole, however, which can raise the distance travelled by the golfer to more than 11km (7 miles). A round of golf can last between three and five hours depending on the number of players, their ability and speed of play.

Single glove
Often worn for better grip; worn on the left hand by righthanders, and the right hand by lefthanders

Shaft technology
Club shafts need to be both strong and lightweight; they are usually made either of steel or graphite

Clubheads
The heads of all golf clubs are metal, even those known for historical reasons as "woods"

Course clothing
Collared or polo shirts and trousers in any colour or combination of colours; the look is stylishly casual; no t-shirts or jeans are allowed

PLAYER PROFILE
Good concentration and hand-eye coordination are vital. Upper body strength and all-round flexibility are an advantage. So, too, is confidence: golf is a game of psychology, and self-belief is as important as talent.

Stylish footwear
Golf shoes have cleats that provide grip but do not damage the course. The uppers are made of leather

Fairway
The grass on the most direct route from tee to green is cut shorter than that of the surrounding areas, rewarding an accurate shot

Natural hazards
The edge of each hole may be marked by trees: these are part of the course, but golfers try to avoid getting stuck in or near them

Men's teeing area
The first stroke has to be taken from a designated part of this zone

Ladies' tee
Women start off ahead of the men; their teeing area may be directly in line with the men's equivalent or set at an angle, as here

Rough
A shot that goes off course may land in the long grass growing along the edges of the fairway, known as rough. Semi rough gives way to heavy rough on the extremes of many holes. Typically it is more challenging to hit a shot from rough than fairway

The ultimate objective
The hole is 10.8cm (4¼in) in diameter and at least 10cm (4in) deep. A flag bearing the number of the hole is often temporarily placed into the hole

Putting green
The area around the hole featured very closely cut grass which facilitates smooth putting

THE HOLES

Each of the 18 holes must comprise a teeing area, a fairway, a putting green, and a hole with a removable flag in it. There may be any number of surrounding hazards: these include artifical bunkers (large depressions filled with sand), and natural features, such as trees, lakes, and streams. The most economical route around the golf course is by keeping the ball on the fairway, but this is far easier said than done. Golf courses are made up of an unregulated variety of par 3, 4, and 5 holes. Par is determined by the hole's length. Par 3s can be any distance to 240yd, par 4s 241–474yd, and par 5s over 475yd. When calculating par it is assumed the player will take two putts on the green. Therefore a par 3 should require one shot to reach the green, par 4 two shots to the green, and par 5, three. However, the player can make a score in any way they choose, or manage.

HANDICAP
Each hole is given a par rating, based on its length. This is the number of strokes that are deemed reasonable for its completion. A player's handicap is calculated using the average number of strokes over par taken over a series of rounds of golf.

TYPES OF GOLF COURSE

Golf's popularity around the world is reflected in the vast diversity of the physical landscapes in which it is played. Golf course types range from the open, windswept coastal "links" of Scotland, where the game evolved, to the perfectly manicured resort courses of the Middle East, set in a sea of desert sand. Golf courses can be found in almost every environment that can afford the space. Probably the most accessible and popular types of course are the tree-lined parkland courses that are features of many city suburbs.

Out of bounds
Land adjacent to the golf club is marked by a series of white posts, beyond which is deemed to be out of bounds. If a ball goes OB a player is penalised one stroke

Sand trap
Bunkers are strategically positioned by course designers to give players extra problems: this one guards the front of the green

Water hazard
If the ball lands here and is irretrievable, the player forfeits a stroke

Back nine
Holes 10–18 cover a total length of 3,710yd (3,392m)

Front nine
Holes 1–9 cover a total distance of 3,735yd (3,415m)

CLASSIC COURSE
Venue for the annual Masters Tournament, one of golf's four Major Championships, the Augusta National Golf Club is one of the world's most exclusive and naturally beautiful courses. Situated on the site of a former tree nursery, Augusta is a prime example of a parkland course with lush fairways bordered by trees and shrubs from which the holes take their names.

Par threes
Four of them: holes 4, 6, 12, and 16; the shortest is 155yd (142m), the longest 240yd (219m)

Par fours
Ten in all: 1, 3, 5, 7, 9, 10, 11, 14, 17, and 18; lengths between 350–505yd (320–462m)

Par fives
A total of four: holes 2 (575yd/526m); 8 (570yd/521m); 13 (510yd/466m); and 15 (530yd/485m)

GOLFING GEAR

A selection of clubs and a good supply of balls are the essentials for a round of golf, and the well-equipped player needs tees (see opposite page), ball markers (to mark the position of the ball if it has to be picked up), and a pitch-mark repairer. As a golfer may be on the course for some hours, he or she may also want to take food and energy drinks, an umbrella and waterproofs, a towel, gloves, and other assorted items. To carry all this gear, golfers use a purpose-made carry-bag or trolley. For the serious golfer, a battery-powered trolley takes over the role of the traditional caddy.

Golf clubs usually have dress rules requiring players to wear smart-casual clothing. Special golf shoes, with spiked or rubber soles to provide grip during the swing, are indispensable.

TOO MANY CLUBS

IN 2001 WELSH PROFESSIONAL IAN WOOSNAM BEGAN THE LAST DAY'S PLAY IN THE BRITISH OPEN GOLF CHAMPIONSHIP WITH A GREAT CHANCE OF WINNING. HE STARTED WELL, BIRDIEING THE FIRST HOLE, BUT ON THE SECOND TEE HIS CADDY NOTICED AN EXTRA CLUB IN THE BAG. THE TWO-SHOT PENALTY HE INCURRED AS A RESULT PROBABLY COST HIM VICTORY.

SELECTION OF CLUBS

A golfer can use up to 14 clubs in any combination to deal with the varying situations likely to be encountered on the course. Most players carry two to three "woods", including a driver to deliver long shots; six or seven irons for play from the fairway and rough; two of the type of irons known as "wedges" for shorter shots; and a putter for playing strokes on the green. All clubs are numbered according to a system designed to help the player select the right tool for the job. Generally, clubs with low numbers send the ball the greatest distances (see opposite page). Modern club designs and materials give golfers greater control over their game than in the past. Personal choice of clubs depends largely on the level of a player's proficiency and style of swing.

CLUBHEAD

Originally made of wood and later of steel, clubheads are now often made of titanium. Because this is lighter, modern clubheads can be made larger and more efficient.

Hosel
The neck of the clubhead where it joins the shaft

Toe
The area of the clubhead furthest from the shaft is called the toe

Face
The side of the club used to strike the ball

DRIVER
The driver is the biggest club in the bag, and is used for long-distance shots. The shape of the face is designed to elevate the ball as it is struck.

7–11°

IRON
Generally used for medium-length shots, irons are the most versatile club in a golfer's armoury. They range from 1 irons (16° loft) to 9 irons (44° loft).

16–44°

WEDGE
Pitching wedges, for short shots from grass, and sand wedges for bunkers have recently been joined on the market by highly lofted lob wedges.

45–60°

PUTTER
The shallowest-faced club in the bag, the putter is used for stroking the ball on the green and sometimes from short grass just off the green.

4–7°

MORE RULES THAN MOST

Golf has many more rules than most sports – 34 plus various sub-clauses – but this reflects the nature of the game. There is clearly more scope for incident on an extensive playing area that includes trees and rivers than on, say, a tennis court. The Rules of Golf are enforced by the Royal and Ancient Golf Club of St Andrews (R&A) in all golf-playing nations of the world, apart from the US and Mexico where the United States Golf Association (USGA) governs.

STRIKING THE BALL
A stroke is defined as the forward momentum of the club with the intention of striking it. If a player makes an attempt to hit the ball, but misses it, that counts as one shot.

ON THE GREEN
On the green only, it is permitted to mark the position of the ball, lift it, and clean it. Golfers can also brush aside loose leaves or sand that might be on their "line". There is a two-stroke penalty in strokeplay for holing a putt without first removing the flag.

HAZARDS AND UNPLAYABLE LIES
There is no penalty for going in a bunker but players must not ground their clubs before making contact with the ball. It is also permitted to play a shot from a water hazard (a more practical

option is to either replay the shot from the original position or take a drop, but not nearer the hole – both options incur a one-stroke penalty). If there is an unplayable lie, such as the ball in a bush, a player can drop the ball at a distance of up to two club-lengths, but not nearer the hole. This also incurs a one-shot penalty.

IMPEDIMENTS AND OBSTRUCTIONS
Moveable natural objects, such as stones and leaves, are defined as loose impediments and can be moved from around the ball without penalty. Obstructions, such as bunker rakes, can also be moved. If the ball moves during the course of this action it counts as one shot. Immovable obstructions are items such as sprinkler heads. Free relief can be taken from these – if they interfere with the player's stance or swing – up to one club's length, not nearer the hole.

BALLS

Although there are strict rules covering the specifications of golf balls, there are many different models to choose from, each of which performs differently in terms of spin, speed, and trajectory. Some balls have multiple inner layers round a small core, while others have a single large core.

White missile
The hard outer layer of a golf ball is covered in small dimples for aerodynamic purposes. To an experienced golfer, slight differences in the dimple pattern give each model a characteristic "feel"

Tee time
For the first stroke at each hole, golfers are allowed to place the ball on a small plastic or wooden peg – the tee – to make the shot easier

LOFT AND LIE

Different lies require different clubs. Balls that lie well on the short grass of the fairway have the greatest range of options. Shots that lie poorly in the rough often demand a mid- to short iron or a utility wood – something with sufficient loft to get the bottom of the blade under the ball. When chipping onto the green over a bunker, the player will opt for a lofted iron – affording maximum height and a soft landing. When there is no obstruction, a shallower-faced club can chip-and-run the ball onto the green.

DISTANCE GUIDE

CLUB	DISTANCE	LOFT
D	230–290 YARDS	7–11°
3-W	210–240 YARDS	13–16°
5-W	200–220 YARDS	19–21°
3	180–205 YARDS	18°
4	170–200 YARDS	22°
5	160–195 YARDS	26°
6	150–180 YARDS	30°
7	140–170 YARDS	34°
8	130–155 YARDS	38°
9	120–145 YARDS	42°
PW	110–130 YARDS	46°
SW	90–100 YARDS	56°

TRAJECTORY

The flight of the golf ball is determined by the degree of loft of the club used. The driver, which has the shallowest face, propels the ball low and far. Wedges, with the steepest loft, lift the ball in a higher trajectory but over a shorter distance. The diagram here shows lofts and distances for a range of irons.

IRON	LOFT	SW 56°	PW 46°	9 42°	8 38°	7 34°	6 30°	5 26°	4 23°	3 22°	2 18°	1 16°
	YARDAGE	90	110	120	130	140	150	160	170	180	190	200

TYPES OF PLAY

There is more than one way of playing golf. In strokeplay, golfers record their score for each hole and add the totals at the end. In Stableford, points are awarded for scores gained on each hole. Matchplay singles is head-to-head competition played hole by hole. Fourball betterball has the same principle as singles but is played in pairs. In foursomes, pairs compete with only one ball shared between partners.

SCORING

Players mark each other's scorecard, never their own. Certain scores are given names, as below.

PAR A score equal to the par of a hole.

BIRDIE A score one less (or under) the par such as a three on a par four.

EAGLE Two under the par. A hole in one on a par three is an eagle.

ALBATROSS Three under par, an extremely rare occurrence, even for the world's best.

BOGEY One more than (over) the par, for instance a six on a par five.

DOUBLE BOGEY Two over par. Too many double bogeys result in a very poor score.

ETIQUETTE

Etiquette on the golf course ensures that everyone enjoys the game and plays in safety. Examples include: keeping quiet when a fellow player is taking a shot; raking bunkers after a shot to remove footprints; replacing divots; and not delaying other players. On the green, players should repair pitch-marks and avoid standing on a fellow player's line.

STAT CENTRAL

MAJOR WINNERS

PLAYER	TOTAL
JACK NICKLAUS	18
TIGER WOODS	14
WALTER HAGEN	11
BEN HOGAN	9
GARY PLAYER	9
TOM WATSON	8
HARRY VARDON	7
GENE SARAZEN	7
BOBBY JONES	7
SAM SNEAD	7
ARNOLD PALMER	7
NICK FALDO	6
LEE TREVINO	6

THE GOLF SWING

All good golf swings start with a good setup and it is impossible to overstate the importance of a good grip, alignment, stance, and posture for beginners. In fact, it is possible to hit the ball well with a good setup and a mediocre swing, but you can make the best swing the world and not hit the ball consistently with a poor setup. The golf swing itself is a question of repetition. The backswing and follow-through should be almost a mirror image of one another.

STANCE

Feet should be shoulder-width apart, with legs slightly bent, and the ball positioned roughly midway between the feet. The player bends forward from the waist towards the ball.

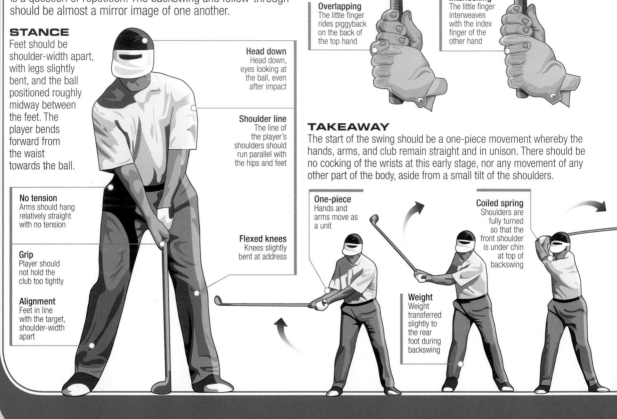

Head down
Head down, eyes looking at the ball, even after impact

Shoulder line
The line of the player's shoulders should run parallel with the hips and feet

No tension
Arms should hang relatively straight with no tension

Grip
Player should not hold the club too tightly

Alignment
Feet in line with the target, shoulder-width apart

Flexed knees
Knees slightly bent at address

GRIP

A good grip is a player's only means of controlling the clubhead and bringing it into impact in a square (straight) position. There are two, equally popular styles of grip (below) and a third, the baseball grip, suitable for junior golfers or those with arthritic problems.

Overlapping
The little finger rides piggyback on the back of the top hand

Interlocking
The little finger interweaves with the index finger of the other hand

TAKEAWAY

The start of the swing should be a one-piece movement whereby the hands, arms, and club remain straight and in unison. There should be no cocking of the wrists at this early stage, nor any movement of any other part of the body, aside from a small tilt of the shoulders.

One-piece
Hands and arms move as a unit

Weight
Weight transferred slightly to the rear foot during backswing

Coiled spring
Shoulders are fully turned so that the front shoulder is under chin at top of backswing

PITCHING AND CHIPPING

For shots of about 90yd (80m) and less players do not need to make a full swing; an abbreviated version, executed with an open stance, is more suited. Pitching shots are very much a question of "feel" – being able to judge specific distances – and this comes down to experience of play and trial and error. Chip shots are played from very close to the green and are either struck at a low trajectory, running along the ground towards the hole (a chip-and-run), or with great height and consequently a soft landing with minimal forward roll (a lob). Executing these type of shots well will result in many short putts, ultimately saving players a number of strokes per round.

PUTTING

Often described as "the game within the game", putting is an art in itself. Players should stand more upright than for a regular shot, keep their head still and move only their hands and arms in a solid unit. However, a good putting stroke and a good judgement of distance is not enough. Players need to have a good appreciation of the contours of the green, how the ball will "break" (move in relation to the slopes), and the speed at which it will travel, after it is struck. A good understanding of these factors is known as being able to "read" the green and this is something that only comes with experience.

Keep still
Head is kept still and eyes are focused on the ball

Smoothly back...
The putter is taken back in a deliberate one-piece motion with hands and arms straight

...and through
The player continues the same smooth motion through impact without looking up

HOLE IN ONE
The Holy Grail of golf for many players, holes in one are normally only ever achieved on par 3s but can also occur on short par 4s and often by chance. Because of their propensity to consistently hit the ball close to the flag professionals score a much higher number of holes in one than amateurs. Many professionals' hole-in-one tallies are well into double figures.

BACKSWING
When the club is at about 45 degrees to the starting position, the player begins to cock the wrists and turn the upper body, pivoting it against the hips. It is essential the head remains still and does not sway or tilt as the shoulders turn.

DOWNSWING AND IMPACT
The downswing is essentially about mirroring, as closely as possible, the movements made in the backswing. The shoulders and upper body should uncoil as all the weight previously loaded onto the rear side redistributes. The hands and arms follow, not lead, this movement to ensure that the clubface reaches impact in a square (straight) position.

TROUBLE SHOTS
Of course, players do not always find themselves with a flat lie on short grass and there is little option when the player finds him or herself in, for instance, a clump of trees, than to chip the ball sideways. However, most situations can be overcome with minor adjustments to the setup. For example, when on uphill or downhill lies players redistribute their weight and alter the position of ball in their stance. On sidehill lies players aim more to the left or right of the target to compensate for the slope. Escape from bunkers is one of the shots that golfers struggle with most commonly. It is key to remember to open the clubface and make a normal swing, making contact with the sand first, not the ball.

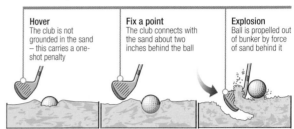

Hover The club is not grounded in the sand – this carries a one-shot penalty

Fix a point The club connects with the sand about two inches behind the ball

Explosion Ball is propelled out of bunker by force of sand behind it

Mirror image Hands are in same position as in backswing

Neutral hands At impact, neutral hands (a product of a good grip) increase the likelihood of a square club face

Eyes down Head is kept still and eyes remain looking at the place where the ball was lying

Textbook finish From a good high finish the player can admire the ball's flight down the fairway

SIDELINES

4 The highest number of major tournaments won consecutively by a single player. Tiger Woods achieved this feat with the British Open, the US Open, and the USPGA in 2000, followed by the US Masters in 2001. In the modern era, a player has never won all four within the same calendar year – known as the Grand Slam of Golf.

1,007 The length, in yards (900m) of the par-6 sixth hole at Chocolay Downs, Marquette, Michigan, the longest hole in world golf.

59 Shooting a round under 60 (usually about ten under the par for the course) is one of the rarest feats in golf. Only five players have ever achieved this on the US Tour – Stuart Appleby, at the 2010 Greenbrier Classic, being the most recent.

INSIDE STORY
The Royal and Ancient (R&A) and the US Golf Association oversee the governance of the sport. They enforce the Rules of Golf, test golf equipment for conformity, implement a handicapping system, and host national championships for men's, women, and junior golf. Professional golf is organised by the Professional Golf Association European Tour (which includes some events in Africa, Asia, and Australasia) and the US Tour which organizes competition in North America. Since 1999 the International Federation of PGA Tours have run three World Golf Championship events.

THE MAJORS
In male professional golf the major championships are the most prestigious tournaments of the season and the benchmark by which players are judged. There are four and they run in order of play as follows: The Masters, held every April at the Augusta National Golf Club, Georgia, a strictly invitational tournament run by the club; the US Open, the flagship event of the USGA, in June; the Open Championship, organized by the R&A in July; and finally the USPGA Championship, in August.

CROQUET

GAME OVERVIEW

Croquet involves hitting balls with a mallet through hoops embedded in the grass playing arena. The winner is the first person or team to hit a centrally located pole. Association Croquet, described here, is the version of the sport played at most international tournaments. The game offers many opportunities to punish opponents and has even been described as one of the world's most aggressive recreational activities – a far cry from the rather staid, genteel stereotype.

The white stuff
Players must wear shirts and trousers, shorts, or skirts, and every piece of clothing must be white

Croquet mallet
The mallet may be gripped anywhere on the handle, but players must not touch the head of it while playing a stroke

Wire wickets
The croquet balls must be struck through wire hoops embedded in the grass court

9.5cm (3¾in)

30cm (12in)

Coloured balls
They are only 3mm (⅛in) smaller than the wickets, so there's very little margin for error

Soft shoes
Players must wear shoes with smooth soles in order to minimise damage to the manicured playing surface

PLAYER PROFILE

Many of the skills required by a croquet player are the same as those needed for proficient putting at golf. Both games require good judgment of the lie of the playing surface and of the weight of each shot. The croquet lawn is smaller than many putting greens, and the balls have relatively short distances to travel, so physical strength is rarely important. The player's age is hardly a consideration either, as seasoned hands may easily outsmart younger, fitter pretenders.

NEW BALLS, PLEASE

FOUNDED IN 1868, THE FIRST NATIONAL HEADQUARTERS OF CROQUET IN GREAT BRITAIN WAS THE WIMBLEDON ALL ENGLAND CROQUET CLUB. HOWEVER, JUST NINE YEARS LATER, THE CLUB WAS RE-NAMED THE WIMBLEDON ALL ENGLAND CROQUET AND LAWN TENNIS CLUB AND PLAYED HOST TO THE FIRST EVER LAWN TENNIS CHAMPIONSHIPS. AS THE POPULARITY OF TENNIS GREW, CROQUET WAS SIDELINED. THE CLUB EVEN DROPPED "CROQUET" FROM ITS NAME FOR A WHILE, AND STOPPED HOLDING CROQUET TOURNAMENTS.

NEED2KNOW

→ A croquet match is played by two sides, made up of either single players or two teams of two. Each side has two balls: one blue and black, the other red and yellow.

→ The world's leading international men's contest is the Croquet World Series for the MacRobertson Shield. The competition takes place over two weeks every three or four years between Australia, Great Britain, New Zealand, and the United States.

→ In addition to the basic Association Croquet, there are several variant forms, including Mondo Croquet, played with sledgehammers and 10-pin bowling balls, and a mounted version on bicycles.

SIDELINES

1 The total number of paying spectators at the Olympic croquet final in 1900, the first and last time the sport was played at the Games. The event was held in Paris, nine out of the 10 croquet competitors were French and, perhaps not surprisingly, France took all the medals in both the singles and doubles competitions.

80 The number of players that entered the 2012 Association Croquet World Championships. In addition to the MacRobertson big four, there were some surprises for anyone who thinks of croquet as the quintessence of Englishness: other contestants hailed from nations not usually associated with croquet, such as Japan and Sweden.

9 The number of times Great Britain has won the MacRobertson Shield, more than any other nation in the history of the competition; two of these victories came as part of a combined team with Ireland. New Zealand and Australia have both won the MacRobertson Shield three times.

COURT CLIPPINGS

The playing surface is a level, well-manicured lawn approximately the size of two tennis courts. Play begins from behind the baulk line at one end of the court. The first hoop has a blue top and the last hoop, known as the "rover", has a red top. To remind players of the direction of play, and to show spectators whether a hoop is being played forwards or backwards, four coloured clips are placed on top of each hoop at the start of the game. The clips indicate the next point for each ball, and are moved to the side of the hoop after the corresponding ball has passed through it once.

MALLET AFORETHOUGHT

Each player has two coloured balls, which must pass through six hoops twice in the correct order and direction, and then hit the central peg. Croquet is a tactical game, and players can sabotage their opponent's position while completing the course.

CONTINUATION STROKES

Twenty-six points are needed to win (12 hoop points and one peg point per ball) and players normally have just one strike per turn. However, if they send the ball completely through a hoop they get another shot ("a continuation stroke"). If the shot hits an opponent's ball ("makes a roquet"), the striker gets two more shots: he or she first places the ball by hand against the opponent's ball, and then strikes his or her own ball. The opponent's ball may thus be sent out of bounds, which is how croquet got its reputation for aggression.

PEELINGS AND OFFSHOOTS

If the striker's ball knocks an opponent's ball through a hoop, the latter is said to have been "peeled": the other side benefits, but does not get a continuation stroke. If a ball rolls off the court, it is replaced on the boundary line at the point where it went out of play.

EQUIPMENT

When not in use, the mallets, balls, hoops, and peg are stored in a long wooden box with rope handles at either end and a lid. It looks like a cross between a shipping crate and a coffin.

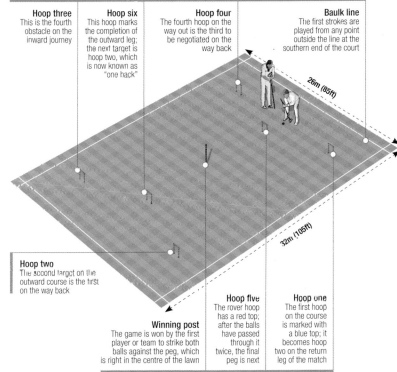

Hoop three
This is the fourth obstacle on the inward journey

Hoop six
This hoop marks the completion of the outward leg; the next target is hoop two, which is now known as "one back"

Hoop four
The fourth hoop on the way out is the third to be negotiated on the way back

Baulk line
The first strokes are played from any point outside the line at the southern end of the court

26m (85ft)

32m (105ft)

Hoop two
The second target on the outward course is the first on the way back

Winning post
The game is won by the first player or team to strike both balls against the peg, which is right in the centre of the lawn

Hoop five
The rover hoop has a red top; after the balls have passed through it twice, the final peg is next

Hoop one
The first hoop on the course is marked with a blue top; it becomes hoop two on the return leg of the match

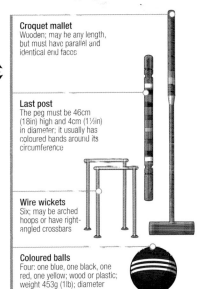

Croquet mallet
Wooden; may be any length, but must have parallel and identical end faces

Last post
The peg must be 46cm (18in) high and 4cm (1½in) in diameter; it usually has coloured bands around its circumference

Wire wickets
Six; may be arched hoops or have right-angled crossbars

Coloured balls
Four: one blue, one black, one red, one yellow; wood or plastic; weight 453g (1lb); diameter 9.2cm (3⅝in)

ROQUET SCIENCE

Unlike most target games, croquet allows players to actively hinder their opponents' progress. This is done in two stages. First, a player performs a roquet stroke, which simply involves striking the other player's ball. The player then picks up their ball, places it in direct contact with the "roqueted" ball, and takes a croquet stroke.

CROQUET STROKE

The purpose of the stroke from which the game gets its name is to send the opponent's ball as far off course as possible. But the best offensive players work out angles that enable them simultaneously to gain advantage for themselves. The perfect croquet is a shot that knocks the opponent's ball a long way off course and sends the player's own ball through a hoop, thus earning a continuation stroke. The diagram on the right shows a typical example.

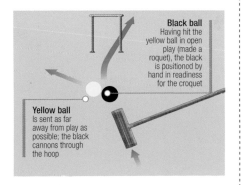

Black ball
Having hit the yellow ball in open play (made a roquet), the black is positioned by hand in readiness for the croquet

Yellow ball
Is sent as far away from play as possible; the black cannons through the hoop

INSIDE STORY

Croquet began in Ireland in the 1830s, later spreading to Great Britain where it quickly grew in popularity. At the time, croquet was the first outdoor sport that could be played by both men and women on an equal footing, and its popularity was sealed when a London sporting goods manufacturer began producing and selling croquet equipment. The sport soon caught on throughout the British colonies, most notably in Australia and New Zealand.

GOVERNING BODY

In England, Wales, and Northern Ireland, the Croquet Association makes the rules, awards top players' seedings, and promotes and regulates the game.

CURLING

GAME OVERVIEW

Sometimes referred to as "chess on ice", curling is a game of skill, precision, and strategy. It began as a Scottish outdoor winter sport before spreading across the globe and becoming one of the highlights of the Winter Olympics. Curling is played on a sheet, or rinks, of ice by two teams of four players. The aim of the game is for a team to place its stones closer to the tee, the centre of a circular target, than the closest stone of the other team. One game is made up of 10 rounds, or ends, and each player delivers two stones, making a total of 16 stones per end. Under the direction of the "skip", the team sweeps the ice directly in front of the stone to adjust the speed and direction of each stone as it slides toward the tee.

THE SHEET

The playing area is known as the sheet and has a circular scoring area, or house, at each end. The house consists of four concentric circles dissected by the centre and tee lines. The largest circle has a diameter of 3.6m (12ft) and the smallest circle, called the button or tee, has a diameter of 30cm (12in). The hog line marks the point by which the stone must be released during a throw, or delivery. A stone is out of play if it crosses the back line behind the house.

TURNING THE STONE

A stone can be made to spin as it moves along the sheet. The direction of rotation a stone is given as it is released determines how it travels along the ice. The direction of the spin determines whether the stone will curl (curve) to the left or right: clockwise spin curls right and anti-clockwise curls left. The greater the amount of spin which is given, the less the stone will curl. On some ice sheets which may not be perfectly level the stone may even travel against the spin.

KEEPING IT COOL

The surface of the sheet needs to be kept at a constant temperature of –5ºC (23ºF). The sheet is sprayed with water before every game. The droplets freeze into tiny bumps on the surface, known as pebble. It is the friction between the stones and pebble that causes curling.

House
The scoring area; a stone must sit within the house (rings) to stand a chance of scoring

Back line
A stone is deemed out of play if it crosses the line touching the back of the house

NEED2KNOW

→ Curling is popular in northern countries, especially Canada and Scotland, where cold weather creates the natural conditions for an ice-based sport. It is now played more widely, including in warmer countries, from Spain to China and Japan.

→ Teams are made up of a lead who throws first, a second who throws second, a vice-skip who usually throws third, and a team captain, called the skip, who directs play and usually throws last.

→ The best stones are made from granite from the Ailsa Craig Island off the coast of Ayrshire, Scotland. Olympic grade stones cost up to US$1,500.

PLAYER PROFILE

All players need to have a fine sense of balance, good flexibility, hand-eye coordination, and control on the ice. The skip and vice-skip also need a sharp mind for tactics and strategy as they direct their teammates to deliver stones in to winning positions.

On the slide
A player does not use his or her arm to propel the stone. The speed of a throw depends on how hard he or she thrusts forwards with the trailing leg. Once released, the player slides along behind the stone

Handle sensor
At elite level, the handles contain sensors that indicate whether a stone has crossed the hog line before being released. A green light flashes at the base of the handle if the release is good, red for a foul throw

Lead shoe
A "slider", a shoe with a smooth sole, is worn on the lead foot during delivery of the stone. At other times the curler wears a thin rubber "gripper" over the slider for traction

Stone
Ailsite granite stones weigh a maximum of 20kg (44lb). The bottom of the stone is concave, and the running surface is a circle 6–12mm (¼–½in) wide

Broom
A versatile piece of kit, it is used to melt the ice, indicate where to aim the stone, or to balance the curler during throws

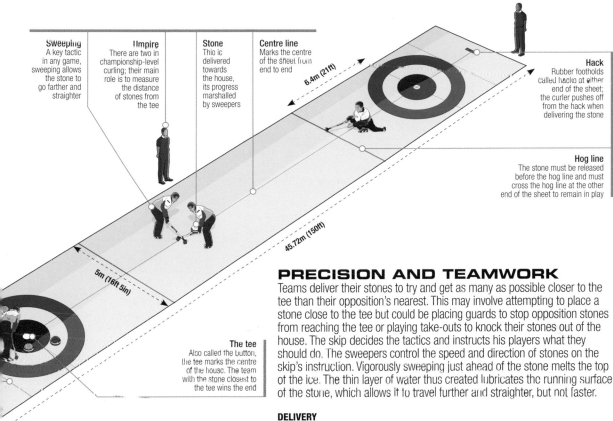

Sweeping
A key tactic in any game, sweeping allows the stone to go farther and straighter

Umpire
There are two in championship-level curling; their main role is to measure the distance of stones from the tee

Stone
This is delivered towards the house, its progress marshalled by sweepers

Centre line
Marks the centre of the sheet from end to end

6.4m (21ft)

45.72m (150ft)

5m (16ft 5in)

Hack
Rubber footholds called hacks at either end of the sheet; the curler pushes off from the hack when delivering the stone

Hog line
The stone must be released before the hog line and must cross the hog line at the other end of the sheet to remain in play

The tee
Also called the button, the tee marks the centre of the house. The team with the stone closest to the tee wins the end

PRECISION AND TEAMWORK

Teams deliver their stones to try and get as many as possible closer to the tee than their opposition's nearest. This may involve attempting to place a stone close to the tee but could be placing guards to stop opposition stones from reaching the tee or playing take-outs to knock their stones out of the house. The skip decides the tactics and instructs his players what they should do. The sweepers control the speed and direction of stones on the skip's instruction. Vigorously sweeping just ahead of the stone melts the top of the ice. The thin layer of water thus created lubricates the running surface of the stone, which allows it to travel further and straighter, but not faster.

DELIVERY
The player crouches on the slider shoe and pushes against the hack with his or her other foot. He or she slides with the stone, controlling its speed, direction, and rotation, before letting go just before it crosses the hog line. Once the stone is released, it must not be touched by a broom or player.

Balanced delivery
The player aims the stone at a position indicated by the skip's broom

ON THE ICE
Stones can curve, or curl, up to 2m (6ft 6in) to the side as they glide down the rink. The curling is caused by the bumpy pebble surface on the ice. Melting the pebble by sweeping stops the stone from curling. As a game progresses, the pebble rubs away and stones may curl more or less than previously.

Quick sweep
Sweepers adjust the pressure on their brooms according to how much they want to redirect the stone

IN THE HOUSE
Inside the house, the skip helps sweep the stone to its desired resting place, either closest to the tee or in a blocking, or guarding, position to prevent the opponents' stones reaching the tee. The last stone to be thrown is called the hammer. The team with the hammer is more likely to win the end.

On the button
The skip also sweeps in front of the opponents' stones that are knocked around inside in the house

ROCK STEADY

Alternating between teams, each player delivers two stones until all 16 have been thrown. Only the team with the stone closest to the tee scores. It scores one point for each stone closer to the tee than any of their opponents' stones.

DRAW
A draw is a throw that lands the stone in the house. A guard sits in front of the house to block opponents' shots. A raise shot promotes a stone into the house from outside, or one in the house closer to the tee.

Raise shot
This stone has been knocked into a winning position closer to the tee by a teammate's stone

TAKEOUT
A takeout is a shot that removes another stone from play – ideally the opposition's! A raise takeout is when the thrown stone uses an intermediate stone to take out the target stone.

Direct hit
The incoming stone strikes the opponents' stone and knocks it out of the house

INSIDE STORY

Curling originated in Scotland, where the outdoor game was popular between the 16th and 19th centuries. The Royal Caledonian Curling Club, curling's oldest society, was established in 1843. The first world championships were held in 1959 (1979 for women); men's and women's events have featured in the Winter Olympics since 1998.

GOVERNING BODIES
The Royal Caledonian Curling Club, the original governing body for curling, and the World Curling Federation (WCF) are based in Scotland. The WCF runs the World Men's and World Women's Curling Championships, as well as the World Junior Curling Championships, and has 50 national members.

LAWN BOWLING

NEED2KNOW

➡ Lawn bowling is one of the world's most popular games for the over 60s, but at a competitive level, the sport is dominated by younger players.

➡ Bowls is most popular in Australia, Canada, New Zealand, the United Kingdom, and UK territories.

➡ All but one of the men's indoor bowls world champions have come from England, Ireland, Scotland, or Wales. The 1992 winner was an Australian.

Formal flourish
Although a player's attire is not a significant part of the game, in competitions men will usually wear white clothes and a tie

Rubber mat
Bowlers must stand with at least one foot on a rubber mat in the centre of their rink

GAME OVERVIEW

Lawn bowling – aka bowls – is a precision sport in which players roll slightly asymmetrical balls, called bowls, along a green. The winner is the person with whose bowls land closest to the target – the "kitty" or "jack".

THE BOWLS

Although bowls were traditionally made of wood or rubber, or a composite, modern bowls are made of lignite. They are designed to travel a curved path, referred to as their bias, produced by the asymmetrical shape of the bowl. The jack is perfectly spherical and usually coloured white.

BIASED BOWL
The bowls are black or brown, weigh about 1.5kg (3.3lb), and are 12–14.5cm (4½–5½in) in diameter. The bowls are not quite round: their bias gives them a slight bulge on one side.

THE GREEN

Bowls is usually played on a manicured grass or synthetic surface known as a bowling green, which is divided into parallel playing strips known as rinks. An indoor variation on carpet is also played. Outdoor greens have a uniform length, but may be of varying widths, depending on the number of rinks. Indoor greens are usually smaller, their dimensions being set by organizers.

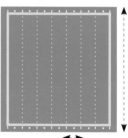

37–40m (120–130ft)

5.5–5.8m (18–19ft)

LAWN RULES

In the simplest singles competition, on the toss of a coin one player begins by placing his rubber mat and rolling the jack to the other end of the green. Once the jack has come to rest, it is aligned to the centre of the rink before the players take turns to roll their bowls. A bowl is allowed to curve outside the rink boundary, but must come to rest within the boundary to remain in play.

After the competitors have delivered all their bowls – four each in singles – the distance of the closest bowl to the jack is determined. Then a point is awarded for each bowl the winning competitor has between the jack and his opponent's closest bowl. This passage of play is known as an end.

BOWL DELIVERY

There are several types of delivery. For a right-hander, a "forehand draw" is aimed to the right of the jack, and curves in to the left. The same bowler can deliver a "backhand draw" by turning the bowl over in his hand and curving it the opposite way. A "drive" involves bowling with force with the aim of knocking either the jack or a specific bowl out of play.

SCORING
Scoring systems vary – either the first to a specified number of points, or the highest scorer after a number of ends. Some competitions use a "set" scoring system, with the first to seven points awarded a set in a best-of-five match.

AND THRASH THE SPANIARDS TOO

THE MOST FAMOUS STORY IN LAWN BOWLS INVOLVES SIR FRANCIS DRAKE. ON 18 JULY 1588, DRAKE WAS INVOLVED IN A GAME AT PLYMOUTH HOE WHEN HE WAS NOTIFIED THAT THE SPANISH ARMADA WERE APPROACHING. HIS IMMORTALIZED RESPONSE WAS THAT "WE STILL HAVE TIME TO FINISH THE GAME AND TO THRASH THE SPANIARDS, TOO." HE THEN PROCEEDED TO FINISH THE MATCH – WHICH HE LOST – BEFORE EMBARKING ON THE BATTLE WITH THE ARMADA – WHICH HE WON.

PÉTANQUE

→ Pétanque is generally associated with southern France, particularly Provence, from where it originates. It is the most played sport in Marseille.

→ The casual form of the game of pétanque is played by about 17 million people in France – mostly during their summer vacations.

→ The International Pétanque Federation was founded in 1958 in Marseille and has about 530,000 members in 88 countries. It is the fourth-largest sports federation in the whole of France.

THE BOULES

Boules are traditionally made of steel and have a chrome outer finish. They each weigh 650–800g (1½–1¾lb), and have a diameter of 7.1–8.0cm (2¾–3in). The jack is made of wood or synthetic material and has a diameter of 2.5–3.5cm (1–1¾in). On the sides they bear engravings indicating the manufacturer's or player's name and the weight of the boule.

THE TRACK

The game is normally played on hard dirt or gravel, but can also be played on grass or other surfaces. The dimensions shown below are the recommended minimum.

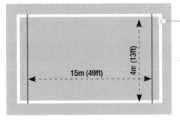

15m (49ft) 4m (13ft)

Flat surface
The game can be played almost anywhere there is a flat surface

BOULES RULES

The game is played in singles or by teams of two or three. The side that wins the toss starts the game by drawing a circle on the playing field 35–50cm (14–20in) in diameter. Both feet must remain inside this circle, touching the ground, when the player is throwing.

The player then throws the jack to a distance of 6–10m (20–30ft) from the starting circle. The jack must be visible (not, for example, buried in gravel), and at least 1m (3ft) from any boundary, otherwise it must be thrown again.

A player from the same team plays the first boule, trying to place it as close to the jack as possible. Then the opposing team must get one of its boules closer to the jack, and they keep playing until they succeed. When they do, it is back to the first team for them to do better. When one team runs out of boules, the other team plays its remaining boules.

GAME OVERVIEW

Pétanque is a form of boules where the goal is to throw metal balls as close as possible to a small wooden ball called a cochonnet ("piglet"). The game is normally played on hard dirt or gravel, but can also be played on grass or other surfaces.

POINTING AND SHOOTING

Players may choose to place or "point" a boule – get it as near as possible to the jack – or "shoot" it – attempt to displace another boule. A successful pétanque team has players who are skilled at shooting as well as players who only point.

For obvious reasons, the pointers play first – the shooter or shooters are held in reserve in case the opponents place well. In placing, a boule in front of the jack has much higher value than one at the same distance behind the jack, because the pushing of a front boule generally improves its position. At every play after the very first boule has been placed, the team whose turn it is must decide whether to point or shoot.

ROLLING IN
This is the easiest shot to play. The ball in thrown about halfway down the track and rolls the rest of the way.

ROLLING IN FOR A HIT
With this shot you land your boule early and make it roll along the ground into your opponent's boule.

SHORT LOB
This shot requires quite a high trajectory with just the right amount of backspin on the boule.

LONG LOB
Going in high is the only way when the ground is rough. The boule lands just about where you want it to lie.

SHOOTING IN
This shot is played fairly low and hard and enables you to move your opponents boule out of position.

CARREAU
This is the hardest shot in pétanque. Hit the opponent's boule and make sure that yours sits in its place.

10-PIN BOWLING

GAME OVERVIEW

Worldwide, 10-pin bowling is possibly second in popularity only to football as a participation sport. While for millions of people this indoor sport is a great way to relax and socialize, it can also be extremely competitive. Bowlers roll a heavy ball along a smooth lane and try to knock down as many of the 10 pins as possible. Points are awarded for the number of pins demolished. Bonuses are given for a "strike" – when every pin is knocked over in one attempt.

Come as you are
The only clothing requirement is that it allows easy movement of the arms and legs

Sure footing
The shoe on the leading foot has a rubber sole to give traction; that on the back foot has a leather sole to permit sliding

PLAYER PROFILE
The only essential is the ability to learn, through endless practice, the techniques of ball control. Age is no barrier: American Dick Weber was 72 when he won a 2002 Professional Bowlers' Association Senior title.

Bowling ball
Balls are traditionally plain black, but may now be finished in any colour and sometimes have patterned designs

18m (60ft)

1.05m (41¼in)

4.6m (15ft)

Foul line
The arm may go beyond this mark, but if the player touches it, the ball bowled counts zero

Approach area
Players use this area to gain speed and leverage on the ball before it is bowled

NEED2KNOW

→ The game emerged in the United States in the early 1900s. The first British alleys opened in London in 1960.

→ One of the sport's annual competitions is the Weber Cup. Team Europe compete against Team USA in the equivalent of golf's Ryder Cup.

PINS AND BALLS

Pins and balls were once made simply of wood, but the former are now synthetic or plastic-coated wood, while the latter are made of plastic, urethane, epoxy or a combination of these materials. For recreational 10-pin bowling, balls come in various weights to suit the strength of the player.

THE BALL
A full-size competition ball weighs 7.25kg (16lb). Its surface is entirely smooth apart from grip holes for the thumb, middle finger, and ring finger.

21.5cm (8½in)

THE PINS
The pins are all of uniform height and should be 11.4cm (4¾in) wide at the belly. They each weigh 1.47–1.64kg (3lb 6oz–3lb 10oz).

38cm (15in)

LIFE IN THE FAST LANE

The bowling lane is made of 39 planks of polyurethane or wood. On either side of it are semicircular gutters to collect off-target balls. Most public bowling alleys have retractable guard rails that can be lowered into place on the lane-side of the gutters; these are normally brought down only to assist young children who lack the strength to control the balls. Contestants must release the ball before reaching the foul line, and, having bowled, they must not overstep onto the lane.

After every turn, the balls are automatically returned to the approach area by an underlane system or along a raised, sloping trackway mounted on the righthand side of the lane.

LANE LAW

In competitive 10-pin bowling, each player has 10 frames, each of which consists of two attempts to knock down as many pins as possible. One point is scored for every pin that is knocked down. Contestants who demolish all 10 pins at the first attempt are awarded a strike, for which they earn a score of 10 points plus a bonus of the total of their next two shots. If the player knocks down all 10 pins in two attempts, he or she is awarded a spare and earns 10 points plus a bonus of the pins knocked down on the next shot. If there is still at least one pin standing after the second attempt, it is called an open frame.

Pin point
The pins are arranged to form a triangle with the apex facing the bowler and four pins in the back row. The pins stand 30cm (12in) apart (measured from the centre of each pin). After each frame, the pins are automatically re-racked by a machine known as a pinsetter

60cm (2ft)

Smooth surface
The surface of the lane is polished with oil before a competition to keep friction to an absolute minimum. The amount of oil used depends on the type of event

The low road
A ball that enters the gutter cannot leave it again; it runs straight down the side, missing all the pins

BALL CONTROL

Since it is physically impossible for the ball itself to strike every pin, the player needs to create a chain reaction of one pin hitting its neighbour, and so on, to get a good score. Experienced bowlers curve the ball's trajectory, or "roll a hook", to achieve maximum effect. The ball starts on a straight course but then curves to the left or right as it approaches the pins. Players whose first throw does not travel according to plan may end up with two or more remaining pins (7 and 10, for example) that are almost impossible to be felled with a single ball. In this instance, the player will choose one of the remaining pins to fell and settle for an open frame.

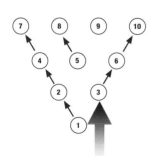

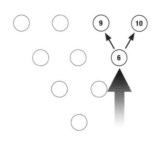

A PERFECT STRIKE
The ideal shot need only hit pins 1, 3, 5, and 9 (for right-handers) because these pins can then take out all the others. The same should also be true of a shot that hits pins 1, 2, 5, and 8 (for left-handers). It is usually important to avoid hitting pin 1 head-on.

MOP-UP OPERATION
In this example, the bowler failed to knock down all the pins at the first attempt; three (6, 9, and 10) were left standing. The player delivers a straight ball just to the right of pin 6, which in turn knocks down 9, and the ball continues and demolishes 10.

STROKERS AND CRANKERS

Bowlers will always argue over the best method of delivery, and the reality is that each has its masters. Many top players use the graceful and stylish stroker, while others prefer the powerplay of cranking. And in East Asia, the spinning or "helicopter" delivery is popular.

STROKER
The stroker is the classic style of hook bowling. The player's sliding foot stops just before the ball reaches the lowest point of the swing, and his or her shoulders are square at the point of release.

CRANKER
The bowler produces the maximum amount of spin on the ball. When delivering the ball, he or she quickly pulls the arm through, bending the elbow to keep the hand behind and under the ball.

THE PERFECT GAME

Bowlers who score a strike every time they throw will score 30 points per frame. If they then get another strike in the tenth and final frame, they are awarded two extra balls. If these are also strikes, the bowler scores the maximum 300 points and has played the perfect game. In 1997, a Nebraska student became the first person to accomplish three consecutive perfect games in an approved series. Perfect games remain rare occurrences.

INSIDE STORY

There are many historical references to bowling, but the first indoor bowling alley was not opened until 1840 – Knickerbockers in New York City. Today, the sport is played in more than 100 countries. The game developed greatly in the second half of the 20th century. While still a relaxed leisure activity for millions, it is now also a recognized competitive sport played by highly paid full-time professionals. Positions on the world ranking system are determined by players' performances in the American, Asian, and European tours.

GOVERNING BODIES
The World Tenpin Bowling Association (WTBA) governs the sport internationally, while the United States Bowling Congress (USBC) and the British Tenpin Bowling Association (BTBA) control the game in their respective countries.

5-PIN BOWLING

GAME OVERVIEW

Individuals or teams take turns to roll a ball at a group of pins; whoever knocks over the most pins after an agreed number of attempts wins the match. The game began as a gentle alternative to 10-pin bowling (see pp.332–33), but soon acquired a devoted following of its own.

V-formation
At the start of every frame, the skittles are set in a V-formation

1.07m (3ft 6in)

18.3m (60ft)

NEED2KNOW

→ The pins are 25 per cent smaller than those used for 10-pin bowling, and the ball can be held in the palm of the hand.

→ The game originates from – and is still almost exclusively confined to – Canada. There, some public bowling alleys offer both 5-pin and 10-pin.

→ Canada has three main annual knockout competitions: an open event, a youth challenge, and a doubles tournament. There is also a league programme.

EQUIPMENT

Originally carved out of maple wood, 5-pin skittles are now almost invariably mass-produced from plastic. The balls are made of solid rubber. Historically, they were of a uniformed design and colour, but since 1990 players have been allowed to personalize their balls with engravings and ID.

BOWLING BALLS
Unlike its 10-pin bowling equivalent, the 5-pin ball has no finger holes, so maintaining a good grip is important.

12.7cm (5in)

Easy to grip
The 5-pin ball weighs 1.6kg (3½lb) and is easy to grip

SHAPELY PIN
The 5-pin skittle is shorter and thinner than the equivalent used in 10-pin bowling. The ring around the bottom of the widest part of its circumference lowers the centre of gravity.

28.5cm (11¼in)

Belly band
The heavy rubber belly-band makes the pin bounce farther than a 10-pin when hit

9cm (3½in)

ATLATL

SPORT OVERVIEW

Atlatl involves using a sling device of the same name to throw a dart or light spear at a target. It combines the physical demands of the javelin in athletics (see p.70) with the accuracy of darts (see pp.342–43).

NEED2KNOW

→ Sling devices were used in many parts of the world until they were superseded by bows and arrows. Atlatl (pronounced "ott-lottle") is an Aztec word. The Aztecs were using the weapon for hunting up to the 16th century.

→ The International Standard Accuracy Competition (ISAC), established in 1996, is a standardized event for atlatlists from around the world.

→ Top players can hit targets up to 100m (325ft) away.

THROWING THE DART

The thrower, or atlatlist, holds the shaft by the handle and grips the dart, usually with his or her thumb and forefinger. As if throwing a javelin or a spear, the thrower brings their arm back and then swings it forwards. Finally, with a flick of the wrist the dart is released at the target.

ATLATL EVENTS

Atlatl events take place around the world, particularly in the US and Europe. Contests are held on dedicated ranges or in open country; each target is set at a different distance from the firing line, both for variety and to test a range of skills. The winner of an event scores the most points after shooting at all the targets.

HITTING THE TARGET
The targets may be any shape or size, but are usually similar to archery targets; others bear the outlines of wild animals. They all have marked areas that score varying numbers of points.

SLING DEVICE
An atlatl is a sling device composed of a single shaft of wood. Any type of wood can be used. At one end is a handle and at the other a means of holding the dart.

Get a grip	Large dart	Holding a dart
The thrower holds the atlatl by the handle	The dart resembles a large arrow and is at least 1.25m (4ft) long	A dart fits into a hook, pin, or socket

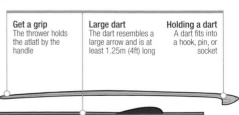

Foul line
Players must release the ball before they reach this mark

Height restriction
To ensure that balls are rolled, not thrown, a perspex sheet is placed across the lanes at a height of 15cm (6in)

SCORING
Players play ten frames per game, with up to three attempts per frame. If a player makes a strike, his or her scores on the next two attempts count double. The maximum game score is 450.

DECREASING VALUE
The foremost pin in the V-formation counts five points; the two behind it score three points each; the backmarkers are each worth two points.

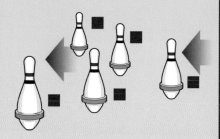

LANE DISCIPLINE
Players must not overstep the foul line at the start of the lane: any violation incurs a 15-pin penalty, which is deducted at the end of the game.

SKITTLES

GAME OVERVIEW
Skittle players or teams take turns to use a ball to knock down a diamond-shaped set of nine skittles at the end of an alley. The player or team that scores the most wins the match. Skittles has many variations; in some the skittles have to go down in a particular order. It is a traditional game that is popular in pubs in parts of England, and is also played in Germany and Austria.

VARIATIONS
Skittle alleys always have a smooth surface, often wooden, and are usually 6.4–11m (21–36ft) from the throwing mark to the front pin. Skittles vary in size and shape, and may include a kingpin. Balls also vary (one rare game uses a discus-shaped cheese) and are usually made of hardwood or rubber. They should be 10–15cm (4–6in) in diameter. The pins are 15–40cm (6–16in) high, and may weigh up to 3kg (6lb 10oz).

Depending on the local rules, the ball may be rolled along the floor, bowled underarm – either with or without a bounce – or simply thrown at the skittles. A match usually consists of 12 hands (turns), and each hand comprises three throws. A point is gained for every skittle knocked over, so the maximum score per hand is 27.

PIN LAYOUT
At the start of each turn, the nine skittles are set out in three rows of three as shown; they should be positioned no more than their own length apart.

HORSESHOE PITCHING

GAME OVERVIEW
Two players or two teams of two players take it in turns to pitch horseshoes at stakes in the ground. The winner scores the highest number of points or near misses. Horseshoe pitching is very popular in rural parts of the US.

LAW AND SCORE
Competitors stand at opposite ends of the playing area and aim their horseshoes at the stake next to their opponent's throwing position. They change ends after every turn, which consists of two throws.

A ringer (a horseshoe that lands around the stake) normally counts three points. The exception is when both players throw a ringer on the same turn, in which case nothing is scored. On each turn, the closest horseshoe to the stake (a near miss) scores one point. The winner is normally the first to 21, although some matches are played in sets.

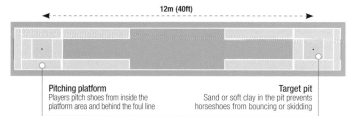

12m (40ft)

Pitching platform
Players pitch shoes from inside the platform area and behind the foul line

Target pit
Sand or soft clay in the pit prevents horseshoes from bouncing or skidding

PLAYING AREA
A stake stands in the centre of the target pit at each end of the playing area. There is a pitching platform on each side of a target pit.

High stakes
Stakes are 2.5cm (1in) in diameter and 37.5cm (15in) high

Sloping stake
A stake slopes at 7.5cm from the perpendicular towards the thrower

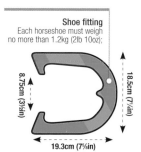

Shoe fitting
Each horseshoe must weigh no more than 1.2kg (2lb 10oz);

8.75cm (3½in)

18.5cm (7¼in)

19.3cm (7⅝in)

PITCHING A SHOE
The horseshoes used in modern horseshoe pitching are usually about twice the size of a real horseshoe. A player stands inside one of the two pitching platforms beside the target pit and pitches at the stake at the far end. For a throw to score points, the stake must be wholly inside an imaginary line between the ends of the horseshoe.

GAME OVERVIEW

With its roots in the game of billiards (see p.339), snooker is a sport where two players use cues and a cue ball to pot as many coloured balls as possible on a table with six pockets. Each of the balls has a points value and must be potted in a particular order. The player with the highest number of points wins the frame (game). Each match consists of an agreed odd number of frames, the winner being the player who secures the most frames.

SNOOKER

THE TABLE

A snooker table is made of a wooden frame within which sits a slate bed that is covered by a wool-based cloth known as baize. The table has six pockets with curved openings: two at the top cushion ("spot" end) corners, two at the bottom cushion ("baulk" end) corners and two in the middle of the side cushions (the centre pockets).

THE BAULK AND THE D

The area between the bottom cushion and a line (baulk line) 74cm (29in) along the table is known as the baulk. At the centre of the baulk line is a semi-circle with a radius of 29cm (11½in) that is called the D.

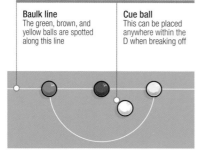

Baulk line
The green, brown, and yellow balls are spotted along this line

Cue ball
This can be placed anywhere within the D when breaking off

Pocket size
Each pocket has an opening of about 9cm (3½in)

Cushions
Also known as rails or bumpers, these are usually made of rubber

Slate bed
Pieces of slate up to 5cm (2in) thick provide the base for the playing surface

Green baize
The green cloth that covers the playing surface and cushions is made of wool

357cm (11ft 8½in)

Foot position
It is important to have a solid stance when playing a shot

Sighting the cue
Looking down the length of the cue helps with shot accuracy

Table frame
This can be made of a variety of materials, usually woods such as mahogany and ash

PLAYER PROFILE
As well as good hand-eye coordination, a snooker player needs to have a steady arm and a firm wrist to achieve total control of the cue and enable shots to be played with accuracy and precision. Mental agility, tactical awareness, and technical consistency are other useful attributes.

EQUIPMENT

A table, balls, and cues are the minimum equipment needed for a game of snooker. Rests, spiders, and extensions are specialist items used to help players execute difficult shots, while chalk adds control to the tip of the cue. For practical purposes, an overhead lamp provides additional lighting over the table.

CUES

These tapered shafts of wood come in one or two pieces and are traditionally made to a standard length of 147cm (4ft 10in), though slightly shorter varieties are also available.

Cue length
Under official rules, a snooker cue must be at least 91.5cm (3ft) long

RESTS AND SPIDERS

Usually constructed from a wooden shaft with a brass or nylon attachment, rests and spiders come in a range of shapes and sizes to suit different hard-to-reach shots.

Rest assured
The rest provides a raised bridge over balls adjacent to the cue ball

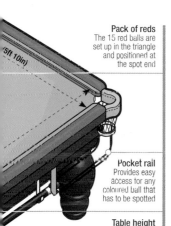

Pack of reds
The 15 red balls are set up in the triangle and positioned at the spot end

(5ft 10in)

Pocket rail
Provides easy access for any coloured ball that has to be spotted

Table height
The distance between the top of the cushion and the floor must be between 85cm and 87.5cm (2ft 9½in and 2ft 10½in)

THE BALLS

Modern snooker balls are made of a plastic called phenolic resin. In addition to the non-value white cue ball, there are 21 other balls on a snooker table: 15 reds (worth 1 point each), plus one each of yellow (2 points), green (3 points), brown (4 points), blue (5 points), pink (6 points), and black (7 points). Full-size balls measure 52mm (2in) in diameter but smaller balls can be used on reduced-sized tables.

1   2   3   4   5   6   7

TRIANGLE

Made of plastic or wood, a triangle is used to place the 15 red balls in their correct position on the table at the start of a frame. A tournament triangle is mounted on rollers for ease of positioning.

CHALK

This is applied to the cue tip, with the thin film of chalk providing grip on the ball when it is struck.

REFEREE

The referee has a variety of roles in a game of snooker including the placing of the balls in their correct position at the start of a frame and repositioning coloured balls – other than reds – after they have been potted during a frame (known as "spotting"). The referee also adjudicates on foul shots, supplies rests, spiders, and extensions when needed, and cleans a ball.

POCKET ROCKET

RONNIE "THE ROCKET" O'SULLIVAN IS THE MOST NATURALLY GIFTED PLAYER TO HAVE EMERGED IN THE SPORT FOR A GENERATION. SINCE TURNING PROFESSIONAL IN 1993 HE HAS WON EVERY MAJOR TOURNAMENT AT LEAST ONCE. EQUALLY ADEPT AT PLAYING RIGHT- AND LEFT-HANDED, THE CHARISMATIC O'SULLIVAN HAS SET NEW STANDARDS IN THE SPORT.

PLAYING BY THE RULES

At the heart of the sport of snooker is the sequence in which the balls must be potted. A red ball has to be potted alternately with a coloured ball until all the reds have been cleared from the table. After this, the colours must be potted in ascending order of their value – yellow, green, brown, blue, pink, and black.

FOULS

Foul shots generally incur a penalty of four points, which are added to the tally of the opposing player. Fouls can take place for a number of reasons including a player striking the ball with both feet off the ground (at least one foot has to be on the floor at all times), hitting a ball that is not "on" (an "on" ball is one that is valid for a player to strike, whether red or another colour), and missing a ball completely. A foul involving a high-scoring colour incurs a penalty to the value of the colour, so a foul on the black incurs a seven-point penalty.

BALL PLAY

There are a whole set of regulations regarding what can and cannot be done with the balls at any given time. One example is a touching ball, a situation that arises after a player plays a shot and the cue ball stops next to – and is touching – one of the other balls. In this case, a player has to strike the cue ball away from the touching ball without moving it otherwise a foul will be called.

SIDELINES

147 The maximum number of points that can be scored on a snooker table if every red ball potted is followed by a black.

15 The number of times Joe Davis won the World Championship (1927–40 and 1946).

4 The number of consecutive century breaks scored by John Higgins in his match against Ronnie O'Sullivan at the 2005 Grand Prix, the first time this had been done at a major tournament. The feat was equalled by Shaun Murphy when playing against Jamie Cope in the 2007 Welsh Open.

105,000,000 The number of Chinese television viewers who watched live as countryman Ding Junhui beat Stephen Hendry in the 2005 China Open.

POTTING TECHNIQUES

A good stance is a key factor in being able to attain the balance needed to play shots with confidence, and this can be achieved by bending the front leg but keeping the back leg straight. A player holds the cue with enough grip to be fully in control of it, but not too tightly – he will then be in an ideal position to place the cue in the "bridge" (hand position on the table) and line up a shot. Having decided which ball he is going to attempt to strike (the "object" ball) and what type of spin he is hoping to impart, he will pull the cue back and then forward onto the cue ball in one smooth motion.

CUEING

An effective cueing action will lead to consistently accurate shots that will enable a player to accumulate the points needed to win a frame. Keeping his arm over the cue as he is about to strike the ball ensures that the elbow with which he is holding the cue is in a straight line with the cue. Maintaining this position through the shot will enable him to hit the ball straight.

OPEN BRIDGE

To do this a player puts his hand flat on the table and positions the cue between his raised thumb and index finger. He raises his palm to follow-through on a shot or keeps it flat to screw the ball back.

CLOSED BRIDGE

Again a player puts his hand flat on the table, but this time he feeds the cue under his index finger and moves his thumb up so that there is a complete circle around the cue. The cue should be able to move smoothly through the circle.

ADDING SPIN

The most important technical ability in snooker is using spin to control the direction of the cue ball and its final resting position. Striking the cue ball on different areas will generate one of three types of spin – back spin, side spin, and top spin – that each have a particular effect on the behaviour of the ball.

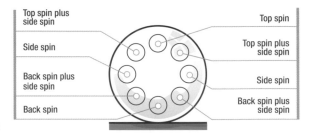

Top spin plus side spin	Top spin
Side spin	Top spin plus side spin
Back spin plus side spin	Side spin
Back spin	Back spin plus side spin

SWERVE

Swerve is a skill that can help to get a player out of a tricky situation or even make a difficult pot. The shot is played by lifting the back of the cue and hitting down on the cue ball either just left or right of centre. Combined with spin, it is an effective weapon in a player's armoury.

Hand position
Raising the palm off the table creates a high bridge

Strike down
A player strikes down on the cue ball, to the left of centre for left swerve as here, or right of centre for right swerve

Object ball
With a little luck and a lot of practice a player should be able to hit the object ball and either steer himself out of trouble or make a pot

BREAKING OFF

The break takes place at the start of each frame, with the basic premise that the player breaking off must strike one of the red balls. A good break will see the cue ball hitting a red ball with the minimum disruption to the pack of reds and then coming back up the table to rest as close to the baulk cushion as possible. This will then put pressure on the opposing player.

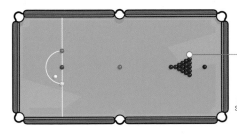

Corner ball
The cue ball should strike the base of the pack and have enough side spin to return to a safe position

BUILDING A BREAK

The most important aspect of amassing points in one visit to the table is thinking ahead to the next shot and the cue ball position needed to get on that shot. A player may well forego an easy shot in order to get position on or pot a ball of higher value. Getting balls into pottable positions is also vital, so a shot that opens up the pack of reds can pay rich dividends.

SAFETY SHOTS

A successful game of snooker is not just about potting the balls. In certain situations it is more beneficial to play a shot that will leave the cue ball in a difficult position for an opponent and open up the possibility of him playing a foul stroke. The ultimate safety shot is a "snooker", when a player's stroke leaves his opponent unable to get a direct line to a red or coloured ball that he must play. Frames can easily be won with strong safety play.

INSIDE STORY

Snooker developed out of variants of the game of billiards that were played by British Army officers stationed in India in the 1870s, with coloured balls added to games previously consisting solely of 15 reds and a black. The word snooker itself came from a term for a new army recruit and was reputedly first used in 1875 by a Colonel Neville Chamberlain to describe the (inexperienced) players of this new game.

WORLD ASSOCIATION

Snooker's governing body is the World Professional Billiards and Snooker Association (WPBSA). It has a commercial arm known as World Snooker that runs the professional tournament circuit and negotiates television rights around the world. The body has had great success in developing the Far Eastern market where the sport is gaining rapidly in popularity. This is due partly to the rise through the ranks of a number of high-quality players from the region, such as Ding Jinhui from China and James Wattana from Thailand.

BILLIARDS

GAME OVERVIEW

There are many different types of billiards, the most popular forms being carom billiards and English billiards. A carom table has no pockets – scoring is achieved by striking two balls onto one another. An English table does incorporate pockets, and scoring takes place either in the carom style or by potting the balls.

THE TABLE

A billiards table is made up of a raised flat slate bed that is covered with fine woollen cloth. The playing surface is surrounded by cushioned edges that are flush around the table for carom but have six pockets set within them for English billiards.

SCORING

In carom, a "count" (point) is scored when a player hits the object ball and the opponent's cue ball in one stroke. In English billiards, this is known as a "cannon" and is worth two points. Extra points are scored by potting or going in off the red ball (three points) or an opponent's cue ball (two points). A single stroke can amass different types of points. For example, a cannon followed by potting the red will secure five points.

THE BALLS

Both carom and English billiards use just three balls: two cue balls (one white and one spotted white or yellow ball) and one red object ball. Each player is assigned his or her own cue ball and keeps it throughout the game.

Spotted white cue ball

Yellow cue ball

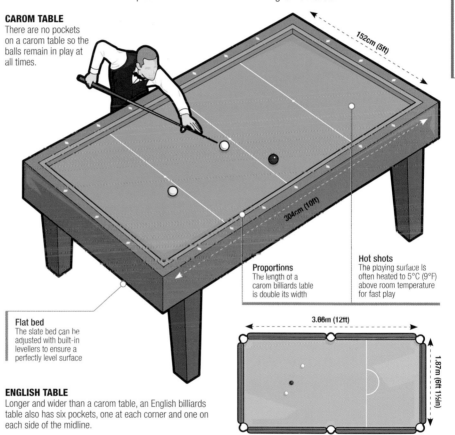

CAROM TABLE
There are no pockets on a carom table so the balls remain in play at all times.

152cm (5ft)

304cm (10ft)

Proportions
The length of a carom billiards table is double its width

Hot shots
The playing surface is often heated to 5°C (9°F) above room temperature for fast play

Flat bed
The slate bed can be adjusted with built-in levellers to ensure a perfectly level surface

ENGLISH TABLE
Longer and wider than a carom table, an English billiards table also has six pockets, one at each corner and one on each side of the midline.

3.66m (12ft)

1.87m (6ft 1½in)

PLAYING BY THE RULES

At the start of a game of carom billiards the balls are placed on three spots on the table: the red ball on the foot spot, the opponent's cue ball on the head spot, and the breaker's cue ball no more than 15cm (6in) from the centre spot on the head string. The only rule is that the breaker must hit the red ball first. Foul shots include striking the wrong cue ball and playing two safety shots in succession. These incur a penalty of missing a turn and losing any count that resulted from the foul stroke.

In English billiards, the red ball is positioned on a spot at the top of the table and the breaker's cue ball is placed within the D (the opponent's cue ball is left off until his or her turn). Penalty points are added to the opponent's score for failing to strike a ball (one point) and for pocketing the cue ball without hitting a ball (three points).

STRINGING
This is the method used to determine the order of play in English billiards (known as "lagging" in carom). Before a game, the players take an as-yet-unassigned cue ball each and hit it from the baulk line so that it rebounds off the top cushion. The player whose ball stops closest to the baulk cushion has the choice of which cue ball to use and the option of shooting first.

OBJECT BALLS

In all forms of pool the cue ball is white and the object balls are coloured and usually numbered. In 8-ball pool and blackball pool, there are 15 object balls: those numbered 1 to 7 have different solid colours, while balls numbered 9 to 15 are white with different coloured stripes and the 8-ball is a solid black. (The numbers on the 6 and 9 balls are underscored to avoid possible confusion.) One variation of 8-ball pool which is common in Great Britain uses seven red and seven yellow balls without numbers but a numbered black.

Players of 9-ball pool use 9 of the numbered object balls – 1 to 8 are solid colours and the 9-ball is striped. In the game of 14:1 continuous pool the 15 object balls are numbered.

POOL

GAME OVERVIEW

Popular in clubs and bars around the world, pool is a cue sport played with a set number of balls on a dedicated table with six pockets. Various forms include 8-ball, 9-ball, blackball, and 14:1 continuous pool (straight pool). Rules may vary from place to place. There are many local, national, and world championships for individuals and teams in men, women, and junior categories.

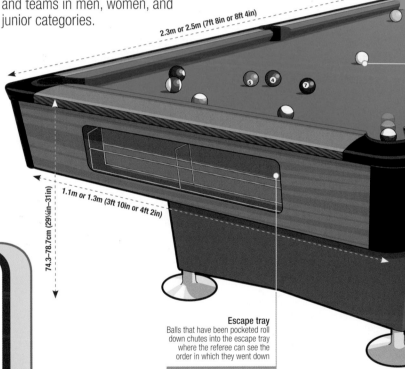

2.3m or 2.5m (7ft 8in or 8ft 4in)

1.1m or 1.3m (3ft 10in or 4ft 2in)

74.3–78.7cm (29¼in–31in)

Escape tray
Balls that have been pocketed roll down chutes into the escape tray where the referee can see the order in which they went down

Cue tip
The cue tip may be no more than 14mm (½in) in diameter

Cue shaft
The wooden shaft must be at least 1m (39½in) long. It may have an internal ferrule for weight and balance

Chalk cube
Players apply chalk to the tip of their cue for "true" contact with the white ball

Rest for support
To help them with shots that are hard to reach players use a rest (also known as a rake or crutch) to support their cue

Racking up
In 8-ball a triangle is used to arrange the object balls at the start of each game

STAT CENTRAL

WPA WORLD 9-BALL CHAMPIONS		
YEAR	NAME	COUNTRY
2012	D. APPLETON	(GBR)
2011	Y. AKAGARIYAMA	(JPN)
2010	F. BUSTAMENTE	(PHI)

WEPF WORLD 8-BALL CHAMPIONS		
YEAR	NAME	(COUNTRY)
2012	JOHN ROE	(ENG)
2011	ADAM DAVIS	(ENG)
2010	MICK HILL	(ENG)
2009	PHIL HARRISON	(ENG)
2008	GARETH POTTS	(ENG)
2007	GARETH POTTS	(ENG)
2006	MARK SELBY	(ENG)
2005	GARETH POTTS	(ENG)
2004	MICK HILL	(ENG)
2003	CHRIS MELLING	(ENG)
2002	JASON TWIST	(ENG)

FAIR AND FOUL

In 8-ball pool the player who pots the first ball must continue potting balls of the same type (either solids or stripes). A player who pots all seven of their balls can then try to pot the black. Whoever pots this 8-ball in a nominated pocket wins the game. In 9-ball pool players have to hit the lowest numbered ball on the table but do not have to pocket the balls in sequence. The 9-ball must be pocketed last. In 14:1 continuous pool players nominate a ball and a pocket, scoring a point each time they achieve it.

Players continue shooting until they either fail to pot an object ball or commit a foul – for example, by potting the white ball or an opponent's ball. Any player who prematurely pots the 8-ball in 8-ball pool or the 9-ball in 9-ball pool automatically forfeits the game.

DO THE HUSTLE

HUSTLERS HANG OUT IN POOL HALLS LOOKING FOR PLAYERS WHO FANCY THEMSELVES BUT AREN'T PARTICULARLY GOOD. THEY SUGGEST A GAME, LOSE IT, THEN PLAY ANOTHER ONE FOR MONEY. AT THIS POINT THEY START PLAYING PROPERLY, COMPREHENSIVELY BEAT THEIR OPPONENT, AND POCKET THE STAKES. THE "ART" WAS IMMORTALIZED BY PAUL NEWMAN IN THE FILM *THE HUSTLER*.

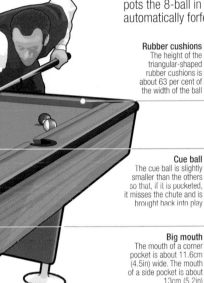

Rubber cushions
The height of the triangular-shaped rubber cushions is about 63 per cent of the width of the ball

Cue ball
The cue ball is slightly smaller than the others so that, if it is pocketed, it misses the chute and is brought back into play

Big mouth
The mouth of a corner pocket is about 11.6cm (4.5in) wide. The mouth of a side pocket is about 13cm (5.2in)

SPIN AND SWERVE

Pool players, like snooker players, can spin the cue ball in a number of ways. As they pot an object ball they may apply top spin, back spin, or side spin to help them gain a good position for their next shot. Sometimes, the path of the cue ball is blocked by an opponent's ball or by the black, preventing a player from hitting their object ball easily. Skilled players get round this by hitting the ball off-centre, causing it to swerve: the further to the left or right of centre, the greater the deviation. This is known as "putting side on it". To swerve round a ball that is very near the cue ball, players use the massé shot (from the French "to rub"), hitting the white off-centre with a downward movement.

TOP SPIN

Top spin makes the white ball run on after it has hit the object ball. Players hit the cue ball above its "equator", causing it to revolve forwards on its axis faster than normal.

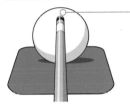

Run on
For top spin, players hit the top of the cue ball

BACK SPIN

Back spin makes the white ball move backwards after hitting the object ball. Players hit the cue ball below the middle – its "equator" – causing it to return towards them.

Pullback
For back spin, players hit the bottom of the cue ball

Corner balls
The two corner balls at the base of the 8-ball rack must be of different types

Foot spot
The apex ball sits on the foot spot when the balls are racked in 8-ball

Playing surface
Baize made of 85 per cent combed worsted wool, and no more than 15 per cent nylon

Head string
The opening break is made from behind the line of the head string

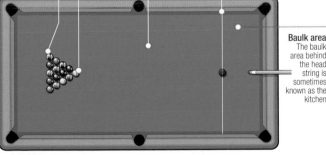

Baulk area
The baulk area behind the head string is sometimes known as the kitchen

INSIDE STORY

Eight-ball pool is most popular in Great Britain and Europe, where it is played in clubs and pubs as well as in dedicated pool halls. Variations in the rules of 8-ball, particularly in Britain, include positioning the black on the foot spot when the balls are racked at the start of a game and giving two shots to an opponent after committing a foul. The World Eightball Pool Federation (WEPF) was set up in 1992 to unite the various organizations who promote 8-ball pool, to set criteria for the players, and to organize an annual World Championship.

WORLD POOL-BILLIARD ASSOCIATION (WPA)

The WPA was founded by members of the World Confederation of Billiard Sports (WCBS) in 1990. The WPA organizes a World 9-ball Championship and an annual World 8-ball Championship that rivals the event organized by the WEPF.

SIDELINES

526 The number of balls pocketed consecutively without a miss by one player in a single session. This record high run was achieved by US champion Willie Mosconi while playing an exhibition match of 14:1 continuous pool in 1954.

128 The number of finalists (from more than 40 countries) in the men's 2011 World Pool Championships in Qatar. The competition opened with 16 groups of eight; the top four in each went forward to a knockout. The first prize was US$36,000.

DARTS

NEED2KNOW

→ Although the starting score is usually 501, it can also be 301, 601, 801, or even 1,001.

→ The throwing line is known as the oche (pronounced "okky"), from the French "ocher", to cut a groove.

→ More than six million people regularly play darts.

→ The quickest way to get down from 501 is in nine darts.

→ Darts is a popular TV sport, with audiences of up to five million in countries such as Britain and the Netherlands.

GAME OVERVIEW

In this enthralling and popular game, two players – male or female – take turns to throw three arrow-like projectiles at a circular board. The target area is divided into a total of 62 sections, each of which counts a different number of points when a dart sticks in it. The object is to score from 501 to zero in fewer throws than the opponent, with the last dart hitting one of the sections that scores double points or, less commonly, the bullseye. The game is mainly about accurate aim and steel nerves, but it is also about mathematics: players need to be able to work out how best to reach the target score.

Follow through
After the throw, the arm is fully extended

Non-throwing hand
The player holds the remaining darts with their points in his palm

Personalized shirts
Loose-fitting shirts may be personalized with the player's name on front and back or in national colours

Toeing the line
A throw does not count if the player oversteps the oche

HARROWING ARROWING

ALL PLAYERS DREAD "DARTITIS", OR THE YIPS, A NERVOUS CONDITION THAT PREVENTS THEM THROWING SMOOTHLY. NO ONE KNOWS WHAT CAUSES IT – OR HOW TO CURE IT. ONE HIGH-PROFILE VICTIM WAS FORMER WORLD CHAMPION ERIC BRISTOW, WHO WAS EVENTUALLY FORCED TO GIVE UP THE GAME IN THE 2000.

PLAYER PROFILE

Darts still has a close link with bars, although professionals no longer drink or smoke on the oche. Today, more and more young players are attracted to the sport. Concentration and hand-eye coordination are keys to success, along with being able to repeat the same movement countless times with only tiny adjustments.

STAT CENTRAL

TOP CHECKOUTS

SCORE	OUTSHOT
170	TREBLE 20, TREBLE 20, BULL
167	TREBLE 20, TREBLE 19, BULL
164	TREBLE 20, TREBLE 18, BULL
161	TREBLE 20, TREBLE 17, BULL
160	TREBLE 20, TREBLE 20, DOUBLE 20
158	TREBLE 20, TREBLE 20, DOUBLE 19
157	TREBLE 20, TREBLE 19, DOUBLE 20
156	TREBLE 20, TREBLE 20, DOUBLE 18
155	TREBLE 20, TREBLE 19, DOUBLE 19
154	TREBLE 20, TREBLE 18, DOUBLE 20
153	TREBLE 20, TREBLE 19, DOUBLE 18
152	TREBLE 20, TREBLE 20, DOUBLE 16
151	TREBLE 20, TREBLE 17, DOUBLE 20
150	TREBLE 20, TREBLE 18, DOUBLE 18
149	TREBLE 20, TREBLE 19, DOUBLE 16
148	TREBLE 20, TREBLE 16, DOUBLE 20

Scorer or referee
May be two officials; sometimes both roles are performed by one person

Announcer
Announces the score after every three darts and the score still required at the start of what may be the last three darts

Oche
Feet must be behind the oche, but the thrower may lean across it

Thrower
Throws from as close as possible to eye level

Non-thrower
Must not obstruct or be in the thrower's field of vision

1.73m (5ft 8in)

2.37m (7ft 9¼in)

BOARD DISCUSSION

The bed of a dartboard is made of cork, sisal, and synthetic materials to give it a "bristle" appearance. Wire separates each scoring section; a dart that lands within a section scores the points, even if it bends the wire out of place. A dart that bounces back off the wire does not count.

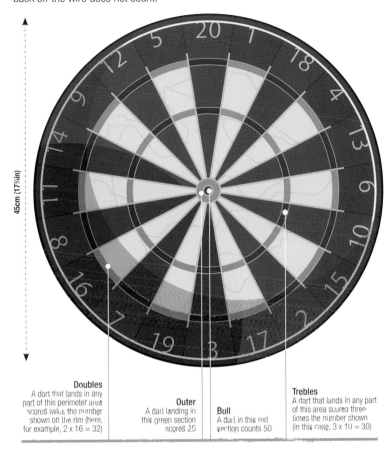

45cm (17¾in)

Doubles
A dart that lands in any part of this perimeter area scores twice the number shown on the rim (here, for example, 2 x 16 = 32)

Outer
A dart landing in this green section scores 25

Bull
A dart in this red section counts 50

Trebles
A dart that lands in any part of this area scores three times the number shown (in this case, 3 x 10 = 30)

CHECKOUT TIME

For the first few darts, players try to score as high as possible, normally going for treble 20 each time. Nearing zero, they often try to leave themselves 32, so they can throw at double 16. This is the checkout of choice because a narrow miss that scores a single 16 leaves them on double 8, which is adjacent on the board. If that fails and they get a single 8, they can go for a double 4, and in turn double 2 and then double 1.

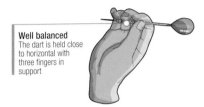

Well balanced
The dart is held close to horizontal with three fingers in support

STANDARD GRIP

The shaft is gripped between thumb and index finger, and steadied on the middle and third fingers; the little finger is withdrawn slightly out of the way.

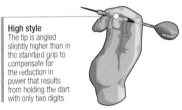

High style
The tip is angled slightly higher than in the standard grip to compensate for the reduction in power that results from holding the dart with only two digits

PENCIL GRIP

The dart is held between thumb and forefinger alone. This common variant of the standard grip is used by many leading players, including 16-times world champion Phil "The Power" Taylor.

ARROWS OF DESIRE

The maximum permitted weight of a dart is 50g (1.8oz). The pointed tip may be made of brass (the cheapest material), alloys of nickel and silver, or tungsten (the most expensive). The shaft is made of plastic or solid aluminium. The flight is detachable and replaceable; it is either tough nylon or flexible plastic.

Types of tip
The choice between hard (tungsten) and other "soft" tips is a matter of individual preference

Finger grip
The thick cylindrical casing around the middle section of the shaft helps balance the dart and makes it easier to hold

Spinning shafts
Some darts have shafts that spin while in flight. Although this does not make them fly truer, it does help the thrower to get close groupings on the board because it enables the flights to slip in next to each other. Rigid shafts increase the likelihood of rebounds

Stabilizing end
The flight has four tailplanes at 90 degrees to each other

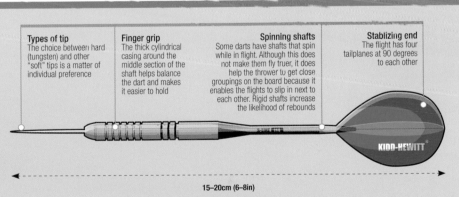

15–20cm (6–8in)

INSIDE STORY

Darts may have developed from archery – early dartboards had concentric targets, as in archery, and darts is still known as "arrows". Darts was a regional game in Britain until the rules were codified in the 1920s. The sport enjoyed a heyday in the 1930s – helped when King George VI and his wife, Queen Elizabeth, were photographed throwing darts in a pub near Windsor. The sport's next boom came in the 1970s, with the introduction of TV games, the emergence of the first darts stars, and the establishment of the World Darts Federation (WDF) and the British Darts Organisation (BDO). The WDF now has 68 member nations.

PROFESSIONAL DARTS CORPORATION (PDC)

In 1992, one of the world's leading players, Phil Taylor, led 15 other top players out of the BDO to form a rival body, the Professional Darts Council, later corporation, (PDC). The PDC has held its own world championship since 1994. It now runs a thriving tour with competitions as far afield as Blackpool and Las Vegas. Top BDO player Raymond van Barneveld defected to the PDC in 2006.

SPORT OVERVIEW

Archery today is far-removed from its roots in hunting and warfare. As a modern sport it involves two or more archers competing against each other to get the highest score by hitting a target that is usually circular, but may also be the outline of a wild animal. Most competitions are held in several stages, at each of which the archers shoot from different distances to display their versatility. Round targets are marked in rings: the closer the ring to the centre, the greater the number of points for a hit. On animal targets, the top scoring areas are those in which a blow to a real animal would be lethal. The winner of an archery tournament is the contestant with the highest points total after a previously agreed number of shots.

ARCHERY

NEED2KNOW

→ The World Archery Federation is the world governing body for archery, and has held annual world championships since 1931.

→ Archery for hunting and warfare has been practised for at least the last 5,000 years. As a sport, archery developed from military training exercises.

→ There are four Olympic events, all over 70m: men's individual, women's individual, men's team, and women's team.

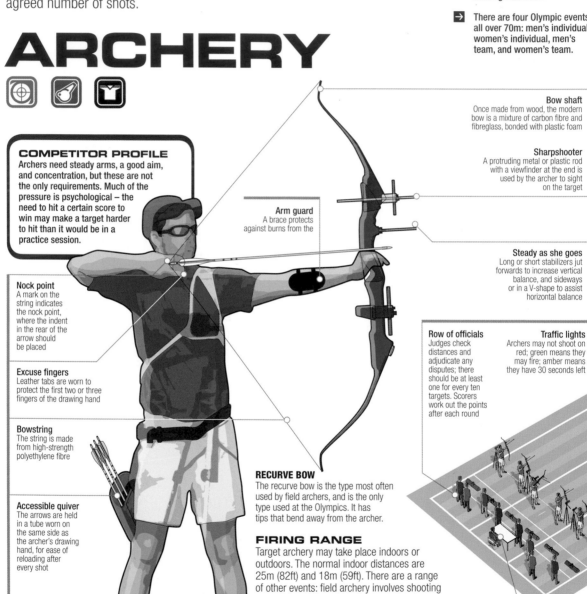

COMPETITOR PROFILE
Archers need steady arms, a good aim, and concentration, but these are not the only requirements. Much of the pressure is psychological – the need to hit a certain score to win may make a target harder to hit than it would be in a practice session.

Nock point
A mark on the string indicates the nock point, where the indent in the rear of the arrow should be placed

Excuse fingers
Leather tabs are worn to protect the first two or three fingers of the drawing hand

Bowstring
The string is made from high-strength polyethylene fibre

Accessible quiver
The arrows are held in a tube worn on the same side as the archer's drawing hand, for ease of reloading after every shot

Stand fast
Archers wear sturdy shoes with smooth soles to maximize the area in contact with the ground

Arm guard
A brace protects against burns from the

Bow shaft
Once made from wood, the modern bow is a mixture of carbon fibre and fibreglass, bonded with plastic foam

Sharpshooter
A protruding metal or plastic rod with a viewfinder at the end is used by the archer to sight on the target

Steady as she goes
Long or short stabilizers jut forwards to increase vertical balance, and sideways or in a V-shape to assist horizontal balance

RECURVE BOW
The recurve bow is the type most often used by field archers, and is the only type used at the Olympics. It has tips that bend away from the archer.

FIRING RANGE
Target archery may take place indoors or outdoors. The normal indoor distances are 25m (82ft) and 18m (59ft). There are a range of other events: field archery involves shooting up and downhill, making the target harder to sight. In ski and run archery, competitors shoot at targets after skiing or running a set course, a little like the biathlon (see pp.306–307). Flight archery, although rarely seen in competition, is one of the purest forms of the sport. There is no target: the aim is simply to fire an arrow as far as possible.

Row of officials
Judges check distances and adjudicate any disputes; there should be at least one for every ten targets. Scorers work out the points after each round

Traffic lights
Archers may not shoot on red; green means they may fire; amber means they have 30 seconds left

Director's chair
The director of shooting controls the competition, and receives points tallies from the scorers

Visual aid
A telescope helps archers see what they have scored and calculate what they still need

A ROBIN HOOD

ONE OF THE RAREST ACHIEVEMENTS IN ARCHERY IS SPLITTING THE SHAFT OF AN ARROW ALREADY IN THE TARGET WITH A LATER SHOT. ARCHERS WHO PERFORM THIS FEAT – KNOWN AS "A ROBIN HOOD" AFTER THE LEGENDARY 12TH-CENTURY ENGLISH BOWMAN – GET TO KEEP THE ARROWS AS A PROUD TROPHY OF THE FEAT.

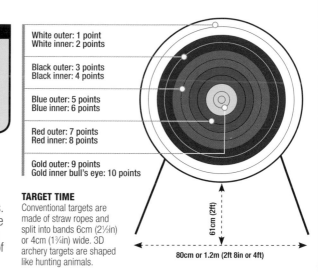

White outer: 1 point
White inner: 2 points

Black outer: 3 points
Black inner: 4 points

Blue outer: 5 points
Blue inner: 6 points

Red outer: 7 points
Red inner: 8 points

Gold outer: 9 points
Gold inner bull's eye: 10 points

61cm (2ft)

80cm or 1.2m (2ft 8in or 4ft)

FLIGHT CONTROL

In FITA tournaments archers have a fixed amount of time to shoot 12 rounds (a total of 36 arrows) at targets between 30m (98ft) and 90m (295ft) away. Scores are updated after six arrows at longer distances and three at shorter distances.

An arrow touching two colours or a dividing line scores the higher value, and one that rebounds from or passes through the target counts only if it leaves a clear mark. In the event of a tie, the winner is the archer with the most scoring hits.

TARGET TIME
Conventional targets are made of straw ropes and split into bands 6cm (2½in) or 4cm (1¾in) wide. 3D archery targets are shaped like hunting animals.

Nock
A V-shaped indentation in the end of the shaft holds the arrow steadily in place on the bowstring

Fletching display
Once made of feathers, modern flights are made of plastic; they help arrows maintain speed and direction

Shaft structure
Arrows used to be made from wood, but are now usually made of carbon fibre or an alloy of carbon and aluminium

Top tip
The sharp point screws onto the arrow, so that it can be adjusted forwards or backwards, as the archer prefers

---

60m line
Only used in women's events

2.5–15m (8–50ft) per target

90m line

80m line

70m line

60m line

50m line

40m line

90m (295ft) line
Only men shoot at this range

30m (98ft) line
The shortest outdoor range

50m (164ft) line
A common range for men and women

70m (230ft) line
The outdoor Olympic distance for both men and women

INSIDE STORY

Archery featured in the Olympics from 1900, but was dropped after 1920 because there were no internationally agreed rules. The establishment of FITA in 1931 changed all that, and the sport was reintroduced at the 1972 Games for both men and women. FITA was established by seven countries, but now has members from 149 countries.

ON TARGET

Archers with a dominant right eye hold the bow in their left hands, and vice versa. Each shot takes only about 15–20 seconds from loading to firing, but holding the bow and pulling the string is still tiring. Archers rest ("let down") their bows in between shots to conserve their strength.

PREPARATION FOR SHOT
The archer stands with the leading shoulder towards the target and the feet set shoulder-width apart. He or she points the bow at the ground and loads the arrow by placing the front of its shaft on the arrow rest and the bowstring into the v-shaped nock at its fletching end.

DRAWING AND TAKING AIM
Holding the string between the index and middle fingers, or the index and middle and ring fingers, the archer pulls it back, raises the bow, and looks down the sight at the target. This position is held at the "anchor point". Some bows have a clicker that sounds when the archer reaches the right draw length.

FOLLOW THROUGH
As the archer prepares to fire, his or her bowstring hand should be resting against the cheek. The arrow is fired by relaxing and straightening the fingers of the drawing hand. Once the shot has been made, the archer "lets down" the bow to rest, and reaches into the quiver for the next arrow.

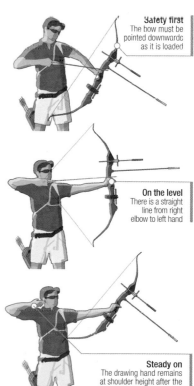

Safety first
The bow must be pointed downwards as it is loaded

On the level
There is a straight line from right elbow to left hand

Steady on
The drawing hand remains at shoulder height after the arrow has flown

→ Pistol shooting featured in the first Olympic Games of 1896. The events have evolved as the manufacture of guns has developed and changed.

→ Some nations with strict gun control laws, including the UK, do not televise shooting events.

→ Target pistol shooting in its modern form is the conservationist's alternative to pigeon shooting.

→ There are five pistol events at the Olympic Games.

COMPETITOR PROFILE

Pistol shooters need extraordinary powers of concentration and mental focus to remain relaxed under pressure, as any nervous tension in the shooting arm will cause the shot to go off-centre of the target. Shooters also need strength and stamina.

PISTOL SHOOTING

SPORT OVERVIEW

In this sport, competitors stand and, with one hand, fire a pistol at a circular target divided into ten concentric rings; the nearer to the centre the shots land, the higher they score; the centre (the bull's-eye) scores ten. The sport takes place on a shooting range. There are a number of events, which are distinguished by the type of pistol used and the distance the competitor stands from the target.

Ear protection
Contestants wear ear plugs, ear muffs or some other form of ear protection while in the vicinity of the firing line

Shooting arm
The arm that holds the pistol is extended and must be completely unsupported

Eye protection
Competitors wear shatterproof safety glasses or similar protection to guard their eyes during the event

Competitor's gun
Three types of pistol are used, depending on the event

Competitors' clothing
No specific clothing is required, but garments that would help immobilize the arms, legs or body are not allowed, and only low-sided shoes, without ankle supports, can be worn

Free hand
The non-shooting hand must not be used in any way; it is usually tucked into a pocket or belt

SHOOTING RANGE

Pistol shooting events take place on a shooting range. Safety is of paramount importance, and officials are on hand to check the competitors' pistols, check the targets, and sometimes to keep a note of the scores after each round of shooting.

CONCENTRIC RINGS

The target is composed of concentric rings. The numbers are the points scored when a shot falls in a ring. Shots hitting a line are awarded the higher point. Targets and the central ring (the 10 ring) vary in size.

SIDELINES

154 The number of national federation members from five continents that are affiliated to the International Shooting Sports Federation.

3 The number of Olympic golds won by German sportsman Ralf Schumann, the most successful pistol shooter to date in the 25m rapid-fire event. His victories came in 1992, 1996, and 2004.

581 The world record score for the 50m pistol event, set by Russian sportsman Alexander Melentiev at the 1980 Olympic Games. A perfect score would be 600; a score of around 570 is considered to be world-class.

Outer rings
Rings scoring 1 to 6 are white

Inner rings
Rings scoring 7 to 10 are black

Shooting station
Each shooting station is 1.25m x 2.5m (4ft 1in x 8ft 2in)

Group of competitors
A group of competitors will all compete at the same time. In Olympic finals, there will be six to eight competitors at the shooting station

TYPES OF PISTOL

Different types of pistol are used for the different events – the 10m air pistol, the 25m pistol, and the 50m pistol. A pistol's calibre is the diameter of its bore. For safety reasons, the ammunition must be made of lead or a similarly soft material. Regulations only allow open sights on the guns so mirrors, optical sights, and telescopic sights are all prohibited. Officials carefully check each competitor's gun before an event begins to make sure the pistol complies with the event's regulations. If a competitor's gun malfunctions during an event he or she has 15 minutes in which to repair or replace it.

10M AIR PISTOL

Competitors use 4.5mm (.177in) calibre pistols that fire lead pellets at targets 10m (32.8ft) away. The maximum allowable weight of the pistol is 1.5kg (3lb oz). The diameter of the 10 ring is 11.5mm (½in).

Ammunition propulsion
The ammunition is propelled by pre-compressed air or by a carbon dioxide cylinder

25M PISTOL

The same requirements govern the women's 25m pistol and the men's 25m rapid-fire pistol events. The guns have a calibre of 5.6mm (.22in) with a maximum weight of 1.4kg (3lb). The diameter of the 10 ring in the rapid fire target is 10cm (4in).

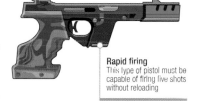

Rapid firing
This type of pistol must be capable of firing five shots without reloading

50M PISTOL

Competitors use 5.6mm (.22in) calibre pistols, which may have a special customized grip but no maximum weight regulation. The precision target stands 50m (164ft) away and the diameter of its 10 ring is 5cm (2in).

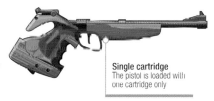

Single cartridge
The pistol is loaded with one cartridge only

OLYMPIC EVENTS

There are five Olympic pistol shooting events, two for women and three for men. The 10m air pistol event, which first featured in the Olympic Games in 1988, is contested by both men and women (in separate events). Men shoot 60 shots within 105 minutes, while women shoot 40 shots within 75 minutes. Women contest the 25m pistol event, in which two rounds of 30 shots are fired. Men contest the 25m rapid-fire pistol event, which also consists of two rounds of 30 shots. Men contest the precision 50m pistol event, in which they fire 60 shots within 120 minutes.

OVERALL WINNER

In each event all competitors take part in a qualification round, from which the best eight (or six for 25m Rapid Fire Men event) proceed to the final. The scores they achieve in the qualification round are added to their final round – whoever has the most points overall is the winner.

PERFECT SCORES

Scoring in the events can be complicated but competitors aim for perfect scores. For example, in the 25m rapid-fire event, the perfect match score is 600 for qualification rounds and a score of 592 is categorized as world class.

ONE-HANDED CHAMPION

KAROLY TAKACS WAS A MEMBER OF THE HUNGARIAN PISTOL SHOOTING TEAM WHEN, IN 1938, HE LOST HIS RIGHT HAND IN A GRENADE EXPLOSION. HE TAUGHT HIMSELF TO SHOOT LEFT-HANDED AND BECAME HUNGARIAN PISTOL SHOOTING CHAMPION IN 1940. HE WENT ON TO WIN GOLD MEDALS IN THE RAPID-FIRE PISTOL EVENT AT THE OLYMPIC GAMES IN LONDON IN 1948 AND AGAIN IN HELSINKI IN 1952.

Target distance
The targets are 10m, 25m, or 50m away from the competitors, depending on the event

25m (82ft)

15m (49ft 6in)

10m (33ft)

Length of the range
The target range has no stipulated overall length, but will be more than 50m (164ft) long to allow sufficient room for targets to be set up for the 50m pistol event

Competitors' targets
Each competitor has his or her own target to fire at. A competitor is penalized if one of their shots accidentally hits a neighbouring target

INSIDE STORY

Along with other target shooting disciplines, pistol shooting is governed by the International Shooting Sports Federation (ISSF), which was established in 1998 and was formerly the International Shooting Union (ISU). The ISSF supervises the World Championships every four years, two years after the Olympic Games. Pistol shooting events in the World Championships are organized for individuals and teams in men, women, and junior categories. The ISSF also supervises World Cups, Continental Championships, and Continental Games. The introduction, in 1989, of a new electronic scoring system superseded paper targets at major competitions and enabled spectators to know results immediately. A new television era was born at the Olympic Games in Barcelona in 1992 when many viewers around the world witnessed coverage of the shooting events for the first time.

INTERNATIONAL SHOOTING SPORTS FEDERATION (ISSF)

The target shooting sport throughout the world is governed by the International Shooting Sports Federation, which is based in Germany.

SHOTGUN SHOOTING

SPORT OVERVIEW

Shotgun shooting is an event in which competitors use a smooth-bored (unrifled) shotgun to shoot at clay targets that are released from a machine called a trap. Clay Target shooting can be broadly split into three categories – trap, skeet, and sporting. Trap and skeet are both performed at the Olympic Games, while sporting involves shooting at targets designed to simulate those found in nature.

Optical sights
Any devices that can be fitted to the gun to help the shooter sight the target, such as magnifying lenses, are prohibited

Shotgun barrel
Skeet-shooting guns often have a shorter barrel than trap-shooting guns (60–71cm/24–28in compared to about 71–86cm/28–34in), because of the shorter-range targets

Ear protection
Competitors are advised to wear ear muffs or some other form of protective gear to protect their hearing

Shotgun gauge
The shotguns used are generally of 12-gauge calibre. Smaller-gauge guns can be used, but anything larger than 12-gauge is not allowed

Sleeveless jacket
No specific clothing is required, but shooters tend to wear a loose sleeveless jacket with large pockets in which to store their cartridges. Shooters generally wear a fairly loose-fitting t-shirt or shirt so their arm movements are not restricted

Shooting position
In all shotgun shooting events the competitors fire at the targets from a standing position

COMPETITOR PROFILE
Shotgun shooters need to focus, both mentally and physically. They need excellent hand-eye coordination and visual–spatial skills. They need to be able to anticipate the trajectory of a fast-moving target and shoot slightly ahead of it, so that they can hit it.

FIELDS OF PLAY

The skeet and the trap events utilize different fields of play. The Olympic skeet field features eight shooting stations arranged in a semi-circle. The competitors shoot from each station in turn. The targets are released from a high and a low trap house at either side of the semi-circle. The trap field features five banks of three traps that sit within a trench that is 15m (49ft) from the shooters. In the double trap event (not illustrated here), two targets are released simultaneously at different heights and angles from the centre bank of traps, with competitors getting one shot at each target. There are five shooting stations, but unlike the trap field, they set in a straight line.

NEED2KNOW

→ The modern sport of shotgun shooting (both trap and skeet) is derived from the custom of shooting birds, in particular pigeons and pheasants, for sport.

→ Skeet shooting was invented in 1915 as a recreational sport. Live pigeons were used at first, but they were eventually replaced with clay targets.

→ Trap shooting has been part of the Olympics since 1950, whereas skeet shooting appeared at the Games for the first time in 1968.

→ The word "skeet" is derived from an old Scandinavian word which means "shooting". The term was adopted by the sport in 1926.

SPORTING CONTROVERSY

IN 1992, CHINA'S SHAN ZHANG BECAME THE FIRST WOMAN TO WIN A MIXED-SEX SHOOTING EVENT IN THE OLYMPIC SKEET. THE EVENTS WERE SUBSEQUENTLY SEGREGATED, AND SHAN WAS NOT ALLOWED TO DEFEND HER TITLE.

THE OLYMPIC SKEETFIELD

A standard round of 25 targets are shot from eight stations in a semi-circle. At the ends of the semi-circle are the high and low trap houses from which targets are released on a fixed trajectory and within defined limits. A set combination of single and double targets are shot from each station and scored on the basis of one point per target hit, and the shooter is only allowed one shot at each target. All shooters on the squad (up to six people) must have have completed the station before moving to the next one.

High trap house
Targets from the high trap house emerge at a height of 3.05m (10ft) and can travel about 65m (213ft)

Positions 1 to 7
The competitor will start at station one and progress from station to station. These stations are 8.1m (26ft 6in) apart

Single and double targets
The round features both single and double targets. A single target is released from either the high or the low trap. Doubles mean that targets are released simultaneously from both the high and the low trap

COMPETITION
There are currently five shotgun shooting events at the Olympics, but the schedule of events has changed in the past. There have been more events in the past; the women's double trap event was dropped after 2004. The world championships feature a greater range of events, including skeet, trap, and double trap for both men and women.

Target crossing point
Targets properly released must pass through a circle located above the target crossing point

Position 8
The 8th shooting station is the largest – it is 90cm x 185cm (35½in x 73in). The other stations are 90cm x 90cm (35½in x 35½in)

Low trap house
The low trap house releases targets at a height of 1.05m (3½ft). The targets may travel at about 88kph (55mph)

TRAP FIELD

In the Trap event, six shooters (a squad) are on the field at any one time. The targets are released immediately on the shooter's call but the shooter does not know which trap in a group of three will release the target. The target reaches an exit speed of about 130kph (80mph). Each shooter is permitted two shots at each target. Each shooter fires in turn from the shooting station until 25 targets (a round) have been shot at by all of the squad members.

Clay targets
The traps are set to shoot out the targets at a variety of heights, speeds, and angles (between 0 and 45 degrees, to both left and right). The competitors can take two shots at each target

Target distance
The trench containing the target-pullers is 15m (40ft) away from the shooting stations

Shooting stations
There are five shooting stations. Each is served by three traps (hence there are a total of 15 traps in the trench)

Field width
The total width of the field of play is 20m (65ft 6in)

Target-puller trench
The trench contains 15 target-pullers, arranged in five groups of three. The trench is 2m (6ft 6in) deep and 2m (6ft 6in) wide

SIDELINES

198 The current world record score for double trap shooting. This record was set by Great Britain's Peter Wilson at a World Cup event in 2012 and is the combined score out of 200 from the qualifying round and final. A perfect score in the qualifying round would be 150; the highest score recorded so far is 148. This score has been achieved by several shooters so there is no overall record holder.

55 The distance in metres the targets in double trap shooting are set to travel when released from the trap (equivalent to 180ft). Double trap shooters generally hit the targets from a distance of 25–40m (82–131ft).

3 The number of shotgun events that have been discontinued at the Olympics. This includes live pigeon shooting. Clay targets were substituted for live birds, and the traps simulate birds in flight.

0–3 The maximum number of seconds between a skeet shooter calling for the target and the target being released. The time interval is deliberately random to increase the difficulty of the shooting challenge.

324 The number of gold medals won by Russia at the ISSF World Championships since 1897. The World Championships are held in a different country every four years, two years after each Olympic Games.

GUNS AND GEAR

Competitors in shotgun events commonly use 12-bore shotguns which fire cartridges containing small pellets. Guns used for trap shooting are the heaviest at around 4kg (9lb), have the longest barrels, and are fitted with a single trigger for rapid firing. Shotguns used for skeet shooting weigh about 3kg (6lb 8oz) and a shorter barrel for better manoeuvrability. Double trap guns are similar to those used in trap, but the pellets have a wider spread.

Butt plates
These plates are movable so the length and height of the buttstock can be adjusted to suit the shooter

Barrel length
Shotguns for skeet have a shorter barrel for quicker, close-range shooting. Trap shotgun barrels are longer

Barrel choke
The choke (constriction at the end of the barrel) can be tailored to the range of the targets. Shotguns for skeet shooting give a wider shot pattern as the targets are shot at closer range; shotguns for trap give a tighter shot pattern

Stock changes
The adjustable comb allows the head of the shooter to be comfortable

SHOTGUN

Shotguns differ from pistols and rifles as they are smooth-bored rather than rifled and are sometimes built with more than one trigger. In shotgun shooting events the guns are loaded with two cartridges.

CLAY TARGET

The saucer-shaped "clay" target is in actual fact made from pitch and chalk. They are approximately 11cm x 2.5cm (4in x 1in); most are coloured for better sighting.

SHOTGUN CARTRIDGES

The cartridges are loaded with buckshot (lead pellets) and weigh 24g (⁷⁄₈oz). The exit speed of the cartridge will be close to 1,530kph (950mph).

TRAP MACHINES

The trap releases the targets automatically via a microphone system that responds to the shooter's call. Traps can be modified to adjust the height, throwing angle, and speed of a target. Some traps can hold as many as 400 targets.

OLYMPIC COMPETITION

In the Olympic competition, there are preliminary rounds from which six competitors proceed to the final. For the men's skeet and trap events, there are five rounds of 25 targets, followed by a final round of 25 targets. In the women's skeet and trap events, there are three rounds of 25 targets culminating in a final round of 25 targets. In the double trap (contested by men only), there are three rounds of 50 targets leading to a final round of 50 targets.

In Olympic skeet shooting, competitors have one shot at each target and there is a delay of up to three seconds before the clay appears. In trap shooting, contenders can take two shots at each target. In double trap, two targets are released simultaneously, so the shooter takes one shot at each.

SCORING

One point is scored for every target hit. To qualify for a hit, the target must be seen to be broken – the referee must see at least one piece fall from it. The referee indicates a target "dead" or "lost" and the scorer marks a "/" or "x" for dead and the figure "0" for lost. The targets used in finals rounds also contain a powder which is more easily seen by spectators and on television when the target is hit.

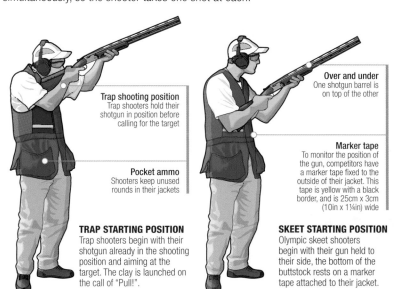

Trap shooting position
Trap shooters hold their shotgun in position before calling for the target

Pocket ammo
Shooters keep unused rounds in their jackets

Over and under
One shotgun barrel is on top of the other

Marker tape
To monitor the position of the gun, competitors have a marker tape fixed to the outside of their jacket. This tape is yellow with a black border, and is 25cm x 3cm (10in x 1¼in) wide

TRAP STARTING POSITION
Trap shooters begin with their shotgun already in the shooting position and aiming at the target. The clay is launched on the call of "Pull!".

SKEET STARTING POSITION
Olympic skeet shooters begin with their gun held to their side, the bottom of the buttstock rests on a marker tape attached to their jacket.

STAT CENTRAL

OLYMPIC SKEET CHAMPIONS

YEAR	NAME (COUNTRY)
2012	VINCENT HANCOCK (USA)
2008	VINCENT HANCOCK (USA)
2004	ANDREA BENELLI (ITA)
2000	MYKOLA MILCHEV (UKR)
1996	ENNIO FALCO (ITA)
1992	SHAN ZHANG (CHN)
1988	AXEL WEGNER (GDR)
1984	MATTHEW DRYKE (USA)
1980	HANS KJELD RASMUSSEN (DEN)

OLYMPIC TRAP CHAMPIONS

YEAR	NAME (COUNTRY)
2012	GIOVANNI CERNOGORAZ (CZE)
2008	DAVID KOSTELECKY (CZE)
2004	ALEXEI ALIPOV (RUS)
2000	MICHAEL DIAMOND (AUS)
1996	MICHAEL DIAMOND (AUS)
1992	PETR HRDLICKA (CZR)
1988	DMITRI MONAKOV (USR)
1984	LUCIANO GIOVANETTI (ITA)
1980	LUCIANO GIOVANETTI (ITA)

INSIDE STORY

Shotgun shooting with clay targets first emerged in the 1880s. Shotgun shooting featured at the first Olympics in 1896, and the line-up of events has changed frequently since then. The first world championships featuring shotgun shooting were held in 1897.

SHOOTING FEDERATION

The International Sports Shooting Federation (ISSF) is the governing body of shotgun shooting. The ISSF holds world championships every four years (two years after the Olympics), featuring more events than the Olympics.

RIFLE SHOOTING

EVENT OVERVIEW

The aim of the competition is to shoot as many bullets into the centre of the target, within a specific time frame. The shooters must take account of the number of shots they fire, and the amount of time they have to do so, both of which are governed by distance. There is a qualifying round, followed by a final, and the winner is determined by adding a competitor's qualification and final scores together.

NEED2KNOW

→ Rifle shooting is administered by the International Shooting Sports Federation (ISSF). There are six rifle-shooting classes at the ISSF World Championships, and three at the Olympics: 50m Rifle Three Positions, 50m Rifle Prone, and 10m Air Rifle.

→ Dismayed by the lack of marksmanship shown by their troops, Union veterans Colonel William C. Church and General George Wingate formed the National Rifle Association (NRA) in 1871.

→ Only bullets made of lead or similar soft material are permitted competition shooting. Tracer, armour piercing, and incendiary ammunition is prohibited.

→ Women were first allowed to compete in Olympic shooting in 1968. Mexico, Peru and Poland each entered one female contestant.

COMPETITOR PROFILE
Rifle shooters need to have extraordinary powers of concentration and mental focus. They also need to be able to control their breathing and hold their hands and body very still for sustained periods of time. Their eyesight must be extremely good as should be their judgement of the elements.

Patched up The jacket and trousers worn by shooters are made of canvas and leather, with non-slip rubber parts to aid steadiness

Tunnel vision Sun visors and other devices are sometimes affixed to the sides of shooting glasses to keep the wind and sun out of shooters' eyes

Wooden stock This part of the rifle can be wooden, metal, plastic, or fibreglass. It is the part of a rifle to which the barrel, action, and trigger are attached, and is used by the shooter to support the gun

Gun metal The barrel is the heaviest component of the rifle. It is usually made from steel

Out of sight The fore sight must not extend beyond the apparent muzzel

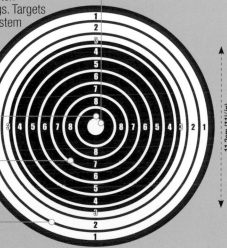

TARGET
For rifle, pistol, and running-target events, shooters fire at round black aiming areas displayed on white backgrounds. The 50m rifle target (right) is divided into ten concentric scoring zones or rings. Targets are electronic with computer system to instantly score each shot. Television monitors will enable spectators to see the impact point of each shot fired.

Targetting the inner circle The inner 10 (a circle inside the 10 ring) is 0.5cm (¼in) in diameter

Missing numbers The 9- and 10-point zones are not marked with a number

Magic numbers Scoring ring values 1 to 8 are printed in the scoring zones in vertical and horizontal lines, at right angles to each other

A fine line The thickness of the circles separating the scoring zones is between 0.2mm and 0.3mm

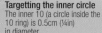

15.4cm (11¼in)

11.2cm (11¼in)

OLYMPIC SCORING
In the Olympics, the 10 rings on the target are sub-divided into ten "decimal" score zones (10.0 to 10.9), the highest score is achieved for hitting the 10 ring.

Score 10.9 10 Ring: width 1cm (⅝in) Inner 10 0.5cm (³⁄₁₆in)
Score 10.8 9 Ring: width 2.6cm (1in)
Score 10.7 8 Ring: width 4.2cm (1½in)
Score 10.6 7 Ring: width 5.8cm (2½in)
Score 10.5 6 Ring: width 7.4cm (3½in)
Score 10.4 5 Ring: width 9.4cm (3½in)
Score 10.3 4 Ring: width 10.6cm (4½in)
Score 10.2 3 Ring: width 12.2cm (4⅝in)
Score 10.2 2 Ring: width 13.8cm (5½in)
Score 10.0 1 Ring: width 15.4cm (6in)

WHERE THEY SHOOT

New outdoor ranges must be constructed in such as way that the sun is behind the shooter as much as possible during the competition day. Also, 50m ranges should have at least 45m open to the sky, while the 300m ranges should have at least 290m open to the skies.

RIFLE RANGE
The firing line must be parallel to the line of targets, and wind flags must be placed at designated distances between the shooter and the targets.

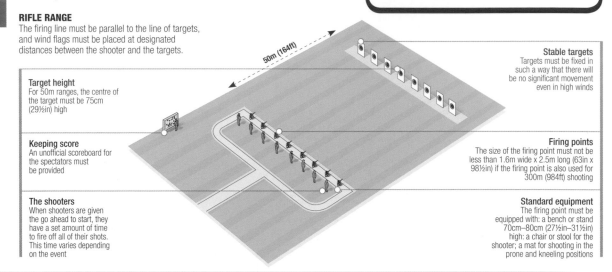

50m (164ft)

Target height
For 50m ranges, the centre of the target must be 75cm (29½in) high

Keeping score
An unofficial scoreboard for the spectators must be provided

The shooters
When shooters are given the go ahead to start, they have a set amount of time to fire off all of their shots. This time varies depending on the event

Stable targets
Targets must be fixed in such a way that there will be no significant movement even in high winds

Firing points
The size of the firing point must not be less than 1.6m wide x 2.5m long (63in x 98½in) if the firing point is also used for 300m (984ft) shooting

Standard equipment
The firing point must be equipped with: a bench or stand 70cm–80cm (27½in–31½in) high: a chair or stool for the shooter; a mat for shooting in the prone and kneeling positions

GUNS AND AMMO

All rifles chambered for rimfire 5.6mm (.22in) long rifle cartidges, and 8mm ammunition are permitted, provided they do not exceed 8kg (17½lb) for men or 6.5kg (14lb) for women, with all accessories used including palm rest or hand stop. In the 10m air rifle event any type of compressed air or gas rifle which fires 4.5mm (.177in) calibre ammunition can be used, as long as it weighs 5.5kg (12lb).

RIFLE SIGHTS
Only "metallic" sights are permitted, which have no lenses or system of lenses.

Looking glass
The sight cannot be enhanced in any way

CARTRIDGE
The required rifle ammunition must be between 5.6mm and 8mm calibre

Igniting the cartridge
The striking pin hits rim of the cartridge it ignite it

.22 CALIBRE RIFLE
This rifle is a small bore, single-loaded rifle in 5.6mm (.22in) calibre ammunition. One of its many features is a shaped stock incorporating adjustments to suit the individual, which include a hook-type butt plate, and a palm rest.

Metal sight
Coloured filters are permitted and the rear sight has fine adjustments for windage and elevation

Palm rest
A palm rest is any attachment or extension below the fore-end which aids the support of the rifle by the forward hand

Gun sling
The maximum width that a sling can be is 4cm (1½in)

The barrel tube
The rifled barrel improves accuracy over long distances

Fore sight
Length of front sight tunnel must be 5cm (2in), and its diameter needs to be 2.5cm (1in)

Butt hook
The total length of the hook, around any curve or bend must not be more than 17.8cm (7in)

.177 AIR RIFLE
The main air rifle competition is the 10m 60 shot for men and the 10m 40 shot for women. Rifles are usually single shot, with a rifled barrel, and a wooden or synthetic stock.

Breech capacity
The gun is single shot, so no magazine needed

Rear sight
Any sight not containing a system of lenses is permitted

Max velocity
Bullet velocity is up to 148mps (485fps)

Barrel length
The maximum length of the barrel is 76cm (30in)

Comfort stock
The stock may have an adjustable rubber pad attached for comfort

TAKING YOUR SHOTS

In all events the format is the same, only the number of shots fired, and the time in which to take the required number of shots will change. In the 50m Rifle Three Positions men's competition the shooter fires 40 shots each in the prone, standing and kneeling positions at a target 50m away. The centre ten must be hit at a distance of 50m within a time limit of 45 minutes in the prone position, 75 minutes in the standing position and 60 minutes in the kneeling position. The best eight shooters qualify for the final. The final consists of ten shots in the standing position with a time limit of 75 seconds per shot.

THREE POSITION TECHNIQUES

In the 50m Rifle Three Positions, illustrated below, shooters fire shots from three different positions: prone, standing, and kneeling. They have to take in to account the climatic conditions at the time, utilizing the wind flags on the range, while being mindful of the time restrictions that are placed on each shooting position.

STANDING

In the standing position for all rifle events, the rifle is held with both hands and rests on the shoulder. The left arm may be supported on the chest or hip. The maximum changeover time between positions is ten minutes for 50m-rifle events.

Shoulder patch
Reinforcement on the shoulder where the butt plate rests must not be longer than 30cm (12in) either vertically or horizontally

Knee patches
Knee patches may have a maximum length of 30cm (12in). Knee reinforcements must not be wider than half the circumference of the trousers leg

KNEELING

When kneeling, the right-handed shooter may touch the ground with the toe of the right foot, the right knee and the left foot. The left knee may support the left elbow, but must be no more than 10cm (4in) past or 15cm (6in) behind the knee cap.

Shooting gloves
The total thickness must not exceed 1.2cm (½in) when measuring front and back materials together

Knee roll
Rifle shooters may use a soft, cylindrical roll to support the instep when kneeling

PRONE

This is the first position that the shooter adopts. A shooter may not let the rifle rest against, or touch, any object. The right-handed shooter's left forearm must form an angle of at least 30 degrees from the horizontal.

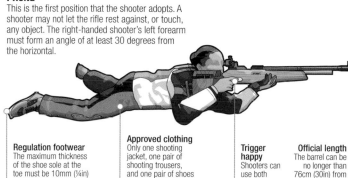

Regulation footwear
The maximum thickness of the shoe sole at the toe must be 10mm (¼in) and the upper part of shoe material must be 4mm (⅛in)

Approved clothing
Only one shooting jacket, one pair of shooting trousers, and one pair of shoes may be approved for each shooter for all rifle events

Trigger happy
Shooters can use both electronic, and traditional triggers

Official length
The barrel can be no longer than 76cm (30in) from breech face to the end of the barrel

STAT CENTRAL

OLYMPIC RIFLE / SHOTGUN EVENTS
50M RIFLE 3 POSITIONS (3X40 SHOTS) MEN
50M RIFLE PRONE (60 SHOTS) MEN
DOUBLE TRAP (150 TARGETS) MEN
SKEET (125 TARGETS) MEN
TRAP (125 TARGETS) MEN
50M RIFLE 3 POSITIONS (3X20 SHOTS) WOMEN
SKEET (75 TARGETS) WOMEN
TRAP (75 TARGET) WOMEN

OLYMPIC BLOOD SPORT

OSCAR SWAHN WAS ALREADY 60 YEARS OLD WHEN HE WON HIS FIRST OLYMPIC GOLD MEDAL. HE WON THE RUNNING DEER SINGLE-SHOT EVENT AND TOOK HIS SECOND GOLD OF THE GAMES THE NEXT DAY IN THE TEAM EVENT. SWAHN ALSO EARNED A BRONZE MEDAL IN THE RUNNING DEER DOUBLE-SHOT CONTEST. TARGETS RATHER THAN LIVESTOCK ARE SHOT AT.

INSIDE STORY

Shooting originated as a means of survival, as it was practised in order to hunt game for food. In the 19th century, however, as the industrial revolution made hunting for food less necessary for many people, shooting evolved into a sport. The sport was first popular in English-speaking countries, notably England and the United States, as well as Ireland and South Africa.

SPORTS
ON WHEELS

Head protection
Riders must wear a full-
or open-face helmet
with a fastened
mouth guard

BMX

Padded shirt
Long-sleeved shirts
with padded elbows
are required for
most track races

Padded trousers
Race riders must
wear full-length
BMX racing trousers
with padded knees

Gloves
Gloves stop
hands slipping on
the bars and prevent blisters

Bike pads
Pads can be placed on the
top tube of the frame and
the neck of the handlebars
to protect the rider in a fall

Race wheels
A typical BMX race bike
has 51-cm (20-in) wheels.

SPORT OVERVIEW

Developed in the United States in the late-
1960s, BMX (bicycle motocross) is a pedal-
powered alternative to motocross (see
pp.395–97). BMX may look like adults racing
on kids' bikes, but nerve and skill are needed
in a sport that includes dirt-track races and
freestyle events, sometimes over huge jumps,
when riders perform awesome acrobatic tricks.

Knobs or smooth
Riders tend to use rough
tyres for dirt jumps. Vert riders
on ramps use tyres that are
almost smooth

Can-can
At the top of the jump the rider
kicks his legs out to the side – a
move known as a no-footed can-can

TRACKS AND RAMPS

BMX races take place on purpose-built dirt tracks. Riders
complete one lap of the circuit and contend with various jumps
and turns as they progress to the finish line. Ramps are used in
freestyle BMX events, of which the "vert" ramp is perhaps the
most extreme example (see below).

DIRT TRACK
A typical BMX track consists of
a starting gate, a dirt track that
includes jumps and banked
and flat corners, and a finish
line. Riders complete the
course in 30 to 45 seconds.

Jumps
Jumps on most tracks are fairly
small, but Supercross tracks
include extreme 13m (40ft) jumps

Banked turn
Banked turns
or corners are
called "berms"

Starting gate

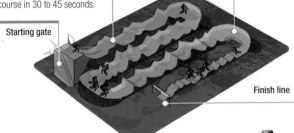

Finish line

Brakes
The bikes used for
dirt jumps do have
brakes: they're not
much use in the air

VERT RAMP
Often used in freestyle
events, a "vert" ramp is
a half pipe with a vertical
section at the top of the
ramp. The tallest ramps
may be up to 4m (13ft)
tall, with a 1m (3ft) vert
section. Riders run up
each side, performing
aerial stunts.

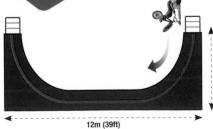

5m (16ft)

12m (39ft)

FLIPWHIP
Riders pull some amazing tricks on dirt jumps. In the flipwhip, the
rider flips the bike backwards in the air while maintaining enough
forward momentum to land and continue the routine.

→ The Union Cycliste Internationale (UCI) is the international governing body for BMX events.

→ BMX pioneer Scot Breithaupt organized some of the first races at Long Beach, California, in 1970.

→ BMX racing was included in the Olympics for the first time at the 2008 Games in Beijing, China.

RACING RULES

In a typical track competition, eight riders race in a series of qualifying heats, called motos. The riders in each moto race against riders of a similar age and ability. In world competition, the elite or pro category consists of top-level riders aged 19 and over. Riders aged 17 and 18 compete in the junior category. After the elimination heats, the fastest four riders progress to the finals, called mains. The fastest rider in the mains wins the overall competition.

TURN A TRICK

Tricks are divided into four main styles: base, grind, aerial, and lip tricks. Base tricks are the basic moves and include bunny hops, wheelies, and fakie, or riding backwards. Riders use footpegs to perform grind and lip tricks on railings or the edge of a half pipe. Aerial tricks on dirt jumps and vert ramps combine huge height with acrobatic twists and turns.

FREESTYLE ARENA

Freestyle events have five disciplines, based on where riders do their tricks: street, park, vert, trails, and flatland. Street riders improvise in the urban landscape – steps, rails, slopes – while park riders use pipes and ramps in skate parks. In vert competitions, riders use a large half pipe with vertical sides to perform jumps or do tricks on the lip of the pipe. Trails are a series of dirt jumps where riders perform tricks. Flatland is the purest form of freestyle: a bike, a rider, a piece of flat ground with nothing to help – or hinder – him or her, and a lot of imagination and skill.

Stretch out
As the descent begins, the rider uses momentum and arm strength to pull the bike beneath him

Round and round
A special rotor in the stem allows the handlebars to rotate indefinitely without tangling the rear brake cable

FLATLAND
Flatland riding is probably the most technically demanding of all the freestyle BMX sports. The rider here is "scuffing" the rear tyre to keep the bike moving as he pulls a trick.

Perfect balance
Keeping the bike in motion makes it far easier to balance than if it became stationary

DIRT JUMPS

The dirt jump is a popular trails freestyle event in which riders make a series of jumps over a mound of dirt. While airborne, the rider pulls a trick to impress the judges. The judges mark jumps according to the rider's style and the level of difficulty. At the end of the competition, the rider with most points wins.

URBAN GAMES

Freestyle riders often see BMX as a way of life rather than a competitive sport, but many riders still take part in major international contests such as the BMX Freestyle Worlds, which were first held in 1986, the Metro Jams, the Backyard Jams, and the X-Games.

Peg-less
Axle pegs are used on ramps and for grinding

Happy landings
BMX bikes have no suspension, which makes the bike "bob" during pedalling. Riders absorb the landing in their legs

INSIDE STORY

BMX was developed in the 1960s by young Americans who wanted to use their pushbikes to copy motorcycle riders. The sport rapidly caught on among the skateboard generation. Today the sport is so popular that it has spawned an industry. Many riders earn a living from their bikes, and the best pros are international celebrities, earning huge sponsorship deals from bike manufacturers and clothing companies.

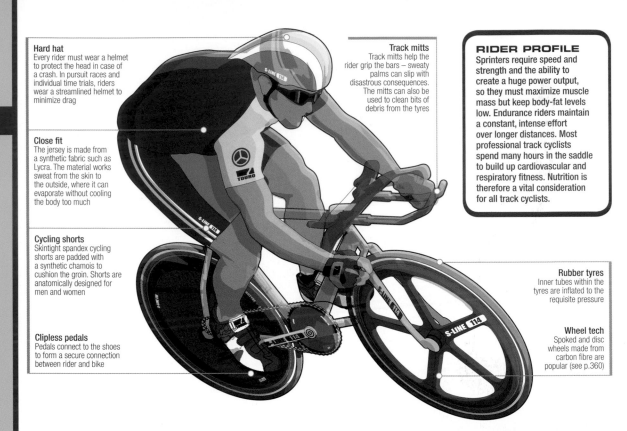

Hard hat
Every rider must wear a helmet to protect the head in case of a crash. In pursuit races and individual time trials, riders wear a streamlined helmet to minimize drag

Close fit
The jersey is made from a synthetic fabric such as Lycra. The material works sweat from the skin to the outside, where it can evaporate without cooling the body too much

Cycling shorts
Skintight spandex cycling shorts are padded with a synthetic chamois to cushion the groin. Shorts are anatomically designed for men and women

Clipless pedals
Pedals connect to the shoes to form a secure connection between rider and bike

Track mitts
Track mitts help the rider grip the bars – sweaty palms can slip with disastrous consequences. The mitts can also be used to clean bits of debris from the tyres

Rubber tyres
Inner tubes within the tyres are inflated to the requisite pressure

Wheel tech
Spoked and disc wheels made from carbon fibre are popular (see p.360)

RIDER PROFILE
Sprinters require speed and strength and the ability to create a huge power output, so they must maximize muscle mass but keep body-fat levels low. Endurance riders maintain a constant, intense effort over longer distances. Most professional track cyclists spend many hours in the saddle to build up cardiovascular and respiratory fitness. Nutrition is therefore a vital consideration for all track cyclists.

SPORT OVERVIEW

Track cycling comprises a number of different races that take place on a closed, banked circuit called a velodrome. The sport originated in Europe as winter training for road cyclists but soon became a spectator-friendly sport in its own right. Today, race formats vary from individual races against the clock to group events that end in breathtaking sprints off the final bend. Short-distance events are tests of sprinting ability, while endurance events take place over longer distances.

THE HARDEST RIDE

THE MOST COVETED PRIZE IN TRACK CYCLING IS THE HOUR RECORD, OF WHICH EDDY MERCKX SAID ON HIS RECORD-BREAKING ATTEMPT IN 1972, "THAT WAS THE HARDEST RIDE I HAVE EVER DONE". COMING FROM THE WINNER OF 11 GRAND TOURS AND THREE WORLD CHAMPIONSHIPS, THAT WAS REALLY SAYING SOMETHING!

NEED2KNOW

→ There are 10 track events currently on the Olympic Games programme. From the London 2012 Games onwards, male and female riders each compete in five events.

→ The UCI organizes a series of World Cup races and a one-off World Championships.

TRACK CYCLING

SIDELINES

93,000,000
The total cost in pounds sterling to build the velodrome for the 2012 London Olympic Games.

42
The average steepest gradient, in degrees, of a typical track. The track is banked to allow racers to ride the 180-degree bends without slowing down.

1
The number of gears on a track bicycle. Rather than start in an easy gear and change to harder gears, riders must start the race in a high gear, requiring a huge push to get the pedals turning.

THE VELODROME

A velodrome track is a banked oval circuit, consisting of two straights connected by two 180-degree bends. The black pole line that runs around the track defines the length of circuit, which varies from 150–500m (492–1,640ft) and may be between 7–9m (23–29½ft) in width, depending on the velodrome. Since January 2000, major events such as the Olympic Games and world championship races have been held exclusively on 250m (820ft) tracks.

CYCLING SCIENCE

Track designers aim to build the banking of the track at precisely the right angle. Straight sections have a relatively gentle angle, but the angle must be sufficiently steep on the bends to allow riders to keep their bikes close to 90 degrees to the track surface, at speeds of up to 70kph (45mph). If there was no banking on the track, the riders would either be forced to deviate from the shortest path around the track, or slow down dramatically.

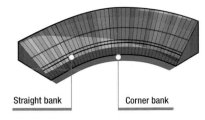

Straight bank   Corner bank

BANKING ANGLES

The banking angle depends on the length of the track. On a standard Olympic 250m track, the angle can be as steep as 45 degrees, while on a 400m track it's around 22 degrees. Even on the straights, the track slopes at an angle of about 12 degrees.

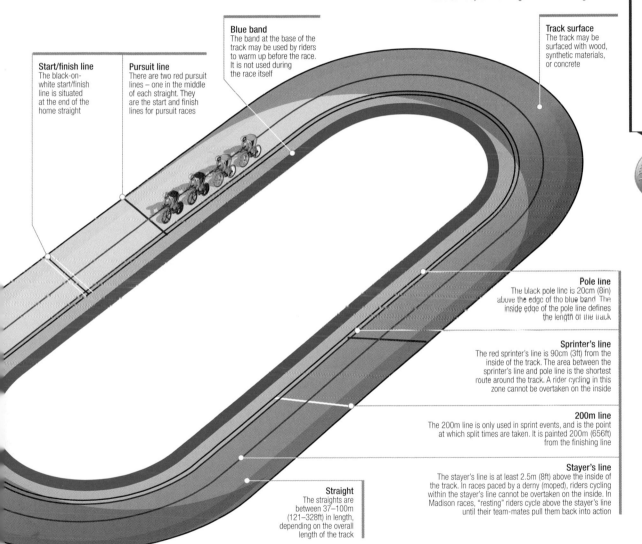

Blue band
The band at the base of the track may be used by riders to warm up before the race. It is not used during the race itself

Track surface
The track may be surfaced with wood, synthetic materials, or concrete

Start/finish line
The black-on-white start/finish line is situated at the end of the home straight

Pursuit line
There are two red pursuit lines – one in the middle of each straight. They are the start and finish lines for pursuit races

Pole line
The black pole line is 20cm (8in) above the edge of the blue band. The inside edge of the pole line defines the length of the track

Sprinter's line
The red sprinter's line is 90cm (3ft) from the inside of the track. The area between the sprinter's line and pole line is the shortest route around the track. A rider cycling in this zone cannot be overtaken on the inside

200m line
The 200m line is only used in sprint events, and is the point at which split times are taken. It is painted 200m (656ft) from the finishing line

Stayer's line
The stayer's line is at least 2.5m (8ft) above the inside of the track. In races paced by a derny (moped), riders cycling within the stayer's line cannot be overtaken on the inside. In Madison races, "resting" riders cycle above the stayer's line until their team-mates pull them back into action

Straight
The straights are between 37–100m (121–328ft) in length, depending on the overall length of the track

INDOORS AND OUTDOORS

In the heyday of track cycling in the early 20th century, most velodromes were built as indoor arenas. Not only did an indoor track guard against bad weather and offer a smoother ride for the competitors, they made ideal venues for late-night revellers and socialites who would come and watch the six-day races in the early hours, when most pubs and bars were shut. More recently, purpose-built velodromes are commonly built outdoors to reduce construction costs.

THE KEIRIN

Originating in Japan in 1948, the keirin is a sprint over 2km (1¼ miles). Up to eight riders cycle behind a moped called a derny. The derny paces the first few laps of the race. The riders then sprint to the finish line. In Japanese, keirin means "fight," and the races often live up to the name, with high-speed crashes common.

TRACK BIKES

Two types of bike are used on the track: a pursuit bike for endurance events and time trials, and a standard bike (shown below) for shorter sprints and points races. At the highest level of competition, bike frames are made from ultra-light carbon fibre or titanium, with a single fixed gear and no brakes. However, aluminium and steel frames are a much cheaper alternative. The main difference between the two types of bike is in the aerodynamics. Pursuit bikes generally have a highly efficient – but less comfortable – aerodynamic position, while standard track bikes are strong and lightweight and more suitable for quick sprints. Pursuit bikes may have tri-bars to help keep the front of the body as small as possible to reduce drag.

Fixed gear
Track bikes have a single fixed gear and no freewheel, which means the rider must keep pedalling until the bike stops

Fibre frame
Track frames are light and stiff. Carbon fibre is the material of choice for elite riders

Handlebars
Riders use drop bars for endurance events, similar to those found on road bikes

Lightweight wheels
Disc wheels reduce drag, allowing faster speeds than traditional spoked wheels

Steep forks
Track bikes have a steep fork angle (rake), which provides stiff handling and stable steering at high speeds

Tyres
Lightweight tubular tyres are popular. The smooth track reduces friction and increases speed

TRACK EVENTS

There is a range of formats of track races. The races are either sprint events, ranging from 500m (550yd) to 2km (1¼ miles), or endurance events, which can be up to 60km (38 miles). The Olympic programme has included different events over the years, and was revised ahead of London 2012 to achieve gender parity, with men's and women's races in each of the following:

INDIVIDUAL SPRINT Also known as the "match" sprint, this race pits two riders against each other over three laps of the track. The rider who starts on the inside lane leads for the first lap. The individual sprint is a game of "cat-and-mouse" until the final 200m, when one rider breaks for the finish line to steal the victory.

TEAM SPRINT Two teams of three riders sprint over three laps. Each rider must lead for one complete lap.

TEAM PURSUIT Track cycling's blue-riband event, the team pursuit involves two teams of four riders race over 4km (2½ miles) in this men-only version of the pursuit.

KEIRIN A mass-start race where riders are paced by a "derny" moped up to a speed of 50kph (31mph), then left to race alone for two laps.

OMNIUM In cycling's equivalent of the heptathlon and decathlon, 24 riders contest six different events – three sprints and three endurance races – with the strongest overall rider taking the win. Events included are a 250m "flying lap" time trial, a points race (30km for men, 20km for women), an elimination race, a pursuit race (4km for men, 3km for women), a scratch race (15km for men, 10km for women), and a time trial (1km for men, 500m for women).

TRACK RULES

In international track meets such as the Olympics and World Championships, track cycling is governed by the rules of the Union Cycliste Internationale (UCI), which is the world governing body for all cycling sports. Domestic competitions are run according to the rules of the relevant national governing body.

OUT OF POSITION

In the early 1990s, Scottish cyclist Graeme Obree developed a unique riding position with his chest tucked low over the handlebar and his elbows up at his sides. He used this "crouch" or "tuck" position to break the nine-year-old World Hour Record in 1993 and to win the individual pursuit World Championships in the same year. When the UCI banned the position, Obree experimented with a new "superman" position, in which his arms were fully extended in front of his body; in 1995, he used it to win the individual pursuit World Championships. When English cyclist Chris Boardman set a new hour record in 1996 using the same superman position, the UCI banned the superman position from competitive track cycling.

WORLD HOUR RECORD

As well as races, velodromes also stage many cycling world-record attempts. The world hour record is one of the most coveted titles. The aim is simple – cycle as far as you can in one hour – but the rules governing the record are anything but. The problem lies with the rapid advances in bike technology. When the great Belgian cyclist Eddy Merckx set a new hour record (49.431km) in 1972, he did not have aerodynamic gear, such as disc wheels and tri bars. So the UCI now recognizes two hour records: the official "UCI Hour Record," which uses Merckx's bike as a standard, and an unofficial "Best Human Effort" record, which allows the use of the latest in bicycle technology.

SIDELINES

49.7 The distance in kilometres (30.882 miles) cycled by Czech cyclist Ondrej Sosenka when he broke the UCI Hour Record in 2005.

20 The distance in centimetres (8in) a rider is legally allowed to roll back in a standstill before being disqualified from the individual sprint.

6,000 The capacity of the Olympic Velodrome in London, the venue for track cycling at the 2012 Games.

TIMING THE TIME TRIAL

The time trial is the only track event in which the rider starts the race from a starting block. Once the back wheel is fixed in the starting block, a clock placed in front of the rider counts down 50 seconds before the start. At the end of the countdown, the brake on the starting block is then released, triggering the chronometer. A transponder on the bike registers the time as the rider crosses the finish line. The timings are accurate to one-hundredth of a second.

Standing start
The rider powers out of the starting block from a standing start

TRACK TECHNIQUES

Riders use a range of different techniques according to the event they are competing in. Individual efforts such as the time trial are exhibitions of strength, speed, and stamina, so there is little room for tactical game play. Other races are a battle of wits, with riders jostling for the best position.

Slingshot
A slingshot effect propels the incoming rider into the race

HELPING HAND

One of the most remarkable sights at a Madison race is the changeover. While one member of the team of two riders is racing, the other team member catches their breath by cruising at the top of the track until it's time to race again. Then he or she rides back down onto the racing line, where the racing partner uses a handsling to propel the non-racing partner up to speed.

Paceline purists
Riders race in a long line, drafting in the slipstream of the rider in front

Up to speed
The derny paces the riders at speeds of up to 45kph (28mph)

DRAFTING THE DERNY

The derny, the moped that paces the first few laps of the keirin, has a flying start, so riders sprint to catch up with it. The derny steadily increases speed, then withdraws, leaving the riders to fight it out over the last two laps.

STANDING STILL

The individual sprint, also called the match sprint, is a three-lap race between two riders. The rider on the inside – decided by the toss of a coin – must lead the race on the first lap. Taking the lead is seen as a disadvantage, because the trailing rider then has the chance of launching a surprise attack. When the final sprint starts, the trailing rider also has the advantage of riding in the opponent's slipstream. On the second lap, therefore, the leading rider will often slow to a complete stop, balancing on the bike in an attempt to force the opponent to the front. On the final lap, one of the riders will crack and sprint for the finish line. The individual sprint is decided on the best of three heats. The winner then progresses to the next round.

Finely balanced
Riders balance on the bike and may gently rock back and forwards

Pedal power
The pedals are kept in a horizontal position, with the bars at a slight angle

STAT CENTRAL

SLIPSTREAM

Drafting is an important element of most cycle races. When drafting, a rider sits a few centimetres behind the rear wheel of the leading racer. The leader does all the work to overcome the forces of drag, while the drafting rider saves up to 40 per cent of his or her energy output by riding in the leader's slipstream. Sometimes, a group of cyclists will bunch together to form a "paceline." Each rider takes a turn at the front, towing the pack behind. The leader then drops off, and the rider behind takes a turn at the front, setting the pace. Riders who do not contribute get a free ride, but are likely to receive stern words from the rest of the pack.

INSIDE STORY

Track racing originated in response to the overwhelming popularity of the bicycle at the end of the 19th century. Track events brought the excitement of road racing to the confines of a closed circuit. It also became a popular method of training for road cyclists. The first documented track race took place in Saint-Cloud, France, in 1868, and velodromes soon cropped up all over Europe and the United States. Mirroring the great road races, some of the early track events were monumental challenges of endurance, including 24-hour races and the notorious Six Days, in which teams of two took it in turns to race over six days and six nights. Sprint events were also popular, and the individual sprint and track time-trial featured in the first Olympic Games in Athens in 1896.

UNION CYCLISTE INTERNATIONALE (UCI)

Founded in 1900, the Union Cycliste Internationale (UCI) is the governing body for all cycling, from BMX to the track. The UCI organizes the Track Cycling World Cup Classics series and the annual Track Cycling World Championships, and collaborates with the International Olympic Committee (IOC) on the Olympics. Each year, the UCI also publishes elite rider rankings for each event.

→ Road racing is popular all over the world, but the most prestigious professional races take place in continental Europe.

→ There are many different road racing formats, including multi-day stage races, and one-day Classics, time trials, and criteriums.

→ The Union Cycliste Internationale (UCI) is the sport's international governing body.

→ Elite riders compete in the UCI World Tour, a series of ranking races held around the world from January to October.

ROAD RACING

SPORT OVERVIEW

Road racing is one of the toughest of all sports. In the major stage races, such as the world-famous Tour de France, elite riders compete at the absolute limits of physical endurance, covering thousands of miles in just a few weeks of racing. A rider must be able to sit in the saddle for a full day's riding, accelerate to speeds of 80kph (50mph) or more, and climb the steepest of mountain passes. But the strangest part of the sport is that most riders must be willing to sacrifice individual glory to help their team leader win the race.

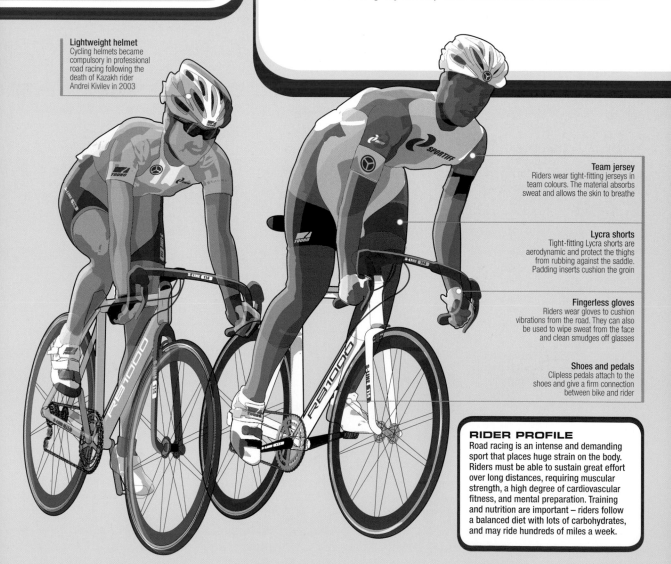

Lightweight helmet
Cycling helmets became compulsory in professional road racing following the death of Kazakh rider Andrei Kivilev in 2003

Team jersey
Riders wear tight-fitting jerseys in team colours. The material absorbs sweat and allows the skin to breathe

Lycra shorts
Tight-fitting Lycra shorts are aerodynamic and protect the thighs from rubbing against the saddle. Padding inserts cushion the groin

Fingerless gloves
Riders wear gloves to cushion vibrations from the road. They can also be used to wipe sweat from the face and clean smudges off glasses

Shoes and pedals
Clipless pedals attach to the shoes and give a firm connection between bike and rider

RIDER PROFILE
Road racing is an intense and demanding sport that places huge strain on the body. Riders must be able to sustain great effort over long distances, requiring muscular strength, a high degree of cardiovascular fitness, and mental preparation. Training and nutrition are important – riders follow a balanced diet with lots of carbohydrates, and may ride hundreds of miles a week.

OPEN ROAD

Road races are contested on normal roads. With the exception of time trials, riders start together in a mass bunch. The race takes place over a set course, which varies in distance depending on the type of race. The aim is to cross the finish line first. Riders race in teams of eight to 10 cyclists, and team-members cooperate to help their leader win the race.

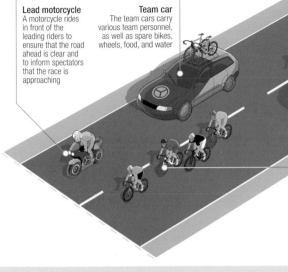

Peloton
The peloton is the name given to the main group of riders in the race. When there is an attack, the riders in the peloton organize the chase

Lead motorcycle
A motorcycle rides in front of the leading riders to ensure that the road ahead is clear and to inform spectators that the race is approaching

Team car
The team cars carry various team personnel, as well as spare bikes, wheels, food, and water

Race director
The race director organizes the whole event and keeps track of the race from a car that follows the lead riders

Breakaway
A handful of riders work together to try to pull away from the rest of the bunch. Cooperating with a few like-minded others to break away from the main peloton is the best method to gain time and win points

TOUR CARAVAN

THE PUBLICITY CARAVAN ADDS A CARNIVAL ATMOSPHERE TO THE TOUR DE FRANCE. A PARADE OF SPONSOR VEHICLES TRAVELS THE SAME ROUTE AS THE TOUR, HANDING OUT FREE GIFTS TO SPECTATORS AS THEY WAIT FOR THE RACERS TO ARRIVE.

BIKE TECHNOLOGY

Form and fitness are the benchmarks of success in the ProTour, but riders also owe much to developments in bike technology. Carbon fibre and high-grade metals, such as titanium, are commonly used for the bike frame, reducing weight but retaining stiffness and strength. For the time trial, riders use dedicated bikes that offer greater aerodynamic advantage than conventional road bikes.

COMMUNICATION

The directeur sportif radios orders to the team during the race. Riders strap a radio under their jersey, and place an earpiece in one ear.

ROAD BIKE

Professional road racers use bikes that are built to be light and strong, and comfortable enough to be ridden for hours on end. Quick-release fixings allow wheels to be swapped quickly in case of punctures.

Lightweight wheels
Deep-section rims combine the aerodynamics of discs and the weight-saving of spokes

Frame and forks
Most road bikes use the diamond-frame design. Stiff, carbon-fibre forks attach to the head tube and absorb minor bumps

Tubular tyres
The inner tube is sewn into the tyre and glued to the wheel rim with rubber cement

Clipless pedals
Cleats on the soles of the shoes clip into the pedals to allow maximum energy transmission for each pedal stroke

Brake/gear shifters
Integrated brake/gear levers allow braking and gear-shifting with minimum effort

TIME-TRIAL BIKE

Used for individual and team time-trial races, time-trial bikes are built for out-and-out speed. Comfort is sacrificed for an aerodynamic riding position, while bigger gears are used to enable the rider to go faster.

Disc wheel
Disc wheels offer an aerodynamic advantage over the traditional spoked variety

Seat tube
Steeper seat-tube angles than on a road bike help the rider tuck into an aerodynamic position

Tri bars
Tri bars help to keep the front of the body as small as possible, to reduce drag

Gear ratio
Riders match the ratio to the course profile. A low ratio is suitable on the flat, while a high ratio is best for hills

Easy-access shifters
Bar-end shifters help the rider maintain an aerodynamic position while changing gear

STAT CENTRAL

TOUR DE FRANCE WINNERS

WINS	WINNER (COUNTRY)
5	JACQUES ANQUETIL (FRA)
5	EDDY MERCKX (BEL)
5	BERNARD HINAULT (FRA)
5	MIGUEL INDURAIN (SPA)
3	PHILIPPE THYS (BEL)
3	LOUISON BOBET (FRA)
3	GREG LEMOND (USA)
2	ALBERTO CONTADOR (SPA)
2	LAURENT FIGNON (FRA)
2	BERNARD THÉVENET (FRA)
2	FAUSTO COPPI (IT)
2	GINO BARTALI (IT)
2	SYLVERE MAES (BEL)
2	ANTONIN MAGNE (FRA)
2	LUCIEN PETIT-BRETON (FRA)

UCI MEN'S WORLD CHAMPIONSHIPS

YEAR	WINNER (COUNTRY)
2012	PHILIPPE GILBERT (BEL)
2011	MARK CAVENDISH (GBR)
2010	THOR HUSHOVD (NOR)
2009	CADEL EVANS (AUS)
2008	ALESSANDRO BALLAN (ITA)
2007	PAOLO BETTINI (ITA)
2006	PAOLO BETTINI (ITA)
2005	TOM BOONEN (BEL)
2004	ÓSCAR FREIRE (ESP)
2003	IGOR ASTARLOZA (ESP)
2002	MARIO CIPOLLINI (ITA)
2001	ÓSCAR FREIRE (ESP)

MEN'S OLYMPIC ROAD RACE

YEAR	WINNER (COUNTRY)
2012	ALEXANDER VINOKOUROV (KAZ)
2008	SAMUEL SANCHEZ (ESP)
2004	PAOLO BETTINI (ITA)
2000	JAN ULLRICH (GER)
1996	PASCAL RICHARD (SUI)
1992	FABIO CASARTELLI (ITA)
1988	OLAF LUDWIG (GDR)
1984	ALEXI GREWAL (USA)
1980	SERGEY SUKHORUCHENKOV (URS)
1976	BERNT JOHANSSON (SWE)
1972	HENNIE KUIPER (NED)
1968	PIERFRANCO VIANELLI (ITA)

MEN'S OLYMPIC TIME TRIAL

YEAR	WINNER (COUNTRY)
2012	BRADLEY WIGGINS (GBR)
2008	FABIAN CANCELLARA (SUI)
2004	TYLER HAMILTON (USA)

RACE FORMATS AND SERIES

There are several different race formats, ranging from three-week stage races to hour-long criteriums. The most prestigious elite races are grouped together in the UCI World Tour, including the Grand Tours, the spring Classics, as well as some smaller races. Riders and teams accumulate points in the series, and at the season's end, those with the most points take the win. The other major contests are the UCI World Championships, which takes place annually, and the Olympics, contested every four years.

STAGE RACES

Stage races are the ultimate in cycling endurance. Each stage is either a day-long point-to-point race or a team or individual time trial. The rider who completes all the stages in the quickest time is the winner. The most prestigious three-week stage races – the Giro d'Italia, Tour de France, and Vuelta a Espanã – are known as the Grand Tours.

CLASSICS

The Classics are one-day, one-off races held in the spring, before the Grand Tours take place. They are usually long races, up to 270km (170 miles) in length, and often feature gruelling climbs or difficult surfaces, such as the cobblestones of Paris–Roubaix.

TIME TRIALS

There is no hiding in the bunch in this so-called "race of truth". In the individual time-trial, competitors ride individually, against the clock. Most stage races also include team time-trials, in which the whole team races as a unit.

Time-trial start
The rider sprints out of the starting gate and accelerates up to race speed

INDIVIDUAL TIME TRIAL
The individual time trial is a tough test of strength and endurance, fought against the clock.

CRITERIUMS

A criterium, or crit, is a high-speed race held in a closed-off city centre or on purpose-built cycling circuits. The circuit is usually less than 5km (3 miles), and the race is held over a set time (commonly one hour) or a set number of laps. As well as the overall victory, riders can win cash prizes, called primes, for intermediate sprints.

THE TOUR DE FRANCE

The Tour de France is the original, toughest, and most prestigious cycling race on the planet. First raced in 1903, it consists of 21 day-long stages over flat, fast roads or vertigo-inducing mountain passes, circumnavigating the French nation and covering around 3,500km (2,175 miles) in the process. The ultimate prize is the "maillot jaune" – the yellow jersey worn by the rider who completes all the stages in the shortest accumulated time.

COLOURED JERSEYS

The leading rider in each category wears a coloured jersey and defends it until the peloton finishes the Tour in Paris. The strongest riders go for the overall victory, climbers focus on the "king of the mountains," sprinters challenge for the points competition, and riders under 25 fight for the best young rider award.

YELLOW JERSEY
The "maillot jaune" is awarded to the highest-placing rider in the general classification.

GREEN JERSEY
The green jersey goes to the rider with the most points in the sprint competition.

POLKA-DOT JERSEY
The polka-dot jersey is awarded to the king of the mountains – the best climber.

WHITE JERSEY
The white jersey goes to the highest-placing young rider in the general classification.

MEET THE TEAM

Most teams are organized around the leader, a dominant rider who has the best chance of winning the race. The priority for the other riders in the team is to support their leader. Within each team, there will be strong climbers and sprinters, time-trial specialists, and domestiques – the workers who guard against breakaways and supply the team with food and water during the race. Top-level teams also have a range of support personnel, including the directeur sportif, mechanics, doctors, and general assistants called soigneurs.

CONTROLLING TACTICS

Road racing is as tactical as it is physically demanding. In a typical race, one or a group of riders may launch a breakaway, in which they cooperate to escape from the peloton and gain as much time as possible. Cooperation in the peloton then plays an important part in determining the result of the race. Riders from some teams will organize a chase, while other teams may slow the pace deliberately to help a teammate in the breakaway gain ground.

DRAFTING

As in track racing, drafting is the most important way to save energy during a road race. The rider at the front of a group uses up a lot of energy to overcome the forces of drag. By sitting on the back wheel of the leading bike, the drafting rider can save as much as 30 per cent of the energy used to cycle at exactly the same speed. Cycling etiquette demands that each rider takes a turn at the front to share the workload, forming what is known as a paceline (see below).

HILL CLIMBING

Good climbing ability is crucial in multi-day stage races, as inclines are the most likely point at which time may be lost or gained. How well a rider climbs depends largely on their power-to-weight ratio. A lighter rider does not need to generate as much power as a heavier rider because they carry less weight up the hill. For this reason, most of the top climbers are lean and light, whereas specialist sprinters are more muscular, and tend to suffer on mountain stages. On long climbs, riders generally stay seated and maintain a high cadence (pedal rate) all the way up the hill. Climbing out of the saddle is reserved for short hills, steep gradients, or an attack to drop a weaker rider.

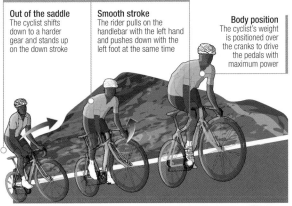

Out of the saddle
The cyclist shifts down to a harder gear and stands up on the down stroke

Smooth stroke
The rider pulls on the handlebar with the left hand and pushes down with the left foot at the same time

Body position
The cyclist's weight is positioned over the cranks to drive the pedals with maximum power

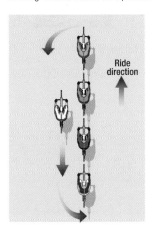

SINGLE PACELINE
In a single paceline, all the cyclists ride in single file. One rider takes a turn at the front and then drops to the back. The next rider then moves up to take his or her place.

Ride direction

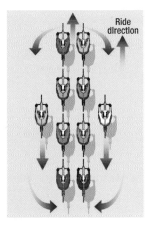

DOUBLE PACELINE
Most common in team time-trials, double pacelines have two parallel lines of riders. Two riders take a turn at the front and then peel off. The riders behind move up to take their place.

Ride direction

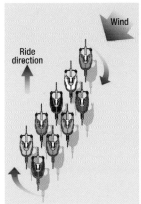

ECHELON
The echelon is a type of paceline used in strong crosswinds. Riders form diagonal lines across the road and peel away from the direction of the prevailing wind.

Wind

Ride direction

ARMSTRONG'S SHAME

CYCLING HAS A HISTORY OF DOPING SCANDALS, NONE BIGGER THAN THAT INVOLVING LANCE ARMSTRONG, A SEVEN-TIME WINNER OF THE TOUR DE FRANCE. IN 2012, THE UNITED STATES ANTI-DOPING AGENCY FOUND HIM GUILTY OF SUSTAINED AND SYSTEMATIC DOPING AND STRIPPED HIM OF ALL HIS TOUR DE FRANCE TITLES. IN 2013, AFTER YEARS OF DENIAL, ARMSTRONG CONFESSED TO DOPING IN AN INTERVIEW WITH OPRAH WINFREY.

SIDELINES

34 The record number of Tour de France stage wins, held by the Belgian Eddy Merckx, an all-round cycling legend.

123,900 The average number of calories burned by a typical racer during the three-week-long Tour de France.

38,155 The minimum wage (in US dollars) for pro cyclists. The best can earn up to US$1 million.

6.8 The minimum permitted weight (in kg) of a professional road bike, according to UCI regulations.

INSIDE STORY

The history of road racing is almost as long as the history of the bicycle itself. The first road race took place in 1869, between Paris and Rouen in France. By the time the first Tour de France was held in 1903, road racing was already a men's Olympic sport, and its popularity had spread across Europe. Following on from the success of riders from America and Australia, road racing has reached out to a wider audience, but recent doping scandals have brought the sport into disrepute.

UCI
Founded in 1900, the Union Cycliste Internationale (UCI) is the international governing body for all cycling sports. The UCI is based in Aigle, Switzerland.

NEED2KNOW

→ There are four main disciplines in competitive mountain biking: cross-country (XC), downhill (DH), four-cross (4X), and trials. Endurance racing, a long-distance form of cross-country racing, is also growing in popularity.

→ Each discipline has an annual World Cup – a series of races held in locations around the world – and a one-off annual World Championships. Both are sanctioned by the Union Cycliste Internationale (UCI).

→ XC racing has been an Olympic sport since 1996, but the other disciplines aren't included in the Olympics.

→ The origin of the mountain bike (MTB) is hotly contested, with cyclists in several countries claiming it as their own. But most agree that the "clunker" bikes built by Californian cyclists in the late 1970s were the creative impetus behind the birth of the sport.

RIDER PROFILE
Each branch of mountain biking requires different physical attributes. XC racers need a high level of cardio-vascular fitness and stamina to last the whole race, DH and 4X racers must have good upper- and lower-body strength for jumping the bike and delivering intense bursts of pedalling, and trials riders need perfect balance and impeccable bike-handling skills.

Lightweight lid
All mountain bikers must wear a helmet. XC, trials, and 4X riders wear lightweight polystyrene types, while DH racers wear full-face helmets for extra protection

Breathable clothing
MTB racing is intensive exercise, so breathable clothing is essential. XC racers wear close-fitting lycra, while baggy attire is more popular in other disciplines

Multiple gears
MTBs have up to 27 gears. XC bikes have more (for riding up and downhill); DH, 4X and trials bikes have fewer

Clipless pedals
Mountain bikers use clipless pedals that fix their feet to the bike, similar to a ski binding

Fat tyres
Tyres with big knobbles give extra grip for riding over loose surfaces

MOUNTAIN BIKING

SPORT OVERVIEW
Mountain biking is the most recent form of cycling to emerge. From its late-1970s origins to the first UCI-sanctioned World Championships in 1990, it rocketed in popularity and became an Olympic sport in 1996. The essence of the sport is in pitting the rider's technical and physical skills against the trail. Most events are against the clock, but trials are scored by judges.

HARD-TAIL MTB
Bikes with suspension forks but no rear shock are known as hard tails. They're great for XC and 4X riding.

Swift stoppers
Hydraulic disc brakes, similar to motorbike brakes, give reliable braking

HI-TECH KIT
In its short lifetime, mountain biking has seen more technological quantum leaps than any other branch of cycling. From carbon fibre and titanium frames, to hydraulic disc brakes and internal gearbox transmissions, the quest for lighter, faster bikes has fuelled huge innovation. Nothing epitomizes this more than suspension – once jeered at as heavy and unnecessary, no bike is now complete without it.

Big travel
Dual-crown forks are designed to take big hits

FRONT SUSPENSION
A suspension fork allows the bike to be ridden faster over rough terrain.

FULL-SUSPENSION MTB
Long-travel suspension forks, a rear shock, and hydraulic disc brakes make this bike great fun for riding downhill hard and fast.

Fully sprung
The heart of a full-suspension bike is the shock, which absorbs bumps from the rear wheel

CROSS-COUNTRY

Racing cross-country is arguably the most popular type of competitive mountain biking, due to the relative lack of specialist equipment and skills compared to other disciplines. Riders race each other over an undulating circuit for a fixed number of laps – first across the line wins. A recent variant of XC racing is the mass-start endurance event, ranging from 6-, 12-, and 24-hour races, to "dusk til dawn" races, 25km (15½-mile), 50km (31-mile), 75km (46½-mile), and 100km (62-mile) "marathons", and multi-day, multi-stage events.

SIDELINES

0 The best score for a trials rider, awarded for a "clean" round. Dabbing the ground with one or both feet, or running out of time, carries a penalty of 5 points – the worst possible score.

19,500 The vertical height gain in metres (63,980ft) of the TransAlp race – more than twice the height of Mount Everest. One of the toughest multi-day mountain bike stage races, competitors race for eight days across the Alps.

10 The amount of suspension travel, in inches (254mm), of a typical downhill full-suspension mountain bike.

DOWNHILL AND 4X

Downhill racing is the mountain biking equivalent of downhill skiing – each rider races individually, against the clock, down a course that runs from the top to bottom of a hillside, and the rider with the fastest time wins. Choice of tyres and suspension can be crucial, as can the precise line taken over the course – seconds can be won and lost by cutting corners or jumping obstacles. Four-cross is a DH variant with four riders racing against each other on a short, downhill course, with jumps, drops, and banked corners thrown in to test the riders' skill.

TRIALS

Mountain bike trials are a form of competition that tests poise, nerve, and artistry. Riders compete in two classes, for bikes with 20 or 26in wheels, and negotiate a series of obstacles without dabbing the floor with their feet, using bunnyhops, wheelies, stationary trackstands, and other balletic manoeuvres. Riders are scored on their skill, style, and invention, and penalized for dabbing their feet.

ARISE, SIR BART

THE FIRST MAN TO BECOME AN OLYMPIC CHAMPION WAS BART BRENTJENS, AT THE ATLANTA GAMES IN 1996. HE WENT TO THE GAMES A COMMONER, BUT SOON AFTER RETURNING TO HIS NATIVE HOLLAND WITH THE GOLD MEDAL, HE WAS REWARDED WITH A KNIGHTHOOD.

BUNNYHOPPING

One of the most fundamental techniques of mountain biking is the bunnyhop. It can be used in any riding situation to jump over rocks, logs, or other obstacles, saving valuable time in a competitive race. It's also crucial for trials riding, as it allows the competitor to hop from one obstacle to the next.

COASTING ALONG
The rider coasts along at a steady speed, standing out of the saddle in a crouched position, with cranks level.

FRONT WHEEL LIFT
The rider pushes down on the bars then pulls up quickly, throwing their upper body to the rear of the bike.

BACK WHEEL TUCK
The back wheel is lifted by tucking the feet up, while pushing them towards the back of the bike, clearing the log.

SMOOTH TOUCHDOWN
Both wheels touch the ground at once, and the impact is absorbed by bending the elbows and knees.

CLIMBING HIGH

Cross-country mountain biking takes place on hilly, often mountainous terrain, so riders must be able to climb efficiently as well as descend quickly. Although standing up while pedalling delivers short bursts of speed, the best method is to stay seated and pedal smoothly, conserving energy.

EFFICIENT ASCENDING
The key to efficient climbing is for the bodyweight to be distributed over the bike so that both wheels maintain maximum grip on the ground.

Weight centred
The rider's bodyweight is centred between the front and back wheels

Round in circles
The pedals are spun in consistent circles, delivering a steady power supply to the wheels

INSIDE STORY

Competitive mountain biking is governed by the UCI, which is based in Switzerland. It organizes the international World Cup and World Championships, while national series are organised by the relevant national body, which must be affiliated to the UCI.

SIDELINES

16.2 The number of seconds Gregory Duggento (Italy) took to skate 200m (219yd) at the World Speed Skating Championships in 2006, breaking the world record.

8,000 The number of participants who competed over 40km (24.8 miles) in the 2007 World Inline Cup curtain raiser in Seoul, South Korea.

12,000 The number of square metres in the world's biggest skate park, complete with bowls, banks, and rails, that was opened in Shanghai, China, in 2005.

24.1 The number of Americans in millions who participated in inline skating in 1999, at the height of the sport's popularity. By 2010, that number had fallen to an estimated 10 million.

ROLLER SKATING

SPORT OVERVIEW

From its humble beginnings in the 19th century, roller skating has evolved into a remarkable number of disciplines. These include inline skating, speed skating, quad skating, aggressive skating, roller derbies, roller hockey, freestyle, and artistic skating. Roller skaters practise on city streets or on country roads, on indoor or outdoor tracks or trails, either recreationally or professionally in races and championships organized on a local, regional, or international level.

SPEED AND STAMINA
Inline roller skaters who want to compete with others, as opposed to enjoying leisurely recreational activities, can enter sprint races to test their speed or marathons that explore the limits of their stamina and endurance.

Sharp angles
As they career around a bend on a track, speed skaters will adopt sharper angles to maintain their momentum

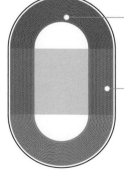

Streamlined helmet
Speed skaters wear streamlined helmets to reduce air resistance – they also offer protection for the head in case of accidents

Close-fitting strip
Speed skaters reduce air resistance by wearing a close-fitting jersey and shorts

Socks
Speed skaters often wear special socks that are durable and comfortable but not bulky

SPEED TRACKS

Speed skaters often race on indoor and outdoor tracks, with two straightaways of the same length and two symmetrical bends of the same diameter. The tracks can be level or have banked bends.

Total length
The minimum length of a track is 125m (42yd) and the maximum length is 400m (437yd)

Track surface
Any material can be used for the track surface as long as it is smooth and not slippery

NEED2KNOW

→ Quad roller skates, invented by James Plimpton in 1863, had two sets of parallel wheels that enabled skaters to go backwards, make turns, and move in a smooth curve.

→ For years after Scott Olson founded Rollerblade Inc. and mass produced skates, the term "rollerblading" was synonymous with inline skating.

TYPES OF SKATE

Variations in the boot, frame, and wheels mean that skates are available in many types and can be made to suit the kind of roller skating and the conditions of the surface on which they are used. Inline skates have aluminium frames that are usually fitted with a maximum of six wheels. Polyurethane wheels vary in diameter between 7.8cm (3in) and 10cm (4in). Skates can be fitted with a brake.

AGGRESSIVE SKATES

Aggressive skaters use inline skates that are tough and equipped with grind plates because of the regular impact of their various tricks and stunts.

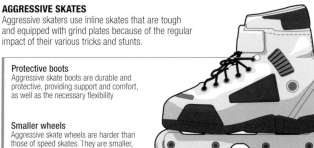

Protective boots
Aggressive skate boots are durable and protective, providing support and comfort, as well as the necessary flexibility

Smaller wheels
Aggressive skate wheels are harder than those of speed skates. They are smaller, giving the skater more manoeuvrability

SPEED SKATES

Skaters make sure they customize their skates to suit their needs, but overall they are lightweight and are as close fitting as possible.

Close-fitting boot
The soft boots that speed skaters wear are usually made of leather and have a lower ankle height

Harder wheels
The wheels on speed skates are harder than those on recreational skates, giving the skater greater speed

VERT, STREET, AND PARK

There are three kinds of aggressive inline skating. Vert is usually aerial trickery done in a half pipe. Street needs obstacles, such as kerbs, rails, and steps. Park is performed in skate parks, often beside skateboarders and BMX bikers.

TRICKS AND STUNTS

A feature of aggressive skating, also called freestyle rollerblading, is the wide repertoire of tricks and stunts, many of which are dangerous. These include grinds, which are sliding manoeuvres along the top of an obstacle such as a handrail or concrete ledge.

Wrist guards
Aggressive skaters often wear wrist guards when they ramp skate or street skate, or if they simply need bulked-up protection

Knee pads
Skaters attempting various stunts need velcro-fixed knee pads that don't slip

WORLD SPEED RACING

The World Championships in inline speed skating are organized by the International Speed Skating Committee (known as Comité International de Course, or CIC). CIC is a technical body of the Fédération International de Roller Sports (FIRS). Inline speed skating competitions, which are held for men and women in junior and senior categories, include sprints, time trials, elimination races, relays, and marathons. Team races include time trials, pursuits, and relays.

AGGRESSIVE INLINE SKATING

For years, the extreme sport of aggressive inline skating has been an underground culture with groups and communities existing and competing on a local and national level. It is popular in the US, Australia, Brazil, Japan, and various European countries, such as The Netherlands, Spain, and the UK. Inline skating events, such as vert, street, and downhill, used to feature at the X Games – a competition of action sports in the US that is held in winter and summer – but was eventually removed from the competition in 2005. In that year, about 50 aggressive skaters and promoters from nine countries set up the International Inline Stunt Association to develop the sport.

MASS STREETSKATING THROUGH THE CITY

SKATERS REGULARLY MEET FOR MASS PARTICIPATION EVENTS THAT FOLLOW A COURSE THROUGH BUSY METROPOLITAN STREETS. IN THE LONDON STREETSKATE, WHICH BEGAN IN 2000, AS MANY AS A THOUSAND SKATERS ARE LED BY UP TO 50 TRAINED MARSHALS WHO KEEP THE TRAFFIC AT BAY. THE LARGEST STREETSKATE IN THE WORLD IS THE PARI ROLLER IN PARIS, WHICH STARTED IN 1994.

STANDING AND MOVING

Individual inline skaters develop their own techniques, depending on what they are trying to do and how experienced they are. However, there are a few basic techniques that are universal. These include standing, stopping, turning, striding, and gliding. Many skates have a heel brake at the back – some are equipped with a leash which the skater pulls. Learning to use the brake can help to avoid accidents.

SKATING FASTER

Speed skaters in motion rarely have both feet on the ground at the same time. They do not twist or turn their shoulders but move their arms forwards or backwards to add to their momentum. They have mastered the art of using their legs independently. As they stride forwards they set each skate down in turn on a line that is central to their body and then push their feet out to the side – rather than pushing backwards behind them. At the end of the stride they flick their heel outwards and begin the cycle again in a relaxed, effortless motion.

INSIDE STORY

Inline skaters from many teams compete for the annual World Inline Cup, which is organized under the auspices of Fédération International de Roller Sports (FIRS). Competitors accumulate points as they move from one location to another through the year. Whoever has the most points by the end of the year is the champion.

Playing kit
Rink hockey players wear lightweight, short-sleeved tops and shorts, similar to those worn in football

Leg protection
Players wear shin guards under their long socks, and knee pads

Hand protection
Padded gloves protect the players' hands

Hockey stick
Players control the ball with a long, slim wooden stick that has a curved end

Skates
Rink hockey players wear traditional-style skates (quads)

ROLLER HOCKEY

SPORT OVERVIEW

Roller hockey is a fast, exciting game played on skates. There are two types: rink hockey and inline hockey. They have similar tactics and principles – two teams compete to score goals by hitting a ball or puck into the opposing team's goal – but differences in rinks and equipment. Rink hockey is a popular professional sport in southern Europe while inline hockey is more common in North America.

INLINE HOCKEY EQUIPMENT

There are differences between inline and rink hockey equipment. Inline players wear helmets and skates with wheels in a line. They use longer sticks and a puck or a ball. Inline goalkeepers use a glove for catching rather than a flat glove for rebounding.

INLINE SKATES
Inline hockey skates have a metal chassis usually fitted with four wheels, but may have five. The wheels at the back may be larger than those in the front. Unlike normal inline skates there is no brake.

PUCK AND STICK
Players use a hard puck (made of plastic or other material) or a ball about 7cm (2¾in) in diameter. The stick can be made of wood, aluminium, carbon composite or graphite.

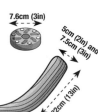

7.6cm (3in)

5cm (2in) and 7.5cm (3in)

32cm (13in)

163cm (65in)

FIELD OF PLAY

Inline roller hockey is played on rinks with the same dimensions as ice hockey rinks (see pp.150–55). The standard size of the rink for rink hockey is shown below. This rink has rounded corners and is surrounded by a wall about 1m (3ft) high.

1 Goalkeeper
The heavily padded goalkeeper (the only player to wear a helmet in rink hockey games) attempts to block the opponent's ball from entering the goal

2 Centre
The centre is an attacker who takes part in face-offs on the centre line at the start of a match and after a goal is scored

3 Winger
The winger is the main attacker and is the most likely player to score goals

4 Defenders
The two defenders try to prevent the opposing team from scoring

5 Referees
Two referees are present on the field of play during the match to administer the rules and award penalties

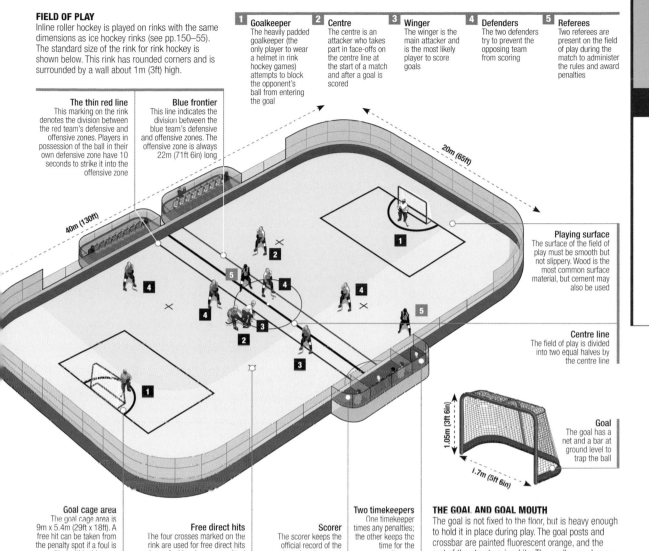

The thin red line
This marking on the rink denotes the division between the red team's defensive and offensive zones. Players in possession of the ball in their own defensive zone have 10 seconds to strike it into the offensive zone

Blue frontier
This line indicates the division between the blue team's defensive and offensive zones. The offensive zone is always 22m (71ft 6in) long

40m (130ft)

20m (65ft)

Playing surface
The surface of the field of play must be smooth but not slippery. Wood is the most common surface material, but cement may also be used

Centre line
The field of play is divided into two equal halves by the centre line

1.05m (3ft 6in)

1.7m (5ft 6in)

Goal
The goal has a net and a bar at ground level to trap the ball

Goal cage area
The goal cage area is 9m x 5.4m (29ft x 18ft). A free hit can be taken from the penalty spot if a foul is committed within this area

Free direct hits
The four crosses marked on the rink are used for free direct hits when a foul has been committed

Scorer
The scorer keeps the official record of the number of goals scored

Two timekeepers
One timekeeper times any penalties; the other keeps the time for the overall game

THE GOAL AND GOAL MOUTH
The goal is not fixed to the floor, but is heavy enough to hold it in place during play. The goal posts and crossbar are painted fluorescent orange, and the rest of the structure is white. The goalkeeper keeps position in a semi-circle with a radius of 1.5m (5ft).

RINK HOCKEY
Rink hockey is played with two teams of five players (one goalkeeper and four skaters – a centre, a winger and two defenders). A team can have a maximum of ten players, including a back-up goalkeeper, which means that substitutions are frequent. Rink games are played in two halves of 25 minutes each, with a ten-minute half-time break. Offside rules vary from country to country. For example, there is no offside in the US.

INLINE HOCKEY
Inline hockey also has five players per team on the field, with a maximum of 14 players on the team. Matches are played in two 20-minute halves with a five-minute half-time. In the event of a tie, overtime is played, followed by a shoot-out if the match is still undecided. Inline hockey has similar rules to ice hockey (see pp.150–55) but has no offside, resulting in more free-flowing play. As with rink hockey, players can incur penalties for fouls such as intentional body-checking and physical contact.

ROAD HOCKEY
ROAD HOCKEY IS A VARIATION ON ROLLER HOCKEY THAT EVOLVED AS A GAME PLAYED IN THE STREETS OF THE UNITED STATES AND CANADA. ALSO KNOWN AS DEK HOCKEY AND BALL HOCKEY IT STARTED AROUND 1970 AND HAS BEEN ORGANIZED INTO LEAGUES AND CHAMPIONSHIPS AND CAN BE PLAYED MORE FORMALLY ON INDOOR AND OUTDOOR RINKS.

INSIDE STORY
The sport of roller hockey dates back to the 1870s and 1880s in Britain. By 1901, teams were playing throughout Europe. Inline roller hockey developed in the 1990s, following the invention of inline skates in the 1980s. The first World Inline Roller Hockey Championship for Men took place in Chicago in 2005, while the first such championship for women took place in Rochester, New York, in 2002. Inline roller hockey was introduced to the World Games in 2005.

FEDERATION INTERNATIONALE DE ROLLER SPORTS (FIRS)
FIRS is the governing body for both rink hockey and inline roller hockey (it also governs speed skating and artistic skating). The World Championship for rink hockey takes place every two years, and that for inline roller hockey annually.

SKATEBOARDING

SPORT OVERVIEW

Millions of people worldwide practise skateboarding as a hobby or even a means of transport; an elite few also participate in skateboarding as a competitive sport. Individual athletes in skateboarding competitions are judged on their ingenuity and skill at performing inventive acrobatic tricks and flips, or their balance and control at negotiating a field of obstacles. Skateboarding is a media-friendly and well-sponsored sport, and high-profile international competitions attract large audiences both at the venue and on television.

HALF PIPES & RAILS

There are various types of skateboard competition, each taking place on a different field of play. Perhaps the most spectacular is the half pipe. This is a U-shaped trough with steeply sloping walls called verts (short for verticals). Skaters ride back and forth along the half pipe, propelling themselves off the verts and performing tricks while airborne. Freestyle contests are also a showcase for tricks, but take place on a flat surface. Street competitions test skaters' skills on features such as curbs and handrails. There are also slalom contests, in which skaters manoeuvre around courses set by cones.

NEED2KNOW

➡️ Rudimentary skateboards were improvised in the 1940s and 1950s by fixing roller-skate wheels to boards, or taking the handlebars off scooters.

➡️ Skateboarding surged in popularity in California in the 1950s and 60s. It had strong ties to surfing culture, and was often called "street surfing" or "sidewalk surfing".

➡️ Skateboarding as a sport really took off in the 1970s, when innovations in manufacture gave skaters more mobility and control, leading them to develop more daring and inventive acrobatic stunts.

SIDELINES

18,500,000 The estimated number of people who take part in skateboarding worldwide (according to a US report in 2002).

10 The number of gold medals Tony Hawk has won for vert skating at the X Games, one of the most high-profile competitions. Hawk is probably the world's best-known and most successful skater.

900 The first 900-degree turn was performed by Tony Hawk in 1999. 720- and 540-degree turns are more common.

THE ZEPHYRS

THE Z-BOYS OF CALIFORNIA, MEMBERS OF THE LEGENDARY ZEPHYR TEAM OF THE 1970S, USED THE WALLS OF EMPTY SWIMMING POOLS TO PRACTICE THEIR TRICKS – AND INTRODUCED VERT SKATING TO THE WORLD.

GRAB 540 BACKSIDE TRICK

The trick illustrated here is the grab 540 backside. The skateboarder performs a 540-degree turn while airborne, with one hand holding onto the board and the other arm providing the impetus for the rotation. The board is released before the skater comes back into contact with the half pipe.

Protective helmet
A crash helmet is essential to prevent injury. Most consist of a rigid plastic exterior with a padded interior to fit closely to the skull

Knee pad
Knee pads consist of a flexible foam part that extends from below the knee to above it, with a tough plastic part to protect the knee itself

Vert lip
Some skateboarders perform tricks on the lip of the vert, such as grinds or one-handed handstands

Vert walls
The total height of the vert (short for vertical) section is usually 3–4m (10–13ft)

Half-pipe surface
The half pipe is usually a wooden frame covered with a smooth surface of masonite (fibreboard)

COMPETITOR PROFILE

Skateboarders need a great sense of balance, perfect timing, coordination, and muscle control to perform the technically demanding tricks. They also need creative flair and imagination to come up with original tricks to impress contest judges. Skateboarders are often fairly lightly built rather than muscle-bound, which gives them greater mobility and control, particularly when airborne.

Skateboard
Skateboards are typically 76–79cm (30–31in) long and 20cm (8in) wide. The deck is surfaced with grip tape to prevent the skater slipping off the board

Elbow pads
Elbow pads have a similar construction to the protective knee pads. Many skaters also wear wrist guards

BOARDS & BODY ARMOUR

Developments in competitive skateboarding have evolved as the technology has improved. The introduction of polyurethane wheels in the early 1970s was a landmark that significantly improved the performance of skateboarders and helped greatly popularize the sport. Apart from the skateboard, protective gear is essential equipment as injuries are common; a helmet, knee pads and elbow pads, and shoes or trainers with a good grip are all key items.

SKATEBOARD
Skateboards can be made from fibreglass or polypropylene, but are most commonly wooden. Maple is the favoured material, and boards are generally made of seven layers of veneer pressed together.

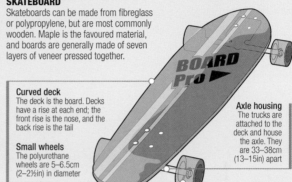

Curved deck
The deck is the board. Decks have a rise at each end; the front rise is the nose, and the back rise is the tail

Small wheels
The polyurethane wheels are 5–6.5cm (2–2½in) in diameter

Axle housing
The trucks are attached to the deck and house the axle. They are 33–38cm (13–15in) apart

TRICKS OF THE TRADE

Street skateboarding techniques appear less spectacular than half-pipe tricks, because they take place on a flat plane, but still require supreme technical ability. The ollie (described below) and grind are core tricks. The grind involves ollieing onto a rail and sliding along it on the trucks of the skateboard.

THE OLLIE
The ollie is a trick in which the skater propels himself off the ground to move airborne vertically, particularly to jump over obstacles on a street course.

Popping the tail
The skater lifts into the air by putting pressure on the tail

Front foot forward
The front foot moves to the nose of the deck to pull up the board

Levelling out
The back foot is lifted up to level out the skateboard

INSIDE STORY

There is no international governing body for skateboarding, and there has been some resistance within the community to having a regulating body for a sport with such strong roots in non-conformist youth culture. However, competitions are vital to the sport. The first official contest was held in California in 1965, and the first European event took place in Germany in 1977. Today, the X Games are one of the most popular events.

X GAMES
The X Games are one of the most high-profile international contests featuring skateboarding along with other "extreme" sports such as snowboarding. The games began in 1995 and take place annually.

MOTOR SPORTS

10

NEED2KNOW

➡️ Each Grand Prix is watched by enormous crowds of enthusiastic spectators and by hundreds of millions of television viewers in nearly every country in the world.

➡️ Formula One was established in 1946 and the first race was in 1947. The first Formula One World Championship was held in 1950.

➡️ The Fédération Internationale de l'Automobile (FIA) is the governing body of Formula One racing.

DRIVER PROFILE
Drivers need to be physically fit and mentally tough to cope with the rigours of competing at high speed in hot, cramped, noisy, and extremely dangerous conditions. Together with supreme driving skills, great courage, and rapid reflexes, drivers need to work closely with their team and quickly adapt their tactics to the circumstances of a race.

SPORT OVERVIEW
The pinnacle of the motor sport calendar, Formula One is an annual series of thrilling, high-speed Grand Prix races held on circuits around the world. Car constructors and drivers conform to a strictly enforced set of regulations – a formula of specifications that is continually adapted to the changing needs of safety and fairness – as they compete for the technological edge that sees them triumph over their rivals. The drivers and constructors who accumulate the most points throughout the season are crowned Formula One World Champions.

DRIVER SAFETY
Racing regulations make driver safety a top priority. The safety cell, seatbelts, and the carbon fibre chassis and body protect drivers from injury in the event of an accident. Drivers have to wear suits and other kit made out of Nomex, a remarkable flame-resistant fabric that withstands hydrocarbon fires.

THE FORMULA ONE CAR
The product of brilliant engineering design and cutting-edge technology, Formula One cars rely on a finely tuned balance of aerodynamics, electronics, tyres, and suspension.

BOW TIE
FLAMBOYANT BRITISH DRIVER MIKE HAWTHORN, WHO BECAME FORMULA ONE CHAMPION IN 1958, OFTEN COMPETED IN RACES WEARING A BOW TIE TO GO WITH HIS DISTINCTIVE SMILE.

Driving gloves
Fireproof gloves are thin to give the driver the feel of the wheel

Crash helmet
Helmets and visors can withstand an object travelling at 480kph (300mph)

Shoulders
Handles on the shoulders enable the driver to be lifted free

Racing boots
Fireproof shoes have a good grip and are thin to give the best control of the pedals

HANS collar
Reduces load on head and neck, and protects them from injury

Air intake
The engine's air intake is just above the driver's head

Safety cell
Built into the chassis, the safety cell contains the cockpit with the fuel tank behind and a protective structure in front

Under the suit
Underwear beneath the suit provides more fireproof protection

Braking system
Carbon fibre disc brakes enable the driver to stop a car travelling at 110kph (70mph) within 18m (60ft). Cars are fitted with a failsafe back-up braking system

Gripping tyres
Precision moulding of tyres increases grip and improves cornering speeds

Rear wing
The aerodynamic effect of a rear wing increases the downward force on the car

Powerful engine
A four-stroke V-8 engine has 2.4 litres (½g) of displacement

Front suspension
The front suspension supports the front of the car and determines how the tyres contact the road

FORMULA ONE

SIDELINES

5 The number of seconds it takes a Formula One car to accelerate from a standing start to 160kph (100mph) and then decelerate to 0 again. A Formula One car travelling at 300kph (186mph) can come to a complete stop in less than 3.5 seconds.

320 The speed in kph (200mph) that Formula One cars can reach on a straight track.

20 The number of Grand Prix races in Formula One's 2012 season, 12 of which – including India, Malaysia, China, Australia, and Bahrain – were outside Europe.

23 The age of the youngest driver – Sebastien Vettel – ever to win the Formula One World Championship. He won it in 2010, his third full Formula One season.

7 The record number of times Michael Schumacher has been Formula One World Champion. Statistically he is the greatest driver the world has ever seen.

POINTS OF CONTACT

Formula One cars are fitted with tyres that maximize the points of contact with the track surface while withstanding massive downforce loads. Hard tyres are more durable and longer lasting than soft tyres, which give more grip. Tyres work best at certain temperatures and are designed to last for one race at the most. Restrictions tend to be reviewed regularly and may change from year to year. Treadless, or slick, tyres were allowed back in 2009, having been banned in 1998. In dry conditions, teams must use both a hard and a soft compound during each race.

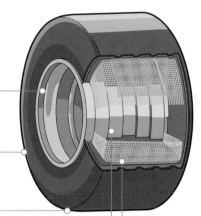

INTERACTIVE STEERING WHEEL

Inside the cockpit the interactive steering wheel provides the driver with various details about the car's performance, as well as the ability to fine-tune and control a number of settings, and the means to communicate via radio with his team in the pits.

Wheel dimensions
The maximum diameter of wheels with wet tyres fitted is 66cm (26½in) and 67cm (26¾in)

Tyre dimensions
The maximum width of front tyres is 35.5cm (14¼in) and of rear tyres is 38cm (15¼in)

Contact surface
The outer surface of the tyre is made of a rubber compound

Bracing plies
In the middle layer bracing plies are embedded in rubber

High-tech mesh
The inner layer is a high-tech mesh of polyester and nylon

Light sequence
A sequence of lights helps the driver time a gear change to perfection

Main display
Information about gears, temperatures and brakes appears on a large screen. At the bottom of the screen the FIA can show the driver the colour of a flag (such as yellow, red, or black) which trackside marshals might be waving

Right button bank
The buttons on the right side of the wheel include the pit lane speed limiter (LIM) and the radio (RAD) which connects the driver with engineers on the pit wall

Gear change/clutch
Drivers can change gear easily by flicking a paddle behind the steering wheel with their fingers. There are usually eight gears (seven forward and one reverse).

Left button bank
The buttons on the left side of the wheel include the neutral setting (N) for the gearbox, the calibration (CAL) of the clutch, menu display on the screen, and the ACK button, which the driver presses when he is unable to talk but wants to acknowledge a radio message he has received from the pits

Traction control
This alters the traction control settings during the race, depending on the grip level required and the changing track conditions

CHOOSING TYRES

Some of the most important decisions a Formula One team must make are focused around choosing the tyres. At the start of a race weekend teams have a supply of ready to go sets of tyres: 14 sets of dry-weather tyres, four sets of wet-weather tyres, and three sets of extreme-weather tyres. If there has been heavy rain, teams may be obliged to use extreme weather tyres for safety.

Dry-weather tyres
These are "slicks", meaning that they have no tread at all. There are two kinds of dry-weather tyre – soft rubber and hard rubber.

Wet-weather tyres
For wet conditions, teams keep tyres with a tread at the ready. They keep a close eye on the weather forecast in case rain is on its way.

Extreme-weather tyres
Tyres for very wet conditions have a deep tread, which improves grip by clearing water from the tyre where it meets the track.

STICKS LIKE GLUE

Designers of Formula One racing cars aim to create a light car that increases mechanical grip and "sticks like glue" to the track. This is achieved by minimizing wind resistance and aerodynamic drag and maximizing the downward force on the car. Over the years, design innovations included the upswept tail, small wings either side of the nose, flexible skirts, and rear wings. In the 1980s the whole car became like a wing, creating a "ground effect" that increased speeds dramatically but made cornering dangerous, so it was banned. Almost every surface on a modern Formula One car is designed to produce downforce.

Front aerofoils
Aerofoils at the front of the car create downforce on the front tyres and aerodynamically channel the air flow to the rest of the car

Barge boards
On the side of the car barge boards shape air flow and reduce turbulence

Shaped helmets
Aerodynamically shaped helmets can improve the air flow into the air intake above the driver's head

Rear wing
The downward force from the adjustable vanes on rear wing increases the grip between rear tyres and track

RACE WEEKEND

Each of the season's Grand Prix races takes place over a weekend. On Friday (Thursday in Monaco), drivers have two free practice sessions. On Saturday, they have another practice, then qualifying sessions to determine where they start Sunday's race. The rules stipulate that there must be a minimum of 20 cars and a maximum of 24 cars in a race.

FREE PRACTICE

The aim of the practice sessions is to give teams experience of the particular circuit: drivers become familiar with the track's idiosyncrasies while engineers and directors make critical tyre and fuel decisions, and adjust the settings of their cars and adapt them to the local conditions.

QUALIFYING FOR THE RACE

In three 15-minute qualifying sessions the drivers compete against the clock to complete the fastest lap and establish the order of the starting line-up for Sunday's race. All the drivers race against each other in the first session – the slowest (usually six) occupy the last places on the grid and take no further part in qualifying. In the second session, the slowest (usually six) go on to occupy the next places (usually 11 to 16) on the grid. In the third session, the remaining drivers compete for the top places on the grid, with the fastest taking pole position.

THE CIRCUITS

The 2011 season saw 20 races around the world, including the Istanbul circuit in Turkey, which was built in 2005. The illustration of this circuit (see below) provides an aerial view of the circuit, and highlights some of the more important aspects of the racetrack.

THE RACE BEGINS

Drivers and cars must be on the grid 15 minutes before the start of the parade lap. During this time, refuelling is finished, tyres are put on the cars, engines are running, and the track is cleared. Two green lights signal the start of the parade lap, which ends with drivers taking up their alloted grid positions. The countdown to the race begins.

GO! GO! GO!

At one-second intervals, red lights come on from left to right and one at a time. After a few seconds all five go out simultaneously – and the sprint for the first corner begins.

SCORING

Drivers are awarded points if they finish a Grand Prix race in the top 10 positions. The winner in first place receives 25 points, the runner-up in second place receives 18 points, third place gets 15 points, fourth place 12 points, through to tenth place with one point. Constructors that have two drivers in a race are awarded their points according to how many their drivers score together. A team that comes first and second is awarded 43 points, for example.

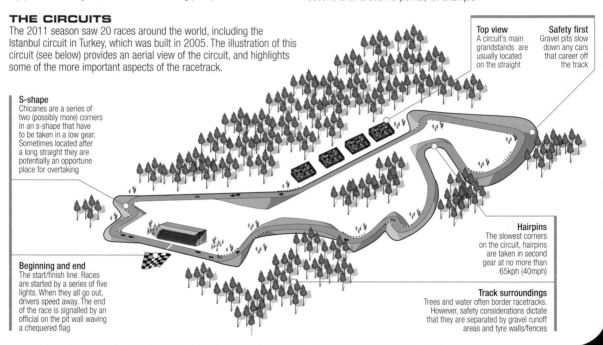

Top view
A circuit's main grandstands are usually located on the straight

Safety first
Gravel pits slow down any cars that career off the track

S-shape
Chicanes are a series of two (possibly more) corners in an s-shape that have to be taken in a low gear. Sometimes located after a long straight they are potentially an opportune place for overtaking

Beginning and end
The start/finish line. Races are started by a series of five lights. When they all go out, drivers speed away. The end of the race is signalled by an official on the pit wall waving a chequered flag

Hairpins
The slowest corners on the circuit, hairpins are taken in second gear at no more than 65kph (40mph)

Track surroundings
Trees and water often border racetracks. However, safety considerations dictate that they are separated by gravel runoff areas and tyre walls/fences

SIGNAL FLAGS

Marshals are stationed at various points around a track, ready to wave flags to attract the drivers' attention. Flags are coloured differently according to the particular signal they are sending, such as danger on the track ahead, an interruption to the race, or all clear.

DANGER ON TRACK
Single yellow means danger; drivers slow down and don't overtake.

DIRTY TRACK
Yellow with red stripes means a slippery track surface ahead.

SLOW CAR
White warns of a slow moving vehicle on the track; drivers slow down.

ALL CLEAR
Green means all clear and yellow flag warnings have been lifted.

LET CAR PASS
Blue warns of a faster car behind; driver to let the car overtake.

TECHNICAL PROBLEM
Black with orange circle and car number warns a driver to return to his pit.

WARNING
Black and white with car number warns of unsporting behaviour.

DISQUALIFICATION
Black with car number orders a driver to his pit; possible disqualification.

RACE INTERRUPTED
Red means the race, practice, or qualifying session is stopped.

RACE OVER
Chequered means the race has ended; shown first to the winner.

TEAM WORK

Many people contribute their services and expertise to the smooth running of a Formula One team. The drivers may become the most visible member, but everybody – from senior managers, designers, and engineers to test drivers, logistical support, and pit crew – is crucial to the team's success.

PIT CREW

When a driver brings his car into the pits for a pit stop, a large team of helmeted mechanics swarm around him in a carefully synchronized flurry of activity. Every split second counts. Each mechanic knows exactly what to do, such as filling up the tank with fuel, jacking up the front, or changing a tyre.

Starter motor
Standing at the ready, a mechanic holds a power-operated starter motor in case the engine stalls

Sidepod cleaning
A mechanic on either side of the car cleans debris out the sidepods

Lollypop man
The lollypop is lowered during the stop and raised when the crews have stood back with their jobs done

Front jack
A front jack man raises and lowers the front of the car in time with the tyre crews

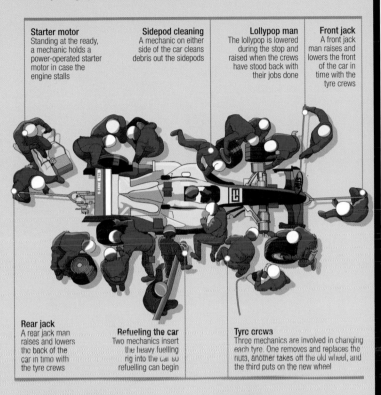

Rear jack
A rear jack man raises and lowers the back of the car in time with the tyre crews

Refueling the car
Two mechanics insert the heavy fuelling rig into the car so refuelling can begin

Tyre crews
Three mechanics are involved in changing each tyre. One removes and replaces the nuts, another takes off the old wheel, and the third puts on the new wheel

THE PIT LANE

The pit lane separates the pit wall from the team garages and is divided into two lanes – the fast lane nearest the pit wall and the inner lane beside the garages. The pit crew emerges from the garages when one of their cars arrives on the inner lane during a pit stop. Teams install their control centres beside the pit wall. These centres become the hub of the team's activity during the race – directors, engineers, and others discuss tactics and strategy, refer to computers, watch monitors and screens, and use the communications equipment that keeps the team in touch with a driver and with analysts back at headquarters.

PIT-BOARD

The pit board tells a driver his race position, laps completed, and the time between him and the car in front and the car behind.

TIMING WALL

Each Formula One team is equipped with a timing wall in the pits where computers analyse the performance of their cars. The team monitors lap times, telemetry, and television feeds on a bank of screens. Between test laps, drivers can watch displays of their laps. The brightness of the screen images is unaffected by strong sunlight or the smoky atmosphere of the garages and pit lane.

STAT CENTRAL

DRIVERS CHAMPIONSHIP

YEAR	NAME	COUNTRY
2012	SEBASTIEN VETTEL	(GER)
2011	SEBASTIEN VETTEL	(GER)
2010	SEBASTIEN VETTEL	(GER)
2009	JENSON BUTTON	(GBR)
2008	LEWIS HAMILTON	(GBR)
2007	KIMI RAIKKONEN	(FIN)
2006	FERNANDO ALONSO	(ESP)
2005	FERNANDO ALONSO	(ESP)
2004	MICHAEL SCHUMACHER	(GER)
2003	MICHAEL SCHUMACHER	(GER)
2002	MICHAEL SCHUMACHER	(GER)

CONSTRUCTORS CHAMPIONSHIP

YEAR	NAME	POINTS
2012	RED BULL	460
2011	RED BULL	650
2010	RED BULL	498
2009	BRAWN	172
2008	FERRARI	172
2007	FERRARI	204
2006	RENAULT	206
2005	RENAULT	191
2004	FERRARI	262
2003	FERRARI	158
2002	FERRARI	221

ALL-TIME RACE WINS

WINS	NAME	COUNTRY
91	MICHAEL SCHUMACHER	(GER)
51	ALAIN PROST	(FRA)
41	AYRTON SENNA	(BRA)
31	NIGEL MANSELL	(GBR)
30	FERNANDO ALONSO	(ESP))
27	JACKIE STEWART	(GBR)
26	SEBASTIEN VETTEL	(GER)
25	JIM CLARK	(GBR)
25	NIKI LAUDA	(AUT)
24	JUAN MANUEL FANGIO	(ARG)

INSIDE STORY

Retired Formula One drivers started competing against each other in 2005 in a series of races called the Grand Prix Masters. Driving identical open-wheel vehicles based on the 1999 Reynard Champ cars and powered by 3.5-litre V-8 engines, all entrants must be medically fit, more than 45 years of age, and veterans of two or more Formula One seasons. Nigel Mansell won the inaugural event at Kyalami, South Africa.

→ Indy car racing is the American equivalent to Formula One.

→ Indy car racing gets its name from the sport's most prestigious race – the Indianapolis 500.

→ Most Indy car racing takes place in the United States, but there are also races in Australia, Brazil, Canada, and Japan.

380

Two-element wing
This type of rear wing is used to increase downforce and drag, limiting the speed of the car and holding it to the road

Air intake
Air feeds directly into the V-8 engine block through the airbox

Smooth tyres
The tread is only the thickness of a credit card. Front tyres have a diameter of 66cm (26in), and those at the rear are 70cm (27½in). They reach 100°C (212°F) during a race

Carbon fibre chassis
This material is strong and light. The minimum weight for an oval-racing car is 708kg (1,530lb) and for a road-racing car it is 726kg (1,600lb)

Front wing
Guides the air over the car to produce the downforce needed to keep it on the track

BUILT FOR SPEED
Indy cars are open-wheel single seaters with an open cockpit and outboard wings at front and rear. Chassis and engine manufacturers supply vehicles on three-year cycles. Restrictions are placed on the power output of the engine and the weight and dimensions of the cars. Engines are 3.5litre V-8s, fuelled by ethanol. The chassis can be no longer than 4.88m (16ft) and no wider than 1.98m (6½ft).

Suspension
Springs and shock absorbers support the weight of the car and smooth out bumps on the road

Cockpit cushion
A cockpit head guard protects the head by absorbing the impact of a collision

Spectator seating
Depending on the circuit, crowds of 100,000 or more can watch from grandstands placed around the circuit

Pits area
This is where mechanics refuel cars, change tyres, and conduct minor repairs

DRIVER PROFILE
Some qualities seem obvious: excellent concentration, vision, and coordination; ample supplies of courage; and long experience of race conditions. Additionally, a driver needs staying power for a long race in a hot car, with toned neck, forearm, and leg muscles to deal with hours of steering, braking, and gear changing.

SPORT OVERVIEW
The Indy car format is overwhelmingly a North American phenomenon that involves open-wheel cars racing at tremendous speeds, often on compact, steeply banked oval tracks but also on road and street courses. The IndyCar® Series is one of the most popular spectator motor sports in the United States, with races attracting bumper crowds to watch exciting and often hard-fought competitions. Races vary in length, the longest being the internationally famous 800km (500 miles) Indianapolis 500.

INDY CAR RACING

RACE CIRCUITS

Indy car races are contested on three main types of race track: ovals (speedways), longer superovals (superspeedways), and street circuits. Drivers may cover up to 800km (500 miles) in the longest races. The most famous of all the Indy car circuits is the Indianapolis Motor Speedway, where drivers battle it out over 200 laps of the 4km (2½ miles) superoval to become the Indy 500 champion. The streets of St. Petersburg, Florida, provide an urban circuit for another leg of the IndyCar Series calendar. This series also features a race in Japan – at the Twin Ring Motegi, which includes both an oval speedway and a road course.

SIDELINES

257,325 The capacity of the stadium at Indianapolis Motor Speedway, the home of the Indianapolis 500.

675 The number of horsepower generated by the 3.5-litre, methanol-powered engine of an Indy car.

5,000 The number of pounds of downforce produced by an Indy car travelling at 350kph (220mph).

POLE POSITION

During qualification, drivers race against the clock to earn a spot on the starting grid. The rules for qualification vary from race to race. For oval races, drivers complete up to three qualification laps. The driver who records the fastest lap takes pole, the next fastest takes second spot, and so on until the starting grid is full. After a couple of warm-up laps, the race has a rolling start behind a pace car. For road races, the six fastest drivers in the qualification laps race head to head to determine the first three rows on the starting grid.

INDY CAR VERSUS FORMULA ONE

There are a number of differences between Indy car racing and Formula One racing (see pp.376–79). Indy car races are usually held on oval circuits and begin in a flying start with the cars in position but on the move. Formula One races are held on non-oval circuits and begin from a standing start with all the cars in position on a formal grid. Indy cars are heavier but faster on the straights than Formula One racers, but the latter are more agile and accelerate more quickly. Indy cars can use slick tyres that are flat and without grooves, whereas Formula One dry weather tyres must have grooves. Traction control and semi-automatic gearboxes are permitted in Formula One cars but not in Indy cars, which have engines limited to 10,300rpm. Indy cars have been fuelled with methanol or a mixture of methanol and ethanol, but in 2007 switched to 100 per cent ethanol. Formula One cars are fuelled with unleaded racing petrol.

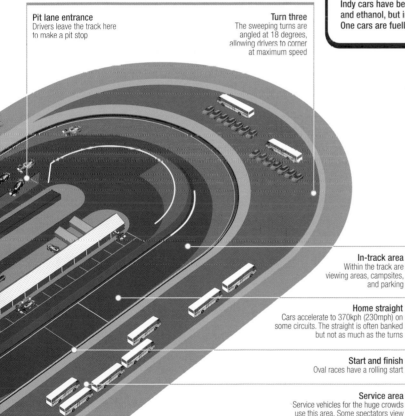

Pit lane entrance
Drivers leave the track here to make a pit stop

Turn three
The sweeping turns are angled at 18 degrees, allowing drivers to corner at maximum speed

In-track area
Within the track are viewing areas, campsites, and parking

Home straight
Cars accelerate to 370kph (230mph) on some circuits. The straight is often banked but not as much as the turns

Start and finish
Oval races have a rolling start

Service area
Service vehicles for the huge crowds use this area. Some spectators view from motorcoaches parked here

Turn two
Drivers slow only marginally as they negotiate this banked corner. Steel and foam energy reduction (SAFER) barriers cushion the impact of cars during crashes

STAT CENTRAL

DRIVERS WITH MOST IRL VICTORIES

WINS	DRIVER (COUNTRY)
28	SCOTT DIXON (NZL)
21	DARIO FRANCHITTI (GBR)
21	HELIO CASTRONEVES (BRA)
19	SAM HORNISH JR. (USA)
16	WILL POWER (AUS)
16	DAN WHELDON (GBR)
14	TONY KANAAN (BRA)
9	SCOTT SHARP (USA)
8	BUDDY LAZIER (USA)
7	RYAN HUNTER-REAY (USA)

INSIDE STORY

Indy car racing has its origins at the Indianapolis Motor Speedway course. For many years, Championship Auto Racing Teams (CART) ran Indy car racing, but after an acrimonious split in 1994, the "Indy" name was taken by the Indy Racing League. CART now runs the Champ Car World Series, an Indy format similar to F1.

GOVERNING BODY

The Indy Racing League (IRL) is the North American organization that sanctions the IndyCar Series. It also runs the developmental Indy pro series.

RACING AN OVAL

Many Indy car races are held on banked ovals. One of the regulars on the IRL schedule is Michigan International Speedway, at Brooklyn, Michigan. This 3.2km (2-mile) D-shaped oval has turns with 18-degree banks, a front straight cambered at 12 degrees, and 5-degree banking on the back straight. On some circuits, drivers' speeds never fall below 320kph (200mph), with faster top speeds on straights.

GP2

NEED2KNOW

→ Televised GP2 races take place in Bahrain, Malaysia, and European countries such as Spain, Italy, France, Hungary, Germany, Belgium, Monaco, and the UK.

→ GP2 cars can reach speeds of 320kph (200mph). They can travel from 0–100kph (62.5mph) in 2.95 seconds and from 0–200kph (123mph) in 6.7 seconds.

SPORT OVERVIEW

Introduced to the motor sports calendar in 2005, the GP2 Series – often abbreviated to GP2 – is a new form of motor racing that replaces Formula 3000 as a means of preparing drivers and their teams for life in the fast lane of Formula One. The GP2 championship is an annual series of races that accompany Formula One races in certain countries. To ensure the best driver prevails in the series, each participating team shares the same engine, chassis, gearbox, and tyres.

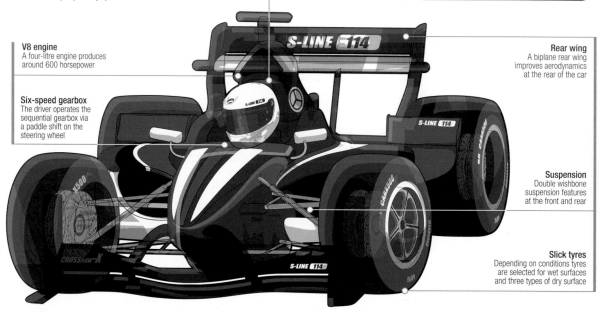

HANS device
Every driver wears a HANS device to protect and support their head and neck

DRIVER PROFILE
The young competitors who participate in GP2 races need driving skill and talent above all else because the car they all drive has no additional technological advantages to help them with handling.

V8 engine
A four-litre engine produces around 600 horsepower

Six-speed gearbox
The driver operates the sequential gearbox via a paddle shift on the steering wheel

Rear wing
A biplane rear wing improves aerodynamics at the rear of the car

Suspension
Double wishbone suspension features at the front and rear

Slick tyres
Depending on conditions tyres are selected for wet surfaces and three types of dry surface

WEEKEND FORMAT

Drivers compete in races which take place at 11 locations. There are two races on each weekend of the series – these follow the same pattern (except at Monaco, which has no Sunday race). Drivers practice and then qualify for their grid position on the Friday, race for 180km (112 miles) on Saturday and then for 120km (75 miles) on Sunday. The top eight results on Saturday determine the order of Sunday's grid in reverse order – 8th takes pole position and the winner starts in 8th place. In Saturday's race there is one compulsory pit stop when teams must change at least two tyres.

POINT SCORING

In the Saturday race 2 points are awarded for achieving pole position and then 10 points to the winner, with 8, 6, 5, 4, 3, 2, and 1 point going to the following 7 finishers. In the Sunday race, the winner receives 6 points, with 5, 4, 3, 2, and 1 point going to the next five finishers. In each race 1 point is awarded for the fastest lap. When Lewis Hamilton won the series in 2006 he amassed 113 points, 12 ahead of Nelson Piquet Jr.

SERIES WINNERS

GERMAN DRIVER NICO ROSBERG WAS THE CHAMPION IN THE INAUGURAL GP2 SERIES IN 2005 AND BRITISH DRIVER LEWIS HAMILTON WON IN 2006. BOTH HAVE GRADUATED TO FORMULA ONE. ART GRAND PRIX WON THE TEAM PRIZE IN BOTH YEARS.

INSIDE STORY

Five essential values help to shape GP2 racing and the regulations that govern it. These are high performance of the GP2 car, control of competition costs, driver safety, training of every team member and, finally, putting on an entertaining and exciting show. Controlling costs became vital with the demise of Formula 3000, which became too expensive for teams to enter. The GP2 series is the first motorsport with a fully integrated strategy – for example, centralized purchasing enables teams to buy cheaper parts.

DTM RACES

The Deutsche Tourenwagen Masters (DTM) is hugely popular in Germany and features a top-class international grid driving works-backed touring cars with V8 engines generating a maximum of 470hp. The cars share standardized tyres, brakes, transmissions, dimensions, and aerodynamics.

DRIVERLESS CAR

SEAT UNVEILED THE WORLD'S FIRST DRIVERLESS TOURING CAR IN 2007. DRIVEN BY REMOTE CONTROL FROM THE PITS, THE CAR CAN PRODUCE CONSISTENTLY FAST LAPS WHILE ELIMINATING RISK.

INSIDE STORY

In 2005, the Fédération Internationale de l'Automobile (FIA) replaced the European Touring Car Championship with the World Touring Car Championship. Drivers compete at 12 tracks in various countries such as Brazil, Italy, and Russia. The races are usually for Super 2000, Diesel 2000, and Super Production cars.

BRITISH TOURING CAR CHAMPIONSHIP

Since its inauguration in 1958, the British Touring Car Championship (BTCC) has been attracting large crowds eager to watch their favourite production models career around race tracks with top drivers at the wheel. Manufacturers were equally keen to showcase their new models, especially with regular television coverage bringing the championship to millions of viewers. Teams using two-litre saloon cars compete in three races at each of nine tracks in the UK and the Republic of Ireland. In 2007, the touring cars were required to conform to the FIA's Super 2000 regulations as a step towards harmonizing technical specifications across the sport.

NEED2KNOW

→ Some touring car races last for 24 hours and are tests of endurance for crew and driver.

→ Drivers coming to touring car racing from Formula One include Mika Häkkinen and Jean Alesi. Drivers who raced in touring cars and graduated to Formula One include Michael Schumacher and Alexander Wurz.

SPORT OVERVIEW

Touring cars are essentially four-door saloon cars or two-door coupés that have been thoroughly modified for competitive racing on road courses and street circuits. Touring cars are different from sports cars, which are often purpose built. Various types of touring car compete in a number of major championships and series around the world, especially in Britain, Germany, and Australia.

TOURING CAR RACING

Rear wing
The adjustable rear wing has a number of different settings

Traction
Cars can be front-wheel, rear-wheel, or four-wheel drive

Driver safety
A roll cage protects the driver in the event of an accident

Front splitter
The aerodynamic front splitter protruding from the front of the car helps to direct air flow

DRIVER PROFILE

Drivers need to be physically fit and mentally tough, with a range of skills – from close-quarter cornering at speed and negotiating chicanes to the tactical knowhow of making tyres last for a whole race – to succeed in fast and furious races on tracks that differ significantly from each other.

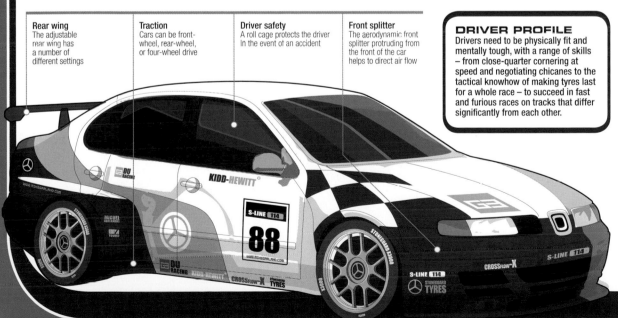

NEED2KNOW

→ Drag racing originated in the United States and is still most popular in North America. It also has a big following in many European countries, Brazil, Mexico, Canada, South Africa, and Australia.

→ Worldwide, there are more than 300 drag strips.

→ The annual US Nationals six-day event organized by the National Hot Rod Association (NHRA) at Indianapolis attracts more than 100,000 spectators and is the richest drag-racing competition in the world.

384

DRAG RACING

SPORT OVERVIEW

Drag racing is about speed, pure and simple. It is the fastest land-based sport. The competition is basic: two motor vehicles race along a relatively short, straight, and level track, and the first to cross the finishing line is the winner. Vehicles are classified according to various criteria, including vehicle type, engine size, wheelbase, and frame type.

Rear wings
Carbon-fibre wings exert a massive downward pressure on the dragster and keep it from taking off when the engines fire up

Supercharger
This rams air into the engine at a staggering rate to keep the fuel burning

Parachutes
Twin chutes are needed to bring the dragster to a halt after a race

Rear tyres
These are massive: 46cm (18in) wide and 95cm (37.5in) in diameter

Front wings
The canard wings help keep the dragster on the track when it is moving

Low clearance
The front of the car must be at least 8cm (3in) off the ground

Powerhouse
The fuel pump supplies the powerful engine with 227 litres (50 gals) of nitromethane per minute

COMPETITOR PROFILE
Total lack of fear is the number one requirement. The ability to focus completely is also crucial, since a fraction of a second's delay when the starting lights change will probably mean the difference between winning and losing. Drag racers have to have the mental strength to psych out their opponents, and resist these tactics from their rivals.

TOP FUEL DRAGSTER
No car in the world can accelerate faster than a top fuel dragster. They are often powered by 426 Chrysler Hemi engines, which have hemispherical combustion chambers with large valves and a more central spark plug to improve ignition and performance and generate 8,000 horsepower. Top fuel dragsters need special fuel, enormous tyres, and wings to keep them firmly on the ground.

GLOVE
The gloves offer all-round, fire-resistant protection for the hands and wrists.

Wrist protection
The glove extends well up the arm

LAYERED HELMET
The helmet has three layers to protect the head from trauma and fire: an outer shell, a foam liner, and an inner fire-resistant layer. To help counter the massive G forces, a 360-degree neck collar provides vital support.

Foam liner
A thick layer of foam helps absorb any impact to the helmet

Outer shell
Provides trauma protection

SIDELINES

3.58 The time in seconds it took Sammy Miller to complete the Santa Pod strip in England in 1984 when he broke the world record in his car Vanishing Point. His average speed over the 400m course was 621.61kph (386.26mph).

15 The number of times American driver John Force has been crowned winner in the NHRA's Funny Car championship. With more than 130 career victories and the holder of the record for qualifying in 395 consecutive events, he is one of the sport's most successful competitors.

SPEEDWAY

The drag-racing speedway strip is straight, level, and short. A special seal applied to the surface of the track increases tyre traction. The standard strip lengths are 400m (¼ mile) or 200m (⅛ mile). Electronic beams at the start and finish record the times of contestants. Drivers accelerate across the starting line as soon as they see the green light appear on the "Christmas tree" in front of them. There is a deceleration section at the end of the track equal in length to one-and-a-half times the race distance.

Signal lights
Drivers prepare to move when the last of the orange lights comes on. A split second later, the green light shows and the race is underway

ROCKET RACERS

THE FASTEST TOP FUEL DRAGSTERS COVER A 400M (¼ MILE) COURSE IN LITTLE MORE THAN FOUR SECONDS, HITTING 530KPH (330MPH) OR MORE. THE 5G DECELERATION EXPERIENCED BY DRIVERS AS PARACHUTES SLOW THEM TO A STOP CAN CAUSE EYE PROBLEMS.

CHRISTMAS TREE

An array of signal lights – from yellow to orange to green – in front of the starting line lets the driver know when the race is ready to begin.

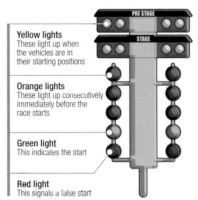

Yellow lights
These light up when the vehicles are in their starting positions

Orange lights
These light up consecutively immediately before the race starts

Green light
This indicates the start

Red light
This signals a false start

Line-up
The vehicles line up side by side in all competitions except handicap races, when vehicles with poorer performance potentials are allowed to compete against faster cars. The slower of the two is given a handicap head start

Lanes
Drivers are not permitted to move from their own lane into that of their opponent. If they do so, they are disqualified

Track surface
A cement surface at the start of the track gives the tyres good traction. The rest of the track may be asphalt

WHAT THEY DRIVE

There are more than 200 different vehicle classes, each with different requirements in terms of engine size, weight, fuel, and chassis style. The main classes are: top fuel dragsters (see p.384), pro stock cars, pro stock bikes, top fuel funny cars, top methanol dragsters, and pro modifed cars.

PRO STOCK CAR
Vehicles must resemble production models but can cover 400m (¼ mile) in six seconds. NHRA cars are allowed an engine capacity of up to 8.2 litres, and IHRA engines may be up to 13.1 litres.

Broad tyres
The rear tyres are almost as large as those of dragsters, 43cm (17in) wide and 82cm (33in) in diameter

PRO STOCK BIKE
Heavily modified motorcycles race in NHRA competitions. Most pro stock bikes are powered by 1,500cc Suzuki engines that can generate 300 horsepower and rev to 13,500rpm.

Wheelie bar
The long aluminium wheelie bar keeps the bike from flipping over backwards when it accelerates

TOP FUEL FUNNY CAR
These vehicles vaguely resemble production cars, but they are nearly as fast as the dragsters. The chassis is light fibreglass and the body is made of aerodynamically enhanced carbon fibre.

Nitromethane fuel
The supercharged, fuel-injected engine runs on nitromethane

THE RACE IS ON

Typically, pairs of drivers race against each other, with winners proceeding to future rounds to battle it out in a knockout. There are few rules, but a driver is disqualified for a foul start or for crossing lanes. Once the green light goes on, the tactic is maximum speed as fast as possible until the first car crosses the finishing line. Sometimes, an engine blows before the vehicle reaches the end of the track, but it can still coast home before its rival. This is called "heads-up racing" and is relatively common.

JUMPING THE LIGHTS
Technically, the car should not move before the green light comes on the Christmas tree. In practice, the driver starts to move his car in the fraction of a second between the last orange light going out and the green flashing on. However, if the car passes the electronic eye in front of the start before the green shows, the driver is said to have "red-lighted" and is disqualified. In the event that both drivers "red-light" then only the first to cross the beam is disqualified.

GOVERNING BODIES
In North America, the sport is governed by The National Hot Rod Association (NHRA) and the International Hot Rod Association (IHRA). Elsewhere, it is governed by the Fédération Internationale de l'Automobile (FIA). These bodies organize championships for various vehicle classes. For example, the NHRA, the world's biggest drag racing organization, organizes the Mello Yello series of races in the United States.

NEED2KNOW

→ The engine sizes of karts range from 80cc to the 250cc of superkarts, some of which have two engines. Two-stroke engines are more widely used than four-stroke engines as they provide a good power-to-weight ratio and are mechanically simple.

→ Karting began in the 1950s when enthusiasts wanted to make the thrill of motor racing accessible for young people and successfully assembled homemade machines from lawnmower engines, simple steering equipment, and small wheels.

→ Formula One champions Fernando Alonso, Michael Schumacher, and Ayrton Senna all began their racing careers in karting.

KARTING

SPORT OVERVIEW

In karting, which is also called go-karting or kart racing, drivers speed around a track and compete with each other to be the first past the finishing post. Often thought of as the simplest form of motor racing yet an important stepping stone for aspiring Formula One drivers, karting is an ideal recreation for both young and old, men and women. Seasoned drivers can take part in junior or senior competitions in which races are organized according to a range of different divisions and classes.

COMPETITOR PROFILE
Drivers need to be fit, mentally strong and be determined to win. They need to develop plenty of skill in techniques such as accurate steering, cornering, acceleration, overtaking, and braking.

Special suits
Drivers wear outfits that resist abrasion and are flame retardant

Engine type
Kart engines are either two stroke or four stroke

Head protection
Kart drivers wear a helmet, often with a transparent visor, and a neck support

Rib protector
Drivers don't wear seat belts but may wear a rib protector under their suit

Ground level
The chassis may be 1.5cm (²/3in) above the ground

TYPES OF KARTING
The most common type is sprint karting, in which drivers compete on twisty tracks between 400m (437yd) and 1,500km (1,640yd) in length. Road-racing karts reach higher speeds and are used on larger tracks with longer straights. Shifter karts have a sequential gearbox and are usually raced on sprint tracks.

INTERNATIONAL COMPETITIONS
International karting competitions, such as the World Championship and the European Championship, are organized by the Commission Internationale de Karting (CIK). This sanctioning body is associated with the Fédération Internationale de l'Automobile (FIA), which organizes Formula One and many other races.

SPEEDWAY KARTS

SPEEDWAY KARTING RACES ARE HELD ON SHORT OVAL TRACKS WITH A DIRT OR ASPHALT SURFACE. KARTS ARE PURPOSE BUILT FOR LEFT-TURN ONLY RACING – THE REAR IS NOT ALIGNED WITH THE FRONT AND THE OUTSIDE REAR WHEEL IS LARGER THAN THE INSIDE REAR WHEEL.

SIDELINES

19 The thousands of rpms that some two-stroke engines can reach.

8 The minimum age for driving a kart in most countries.

80 The speed, in kph (50mph), of a kart on a short track. On longer straight tracks karts may reach twice this speed.

4.5 The number of seconds a 100cc two-stroke engine, weighing 150kg, takes to go from 0–97kph (0–60mph).

INSIDE STORY
Traditionally, karts need to be started by an external starter or a push start. By contrast, touch-and-go (TaG) karts are equipped with a push-button starter, are long-lasting and are used in many clubs around the world. The Rotax Max was the first successful TaG kart and the Austrian manufacturer organizes national competitions in a number of countries.

COMPETITOR PROFILE
Stock car drivers need to be tactically clever during a race so they can judge the most opportune moments to overtake, to fall in line to reduce drag, and to break out of the group to win the race.

Roll cage
The middle section of the car has a roll cage that keeps its integrity to protect the driver in the event of an accident

Rook flaps
If a car spins out of control a set of flaps at the back of the roof reduces lift and prevents the car from taking to the air

Radial tyres
Stock cars have radial tyres that are stable at high temperatures and give good traction – many are filled with nitrogen instead of air

Powerful engine
Stock car engines have a large displacement, generate as much as 750 brake horsepower, and reach speeds of 320kph (200mph)

SPORT OVERVIEW

Stock car racing is a predominantly North American motor sport in which drivers in various vehicle categories compete on oval tracks. Originally, the cars had to be models that were part of the stock which manufacturers sold to the public. In 1973 the rules changed so that cars may look like production models but their specifications conform to the standards laid down by NASCAR, the governing body.

STOCK CAR RACING

NASCAR RACES

The National Association for Stock Car Racing (NASCAR) was formed in 1948 and regulates the sport in the US. It organizes the two main series of races – the Sprint Cup (which includes the Daytona 500) and the Nationwide series – and sanctions 1,500 races at 100 tracks in the US, Canada, and Mexico.

OVAL TRACKS

Races are usually held on oval tracks between 400m (437yd) and 4.26km (2²/₃ miles) in length. Some are banked and others, known as dirt tracks, are unpaved short tracks. Long tracks, such as the one at Talladega in Alabama, are called superspeedways.

IN THE SLIPSTREAM

During a race drivers tend to make the best use of the aerodynamics of slipstreaming. They bunch together or follow each other closely in a line to reduce the drag on their vehicles and save fuel. Such dangerous manoeuvres make the sport exciting and entertaining. Although accidents are common, severe injuries to the drivers are rare.

WIN ON SUNDAY, SELL ON MONDAY

THE FIRST MODERN OVERHEAD VALVE ENGINE TO GO ON SALE TO THE GENERAL PUBLIC WAS THE OLDSMOBILE ROCKET V8. ITS SUCCESS IN THE STOCK CAR RACES OF 1949 AND 1950 ENCOURAGED MORE AND MORE PEOPLE TO BUY THE CAR, LEADING TO THE SAYING "WIN ON SUNDAY, SELL ON MONDAY".

INSIDE STORY

Stock car racing arrived in Britain in 1954, using slightly modified saloon cars. Contact between cars became part of the sport so bumpers and roll bars were added. The British Stock Car Association (BriSCA) is the sport's governing body. Formula One stock cars look nothing like production models and have open wheels and a centrally located driver.

→ The Fédération Internationale de l'Automobile (FIA) sanctions the Cross-Country Rally World Cup, which is made up of a maximum of eight events each season.

→ Early cross-country rally events included the Peking to Paris race of 1907, which involved just five cars covering the 96,560km (60,000-mile) distance in 60 days.

→ Although it is no longer a World Cup event, the Dakar Rally remains the biggest, most dangerous, and most prestigious of all cross-country rallies. In 2012, 171 cars, 218 motorcycles, and 76 trucks started the race.

ROUGH RIDES
In cross-country rallying, anything goes. From the sands of the Sahara to the rocky, steep terrain of the Atlas mountains, and the savannas of the Pampas, it's a test of endurance and navigation – the tougher the better.

Helmet
Along with a neck brace, provides rider with head protection

In the frame
A robust frame provides optimal weight distribution

DESERT BIKES
Off-road motorbikes need to have a combination of robustness, power, and light weight. Ground clearance is high to avoid hitting obstacles such as rocks, while the suspension is beefed up to enable riding over rough terrain.

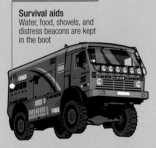

Survival aids
Water, food, shovels, and distress beacons are kept in the boot

KEEP ON TRUCKIN'
For most cross-country endurance rallies trucks are defined as vehicles with a total weight of 3.5 tonnes or more. They can carry up to three people and have a fuel capacity in excess of 820 litres (180 gals).

OFF-ROAD RALLYING

SPORT OVERVIEW
This is the ultimate form of endurance racing, requiring the spirit of an adventurer as much as that of a sportsperson. Once exclusively a car sport, motorcycles and trucks now also race point-to-point routes that traverse hundreds or thousands of kilometres of desert, mountain, or other wild terrain. Winning drivers are those with the quickest aggregate times over several legs, sometimes raced daily over a week or more. The most famous event is the Dakar Rally, which starts in Europe and ends in Dakar, Senegal.

PENALTIES
Drivers do not have to follow precisely the same route, but they must get from the start to the finish of a section by passing one or more checkpoints. Failure to do so results in time penalties.

> **DRIVER PROFILE**
> Drivers, co-drivers, and riders in this motor sport need all the attributes of adventurers as well as athletes.

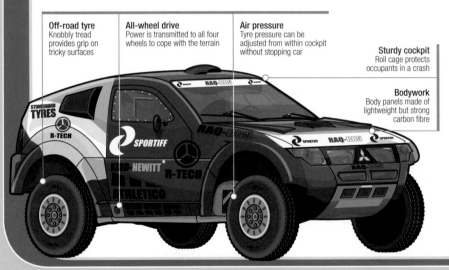

Off-road tyre
Knobbly tread provides grip on tricky surfaces

All-wheel drive
Power is transmitted to all four wheels to cope with the terrain

Air pressure
Tyre pressure can be adjusted from within cockpit without stopping car

Sturdy cockpit
Roll cage protects occupants in a crash

Bodywork
Body panels made of lightweight but strong carbon fibre

SIDELINES

26 The number of competitors who have died in the Dakar Rally since its first running in 1978.

1,000,000 The number of Portuguese spectators who came to watch the 2007 Dakar Rally over its first two days as the race left the capital Lisbon and worked its way across into Spain.

5 The number of times the Dakar Rally has been held in South America. The race was relocated in 2009 due to fears of terrorist attacks along the route through North Africa.

DAKAR INSPIRATION
FRENCHMAN THIERRY SABINE CAME UP WITH THE IDEA OF THE DAKAR RALLY AFTER GETTING LOST IN THE LIBYAN DESERT DURING THE 1977 ABIDJAN TO NICE RALLY. HE ORGANIZED THE FIRST DAKAR RALLY IN 1978. THERE WERE 170 ENTRIES. THIERRY WAS KILLED IN A HELICOPTER CRASH DURING THE 1986 EVENT.

NEED2KNOW

→ When European truck racing started in the 1980s, road-going, working vehicles were used.

→ The Camping World Truck Series first began in 1995.

→ A racing truck can accelerate to 161kph (100mph) quicker than a Porsche 911 sports car.

→ The minimum weight for a truck is 5,500kg (5.5 tonnes).

→ For safety reasons, there is maximum speed limit of 160kph (100mph).

ON THE TRACK

The European race series is controlled by the Fédération International de l'Automobile (FIA), and it has limited the top speed of the trucks to 161kph (100mph). Rather than the static grid used in other types of motor sport, races commence with a rolling start and last for a predetermined number of laps. Points are given to trucks finishing in the top positions and are accumulated from the two races held at each circuit over one weekend.

DRIVER PROFILE

Driving a 5.5-tonne truck around a racing circuit at high speed is not for the faint-hearted. Lightning-quick reactions and nerves of steel are essential requirements. To race a truck, drivers must be at least 21 years old and hold a race licence.

TRUCK TRACKS

In both Europe and the US, truck racing is held at a variety of tracks, from "road courses" that incorporate both left- and right-handed turns to oval circuits that only include left-handed bends. Fewer than 10 tracks host the European Truck Racing Championship (ETRC) each season, but the Camping World Truck Series visits up to 25 circuits a year.

RACING RULES

As well as conventional motor sport penalties, such as for speeding in the pit lane, truck racing drivers are disciplined for infringements like emitting excessive exhaust smoke and exceeding the 161kph (100mph) speed limit.

WHEEL TO WHEEL

While truck racing is not meant to be a contact motor sport, the massive size of the vehicles and limited width of the tracks produces plenty of close-quarter action.

Racing tyre
Special "sticky" rubber is used to help grip the track

Pulling power
Turbocharged diesel engine is able to generate 1,050bhp

Driver safety
The cab has a built-in roll cage to protect the driver

Modified suspension
Racing shock absorbers enable the truck to corner at high speed

Vehicle weight
European racing trucks must weigh at least 5,500kg (5.5 tonnes)

Tuned-up power
Most trucks have 12-litre turbocharged diesel engines

Truck stop
Water-cooled disc brakes are needed to slow the truck down

TRUCK RACING

SPORT OVERVIEW

Truck racing may not be the most high-profile of motor sports but it is certainly one of the most exciting. The European Truck Racing Championship (ETRC) takes place on some of the world's best-known motor-racing circuits, such as the Nürburgring in Germany and Le Mans in France. In the United States, the Camping World Truck Series draws massive crowds to tracks all over the country to watch modified pick-up trucks go head-to-head in races of up to 400km (250 miles).

TOP TRACK

THE NÜRBURGRING IN GERMANY IS THE LONGEST AND MOST EXCITING TRACK IN EUROPE. IT IS A VENUE FOR THE BRITISH TRUCK RACING CHAMPIONSHIP (BTRC) DURING WHICH OVER 150,000 FANS GATHER TO WATCH THE ACTION.

RALLYING

SPORT OVERVIEW

Rallying is a fast and furious point-to-point motor sport raced on public and private roads, usually against the clock. The World Rally Championship (WRC) is the sport's premier event, featuring races on a wide range of courses all around the world that test the reliability of the cars and the nerves and skills of the driver and co-driver.

Crew protection
Extra-strong roll cage is welded into the frame of the car

Removable panels
Body panels are made of pressed steel and can be replaced during a race

Onboard data
Crew can access technical data about the car

Rallying powerplant
All WRC cars incorporate two-litre, turbocharged engines

Braking system
Massive ventilated disc brakes provide the stopping power

Racing rubber
Tyres can be up to 46cm (18in) wide to provide extra grip

Transmission
Six-speed gearbox is operated via a semi-automatic shifter

Racing chassis
Hand-built chassis is stiffened to create a rigid car able to withstand the extreme forces of a rally

Aerodynamic aid
Rear spoiler creates downforce that helps to control the car when cornering at high speeds

NEED2KNOW

→ Until private routes were used in the 1950s, rallying events took place on public roads.

→ Swede Björn Waldegard won the first World Rally Championship for Drivers in a Ford Escort in 1979.

CLASSIC RALLY

LAST RUN AS A WRC EVENT IN 2002, THE SAFARI RALLY IS REGARDED AS THE TOUGHEST OF THEM ALL. HELD ON THE OPEN ROADS OF EAST AFRICA, HAZARDS INCLUDED WILD ANIMALS AND SEVERE DUST STORMS.

ALL-TERRAIN DRIVING

From the icefields of Sweden to the high-altitude mountain passes of Argentina and the forest tracks of Wales, WRC races take place over every conceivable type of course. Only by being able to master terrain as varied as ice, mud, gravel, and sand do drivers stand a chance of challenging for the Championship. The rallies are made up of short, timed special stages where the§ points are won, and liaison stages that enable the manufacturer-backed teams to get to the start of the next special stage.

RALLY FORMAT

Each rally has up to 25 special stages, ranging in length from just a few kilometres up to 60km (37 miles). Stages have a staggered start, with cars sent off at a time interval of one or two minutes to race over a mixture of (closed) public and private roads. Drivers aim to cover the course as quickly as possible, with the winning car the one that completes all the stages in the least overall time.

TIME PENALTIES

Rallying has a strict system of time penalties. These are imposed on drivers for reasons such as being late for the start of a stage and if team mechanics spend longer than the allotted time allowed to check a car at the end of a stage.

THE CO-DRIVER

The eyes of a rally car team, the co-driver provides his or her driver with all the navigational information needed to complete a stage. Before a stage, the co-driver surveys the course and takes detailed notes on the location of bends, type of road surface, and any potential hazards. These are then read out to the driver during the race.

CARS UNDER SCRUTINY

According to the rules laid down by the sport's governing body, the Fédération International de l'Automobile (FIA), World Rally cars must be based on their passenger car equivalents and be available – albeit in limited numbers – to the public. But that's where similarities end, as teams then modify the cars within the limits set by the FIA. At WRC events, a team of official scrutineers checks the cars for legality before, during, and after the race, with drivers sometimes disqualified from a rally for contravening technical regulations.

SPEED FREAKS

Maintaining momentum is the key to fast times out on the course. Accelerating into jumps and water troughs keeps the car "nose up", which is vital if the driver is to execute a safe landing. Drivers take advantage of the extra traction in dips and troughs to use heavier braking and steering to maintain a smooth line through the course. Most rally cars incorporate four-wheel drive, where power is transmitted to each wheel, and this provides extra traction for the tyres to grip to the surface.

CORNERING TECHNIQUES

Cornering is a fine balance of play between the brakes, throttle, accelerator, and clutch. The art of drifting – setting a car sideways through a corner to enable a faster exit – is a crucial rally technique, and it can be carried out in a number of different ways.

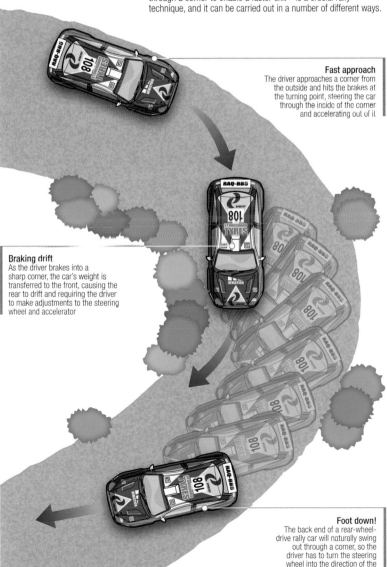

Fast approach
The driver approaches a corner from the outside and hits the brakes at the turning point, steering the car through the inside of the corner and accelerating out of it

Braking drift
As the driver brakes into a sharp corner, the car's weight is transferred to the front, causing the rear to drift and requiring the driver to make adjustments to the steering wheel and accelerator

Foot down!
The back end of a rear-wheel-drive rally car will naturally swing out through a corner, so the driver has to turn the steering wheel into the direction of the corner and then accelerate hard out of it

STAT CENTRAL

MOST WRC WINS – DRIVER

WINS	DRIVER
77	SEBASTIEN LOEB
30	MARCUS GRONHOLM
26	CARLOS SAINZ
25	COLIN MCRAE
24	TOMMI MAKINEN
23	JUHA KANKKUNEN
20	DIDIER AURIOL
19	MARKKU ALEN
18	HANNU MIKKOLA
17	MASSIMO BIASION

MOST WRC WINS – MANUFACTURER

WINS	MANUFACTURER
87	CITROËN
79	FORD
74	LANCIA
48	PEUGEOT
47	SUBARU
43	TOYOTA
34	MITSUBISHI
24	AUDI
21	FIAT
9	DATSUN/NISSAN

BEHIND THE SCENES

PROFESSIONAL TEAMS ENTER UP TO THREE CARS IN A RACE, AND THEY ARE ALL BACKED UP BY A TECHNICAL SUPPORT CREW THAT KEEPS THEM AT PEAK PERFORMANCE DURING THE RALLY. BETWEEN STAGES EACH CAR IS INSPECTED BY THE SUPPORT CREW.

INSIDE STORY

The concept of rallying dates back to competitions between the first horseless carriages in the 19th century. Early motorized rallies included the Monte Carlo Rally, which was first held in 1911 and is still raced today. Longer events then sprang up, such as the 16,000km (10,000-mile) Méditeranée-le Cap held in Africa in the 1950s. It is a far cry from professional modern rallying and its highly tuned cars racing over short distances.

GOVERNING BODY

Rallying comes under the auspices of the FIA World Motor Sport Council that governs all motor sports. The Council organizes the WRC that takes place annually over 13 courses worldwide.

RACER PROFILE

With races running for roughly an hour, endurance is a must-have capability, together with strength and low body weight. Riders also need the courage to take their bikes as fast as 320kph (200mph) or more.

Engine power
Engine size varies according to the race specs. For MotoGP races they are state-of-the-art 800cc four-stroke engines

One-piece suit
A padded, abrasion-resistant, one-piece bodysuit and gloves are obligatory

Safey Helmet
These are designed to absorb one incident only

THE CIRCUIT

Circuits are usually specially built tracks, and while each one has its own layout and special character, they all have common features. These include gentle and hairpin bends, straights, ascents and descents (sometimes), a run-off area, and gravel beds for safety. The track must be sufficiently wide for bikes to corner and pass each other, and barriers and off-track emergency zones are placed appropriately. Spectators watch races from various stands and grandstands, and safety marshalls are positioned around the track to help riders who have had accidents.

OTHER COURSES

Road races are not always held on specially built circuits. Races sometimes take place on public roads, airfields, or a combination of public roads and off-road tracks.

DRAG RACING Two contestants race each other along a straight, paved strip of road, such as a dragster track, that is commonly 400m (¼mile) long.

HILL CLIMB Single riders race the clock along uphill stretches of road.

ROAD RALLY Competitors drive along open public roads between a fixed start and finish, visiting checkpoints along the route. The riders must obey speed restrictions and other rules of the road.

Broad tyres
Rear tyres are wider than the front for extra grip, as all the power goes through this wheel

Aerodynamic design
A powerful engine and aerodynamic design allow MotoGP bikes to hit speeds of 350kph (215mph)

PUSHING TOO HARD

ON 7 MARCH 2007 SHINYA NAKANO CRASHED DURING PRACTICE AT THE SPANISH GP. TRAVELLING AT MORE THAN 320KPH (200MPH) HE LOST CONTROL OF THE FRONT END OF HIS BIKE WHILE GOING INTO A TURN.

NEED2KNOW

→ Track motorcycle racing is a massively popular spectator sport around the world, particularly on television. An estimated 300 million people worldwide watch each Moto Grand Prix.

→ The most presitigious races are those of the MotoGP World Championship, which is contested at 18 circuits around the world every year.

→ In 2001 Valentino Rossi, conqueror of the 125, 250, and 500 World Championships in his second season in each class, became only the second rider in history (after Phil Read) to achieve this feat.

ROAD RACING

SPORT OVERVIEW

The most popular road racing events involve competitors riding motorcycles on tarmac circuits or closed public roads. The most illustrious circuit races are the 125cc, 250cc, 800cc GP World Championships, and the World Championships for Superbike, and Supersport, Endurance, and Sidecar categories, but Motocross and Supercross events have increased in popularity, especially in the US.

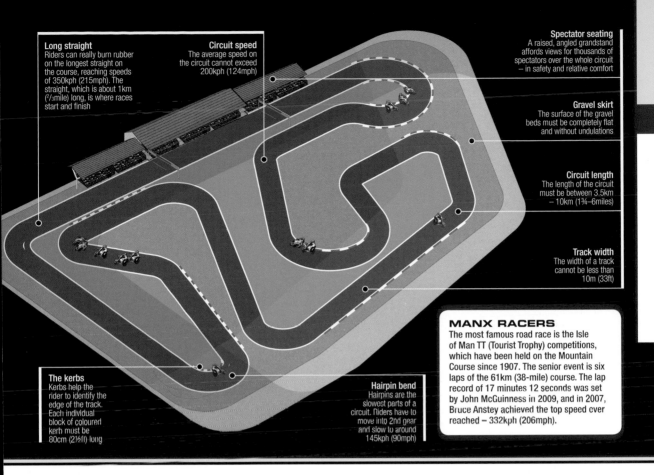

Long straight
Riders can really burn rubber on the longest straight on the course, reaching speeds of 350kph (215mph). The straight, which is about 1km (²/₃mile) long, is where races start and finish

Circuit speed
The average speed on the circuit cannot exceed 200kph (124mph)

Spectator seating
A raised, angled grandstand affords views for thousands of spectators over the whole circuit – in safety and relative comfort

Gravel skirt
The surface of the gravel beds must be completely flat and without undulations

Circuit length
The length of the circuit must be between 3.5km – 10km (1¾–6miles)

Track width
The width of a track cannot be less than 10m (33ft)

The kerbs
Kerbs help the rider to identify the edge of the track. Each individual block of coloured kerb must be 80cm (2½ft) long

Hairpin bend
Hairpins are the slowest parts of a circuit. Riders have to move into 2nd gear and slow to around 145kph (90mph)

MANX RACERS
The most famous road race is the Isle of Man TT (Tourist Trophy) competitions, which have been held on the Mountain Course since 1907. The senior event is six laps of the 61km (38-mile) course. The lap record of 17 minutes 12 seconds was set by John McGuinness in 2009, and in 2007, Bruce Anstey achieved the top speed ever reached – 332kph (206mph).

ESSENTIAL RIDING KIT

Protective clothing is not optional: all racing motorcyclists crash, and most suffer injuries from time to time. Wearing the proper gear can make the difference between some bad bruising and broken bones, or worse. A full face helmet, one-piece racing leathers, gloves, knee sliders, and boots are all compulsory, and all racers must wear a metal identification tag with blood-group details. Riders must be in peak physical condition to race with all the required safety equipment.

GLOVES
The outer leather skin is reinforced, and a foam lining gives extra protection and comfort. There can be sticky-grip material on the palms.

HELMET
In addition to absorbing impacts and shielding the face, the helmet is designed to draw in fresh air, and allow exhaled air and humidity out.

BOOTS AND KNEE-SLIDERS
A number of independent plates offer special protection for the Achilles heels, ankle balls, toes, and lower shins. These give extra protection for the vulnerable knees and shins.

Stick-ons
The knee-slider pad is attached to the leg with velcro

Shin covers
Give extra protection to one of the most damaged parts of the body

Tough panels
Carbon-fibre sole inlays provide additional safety

Shoulder pad
Titanium shoulder pads are necessary insurance against a broken clavicle (shoulder bone)

Chest protector
Integrated panels guard against impacts around the chest and rib areas

Elbow guard
A damaged elbow will hamper a rider's ability to race, so they must be protected

ADDITIONAL PROTECTION
Titanium shoulder, elbow, and knee guards are integrated into the contruction of the leathers. Stretch fabric provides more comfort for the crotch and inner thighs.

Knee protection
Knee sliders are attached to the side of the knee pad

Damage limitation
Shin-length boots are worn over the top of the full-lengh suit

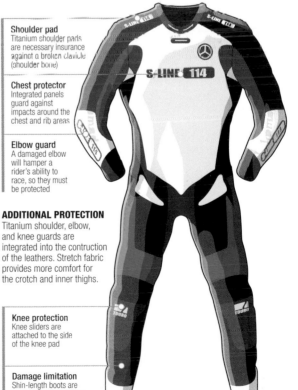

RULES OF THE ROAD

World championship 125cc, 250cc, and MotoGP races, run by the Fédération Internationale de Motocyclisme (FIM), are between 95–130km (59–81miles) long. The number of laps to be raced will depend on the length of the track. Positions on the starting grid are decided by the fastest lap time recorded during qualifying and to qualify for the race proper, a rider must achieve a time at least equal to 107 per cent of the time recorded by the fastest rider of their class. Before the start, race officials declare a race "dry" or "wet" so riders can decide which tyres to use. Tyres can be changed on the grid before the start of the race. After one warm-up lap, the race is started by lights. A red light will be displayed for between two and five seconds, and when it goes out, the race will start. If two riders cannot be separated at the finish, the one who achieved the fastest lap time during the race wins.

TAKING A CORNER

While overtaking is the skill that marks out a championship winner from an also-ran, cornering hard and fast will enable a rider to achieve top lap times. The more time the bike spends upright, the quicker it will go, so being able to get in and out of corners quickly will allow the rider to improve upon lap times, and therefore be competitive in a race.

STAT CENTRAL

GRAND PRIX WINNERS

RIDER (NATIONALITY)	TITLES	WINS
GIACOMO AGOSTINI (ITALY)	15	122
ANGEL NIETO (SPAIN)	13	90
VALENTINO ROSSI (ITALY)	9	105
MIKE HAILWOOD (UK)	9	76
CARLO UBBIALI (ITALY)	9	39
JOHN SURTEES (UK)	7	38
PHIL READ (UK)	7	52
GEOFF DUKE (UK)	6	33
JIM REDMAN (RHODESIA)	6	45
MICK DOOHAN (AUSTRALIA)	5	54
ANTON MANG (GERMANY)	5	42

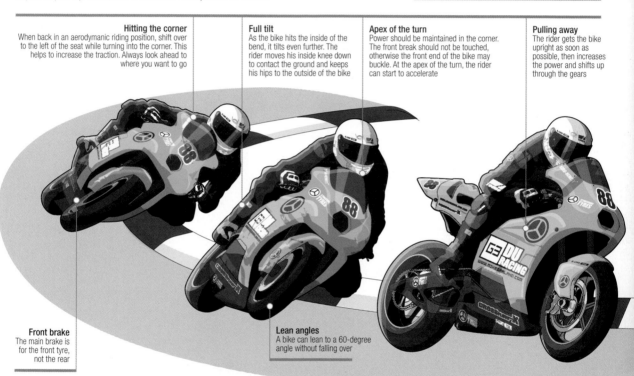

Hitting the corner
When back in an aerodynamic riding position, shift over to the left of the seat while turning into the corner. This helps to increase the traction. Always look ahead to where you want to go

Full tilt
As the bike hits the inside of the bend, it tilts even further. The rider moves his inside knee down to contact the ground and keeps his hips to the outside of the bike

Apex of the turn
Power should be maintained in the corner. The front break should not be touched, otherwise the front end of the bike may buckle. At the apex of the turn, the rider can start to accelerate

Pulling away
The rider gets the bike upright as soon as possible, then increases the power and shifts up through the gears

Front brake
The main brake is for the front tyre, not the rear

Lean angles
A bike can lean to a 60-degree angle without falling over

VALENTINO, NUMERO UNO

ITALIAN RIDER VALENTINO ROSSI IS THE WORLD'S NUMBER 1 MOTORCYCLING SUPERSTAR. NICKNAMED "THE DOCTOR" FOR HIS CLINICAL DISMANTLING OF OPPONENTS, ROSSI HOLDS THE RECORD FOR THE MOST CONSECUTIVE PODIUM APPEARANCES. BETWEEN 8 SEPTEMBER 2002 AND 18 APRIL 2004, HE STOOD ON THE PODIUM ON 23 OCCASIONS. HIS SUCCESS ON THE TRACK HAS BROUGHT HIM FORTUNE AS WELL AS FAME, AND BY 2009 HIS ANNUAL EARNINGS AMOUNTED TO A MONUMENTAL $35 MILLION. THAT'S A LOT OF LOOT.

INSIDE STORY

The origins of road racing go back to the 1894 Paris–Rouen race, which saw motorcycles and cars racing side by side. The first Isle of Man TT took place in 1907. Circuit racing did not start until 1949, when the FIM launched the Road Racing World Championship Grand Prix for 125cc, 250cc, 350cc (now discontinued), and 500cc bikes, and sidecars. The early years were monopolized by Italian and British riders, but Australians, Americans, and Spanish riders now dominate the sport. The Superbikes (1000cc) championship began in 1988, and MotoGP, which replaced the 500cc class, was launched in 2002.

GOVERNING BODY

The FIM was founded in 1904 by representatives of motorcycle clubs from Austria, Belgium, Denmark, France, Germany, and Great Britain. Today, it represents 103 national motorcycle federations divided into six regional groups: Africa, Asia, Europe, South America, North America, and Oceania. The FIM is recognized by the IOC.

SPORT OVERVIEW

Off-road motorcycle racing includes any competition that is not raced on tarmac circuits or roads. The most popular events are motocross (MX), supercross (SX), speedway, enduro, cross-country, and trials. In recent years, variants such as beachcross have developed a large following. Apart from the race surface, the big difference from track racing is the style of the bikes.

OFF-ROAD MOTORCYCLE RACING

NEED2KNOW

→ Speedway took Britain by storm when it was introduced in the 1920s. In its heyday, crowds of 80,000 or more attended races. Today a popular GP series takes place throughout Europe.

→ In North America, indoor supercross on man-made courses is more popular than motocross, attracting massive crowds at indoor arenas. More than 70,000 spectators have packed the Georgia Dome for a World Supercross Series event.

→ In the early years of motocross, the 500cc class was considered the premier division. However, as technology progressed, the 250cc bikes became faster and more manageable, and eventually superseded the 500cc bikes to became the premier class event.

Head gear
Riders cannot compete without an approved helmet

Goggles
must be removable since they are likely to get muddy

Body protection
The body armour worn outside of the jersey is usually made from a hard plastic

Lever setup
The clutch lever and brake lever should be angled down slightly so that the forearms are in a straight line with the levers

RIDER PROFILE

Off-road racing requires skill, strength, stamina, and concentration. Riders must be prepared to take knocks and get muddy. Trials riders must be especially skilful, have tremendous balance, throttle control, and vision to negotiate the demanding obstacles, steep slopes, and sharp turns.

Controlling suspension
Rebound dampening controls how fast the suspension returns to its full length after it's been compressed by hitting an obstacle or bump. If the rebound dampening is set too fast the bike may have a tendency to kick up when accelerating out of corners

Deep blocks
Tyre patters differ depending on the terrain. For deep mud, tall blocks give good grip and resist slippage when the bike is cornering. On front tyres, the blocks are sometimes turned 45 degrees to evacuate mud quickly

Engine power
Motocross bikes are usually powered by single-cylinder, two-, or four-stroke engines

Quick change
Wheelbase is the measure of the distance between the front wheel and back wheel. Bringing your rear wheel forward will decrease the wheelbase and will make the bike quicker to turn in a corner

A TEAM MOTOCROSS COMPETITION TOOK PLACE IN HOLLAND IN 1947. THE RACE COMPRISED TWO HEATS OF EIGHT LAPS EACH OVER A TWO-MILE COURSE, WITH TEAM SCORES BASED ON THE TIMES OF THE THREE FASTEST RIDERS. THE BRITISH TEAM WON BY JUST NINE SECONDS OVER BELGIUM.

WHAT THEY RIDE

Off-road bikes come in many different sizes and shapes, but all need super-responsive engines for quick acceleration, tyres that can grip difficult terrain, and suspension that is able to cope with the bumps and jolts. Race classes generally divide on the basis of engine size.

ENDURO

The biggest difference between an enduro bike and MX and SX machines is that enduros have to be street-legal. Engine size ranges from 100cc to 650cc, and races are classified accordingly.

Lit up
Front and rear lights are fitted for safe racing at night

Narrow handlebars
These give the bike a little more versatility when racing through obstacles

TRIAL BIKES

Trial motorcycles are extremely lightweight, are designed to be ridden standing up, and have suspension travel that is short, relative to a motocross or enduro motorcycle.

ALL-TERRAIN VEHICLES

Riders of all-terrain vehicles (ATVs) have their own motocross competition. Engines used in sanctioned competition must be production model ATV engines available to the public.

Power pack
A four-stroke engine and electronic fuel injection provide top performance

Super-shocks
Sport ATVs have shock absorbers with a much-needed 25cm (10in) of travel

MX CIRCUIT

Races are held on a marked and fenced circuit, often 1.5–2km (1–1¼ miles) long, that combines steep drops and climbs, with fast straights, artificial jumps, and steep turns to create a varied and exciting racing environment. In accordance with FIM rules, the track materials should be natural and must be capable of retaining water, easily maintained, and give traction. Races run for a fixed period, usually 30 minutes plus two further laps, with a maximum of 30 competitors riding in each race.

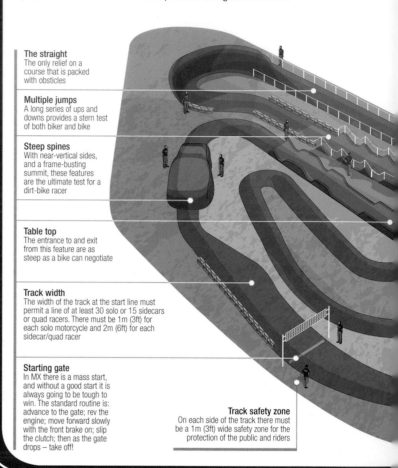

The straight
The only relief on a course that is packed with obstacles

Multiple jumps
A long series of ups and downs provides a stern test of both biker and bike

Steep spines
With near-vertical sides, and a frame-busting summit, these features are the ultimate test for a dirt-bike racer

Table top
The entrance to and exit from this feature are as steep as a bike can negotiate

Track width
The width of the track at the start line must permit a line of at least 30 solo or 15 sidecars or quad racers. There must be 1m (3ft) for each solo motorcycle and 2m (6ft) for each sidecar/quad racer

Starting gate
In MX there is a mass start, and without a good start it is always going to be tough to win. The standard routine is: advance to the gate; rev the engine; move forward slowly with the front brake on; slip the clutch; then as the gate drops – take off!

Track safety zone
On each side of the track there must be a 1m (3ft) wide safety zone for the protection of the public and riders

MAYHEM ON FOUR WHEELS

All-terrain vehicle (ATV) racing is especially popular in North America, with engine size starting at 50cc. Four-wheeled ATVs are raced in a similar format to their two-wheeled equivalents: MX, MS, enduro, and hare and hounds. Additionally, ATV tourist trophy scrambles are held on prepared dirt tracks with right and left turns and jumps, and on a short track. The racing is similar to speedway, with competitors battling it out on oval tracks roughly 400m (¼ mile) long. For the really brave, there is ATV racing on ice!

KEY SKILLS

The skills required to be an off-road racer are numerous, but a must-have is the ability to corner at speed on a surface with little traction. Particularly hard to negotiate are turns without a camber, such as those of a speedway circuit or an MX course. For MX, SX, and any cross-country discipline, the ability to negotiate the jumps skilfully is especially crucial.

TAKING OFF

To be an effective jumper the rider has to be able to generate enough lift to get over an obstacle. They also have to land without breaking the momentum of the bike. Skilled riders alter their direction while in mid-air, making the jump look even more spectacular.

OTHER COURSES

A number of new motor sports developed from speedway and arguably from the exploits of Evel Knievel. What they have in common is that the races (usually) take place on dirt courses with various obstacles in the form of jumps. Different courses require different bikes. For instance, because of the restricted space available on Supercross circuits, 250cc bikes are the main racing class of bike.

SUPERCROSS SX is indoor MX and has all the features of the latter – climbs, jumps, hairpin turns, and fierce racing competition – packed into a tight stadium circuit. This derivative of MX provides spectacular viewing. Qualifying rounds are followed by semifinals and the "main event".

ENDURO Riders are timed over a rough course of up to 160km (100 miles) long. Racers set off at intervals along boulder-strewn riverbeds, along forest tracks, and up steep muddy banks, checking in at time stations along the route. Penalties are awarded for slow times.

TRIALS Each course is different and is designed to challenge riders' bike control to the limit. Competitors have to negotiate a circuit of large boulders, ledges, water, logs, and pallets without touching their feet on the ground. If they do touch, the "dab" or "prod" is penalised.

SPEEDWAY Four riders, two from each team, race over four laps of an oval track and each race is over in less than a minute. They race 500cc single-geared machines with no brakes.

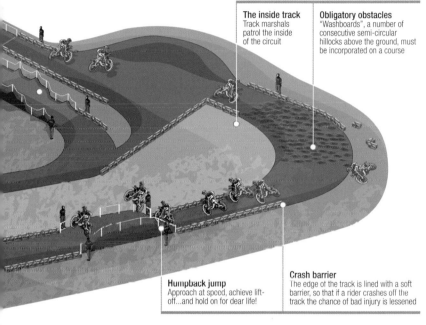

The inside track
Track marshals patrol the inside of the circuit

Obligatory obstacles
"Washboards", a number of consecutive semi-circular hillocks above the ground, must be incorporated on a course

Humpback jump
Approach at speed, achieve lift-off...and hold on for dear life!

Crash barrier
The edge of the track is lined with a soft barrier, so that if a rider crashes off the track the chance of bad injury is lessened

DIRT BIKE RULES

Each discipline has its own rulebook enforced by the governing body (the FIM), but foul, unfair, or dangerous riding always results in disqualification. Exacting regulations control the machines ridden, the equipment worn by the racer, and the fuel used. In six-day enduro events, the bikes are in the possession of the race organizers; this is called parc fermé, or closed control, and prevents work being carried out on vehicles between different days of a race. Starts vary between disciplines, so MX and speedway have mass starts, but solo racers start at timed intervals in enduro.

STAT CENTRAL

WORLD MOTOCROSS CHAMPIONS	
TITLES	**RIDER (COUNTRY)**
FIM MX1 WORLD MOTOCROSS (250cc)	
7	STEFAN EVERTS (BEL)
6	JOEL ROBERT (BEL)
4	TORSTEN HALLMAN (SWE)
FIM MX2 WORLD MOTOCROSS (125cc)	
3	ALESSION CHIODI (ITA)
3	HARRY EVERTS (BEL)
FIM MX3 WORLD MOTOCROSS (500cc)	
5	ROGER DE COSTER (BEL)
4	JOEL SMETS (BEL)
3	GEORGES JOBE (BEL)
AMA USA MOTOCROSS (125cc)	
5	RICKY CARMICHAEL (USA)
3	RYAN VILLOPOTO (USA)
AMA USA MOTOCROSS (250cc)	
7	RICKY CARMICHAEL (USA)
4	GARY JONES (USA)

JUMPING TECHNIQUE

There are quite a few different types of obstacle found on a track but the basic skills remain the same regardless of what the rider is trying to jump.

The approach
When approaching dirt-bike jumps the rider should be standing up on the bike in a crouched position gripping the bike with the legs

The take off
The rider should pick a line on the up ramp, keeping an even throttle on approach. Some dirt-bike jumps, like tabletops or gap jumps, need to be hit at a certain speed to clear them, so the speed must be good before the rider gets to them

Hit the ground racing
Once in the air, the rider looks where to land. If landing on the flat, land with the rear wheel down first. When landing on a down ramp, the bike must land at the same angle as the down ramp. Get on the throttle just before landing

INSIDE STORY

Motocross was first known as a British off-road event called Scrambles, which was itself an evolution of Trials events popular in northern Britain. During the 1930s the sport grew in popularity, especially in Britain. In 1952 the FIM created an individual European 500cc Championship and in 1962, a 250cc world championship was created. It was in the smaller 250cc category that the sport came into its own. It has evolved with sub-disciplines such as stadium events known as Supercross and Arenacross. Freestyle (FMX) events, where riders are judged on their aerial acrobatic skills, have gained popularity, as has Supermoto (Motocross style racing on both tarmac and off road).

→ Powerboat racing is an expensive sport – the cost of equipment, fuel, and maintenance can reach seven-figure sums.

→ Formula One powerboat races attract live audiences of up to 70,000 spectators – who all get to watch for free.

→ Some powerboats can accelerate to 160kph (100mph) in 4 seconds.

→ Crews all need a licence to thrill. Part of the exam requires them to escape from a cockpit that has been submerged in water, and they must also undergo a rigorous medical examination.

CREW PROFILE

Formula One and Class 1 powerboats have two-person crews of a driver and a throttle operator. Though lifejackets are compulsory, the crew should be strong swimmers, and must be able to manoeuvre the craft safely at high speeds. The ability to "read" the water is essential, as is having a constant awareness of the boat's position on the course.

POWERBOAT RACING

SPORT OVERVIEW

With vessels able to reach speeds up to 225kph (140mph), powerboat racing is the fastest, most dangerous, and most glamorous of all watersports. Boats race in various classes depending on their engine size and travel around a defined course – either circular or point-to-point. Other races focus on endurance and are designed to test the resilience of vessels and crews. Crashes are rare, but can be fatal.

WATER COURSE

Powerboat races can be held on any suitable expanse of water such as a bay, fjord, lake, or river, or sometimes open sea. The course may be around natural features, such as rocks and islands, or marked out with buoys.

Boats usually go round a course anticlockwise, but the direction may be reversed if tide or weather conditions dictate. At inshore races the starting jetty must be no less than 75m (246ft) long, and should be positioned at least 300m (328yd) from the first turn for safety reasons. No straight should be longer than 850m (930yd).

On a straightforward race course the winner is the boat that first crosses the finishing line after completing a certain number of laps. Slalom courses have a much larger number of buoys to mark out all the necessary turns.

Propeller
Various types are used depending on the condition of the water; propellers are made of stainless steel, and can have three, four, or six blades

Design values
The two main construction criteria of a modern powerboat are aerodynamic efficiency (hence the streamlining), and safety

Adjustable wings
The crew can adjust the angle of the wings on each of the parallel hulls to control the amount of lift created by the oncoming air

Cockpit
This self-contained protective "cell" is made of carbon fibre and Kevlar® and is not part of the boat's structure, so as to reduce the effects of an impact on the crew

Auxiliary power
Two batteries are located in the left picklefork (hull), one to start the engine and another main battery to provide electrical power for the engine

Nose
The nose is filled with plastic foam that enables the boat to absorb the energy created by rough water

FORMULA ONE POWERBOAT RACING

Formula One (F1) is the most prestigious competition in powerboat racing, with events taking place in countries around the world that include Brazil, Ukraine, China, and the United Arab Emirates (UAE). It attracts thousands of spectators to each event.

COURSE LAYOUTS

Although F1 courses vary in type, they are all about 2,000m (6,560ft) long. Each circuit incorporates at least one long straight where the boats reach their top speeds, with Doha in Quatar even having two 650m (2,133ft) straights. Other circuits include hairpin turns that test the ability of drivers to steer their boats around buoys without the assistance of brakes or gears.

SHARJAH CIRCUIT

This course in the UAE has hosted F1 races since 2000, and is also the venue for other classes of powerboat racing. The race is held on an artificial stretch of water called Khalid Lagoon.

RACE QUALIFICATION

Each F1 event runs over two days, with the first day set aside for teams to post the fastest time possible during time trials. This generally determines the grid positions in the main race on day two, though an extra race (a "shootout") is held at the end of the first day between the top six boats to see which one starts on pole.

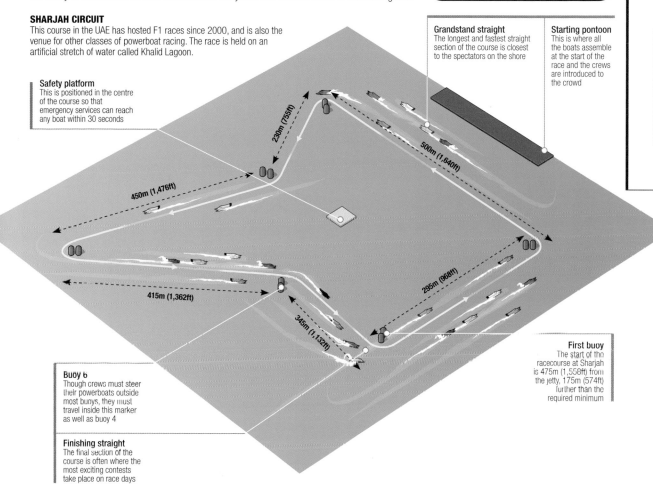

Safety platform
This is positioned in the centre of the course so that emergency services can reach any boat within 30 seconds

Grandstand straight
The longest and fastest straight section of the course is closest to the spectators on the shore

Starting pontoon
This is where all the boats assemble at the start of the race and the crews are introduced to the crowd

230m (755ft)

450m (1,476ft)

500m (1,640ft)

415m (1,362ft)

295m (968ft)

345m (1,132ft)

First buoy
The start of the racecourse at Sharjah is 475m (1,558ft) from the jetty, 175m (574ft) further than the required minimum

Buoy 6
Though crews must steer their powerboats outside most buoys, they must travel inside this marker as well as buoy 4

Finishing straight
The final section of the course is often where the most exciting contests take place on race days

F1 BOATS

The catamarans that compete in F1 are 6m (20ft) long and 2.1m (6.9ft) wide. Their design allows the hulls to lift out of the water at high speeds; the idea is for the boat to sit on a cushion of air on the tunnel of water formed between the two hulls, with just a small section of the boat actually remaining in the water. This enables the 350bhp engines to propel the boat to exceptionally high speeds, and has led some people to say that the sport has almost as much in common with flying as it does with boating. In addition the boat – as well as the crew – has to be strong enough to survive large G-forces at the turns.

SAFETY FEATURES

As well as operating the boat from inside a strengthened cockpit "capsule", the crew are protected by safety belts, head and neck harnesses, and an airbag system that inflates if the vessel crashes. As recently as the 1980s, F1 boats were made of fragile plywood and the unharnessed crew sat in open cockpits.

STAT CENTRAL

FORMULA 1 WORLD CHAMPIONS	
YEAR	WINNER
2012	ALEX CARELLA (ITA)
2011	ALEX CARELLA (ITA)
2010	SAMI SELIO (FIN)
2009	GUIDO CAPPELLINI (ITA)
2008	JAY PRICE (USA)
2007	SAMI SELIO (FIN)
2006	SCOTT GILLMAN (USA)
2005	GUIDO CAPPELLINI (ITA)
2004	SCOTT GILLMAN (USA)
2003	GUIDO CAPPELLINI (ITA)
2002	GUIDO CAPPELLINI (ITA)

EQUIPMENT

Although the various types of boats have different technical and safety specifications, all use a global positioning system (GPS) as the standard method for navigation. Timing equipment is installed into the cockpits, as is a system of lights that are activated by race coordinators in the event of all boats having to slow down – or even stop completely – after an incident or rule violation. The crew members themselves must wear clothing that is both waterproof and fireproof, as well as protective helmets and lifejackets.

TALK ON WATER

The roar of the engines and the slap of the water make it hard for the crew to hear each other, so they usually communicate by radio even when sitting side by side in the cockpit. This method is also used to pass tactical and other messages between the boat and the team engineers and directors located on the shore.

BOAT TYPES

Powerboats come in various designs, with the smallest vessels found in Formula One (F1). Offshore racing uses the largest boats with the most powerful engines, some of which are made by the Italian supercar manufacturer, Lamborghini. For speed, nothing can beat unlimited hydros, which can reach 300kph (187mph).

Bodyshell
Made of carbon fibre and other composite materials

Windscreen
Material is the same as that used in military aircraft windscreens

Picklefork
The two forks are designed to crumple in the event of contact with another boat

FORMULA ONE OUTBOARD
At the heart of the catamarans used in F1 are 2-litre gas-powered engines that can generate up to 425bhp. The boats have a crew of two, weigh 390kg (860lb) and are able to carry 120 litres (26 gals) of fuel.

6m (19ft 6in)

OFFSHORE CLASS 1
Boats racing in this class can be monohulls or catamarans. Powered by two or three 8-litre gas engines or 10-litre diesel units, they are able to average 200kph (125mph) over a race and hit maximum speeds of 250kph (156mph). The crew is made up of a driver and a throttle controller.

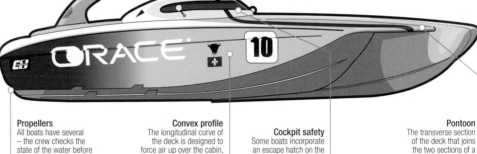

Propellers
All boats have several – the crew checks the state of the water before deciding which one to use

Convex profile
The longitudinal curve of the deck is designed to force air up over the cabin, then fall directly behind it

Cockpit safety
Some boats incorporate an escape hatch on the floor of the cockpit

Pontoon
The transverse section of the deck that joins the two sections of a catamaran hull

14m (46ft)

UNLIMITED HYDRO
These boats are propelled by inboard turbine or piston engines similar to those used in aircraft. The adjective refers to their top speed of 300kph (187mph), which makes them the fastest of all powerboats. What is not unlimited, however, is the size of their propellers, which may be no more than 40cm (16in) in diameter.

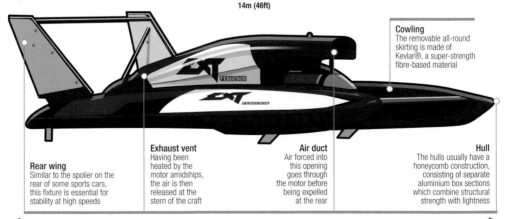

Cowling
The removable all-round skirting is made of Kevlar®, a super-strength fibre-based material

Rear wing
Similar to the spolier on the rear of some sports cars, this fixture is essential for stability at high speeds

Exhaust vent
Having been heated by the motor amidships, the air is then released at the stern of the craft

Air duct
Air forced into this opening goes through the motor before being expelled at the rear

Hull
The hulls usually have a honeycomb construction, consisting of separate aluminium box sections which combine structural strength with lightness

8.5–9.75m (28–32ft)

SIDELINES

511.11 The highest speed in kilometres per hour (317.6mph) ever achieved in a powerboat. The record, set in 1978, belongs to Ken Warby of Australia.

40 The distance in nautical miles (74km/46 miles) over which motor boats raced at the 1908 Olympics, the last time the sport featured in the Games. There were three events – under 18m (60ft), 8m (26ft), and open – and in each there was only one finisher.

12 The number of victories achieved by American Lee Edward "Chip" Hanauer since 1982 in the Gold Challenge Cup. This prestigious American Power Boat Association (APBA) event is held annually in the United States, often on the Detroit River.

BIRTH OF INTERNATIONAL POWERBOATING

THE FIRST ANNUAL INTERNATIONAL POWERBOAT COMPETITION, THE HARMSWORTH CUP, WAS SET UP IN 1903 BY THE OWNER OF THE BRITISH *DAILY MAIL* NEWSPAPER, ALFRED HARMSWORTH, DURING THE 1920S. THE ANNUAL RACE WAS WON NINE TIMES BY GAR (SHORT FOR GARFIELD) WOOD, AN AMERICAN INVENTOR WHO AT HIS DEATH IN 1971 HELD MORE PATENTS THAN ANYONE ELSE IN HISTORY. WOOD LOOKED OLDER THAN HIS YEARS, AND SPORTS JOURNALISTS DUBBED HIM "THE GREY FOX".

AQUA TACTICS

While in Formula One motor racing it is advantageous to tuck in close behind a rival, and overtake as late in the race as possible, the wake of a speeding launch makes powerboat racing a sport in which it is desirable to lead from the front.

BUOY-WATCHING

Drivers must not give buoys or markers too wide a berth, for fear of losing precious time (see the Bad Line in the illustration on the right), but equally they should not touch them. If they go inside a course marker that should have been rounded they are given a penalty that can range from a one-lap deduction to disqualification from the race. As in motor racing, there is an art to cornering efficiently, with drivers attempting to travel in as straight a line as possible around the buoys while at the same time maintaining a high speed.

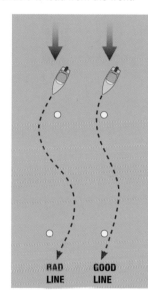

BAD LINE   GOOD LINE

FULL THROTTLE

There's more to powerboat racing than steering the vessel and flooring the throttle. Crews must constantly balance the power generated by the engine against the angle of the bow or bows and the propeller, adjusting the former to maximize the benefits of the latter. The revs generated by the motor count for nothing if the bow is hitting, rather than cutting through, the air and water ahead. Energy is also wasted if the propeller is not cutting as deep as possible below the surface of the water.

MONEY MATTERS

Although there are some similarities between powerboat racing and motor sport, especially in the way they are marketed, there is one major difference – fans of the water-based sport don't have to pay to spectate.

At the top level of the sport, vast sums of money are generated by television deals secured with broadcasters around the world and through the sponsorship of teams by some of the world's most high-profile companies. The globalization of Formula One really began in the early 1990s when Nicolo di San Germano took over as head of marketing for the discipline. He oversaw the expansion of the sport into new, untapped areas of the world such as Asia.

RULING THE WAVES

Competitions are held in various categories, often according to engine size. What is common to all events is that races begin on a jetty away from the circuit and engines must remain switched off until officials give a green light for the start.

FORMULA ONE

Formula One events are for boats with 2000cc engines. There are up to ten Grands Prix a year, each with 24 participating boats. The top ten boats that post the most amount of laps after 45 minutes get points on a sliding scale, from 20 points for a win to one point for coming tenth.

CLASS 1

The Class 1 World Offshore Championship is contested over ten events spread throughout the year. Each race is over approximately 182km (115 miles) around a circuit measuring 9km (5¾ miles) or for a period of no more than one hour. The points system is the same as that used in Formula One.

HARMSWORTH CUP

Among the many regional races held around the world is the Harmsworth Cup, which is held over point-to-point courses such as Cowes–Torquay–Cowes along the south coast of England. There is no limitation on engine size, and the most successful boats in the modern era have been powered by units based on helicopter engines.

OTHER RACING TYPES

Hydroplane racing takes place on relatively short courses in the United States and Australia, while P1 is a Europe-based endurance series made up of races that cover 148km (92 miles).

KING OF THE WATER

GUIDO CAPPELLINI IS REGARDED AS ONE OF THE ALL-TIME GREAT DRIVERS IN F1 POWERBOAT RACING. THE FORMER SHIPBUILDER FROM COMO IN ITALY BEGAN HIS RACING CAREER IN LAND-BASED GO-KARTS AND HAS WON MORE INDIVIDUAL F1 GRANDS PRIX RACES AND MORE WORLD CHAMPIONSHIPS THAN ANY OTHER COMPETITOR. HE SECURED HIS FIRST WORLD TITLE IN 1993 AND HAS SO FAR WON A FURTHER NINE WORLD CHAMPIONSHIPS.

INSIDE STORY

Powerboat racing changed radically in 1981 when the International Powerboating Union recognized the Formula One class. What had previously been a minority sport was quickly transformed into a major attraction for spectators and sponsors alike. Races that had formerly been held on any suitable body of water now had to take place in sight of a shore that housed the full range of service industries – such as hotels, restaurants, and marine engineering works – and which had good transport links.

AMERICAN POWER BOAT ASSOCIATION (APBA)

The first official powerboat race was held in 1903 on New York's Hudson River under the auspices of the American Power Boat Association (APBA). The APBA held sway in North America, but had little influence in the rest of the world, and this schism slowed the growth of the sport internationally.

UNION INTERNATIONALE MOTONAUTIQUE (UIM)

The Union Internationale Motonautique (UIM) was the rest of the world's response to the APBA. Formed in 1927, its founder members were Argentina, Belgium, France, Germany United Kingdom, Holland, Ireland, Monaco, Norway, Poland, and Sweden. The United States finally joined on the eve of World War II.

AIR RACING

NEED2KNOW

→ The first event in air racing history was the 1909 Reims Air Race. Pilots raced from Reims, in France, to England.

→ The competitors use high-end aerobatics planes, all of which are equipped with Lycoming engines.

→ If a pylon gets hit, the crew can set up another one to replace it in less than three minutes.

SPORT OVERVIEW

Air racing features a dynamic new discipline, where the objective is to navigate a challenging race course in the sky, in the fastest possible time. Flying individually against the clock, the pilots have to execute tight turns through a slalom course consisting of specially designed pylons, called "Air Gates". But the air race is not just about speed. Precision flying is crucial to success because any mistakes made by a pilot will incur penalty points, which are added to the pilot's final lap time.

SPEED RACING

This racing was the forerunner to air racing and is all about speed. In closed-circuit air racing, as it is known, the course is marked out by six, 9m (30ft) high pylons. There are two parallel straights, with a semi-circle at each end, which the pilots race around. Only eight race at one time, and the race distance in blue riband class is usually 39km (24 miles).

Wing span
The wings are 100 per cent carbon fibre and have a span of 8m (26ft)

The driving force
Three-blade propellers are most widely used. The maximum rotation is 2,700rpm

Engine power
Planes are commonly powered by fuel-injected, six-cylinder 8.8-litre engines, which are capable of producing 260–310hp

Changing lanes
Ailerons are used to change direction. They are mounted on the trailing edge of each wing

The main body
The fuselage should be strong and lightweight. It can be made of carbon fibre, steel tubing, or a mixture of the two

Pilot seats
The canopy can be jettisoned if the pilot has to eject, but race planes do not have ejector seats

SIDELINES

8 The average length, in miles, over which the pilots race during each air racing session. This translates to approximately 13km.

400 The average speed, in kilometres per hour (250mph), that the planes reach during the qualifying sessions, and during the race.

10 Race competitors perform challenging manoeuvres and fly close to the ground. During some turns, pilots have to withstand forces of almost 10G – 10 times their own bodyweight. All this must be endured without the help of a G-suit.

2003 The year that the first Red Bull air race took place. There were only two races in that first year, but the number of races has increased over the years.

FLYING THE COURSE
The Qualifying consists of two Qualifying sessions, with the pilot's fastest result being used. The quickest 12 pilots take part in the Elimination session, from which eight pilots will take part in the Race Finals. Penalty seconds are added for an incorrect passing of a Gate. A three-second penalty is incurred when a pilot passes a gate too high, performs the wrong type of crossing, or fails to perform a manoeuvre correctly. A ten-second penalty is incurred when a pilot touches a pylon.

AIR GATE
Standing at 20m (66ft) high, an Air Gate consists of two pylons (only the Quadro, a special air gate, has four), which are made of a light spinnaker material that rips if it is touched by an aircraft. Colliding with the gates is not dangerous to the pilot or the plane, but it does produce a bang, because the pylons are filled with compressed air. The Air Gates are resilient and can withstand wind-speeds of up to 54kph (34mph). At their base they measure 5m (16ft) across, and at their tip measure 75cm (29½in).

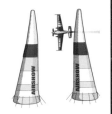

SAFETY AND SUPERVISION
The Air Race World series is governed by the FAI (Fédération Aéronautique International). All the tracks must comply with the governing body's regulations.

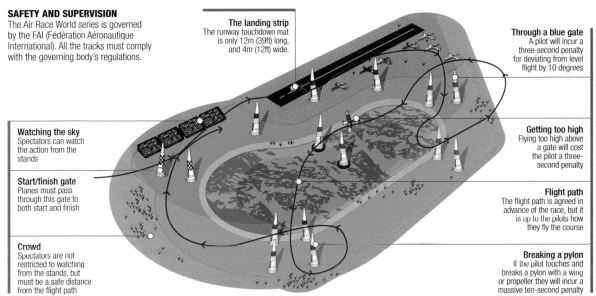

The landing strip The runway touchdown mat is only 12m (39ft) long, and 4m (12ft) wide.

Watching the sky Spectators can watch the action from the stands

Start/finish gate Planes must pass through this gate to both start and finish

Crowd Spectators are not restricted to watching from the stands, but must be a safe distance from the flight path

Through a blue gate A pilot will incur a three-second penalty for deviating from level flight by 10 degrees

Getting too high Flying too high above a gate will cost the pilot a three-second penalty

Flight path The flight path is agreed in advance of the race, but it is up to the pilots how they fly the course

Breaking a pylon If the pilot touches and breaks a pylon with a wing or propeller they will incur a massive ten-second penalty

THE COURSE
The race track is approximately 1.4km (1mile) long and consists of a series of inflatable gates (air gates). Pilots complete one of three predetermined flight plans in each session. They must pass between the gates, making either a horizontal crossing (through gates marked in blue) or a vertical crossing (through gates marked in red). Pilots must fly through the slalom gates which consist of three single Air Gates. The courses will differ slightly from event to event. Each round has new challenges and varying enviromental factors.

A WORLD-WIDE EVENT
From its humble beginnings in 2003, the Red Bull Air Race World Series grew into a global phenomenon. This development was halted by a hiatus in championships between 2011–13, although the series is expected to recommence in 2014. The locations used for the 2007 series are shown below. In the US, closed-circuit racing is still the most popular form of the sport (see opposite page).

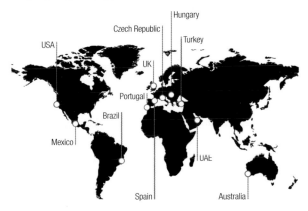

ESSENTIAL TECHNIQUES
The Air Race is not just about speed, it is as much about accurate low-level flying. The pilots are required to execute specific "turning manoeuvres", such as the knife edge manoeuver, the horizontal crossing, and the half Cuban eight, in order to navigate the track. The slightest mistake in the execution of the manoeuvre can result in penalty points being incurred. Other manoeuvres that the pilot may execute during a racing or qualification lap include, tailslides, vertical roll, horizontal round, and the loop.

BLUE-COLOURED PYLONS
When positioned parallel to each other, the blue-coloured pylons, which stand approximately 14m (46ft) apart, form an air gate. The pilots must fly through the blue gates horizontally. This is called a horizontal crossing.

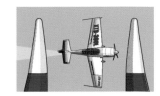

THE KNIFE EDGE MANOEUVRE
The red-coloured pylons that stand just 10m (33ft) apart, form an even tighter Air Gate that pilots must pass in a "knife edge" (or vertical) position – with one wing pointed towards the sky and the other towards the earth.

THE HALF CUBAN EIGHT
This particular manoeuvre is used to reverse the direction of the plane. To execute the manoeuvre, the pilot performs a pull-up and five-eighths inside loop to a 45 degrees, followed by a half roll, and a one-eighths inside loop to level flight.

SNOWMOBILING

SPORT OVERVIEW

In the snowbelt communities of the Northern Hemisphere, particularly the United States and Canada, snowmobiling is a popular motor sport with exciting – and fiercely competitive – winter races held on ice ovals and over cross-country trails. Snowmobiles grew in popularity when the invention of the Ski-doo in the late 1950s brought smaller and lighter engines to the rear-track, front-ski system of the earlier and larger snow vehicles that had been used by the military, postal services, ambulances, and the forestry industry.

Banked corners
At each end of the ice oval heavily cambered corners keep the snowmobiles on track

ICE OVAL
At many venues, including the famous Eagle River in Wisconsin, snowmobilers compete in races round oval ice tracks.

NEED2KNOW

→ The average age of a snowmobiler is 41 years. Around 17 per cent of all snowmobilers are 60 or older.

→ In summer, instead of missing their sport, many snowmobilers modify their vehicles for racing on grass or water.

COMPETITOR PROFILE
Snowmobile races can be hard work so riders must be physically fit, with the strength to control a powerful precision machine at high speeds. Mental alertness and a cool nerve are also needed to cope with the thrills and spills of racing on snow and ice over often hazardous terrain.

Snowmobile windscreen
The windscreen stops the rider being buffeted too much when racing

Protective clothing
A waterproof jacket and trousers keep the rider dry and warm. Gloves and boots protect the hands and feet

Driving force
The two-stroke or four-stroke engines that power modern snowmobiles are increasingly clean and efficient

SNOWMOBILE
Made of light, durable materials, modern snowmobiles accelerate quickly and can reach speeds of 190kph (120mph). The vehicles are noisy and there are concerns about the impact of their exhaust fumes on the environment.

Track drive
The engine is connected to the track drive which, in turn, moves the tracks

Light tracks
The tracks, which are made of a light material such as rubber, spread out the weight to stop the snowmobile sinking

Comfort and stability
Shock absorbers, springs, and dampers fitted to each ski provide a comfortable and stable ride

Skis
The skis can be either double or single, and are produced in various sizes and widths for different terrains

SIDELINES

129,087 The number of snowmobiles sold throughout the world in 2012: 48,689 of them in the United States and 40,165 in Canada.

1,481 The approximate number of kilometres (920 miles) per year an average snowmobiler rides. In the same period, he or she spends $4,000 (£3,000) on the sport.

80 The percentage of snowmobilers who use their snowmobile for trail riding or for touring on the many trails that have been specially groomed and marked. Around 20 per cent use their snowmobile for transport, fishing, or work.

23 The billions of US dollars (£20 billion) that snowmobilers in the United States and Canada spend annually on their sport. In Europe and Russia, the corresponding figure is $4 billion.

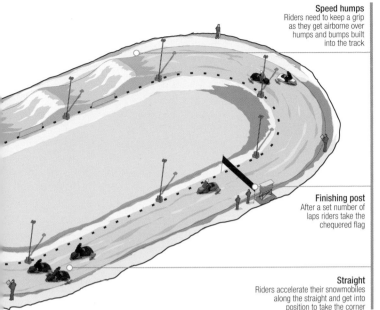

Speed humps
Riders need to keep a grip as they get airborne over humps and bumps built into the track

Finishing post
After a set number of laps riders take the chequered flag

Straight
Riders accelerate their snowmobiles along the straight and get into position to take the corner

TYPES OF SNOWMOBILE

There are five main types of snowmobile, starting with the light, easy-to-handle, entry-level machines (also called trail models). Performance machines are heavier, have a little more horsepower (85+hp) and are more responsive. Touring snowmobiles are even larger and heavier, have longer tracks and can carry two people in comfort over long distances. Mountain snowmobiles are longer, narrower, more powerful, and have special tracks that enable various manoeuvres in deep powder snow. Utility machines, which are heavier, longer, and a little wider than other types, are good for trails and working in heavy snow.

TREK OVER THE TOP

Each February snowmobilers can trek along 322km (200 miles) of groomed trails from Tok in Alaska to Dawson City in the Yukon. Also called the Tok to Dawson Poker Run, the trek allows touring snowmobilers to travel along the Top of the World Highway, with steep hills, howling winds, twisting turns, and breathtaking views.

EAGLE RIVER

The Derby Track at Eagle River in northern Wisconsin plays host to the annual World Snowmobiling Championships. Snowmobile racing started here in 1964, with events such as hill climbing, cross-country races, and sprint races on a track laid out on a lake and drawing a crowd of around 3,000. As the years went by, new courses and facilities attracted prize money, television coverage, professional riders, and crowds of 50,000 or more. In the 40th Eagle River World Championship, which was held over seven days, riders competed for the World Championship Oval, the World Championship Snocross, and the Vintage World Championship. In 2007 Eagle River held the 44th World Championship Derby, the Loadmaster Classic Vintage weekend, and a World Power Sports Association National Snocross event.

SNOCROSS

The thrilling sight of snowmobiles negotiating a snocross course (a track resembling a motocross course with snow) attracts large numbers of spectators. The short track, which is composed of various bumps, banked corners, and tight turns, encourages the riders to catch "big air" and perform breathtaking aerial manoeuvres. Snocross classes may vary from region to region. In some championships the classes cater for a whole range of abilities from Mini, designed for children up to the age of 11, to Pro, for entrants who already have experience of competing at expert level (see stat table below).

IRON DOG CLASSIC

RENOWNED AS THE LONGEST AND TOUGHEST SNOWMOBILE RACE IN THE WORLD, THE IRON DOG GOLDRUSH CLASSIC IS SOME 3,220KM (2,000 MILES) LONG AND LINKS WASILLA WITH NOME AND FAIRBANKS IN ALASKA. COMPETITORS RIDING SNOWMOBILES USING SPECIAL FUEL TRAVEL AT SPEEDS OF UP TO 160KPH (100MPH) ACROSS EXTREMELY RUGGED TERRAIN IN TEMPERATURES FAR BELOW ZERO.

GROOMING THE TRAILS

Throughout the snowbelt of North America an army of volunteers from snowmobiling clubs and other organizations work with provincial, state, or local governments, and private landowners to design, map, construct, and groom marked trails. It has been estimated that more than 362,000km (225,000 miles) of groomed – and maintained – trails are accessible to the 4 million or more snowmobilers in Canada and the United States.

STAT CENTRAL

SNOCROSS CLASSES	
CLASS	**AGE RANGE**
MINI	5–11 YEARS
YOUTH 1	9–13 YEARS
YOUTH 2	13–17 YEARS
SPORT	13 + YEARS
PLUS 30	29 + YEARS
MASTERS	39 + YEARS
SEMI PRO	13 + YEARS
PRO	13 + YEARS

SNOWMOBILE ENGINE
CYLINDER VOLUME
125CC (MAX SPEED OF 15KPH (10MPH)
500CC MAX (INC. LIQUID COOLED)
500CC MAX (PRO UP TO 800CC)
600CC MAX (NOT LIQUID COOLED)
800CC MAX

INSIDE STORY

The United States Snowmobiling Association (USSA) is the sports' oldest sanctioning body. Founded in 1965, it took on the organization of a chaotic sport – there were nearly 120 brands of snowmobiles with more than 25 different engines, and races were held everywhere at the same time. The USSA established uniformity of rules, specifications, and track safety, and ordered the events calendar.

WORLD POWER SPORTS ASSOCIATION (WPSA)

The WPSA is a a governing body that organizes, regulates, and promotes various snowmobiling competitions.

ANIMAL
SPORTS

Crash cap
The protective crash cap is masked by the owner's colours – here a green silk

Goggles
Eye protection is essential as galloping horses kick back dirt and mud that can obscure jumps and may cause injury

Owner's colours
Jockeys wear the "colours" of the owner of the horse over their body protectors

Racing saddle
Saddles are smaller and lighter than ordinary saddles. Jockeys also ride with very short stirrups

Breast plate
Narrow horses have these attached to the saddle to prevent it from slipping back during the race

Safety girth
A second girth helps to ensure that the saddle and weight cloth remain in place throughout a race

Brushing boots
These wrap around the horse's forelegs and protect them if they hit a hurdle during a race

HORSE RACING

SPORT OVERVIEW

Race meetings usually comprise six races run over various distances. In summer all the meetings are flat; in winter there are also jump meetings in some countries. Horses are trained to race according to their age and experience; younger horses usually run shorter distances and carry less weight. Jockeys are small, light, and highly competitive, and injuries are not uncommon, particularly for jump jockeys. As a spectator sport, racing is extremely popular – classic races are watched by millions, many of whom gamble on the outcome.

PROLIFIC ARKLE

ARKLE WON HIS RACES IN THE UK AND IRELAND SO CONVINCINGLY THAT THE HANDICAPPER WAS FORCED TO ISSUE TWO WEIGHT RATINGS – ONE APPLIED IF HE RAN AND ANOTHER IF HE DID NOT. USUALLY ARKLE CARRIED OVER TWO STONE MORE THAN HIS RIVALS.

NEED2KNOW

→ Most horse races are run over special courses either on the flat, over hurdles, or over jumps. The Palio horse race in Sienna is held in the town square twice a year.

→ Bred for its speed, the Thoroughbred horse descended from three stallions – the Byerley Turk (1689), the Darley Arabian (1704), and the Godolphin Arabian (1730).

→ The most famous steeplechase is the Grand National run over 4½ miles at Aintree, England, in April each year.

FLAT RACECOURSES

There are two types of flat racecourse. Grass tracks are sited on undulating natural terrain and vary considerably in shape and size. Some operate in a clockwise direction and others in an anticlockwise direction, and many have straight sections that are long enough to accommodate shorter five furlong races. All-weather dirt tracks are man-made, flat, and in many countries operate only in an anticlockwise direction. The starting stalls are mobile and can be set up at the appropriate distances on race days. The finishing post is permanent and usually sited in front of the grandstands. Most tracks have a camera that photographs the first horse past the post. In a close finish, the picture is used to decide the winner.

STEEPLECHASE COURSES

National hunt racing is centred mainly in the UK, Ireland, and France. Racing is on grass over either brush fences or over hurdles, which are flexible and lower in height. The two courses are usually side by side. Racing can be either clockwise or anticlockwise depending on the course and some racecourses have both jumping and flat facilities. The amateur equivalent of the steeplechase is called a point-to-point – these courses are usually on farms and only used once or twice a year. Other countries, such as the US, do have jump races but often the fences are more varied and include natural hedges and timber obstacles.

Hurdle

Wing

HURDLES

A minimum of 3ft 6in high, hurdles are made up of brush sections – three are shown here. The sections slope away from approaching horses and each will flex downward independently if a horse hits it. The white "wing' to the left guides horses into the jump.

Plain fence

CHASE JUMP

Plain fences are usually made of brush and a minimum of 4ft 6in high. A couple of fences on the circuit will be open ditches with a ditch on the take off side. There is usually one water jump.

Wing

AMERICAN QUARTER HORSE

Most racehorses are Thoroughbreds but Quarter Horse, Arab, and pony racing are also very popular. The Quarter Horse, named for its speed over a quarter mile, is the dragster of the horse world. It can cover 440 yards in less than 21 seconds from a standing start. This makes the Quarter Horse faster than a Thoroughbred over short distances. Quarter Horses race on the flat over one eighth to a half a mile. In contrast Thoroughbred races range from five furlongs to about two and a half miles.

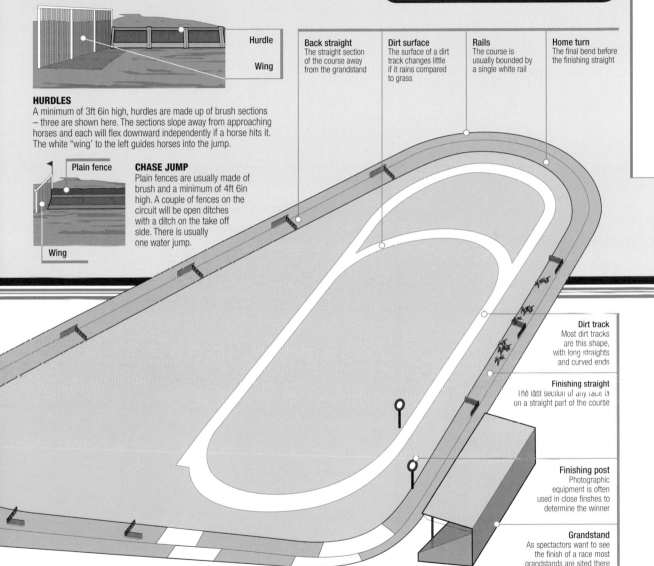

Back straight
The straight section of the course away from the grandstand

Dirt surface
The surface of a dirt track changes little if it rains compared to grass

Rails
The course is usually bounded by a single white rail

Home turn
The final bend before the finishing straight

Dirt track
Most dirt tracks are this shape, with long straights and curved ends

Finishing straight
The last section of any race is on a straight part of the course

Finishing post
Photographic equipment is often used in close finshes to determine the winner

Grandstand
As spectactors want to see the finish of a race most grandstands are sited there

HANDICAP RACES

Horses sometimes run in handicap races which aim to give all horses entered a fair chance of winning. Essentially, more successful horses carry more weight, one pound being equivalent to about one length in distance. If necessary, lead weight is carried in a weight cloth under the saddle. Jockeys are "weighed in" with their saddles and weight cloths before and after the race to confirm the correct weight is carried.

START GATE

Used in flat racing, horses are loaded into the back of the stalls and then released together from the front when the race starts. In the US, the opening of the gates coincides with the ringing of a bell.

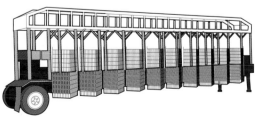

JOCKEY KIT

All jockeys carry a whip and most wear goggles to protect their eyes. They wear the same basic clothing (shown here) but change their "colours" depending on the owner of the horse they are riding.

HEAD GEAR

The crash cap is designed to cushion the skull during a fall, and to protect the head from being kicked by other horses, both of which are more likely to happen in jump racing.

The helmet
The hard outer casing is padded on the inside

Chin harness
The harness holds the crash cap firmly in position

RACING SILKS

The lightweight coloured silks help spectators to distinguish the runners during a race.

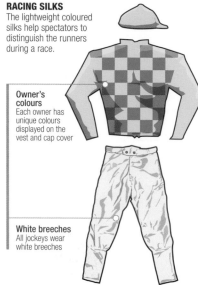

Owner's colours
Each owner has unique colours displayed on the vest and cap cover

White breeches
All jockeys wear white breeches

Shoulder pad
Protects the upper arm

Padded panels
Protect the body but allow movement

BODY PROTECTORS

Mainly worn to help prevent back injuries, body protectors are mandatory for all jockeys.

Boot tops
White breeches tuck into the soft tops of the boots

LONG BOOTS

Soft leather hunting boots protect the lower leg and are often made to measure for extra comfort.

RULES OF RACING

Because large amounts of money can be won or lost on a single race, there are many rules and regulations in place to reduce the likelihood of fraud. For example, no race can start before the time stated, and winning horses, like athletes, are tested for drugs. Horses that are expected to do well but run badly are also tested to check they have not been "nobbled" and sometimes the trainer and jockey are interviewed by the racecourse stewards to explain the poor running of a horse. Whipping is always a contentious issue and so in the UK excessive use of the whip carries a penalty – jockeys found guilty of this are suspended for several days.

AGES AND RACES

Thoroughbreds are all aged from 1 January of each year regardless of the month in which they are born. Flat horses can race as early as two over a distance of five furlongs but those destined for hurdling and chasing careers cannot start racing until they are at least four years old. Some flat races are restricted to fillies only and others to colts. Maiden races are restricted to horses that have never won a race.

BREEDING

Thoroughbred bloodlines are very important in the breeding of racehorses. The matching of a mare with a stallion depends on the sort of racehorse required. For example, fast racehorses are more likely to be produced from horses that were themselves successful in sprint races. Many Thoroughbreds are sold at sales as yearlings; purchases are made on the basis of their bloodlines and conformation.

RACE TECHNIQUES

The key to racing a horse is settling it at the start of the race, so it doesn't waste energy, and knowing how it runs best. Some horses are front runners, others like to make a late challenge, and saving a horse can produce a good enough finish to win the race.

GALLOP

All races are run at the gallop. At first the pace may be quite steady, particularly if the race is a long one. The pace picks up markedly in the last mile, and by the final furlong the horses in contention will be running flat out, encouraged by the hands, heels, and whips of their jockeys.

Sitting quietly
Jockey crouched low and in perfect balance with the galloping horse

JOCKEY AND HORSE IN UNISON

During a race, the jockey crouches low over the horse, keeping his legs still, but moving his arms slightly to accommodate movements of the horse's head as it gallops.

JUMPING

Besides running quickly, jump horses also have to clear a number of fences or hurdles at speed without falling. Even if they negotiate the fence successfully, there is also the risk that they will be brought down by another horse falling in their path.

BECHERS BROOK

This is the second and twenty-second fence in the Grand National. Famous for the drop on the landing side, the fence is named after Captain Becher who fell into the brook during the race in 1839.

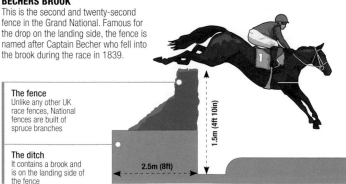

The fence
Unlike any other UK race fences, National fences are built of spruce branches

The ditch
It contains a brook and is on the landing side of the fence

1.5m (4ft 10in)

2.5m (8ft)

WINNING WAYS

Top racehorses are the product of good teamwork. On the day of a race, a horse must be produced in peak condition and this is the responsibility of the trainer. He or she must get the horse fit and ready to race without it succumbing to any injuries. It will be ridden almost every day on the home gallops by a stable lad and its progress is carefully monitored. The amount and type of work a racehorse does depends on the distance of the races it is going to run in and when in the racing season the races take place. Each horse has a stable lad or girl, who is responsible for its care. They groom the horse to tone its muscles, and keep it relaxed and happy. If the slightest thing is wrong, such as a horse not eating its food, it is their job to make the trainer aware of it. If everything goes to plan, the horse will be ready to race.

THE GOING

Some horses run better on hard ground than on soft and so the "going" is an important consideration when deciding to run a horse. Trainers will often enter horses for races at different courses or on different days of the same meeting, so they can run the horse where the going suits it best. It also allows the trainer flexibility if a race meeting is abandoned.

THE JOCKEYS

The jockey is an experienced rider who guides the horse through the race and ensures it has the best chance of winning when the time comes. "Stable jockeys" are retained by a particular stable to ride all their horses, other jockeys have agents and are booked to ride for a variety of owners and trainers. The jockey who rides the most winners in a single season becomes the champion jockey of that year.

THE WEIGHTS

In some flat races, all horses carry the minimum 50kg (7st 12lb), but in handicaps the weight carried ranges from 53kg (8st 4lb) to 64kg (10st). In contrast jump horses carry a mininum weight of 64kg (10st) while the top weighted horse may carry 80kg (12st 7lb). Most professional jockeys are men, but there are a few women who hold licences.

CHAMPION JOCKEY LESTER PIGGOTT

CHAMPION JOCKEY ON ELEVEN OCCASIONS, LESTER PIGGOTT IS ONE OF THE GREATEST FLAT RACING JOCKEYS OF ALL TIME. HE RODE HIS FIRST WINNER WHEN JUST TWELVE YEARS OLD AND RETIRED ON A TOTAL OF 4,493 WINNERS, WHICH INCLUDED NINE DERBYS.

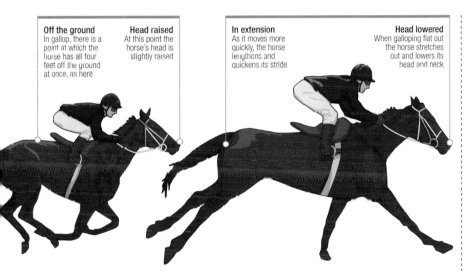

Off the ground
In gallop, there is a point at which the horse has all four feet off the ground at once, as here

Head raised
At this point the horse's head is slightly raised

In extension
As it moves more quickly, the horse lengthens and quickens its stride

Head lowered
When galloping flat out the horse stretches out and lowers its head and neck

RACE TACTICS

Race riding is very tactical but success also depends on finding an opening between tiring horses when making the final challenge. Tactics are more extreme in valuable races where a trainer may enter a horse purely to make the pace for another more fancied runner. Sometimes jockeys are given precise instructions by a trainer on how to ride a race but others are left to decide for themsleves as the race develops.

SETTING THE PACE

The leading horse in a race sets the pace. Jockeys on following horses must be mindful that their horses are not tempted to run faster than they would like, or get left too far behind and lose their chance of winning.

A GOOD START

A good start is essential, particularly in shorter races that include bends. Getting away swiftly allows a jockey time to cross to the inside rails and take the shortest track without impeding other runners in the race.

USING WHIPS

The use of whips in horse racing, like racing itself, varies from country to country, and there are strict regulations regarding a whip's length and weight. Whether hitting a horse makes it go faster or not is much debated. However, "showing" the whip to a horse in the final stages of a race and moving it back and forth without actually making it contact can help to keep a tiring horse running straight.

INSIDE STORY

People have raced horses for over 4,000 years. Flat racing started in the UK when knights brought small, swift Arab horses back from the Crusades. It became more popular in the 1700s, possibly due to royal interest in the sport – a tradition that has continued to the present day. Early European settlers took flat racing to the US, the first race track being built on Long Island in 1665. Today racing is the second most popular spectator sport in the US.

Steeplechasing has its roots in the Irish hunting community, who used to race between landmarks such as church steeples, and gave the sport its name. Racing now has a worldwide following with tracks as far afield as Australia and New Zealand, Hong Kong, Dubai, and South Africa.

THE WORLD'S RICHEST RACE

The Dubai World Cup is held in late March and has prize money of $6 million. It is a flat race run over a 10 furlong (2,000m) dirt track at Nad Al Sheba racecourse in Dubai City, United Arab Emirates. First run in 1996, the Dubai World Cup was created by Sheikh Mohammed bin Rashid Al Maktoum and attracts the best three- and four-year-old Thoroughbreds in the world.

→ The International Equestrian Federation (FEI) is the governing body for Olympic equestrian sports. Dressage has been an Olympic sport since 1912.

→ Dressage grew out of the training methods used to prepare horses for the battlefield.

412

SPORT OVERVIEW

Dressage has been called "horse ballet". It is the ultimate exhibition of horsemanship. In this centuries-old sport, horse and rider are tested on a series of precise movements, with the horse responding to the rider's slightest commands or "aids". Horse and rider are also expected to be well turned out. Dressage has a long military tradition, and riders from the armed forces may compete in uniform.

DRESSAGE

RIDER PROFILE
Dressage requires concentration, patience, and supreme horsemanship. The rider must exhibit complete control over the horse using the most subtle commands. The horse must be obedient, but the rider should not force it against its will. This can only be achieved over years of intensive training.

Formal attire
Military riders may compete in uniform, otherwise riders wear formal attire as stipulated by the FEI and may consist of a top hat and tail coat with white or cream jodphurs and long leather boots. Gloves are compulsory

Good grooming
The horse should be immaculately turned out with the mane plaited

Dressage saddle
The saddle is deep-seated with long, straight flaps. This allows closer contact between riders' legs and horses' flanks

Double bridle
Dressage riders use a double bridle, which has two bits that attach to two sets of reins

Stirrups
Flat-based metal arches are attached to the saddle by adjustable strips of leather

---

THE ARENA
The standard dressage arena is a flat rectangle, usually of sand. Letters mark the points in the arena at which particular movements are made. Those around the edge of the arena are visibly marked. The letters that run down the centre line of the arena are not visibly marked, but are used in the same way.

Soft going
The arena is flat with a sandy footing. Shredded rubber may be added to make the footing softer

Letter markers
Riders use the letter markers as reference points when performing the movements of the test. Horse and rider always enter at A. The origins of the lettering system are uncertain

Judging panel
The chairman of the judging panel sits at letter C. Other judges observe from various points around the arena

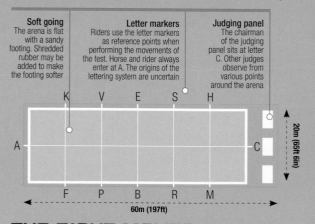

20m (65ft 6in)

60m (197ft)

THE RIGHT MOVES
Each dressage test consists of up to 35 movements. A test is ridden from memory in a set order around points in the arena, which are marked by the letters. The test ends with a halt and salute to the head judge. Up to 20 tests are recognized in FEI international competitions.

ROUNDS AND TESTS
In advanced dressage tests, horse and rider perform a series of movements in an arena like that illustrated (see left). The horse has to show three paces – walk, trot, and canter – as well as smooth transitions within and between these paces. Five judges assess each of the movements from different angles and award a mark from one to ten. Once added, these scores produce a percentage, and the rider or team with the highest marks is the winner. Olympic and World Championship competitions include Grand Prix, Grand Prix Special, and Grand Prix Freestyle (Kür) tests.

THE SPANISH RIDING SCHOOL

THE STALLIONS AND RIDERS OF THE SPANISH RIDING SCHOOL IN VIENNA ARE FAMOUS FOR THEIR PERFORMANCES OF CLASSICAL HORSEMANSHIP. THE HORSES ARE SAID TO DANCE TO THE MUSIC THAT ACCOMPANIES THEIR QUADRILLE RIDES DURING WHICH A GROUP OF HORSES PERFORMS A NUMBER OF DRESSAGE MOVEMENTS IN FORMATION. ONLY OLDER STALLIONS ARE TRAINED TO PERFORM THE COMPLEX MOVEMENTS OF HAUTE ÉCOLE OR "AIRS ABOVE THE GROUND". THE HORSES ARE CHARACTERIZED BY THEIR GOOD NATURE, STAMINA, PERFECT PHYSIQUE, GRACE, AND INTELLIGENCE.

EVENTING

SPORT OVERVIEW

Eventing is the triathlon of equestrian sports. Often taking place over three days, it combines the horsemanship of dressage with the endurance of cross country and the skill of showjumping – all ridden on the same horse. As with many equestrian sports, eventing has a strong military tradition. In recent times, a shorter event has evolved, which has a reduced cross-country section and can be completed in a single day.

NEED2KNOW

→ Before the 1952 Olympics, eventing was only for military athletes. Today men and women compete against each other on an equal footing.

→ The cross-country tests the courage of both horse and rider over 30 to 40 jumps.

→ The most accomplished riders come from Australasia, Europe, and North America.

→ Eventing can take place over one, two, or three days.

PENALTY POINTS

Since 1971, the overall winner of an eventing competition has been decided using a system of penalty points. Penalty points accumulated during the dressage are added to jumping and time faults accrued in the cross-country and show-jumping tests. A rider receives time faults for each second by which he or she exceeds the time limit in each test, while jumping faults are given for knocking down or refusing to jump an obstacle. Depending on the ground – wet or dry – the cross-country test can be very influential when it comes to scoring the competition. The winner is the rider with the least number of penalty points in all three tests.

THREE-DAY EVENTING

Eventing is a complete test of horse and rider over three days of competition. Dressage takes place on the first day, followed by cross-country on day two, with the jumping test on the third and final day. Dressage is covered in detail on the opposite page, and show-jumping on pp.414–15.

CROSS COUNTRY

This is the most demanding test in the competition during which the fitness of horse and rider are tested. Competitors gallop over a set distance jumping a variety of solid obstacles, including water hazards and drop fences.

Natural obstacles
Drystone walls often feature in the cross-country test

JUMPING

Each rider guides his or her horse through a course that includes up to 16 jumps. The course tests the jumping skills of the horse and rider as well as the fitness and stamina of the horse, which will be recovering from the exertions of the previous day.

Show jump
The poles used in show jumping fall when knocked by the horse

ELITE COMPETITION

The numerous competitions in FEI's international eventing calendar are categorized by their star rating, four stars being the highest level of competition, one star the lowest. The most advanced and keenly contested are the four-star Concour Complet International (CCI) events. There are only six four-star events in the world: Adelaide in Australia, Badminton and Burghley in Britain, Kentucky in the United States, Luhmülen in Germany, and Pau in France. The Olympics and World Equestrian Games are equivalent to four-star CCI events.

A SPORT OF PRINCESSES

IN GREAT BRITAIN, EVENTING HAS A NOBLE PEDIGREE. BOTH THE PRINCESS ROYAL AND HER DAUGHTER ZARA PHILLIPS HAVE WON MAJOR EVENTING COMPETITIONS, INCLUDING THE WORLD CHAMPIONSHIPS.

RIDER PROFILE

Eventing is demanding on both horse and rider. The different phases test different skills, and riders must show complete control in the saddle. Each rider develops a close relationship with a horse through many years of training.

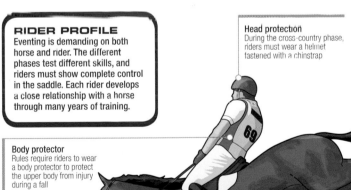

Head protection
During the cross-country phase, riders must wear a helmet fastened with a chinstrap

Body protector
Rules require riders to wear a body protector to protect the upper body from injury during a fall

In the saddle
The saddle used for the cross country is a cross between those used for racing and jumping

Leg protection
The horse's legs are covered with grease to protect them against injury if they collide with obstacles on the course

SHOWJUMPING

SPORT OVERVIEW

Showjumping involves horse and rider partnerships jumping over a course of obstacles in an arena. The rider has to present the horse at the jump (or fence) at a suitable speed and in balance, while the horse has to jump and land cleanly. There are usually two rounds. The second one, the jump-off, involves only those who cleared all the fences the first time and is held against the clock. Competitions range from small local events to the Grand Prix, World Cup, and Nations Cup.

THE ARENA

There is no standard size of arena and courses can be indoors or outside, on sand, earth, or grass. Grand Prix are contested over courses of up to 15 obstacles and a distance of up to 1,000m (3,330ft). The course designer includes a variety of set fences. For example, there will usually be a solid-looking wall, which is intimidating for both horse and rider. The prescribed route involves tight cornering and taxing take-off points. Time penalties increase the pressure.

NEED2KNOW

→ Showjumping has been on the Olympic schedule since 1912.

→ The sport is popular in North America, Australasia, and Europe.

→ Men and women compete against each other as equals in showjumping.

→ The Grand Prix events are the highest level of competition with the most prize money.

Dress up
Riders usually wear white jodhpurs, long boots, and a red or black jacket. Many carry a crop to encourage the horse to make the jump

Head protection
The helmet is an essential item to protect the rider's head from injury in the event of a fall

RIDER PROFILE
An excellent sense of balance, good physical fitness, and the ability to judge distances are crucial in a rider. Determination and boldness are also important as the fences are often designed to be off-putting and can look very high, even from the back of a horse. Close rapport with the horse is essential.

Saddle up
A jumping saddle has flaps that are widely curved at the front to allow the stirrup leathers to be short, while still providing knee support for the rider

Belly pad
A wide belly pad protects the horse's underside from damage by the shoe studs when the horse tucks up its front legs to jump

Leg protection
The legs are usually fitted with boots to protect against knocks and tendon damage

Reining in
The bridle is often fitted with a running martingale, which prevents the horse raising its head too high

Judging panel
A panel of jump judges calculates the results of the competition. In national and international competitions, the panel is headed by a chairperson, approved by the national governing body or by the FEI (International Equestrian Federation)

Water jump
Many larger events include a water jump; most have a small brush fence on the take-off side. It is tempting for both horse and rider to look at the water, which disrupts the flow of the jump. The horse must clear the fence without touching the water

Arena party
Members of the arena party work under the direction of the course steward. They rebuild any obstacles that have been knocked down. When a competitor is on the course, the arena party keep out of the way to avoid causing a distraction

A TINY HERO
STROLLER (1950–1986) IS ONE OF THE MOST FAMOUS SHOWJUMPERS. A PONY ONLY 14.2 HANDS (1.47M) HIGH, HE COMPETED SUCCESSFULLY AGAINST HORSES OVER 16.2 HANDS (1.68M) HIGH. IN 1967 HE AND HIS RIDER MARION COAKES WON THE HICKSTEAD DERBY AND IN THE 1968 MEXICO OLYMPICS THEY WON AN INDIVIDUAL SILVER MEDAL. THEY WON 61 INTERNATIONAL COMPETITIONS IN ALL.

JUMPING RULES
The basic rules of showjumping are quite simple: to clear the obstacles in the order dictated by the course builder. This must be done without the horse knocking down any poles or putting its feet into the water jump, stopping in front of a jump (a refusal) or ducking past it (a run out): any of these earn four penalty points (faults). A third refusal results in elimination, as does following the wrong route, not going through the start and finish, or the rider falling off. The course must be completed within a set time to avoid time faults. Riders who go clear in the first round go on to the jump-off, which is held over fewer jumps. If two or more horses jump clear again, the winner is the one with the fastest time.

SPECTATOR SPORT
With its straightforward rules and fast, furious pace, showjumping makes a good spectator sport. Individual rounds last a matter of seconds and the variety of horses and personalities of the riders add to the interest.

The double
Two fences with space for only a single canter stride between, the double needs accurate riding and athletic ability to clear

Oxer
The front and back poles of an oxer are the same height. A horse finds the width of this type of fence difficult to judge and, therefore, it is harder to ride without incurring faults

SADDLE WORK
Competitive jumping is done at the canter, a fast, bouncy pace that the rider can adjust to achieve a longer or shorter stride. The comparatively short stirrup leathers allow the rider to move fluidly in the saddle. Leaning forward over the jump has the double effect of taking the rider's weight off the horse's back and loosening the reins very slightly, both of which allow the horse to bascule (arc over the jump) more easily.

HORSE PROFILE
Although any horse can jump, not all make good competition jumpers. Key traits in a showjumper are boldness – to jump the fences – and carefulness – not to knock them down. It must also be responsive to the rider's requests, and be highly athletic and fit.

MAKING A GOOD JUMP
A jump can be broken down into five elements: approach, take-off, jump, landing, and getaway. Each one plays a key part in whether the horse jumps successfully or not.

Controlled approach
Impulsion (power in the horse's legs) is crucial in the approach. The rider may also alter the horse's stride length to arrive at the best take-off point

Taking off and jumping
At take-off, the horse tucks up its front legs and powers off with its hind legs. The jump is an extended canter stride

Landing and getaway
On landing, the horse and rider move on to the next jump as smoothly and efficiently as possible

SIDELINES

5 The Olympic record for showjumping golds, held by German Hans Gunther Winkler.

8.4 The longest jump over water in metres (27ft) set by Andre Ferreira of South Africa in 1975.

2.47 The FEI high jump record in metres (8ft) set by Alberto Morales of Chile in 1949.

50,000 The capacity of the equestrian centre built for the 2000 Olympics in Sydney.

INSIDE STORY
The origins of showjumping can be traced to 19th-century Britain when riders regularly negotiated obstacles such as fences and walls during mounted hunts. The riding style then was to have long stirrups and stay upright over the jump. Early competitions were dominated by military riders and it was Italian Captain Federico Caprilli of the Pinerolo Cavalry School who developed the forward jumping seat used today.

Draw reins
The reins run on a pulley design from head to girth to aid control when turning

Martingale
A standing martingale stops the horse from tossing up its head and hitting the rider

PLAYER PROFILE
Polo is a sport that demands high levels of coordination and riding skills. Players attribute much of their success to their horses, traditionally known as ponies.

Mane
The mane is clipped so it does not get caught up with the player's rein hand

Tail
The tail is braided, folded and taped so that it does not obstruct a swinging mallet

Breastplate
The breastplate is used to secure the saddle, preventing it from slipping back

Bell boots
The bell boot protects the sensitive coronet band at the top of each hoof

Polo wraps
The wraps are bandages that protect the cannons (lower legs) from mallet blows

POLO

GAME OVERVIEW

Outdoor polo is an equestrian sport played between two teams of four players. The game is played in time periods called chukkas. There are six chukkas in most matches, and each one lasts for seven minutes of nonstop play. During play, the aim is to score more goals than the opposing team. A player scores using a long wooden mallet to drive the ball through the opposition's goal posts. Polo is played at a breathtaking pace and is an exhilarating sport for spectators and players alike. An indoor variation, called arena polo, is also played.

ARENA POLO
Arena polo is an indoor version of the sport played according to the same basic rules. Each team has three players, and the game is played over four chukkas of seven and a half minutes each. As the size of the playing area is smaller, arena polo is generally much slower than its outdoor counterpart, but it more than makes up for this with its physical nature.

SIDELINES

5 The number of times polo has been included in the Olympics (Paris 1900, London 1908, Antwerp 1920, Paris 1924, and Berlin 1936).

19 The age of Argentine polo player Facundo Pieres when he reached his 10-goal handicap – the youngest player ever to do so.

1875 The year in which the the Hurlingham Polo Committee was established. It continues to govern the game in the United Kingdom, under the name of the Hurlingham Polo Association.

4,307 The elevation (in metres) of the reputed highest polo ground in the world, which is situated on the Deosai Plateau in Pakistan.

NEED2KNOW

→ Polo is one of the oldest team sports in the world. It is thought to have originated in Persia around 600 BCE.

→ The Federation of International Polo (FIP) is the governing body for the sport and organizes the Polo World Championships.

→ Argentina dominates the world of professional polo. Most of the world's ten-goal handicap players (the highest ranking) hail from Argentina.

ESSENTIAL EQUIPMENT

Polo is a tough contact sport, and the saddle and tack must be able to withstand the twists and turns and high-speed chases. Players use a long-handled mallet to hit the ball. The longer sides of the mallet, not the tips, are used to make impact.

SPECIALIZED BALL
In outdoor polo, the ball is made of solid high-density plastic. In arena polo, it is inflated and made of leather (above).

11.5cm (4½in)

POLO SADDLE
Players use an English saddle similar to a jumping saddle without the padded knee rolls.

120–135cm (48–54in)

Rubber grip
A rubber grip helps the player grip the mallet, and a webbed thumb sling wraps around the hand to prevent the player from dropping it

Bamboo shaft
The shaft is made from bamboo cane and may be rigid or flexible. The length depends on the height of the mount

Mallet head
The head is about 25cm (10in) long and tapered at one end to allow for a full swing flush to the ground

MALLET CONTROL
The mallet head is weighted to give a player greater control of the pendulum-like swing. The weight of the head is called the "cigar".

WHAT THEY WEAR

Every player wears a helmet, a polo shirt in team colours bearing the number of the player's position, and traditional white polo breeches. Riding boots may include spurs. Knee pads are compulsory in some clubs, and gloves are optional.

Team colours
Players display their team colours on their helmets

Polo shirt
The number on the shirt indicates the player's position

HEAD PROTECTION
A flying ball could seriously injure a player, so it is compulsory that all players wear a helmet.

COLLARED SHIRT
The collared polo shirt displays the team's colours, and is as popular on the high street as it is on the polo field.

GLOVES FOR GRIP
Most players wear at least one glove (on the right hand) to improve their grip on the mallet.

KNEE PADS
Smooth leather pads protect the players' knees from knocks and flying balls.

Polo boots
Leather boots offer protection from bumps and balls

RIDING BOOTS
Well-fitting boots cut just below the knees protect the lower legs from injury during play.

THE FIELD OF PLAY

Outdoor polo is played on a flat, grass playing field with an area equivalent to nine football pitches. The length of the field is always 300yd (274.3m), but the width can vary. Fields that are enclosed by an upright board are 160yd (146.3m) wide, while unboarded fields, bounded by a white line, are usually 200yd (182.9m) wide. Padded wooden goal posts stand 8yd (7.3m) apart and are centred at each end of the field.

1 Number 1
The number 1 is the main attacker but the least experienced player. He uses the speed of his mount to race upfield and score the goals

2 Number 2
The number 2 is the secondary attacker. He drives into the opposition's half, breaks up defensive plays, and sets up the scoring chances

3 Number 3
The most experienced player of the team, the number 3 is the play maker and the pivot between attack and defence. He hits all the penalty shots

4 Number 4
The number 4, or back, plays defence. He uses the speed and strength of his mount to break up attacking plays by the opposition and to guard the goal

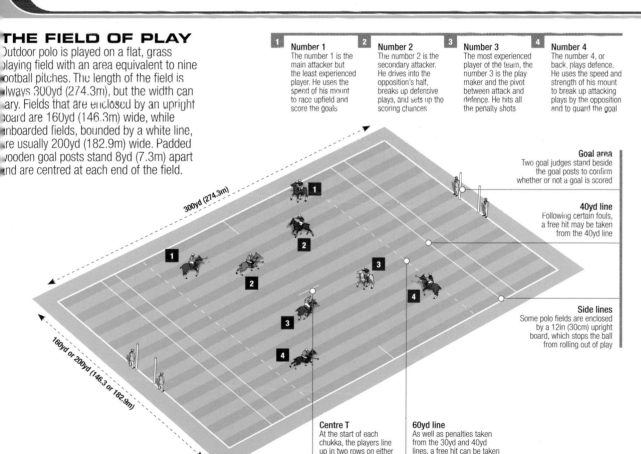

300yd (274.3m)

160yd or 200yd (146.3 or 182.9m)

Goal area
Two goal judges stand beside the goal posts to confirm whether or not a goal is scored

40yd line
Following certain fouls, a free hit may be taken from the 40yd line

Side lines
Some polo fields are enclosed by a 12in (30cm) upright board, which stops the ball from rolling out of play

Centre T
At the start of each chukka, the players line up in two rows on either side of the centre T

60yd line
As well as penalties taken from the 30yd and 40yd lines, a free hit can be taken further away from the goal

PLAY THE GAME

Polo is played at an electrifying pace. A full match may last for eight chukkas, but most games are now played over six chukkas. Play is continuous. Stoppages occur only when there is an injury to a horse or player or if broken tack prevents a player from continuing. The intervals between chukkas usually last four minutes, which allows the riders to change their mounts (although they may do so at any point in the game). There is a longer ten-minute interval at half time.

POLO SPORTS
Many different sports go by the name of polo. One version is played using camels instead of horses, another uses elephants, and there is even a game involving yaks. Other polo sports include canoe polo and cycle polo, but these are generally played for fun. Water polo is a competitive team sport and is played at Olympic level.

HANDICAPS

Polo has adopted a handicap system so that two teams fielding players of differing abilities have an equal chance of winning the game. The handicap is based on a standard six-chukka match and runs on a scale of −2 to +10 goals, with −2 being the lowest and +10 the top end of the scale. A player with a handicap of four is good enough to play in international matches. Before the start of the game, the handicap of each player in the team is added to give the overall team handicap. The difference in the total between the two teams is given as a goal advantage to the team with the lower handicap. So a team with an overall handicap of 30 playing a team with a handicap of 35 starts the match with a five-goal advantage.

LEFT OUT

ALTHOUGH THERE ARE A FEW LEFT-HANDED POLO PLAYERS ON THE INTERNATIONAL CIRCUIT, THE MALLET MUST ALWAYS BE HELD IN THE RIGHT HAND – LEFT-HANDED PLAY WAS OUTLAWED IN 1975 AS IT WAS DEEMED TOO DANGEROUS.

PENALTIES

If one member of a team commits a foul, one of the umpires may call for a free hit or a penalty hit. Minor fouls are usually penalized by a free hit from the 40yd line or the 60yd line, depending on the level of the offence. If the foul prevents a player from scoring a goal, the umpire will call for a penalty hit from the 30yd line. Penalties are usually taken by the most experienced player at number 3, who gallops up to the ball on the line and drives it between the goal posts. The opposing team cannot interfere with play during a penalty hit.

PLAYING POLO

The rules of polo are complex and govern everything from the size of the goal to the team colours. Various field rules cover playing situations. The main aim is to ensure the safety of the players and their ponies. The most common rules cover riding violations and dangerous use of the mallet. Three officials enforce the rules. Two mounted umpires follow the game on each side of the field. A referee presides off the field and settles any disputes between the umpires by watching a video replay of the game.

STARTING PLAY

At the start of each chukka, and after each goal is scored, the teams line up in two rows on either side of the centre T. One of the mounted umpires then bowls the ball in between the two teams to start the game. When the ball goes out of play at the side line, the two teams line up 5yds (4.6m) from the spot where it went out, and the umpire restarts the game in the same way. If an attacking player knocks the ball out past the end line, a defending player hits the ball back into play from the spot where it went out of play.

ATTACKING SHOTS

A professional polo player can hit the ball the full length of the field in just two powerful strokes. Standing in the stirrups increases the power of the shot. A player may hit the ball in any direction. Some shots are much more difficult than others, so polo players of all levels practise their technique on the wooden horse. The hardest shot to play is known as the "millionaire's hit", which is taken under the horse's belly and involves considerable risk of injury if the mallet gets caught in the pony's legs.

FOREHAND
A forehand shot is played with the ball on the offside (right-hand side) of the polo pony. The ball is struck in the direction of travel.

Offside forehand
The offside forehand is the most powerful and widely used shot in polo

Nearside backhand
This is the basic backhand stroke, and is the second most powerful shot in the game

BACKHAND
Backhand shots are played with the ball on the nearside (left-hand side) of the polo pony. The ball is struck backwards, opposite to the direction of travel.

DEFENSIVE PLAY

A variety of defensive techniques are used to contest for the ball in open play. The number 4, or back, is the key defensive player. He or she maintains a solid defence with support from the number 3. Most of the back's shots are backhand strokes to drive the ball away from the goal.

Hooking sticks
A player can use his or her mallet to hook the mallet of an opposing player and block their strike

FOULS AND PENALTIES

Polo is a tough, physical sport and, with ponies travelling at full gallop, the safety of both rider and horse is always paramount. For this reason, the use of excessive force is considered to be unsporting conduct. A player may not use his or her elbows, for example, when riding another player off the ball. This will generally result in a free hit from the spot at which the foul took place.

CROSSING THE LINE

The most important principle in polo is the "line of the ball". This imaginary line represents the path of the ball each time it is hit by a player, and it establishes the right of way for all the players on the field. When a player has the line of the ball, he or she has the right of way – which usually belongs to the player who last struck the ball. If another player crosses the line of the ball in front of the player with the right of way, the umpire will call a foul and award a penalty.

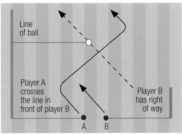

Line of ball

Player A crosses the line in front of player B

Player B has right of way

A B

DANGEROUS RIDING

Dangerous riding is a catch-all for any riding behaviour that is likely to put another player or pony in serious danger. Any exhibition of dangerous riding is strictly prohibited and heavily penalized by the umpires. Examples of dangerous riding include crossing in front of a player riding at a gallop, riding off at an angle greater than 45 degrees, pulling across another player's pony, crossing the hind legs of an opponent's pony or riding in a generally intimidating manner.

TACTICS AND TECHNIQUES

Polo is as much a game of tactics and strategy as it is an exhibition of strength and stamina. A team rarely works out a game plan in advance, but the players do take time to learn about the opposition's strengths and weaknesses in the hope of exploiting them during the match. Players save their best polo ponies for the fourth or sixth chukkas, which are generally the most crucial in deciding the outcome of the game.

TAILING THE BALL

Tailing, or backing, the ball is a backward pass to a team mate. The player who receives the pass can turn into the ball and then drive it into an attacking position. Tailing the ball is an easier option than turning the ball and may also be used when a player steals the ball from an opponent. After the steal, the player may tail the ball to turn it back in the direction of his or her opponent's goal.

TURNING THE BALL

Turning the ball allows a defending player who is chasing a ball in the direction of his or her own goal to turn and get into an attacking position. A player may also turn the ball to allow team-mates to get into better positions. The turn involves cutting the ball back upfield and then turning the horse back onto the new line. This takes time so it is best avoided if opposing players are close to the play.

RIDING OFF

In some circumstances, a player may decide to ride another player off the ball rather than try to hit or chase it themselves. This tactic is often used if a team-mate is in a better field position to take the shot. Riding off is allowed as long as the angle of attack is less than 45 degrees. Although the polo ponies do most of the hard work, each player may also use his or her body to shove the opponent off the ball.

Dangerous play
The use of elbows while riding off is against the rules

RIDING A PLAYER OFF THE BALL
The player in blue is attempting to ride his opponent off the ball. A player may use his or her mount to physically push an opponent off the ball. Riding off is a defensive move that can be used to prevent an opponent striking the ball, or to allow a team-mate a clear shot.

FOUL HOOK

If a player tries to hook by reaching over his opponent's mount, the umpire will call a "cross hook" foul. The hook must be attempted from the same side of the opponent's pony as the ball. Hooking above shoulder level or in front of the horse's legs will result in a penalty call.

Penalty position
A player commits a foul by hooking from the wrong side, with his or her mallet held above shoulder level

INSIDE STORY

Known as the "sport of kings" thanks to its association with royalty, polo is a sport with a long history. The exact origins of polo are unknown, but it is certainly true that a version of the sport was being played in the Middle East as early as 600 BCE. Over the centuries, polo spread throughout Asia and eventually reached Britain through India. The sport was included as an Olympic event from 1900–1939, but has since enjoyed limited growth thanks to the cost of competing at a serious level.

WORLD BODY

Founded in Argentina in 1982, the Federation of International Polo (FIP) is the world governing body for the polo-playing countries of the world. One of the FIP's main aims is to restore the sport's Olympic status.

BRITISH BODY

The Hurlingham Polo Association (HPA) is the ruling body for polo in Britain, Ireland, and 32 overseas associations. The HPA is the oldest polo organization in Britain and has 92 club members in the UK and Ireland.

GREYHOUND RACING

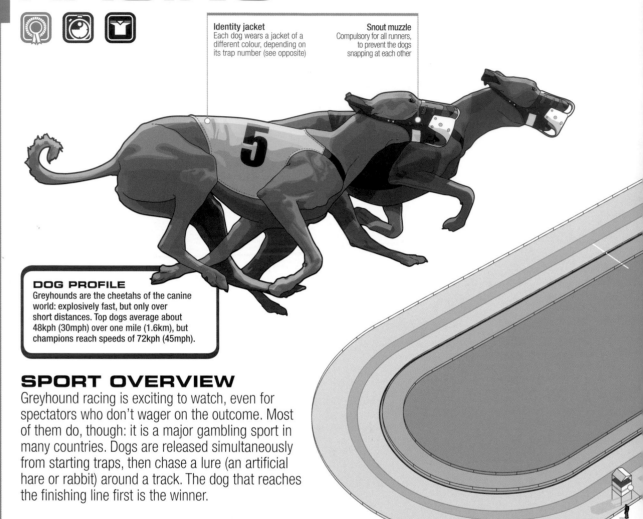

Identity jacket
Each dog wears a jacket of a different colour, depending on its trap number (see opposite)

Snout muzzle
Compulsory for all runners, to prevent the dogs snapping at each other

DOG PROFILE
Greyhounds are the cheetahs of the canine world: explosively fast, but only over short distances. Top dogs average about 48kph (30mph) over one mile (1.6km), but champions reach speeds of 72kph (45mph).

SPORT OVERVIEW
Greyhound racing is exciting to watch, even for spectators who don't wager on the outcome. Most of them do, though: it is a major gambling sport in many countries. Dogs are released simultaneously from starting traps, then chase a lure (an artificial hare or rabbit) around a track. The dog that reaches the finishing line first is the winner.

COURSE OF EVENTS
Dog races are held over distances of between 210m (230yd) and 1,105m (1,208yd). A rubber track surface is covered with a mixture of sand and a binding material, such as polyurethane, that prevents the grains blowing away.

NEED2KNOW

→ Greyhound racing is popular in many countries, but is a major betting sport in Britain, Australia, Ireland, New Zealand, and the United States.

→ An evening at "the dogs" is a popular social activity, with up to a dozen or more races and abundant food and drink.

→ Other racing dogs include whippets and, mainly in the United States, dachshunds.

SIDELINES

29.36 The number of seconds taken by the legendary Mick the Miller to complete the 480m (525yd) Greyhound Derby course at London's White City Stadium in 1929. The half-minute barrier had previously been regarded as unbreakable.

16 The maximum number of characters permitted in the name of a racing greyhound; that includes spaces between the words. "Mick the Miller" was only one letter under the limit.

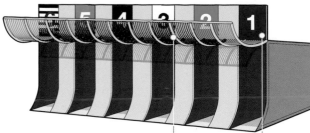

IN THE TRAP
The dogs are loaded into the starting gate according to a draw or current form. When they are in safely, the starter gives the order to start the hare.

Grilles
Open automatically to release the dogs after the lure has passed

Numerical significance
The trap and the dog closest to the inside rail always have the number one

COLOUR CODING
Every dog wears the appropriate jacket for his or her starting trap. Most races have six competitors, but in a seven- or eight-dog race, No.7 wears a leaf green jacket, and No.8 has a coat with yellow and black halves.

No. 1
Often believed to be the best position, because it is on the shortest inside track. In reality, many dogs perform better from a wider start

Outside rail
The greyhound with the highest number starts from the trap closest to this perimeter fence

Speeding lure
Runs on a rail that encircles the inner perimeter of the track; when it reaches a certain point beyond the starting gates, it goes over a tripswitch that opens the grilles and lets the dogs out

Paddock
Between the weigh-in and the off, all the runners must remain in plain view of spectators and officials so that the former can pick the likely winner and the latter can ensure that there are no attempts to tamper with the dogs

Finishing line
Cameras are mounted on the line to help judges call close decisions

Starting traps
These are removed from the track once the race has started and the dogs are clear

Grandstand
The site of most of the amenities – bars, restaurants, toilets. There are betting kiosks here, too, as well as stalls all round the stadium

Starter's rostrum
It is from here that the main course official gives a plainly visible signal to start the hare

THE HARE
The lure is electrically powered and runs on a rail around the edge of the course. Although they are known as hares, lures may come in any shape, within reason.

DOG TAGS
Every greyhound must have an identity book that gives its sex, colour, and markings (including earmarks) to prove that it really is the dog its owner says it is. This ID system is employed to prevent "ringing" (unauthorized substitutions).

RACE REGS
Every greyhound must be a registered weight, which is notified by the owner and agreed in advance by the race organizers. If the dog is more than 1kg (2.2lb) over or under at the weigh-in, two hours before the off, it will be withdrawn from the race.

Some events are open; others are graded. In graded races, the best dogs are seeded, and given the starting trap that most suits their racing style. Those in the outside lane have a "W" (for "wide runner") marked on their trap or beside their name on the race card. Seeded greyhounds with a known preference for the middle of the course are denoted by the letter "M".

No dog may run in more than one race per meeting. In the event of a dead heat, the winner may be decided by drawing lots.

OBSTACLE COURSE
Some dog races are held over a variable number of hurdles, usually between five and seven. Each jump is 75.8cm (2ft 6in) high, and slants forwards at 20–25 degrees from the perpendicular. Like horses, greyhounds tend to be suited to one form of racing or the other, and rarely excel in both. In most dog-racing nations, the premier hurdle event is the Greyhound Grand National; flat-track equivalents are known as Greyhound Derbys.

INSIDE STORY
Greyhound racing has its roots in hare coursing, but it had detached itself from bloodsports by the late 19th century. In Britain, attendances at meetings peaked after World War II, but declined dramatically when off-course betting was legalized in 1961 (the sport still has a huge following among gamblers). Dog racing is also big business in Australia and, increasingly, South Africa. In several European countries, races are popular but less commercial: greyhounds that compete in Belgium, France, Germany, and the Netherlands are still principally pets rather than investments.

34,000,000 The number of spectators who paid to attend greyhound races in Britain in 1946, an all-time high.

34–36 The weight, in kilograms (75–80lb), of a racing greyhound at the peak of its career, between two and three years of age.

7 The number of US states with greyhound racing tracks. There are now only 25 tracks in the US, 13 of which are located in the state of Florida.

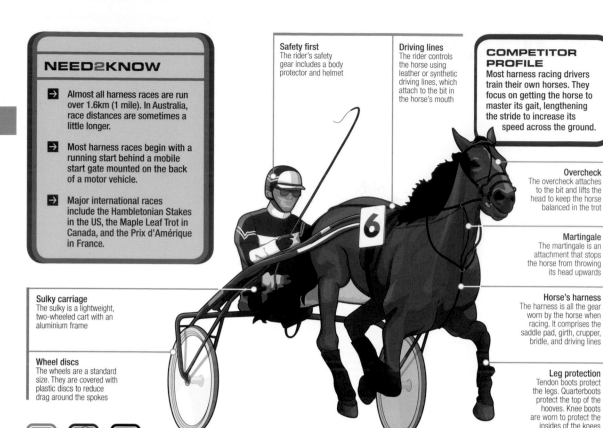

→ Almost all harness races are run over 1.6km (1 mile). In Australia, race distances are sometimes a little longer.

→ Most harness races begin with a running start behind a mobile start gate mounted on the back of a motor vehicle.

→ Major international races include the Hambletonian Stakes in the US, the Maple Leaf Trot in Canada, and the Prix d'Amérique in France.

Safety first
The rider's safety gear includes a body protector and helmet

Driving lines
The rider controls the horse using leather or synthetic driving lines, which attach to the bit in the horse's mouth

COMPETITOR PROFILE
Most harness racing drivers train their own horses. They focus on getting the horse to master its gait, lengthening the stride to increase its speed across the ground.

Overcheck
The overcheck attaches to the bit and lifts the head to keep the horse balanced in the trot

Martingale
The martingale is an attachment that stops the horse from throwing its head upwards

Horse's harness
The harness is all the gear worn by the horse when racing. It comprises the saddle pad, girth, crupper, bridle, and driving lines

Sulky carriage
The sulky is a lightweight, two-wheeled cart with an aluminium frame

Wheel discs
The wheels are a standard size. They are covered with plastic discs to reduce drag around the spokes

Leg protection
Tendon boots protect the legs. Quarterboots protect the top of the hooves. Knee boots are worn to protect the insides of the knees

HARNESS RACING

SPORT OVERVIEW

Harness racing is a popular form of horse racing in Europe and North America. Each horse pulls the driver in a cart called a sulky. Races take place at a trot or pace, and the horse must not change its gait. The winner is the first horse past the finish post.

DUST TRACKS

In the United States, almost all harness races take place on flat dust tracks. The track must form a circuit, but otherwise there are no rules about its shape or dimensions – straights can be long or short, and curves can be tight or sweeping. The mile is widely regarded as the classic distance. In Europe, racetracks are usually covered with grass and can be up to 2.2km (1½ miles) long.

SPECTACULAR STARTS

In the United States, some races have spectacular running starts behind a mobile starting gate. The drivers get their horses up to speed as the gate approaches the starting line. Then, as the gate passes over the starting line, the two wings of the gate fold forwards, leaving the horses free to battle it out over the racetrack.

BREAKING THE GAIT

The most important rules govern the horse's gait during the race. Assisted by the race stewards, the gait judge is responsible for checking gait. He or she follows the race in a car and may use video footage to see if any horse breaks gait. In European races, breaking gait results in immediate disqualification. In the United States, the horse must move to the outside of the track and resume the required gait before continuing to race. The horse then drops one place overall.

HORSE'S GAIT

Harness racing takes place in one of two different gaits, or stride patterns. European races are exclusively trotting. In North America and elsewhere, the faster pacing gait is much more common than trotting.

THE TROT

In the trot, the left front and right hind legs touch the ground at the same time, then the right front and left hind legs.

Lateral legs
The left front and left hind legs touch the ground together

THE PACE

In the pace, the left front and left hind legs touch the ground at the same time, then the right front and right hind legs. Unlike the trot in which diagonal pairs of legs move together, the pace involves coordination of the limbs on each side of the horse in turn. This is not a natural pace for most horses and so it has to be taught or bred to move in this way. To help maintain the pace during races, many horses wear an additional piece of tack called a hobblehanger, which fits loosely around the upper leg.

RODEO

SPORT OVERVIEW

Modern rodeo is an American creation with Mexican origins. There are seven standard events in most professional rodeos. The roughstock events are judged, and the competitor with the most points wins. The timed events are races against the clock, and the fastest competitor wins.

THE ARENA

A rodeo takes place inside a fenced dirt arena. There is no standard size for the arena, which may be indoors or outdoors. At one end is a bucking chute, in which competitors mount for the ride. A gate opens up into the arena when the competitor is ready. The roping chute is a three-sided pen at the opposite end of the arena. It is used to load the animals used for the timed roping events.

COMPETITOR PROFILE
Different rodeo events require different skills. Roughstock events are the most physically demanding and require great strength and agility – and an equal measure of courage! Roping events rely on agility, speed, strength, and timing.

NEED2KNOW

→ The Professional Rodeo Cowboys Association (PRCA) is the largest governing body for the sport.

→ Held in Las Vegas, the National Finals Rodeo is the most prestigious event in the United States.

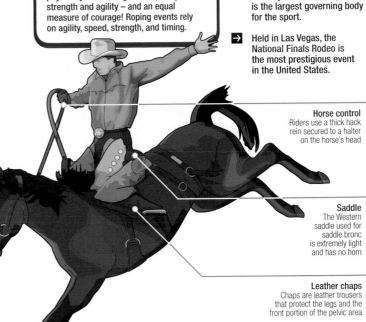

Horse control
Riders use a thick hack rein secured to a halter on the horse's head

Saddle
The Western saddle used for saddle bronc is extremely light and has no horn

Leather chaps
Chaps are leather trousers that protect the legs and the front portion of the pelvic area

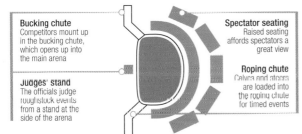

Bucking chute
Competitors mount up in the bucking chute, which opens up into the main arena

Judges' stand
The officials judge roughstock events from a stand at the side of the arena

Spectator seating
Raised seating affords spectators a great view

Roping chute
Calves and steers are loaded into the roping chute for timed events

RODEO RULES

There are three roughstock events: bareback, saddle bronc, and bull riding. Competitors may only use one hand to ride: any use of the free hand results in disqualification. There are four timed events: steer wrestling, barrel racing, tie-down, and team roping. In all but the barrel racing event, a barrier across the bucking chute stops riders from getting a head start on the livestock. Breaking the barrier incurs a time penalty.

ROUGHSTOCK SCORING

Scoring for roughstock events is based on a ride of at least eight seconds without disqualification. There may be two or four judges, each of whom awards up to 25 points to the competitor and the animal. The score for a perfect ride is 100 points.

RODEO TECHNIQUES

While good riding skills are key to all the rodeo events, the tie-down and team roping events require the additional mastery of various roping techniques from the saddle (see below).

RODEO STYLE

Style is an important part of the modern rodeo. Riders wear a traditional cowboy hat made of either tan straw or black felt. A true cowboy would never lose his hat during an event.

BARREL RACING

Traditionally a women's event, a barrel race is timed and involves riding a clover-leaf pattern around three barrels placed in a triangle.

Tight turn
The rider has to navigate the horse around each barrel as tightly as possible

TIE-DOWN

Tie-down involves roping a calf and tying its legs together. The calf must remain tied for six seconds or the competitor will be disqualified.

Off the side
The rider has to dismount to tie off the legs of a roped calf

BULL RIDING

Bull riding is a bareback form of riding using only a thick bullrope to stay on the bull. The event requires coordination and courage.

No saddle
A bull rider has no saddle and holds on with just a rope

CAMEL RACING

Jockey
Riders must be light, well-balanced, and brave.
Traditionally, jockeys were boys of 6–7 years old

Racing bridle
The "al khidham", made
from a rope tied around the
head, provides steering

Racing saddle
Made from a blanket, the
"al shidad" saddle is light and soft

SPORT OVERVIEW

This popular spectator sport, which originated centuries ago among the Bedouin tribes, attracts large prizes. Female camels are preferred for racing. When trained they can sprint at up to 64kph (40mph) and maintain speeds of 28kph (18mph) for an hour.

RACE TRACK
In the United Arab Emirates, races are held over 4–10km (2½–6¼ miles) on purpose-built, circular sand tracks. Australian races are typically "quarter-milers" over 400m (440yds), but longer races are increasingly common as the sport's popularity grows. Tracks can be grass or sand.

ROBOTS AND CAMELS
A racing camel is long-legged and slender with a much reduced hump due to the animal's extreme fitness. Camels begin training at about 13 months old and start racing at three years old. Controversy over the use of child riders led to the development of tiny robotic jockeys, complete with whip, which are controlled from vehicles following behind.

NEED2KNOW

→ Professional camel races are common in North and East Africa, the Arabian Peninsula, particularly in the United Arab Emirates (UAE) and Qatar, and in Australia.

→ The King's Cup Camel Race, held annually in Saudi Arabia, has 2,000 competitors. Most races have 25–30 entrants.

DOGSLEDDING

SPORT OVERVIEW
Sprint or endurance dogsledding races are held worldwide (on wheeled carts if there is no snow). The sled is pulled by teams of up to 24 dogs, usually hitched in tandem. The driver rides behind and directs the dogs.

NEED2KNOW

→ Organized dogsled racing began in Nome, Alaska, in 1908.

→ The Yukon Quest, said to be the toughest race, covers 1,643km (1,020 miles).

RACE TRAILS
Trails are marked out and have regular checkpoints and "dog drops", where tired or injured dogs can be left. Teams are normally started one after the other at timed intervals.

DOGS AND MUSHERS
Endurance, speed, and a close team spirit are key qualities in the dogs. They are trained to work in a specific position in the group and look on the musher as their pack leader.

Musher
The driver is known as the "musher", from the French "marcher", once the command for the dogs to begin pulling

Racing sled
The short-bodied sleds are often wooden. They have carbon fibre runners and aluminium fittings

Sprint team
Each dog wears a well-fitted "x-back" harness with padding over the chest

IDITAROD RACE

THIS ALASKAN RACE IS 1,852KM (1,150 MILES) LONG. JOHN BAKER HOLDS THE RECORD OF 8 DAYS, 19 HOURS, 46.3 MINUTES, SET IN 2011.

HORSEBALL

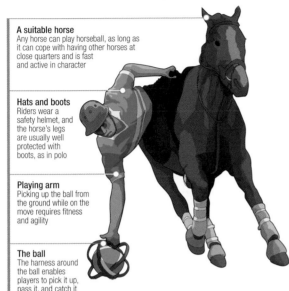

A suitable horse
Any horse can play horseball, as long as it can cope with having other horses at close quarters and is fast and active in character

Hats and boots
Riders wear a safety helmet, and the horse's legs are usually well protected with boots, as in polo

Playing arm
Picking up the ball from the ground while on the move requires fitness and agility

The ball
The harness around the ball enables players to pick it up, pass it, and catch it

SPORT OVERVIEW
This comparatively new equestrian sport has been likened to a combination of polo, rugby, and basketball. It is played by of two sides of four mounted players who can be of any sex and any age over eight years old. The winner is the team that scores the most goals.

FIELD OF PLAY
The arena is 20m x 60m (65ft x 200ft). The two goals are 1m (3ft) circles, fixed 3.5m (11ft 6in) off the ground. The game has two 10-minute halves during which players pass the ball with the aim of scoring – three passes must be made between three team members before scoring.

HORSE AND RIDER
Originally developed to inject new life into riding schools, horseball's fast pace requires good balance and excellent communication between horse and rider. Riders have to be able to control the horse with their legs and without using the reins. The horse must be responsive and fit. Some dressage training is ideal as this increases its agility and suppleness.

NEED2KNOW

→ Horseball was first played in the 1970s in France.

→ The most important events are the World Championship, the European Horseball Championships, and the Champions League.

→ The International Horseball Federation has 19 members.

HORSE DRIVING

NEED2KNOW

→ Harness racing, an ancient sport, dating to Roman chariot races and before, involves racing around a sand or earth track. Speed is key.

→ Trial driving is newer and consists of teams competing in three events – speed, agility, and obedience are important.

SPORT OVERVIEW
Driving activities are very varied, ranging from trotting races where horse and driver teams race each other, to trial driving where teams of four horses complete various tests, including dressage.

HORSE AND DRIVER
Because of its diversity, there is a type of driving to suit any horse, from pony to heavy horse. Pacing races are fast and use ultra-light buggies, while a full-size coach drawn by a team of four horses is slower but requires just as much skill and coordination on the part of the driver. Prince Philip, the Duke of Edinburgh, was a competitive driver for many years.

Scurry harness
This is a simple harness with a wide breastplate for comfortable pulling

Team of two
While the driver steers, the "groom" helps to balance the vehicle

Four wheeler
A low centre of gravity and strong suspension are necessary

SEA MATCH FISHING

SPORT OVERVIEW

Competition fishing from the shore is the logical progression for many pleasure fishermen looking for a competitive side to the sport. Shore-based competitions tend to be split into two distinct types: pegged/fixed venue, and roving, defined boundary/area events, depending very much on where they are held. More so nowadays these competitions are fished in the most conservation-minded way possible, whereby fish are caught, quickly measured and then returned alive to the sea (especially the pegged, fixed-venue matches). Various fish are assigned certain numbers of points according to species and length.

COMPETITOR PROFILE

Sea fishing is a sport where often lengthy periods of inactivity (waiting for fish to bite) are punctuated by short bursts of frenetic activity (when fish are caught, reeled in, weighed, and released in a matter of a few seconds) so anglers need excellent concentration, patience, and quick reflexes. Good upper body strength and balance is important, especially when reeling in (some fish are extremely heavy), as is a willingness to experiment with different equipment, types of bait, and locations to get the best catches.

NEED2KNOW

→ Modern sea match fishing grew out of the "birth" of technically advanced shore fishing in the 1960s. Modern rod-building methods came from the use of fibreglass and this gave rise to pioneering long-range shore fishing techniques to more successfully fish certain parts of the coastline.

→ Due to the need to catch all kinds of fish, sea match fishing tends to be a very technically advanced arm of the sport. These highly specialized fishing methods in turn filter down to certain parts of the pleasure fishing market (rig, rod, transport, and shelter developments for example).

Keeping warm
A snug fleece is usually preferred on cold days when the wind blows in from the sea

Hold tight
Fishermen keep a firm grip on the base of the rod, with the other hand supporting

Hardwearing clothes
Anglers are likely to get dirty fishing from slippery rocks and other terrain so jeans are common

SIDELINES

3,000 The number of competitors at sea match fishing's World Games in Portgual in 2006. The World Games is the sport's flagship event, held every five years.

14 The total number of world championship medals won by England's Chris Clark. Chris retired from competitive fishing in 2006 and is now a member of the international board and a leading referee.

Strong legs
Although hardly athletes, the leg muscles of a fisherman will be strong from many hours spent on their feet

Solid base
Boots with good grip are important, especially when reeling in

CATCHING FISH

There are various fundamentals that are of great importance for successful competition fishing, from bait to location. Two key techniques are casting and playing the fish, described below.

CASTING

The art of using the rod and reel to cast the baited rigs out to sea, sometimes at very long range. The ability to be able to cast further, often into deeper water, can be an advantage. A safe, reliable, and efficient casting technique will pay dividends.

PLAYING THE FISH

Often when a fish is snared the angler will not reel it in straight away. He will allow it to take the line against the reel's drag until it runs out, and then recover line when the fish tires. This allows for heavy fish to be successfully landed.

RODS AND REELS

The majority of shore fishing is carried out using a 3.66m–4.27m (12-14ft) fishing rod, commonly known as a beachcaster. They are designed to cast around 113–170g (4-6oz) of lead weight plus bait; the fisherman then watches the rod tip for signs of a bite. Many open beach- and estuary-style match fishermen will also carry a lighter rod (rated 56–113g [2-4oz]) and reel, principally for fishing at close to medium range for smaller species (called "scratching").

Butt section

2m (6.5ft) approx

Tip section

Secure line
Rings along the tip section hold the line from the reel in place

Reel seat
Also known as a winch fitting, this device fixes the reel to the rod

TRIPOD

A lot of shore fishing, both match and pleasure, is about casting out and waiting for the fish to come to you. Hence the need for putting your fishing rods in a purpose-built tripod and watching the tips for signs of a bite.

FISH TO THE CLOCK

Once the baited rig is cast out, the rod tends to be placed in the tripod. In areas where there are plenty of small fish, many fishermen will "fish to the clock", whereby they reel in at their own set time intervals. This serves both to bring the fish in for measuring and also for a continual changing and renewal of the baits (to keep the freshest, most inviting scent trail out there as possible). But often the fisherman will wait for the rod tip to signal a bite (when the fish picks up a baited hook the movement "rattles" the rod tip) before reeling in the fish.

RIGS

There are countless varieties of rigs for match fishing, mainly working on the principal of baiting up the hooks, casting out the baited rig, and letting the weight (grip or plain) settle on the bottom. Fish home in on the scent from the bait.

BAIT

The successful match fisherman will access the best-quality bait, often carrying many varieties and with plenty of research into local preferences and recent trends. Baits might include various worm species (lugworm, ragworm, white ragworm etc.), crab, fresh and blast-frozen fish (mackerel, sandeel) and squid.

REELS

The reel is a device used for the deployment and retrieval of fishing line using a spool mounted on an axle. In sea match fishing, small multipliers or medium- to large-sized fixed-spool reels are used, depending on preference.

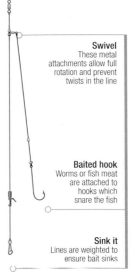

Swivel
These metal attachments allow full rotation and prevent twists in the line

Baited hook
Worms or fish meat are attached to hooks which snare the fish

Sink it
Lines are weighted to ensure bait sinks

Bail arm
This is flicked back to allow line to flow off the spool when casting; it flips forward when the handle is wound on

LAWS OF FISHING

There are two different types of sea match fishing – one based on the sizes (length) of the fish caught, the other on the total weight of all fish caught by the individual fisherman.

ROVING, DEFINED AREA MATCHES

These style of matches tend to be fished in areas where suitable venues for large scale, fixed venue matches do not exist, generally along areas of the coastline made up of rocks, small bays, cliffs, and headlands. The competition is again run to specific times, but due to the roving nature of them, more often than not the fish will be brought back to a central weighing station at the end. The winner tends to be the person with the heaviest "bag" of fish; note that once again the competition will be run on strict size limits of fish.

PEGGED, FIXED VENUE MATCH

A suitable venue is chosen by the committee, often an open beach with sufficient space to be split up into zones and pegs (specific location for the fisherman to fish from). Fishermen tend to gather beforehand at a designated location to pay their subs and pick their peg numbers on a random basis. From here they will spread out to their pegs and await the start time. Once underway, on a measure-and-release competition the fisherman will measure any fish with a fellow competitor or steward as a witness and then return the fish alive before casting out again. Points are awarded on lengths, bearing in mind that species of fish have to attain certain minimum lengths to count. The winner is the fisherman who records the greatest length total at the designated finishing time. There are often cash prizes for zone winners as well as the overall winner.

INSIDE STORY

Match angling is governed by the International Angling Federation (CIPS) which was formed in 1952. A sub-division of CIPS, the International Sea Sport Fishing Federation (FIPS-M) organizes a variety of annual World Championships (shore, boat, big game, long-casting etc) for men, women, and junior competitors. Each competing nation submits a five-man team. There are also prizes for individuals.

EXTREME SPORTS

12

SPORT OVERVIEW

Street luge is an extreme version of the Olympic winter sport luge (see p.310). Riders hurtle down a concrete track or road on a glorified skateboard, at speeds of up to 110kph (70mph), lying just centimetres above the ground. Street luges do not have brakes: riders must use their feet to slow down. The objective is simple: to get to the end of the course first. Every course is different, but most are 1–5km (½–3 miles) long. There are several types of competition, all equally hair-raising. In dual competition, two racers compete for the right to progress to the next round, and there are also competitions where four or six lugers race each other, with frequent spectacular crashes.

SPEEDING TICKETS
IN THE EARLY DAYS OF STREET LUGE, RACERS OFTEN COMPETED ON PUBLIC HIGHWAYS IN CALIFORNIA. THERE WERE NUMEROUS CRASHES INVOLVING SPECTATORS AS WELL AS COMPETITORS, AND THE CALIFORNIA HIGHWAY PATROL EVEN HANDED OUT SPEEDING TICKETS. EVENTUALLY, LOS ANGELES AND OTHER CITIES BANNED RACING ON STREETS WITH A GRADIENT STEEPER THAN 3 PER CENT.

RULES OF THE ROAD
There is no single governing body and no one set of rules, although competitors are never allowed to push or kick each other out of the way. Luges must have bumpers at the front and rear, but regulations governing the weight, length, and width of the luge vary between sanctioning bodies. For example, Gravity Sports International disallows luges heavier than 25kg (55lb).

STREET LUGE

NEED2KNOW

→ Street luge is most popular in the United States, Canada, and some European countries, including Austria, France, Switzerland, and Britain.

→ The sport originated in southern California in the 1970s. Skateboarders discovered that they could go downhill faster if they lay down on their boards.

→ The first competitive race was at Signal Hill, California, in 1978.

→ The major street-luge sanctioning body is the International Gravity Sports Association.

GEAR AND WHEELS
Riders often come off their luges and need to be well protected. Helmets, full leather suits, gloves, and boots are standard. The luge design varies greatly. Some are made of wood, but most are aluminium. They have between four and six wheels, front and rear bumpers, lean-activated trucks (which connect the wheels and axles to the seat pan), and handrails. Luges are up to 2.6m (8ft 6in) long and 40cm (16in) wide.

Head shell
Racers wear a hard shell helmet with a face shield and chin strap

Seat pan
Most of the rider's body is supported on a padded area attached to the aluminium body of the luge

Racing suit
A tough leather or Kevlar body suit is a necessity

PUSH-OFF APRON
A good start is essential if a competitor is going to win a race. Racers use their hands to gain momentum in a zone between the starting line and the beginning of the road course called the push-off apron. Once speeding downhill, experienced racers take advantage of the slipstreams behind other racers to maintain speed.

Safety bumpers
Luges have a bumper at the front and rear

Small wheels
There are four front wheels attached to the truck. The wheels are about 10cm (4in) in diameter

Steering truck
The trucks have lean-activated steering. By leaning the body one way or the other, the rider can change the luge's direction

COMPETITOR PROFILE
Street luge is potentially a very dangerous sport, and competitors need nerves of steel as they corner at great speed. Racers must be totally focused on the course ahead and their fellow racers, since any lack of concentration can result in a costly crash.

No sleeves
A sleeveless shirt gives the athlete freedom of movement and lessens the risk of snagging on obstacles

City wall
The urban equivalent of mountain faces and canyons make an ideal environment for a parkour practitioner

Loose trousers
Loose-fitting trousers or shorts allow the ease of movement necessary for long jumps and difficult climbs

Gripping trainers
A good pair of trainers is important. These should give some grip on brick, concrete, and steel surfaces

NEED2KNOW

→ The word parkour comes from the French "parcours du combattant", the obstacle courses used by French soldiers in training in the early 20th century.

→ Parkour movements have featured in many films, including *Casino Royale* and *Breaking and Entering*, and in the BBC TV trailer Rush Hour.

→ Organizations such as Urban Freeflow offer advice and training to aspiring traceurs.

COMPETITOR PROFILE

Before an aspiring traceur attempts a difficult route, he or she must train for months, if not years. Physically, the sport requires strength throughout the body, balance, and agility. But parkour is just as much about mental strength – the ability to be totally aware of the surrounding environment and the judgement to decide in a split second whether or not a move is feasible.

PARKOUR

SPORT OVERVIEW

Demanding the agility of an acrobat and the spirit of a warrior, parkour has attributes of the martial arts and of dance. It involves uninterrupted motion around, under, over, and through physical obstacles – usually the city environment. The practitioners of parkour are called traceurs. There are no fixed courses, but experienced traceurs stretch themselves by climbing walls, jumping obstacles, and running along the tops of rails. Each new obstacle presents a new challenge. Parkour demands more than simply strength, stamina, and agility. Its adherents also believe it should involve grace and beauty. Most do not compete against each other but against themselves in a constant struggle for self-improvement.

LEAP OF FAITH

Each route presents a different set of difficulties, and an experienced traceur must know hundreds of moves. However, the core skills – jumping, landing, and rolling to absorb impact – are just as important. Precision Jump, or "saut de precision", is a jumping move that combines power, grace, and accuracy (see below).

PRECISION JUMP
For a traceur, the object of a precision jump, as with other parkour moves, is not simply to leap an obstacle, but to do it with style and grace.

Landing
The traceur crouches as he lands, with the legs bent. This position softens the blow of landing. With experience, the jumper can land on the target precisely and be ready to start running to the next obstacle

Take-off
The jumper prepares to leap with the legs bent at the waist and knees and the arms extended behind him

Ascent
The legs are extended suddenly to provide the momentum for a long jump. The arms are raised above the head

Descent
The legs begin to bend in preparation for landing, and the arms are brought to the side of the body

EXTREME CLIMBING

SPORT OVERVIEW

Extreme climbers tackle rock and ice faces that look impossible even to regular climbers. Climbs are divided into aid and free. Aid climbing uses artificial devices for support whereas free climbing uses only natural features. Both free and aid climbers use ropes, however, in free solo climbing, often only climbing shoes and hand chalk are used. The main challenge for most extreme climbers is tackling new and more difficult routes, or completing a route in a faster time.

NEED2KNOW

→ Ice climbing is especially popular in North America, with 220,000 enthusiasts in the USA alone. Ice Climbing World Cup events are held in North America and Europe.

→ A survey in the United States showed that climbing is one of the most popular extreme sports. The average age of climbers was found to be 23 years.

ATHLETE PROFILE
Climbers need great leg and arm strength, muscle coordination, endurance, flexibility, and excellent balance. The ability to remain relaxed and confident on vertical faces and overhangs is equally vital.

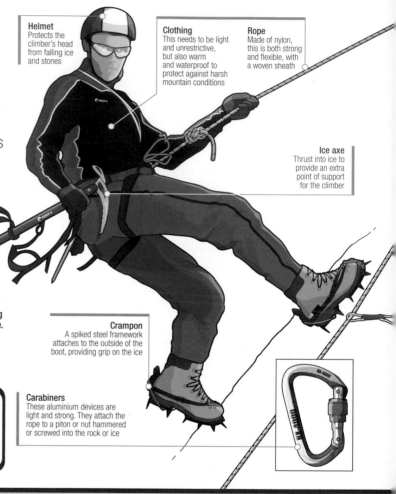

Helmet
Protects the climber's head from falling ice and stones

Clothing
This needs to be light and unrestrictive, but also warm and waterproof to protect against harsh mountain conditions

Rope
Made of nylon, this is both strong and flexible, with a woven sheath

Ice axe
Thrust into ice to provide an extra point of support for the climber

Crampon
A spiked steel framework attaches to the outside of the boot, providing grip on the ice

Carabiners
These aluminium devices are light and strong. They attach the rope to a piton or nut hammered or screwed into the rock or ice

WHERE THEY CLIMB

Anything goes, especially uncharted territory. Vertical faces, crumbling rock, overhangs, and harsh weather all represent new challenges to be overcome. Climbs are graded for difficulty. For example, an A6-graded climb on the "new wave" system is so treacherous that if one member of the team falls, the mistake may kill the whole team.

EQUIPMENT

Equipment varies according to the type of climb. A free climber may use only climbing shoes, gymnastic chalk to dry sweat from his or her hands, and lightweight, non-restrictive clothing. Aid climbers use ropes, carabiners, pitons, and more. Ice climbers wear crampons over their climbing shoes and carry ice screws and ice axes. If a climber is planning to overnight on a mountain, he or she will need a sleeping bag or down jacket; a bivy bag is also useful.

INSIDE STORY

People have climbed mountains for thousands of years, but the first recorded climb of a major peak was of Mont Blanc, France, in 1786. Competition climbing started in Russia in the 1970s.

GOVERNING BODIES
Competitive ice climbing is governed by the International Mountaineering and Climbing Federation (UIAA). Indoor sport climbing is governed by the International Federation of Sport Climbing (IFSC), formed in 2007.

CLIMBING SHOE
The uppers of a climbing shoe are made of supple leather or synthetic material with a sticky rubber sole and toes and heel-liners made of rubber. They should fit snugly around the foot.

Strap in
Tightly fitting shoes are essential

ICE SCREW
Used when crossing over steep ice, ice screws are tubular and can be screwed in and out of the ice for secure attachment of carabiners through which a rope can pass.

Grip it
Some ice scews are as long as 23cm (9in). Long, thick, threads ensure a solid grip

NEED2KNOW

→ More than 70,000 men and women participate in ultramarathons, races defined as longer than the standard 42km (26-mile) marathon.

→ The International Association of Ultra Runners (IAU) organizes annual World Championships for a variety of races, including 50km (30 miles), 100km (60 miles), 24 hour, and 48 hour.

→ It is unquestionably one of the world's most demanding sports, both physically and mentally.

RUNNING BY THE RULES

Rules vary from event to event, but given the high risk of fatigue it is usual for each runner to have his or her own support crew to administer to them during breaks. Runners must progress entirely under their own power and are prohibited from wearing artificial cooling systems, but can and should wear lightweight running gear, a hat and sunglasses, and carry ample water – for obvious reasons. In some races, participants are allowed a fellow runner to set them a pace. On cross-country courses, where it is impossible to continually monitor the progress of competitiors, runners are obliged to check in at regular time stations along the route.

SIDELINES

23,961 The number of competitors in the 75th Comrades Marathon – the world's oldest and largest ultramarathon held in Cape Town.

5,022 The length in kilometres (3,100 miles) of the world's longest certified ultramarathon, the Self-Transcendence in New York. The record for completing the course is 41 days.

9,000 The ascent, in feet (2,744m), of Cumbria's Wasdale Fell Race.

ROUND-THE-WORLD RUN

DANISH ULTRA LONG DISTANCE RUNNER JESPER OLSEN RAN AROUND THE WORLD IN 22 MONTHS IN 2004–2005, ON A ROUTE COVERING 26,000KM (16,250 MILES). FOR MOST OF THE RUN HE PUSHED A BABY-JOGGER CARRIAGE WHICH CONTAINED FOOD, BEVERAGES, A TENT, AND OTHER EQUIPMENT.

WHERE THEY RUN

Ultramarathons are run on athletics tracks, roads, dirt tracks, or open terrain. Some are simply tests of distance endurance while others offer additional challenges. The 215km (135-mile) Badwater Ultramarathon, held in searing temperatures, starts in Death Valley, California, and climbs more than 2,600m (8,600ft). Participants in the Four Deserts series must complete 250km (156-mile) races across the Sahara, Gobi, and Atacama deserts before being eligible for the last race – in Antarctical

SPORT OVERVIEW

Ultra running takes many forms. The most popular races are ultramarathons, extraordinary feats of endurance over distances longer than the traditional 42km (26-mile) marathon, and sometimes over extreme terrain. Events are either run over a fixed distance, for example, 50km (31 miles), or a fixed time period, such as 24 hours, three days, or six days.

ULTRA RUNNING

Shades
These protect the eyes from bright sunshine as well as from any stones or grit that might fly up when negotiating rough terrain

Water bottle
This is vital to keep a runner hydrated on a long race

Number's up
Each runner is assigned a number which is attached to their clothing

Shorts
These should allow unrestricted leg movement but be largely skin tight to avoid repetitive chaffing

Sunblock
Hight exposure to the sun's rays is one of the many problems faced by the long-distance runner. A high-factor sunblock, liberally applied, is vital

Hat
This should have a broad peak and protection from the sun for the back of the neck

Backpack
Contains food supplements and a GPS gives the runner his or her position in featureless terrain

Weather gaiters
They keep water (sweat and rain) and loose debris like mud and twigs from getting into your shoes

Shoes
Comfort is as important as durability for footwear

696

ATHLETE PROFILE

Physical and mental stamina are critical. Training over ever longer periods of time, and in harsher environments, conditions the heart and muscles. Carrying weights also helps to build strength. Acquiring the mental stamina to run for hours or days is not so easy, but without it even the fittest individual will fail an ultra-distance challenge.

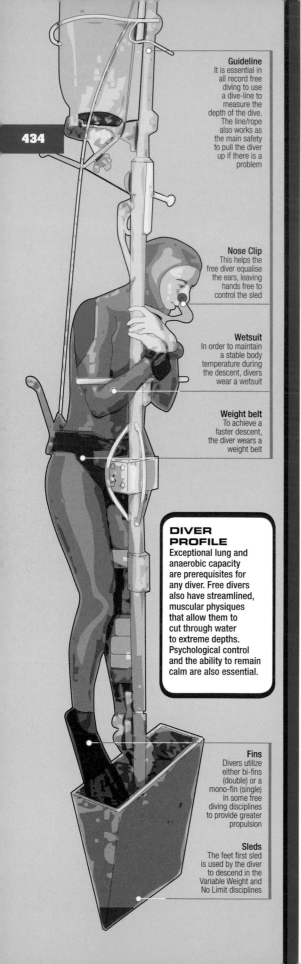

Guideline
It is essential in all record free diving to use a dive-line to measure the depth of the dive. The line/rope also works as the main safety to pull the diver up if there is a problem

Nose Clip
This helps the free diver equalise the ears, leaving hands free to control the sled

Wetsuit
In order to maintain a stable body temperature during the descent, divers wear a wetsuit

Weight belt
To achieve a faster descent, the diver wears a weight belt

DIVER PROFILE
Exceptional lung and anaerobic capacity are prerequisites for any diver. Free divers also have streamlined, muscular physiques that allow them to cut through water to extreme depths. Psychological control and the ability to remain calm are also essential.

Fins
Divers utilize either bi-fins (double) or a mono-fin (single) in some free diving disciplines to provide greater propulsion

Sleds
The feet first sled is used by the diver to descend in the Variable Weight and No Limit disciplines

SPORT OVERVIEW

Free diving is a dangerous sport in which competitors attempt to attain great depths, times, or distances on a single breath, either in open water or a swimming pool. Free divers expose themselves to numerous dangers, such as deep-water blackout and drowning, in pursuit of new records and greater extremes. Free diving is a sport based on individual achievement, with disciplines conducted either as record attempts or competitions where the best individual performances determine the winners.

FREE DIVING

DIVING DISCIPLINES

There are five depth disciplines recognized by the International Association for the Development of Apnea (AIDA), the official governing body of free diving. Constant Weight with fins is the most common free diving event and involves the diver descending to depth with the aid of fins and a set weight. Constant Weight without fins is the most difficult depth discipline and operates under the same rules as Constant Weight with fins, but without the use of swimming apparatus. In the Free Immersion discipline, divers use a guideline to pull themselves to depth and back to the surface. The Variable Weight discipline involves the diver using a weighted sled to descend and their own strength to resurface, either by swimming or pulling on the guideline. No Limit is the absolute depth discipline, where the diver descends using a weighted sled and ascends using a method of their choice.

POOL DISCIPLINES

There are three recognized pool disciplines, and two of these must be conducted in a pool at least 25m (82ft) in length. Dynamic Apnea is swimming underwater to attain the greatest distance; this discipline is divided into two categories: with and without fins. The third discipline, Static Apnea, is timed underwater breath-holding.

NEED2KNOW

→ The first Free Diving World Championship in 1996 involved teams from Germany, Belgium, Colombia, Spain, France, and the inaugural winner, Italy.

→ The current world record for the No Limit discipline stands at a staggering 214m (702ft). It was set by Austrian Herbert Nitsch.

THE BIG BLUE

THE SPORT OF FREE DIVING WAS IMMORTALIZED IN THE 1988 FILM *THE BIG BLUE*. THE FILM DEPICTS A FICTIONALIZED ACCOUNT OF THE REAL LIFE RIVALRY BETWEEN TWO FAMOUS FREE DIVERS: FRENCHMAN JACQUES MAYOL AND ITALIAN ENZO MAIORCA.

TRAINING

Free divers undertake underwater and out-of-water training. One out-of-water exercise is the "Apnea walk". The athlete executes a short breath hold (typically one minute) taken at rest, followed by a walk while maintaining the hold. This exercise accustomize their muscles to anaerobic (meaning "without air") conditions.

INSIDE STORY

Jacques Mayol and Enzo Maiorca were the inspiration for organized competitive free diving. The two athletes frequently broke each other's record attempts and increased public interest in the sport during the 1960s and 1970s. In 1976 Mayol became the first to descend to 100m (328ft). Maiorca held as many as 13 world records between 1960 and 1974. In 1983, at the age of 56, Mayol dove to 105m (345ft).

CLIFF DIVING

SPORT OVERVIEW

Described by the World High Diving Federation (WHDF) as "the acrobatic perfection of diving into water", cliff diving is a high-risk sport in which athletes leap from a steep cliff and performing difficult combinations of twists and somersaults as they plummet to the water below. Competitors aim to execute dives according to a strict criterion that is assessed by a panel of judges, who award points after the successful execution of each dive.

COMPETITION LOCATIONS

Cliff diving events are held at locations that have a sheer vertical cliff face and water with a minimum depth of 5m (16ft). The standard height regulations are 23–28m (75–92ft) for men and 18–23m (59–75ft) for women. For international events, the take-off platform usually stands 1m (3ft) out from the cliff face, although it is common at non-international events for divers to launch directly from the cliff face.

DIFFICULT COMBINATIONS

To gain maximum points a diver must execute difficult combinations of somersaults and twists in performing a dive. Important elements in a successful dive are the height, angle, momentum, and position of the take off; the clear demonstration of announced positions during the dive, such as the "pike", "tuck", or "split"; and the limited amount of splash created on water entry.

Leg position
Points can be deducted if a diver opens their legs during a dive, which they occasionally must do to regain balance

Head First?
It is not standard practice for divers to enter the water head first; most dives are executed by entering the water feet first

Body strength
Divers must use considerable body strength to maintain a vertical body position on entry, which reduces the amount of splash created

DIVER PROFILE
Cliff divers are courageous athletes who have extraordinary physical control. Competitors have lean, muscular bodies that allow them to complete complex mid-air manoeuvres in an average of thee seconds.

NEED2KNOW

→ The inaugural WHDF World Championship was held in Switzerland in 1997. Dustin Webster from the USA emerged the victor with a total score of 248.04.

→ The water entry speed of a cliff diver ranges from 75 to 100kph (46 to 62mph) and has an impact nine times greater than that caused diving from a standard 10m (33ft) platform.

→ The highest score ever received for a single dive is 168.00, recorded by Russian Artem Silchenko at a WHDF International Event in 2006. Silchenko performed a back three somersaults pike with two twists, which has a 5.6 degree of difficulty.

A PERFECT DAY

Colombian Orlando Duque, considered to be one of the most elegant cliff divers ever, performed what has been labelled "the perfect dive" on his way to victory at the 2000 WHDF World Championship in Kaunolu, Hawaii. Duque performed a double back somersault with four twists to receive a perfect "10" from all seven judges. Duque's victory was the first of three consecutive world titles from 2000 to 2002, making him the only athlete to accomplish this feat to date.

RULES AND REGULATIONS

A standard event contains three rounds, with each diver allowed one dive per round. A dive is awarded a score out of ten by a panel of five judges. The highest and lowest marks are eliminated, and the sum of the three remaining scores is multiplied by the degree of difficulty ascribed to the dive attempted. The degree of difficulty for a dive is determined by adding pre-set scores attributed to five different categories: take off; somersaults; twists; number of mid-air positions; and water entry. At the end of the three rounds, the diver with the highest combined total is declared the winner.

INSIDE STORY

King Kahekili (1710–94), the last independent king of Maui, was renowned for *lele kawa*, which in English means: "leaping off high cliffs and entering the water feet first without a splash". A generation later, Hawaiians began practising *lele kawa* as a sport, with judgment passed on the style of the jump and the amount of splash on entry.

WHDF
The World High Diving Federation (WHDF) was founded in 1996 and has its headquarters in Avegno, Switzerland. The WHDF is the current, official governing body of international cliff diving.

FREERIDE MOUNTAIN BIKING

NEED2KNOW

→ The Red Bull Rampage is the gold standard event for the sport, and has been contested at Virgin, Utah, in the US on six occasions between 2001 and 2012.

→ More than 6,000 spectators watched the Monster Park Slopestyle freeride competition at Dana Park, California, in 2004.

SPORT OVERVIEW

Just like freeride snowboarding and freeskiing, freeride mountain biking encompasses a range of riding styles that are all linked by a single theme – riding without boundaries. Bikes with more and better suspension enable longer and faster descents, ever-larger jumps, and more extreme lines to be taken.

FREERIDE BIKES

Full-suspension bikes allow massive shock absorption at high speeds and are capable of traversing obstacles large and small.

Total protection
A full-face helmet is essential to protect the head and face in case of a crash

Gear control
Most freeride bikes have just nine gears; normal mountain bikes have 27

Body armour
Riders wear full-finger gloves and padded protection on the body, especially on the knees and elbows. This will limit injury but not necessarily prevent it

Aluminium frame
Freeride bikes are not the lightest, typically weighing 14–20kg (30–45lb)

Flat pedals
Lightweight, strong alloy pedals provide a stable riding platform

Long-travel suspension
Most designs feature around 23cm (9in) of front and rear wheel travel

Tough tyres
Designed to withstand extreme pressure, the tyres have tread that allows great lean angles

GRABBING BIG AIR

Freeriding is about riders spontaneously pulling jumps and tricks over natural terrain or on urban courses, so it does not lend itself easily to organized contests. The flagship events are invite-only contests where top freeriders compete for cash, and judges award marks for difficulty, speed, fluidity, tricks, and style. One such event is the Red Bull Rampage, which is contested on a predominantly natural course augmented with wooden features. Urban events over man-made courses are also increasingly popular.

NORTH SHORE NIRVANA

An offshoot of freeriding that has grown rapidly is the North Shore style, named after the area of Vancouver, Canada, where it first emerged. The style involves riding over man-made wooden boardwalks, originally built to convey walkers over densely vegetated areas of the forest floor, and has evolved into riding narrow planks called "skinnies", tree trunks, jumps, and drops, and even massive see-saws. The influence of North Shore riding can be seen in mainstream freeriding, with many wooden features evident in freeride contests.

RIDER PROFILE

Riders need upper and lower body strength, a large lung capacity, and technical bike-riding skills – namely balance, jumping technique, the ability to pick a line, and timing. Competitors also need lots of confidence and to be in total control of their bike at all times – one mistake could result in broken bones.

Approach work
Approaching the jump, the freerider brakes and swings the rear wheel around

In rotation
As the rider launches over the edge of the rock, the bike is already rotating. It continues to turn throughout the jump

In control
The rider must maintain control over the bike as it descends and spins

360-DEGREE DOWNHILL JUMP

Not content to race over the edge of near-vertical rocks up to 9m (30ft) high, top freeriders manage to perform aerial stunts at the same time – and come back down to earth with both bike and body intact.

Rear landing
The rider must keep his weight over the bike's rear to ensure the rear wheel touches down first. Front and rear shocks help to absorb the impact

NEED2KNOW

→ Competitive land yachting is most popular in Europe and North America. France dominated the medal ceremonies at the 2010 world championships – held at De Panne, Belgium – winning three of the six racing categories.

→ The International Land and Sandyachting Federation (FISLY), the sport's governing body, organizes world championships every two years.

RULES OF THE BEACH

Pilots must not let their yachts obstruct or touch other craft. If two racers are approaching each other from different angles, the one on the right has priority, and the other must slow down or move aside. An overtaking yacht must not force the slower vehicle to move aside, but the yacht being overtaken is not allowed to manoeuvre into the path of the faster craft.

STARTING FLAG
The start of the race is signalled when the solid red flag is lowered near the starting line.

TURNING MARKER
The layout of the course for a land yacht race is marked by flags, which indicate where pilots have to turn.

FINISH FLAG
The race finishes when the chequered flag is raised as the first competitors crosses the line.

LIE OF THE LAND

Good competition requires two things – a large, relatively flat, open space, and wind – so anywhere that fits this description could host land-yacht racing. Beaches, salt flats, frozen lakes (with skates used instead of wheels), and airfields are all suitable. The beaches at De Panne (Belgium), Le Touquet (France), and Terschelling (Netherlands), and the dry lake at Ivanpah, Nevada (United States), are popular competition venues. Races are usually contested on closed circuits, with turning markers (a flag with red and white diagonals) used to indicate the extremities of the course. The distance between markers must be at least 2km (1¼ miles), and obstacles are coned off.

SPORT OVERVIEW

Pilots race three-wheeled, wind-propelled vehicles across large expanses of flat ground. The pilot steers from a prone position, with the use of pedals or levers. By controlling the angle of the sail, a skilled pilot can attain speeds several times faster than the prevailing wind. With no brakes, pilots must use the wind to stop. Land yachts often turn over, so the sport is potentially dangerous.

LAND YACHTING

LAND YACHT CLASSES

Several different classes of land yacht are recognized for competitions, including:

CLASS 2 The largest and most powerful class, with a fibreglass hull, a wing-shaped mast up to 8m (25ft) high, and a wooden rear axle. Not always the fastest craft, they are sailed mostly in Europe.

CLASS 3 Similar in appearance to Class 2 but smaller, this class of yacht is the most popular craft, and is capable of reaching speeds of 110kph (70mph) or more.

CLASS 5 A smaller class of craft than Classes 2 and 3, the pilot lies in a fibreglass seat suspended from a tubular steel or aluminium chassis, rather than inside the hull.

STANDART Standart yachts are similar to Class 5 craft, with one crucial difference – every yacht is identical. Designed so that pilots cannot rely on technological advantage, Standart yachts allow racers to compare their own performance rather than that of their craft.

PILOT PROFILE
Pilots must have a thorough knowledge of how to harness the wind's energy to best effect, and this skill is not learned overnight. They must also be aware of the dangers inherent in the wind, the surface they are "sailing" over, and other yachts. Lightning reflexes, physical strength, total focus, and lots of courage are also crucial.

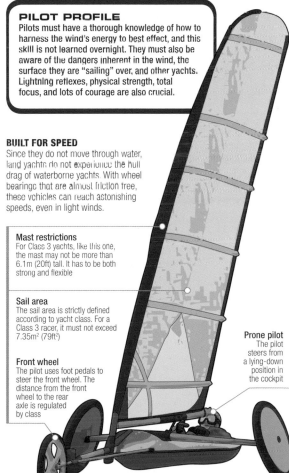

BUILT FOR SPEED
Since they do not move through water, land yachts do not experience the hull drag of waterborne yachts. With wheel bearings that are almost friction free, these vehicles can reach astonishing speeds, even in light winds.

Mast restrictions
For Class 3 yachts, like this one, the mast may not be more than 6.1m (20ft) tall. It has to be both strong and flexible

Sail area
The sail area is strictly defined according to yacht class. For a Class 3 racer, it must not exceed 7.35m² (79ft²)

Front wheel
The pilot uses foot pedals to steer the front wheel. The distance from the front wheel to the rear axle is regulated by class

Prone pilot
The pilot steers from a lying-down position in the cockpit

WHITEWATER RAFTING

SPORT OVERVIEW

Whitewater rafting is an exciting and potentially dangerous recreational and competitive sport in which a small crew uses paddles or oars to control an inflatable raft along a stretch of a turbulent river. Clubs or commercial operators offer adventurous types of all ages the unique opportunity to safely tackle fast-flowing currents and to shoot the rapids on out-of-the-way rivers all over the world. More experienced rafters can compete in national, continental, or international events, including the World Rafting Championships.

TYPES OF RAFT

Paddle boats are the most common type of raft for those who want to participate in directing the craft through the foaming waters of the river. Oar boats use oars to navigate rapids and are generally larger, heavier, and more stable than paddle boats. Another type is the cataraft, which is composed of two parallel pontoons connected by a metal frame and is paddled by a crew of two people.

WORLD CHAMPIONSHIP

Every two years, the International Rafting Federation organizes the World Rafting Championship for men and women. Teams of six rafters compete for points across three disciplines – sprint, slalom, and downriver – to decide the overall winner. They sprint down powerful rapids, slalom through 12 upriver and downriver gates, and finally race downriver for almost an hour.

NEED2KNOW

→ Whitewater rafting grew in popularity during the 1970s after slalom canoeing was included in the 1972 Munich Olympic Games.

→ In the 2011 World Rafting Championship, Japan was the men's overall team winner and the Czech Republic was the women's overall team winner.

CLASSES OF WHITEWATER

Whitewater is graded according to an International Grading System, from the smooth flowing water of Class One, to the extreme water of Class Six, which can only be tackled by teams of experts. Class Two is rougher than Class One, Class Three has some whitewater, and Class Four has plenty of whitewater. Class Five is only for advanced rafters because it has hidden obstacles and hazards.

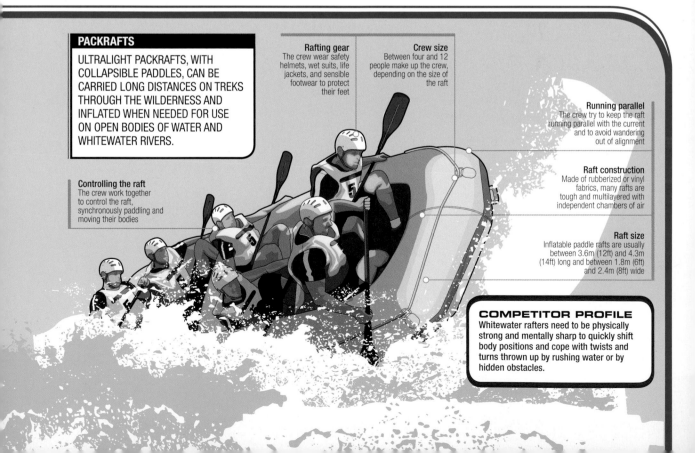

PACKRAFTS

ULTRALIGHT PACKRAFTS, WITH COLLAPSIBLE PADDLES, CAN BE CARRIED LONG DISTANCES ON TREKS THROUGH THE WILDERNESS AND INFLATED WHEN NEEDED FOR USE ON OPEN BODIES OF WATER AND WHITEWATER RIVERS.

Rafting gear
The crew wear safety helmets, wet suits, life jackets, and sensible footwear to protect their feet

Crew size
Between four and 12 people make up the crew, depending on the size of the raft

Running parallel
The crew try to keep the raft running parallel with the current and to avoid wandering out of alignment

Raft construction
Made of rubberized or vinyl fabrics, many rafts are tough and multilayered with independent chambers of air

Raft size
Inflatable paddle rafts are usually between 3.6m (12ft) and 4.3m (14ft) long and between 1.8m (6ft) and 2.4m (8ft) wide

Controlling the raft
The crew work together to control the raft, synchronously paddling and moving their bodies

COMPETITOR PROFILE
Whitewater rafters need to be physically strong and mentally sharp to quickly shift body positions and cope with twists and turns thrown up by rushing water or by hidden obstacles.

NEED2KNOW

→ The triathalon features an open water race of 1.5km (1 mile).

→ The 10km (6¼ mile) open water race was included in the 2008 Beijing Olympics for the first time.

→ In the women's 10km at London 2012, less than 1 second separated Éva Risztov in first from second-placed Haley Anderson.

SIDELINES

5 The number of oceans (Atlantic, Arctic, Indian, Pacific, and Southern) in which the pioneering British swimmer Lewis Gordon Pugh has completed a long-distance swim. He is the first person to achieve this feat.

66 The number of days Slovenian Martin Strel spent swimming down the River Amazon – from Atalaya in Peru to the Brazilian city of Belem – in 2007, setting a new long-distance record of 5,268km (3,273 miles).

1,307 The number of solo swimmers to have crossed the English Channel as of March 2013. The average solo crossing time is approximately 13 hours. Measuring 21¾ miles (35 km) at its narrowest, it is said to be "the Everest of open water swimming" because of tides, winds, and shipping.

42 The number of swimmers from 25 countries who took part in the women's 10km (6¼ mile) race at the 12th FINA World Championships in Melbourne in 2007.

ENDURANCE RACES

Endurance swimmers compete in races of various distances, usually 5km (3 miles), 10km (6¼ miles), and 25km (15½ miles). Other events involve swimmers competing for a set time, usually an hour or more. The Fédération Internationale de Natation (FINA) organizes men's and women's events at the World Championships, the Open Water World Championships, and the Marathon World Cup, which is a series of races of 10km (6¼ miles). In open water races each swimmer is accompanied by an escort safety craft, which contains a judge and a member of the swimmer's team who can give advice and monitor the swimmer's wellbeing.

SPORT OVERVIEW

Endurance swimmers take part in long-distance freestyle events in open water, such as rivers, lakes, or oceans, or in pools or other man-made bodies of water. They compete with each other in various events at local, national, or international championships, such as the biannual World Championships. Swimmers often challenge themselves to conquer a stretch of open water, such as the English Channel, the North American Great Lakes, or a Norwegian fjord.

OPEN WATER CHALLENGES

Many endurance swimmers compete in open water races such as the 20km (12½ mile) Rottnest Channel Swim in Perth, Australia, or in the long lane swimming events in the waterways of The Netherlands. Others successfully take on some remarkable open water challenges. For example, the American Lynne Cox became the first to swim the Bering Strait between Alaska and Russia. She also braved the icy waters of Antarctica to swim 1.7km (1 mile).

ESCAPE FROM ALCATRAZ

SWIMMING FROM THE ISLAND OF ALCATRAZ TO THE SHORES OF SAN FRANCISCO IS A COMMON OPEN WATER EVENT THAT SOME DETERMINED SWIMMERS HAVE COMPLETED MORE THAN 100 TIMES.

ENDURANCE SWIMMING

COMPETITOR PROFILE

Endurance swimmers need to develop a good technique with long, smooth, and strong strokes that form a consistent rhythm and a regular tempo. As well as being physically fit swimmers have to be mentally tough, keeping their minds active. They need to be sure they can complete the required distance and, during events in open water, cope with the cold, tides, and windy conditions.

Bright cap
A brightly coloured cap stands out clearly and can be seen by judges and safety crews

Goggles
Most swimmers wear goggles as well as nose clips and ear plugs

Swim suit
Swimmers often wear a swim suit, but not a wet suit because it increases buoyancy

HANG GLIDING

NEED2KNOW

→ In the 1890s, Otto Lilienthal made and flew pioneering hang gliders in Germany.

→ In 1963, Australian electrical engineer John Dickenson constructed a portable and controllable glider. Later that year Rod Fuller flew it in public while being towed by a motor boat, ushering in the popular era of hang gliding.

→ The Fédération Aéronautique International organize a World Pilot Ranking System (WPRS) so that pilots can score points in the type of hang gliding competition they enter – Aerobatic, Class 1, Class 2, and Class 5.

SPORT OVERVIEW

Powered only by movements of the air, hang gliders and their pilots soar like eagles above the landscape. Either for sheer pleasure or in cross-country and aerobatic competitions, pilots fly their increasingly sophisticated gliders for long distances and to great heights.

A SINGLE WING

Hang gliders have one triangle-shaped wing composed of a fabric sail mounted on an aluminium frame, which may be strengthened with carbon fibre. An enclosed fabric harness hangs from the wing's centre of gravity and fully supports the pilot's weight. The pilot is free to shift his or her weight and so direct the glider through the air.

Non-rip sail
A hang glider's sail is made of a non-rip fabric such as Mylar

Lift off
The aerofoil shape of the wing creates lift as it moves through the air – just like an aeroplane wing

S-LINE 114

Wing frame
The aluminium frame of the wing is both strong and light

Control bar
The pilot steers the hang glider via the control bar, which is attached to the wing

Lying prone
The harness suspends the pilot in a prone position – by moving forward and back, and from one side to the other, the pilot can alter the glider's direction

SIDELINES

8-32 The speed (in km per hour) of the wind needed for ideal launching and landing manoeuvres.

16-90 The age range for pilots learning to fly hang gliders. Women make up about 10-15 per cent of hang glider pilots in the US.

83 The number of active national members registered with hang gliding's governing body, the Fédération Aéronautique International.

INSIDE STORY

National and international competitions regularly take place in countries around the world. Events are organized for different hang gliding classes – flexibles (Class 1) and rigids (Class 2 and 5) – in different categories for both individuals and teams. The world straight distance record is held by Dustin B. Martin who flew 764km (437½ miles) in 2012.

TAKING OFF AND LANDING

Usually, pilots take to the air by foot launching. Carrying the glider on their shoulders they run down a hill or mountain until they reach a sufficient speed for take off. They can also be towed by a boat, truck, or ultralight aircraft, or pulled into the air by a stationary winch. Once airborne they steer the glider by moving their weight, navigating through changing air masses such as thermals, where warm air rises, or ridge lifts, where air masses encounter a cliff, hill, or mountain. To land, the pilot steers the glider earthward, then stalls the wing by rotating it upward and coming to ground on his or her feet.

SENSITIVE TO WIND

An essential instrument for many pilots is the variometer, which is very sensitive to vertical wind speeds. It may "bleep" audibly, have a visual display, and be able to assess height. It measures the rate of climb or fall, enabling a pilot to judge a thermal or ridge lift accurately. A built-in global positioning system (GPS) helps pilots – and judges – to keep track of their course in competitions.

SELF-INFLATING CANOPY

The canopy of a paraglider is designed to fill with air and inflate itself. When the wind is light the pilot runs forward with the canopy behind so that air enters vents in a row of long "cells" that are open at the front and closed at the back. When the wind is stronger the pilot faces the canopy as if it were a kite, controlling it so that it fills with air.

SPORT OVERVIEW

As a sport, paragliding is similar to hang gliding – pilots remain airborne for hours and compete fiercely for cross-country and aerobatic awards. They differ in several ways. Paraglider pilots are usually suspended in a sitting position under a canopy, which is inflated by air pressure and controlled by lines. Paragliders are lighter, more portable, and easier to assemble than hang gliders – but fly more slowly and have lower performance.

PARAGLIDING

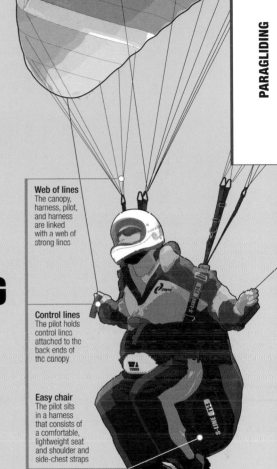

Web of lines The canopy, harness, pilot, and harness are linked with a web of strong lines

Control lines The pilot holds control lines attached to the back ends of the canopy

Easy chair The pilot sits in a harness that consists of a comfortable, lightweight seat and shoulder and side-chest straps

PARAHAWKING

PARAGLIDERS IN NEPAL HAVE DEVISED A UNIQUE DOUBLE ACT KNOWN AS PARAHAWKING, WHICH OFFERS A REMARKABLE AEROBATIC ADVENTURE OF SOARING WITH KITES, EAGLES, AND VULTURES.

DESIGNED FOR SOARING

Paragliders are perfect for effortlessly soaring on air currents, whether they are thermals or ridge lifts. Experienced pilots often stay airborne for three hours on average and may reach altitudes of more than 3,000m (9,842ft). The duration record for staying aloft is 11 hours and the longest distance recorded by a paraglider is 502km (311 miles).

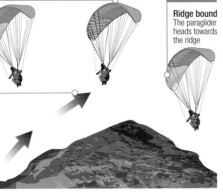

Held aloft The paraglider rides upwards on the air currents

Rising air Air rises as it approaches high ground

Ridge bound The paraglider heads towards the ridge

RIDGE LIFT

Lift is created when prevailing winds come up against hills or sloping ground and are deflected upwards. Paragliders and hang gliders ride this narrow band of rising air to stay airborne for long periods.

INSIDE STORY

Like hang gliding there are both national and international paragliding competitions throughout the world. There are individual and team events for cross-country paragliding, paragliding accuracy, and paragliding aerobatics, each with a World Pilot Ranking System (WPRS) organized by the Fédération Aéronautique International (FAI). The 11th FAI World Championships were held in 2009 in El Peñon, Mexico. Switzerland's Andi Aebi won the overall cross-country event, and Elisa Houdry of France won the cross-country women's event. The inaugural FAI Asian Paragliding Championship was held in Hadong, Korea, in 2004.

SPORT OVERVIEW

Launching themselves into thin air from a great height, usually from an aeroplane, skydivers go into free fall for a period of time before opening a parachute to enable them to land in a drop zone at a safe speed. It is usually a recreational sport, but experienced skydivers take part in competitions and may engage in variations, such as freestyle, formation skydiving, skysurfing, blade running, and freeflying.

SKYDIVING

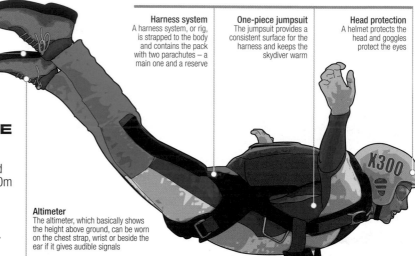

Strong footwear
Skydivers generally wear strong footwear so that they are supported when they come in to land – but also light in weight to prevent them interfering with aerodynamics

Harness system
A harness system, or rig, is strapped to the body and contains the pack with two parachutes – a main one and a reserve

One-piece jumpsuit
The jumpsuit provides a consistent surface for the harness and keeps the skydiver warm

Head protection
A helmet protects the head and goggles protect the eyes

Altimeter
The altimeter, which basically shows the height above ground, can be worn on the chest strap, wrist or beside the ear if it gives audible signals

GOING FOR A DIVE

Skydivers usually jump out of a plane and, generally, need clear skies. Skydivers take off from a small airfield and jump from a plane at about 4,000m (13,000ft). For a while they free fall, often flying in the "belly-to-earth" position. They may perform aerobatic manoeuvres, such as loops and turns. Eventually, they open their parachute so that they are fully inflated at about 760m (2,500ft). Skydivers aim to land in an organized drop zone.

PARACHUTES

Free falling skydivers travel at speeds of 190kph (120mph) or more. The parachutes they use, which are usually self-inflating ram-air wings, are designed to cope with opening in these conditions. The parachutes have steering lines and toggles which the skydivers use to control their flight and to land safely.

Aerofoil shape
The canopy of the parachute is aerodynamic like an aeroplane's wing

Flight control
The skydiver steers the parachute to land in the drop zone

FORMATION SKYDIVING

During the period of free fall skydivers can get together to perform formation skydiving, also called relative work. They come together – sometimes in their hundreds – for a short time and form various patterns which they have first practised carefully on the ground. Canopy formation, also called canopy relative work, is another skill in which skydivers open their canopies as soon as they jump. They come together to create a stack with formations such as biplane and diamond.

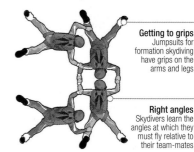

Getting to grips
Jumpsuits for formation skydiving have grips on the arms and legs

Right angles
Skydivers learn the angles at which they must fly relative to their team-mates

COMING TOGETHER
Formation skydivers come together in a prearranged picture. They know exactly the right angle in which to arrive, where to grip the team-mate next to them and what the signals are to progress to the next stage.

INSIDE STORY

World, regional, and national skydiving competitions take place in a number of parachuting disciplines – from artistic events, such as freestyle, skysurfing, and freeflying, to canopy formation, accuracy landing, and formation skydiving. There are usually categories for men, women, teams, and juniors.

INTERNATIONAL PARACHUTING COMMISSION (IPC)
Skydiving and parachuting activities are governed by the International Parachuting Commission, one of several air sports commissions run by the Fédération Aéronautique Internation (FAI). The IPC organizes international championships and is responsible for verifying world records.

NEED2KNOW

→ A range of conditions prevents people from bungee jumping safely. These include high blood pressure, heart problems, back problems, epilepsy, excess weight, and pregnancy.

→ Bungee jumping is practised in many countries around the world, from the US, the UK and most of Europe to South America, Australia, New Zealand, India, Japan, and Korea.

Swallow dive
A leap with arms stretched out wide is popular way to jump

HIGHEST BUNGEE JUMPS

HEIGHT	LOCATION
321M	ROYAL GORGE BRIDGE COLORADO, USA
233M	MACAU TOWER MACAU CHINA
220M	VERZASCA DAM, LOCARNO, SWITZERLAND
216M	BLOUKRANS RIVER BRIDGE, SOUTH AFRICA

Head protection
Bungee jumpers sometimes wear a helmet to protect their heads

Body harness
Straps and webbing provide a secure and comfortable jump

Free arms
With their arms free jumpers can perform twists and turns

Leg harness
Straps of the leg harness are usually attached to both legs – leg harnesses used alone can provide a genuine feeling of flying

High platform
The bungee cord is safely and securely attached to a high platform

BUNGEE JUMPING

SPORT OVERVIEW

Bungee jumping is a thrill-seeking event in which individuals dive headfirst from a high point and plummet to the ground, only to be saved at the last moment by an incredibly elastic rope. Described by many as the ultimate adrenalin rush, this event is almost exclusively a recreational pastime.

HIGH POINTS

Bridges, hot air balloons, cranes, and towers are some of the many high points that bungee jumpers use for their daredevil dives. Some of the renowned include the Bloukrans Rivers Bridge in South Africa, the Verzasca Dam in Switzerland, and the Kawarau Bridge in New Zealand. Commerical bungee operators often use mobile cranes for jumps.

TAKING THE PLUNGE

Totally reliable elastic ropes are vital to the safety of an event that is fraught with danger. Cords made of strands of latex rubber are either enclosed or exposed depending on the kind of extension and bounce required. Bungee jumpers are weighed carefully and equipped with body harnesses before going to the platform where they take the plunge. The jump lasts a few seconds and includes a few rebounds. The cord absorbs most of the g-forces so that the jumper slows down steadily without experiencing a sharp jolt to the system.

INSIDE STORY

Inspired by the land divers of Pentecost Island in the Pacific islands of Vanuatu, four members of the Dangerous Sports Club tied elastic rope to their ankles and jumped off the Clifton Suspension Bridge in Bristol in 1979, so initiating the modern era of bungee jumping.

PROMOTING SAFETY

Many bungee jumping clubs around the world have extremely good safety records because they have introduced failsafe mechanisms to protect their jumpers. In some countries, the sport is regulated. For example, clubs in Great Britain are affiliated to the British Elastic Rope Sports Association (BERSA), which is an organization that promotes safety, training and licensing.

INDEX

I

J

K

CONTACTS

Olympics
Athletics
UK Athletics www.ukathletics.net

Gymnastics
Federation Internationale
de Gymnastique
www.fig-gymnastics.com

Weightlifting/Powerlifting
International Weightlifting Federation
www.iwf.net

Soccer
Federation International de Football Association
www.fifa.com

Basketball
International Basketball Federation
www.fiba.com

American football
National Football League
www.nfl.com

All American Football League
www.aafl.com

Rugby union
International Rugby Board
www.irb.com

Rugby League
Rugby League International Federation
www.rlif.com

Australian Rules football
Australian football League
www.afl.com

Cricket
International Cricket Council
www.icc-cricket.com

Baseball
International Baseball Federation
www.baseball.ch

Softball
International Softball Federation
www.internationalsoftball.com

Rounders
National Rounders Association
www.nra-rounders.co.uk

Ice Hockey
International Ice Hockey Federation
www.iihf.com

Bandy
International Bandy Federation
www.internationalbandy.com

Field Hockey
International Hockey Federation
www.fihockey.org

Floorball
International Floorball Federation
www.floorball.org

Lacrosse
International Lacrosse Federation
www.intlaxfed.org

Volleyball
International Volleyball Federation
www.fivb.org

Footvolley
UK Footvolley Association
www.footvolley.co.uk

Sepak Takraw
English Sepak Takraw Association
www.sepak-takraw.co.uk

Netball
International Federation of Netball Associations
www.netball.org

Handball
International Handball Federation
www.ihf.info

Gaelic Football
Gaelic Athletic Association
www.gaa.ie

Hurling
Gaelic Athletic Association
www.gaa.ie

Shinty
Camanachd Association
www.shinty.com
Dodgeball
International Dodgeball Federation
www.dodge-ball.com

Tug of War
The Tug of War Association
www.tugofwar.co.uk

Ultimate Frisbee
Ultimate Players Association
www.upa.org

Tennis
International Tennis Federation
www.itftennis.com
www.atptennis.com

Real Tennis
International Real Tennis Professional
Association
www.irtpa.com

Soft Tennis
Japan Soft Tennis Association
www.jsta.or.jp

Table Tennis
International Table Tennis Federation
www.ittf.com

Badminton
International Badminton Federation
www.internationalbadminton.org

Jianzi
Jianzi UK
www.jianzi.co.uk

Squash
World Squash Federation
www.worldsquash.org

Racquetball
USA Raquetball
www.usra.org

Racquets
Paddleball
United States Paddleball Association
www.uspaddleballassociation.org

Eton Fives
Eton Fives Association
www.etonfives.co.uk

Pelota
International Federation of Basque Pelota
www.fipv.net

Boxing
International Boxing Federation
www.ibf-usba-boxing.com

World Boxing Organisation
www.wbo-int.com

Fencing
Federation International de Escrime (FIE)
www.fie.ch

Judo
International Judo Federation
www.ijf.org

Sumo
International Sumo Federation
www.amateursumo.com

Wrestling
Federation International de
Luttes Associees
www.fila-wrestling.com

Karate
World Karate Federation
www.wkf.net
Kungfu
International KungFu Federation
www.internationalkungfu.com

Ju-jitsu
International Judo Association
www.ijf.org

Taekwando
Taekwon Do International
www.tkd-international.com
Kickboxing
World Kickboxing Network
www.worldkickboxingnetwork.com

World Kickboxing Association
www.worldkickboxingassociation.com

Sombo
British Sombo
www.britishsombo.co.uk

Kendo
International Kendo Federation
www.kendo-fik.org

Swimming
Federation Internationale de Natation
www.fina.org

Diving
Federation Internationale de Natation
www.fina.org

Water Polo
Federation Internationale de Natation
www.fina.org

Synchronised Swimming
Federation Internationale de Natation
www.fina.org

Underwater Sports
World underwater Federation
www.cmas.org

Sailing
International Sailing Federation
www.sailing.org

Rowing
International Rowing Federation
www.worldrowing.com

Kayaking
International Canoe Federation
www.canoeicf.com

Canoeing
International Canoe Federation
www.canooicf.com

Dragonboat Racing
International Dragonboat Federation
ww.idbf.com

Waterskiing
International Waterski Federation
www.iwsf.com

Windsurfing
International Windsurfing Association
www.internationalwindsurfing.com

Surfing
International Surfing Association
www.isasurf.org

Association of Surfing Professionals
www.aspworldtour.com

Alpine Skiing
International Skiing Federation
www.fis-ski.com

Freestyle Skiing
International Skiing Federation
www.fis-ski.com

Snowboarding
World Snowboard Federation
www.worldsnowboardfederation.com

Cross-country skiing
International Skiing Federation
www.fis-ski.com

Ski jumping
International Skiing Federation
www.fis-ski.com

Nordic Combined
United States Ski Association
www.ussa.org

Biathlon
British Biathlon Union
www.britishbiathlon.com

Bobsledding
Federation Internationale de Bobsleigh et
de Tobaganning

Luge
International Luge Federation
www.fil-luge.org

Skeleton
FIBT www.bobsleigh.com

Speed Skating
International Skating Union
www.isu.org

Figure Skating
International Skating Union
www.isu.org

Ice Dance
International Skating Union
www.isu.org

Golf
International Golf Federation
www.internationalgolffederation.org

United States Golf Association
www.usga.org
PGA www.pga.com

Croquet
The Croquet Association
www.croquet.org

Curling
World Curling Federation
www.worldcurling.org

United States Curling Association
www.usacurl.org

English Curling Association
www.englishcurling.org.uk

Lawn bowling
The English Bowling Association
www.bowlsengland.com

Petanque
International Federation of Petanque
www.fipjp.com

English Petanque Association
www.englishpetanque.org.uk

10-pin bowling
United States Bowling Congress www.bowl.com

5-pin bowling
Canadian 5-pin Bowler's Association
www.c5pba.ca

Skittles
Stroud and District Skittles League
www.stroudskittles.co.uk

Atlatl
World Atlatl Association
www.worldatlatl.org

Horseshoe
National Horseshoe Pitching Association
of America
www.horseshoepitching.com

Snooker
World Snooker Association
www.worldsnooker.com

Billiards
World Pool billiard Association
www.wpa-pool.com

Pool
World Eightball Pool Federation
www.wepf.org

Darts
British Darts
www.bdodarts.com

Archery
International Archery Federation
www.archery.org

Pistol Shooting
International Shooting Sport Federation
www.issf-shooting.org
Shotgun Shooting
International Shooting Sport Federation
www.issf-shooting.org

Rifle Shooting
International Shooting Sport Federation
www.issf-shooting.org

BMX
Union Cycliste Internationale
www.uci.ch

Track Cycling
Union Cycliste Internationale
www.uci.ch

Road Racing
Union Cycliste Internationale
www.uci.ch

Mountain Biking
International Mountain Bicycling Association
www.imba.com

Roller Skating
International Rollersports Federation
www.rollersports.org

Roller Hockey
International Rollersports Federation
www.rollersports.org

Skateboarding
www.gravity-sports.com

Formula 1
International Automobile Federation
www.fia.com

Indy Car Racing
International Automobile Federation
www.fia.com

GP2
International Automobile Federation
www.fia.com

Touring Car Racing
International Automobile Federation
www.fia.com

Drag Racing
International Hot Rod Association
www.ihra.com
Karting
International Kart Federation
www.ikfkarting.com

Stock Car Racing
National Association for Stock Car Auto Racing
www.nascar.com

Off Road Rallying
International Automobile Federation
www.fia.com

Truck Rallying
British Truck Racing Association
www.btra.org

Rallying
International Automobile Federation
www.fia.com

Road Motorcycle Racing
Federation Internationale de Motocyclisme
www.fim.ch

Off-road Motorcycle Racing
Federation Internationale de Motocyclisme
www.fim.ch

Powerboat Racing
Union Internationale Motonautique
www.uimpowerboating.com

American Powerboat Association
www.apba-racing.com

Air Racing
Royal Aero Club Ltd
www.royalaeroclub.org

Snowmobiling
Powersports Entertainment
www.powersportstour.com

Horse Racing
International Federation of
Horseracing Authorities
www.horseracingintfed.com

National Thoroughbred Racing Association
www.ntra.com

Dressage
International Equestrian Federation
www.horsesport.org
Eventing
International Equestrian Federation
www.horsesport.org

Showjumping
International Equestrian Federation
www.horsesport.org

Polo
Federation of International Polo
www.fippolo.com

Hurlingham Polo Association
www.hpa-polo.co.uk

Greyhound Racing
British Greyhound Racing Board
www.thedogs.co.uk

Harness Racing
Harness Racing in Australia
www.harness.org

Rodeo
Australian Professional Rodeo Association
www.prorodeo.asn.au

Horseball
International Horseball Federation
www.fihb-horseball.org

Horsedriving
British Horse Driving Trials Association
www.horsedrivingtrials.co.uk
Camel Racing
Imparja Camel Cup Committee
www.camelcup.com.au

Dog Sledding
International Federation of Sleddog Sports
www.sleddogsport.com
International Sled Dog Racing Association
www.isdra.org

Street Luge
Gravity Sports International
www.gravitysportsinternational.com

Parkour
American Parkour
www.americanparkour.com

Extreme Climbing
International Mountaineering and Climbing
Federation
www.uiaa.com

Ultra Running
International Association of Ultra Running
www.iau.org.tw

Free Diving
International Association for the Development
of Free Diving
www.aidainternational.org

Cliff Diving
World High Diving Federation
www.whdf.com

Mountain Biking
International Mountain Bicycling Association
www.imba.com

Land Yatching
International Land and Sandyachting Federation
www.fisly.org

White Water Rafting
International Rafting Federation
www.intraftfed.com

Endurance Swimming
Midmar Mile
www.midmarmile.co.za

Hang Gliding
British Hang gliding and Paragliding Association
www.bhpa.co.uk

Paragliding
British Hang gliding and Paragliding Association
www.bhpa.co.uk

Skydiving
British Parachute Association
www.bpa.org.uk

Bungee jumping
www.bungeezone.com/orgs/bersa.shtml

ACKNOWLEDGMENTS

Dorling Kindersley would like to thank the following people for their help in the preparation of this book: at DK India – Kingshuk Ghoshal, Govind Mittal, Deeksha Saikia, Bimlesh Tiwary, and Balwant Singh; editorial assistance – Ann Baggaley, Jarrod Bates, Bob Bridle, Kim Bryan, Gill Edden, Anna Fischel, Phil Hunt, Tom Jackson, Nicky Munro, Nigel Ritchie, Manisha Thakkar, Simon Tuite, Miezen Van Zyl, Jo Weeks; for design assistance – Sarah Arnold and Susan St. Louis; for additional illustrations – David Ashby, Kevin Jones Associates, Peter Bull, Brian Flynn, Phil Gamble, Tim Loughead, Patrick Mulrey, Oxford Designers & Illustrators, Jay Parker, and Mark Walker, for index – Ian D. Crane; for flags – The Flag Institute, Chester, UK.

PICTURE CREDITS

The publisher would like to thank the following (a-above; b-below/bottom; c-centre; f-far; l-left; r-right; t-top):

12 Getty Images: IOC Olympic Museum (cra) (crb). 13 Getty Images: IOC Olympic Museum (tr) (crb). PA Photos: (cra); DPA (cl) (c). 14 Getty Images: IOC Olympic Museum (tr) (cr) (crb). PA Photos: (cb); S&G (ca); Topham Picturepoint (fcr) (cl). 15 Getty Images: IOC Olympic Museum (cr) (crb) (tr). 16 Getty Images: IOC Olympic Museum (tr) (cr) (crb). 17 Getty Images: IOC Olympic Museum (crb) (tr). PA Photos: (cr) (cb); AP (ca) (cla) (clb). 18 Corbis: Hulton-Deutsch Collection (tl). Getty Images: IOC Olympic Museum (cr) (tr). PA Photos: (bc). 19 Getty Images: AFP (cla); IOC Olympic Museum (cr) (tr). PA Photos: S&G (br). 20 Getty Images: IOC Olympic Museum (tr). PA Photos: DPA (b); S&G (ca). 21 Corbis: Bettmann (crb). Getty Images: IOC Olympic Museum (tr) (cr). PA Photos: (cla). 22 Getty Images: IOC Olympic Museum (tr) (cr). PA Photos: Robert Rider-Rider/AP (cb); S&G (tl). 23 Getty Images: IOC Olympic Museum (cr). PA Photos: AP (cb); DPA (t). 24 Getty Images: Hulton Archive/Keystone (t); IOC Olympic Museum (cr). PA Photos: S&G (br). 25 Getty Images: IOC Olympic Museum (tr) (cr). PA Photos: AP (cla); DPA (crb). 26 Getty Images: IOC Olympic Museum (tr) (cr). PA Photos: AP (cla); DPA (crb). 27 Getty Images: IOC Olympic Museum (tr); AFP (cla); IOC Olympic Museum (cr) (tr). PA Photos: S&G (br). 20 Getty Images: IOC Olympic Museum (tr). PA Photos: DPA (b); S&G (ca). 21 Corbis: Bettmann (crb). Getty Images: IOC Olympic Museum (tr) (cr). PA Photos: (cla). 22 Getty Images: IOC Olympic Museum (tr) (cr). PA Photos: Robert Rider-Rider/AP (cb); S&G (tl). 23 Getty Images: IOC Olympic Museum (cr). PA Photos: AP (cb); DPA (t). 24 Getty Images: Hulton Archive/Keystone (t); IOC Olympic Museum (cr). PA Photos: S&G (br). 25 Getty Images: IOC Olympic Museum (tr) (cr). PA Photos: AP (cla); DPA (crb). 26 Getty Images: IOC Olympic Museum (tr) (cr). PA Photos: AP (cla); DPA (crb). 27 Getty Images: IOC Olympic Museum (tr); Bob Martin (b). PA Photos: Heikki Kotilainen/Lehtikuva (cla). 28 Getty Images: IOC Olympic Museum (tr). PA Photos: AP (b) (cla). 29 Getty Images: IOC Olympic Museum (tr) (cr). PA Photos: AP (cla); Wilfried Witters/Witters (crb). 30 Getty Images: IOC Olympic Museum (tr) (cr). PA Photos: S&G (cla) (crb). 31 Getty Images: IOC Olympic Museum (cr). PA Photos: Ed Reinke/AP (t); S&G (br). 32 Corbis: Mike King (cr). Getty Images: IOC Olympic Museum (tr) (br). MARTIN/AFP (bl). 33 Getty Images: Clive Brunskill (tr); IOC Olympic Museum (tr) (cr). PA Photos: Michael Probst/AP (bl). 34 Getty Images: Jiji Press/AFP (tr); Mike Powell (cla); Nick Wilson (cr). PA Photos: Neal Simpson (br). 35 Getty Images: Stuart Hannagan (br); IOC Olympic Museum (tr) (cr). PA Photos: Tony Marshall (cla). 36 Corbis: Gero Breloer/EPA (cla). Getty Images: Gabriel Bouys/AFP (br); IOC Olympic Museum (tr) (cr). 37 Getty Images: Frank Fife (b); Clive Rose (cra); IOC Olympic Museum Collections (tr). 38 Getty images: Attila Kisbenedek (b); Getty/AFP (tl). 39 Corbis/Visionhaus (t); Getty/Johannes Eisele (bl). 40 Corbis/Julian Stratenschulte (b). 41 Leo Mason/Corbis (tl); Yang Lei/Xinhua Press/Corbis (tr); AFP/Getty (bl); AFP/Getty (bc); Gallo Images (br). 42 Jean-Yves Ruszniewski/TempSport/Corbis (t); Getty (bl); Julian Stratenschulte/dpa/Corbis (br) 43 Getty Images: Phil Cole

All other images © Dorling Kindersley